Solutions Manual

for use with

Corporate Finance

Seventh Edition

Stephen A. Ross
Massachusetts Institute of Technology

Randolph W. Westerfield
University of Southern California

Jeffrey Jaffe
University of Pennsylvania

McGraw-Hill
Irwin

Boston   Burr Ridge, IL   Dubuque, IA   Madison, WI   New York   San Francisco   St. Louis
Bangkok   Bogotá   Caracas   Kuala Lumpur   Lisbon   London   Madrid   Mexico City
Milan   Montreal   New Delhi   Santiago   Seoul   Singapore   Sydney   Taipei   Toronto

McGraw-Hill
Irwin

Solutions Manual for use with
CORPORATE FINANCE
Stephen A. Ross, Randolph W. Westerfield, Jeffrey Jaffe

Published by McGraw-Hill/Irwin, an imprint of The McGraw-Hill Companies, Inc., 1221 Avenue of the Americas, New York, NY 10020. Copyright © 2005, 2002, 1999, 1996, 1993, 1990, 1988 by The McGraw-Hill Companies, Inc. All rights reserved.

2 3 4 5 6 7 8 9 0 QPD/QPD 0 9 8 7 6 5 4

ISBN 0-07-287192-X

www.mhhe.com

Contents

Part A   **Concept Questions**.. A-1

Part B   **Answers to End-of-Chapter Problems**

Chapter 2:   Accounting Statements and Cash Flow.. B-41

Chapter 3:   Financial Planning and Growth... B-45

Chapter 4:   Net Present Value... B-49

Appendix 4A: Net Present Value: First Principles of Finance....................................... B-74

Chapter 5:   How to Value Bonds and Stocks.. B-75

Appendix 5A: The Term Structure of Interest Rates, Spot Rates, and Yields to Maturity B-90

Chapter 6:   Some Alternative Investment Rules... B-92

Chapter 7:   Net Present Value and Capital Budgeting.. B-116

Chapter 8:   Risk Analysis, Real Options, and Capital Budgeting............................... B-162

Chapter 9:   Capital Market Theory: An Overview.. B-176

Chapter 10:   Return and Risk: *The Capital-Asset-Pricing Model (CAPM)* B-190

Chapter 11:   An Alternative View of Risk and Return: *The Arbitrage Pricing Theory* B-225

Chapter 12:   Risk, Cost of Capital, and Capital Budgeting... B-236

Chapter 13:   Corporate-Financing Decisions and Efficient Capital Markets.................. B-246

Chapter 14:   Long-Term Financing: *An Introduction* B-251

Chapter 15:   Capital Structure: *Basic Concepts* B-257

Chapter 16:   Capital Structure: *Limits to the Use of Debt*.. B-291

Appendix 16B: The Miller Model and the Graduated Income Tax B-310

Chapter 17:   Valuation and Capital Budgeting for the Levered Firm............................ B-316

Chapter 18:   Dividends and Other Payouts.. B-339

Chapter 19:   Issuing Securities to the Public... B-347

Chapter 20:   Long-Term Debt... B-354

Chapter 21:   Leasing B-362

Chapter 22:   Options and Corporate Finance: *Basic Concepts* B-371

Chapter 23:   Options and Corporate Finance: *Extensions & Applications* B-399

Chapter 24:   Warrants and Convertibles.. B-404

Chapter 25:   Derivatives and Hedging Risk.. B-412

Chapter 26:   Short-Term Finance and Planning.. B-424

Chapter 27:   Cash Management... B-431

Chapter 28:   Credit Management.. B-437

Chapter 29:   Mergers and Acquisitions.. B-444

Chapter 30:   Financial Distress B-456

Chapter 31:   International Corporate Finance.. B-458

Part C   **Selected Answers to Numeric Problems**... C-465

CONCEPT QUESTIONS - CHAPTER 1

1.1 • **What are the three basic questions of corporate finance?**
   a. Investment decision (capital budgeting): What long-term investment strategy should a firm adopt?
   b. Financing decision (capital structure): How much cash must be raised for the required investments?
   c. Short-term finance decision (working capital): How much short-term cash flow does company need to pay its bills.

   • **Describe capital structure.**
   Capital structure is the mix of different securities used to finance a firm's investments.

   • **How is value created?**

   • **List three reasons why value creation is difficult.**
   Value creation is difficult because it is not easy to observe cash flows directly. The reasons are:
   a. Cash flows are sometimes difficult to identify.
   b. The timing of cash flows is difficult to determine.
   c. Cash flows are uncertain and therefore risky.

1.2 • **What is a contingent claim?**
   A contingent claim is a claim whose payoffs are dependent on the value of the firm at the end of the year. In more general terms, contingent claims depend on the value of an underlying asset.

   • **Describe equity and debt as contingent claims.**
   Both debt and equity depend on the value of the firm. If the value of the firm is greater than the amount owed to debt holders, they will get what the firm owes them, while stockholders will get the difference. But if the value of the firm is less than equity, bondholders will get the value of the firm and equity holders nothing.

1.3 • **Define a proprietorship, a partnership and a corporation.**
   A proprietorship is a business owned by a single individual with unlimited liability. A partnership is a business owned by two or more individuals with unlimited liability. A corporation is a business which is a "legal person" with many limited liability owners.

   • **What are the advantages of the corporate form of business organization?**
   Limited liability, east of ownership transfer and perpetual succession.

1.4 • **What are the two types of agency costs?**
   Monitoring costs of the shareholders and the incentive fees paid to the managers.

- **How are managers bonded to shareholders?**
  a. Shareholders determine the membership to the board of directors, which selects management.
  b. Management contracts and incentives are build into compensation arrangements.
  c. If a firm is taken over because the firm's price dropped, managers could lose their jobs.
  d. Competition in the managerial labor market makes managers perform in the best interest of stockholders.

- **Can you recall some managerial goals?**
  Maximization of corporate wealth, growth and company size.

- **What is the set-of-contracts perspective?**
  The view of the corporation as a set of contracting relationships among individuals who have conflicting objectives.

1.5 - **Distinguish between money markets and capital markets.**
  Money markets are markets for debt securities that pay off in less than one year, while capital markets are markets for long-term debt and equity shares.

- **What is listing?**
  Listing refers to the procedures by which a company applies and qualifies so that its stock can be traded on the New York Stock Exchange.

- **What is the difference between a primary market and a secondary market?**
  The primary market is the market where issuers of securities sell them for the first time to investors, while a secondary market is a market for securities previously issued.

CONCEPT QUESTIONS - CHAPTER 2

2.1 - **What is the balance-sheet equation?**
  Assets = Liabilities + Stockholders' equity

- **What three things should be kept in mind when looking at a balance sheet?**
  Accounting liquidity, debt vs. equity, and value vs. cost.

2.2 - **What is the income statement equation?**
  Revenue - expenses = Income

- **What are the three things to keep in mind when looking at an income statement?**
  Generally Accepted Accounting Principles (GAAP), noncash items, and time and costs.

- **What are noncash expenses?**
  Noncash expenses are items included as expenses but which do not directly affect cash flow. The most important one is depreciation.

2.3   • **What is net working capital?**
  It is the difference between current assets and current liabilities.

- **What is the change in net working capital?**
  To determine changes in net working capital you subtract uses of net working capital from sources of net working capital.

2.4   • **How is cash flow different from changes in net working capital?**
  The difference between cash flow and changes in new working capital is that some transactions affect cash flow and not net working capital. The acquisition of inventories with cash is a good example of a change in working capital requirements.

- **What is the difference between operating cash flow and total cash flow of the firm?**
  The main difference between the two is capital spending and additions to working capital, that is, investment in fixed assets and "investment" in working capital.

2.5   • **How is the Statement of Cash Flows in Table 2.4 different from cash flow of the firm in Table 2.3?**

CONCEPT QUESTIONS - CHAPTER 3

3.1   • **What are the two levels of the financial planning process?**
  The time frame and the level of aggregation.

- **Why should firms draw up financial plans?**
  It accomplishes various goals:
  1. It improves interactions between investment proposals for the different operating activities of the firm.
  2. It provides opportunities for the firm to work through various investment and financial alternatives
  3. It provides greater flexibility.
  4. It avoids surprises.

3.2   • **When might the goals of growth and value maximization be in conflict and when would they be aligned?**
  They might be in conflict if management is willing to accept negative NPV projects just for the sake of growth. They would be aligned if growth is an indeterminate goal that leads to higher value.

- **What are the determinants of growth?**
  1. Profit margin
  2. Asset utilization
  3. Payout ratio
  4. Debt ratio

CONCEPT QUESTIONS - CHAPTER 4

4.1 • **Define future value and present value.**
Future value is the value of a sum after investing over one or more periods.
Present value is the value today of cash flows to be received in the future.

• **How does one use net present value when making an investment decision?**
One determines the present value of future cash flows and then subtracts the cost of the investment. If this value is positive, the investment should be undertaken. If the NPV is negative, then the investment should be rejected.

4.2 • **What is the difference between simple interest and compound interest?**
With simple interest, the interest on the original investment is not reinvested. With compound interest, each interest payment is reinvested and one earns interest on interest.

• **What is the formula for the net present value of a project?**

$$NPV = -C_0 + \sum_{t=1}^{T} C_t /(1+I)^t$$

4.3 • **What is a stated annual interest rate?**
The stated annual interest rate is the annual interest rate without consideration of compounding.

• **What is an effective annual interest rate?**
An effective annual interest rate is a rate that takes compounding into account.

• **What is the relationship between the stated annual interest rate and the effective annual interest rate?**
Effective annual interest rate $= (1 + (r/m))^m - 1$.

• **Define continuous compounding.**
Continuous compounding compounds investments every instant.

4.4 • **What are the formulas for perpetuity, growing-perpetuity, annuity, and growing annuity?**
Perpetuity: PV = C/r
Growing Perpetuity: PV = C/(r-g)
Annuity: PV = (C/r) [1-1/(1+r)^T]
Growing Annuity: PV = [C/(r-g)] [1-((1+g) / (1+r))^T]

• **What are three important points concerning the growing perpetuity formula?**
1. The numerator.
2. The interest rate and the growth rate.
3. The timing assumption.

• **What are four tricks concerning annuities?**
1. A delayed annuity.
2. An annuity in advance
3. An infrequent annuity
4. The equating of present values of two annuities.

CONCEPT QUESTIONS - Appendix to Chapter 4

• **How does an individual change his consumption across periods through borrowing and lending?**

• **How do interest rate changes affect one's degree of impatience?**

CONCEPT QUESTIONS - CHAPTER 5

5.2 • **Define pure discount bonds, level-coupon bonds, and consols.**
A pure discount bond is one that makes no intervening interest payments. One receives a single lump sum payment at maturity. A level-coupon bond is a combination of an annuity and a lump sum at maturity. A consol is a bond that makes interest payments forever.

• **Contrast the state interest rate and the effective annual interest rate for bonds paying semi-annual interest.**
Effective annual interest rate on a bond takes into account two periods of compounding per year received on the coupon payments. The state rate does not take this into account.

5.3 • **What is the relationship between interest rates and bond prices?**
There is an inverse relationship. When one goes up, the other goes down.

- **How does one calculate the yield to maturity on a bond?**
  One finds the discount rate that equates the promised future cash flows with the price of the bond.

5.8 • **What are the three factors determining a firm's P/E ratio?**
  1. Today's expectations of future growth opportunities.
  2. The discount rte.
  3. The accounting method.

5.9 • **What is the closing price of Gateway, Inc. ?**
  The closing price of Gateway, Inc. is 6 3/16.

- **What is the PE of Gateway, Inc. ?**
  The PE of Gateway, Inc. is 29.

- **What is the annual dividend of General Motors?**
  The annual dividend of General Motors is zero.

CONCEPT QUESTIONS - Appendix to Chapter 5

- **Define the forward rate.**
  Given a one-year bond and a two-year bond, one knows the spot rates for both. The forward rate is the rate of return implicit on a one-year bond purchased in the second year that would equate the terminal wealth of purchasing the one-year bond today and another in one year with that of the two-year bond.

- **What is the relationship between the one-year spot rate, the two-year spot rate and the forward rate over the second year?**
  The forward rate $f_2 = [(1+r_2)^2 / (1+r_1)] - 1$

- **What is the expectation hypothesis?**
  Investors set interest rates such that the forward rate over a given period equals the spot rate for that period.

- **What is the liquidity-preference hypothesis?**
  This hypothesis maintains that investors require a risk premium for holding longer-term bonds (i.e. they prefer to be liquid or short-term investors). This implies that the market sets the forward rate for a given period above the expected spot rate for that period.

CONCEPT QUESTIONS - CHAPTER 6

6.1 • **What is the NPV rule?**

• **Why does this rule lead to good investment decisions?**

6.2 • **List the problems of the payback method.**
1. It does not take into account the time value of money.
2. It ignores payments after the payback period.
3. The cutoff period is arbitrary.

• **What are some advantages?**
1. It is simple to implement.
2. It may help in controlling and evaluating managers.

6.4 • **What are the three steps in calculating AAR?**
1. Determine average net income.
2. Determine average investment
3. Divide average net income by average investment.

• **What are some flaws with the AAR approach?**
1. It uses accounting figures.
2. It takes no account of timing.
3. The cutoff period is arbitrary.

6.5 • **How does one calculate the IRR of a project?**
Using either trial-and-error or a financial calculator, one finds the discount rate that produces an NPV of zero.

6.6 • **What is the difference between independent projects and mutually exclusive projects?**
An independent project is one whose acceptance does not affect the acceptance of another. A mutually exclusive project, on the other hand is one whose acceptance precludes the acceptance of another.

• **What are two problems with the IRR approach that apply to both independent and mutually exclusive projects?**
1. The decision rule depends on whether one is investing of financing.
2. Multiple rates of return are possible.

• **What is MIRR?**

• **What are two additional problems applying only to mutually exclusive projects?**
1. The IRR approach ignores issues of scale.

2. The IRR approach does not accommodate the timing of the cash flows properly.

6.7 • How does one calculate a project's profitability index?
Divide the present value of the cash flows subsequent to the initial investment by the initial investment.

• How is the profitability index applied to independent projects, mutually exclusive projects, and situations of capital rationing?
1. With independent projects, accept the project if the PI is greater than 1.0 and reject if less than 1.0.
2. With mutually exclusive projects, use incremental analysis, subtracting the cash flows of project 2 from project 1. Find the PI. If the PI is greater than 1.0, accept project 1. If less than 1.0, accept project 2.
3. In capital rationing, the firm should simply rank the projects according to their respective PIs and accept the projects with the highest PIs, subject to the budget constrain.

CONCEPT QUESTIONS - CHAPTER 7

7.1 • What are the four difficulties in determining incremental cash flows?
1. Sunk costs.
2. Opportunity costs
3. Side effects.
4.

• Define sunk costs, opportunity costs, side effects, and allocated costs.
1. Sunk costs are costs that have already been incurred and that will not be affected by the decision whether to undertake the investment.
2. Opportunity costs are costs incurred by the firm because, if it decides to undertake a project, it will forego other opportunities for using the assets.
3. Side effects appear when a project negatively affects cash flows from other parts of the firm.
4.

7.2 • What are the items leading to cash flow in any year?
Cash flow from operations (revenue-operating costs-taxes) plus cash flow of investment (cost of new machines + changes in net working capital + opportunity costs).

• Why did we determine income when NPV Analysis discounts cash flows, not income?
Because we need to determine how much is paid out in taxes.

- **Why is working capital viewed as a cash outflow?**
  Because increases in working capital must be funded by cash generated elsewhere in the firm.

7.4 • **What is the difference between the nominal and the real interest rate?**
  The nominal interest rate is the real interest rate with a premium for inflation.

- **What is the difference between nominal and real cash flows?**
  Real cash flows are nominal cash flows adjusted for inflation.

7.5 • **What is the equivalent annual cost method of capital budgeting?**
  The decision as to which of various mutually exclusive machines to buy is based on the equivalent annual cost. The EAC is determined by dividing the net present value of costs by an annuity factor that has the same life as the machines. The machine with the lowest EAC should be acquired.

CONCEPT QUESTIONS - CHAPTER 8

8.1 • **What is a decision tree?**
  It is a method to help capital budgeting decision-makers evaluating projects involving sequential decisions. At every point in the tree, there are different alternatives that should be analyzed.

- **How do decision trees handle sequential decisions?**

8.2 • **What is a sensitivity analysis?**
  It is a technique used to determine how the result of a decision changes when some of the parameters or assumptions change.

- **Why is it important to perform a sensitivity analysis?**
  Because it provides an analysis of the consequences of possible prediction or assumption errors.

- **What is a break-even analysis?**
  It is a technique used to determine the volume of production necessary to break even, that is, to cover not only variable costs but fixed costs as well.

- **Describe how sensitivity analysis interacts with break-even analysis.**
  Sensitivity analysis can determine how the financial break-even point changes when some factors (such as fixed costs, variable costs, or revenue) change.

8.4 • **What are the different types of real options?**

- **Why does traditional NPV analysis tend to underestimate the true value of a capital project?**

CONCEPT QUESTIONS - CHAPTER 9

9.1 • **What are the two parts of total return?**
Dividend income and capital gain (or loss)

• **Why are unrealized capital gains or losses included in the calculation of returns?**
Because it is as much a part of returns as dividends, even if the investor decides to hold onto the stock and not to realize the capital gain.

• **What is the difference between a dollar return and a percentage return?**
A dollar return is the amount of money the original investment provided, while percentage return is the percentage of the original investment represented by the total return.

9.2 • **What is the largest one-period return in the 77-year history of common stocks we have displayed, and when did it occur? What is the smallest return, and when did it occur?**
Largest common stock return: 53.99% in 1933. Smallest common stock return: -43.34% in 1931.

• **In how many years did the common stock return exceed 30 percent, and in how many years was it below 20 percent?**
It exceeded 30% in 16 years. It was below 20% in 39 years.

• **For common stocks, what is the longest period of time without a single losing year? What is the longest streak of losing years?**
There are 6 consecutive years of positive returns. The longest losing streak was 4 years.

• **What is the longest period of time such that if you have invested at the beginning of the period, you would still not have had a positive return on your common-stock investment by the end?**
The longest period of time was 14 years (from 1929 to 1942).

9.4 • **What is the major observation about capital markets that we will seek to explain?**
That the return on risky assets has been higher on average than the return on risk-free assets.

• **What does the observation tell us about investors for the period from 1926 through 1994.**
An investor in this period was rewarded for investment in the stock market with an extra or excess return over what would have achieved by simply investing in T-bills.

9.5 • **What is the definition of sample estimates of variance and standard deviation?**
Variance is given by $\text{Var}(R) = (1/(T-1)) \, \Sigma_t (R_t - R)^2$ where T is the number of periods, R_t is the period return and R is the sample mean. Standard deviation is given by $SD = \text{Var}^{1/2}$. For large T, (T-1) may be approximated by T.

• **How does the normal distribution help us interpret standard deviation?**
For a normal distribution, the probability of having a return that is above or below the men by a certain amount only depends on the standard deviation.

CONCEPT QUESTIONS - CHAPTER 10

10.3 • **What are the formulas for the expected return, variance, and standard deviation of a portfolio of two assets?**

$$E\{R_p\} = X_i R_i + X_j R_j$$

$$\text{Var}_p = (X_i^2 (R_i - R_i)^2 + X_j^2 (R_j - R_j)^2 + 2X_i X_j (R_i - R_i)(R_j - R_j)$$

$$SD_p = \text{Var}_p^{1/2}$$

• **What is the diversification effect?**
As long as the correlation coefficient between two securities is less than one, the standard deviation of a portfolio of two securities is less than the weighted average of the standard deviations of the individual securities.

• **What are the highest and lowest possible values for the correlation coefficient?**
+1 and -1.

10.4 • **What is the relationship between the shape of the efficient set for two assets and the correlation between the two assets?**
The less correlation there is between two assets the more the efficient set bends in toward the y-axis.

10.5 • **What is the formula for the variance of a portfolio for many assets?**

$$\text{Var}_p = \sum_{I=1}^{N} \sum_{j=1}^{N} [X_i X_j (R_i - R_i)(R_j - R_j)]$$

• **How can the formula be expressed in terms of a box or matrix?**
The terms on the diagonal of the matrix represent the variances of each term and the off-diagonal elements represent the covariances.

10.6 • **What are the two components of the total risk of a security?**
Portfolio risk and diversifiable risk.

• **Why doesn't diversification eliminate all risk?**
Because the variances of the portfolio asymptotically approaches the portfolio risk. This risk is the covariance of each pair of securities, which always remains.

10.7 • **What is the formula for the standard deviation of a portfolio composed of one riskless and one risky asset?**

$$SD_P = (X_A^2 Var_A)^{1/2} = X_A SD_A \text{ where A is the risky asset}$$

• **How does one determine the optimal portfolio among the efficient set of risky assets?**
This portfolio lies at the point at which a line drawn from the risk-free rate is tangent to the efficient set.

10.8 • **If all investors have homogeneous expectations, what portfolio of risky assets do they hold?**
The market portfolio.

• **What is the formula for beta?**
$B_i = COV(R_i R_m)/Var(R_m)$

• **Why is the beta the appropriate measure of risk for a single security in a large portfolio?**
Because beta measures the contribution of that single security to the variance of the portfolio.

10.9 • **Why is the SML a straight line?**
Because investors could form homemade portfolios that dominate portfolios that don't lie on a straight line. Buying and selling of these portfolios would then drive any outliers back to the line.

• **What is the Capital-Asset-Pricing model?**
The CAPM is a linear model that relates the expected return on an asset to its systematic risk (beta).

• **What are the differences between the capital market line and the security market line?**
The SML relates expected return to beta, while the CML relates expected return to the standard deviation. The SML holds both for all individual securities and for all possible portfolios, whereas the CML holds only for efficient portfolios.

CONCEPT QUESTIONS - CHAPTER 11

11.1• **What are the two basic parts of a return?**
1. The expected part
2. The surprise part

• **Under what conditions will some news have no effect on common stock prices?**
If there is no surprise in the news, there will not be any effect on prices. That is, the news was fully expected.

11.2• **Describe the difference between systematic risk and unsystematic risk.**
A systematic risk is any risk that affects a large number of assets, each to a greater or lesser degree. An unsystematic risk is a risk that specifically affects a single asset or a small group of assets.

• **Why is unsystematic risk sometimes referred to as idiosyncratic risk?**
Because information such as the announcement of a labor strike, may affect only some companies.

11.3 • **What is an inflation beta? A GNP beta? An interest-rate beta?**
An inflation beta is a measure of the sensitivity of a stock's return to changes in the expected inflation rate. A GNP beta measures the sensitivity of a stock's return to changes in the expected GNP. An interest rate beta reflects the sensitivity of a stock's return to changes in the market interest rate.

• **What is the difference between a k-factor model and the market model?**
The main difference is that the market model assumes that only one factor, usually a stock market aggregate, is enough to explain stock returns, while a k-factor model relies on k factors to explain returns.

• **Define the beta coefficient.**
The beta coefficient is a measure of the sensitivity of stock's return to unexpected changes in one factor.

11.4• **How can the return on a portfolio be expressed in terms of a factor model?**
It is the weighted average of expected returns plus the weighted average of each security's beta times a factor F plus the weighted average of the unsystematic risks of the individual securities.

• **What risk is diversified away in a large portfolio?**
The unsystematic risk.

11.5• **What is the relationship between the one-factor model and CAPM?**
Assuming the market portfolio is properly scaled, it can be shown that the one-factor model is identical to the CAPM.

11.7 • **Empirical models are sometimes called factor models. What is the difference between a factor as we have used it previously in this chapter and an attribute as we use it in this section?**

A factor is generally a market wide or industry wide factor proxying the systematic risk. An attribute is related with the returns of the stocks.

• **What is data mining and why might it overstate the relation between some stock attribute and returns?**

Choosing parameters because they have been shown to be related to returns is data mining. The relation found between some attribute and returns can be accidental, thus overstated.

• **What is wrong with measuring the performance of a U.S. growth stock manager against a benchmark composed of English stocks?**

Using a benchmark composed of English stocks is wrong because the stocks included are not of the same style as those in a U.S. growth stock fund.

CONCEPT QUESTIONS - CHAPTER 12

12.2• **What is the disadvantage of using too few observations when estimating beta?**

Small samples can lead to inaccurate estimations.

• **What is the disadvantage of using too many observations when estimating beta?**

Firms may change their industries over time making observations from the distant past out-of-date.

• **What is the disadvantage of using the industry beta as the estimate of the beta of an individual firm?**

The operations of a particular firm may not be similar to the industry average.

12.3• **What are the determinants of equity betas?**
1. The responsiveness of a firm's revenues to economy wide movements.
2. The degree of a firm's operating leverage.
3. The degree of a firm's financial leverage.

• **What is the difference between an asset beta and an equity beta?**
Financial leverage.

12.6 • **What is liquidity?**
Liquidity in this context means the cost of buying and selling stocks. Those stocks that are expensive to trade are considered less liquid.

- **What is the relation between liquidity and expected return?**
  There is a high expected return for illiquid stocks with high trading costs.

- **What is adverse selection?**
  Adverse selection occurs when individuals have ignorance about traits, trends, or other information hidden in a population. For instance, a trader may suffer from adverse selection if certain market knowledge is hidden from him but is available to some investors.

- **What can a corporation do to lower its cost of capital?**
  A corporation can be proactive in taking actions that will lower trading costs, thereby lowering its cost of capital.

CONCEPT QUESTIONS - CHAPTER 13

13.1• **List the three ways financing decisions can create value.**
1. Fool investors
2. Reduce costs or increase subsidies
3. Create a new security

13.2 • **Can you define an efficient market?**
It is a market where current prices reflect all available information.

- **Name the three foundations of market efficiencies?**

13.3 • **Can you describe the three forms of the efficient-market hypotheses?**
1. Weak-from EMH postulates that prices reflect all information contained in the past history of prices.
2. Semistrong form EMH says that prices not only reflect the history of prices but all publicly available information.
3. Strong form EMH contends that prices reflect all available information, public and private (or "inside").

- **Does market efficiency mean you can throw darts at a Wall Street Journal listing of New York Stock Exchange stocks to pick a portfolio.**
  No. All it says is that, on average, a portfolio manager will not be able to achieve excess returns on a risk-adjusted basis.

- **What does it mean to say the price you pay for a stock is fair?**
  It means that the stock has been priced taking into account all publicly available information.

13.5 • **What do representativeness and conservatisim mean?**

- **What are the risks involved in arbitrage?**

13.6 • Name five empirical challenges to market efficiency.

13.8 • What are the four implications of market efficiency for corporate finance?

CONCEPT QUESTIONS - CHAPTER 14

14.1• What is a company's book value?
It is the sum of the par value, capital surplus and accumulated retained earnings.

• **What rights do stockholders have?**
 1. Voting rights for board members
 2. Proxy rights
 3. Asset Participation in case of liquidation
 4. Voting rights for mergers and acquisitions
 5. Preemptive rights to new shares issued.

• **What is a proxy?**
It is the grant of authority by a shareholder to someone else to vote his or her shares.

14.2• What is corporate debt? Describe its general features.
Corporate debt is a security issued by corporations as a result of borrowing money and represents something that must be repaid. Its main features are:
 1. It does not represent ownership interest in the firm.
 2. Payment of interest on debt is tax deductible because it is considered a cost of doing business.
 3. Unpaid debt is a liability of the firm.

• **Why is it sometimes difficult to tell whether a particular security is debt or equity?**
Because it has characteristics that are particular to both. Companies are very adept at creating hybrid securities that are considered debt by the IRS but have equity features.

14.3• What is a preferred stock?
It is a security that has preference over common stock in the payment of dividends and in the distribution of assets in the case of liquidation.

• **Do you think it is more like debt or equity?**
Preferred stock is similar to both debt and common equity. Preferred shareholders receive a stated dividend only, and if the corporation is liquidated, preferred receive a stated dividend only, and if the corporation is liquidated,

preferred stockholders get a stated value. However, unpaid preferred dividends are not debts of a company and preferred dividends not a tax deductible business expense.

- **What are three reasons why preferred stock is issued?**
  1. Because of the way utility rates are determined in regulatory environments, regulated public utilities can pass the tax disadvantage of issuing preferred stock on to their customers.
  2. Companies reporting losses to the IRS may issue preferred stock.
  3. Firms issuing preferred stock can avoid the threat of bankruptcy that exists that debt financing.

14.4 • **What is the difference between internal financing and external financing?**
Internal financing comes from internally generated cash flows and does not require the issuing securities.

- **What are the major sources of corporate financing?**
  1. Internal financing
  2. External financing (new long-term borrowing, equity)

- **What factors influence a firm's choices of external versus internal equity financing?**
  1. The general economic environment, specifically, business cycles.
  2. The level of stock prices
  3. The availability of positive NPV projects.

- **What pecking order can be observed in the historical patterns of long-term financing?**
The first form of financing is internally generated funds, then external financing; debt is used before equity.

CONCEPT QUESTIONS - CHAPTER 15

15.1 • **What is the pie model of capital structure?**
It is a model in which the value of the firm is pictured as a pie cut into debt and equity slices.

15.2 • **Why should financial managers choose the capital structure that maximizes the value of the firm.**
Because this capital structure also maximizes the value of equity.

15.3 • **Describe financial leverage.**
It is the extent to which a company relies on debt in its capital structure.

- **What is levered equity?**
  The equity of a firm that has debt in its capital structure.

- **How can a shareholder of Trans Am undo the company's financial leverage?**
  By selling shares of Trans Am and buying bonds or investing the proceeds in another company's debt.

15.4 • **Why does the expected return on equity risk with firm leverage?**
  Because increasing leverage raises the risk of equity.

- **What is the exact relationship between the expected return on equity and firm leverage?**
  $R_s = r_o + (r_o - r_b) (B/S)$

- **How are market-value balance sheets set up?**
  They are set up the same way as accounting balance sheets with assets on the left side and liabilities on the right side. However, instead of valuing assets in terms of historical values, market values are used.

15.5 • **What is the quirk in the tax code making a levered firm more valuable than an otherwise-identical unlevered firm?**
  Interest payments are tax deductible and dividend payments are not.

- **What is MM Proposition under corporate taxes?**
  $V_L = V_U + T_C B$

- **What MM Proposition II under corporate taxes?**
  $r_s = p + (B/S)(1 - T_c)(p - r_B)$

CONCEPT QUESTIONS - CHAPTER 16

16.1 • **What does risk-neutrality mean?**
  Investors are indifferent to the presence of risk.

- **Can one have bankruptcy risk without bankruptcy costs?**
  Yes. When a firm takes on debt the risk of bankruptcy is always present but bankruptcy cost may not be.

- **Why do we say that stockholders bear bankruptcy costs?**
  Because in the presence of bankruptcy costs, bondholders would pay less for any debt issued. This then will reduce the value of potential future dividends.

16.2 • **What is the main direct cost of financial distress?**
  Legal and administrative costs of liquidation or reorganization.

- **What are the indirect costs of financial distress?**
  Those that arise because of an impaired ability to conduct business.

- **Who pays the costs of selfish strategies**?
  Ultimately, the stockholders.

16.4 • **List all the claims to the firm's assets.**
  Payments to stockholders and bondholders, payments to the government, payments to lawyers, and payments to any al all other claimants to the cash flows of the firm.

- **Describe marketed claims and nonmarketed claims.**
  Marketed claims are claims that can be sold or bought in capital markets. Nonmarketed claims are claims that cannot be sold in capital markets.

- **How can a firm maximize the value of its marketed claims?**
  By minimizing the value of nonmarketed claims such as taxes.

16.5 • **Do managers have an incentive to fool investors by issuing additional debt?**

16.6 • **What are agency costs?**
  Costs that arise from conflicts of interest between managers bondholders and stockholders.

- **Is there a cost to issuing additional debt?**

- **Why are shirking and perquisites considered an agency cost of equity?**
  Because managers will act in their own best interests rather than those of shareholders.

- **What empirical evidence suggests that managers signal information through debt levels?**

- **How do agency costs of equity affect the firm's debt-equity ratio?**
  The optimal debt-equity ratio is higher in a world with agency costs than in a world without such costs.

- **What is the Free Cash Flow Hypothesis?**
  We might expect to see more wasteful activity in a firm capable of generating large cash flows.

16.7 • **What is the pecking-order theory?**
  This theory states that when a firm seeks new capital it faces 'timing' issues of new stock.

- **What are the problems of issuing equity according to this theory?**
  The theory implies that only overvalued firms have an incentive to issue equity and given market reactions to a stock issue, virtually no firm will issue equity. The model results in firms being financed virtually entirely by debt. Moderating the pure theory and we would predict that debt should be issued before equity.

- **What is financial slack?**
  If a firm expects to fund a profitable project in the future it will start to accumulate a cash reservoir today, thus avoiding the need to go to the capital markets.

16.8 • **How do growth opportunities decrease the advantage of debt financing?**
  Growth implies significant equity financing, even in a world with low bankruptcy costs. To eliminate the potential increasing tax liability resulting from growing EBIT, the firm would want to issue enough debt so that interest equals EBIT. Any further increase in debt would, however, lower the value of the firm in a world with bankruptcy costs.

16.10 • **List the empirical regularities we observe for corporate capital structure?**
  1. Most corporations have low debt ratios.
  2. Changes in financial leverage affect firm value.
  3. There are differences in the capital structure of different industries.

- **What are the factors to consider in establishing a debt-equity ratio?**
  1. Taxes
  2. Financial distress costs
  3. Pecking order and financial slack.

CONCEPT QUESTIONS - CHAPTER 17

17.1 • **How is the APV method applied?**
  APV is equal to the NPV of the project (i.e. the value of the project for an unlevered firm) plus the NPV of financing side effects.

- **What additional information beyond NPV does one need to calculate A|PV?**
  NPV of financing side effects (NPVF)>

17.2 • **How is the FTE Method applied?**
  FTE calls for the discounting of the cash flows of a project to the equity holder at the cost of equity capital.

- What information is needed to calculate FTE?
  Levered cash flow and the cost of equity capital.

17.3 • How is the WACC method applied?
WACC calls for the discounting of unlevered cash flows of a project (UCF) at the weighted average cost of capital, WACC.

17.4 • What is the main difference between AAPV and WACC?
WACC is based upon a target debt rate and APV is based upon the level of debt.

• What is the main difference between the FTE approach and the two other approaches?
FTE uses levered cash flow and other methods use unlevered cash flow.

• When should the APV method be used?
When the level of debt is known in each future period.

• When should the FTE and WACC approaches be used?
When the target debt ratio is known.

CONCEPT QUESTIONS - CHAPTER 18

18.2 • Describe the procedure of a dividend payment.
1. Dividends are declared: The board of directors passes a resolution to pay dividends.
2. Date of record: Preparation of the list of shareholders entitled to dividends.
3. Ex-Dividend date: A date before the date of record when the brokerage firm entitles stockholders to receive the dividend if they buy before this date.
4. Date of payment: Dividend checks are sent to stockholders.

• Why should the price of a stock change when it goes ex-dividend?
Because in essence the firm is reducing its value by the amount paid out in cash for the dividend.

18.3 • How can an investor make homemade dividends?
By selling shares of the stock.

• Are dividends irrelevant?
If we consider a perfect capital market, dividend policy, and therefore the timing of dividend payout, should be irrelevant.

• What assumptions are needed to show that dividend policy is irrelevant?
1. Perfect markets exist.
2. Investors have homogeneous expectations
3. This investment policy of the firm is fixed.

18.4 • In a perfect capital market are repurchases preferred to dividends?

• What are five reasons for preferring repurchases to dividends in the real world?

18.5 • List four alternatives to paying a dividend with excess cash.

• Indicate a problem with each of these alternatives.

18.6 • What are the real-world factors favoring a high-dividend policy?
1. Desire for current income
2. Resolution of uncertainty
3. Brokerage and other transactions costs
4. Fear of consumption out of principal

18.7 • What are tax clienteles?
Different types of shareholders that prefer one kind of dividend policy due to difference in tax brackets.

CONCEPT QUESTIONS - Appendix to Chapter 18

• **What is a stock dividend? A stock split?**
Stock dividend is a dividend in the form of stocks. In a stock split, each shareholder receives additional shares of stock for each one held originally.

• **What is the value of a stock dividend and a stock split?**
It can be positive, zero or negative. The possible benefits are lowered commission in stock trades within the proper trading range. The costs are related to the financial procedures.

CONCEPT QUESTIONS - CHAPTER 19

19.1 • **Describe the basic procedures in a new issue.**
1. Obtain approval of the Board of Directors.
2. File registration statement with the SEC
3. Distribute prospectus
4. Determine offer price
5. Place tombstone advertisements.

• **What is a registration statement?**
A document filed with the SEC containing information relevant to the offering.

19.3 • **Describe a firm commitment underwriting and a best-efforts underwriting.**
In a firm commitment underwriting, the underwriter buys the entire issue and then resells it. In a best efforts underwriting, the underwriter is only legally bound to use "best efforts" to sell the securities at the agreed upon offering price.

   • **Suppose that a stockholder calls you up out of the blue and offers to sell you some shares of a new issue. Do you think the issue will do better or worse than average?**
   It will probably do worse because otherwise it would have been oversold and there would be no need for the broker to try to sell it to you.

19.4 • **What are some reasons that the price of stock drops on the announcement of a new equity issue?**
   1. Managers are disinclined to issue stock when the share price is below their estimate of intrinsic value. Equity offerings signal that management considers the share price high.
   2. Equity offerings are more likely when the firm is over-levered.

19.5 • **Describe the costs of a new issue of common stock.**
   1. Spread: The difference between the offering price and what the underwriter pays the issuing company.
   2. Other direct expenses: Filing fees, legal fees and taxes.
   3. Indirect expenses: Management time spent analyzing the issuance.
   4. Abnormal returns: The drop in the current stock price by 1% to 2% in a seasoned new issue of stock.
   5. Underpricing: Setting the offering price below the correct value in an initial new issue of stock.
   6. Green shoe option: The underwriter's right to buy additional shares at the offer price to cover overallotments.

   • **What conclusions emerge from an analysis of Table 19.5?**
   1. There are substantial financial economies of scale.
   2. Direct costs are somewhat greater than indirect ones.
   3. Higher costs for best efforts offers.
   4. More underpricing for firm commitment than for best efforts offers.
   5. Both direct and indirect costs are higher for initial offerings than for seasoned ones.

19.6 • **Describe the details of a rights offering.**
In a rights offering, each shareholder is issued an option to buy a specified number of shares from the firm at a specified price within a certain time frame. These rights are often traded on securities exchanges or over the counter.

- **What are the questions that financial management must answer in a rights offerings?**

  1. What price should existing shareholders pay for a share of new stock?
  2. How many rights will be required to purchase one share of stock?
  3. What effect will the rights offering have on the price of the existing stock?

- **How is the value of a right determined?**
  Value of one right
  = Rights-on stock price - ex-rights stock price
  = (Ex-rights price - Subscription price) / (rights/share)
  = (Rights-on price - Subscription price) / (rights/share+1)

19.7 • **What are the several kinds of dilution?**
  1. Dilution of ownership
  2. Dilution of market value
  3. Dilution of book value

- **Is dilution important?**
  True dilution, of ownership or market value, is very important because it is an economic loss to current shareholders. Book value dilution, on the other hand, is irrelevant.

- **Why might a firm prefer a general cash offering to a rights offering?**
  1. Underwriters provide insurance regarding the amount raised by the firm regardless of true stock value.
  2. Proceeds are available sooner.
  3. Underwriters will provide wider distribution of ownership
  4. Underwriters provide consulting advice.

19.8 • **Describe shelf registration.**
  It is registration allowed by Rule 415 of the SEC whereby a corporation registers stock that will be sold within two years of registration.

- **What are the arguments against shelf registration?**
  1. The costs of new issues might go up because underwriters may be unable to provide as much information to potential investors as would be true otherwise.
  2. It may cause "market overhand" which will depress market prices.

19.9 • **What are the different sources of venture-capital financing?**
  Private partnerships and corporations, large industrial or financial corporation, and wealthy families and individuals.

- **What are the different stages for companies seeking venture capital financing?**

  Seed money, start-up, and then first through fourth round financing as the company gets off the ground.

- **What is the private equity market?**

  The private equity market involves the issuance of securities to a small number of private investors or certain qualified institutional investors.

- **What is Rule 144A?**

  Rule 144A establishes a legal framework for the issuance of private securities to qualified institutional investors.

CONCEPT QUESTIONS - CHAPTER 20

20.2 • **Do bearer bonds have any advantage? Why might Mr. "I Like to Keep My Affairs Private" prefer to hold bearer bonds?**

  They have the advantage of secrecy.

- **What advantages and what disadvantages do bondholders derive from provisions of sinking funds?**

  They provide additional security as an early warning system if sinking fund payments are not made. But if interest rates are high, the company will buy the bonds from the market, and if rates are low, it will use the lottery, exercising an option that makes sinking fund bonds less attractive to bondholders.

- **What is a call provision? What is the difference between the call price and the stated price?**

  It is an option that allows the company after a certain number of years to repurchase the bonds at the call price. This option will only be exercised if interest rates drop. The difference between the call price and the stated price is the call premium.

20.3 • **What the advantages to a firm of having a call provision?**

  If interest rates go down and the market bond prices are higher than the call price, the firm can exercise its call option and buy the bonds at less than the market price.

- **What are the disadvantages to bondholders of having a call provision?**

  If the firm decides to exercise its option, bondholders will have to sell their bonds to the firm at less than the market price.

20.4 • **List and describe the different bond rating classes.**
1. Investment grade |AAA/Aaa to BBB/Baa: extremely strong to adequate capacity to pay interest and principal.
2. Speculative BB/Ba to CC/Ca: slightly to extremely speculative capacity to pay interest and principle.
3. C: Debt not currently paying interest
4. D: Debt in default.

• **Why don't bond prices change when bond ratings change?**
The bond ratings are based on publicly available information and therefore may not provide information that the market did not have before the change.

• **Are the costs of bond issues related to their ratings?**
Investment –grade issues have much lower direct costs than non-investment grade issues.

20.5 • **Create an idea of an unusual bond and analyze its features**.
The text provides an example of an unusual bond; income bonds are a hybrid between debt and equity. For the firm interest is tax deductible, but the payment depends on income rather than being fixed. This feature makes it riskier than normal bonds, and although the tax deductibility may make them appear cheaper, the market prices them according to risk as well.

20.6 • **What are the differences between private and public bond issues?**
1. Direct private placement of long-term debt does not require SEC registration.
2. Direct placement is more likely to have more restrictive covenants.
3. Distribution costs are lower for private bonds.
4. It is easier to renegotiate a private placement because there are fewer investors.

• **A private placement is more likely to have restrictive covenants than is a public issue. Why?**
It is arranged between a firm and a few financial institutions, such as banks or insurance companies, that are very much interested in avoiding the transfer of wealth from them to stockholders. It is easier for a few financial institutions to renegotiate restrictive covenants if circumstances change.

CONCEPT QUESTIONS – CHAPTER 21

21.1 • **What are some reasons that assets like automobiles would be leased with operating leases, whereas machines or real estate would be leased with financial leases?**
1. Operating leases have a cancellation option that protects the lessee from technological obsolescence in the case of equipment.

2. The service provided by the lessor in an operating lease eliminates the problem of retraining employees to service the new equipment or the problem of repairs in the case of a person leasing a car.

- **What are the differences between an operating lease and a financial lease?**
  1. Operating leases are not fully amortized.
  2. In an operating lease the lessor maintains and insures the leased asset. With financial leases the lessee must do both himself.
  3. Operating leases have a cancellation option.

21.2 • Define capital lease.

Capital leases meet at least one of the following:
1. Transfer of ownership by the end of the lease term.
2. Bargain purchase price option.
3. Lease term at least 75 percent of asset's economic life.
4. PV (lease payments) at least 90 percent of asset's fair value.

- **Define operating lease.**

  "Operating lease" is a general term applied to leases which are typically not fully amortized, are maintained by the lessor, and have a cancellation option.

21.3• What are the IRS guidelines for treating a lease contract as a lease for tax purposes?

Very generally, the guidelines are set up to identify lease contracts which are purely a tax dodge.

21.5 • How should one discount a riskless cash flow?

At the after-tax riskless interest rate.

21.9 • Summarize the good and bad arguments for leasing.

Good Arguments:
a. Leasing reduces taxes because firms are in different tax bracket.
b. Leasing reduces uncertainty by eliminating the residual value risk.
c. Leasing lowers transactions costs by reducing the changes of ownership of an asset over its useful life.

Bad Arguments:
a. Leasing improves accounting income and the balance sheet if leases are kept off the books.
b. Leasing provides 100% financing, but secured equipment loans require an initial down payment.
c. There are special reasons like government appropriations for acquisitions and circumventing bureaucratic firms.

CONCEPT QUESTIONS - CHAPTER 22

22.2 • What is a call option?
A call option is a contract that gives the owner the right to buy an asset at a fixed price within a certain time period.

• How is a call option's price related to the underlying stock price at the expiration date?
If the stock is "in the money" (above the striking price), stock price and option price are linearly related. If it's "out of the money", the call option is worthless.

22.3 • What is a put option?
A put option is a contract that gives the owner the right to sell an asset at a fixed price within a certain time period.

• How is a put option related to the underlying stock price at expiration date?
If the stock is "in the money" (below the striking price), stock price and option price are linearly related. If it's "out of the money", the put option is worthless.

22.6 • What is a put-call parity?
The theorem says that because a call's payoff is the same as payoffs from a combination of buying a put, buying the underlying stock and borrowing at the risk-free rate, the call and the combination should be equally priced.

22.7 • List the factors that determine the value of options?
1. Exercise price
2. Maturity
3. Price of the underlying asset
4. Variability of the underlying asset
5. Interest rate

• Why does a stock's variability affect the value of options written on it?
The more variable the stock the higher the possibility that it will go over the exercise price in the case of a call or under the exercise price in the case of a put. The variability increases the changes of the stocks price extremes.

22.8 • How does the two-state option model work?
It uses the fact that buying call can be made equivalent to buying the stock and borrowing to determine option value.

• What is the formula for the Black-Scholes option-pricing model?
$C = S_o N(d_1) - E e^{-rft} dN(d_2)$

Where $d_1 = [\ln(S/E) + d(r_f + (1/2)\sigma^2)^t] / (\sigma^2 t)^{1/2}$

$d_2 = d_1 - (\sigma^2 t)^{1/2}$

22.9 • **How can the value of the firm be expressed in terms of call options?**
Bondholders own the firm and have written a call to stockholders with an exercise price equal to the promised interest payment.

• **How can the value of the firm be expressed in terms of put options?**
Stockholders own the firm and have purchased a put option from the bondholders with an exercise price equal to the promised interest payment.

• **How does put-call parity relate these two expressions?**
A call option's payoff is the same as the payoff from a combination of buying a put, buying the underlying stock and borrowing at the risk-free rate. Consequently, puts and calls can always be stated in terms of the other.

22.12 • **Why are the hidden options in projects valuable?**
Even the best laid plans of men and mice often go astray. The option to adapt plans to new circumstances is a valuable asset.

CONCEPT QUESTIONS - CHAPTER 23

23.1 • **Why do companies issue options to executives of they cost the company more than they are worth to the executive? Why not just give cash and split the difference? Wouldn't that make both the company and executive better off?**
One of the purposes to give stock options to CEOs (instead of cash) is to bond the performance of the firm's stock with the compensation of the CEO. In this way, the CEO has an incentive to increase shareholder value.

23.2 • **What are the two options that many businesses have?**
Most businesses have the option to abandon under bad conditions and the option to expand under good conditions.

• **Why does a strict NPV calculation typically understate the value of a firm or a project?**
Virtually all projects have embedded options, which are ignored in NPV calculations and likely leads to undervaluation.

CONCEPT QUESTIONS - CHAPTER 24

24.2 • **What is the key difference between a warrant and a traded call options?**
When a warrant is exercised, the number of shares increases. Also, the Warrant is an option sold by the firm.

- **Why does dilution occur when warrants are exercised?**
  Because additional shares of stock are sold to warrant holders at a below market price.

- **How can the firm hurt warrant holders?**
  The firm can hurt warrant holders by taking any action that reduces the value of the stock. A typical example would be the payment of abnormally high dividends.

24.4 • **What are the conversion ratio, the conversion price, and the conversion premium?**
  The conversion ratio is the number of shares received for each debenture. The conversion price is equivalent to the price which the holders of convertible bonds pay for each share of common stock they receive. The conversion premium is the excess of the conversion price over the common stock price.

24.5 • **What three elements make up the value of a convertible bond.**
  Convertible bond value = Greater of (straight bond value and conversion value) plus option value.

- **Describe the payoff structure of convertible bonds?**
  It is the value of the firm if the value of the firm is less than total face value. It is the face value if the total face value is less that the value of the firm but greater than its conversion value. It is the conversion value if the value of the firm and the conversion value are greater than total face value.

24.6 • **What is wrong with the simple view that it is cheaper to issue a bond with a warrant or a convertible feature because the required coupon is lower?**
  In an efficient capital market the difference between the market value of a convertible bond and the value of straight bond is the fair price investors pay for the call option that the convertible or the warrant provides.

- **What is wrong with the Free Lunch story?**
  This story compares convertible financing to straight debt when the price falls and to common stock when price rises.

- **What is wrong with the Expensive Lunch story?**

24.7 • **Why do firms issue convertible bonds?**
  1. To match cash flows, that is, they issue securities whose cash flows match those of the firm.
  2. To bypass assessing the risk of the company (risk synergy). The risk of company start-ups is hard to evaluate.
  3. To reduce agency costs associated with raising money by providing a package that reduces bondholder-stockholder conflicts.

24.8 • **Why will convertible bonds not be voluntarily converted to stock before expiration?**
Because the holder of the convertible has the option to wait and perhaps do better than what is implied by current stock prices.

• **When should firms force conversion of convertibles? Why?**
Theoretically conversion should be forced as soon as the conversion value reaches the call price because other conversion policies will reduce shareholder value. If conversion is forced when conversion values are above the call price, bondholders will be allowed to exchange less valuable bonds for more valuable common stock. In the opposite situation, shareholders are giving bondholders the excess value.

CONCEPT QUESTIONS – CHAPTER 25

25.1 • **What is a forward contract?**
An agreement to trade at a set price in the future.

• **Give examples of forward contracts in your life.**
A forward contract is formed when you contract an artisan to construct a banjo and agree to pay him $1,200 on delivery.

25.2 • **What is a futures contract?**
Futures contracts are like forward contracts except that:
1. They are traded on organized exchanges.
2. They let the seller choose when to make delivery on any day during the delivery month.
3. They are marked to market daily.

• **How is a futures contract related to a forward contract?**
In both contracts, it is the obligation of both the buyer and seller to settle the contract at the future date.

• **Why do exchanges require futures contracts to be marked to the market?**
Because there is no accumulation of loss, the mark to the market convention reduces the risk of default.

25.3 • **Define short and long hedges.**
A short futures hedge involves selling a futures contract. A long futures hedge involves buying a futures contract.

• **Under what circumstances is each of the two hedges used?**
Short hedges are used when you will be making delivery at a future date and wish to minimize the risk of a drop in price. Long hedges are used when you must purchase at a future date and wish to minimize the risk of a rise in price.

- **What is a rolling stock strategy?**
  A rolling stock strategy involves buying a short-term futures contract and simultaneously selling a long-term futures contract. After the short-term elapses, the rolling stock involves buying another short-term futures contract. The strategy is implemented over a series of short-term contracts.

25.4 • **How are forward contracts on bonds priced?**
  The same as any other cash flow stream – as the sum of discounted cash flows:
  $$P_{\text{FORW.CONT}} = (1 + r_1)[\sum_{t=1} (I_t/(1+r_t)^t + PAR/(1 + r_T)^T]$$

- **What are the differences between forward contracts on bonds and futures contracts on bonds?**
  Futures contracts on bonds have the following characteristics:
  1. They are traded on organized exchanges.
  2. The seller can make delivery on any day during the month.
  3. They are marked to market daily.

- **Give examples of hedging with futures contracts on bonds.**
  Your partnership has just leased commercial space in a downtown hotel to a department store chain. The lessee has agreed to pay $1 million per year for 8 years. You can hedge the risk of a rise in inflation (and hence a fall in the value of the lease contract) over this period by forming a short hedge in the T-bond futures market.

25.5 • **What is duration?**
  The weighted average maturity of a cash flow stream in present value terms.

- **How is the concept of duration used to reduce interest rate risk?**
  By matching the duration of financial assets and liabilities, a change in interest rates has the same impact on them value of the assets and liabilities.

25.6 • **Show that a currency swap is equivalent to a series of forward contracts.**
  Assume the swap is for five year at a fixed term of 100 million DM for $50 million each year. This is equivalent to a series of forward contracts. In year one, for example, it is equivalent to a one-year forward contract of 100 million DM at 2 DM/$.

CONCEPT QUESTIONS – CHAPTER 26

26.2 • **What is the difference between net working capital and cash?**
  Net working capital includes not only cash, but also other current assets minus current liabilities.

- **Will net working capital always increase when cash increases?**
  No. There are transactions such as collection of accounts receivable that increase cash but leave net working capital unchanged. Any transaction that will increase cash but produce a corresponding decrease in another current asset account or an increase in a current liability will have the same effect.

- **List the potential uses of cash.**
  1. Acquisition of capital
  2. Acquisition of marketable securities
  3. Acquisition of working capital
  4. Payment of dividends
  5. Retirement of debt
  6. Payment for labor, management and services rendered

- **List the potential sources of cash.**
  1. Sale of services or merchandise
  2. Collection of accounts receivable
  3. Issuance of debt or stock
  4. Sale of marketable securities
  5. Sale of fixed assets
  6. Short-term bank loans
  7. Increased accrued expenses, wages, or taxes.

26.3• **What does it mean to say that a firm has an inventory-turnover ratio of four?**
  It means that on average the inventory is kept on hand for (365 days per year/4 times per year) = 91.25 days.

• **Describe operating cycle and cash cycle. What are the differences between them?**
  The operating cycle is the period of time from the acquisition of raw material until the collection of cash from sales. It includes conversion of raw materials into finished goods, inventories, sales and collection of accounts receivable. The cash cycle is the period of time from the cash payment for raw materials to the collection of cash. The difference between the two is the accounts payable stage, the time between the acquisition of raw materials and the cash payment for them.

26.4• **What keeps the real world from being an ideal on where net working capital could always be zero?**
  A long-term rise is sales level will result in permanent investment in current assets. In addition, any day-to-day and month-to-month fluctuation in the level of sales will produce a nonzero NWC.

- **What considerations determine the optimal compromise between flexible and restrictive net-working-capital policies?**
  1. Cash reserves: How much cash does management want?
  2. Matching of asset and liability maturity (maturity hedging)
  3. Term structure: The difference between short-term and long-term interest rates

26.5 • **How would you conduct a sensitivity analysis for Fun Toys' net cash balance?**
By determining the net cash balance under different scenario assumptions – changing factors that will affects net cash balance and figuring out the result.

- **What could you learn from such an analysis?**
  It will give you an idea of what the range of net cash balances will be under the different scenarios and how sensitive the net cash balance is to each of the factors that affect it.

26.6 • **What are the two basic forms of short-term financing?**
Unsecured bank borrowing and secured bank borrowing.

- **Describe two types of secured loans.**
  1. Accounts receivable financing. In this type of borrowing, accounts receivable are either assigned or factored. In the latter case receivables are actually sold at a discount.
  2. Trust receipt. This is one of the three types of inventory loans in which the borrower holds the inventory in "trust" for the lender.

CONCEPT QUESTIONS – CHAPTER 27

27.1 • **What is the transactions motive, and how does it lead firms to hold cash?**
It is the necessity to hold cash for disbursements to pay wages, trade debts, taxes and dividends. A firm that does not have cash for these transactions will not be able to meet its obligations. Because cash inflows and outflows are seldom synchronized, firms need cash balances to serve as a buffer.

- **What is a compensating balance?**
  It is the amount of cash banks require firms to keep permanently in their accounts to compensate the bank for services rendered.

27.2 • **What is a target cash balance?**
It is a firm's desired level of cash holdings to satisfy the transactions and compensating balance needs.

- **What are the strengths and weaknesses of the Baumol model and the Miller-Orr model?**

  The Baumol model is a very simple and straightforward model with sensible conclusions, but it assumes a constant disbursement rate, lack of cash receipts during the projected period, and makes no allowance for "safety stock." It also assumes discrete, certain cash flows. The Miller-Orr model improves the understanding of the problem by determining the relationships among the different variables, but it neglects other factors that affect the target cash balance.

27.3 • **Describe collection and disbursement float.**

  Collection float is the time that elapses from the moment the customer mails the payment until cash is received. Disbursement float is the time that elapses from the moment a company mails a check and the time cash is withdrawn from the company's bank account.

- **What are lockboxes? Concentration banks? Wire transfers?**

  Lockboxes are postal boxes strategically located in such a way that the mailing time from customers to the box is minimized. The firm's bank has direct access to the boxes, and thus in-house handling is eliminated and collection float is reduced. Concentration banks are regional banks in which the company has accounts and to which it sends excess cash at the end of the day. In this fashion checks obtained from nearby customers can be collected daily. Wire transfers are electronic transfers of surplus funds from local deposit banks to concentration banks.

- **Suppose an overzealous financial manager writes checks on uncollected funds. Aside from legal issues, who is the financial loser in this situation?**

  The bank where the firm has its accounts.

27.4 • **Why do firms find themselves with idle cash?**

  To finance seasonal or cyclical activities (transactions motive), to finance planned expenditures (investment motive), and to provide for unanticipated contingencies (precautionary motive).

- **What are the types of money-market securities?**

CONCEPT QUESTIONS - CHAPTER 28

28.1 • **What considerations enter into the determination of the terms of sale?**
  1. Probability of non-payment
  2. Size of the account
  3. Perishability of goods
  4. Industry standards and competition
  5. Standard speed of collection
  6. Price of the goods

28.2 • **List the factors that influence the decision to grant credit.**
1. The delayed revenues from granting credit
2. The immediate cost of granting credit
3. The probability of non-payment
4. The appropriate required rate of return for delayed cash flows.

28.4 • **What is credit analysis?**
It is the process of trying to determine the probability that a customer will default. It involves:
a. gathering relevant information, and
b. determining creditworthiness

• **What are the five Cs of credit?**
Character, capacity, capital, collateral, conditions.

28.5 • **What tools can a manager use to analyze a collection policy?**
Average collection period, the aging schedule, and the payments pattern.

CONCEPT QUESTIONS - CHAPTER 29

29.1 • **What is a merger? How does a merger differ from other forms of acquisition?**
A merger is the absorption of one firm by another, where the acquiring firm retains its identity and the acquired firm ceases to exist. It differs from other forms of acquisition in that no new firm is created, and there is no need of buying the individual assets of the acquired firm or its stock.

• **What is a takeover?**
It is the transference of control of a firm from one group of shareholders to another by means of a majority vote of the board of directors.

29.8 • **Why can a merger create the appearance of earnings growth?**
If a high price-earnings ratio company acquires a low price-earnings company, the market might assume that the price-earnings ratio does not change.

29.10 •**What can a firm do to make a takeover less likely**?
1. It can change the corporate charter by requiring a higher percentage of share approval for a merger or staggering the election of board members.
2. It can engage in standstill agreements (greenmail).
3. It can make an exclusionary self-tender
4. It can provide golden parachutes to top executives
5. It can sell major assets, i.e., the "crown jewels".

6.   It can use "poison pills".

29.11 •What does the evidence say about the benefits of mergers and acquisitions?
It says that they usually benefit the shareholders of the acquired firm but do not significantly affect the shareholders of the acquiring firm. In terms of the new entity, a monopoly power can be created.

29.12 •Can you describe a Keiretsu?
Networks of Japanese firms usually affiliated around a large bank, industrial firm, or trading firm.

• What is a benefit of Keiretsu?
To reduce the costs of financial distress.

CONCEPT QUESTIONS - CHAPTER 30

30.1 • Can you describe financial distress?
It is a situation where operating cash flows at a firm are not sufficient to satisfy current obligations and the firm is forced to take corrective action.

• What are stock based insolvency and flow based insolvency?
Stock based insolvency occurs when a firm has negative net worth. Flow based insolvency occurs when a firm has a short fall in cash flow.

30.2 • Why doesn't financial distress always cause firms to die?
Financial restructuring may make a firm worth more"alive than dead".

• What is a benefit of financial distress?
It can serve as an early warning system or "wake up call.

30.3 • What is bankruptcy?
Legal bankruptcy occurs when a firm files for bankruptcy under chapter 7 (liquidations) or chapter 11 (reorganization). 1 the Bankruptcy Reform Act, 1978.

• What is the difference between liquidation and reorganization?
Liquidation occurs when the assets of a firm are sold and payments are made to creditors (usually based upon the APR). Reorganization is the restricting of the firm's finances.

30.4 • What are two ways a firm can restructure its finances?
Private workouts may be more expensive because of complex capital structure or conflicts of interest.

- **Why do firms use formal bankruptcy?**
  Equity holdouts
  Private workouts may be more expensive because of complex capital structure or conflicts of interest.

30.5 • **What is a prepackaged bankruptcy?**
  A situation where the firm and most of all creditors agree to a private reorganization before bankruptcy takes place. After the private agreement, the firm files for formal bankruptcy.

- **What is the main benefit of prepackaged bankruptcy?**
  Revco's complicated capital structure.

CONCEPT QUESTIONS - CHAPTER 31

31.1 • **What is the difference between a Eurobond and a foreign bond?**
  A Eurobond is issued by a foreign country, denominated in the currency of its country of origin and sold in a different country. A foreign bond is denominated in the currency of the country in which it is sold, although it is issued by a company from another country.

31.3 • **What is the law of one price? What is purchasing-power parity?**
  The law of one price is the simplest version of PPP. It states that a commodity will cost the same regardless of what currency is used to purchase it. PPP says that different currencies represent different purchasing powers, and the exchange rate adjusts to keep the purchasing power constant.

- **What is the relationship between inflation and exchange-rate movements?**
  This relationship is called "relative purchasing power parity" and states that the rate of inflation in one country relative to the inflation rate in another country determines the rate of change of the exchange rate of the currencies of the two countries.

31.4 • **What is the interest-rate-parity theorem?**
  It is a theorem that implies that if interest rates are higher in one country than another, the latter country's currency will sell at a premium in the forward market. In this way money earns the same regardless of what currency it is invested in.

- **Why is the forward rate related to the expected future spot rate?**
  The trading in forward rates is based on what traders expect the spot rate to be in the future. If the expectation for the spot rate is $X/DM in three months, disregarding risk aversion, the three month forward rate should also be $X/DM.

- **How can one offset foreign exchange risk through a transaction in the forward markets?**
  Through the purchase or sale of a forward contract in a position offsetting that of the firm's liability or promised payment.

31.5 • **What problems do international projects pose for the use of net present value techniques?**
   1. Foreign exchange conversion. What exchange rate should one use, the company's projection or the market's.
   2. Repatriation of funds. Some countries place restrictions on remittance of funds to the investing country.
   3. The appropriate discount rate may be lower than the domestic rate if the firm can diversify in ways that its shareholders cannot. Foreign political risk may raise the required return in some cases.

31.7 • **What issues arise when reporting foreign operations?**
   1. What exchange rate should you use if the exchange rate has changed during the period?
   2. How do you handle unrealized accounting gains or losses from foreign currency?

Chapter 2: Accounting Statements and Cash Flow

2.1   Following the example in Table 2.1:

Assets

Current assets	
Cash	$4,000
Accounts receivable	8,000
Total current assets	$12,000
Fixed assets	
Machinery	$34,000
Patents	82,000
Total fixed assets	$116,000
Total assets	$128,000

Liabilities and equity

Current liabilities	
Accounts payable	$6,000
Taxes payable	2,000
Total current liabilities	$8,000
Long-term liabilities	
Bonds payable	$7,000
Stockholders equity	
Common stock*	$88,000
Capital surplus	19,000
Retained earnings	6,000
Total stockholders equity	$113,000
Total liabilities and equity	$128,000

* You can back this out knowing that Total Assets = Total Liabilities + Equity

2.2

	One year ago	Changes	Today
Long-term debt	$50,000,000	none	$50,000,000
Preferred stock	30,000,000	none	30,000,000
Common stock	100,000,000	10 million new issue	110,000,000
Retained earnings	20,000,000	5 million net income less 3 million paid out dvds	22,000,000
Total	$200,000,000		$212,000,000

2.3   Following the example in Table 2.2:

Income Statement

Total operating revenues		500000
Cost of goods sold	(200000)	
Administrative expenses	(100000)	(300000)
Earnings before interest and taxes (EBIT)		200000
Interest expense		(50000)
Earnings before Taxes		150000
Taxes		(51000) (Taxes = 150,000 x .34)
Net income		99000

2.4   a.

Income Statement
The Flying Lion Corporation

	20X1	20X2
Net sales	$800,000	$500,000
Cost of goods sold	(560,000)	(320,000)
Operating expenses	(75,000)	(56,000)
Depreciation	(300,000)	(200,000)
Earnings before taxes (EBT)	$(135,000)	$(76,000)
Taxes*	40,500	22,800
Net income	$(94,500)	$(53,200)

*The problem states that Flying Lion has other profitable operations. Assume those operations generate at least $135,000 EBT in 20X1 and $76,000 in 20X2. Then, Flying Lion can take advantage of tax losses by deducting these tax liabilities from the other operations that have taxable profits. If Flying Lion did not have sufficient other operations or tax losses could not be carried forward or backward, then tax benefit in each of these years would have been less or zero.

b.   Operating Cash Flow is earnings before interest and depreciation, less taxes. So, since we already have net income from part a, it can be found as

net income + depreciation + interest expense

So for Flying Lion, we have :

Operating cash flow for 20X2 = -$94,500 + $300,000 + $0 = $205,500

Operating cash flow for 20X1 = -$53,200 + $200,000 + $0 = $146,800

2.5   The main difference between accounting profit and cash flow is that non-cash costs, such as depreciation expense, are included in accounting profits. Cash flows do not consider costs that do not represent actual expenditures. Cash flows deduct the entire cost of an investment at the time the cash flow occurs, rather than amortizing over some period, as is done with accounting profit. Look back at the previous problem and notice the differing effects of depreciation, with and without "other operations". Since depreciation is a non-cash expense, it only effects cash flow in that it effects Taxes.

2.6   Note that parts a, b and c are simply asking for sequential pieces of the Income Statement:

a.   Net operating income   = Sales - COGS - Selling expenses - Depreciation
    = \$1,000,000 - \$300,000 - \$200,000 - \$100,000
    = \$400,000

b.   Earnings before taxes   = Net operating income - Interest expense
    = Net operating income - (Notes Payable x Interest Rate)
    = \$400,000 - (\$1,000,000)(0.1)
    = \$300,000

c.   Net income   = Earnings before taxes - Taxes
    = Earnings before taxes - (EBT x TaxRate)
    = \$300,000 - (\$300,000)(0.35)
    = \$195,000

d.   Operating Cash flow   = Net income + Depreciation + Interest expense
    = \$195,000 + \$100,000 + \$100,000
    = \$395,000

2.7   Following the example in Table 2.3:

Total Cash Flow of the Stancil Company

Cash flows from the firm

Operating Cash Flow	0
Capital spending (purchase of fixed assets)	(1000)
Additions to working capital (purchase of inventory)	(4000)
Total	(5000)

Cash flows to investors of the firm

Short-term debt	(6000)
Long-term debt	(20000)
Equity (Dividends paid out less sale of common)	21000
Total	(5000)

2.8   a.   The difference in cash flow is the sum of the differences in cash flows from operations investing activities, and financing activities.

b.   The changes in net working capital can be computed from:

<u>Sources of net working capital</u>

Net income	$100
Depreciation	50
Increases in long-term debt	<u>75</u>
Total sources	$225

<u>Uses of net working capital</u>

Dividends	$50
Increases in fixed assets*	<u>150</u>
Total uses	$200
Additions to net working capital	$25

*Includes $50 of depreciation.

c.

<u>Cash flow from the firm</u>

Operating cash flow	$150
Capital spending	(150)
Additions to net working capital	<u>(25)</u>
Total	$(25)

<u>Cash flow to the investors</u>

Debt	$(75)
Equity	<u>50</u>
Total	$(25)

Chapter 3: Financial Planning and Growth

3.1   From the relationship, S = .00001 x GNP, we can get forecast sales:

S = 0.00001;   GNP = 0.00001 ($2,050 trillion) = $20,500,000

Now, compute the other values:

Projected Current Assets = Current Assets + ΔCurrent Assets:
CA = $500,000   +   0.25 ($20,500,000)   = $5,625,000

Similar for rest:
FA = $1,000,000   +   0.50 ($20,500,000)   = $11,250,000
CL = $100,000   +   0.10 ($20,500,000)   = $2,150,000

and:
NP = 0.02 ($20,500,000)   = $410,000

Compute the new amount of retained earnings:
ΔRE   = NP (1 - dvd payout ratio)
        = NP (1 - 0.34) = $410,000 (0.66) = $270,600
RE   = $3,400,000 + $270,600 = $3,670,600

Compute the new amount of bonds:
Debt-to-Asset Ratio = Total Debt / Total Assets
                  = ($1,100,000 + $2,500,000) / ($3,000,000 + $6,000,000) = 0.40

Bonds = [Total Assets x Debt/Asset ratio] - Current Liabilities
        = [(CA + FA) x 0.40] - CL
        = ($5,625,000 + $11,250,000) (0.40) - $2,150,000 = $4,600,000

Compute the new amount of stock:
Use: Total Assets ≡ Total Liabilities + Total Equity, then

Stock   = [(CA + FA) - (CL + Bonds + RE)]
        = ($5,625,000 + $11,250,000) - ($2,150,000 + 4,600,000 + 3,670,600)
        = $6,454,400

And now we can use the above to fill in the Balance Sheet:

Balance Sheet

Current Assets	5,625,000	Current Liabilities	$2,150,000
Fixed Assets	11,250,000	Bonds	4,600,000
Total Assets	$16,875,000	Common Stock	6,454,400
		Retained Earnings	3,670,600
		Total Liabs & CS	$16,875,000

3.2 First we need to find the change in Sales. Projected Sales are 110% of current sales, so current sales are:

$$S = 330 \text{ million} / 1.10 = 300 \text{ million}$$

and

$$\Delta S = 300 \text{ million} \times 10\% = \$30 \text{ million}$$

a. For external funds needed (in millions):

ΔCurrent Assets	= 25% ΔSales	= .25(30)
ΔFixed Assets	= 150% ΔSales	= 1.50(30)
ΔShort Term Debt	= 40% ΔSales	= .40(30)
ΔLong Term Debt	= 45% ΔSales	= .45(30)

and using the formula from the book:

$$EFN = \left(\frac{Assets}{Sales} \right) \Delta Sales - \left(\frac{Debt}{Sales} \right) \Delta Sales - ProfitMargin(Sales)(1 - DvdPayout)$$

$= (25\% + 150\%) \times 30 - (40\% + 45\%) \times 30 - (12\% \times 330)(1 - 40\%)$
$= \$3.24 \text{ million}$

b. Current assets = 25% x 330 / (1 + 10%) = 75
Fixed assets = 150% x 330 / (1+10%) = 450
Total assets = Current assets + Fixed assets = 75 + 450 = \$525 million
Short term debt = 40% x 330 / (1+10%) = 120
Long term debt = 45% x 330 / (1 + 10%) = 135
Common stock = 50
Retained earnings = 220

Total liabilities = \$525 million

c. Pro Forma Balance Sheet
Current assets = 25% x 330 = 82.5
Fixed assets = 150% x 330 = 495
Total assets = \$577.5 million
Short term debt = 40% x 330 = 132
Long term debt = 45% x 330 = 148.5
Common stock = 50
Retained earnings = 243.76

Total liabilities = 574.26

Note that parts b and c agree with part a:

External funds needed = 577.5 - 574.26 = \$3.24 million

3.3 a. Compute the sustainable growth using the formula from the text.

$$\frac{\Delta S}{S} = \frac{P(1-d)(1+L)}{T - P(1-d)(1+L)} = \frac{0.05(0.5)(2)}{1 - 0.05(0.5)(2)} = 0.0526 = 5.26\%$$

b. Yes, it is possible for the actual growth to differ from the sustainable growth. If any of the actual parameters (P, T, L or d) differ from those used to compute the sustainable growth rate, the actual growth rate will deviate from the sustainable growth rate.

c. Stieben Company can increase its growth rate by doing any of the following.

i. Sell new stock

ii. Increase its debt-to-equity ratio by either selling more debt or repurchasing stock

iii. Increase its net profit margin

iv. Decrease its total assets to sales ratio

v. Reduce its dividend payout

3.4 a. Using the formula from the book:

$$EFN = \left(\frac{Assets}{Sales}\right)\Delta Sales - \left(\frac{Debt}{Sales}\right)\Delta Sales - ProfitMargin(Sales)(1 - DvdPayout)$$

= 1(6,400,000) - .4375(6,400,000) - .0625(38,400,000(1-.7)

= 2,880,000

New Debt = Projected Debt - Current Debt
= 2,800,000 - 2,000,000
= $800,000

3.4   (continued)

b.

Pro Forma Balance Sheet
Optimal Scam Company

Current assets		$19,200,000
Fixed assets		19,200,000
	Total assets	$38,400,000
Current liabilities		$12,000,000
Long-term debt		4,800,000
	Total liabilities	$16,800,000
Common stock		$16,880,000
Accumulated retained earnings		4,720,000
	Total equity	$21,600,000
	Total liabilities and equity	$38,400,000

c.

$$\text{Sustainable growth} = \frac{\Delta S}{S} = \frac{P(1-d)(1+L)}{T - P(1-d)(1+L)}$$

$$= \frac{0.0625(.3)(1.7778)}{1 - 0.0625(0.3)(1.7778)} = 0.0345 = 3.45\%$$

d.   Optimal Scam is far below its growth rate objective. Cutting the dividend to zero will not be enough. It could only attain a 12.5% growth rate by eliminating the dividend. Optimal Scam must increase its asset utilization and/or its profit margin substantially to be able to achieve its objective growth rate. Optimal could also increase its debt load; this action will increase ROE.

Chapter 4: Net Present Value

4.1 a. Future Value $= C_0 (1+r)^T$
         $= \$1,000 (1.05)^{10} = \textbf{\$1,628.89}$

  b. Future Value $= \$1,000 (1.07)^{10} = \textbf{\$1,967.15}$

  c. Future Value $= \$1,000 (1.05)^{20} = \textbf{\$2,653.30}$

  d. Because interest compounds on interest already earned, the interest earned in part (c), $1,653.30 (=$2,653.30 - $1,000) is more than double the amount earned in part (a), $628.89 (=$1,628.89).

4.2 The present value, PV, of each cash flow is simply the amount of that cash flow discounted back from the date of payment to the present. For example in part (a), discount the cash flow in year 7 by seven periods, $(1.10)^7$.

  a. $PV(C_7) = C_7 / (1+r)^7$
       $= \$1,000 / (1.10)^7 = \textbf{\$513.16}$

  b. $PV(C_1) = \$2,000 / 1.10 = \textbf{\$1,818.18}$

  c. $PV(C_8) = \$500 / (1.10)^8 = \textbf{\$233.25}$

4.3 The decision involves comparing the present value, PV, of each option. Choose the option with the highest PV. Since the first cash flow occurs 0 years in the future, or today, it does not need to be adjusted.

   $PV(C_0) = \textbf{\$1,000}$

Since the second cash flow occurs 10 years in the future, it must be discounted back 10 years at eight percent.

   $PV(C_{10}) = C_{10} / (1+r)^{10}$
       $= \$2,000 / (1.08)^{10}$
       $= \textbf{\$926.39}$

Since the present value of the cash flow occurring today is higher than the present value of the cash flow occurring in year 10, you should take the $1,000 now.

4.4 Since the bond has no interim coupon payments, its present value is simply the present value of the $1,000 that will be received in 25 years. Note that the price of a bond is the present value of its cash flows.

   $P_0 = PV(C_{25})$
     $= C_{25} / (1+r)^{25}$
     $= \$1,000 / (1.10)^{25}$
     $= \textbf{\$92.30}$

The price of the bond is $92.30.

4.5   The future value, FV, of the firm's investment must equal the $1.5 million pension liability.

$$FV = C_0 (1+r)^{27}$$

To solve for the initial investment, C_0, discount the future pension liability ($1,500,000) back 27 years at eight percent, $(1.08)^{27}$.

$$\$1,500,000 / (1.08)^{27} = C_0$$
$$= \$187,780.23$$

The firm must invest $187,708.23 today to be able to make the $1.5 million payment.

4.6   The decision involves comparing the present value, PV, of each option. Choose the option with the highest PV.

a.   At a discount rate of zero, the future value and present value of a cash flow are always the same. There is no need to discount the two choices to calculate the PV.

PV(Alternative 1)   **= $10,000,000**

PV(Alternative 2)   **= $20,000,000**

Choose Alternative 2 since its PV, $20,000,000, is greater than that of Alternative 1, $10,000,000.

b.   Discount the cash flows at 10 percent. Discount Alternative 1 back one year and Alternative 2, five years.

PV(Alternative 1) $= C / (1+r)$
                      $= \$10,000,000 / (1.10)^{1}$
                      = $9,090,909.10

PV(Alternative 2) $= \$20,000,000 / (1.10)^{5}$
                      = $12,418,426.46

Choose Alternative 2 since its PV, $12,418,426.46, is greater than that of Alternative 1, $9,090,909.10.

c.   Discount the cash flows at 20 percent. Discount Alternative 1 back one year and Alternative 2, five years.

PV(Alternative 1) $= C / (1+r)$
                      $= \$10,000,000 / (1.20)^{1}$
                      = $8,333,333.33

PV(Alternative 2) $= \$20,000,000 / (1.20)^{5}$
                      = $8,037,551.44

Choose Alternative 1 since its PV, $8,333,333.33, is greater than that of Alternative 2, $8,037,551.44.

d.   You are indifferent when the PVs of the two alternatives are equal.

Alternative 1, discounted at r = Alternative 2, discounted at r
$\$10,000,000 / (1+r)^{1}$ $= \$20,000,000 / (1+r)^{5}$

Solve for the discount rate, r, at which the two alternatives are equally attractive.

$$
\begin{aligned}
\frac{[1/(1+r)^1](1+r)^5}{(1+r)^4} &= \$20,000,000 / \$10,000,000 \\
1+r &= 2 \\
1+r &= 1.18921 \\
r &= 0.18921 = \mathbf{18.921\%}
\end{aligned}
$$

The two alternatives are equally attractive when discounted at 18.921 percent.

4.7   The decision involves comparing the present value, PV, of each offer. Choose the offer with the highest PV.

Since the Smiths' payment occurs immediately, its present value does not need to be adjusted.

$$
\text{PV(Smith)} = \mathbf{\$115,000}
$$

The Joneses' offer occurs three years from today. Therefore, the payment must be discounted back three periods at 10 percent.

$$
\begin{aligned}
\text{PV(Jones)} &= C_3 / (1+r)^3 \\
&= \$150,000 / (1.10)^3 \\
&= \mathbf{\$112,697.22}
\end{aligned}
$$

Since the PV of the Joneses' offer, $112,697.22, is less than the Smiths' offer, $115,000, you should choose the Smiths' offer.

4.8   a.   Since the bond has no interim coupon payments, its present value is simply the present value of the $1,000 that will be received in 20 years. Note that the price of the bond is this present value.

$$
\begin{aligned}
P_0 &= PV(C_{20}) \\
&= C_{20} / (1+r)^{20} \\
&= \$1,000 / (1.08)^{20} \\
&= \mathbf{\$214.55}
\end{aligned}
$$

The current price of the bond is $214.55.

    b.   To find the bond's price 10 years from today, find the future value of the current price.

$$
\begin{aligned}
P_{10} &= FV_{10} \\
&= C_0 (1+r)^{10} \\
&= \$214.55 (1.08)^{10} \\
&= \mathbf{\$463.20}
\end{aligned}
$$

The bond's price 10 years from today will be $463.20.

    c.   To find the bond's price 15 years from today, find the future value of the current price.

$$
\begin{aligned}
P_{15} &= FV_{15} \\
&= C_0 (1+r)^{15} \\
&= \$214.55 (1.08)^{15} \\
&= \mathbf{\$680.59}
\end{aligned}
$$

The bond's price 15 years from today will be $680.59.

4.9   Ann Woodhouse would be willing to pay the present value of its resale value.

$$PV = \$5,000,000 / (1.12)^{10}$$
$$= \$1,609,866.18$$

The most she would be willing to pay for the property is $1,609,866.18.

4.10   a.   Compare the cost of the investment to the present value of the cash inflows. You should make the investment only if the present value of the cash inflows is greater than the cost of the investment. Since the investment occurs today (year 0), it does not need to be discounted.

PV(Investment)   **= $900,000**

PV(Cash Inflows) $= \$120,000 / (1.12) + \$250,000 / (1.12)^2 + \$800,000 / (1.12)^3$
                                  = $875,865.52

Since the PV of the cash inflows, $875,865.52, is less than the cost of the investment, $900,000, you should not make the investment.

     b.   The net present value, NPV, is the present value of the cash inflows minus the cost of the investment.

NPV   = PV(Cash Inflows) – Cost of Investment
          = $875,865.52 – $900,000
          = -$24,134.48

The NPV is -$24,134.48.

     c.   Calculate the PV of the cash inflows, discounted at 11 percent, minus the cost of the investment. If the NPV is positive, you should invest. If the NPV is negative, you should not invest.

NPV   = PV(Cash Inflows) – Cost of Investment
          $= \$120,000 / (1.11) + \$250,000 / (1.11)^2 + \$800,000 / (1.11)^3 - \$900,000$
          = -$4,033.18

Since the NPV is still negative, -$4,033.18, you should not make the investment.

4.11   Calculate the NPV of the machine. Purchase the machine if it has a positive NPV. Do not purchase the machine if it has a negative NPV.

Since the initial investment occurs today (year 0), it does not need to be discounted.

PV(Investment)   = -$340,000

Discount the annual revenues at 10 percent.

PV(Revenues) $= \$100,000 / (1.10) + \$100,000 / (1.10)^2 + \$100,000 / (1.10)^3 +$
                    $\$100,000 / (1.10)^4 + \$100,000 / (1.10)^5$
                    = $379,078.68

Since the maintenance costs occur at the beginning of each year, the first payment is not discounted. Each year thereafter, the maintenance cost is discounted at an annual rate of 10 percent.

$$PV(\text{Maintenance}) = -\$10,000 - \$10,000 / (1.10) - \$10,000 / (1.10)^2 - \$10,000 / (1.10)^3 - \$10,000 / (1.10)^4$$
$$= -\$41,698.65$$

$$NPV = PV(\text{Investment}) + PV(\text{Cash Flows}) + PV(\text{Maintenance})$$
$$= -\$340,000 + \$379,078.68 - \$41,698.65$$
$$= -\$2,619.97$$

Since the NPV is negative, -\$2,619.97, you should not buy the machine.

To find the NPV of the machine when the relevant discount rate is nine percent, repeat the above calculations, with a discount rate of nine percent.

$$PV(\text{Investment}) = -\$340,000$$

Discount the annual revenues at nine percent.

$$PV(\text{Revenues}) = \$100,000 / (1.09) + \$100,000 / (1.09)^2 + \$100,000 / (1.09)^3 + \$100,000 / (1.09)^4 + \$100,000 / (1.09)^5$$
$$= \$388,965.13$$

Since the maintenance costs occur at the beginning of each year, the first payment is not discounted. Each year thereafter, the maintenance cost is discounted at an annual rate of nine percent.

$$PV(\text{Maintenance}) = -\$10,000 - \$10,000 / (1.09) - \$10,000 / (1.09)^2 - \$10,000 / (1.09)^3 - \$10,000 / (1.09)^4$$
$$= -\$42,397.20$$

$$NPV = PV(\text{Investment}) + PV(\text{Cash Flows}) + PV(\text{Maintenance})$$
$$= -\$340,000 + \$388,965.13 - \$42,397.20$$
$$= \$6,567.93$$

Since the NPV is positive, \$6,567.93, you should buy the machine.

4.12   a.   The NPV of the contract is the PV of the item's revenue minus its cost.

$$PV(\text{Revenue}) = C_5 / (1+r)^5$$
$$= \$90,000 / (1.10)^5$$
$$= \$55,882.92$$

$$NPV = PV(\text{Revenue}) - \text{Cost}$$
$$= \$55,882.92 - \$60,000$$
$$= -\$4,117.08$$

The NPV of the item is -\$4,117.08.

b.   The firm will break even when the item's NPV is equal to zero.

$$NPV = PV(\text{Revenues}) - \text{Cost}$$
$$= C_5 / (1+r)^5 - \text{Cost}$$
$$\$0 = \$90,000 / (1+r)^5 - \$60,000$$
$$r = 0.08447 = 8.447\%$$

how to calculate

The firm will break even on the item with an 8.447 percent discount rate.

4.13   Compare the PV of your aunt's offer with your roommate's offer. Choose the offer with the highest PV. The PV of your aunt's offer is the sum of her payment to you and the benefit from owning the car an additional year.

$$PV(Aunt) = PV(Trade\text{-}In) + PV(Benefit\ of\ Ownership)$$
$$= \$3,000\ /\ (1.12) + \$1,000\ /\ (1.12)$$
$$= \$3,571.43$$

Since your roommate's offer occurs today (year 0), it does not need to be discounted.

$$PV(Roommate) = \$3,500$$

Since the PV of your aunt's offer, \$3,571.43, is higher than your roommate's offer, \$3,500, you should accept your aunt's offer.

4.14   The cost of the car 12 years from today will be \$80,000. To find the rate of interest such that your \$10,000 investment will pay for the car, set the FV of your investment equal to \$80,000.

$$FV = C_0\,(1+r)^{12}$$
$$\$80,000 = \$10,000\,(1+r)^{12}$$

Solve for the interest rate, r.

$$8 = (1+r)^{12}$$
$$\mathbf{0.18921} = r$$

The interest rate required is 18.921%.

4.15   The deposit at the end of the first year will earn interest for six years, from the end of year 1 to the end of year 7.

$$FV = \$1,000\,(1.12)^{6}$$
$$= \$1,973.82$$

The deposit at the end of the second year will earn interest for five years.

$$FV = \$1,000\,(1.12)^{5}$$
$$= \$1,762.34$$

The deposit at the end of the third year will earn interest for four years.

$$FV = \$1,000\,(1.12)^{4}$$
$$= \$1,573.52$$

The deposit at the end of the fourth year will earn interest for three years.

$$FV = \$1,000\,(1.12)^{3}$$
$$= \$1,404.93$$

Combine the values found above to calculate the total value of the account at the end of the seventh year:

$$FV = \$1,973.82 + \$1,762.34 + \$1,573.52 + \$1,404.93$$
$$= \mathbf{\$6,714.61}$$

The value of the account at the end of seven years will be $6,714.61.

4.16 To find the future value of the investment, convert the stated annual interest rate of eight percent to the effective annual yield, EAY. The EAY is the appropriate discount rate because it captures the effect of compounding periods.

a. With annual compounding, the EAY is equal to the stated annual interest rate.

$$FV = C_0 (1+ EAY)^T$$
$$= \$1,000 (1.08)^3$$
$$= \$1,259.71$$

The future value is $1,259.71.

b. Calculate the effective annual yield (EAY), where m denotes the number of compounding periods per year.

$$EAY = [1 + (r/m)]^m - 1$$
$$= [1 + (0.08 / 2)]^2 - 1$$
$$= 0.0816$$

Apply the future value formula, using the EAY for the interest rate.

$$FV = C_0 [1+EAY]^3$$
$$= \$1,000 (1 + 0.0816)^3$$
$$= \mathbf{\$1,265.32}$$

The future value is $1,265.32.

c. Calculate the effective annual yield (EAY), where m denotes the number of compounding periods per year.

$$EAY = [1 + (r/m)]^m - 1$$
$$= [1 + (0.08 / 12)]^{12} - 1$$
$$= 0.083$$

Apply the future value formula, using the EAY for the interest rate.

$$FV = C_0 (1+ EAY)^3$$
$$= \$1,000 (1 + 0.083)^3$$
$$= \mathbf{\$1,270.24}$$

The future value is $1,270.24.

d.   Continuous compounding is the limiting case of compounding. The EAY is calculated as a function of the constant, e, which is approximately equal to 2.718.

$$
\begin{aligned}
\text{FV} &= C_0 \times e^{rT} \\
&= \$1,000 \times e^{0.08 \times 3} \\
&= \mathbf{\$1,271.25}
\end{aligned}
$$

The future value is \$1,271.25.

e.   The future value of an investment increases as the compounding period shortens because interest is earned on previously accrued interest payments. The shorter the compounding period, the more frequently interest is paid, resulting in a larger future value.

4.17   Continuous compounding is the limiting case of compounding. The future value is a function of the constant, e, which is approximately equal to 2.718.

a.
$$
\begin{aligned}
\text{FV} &= C_0 \times e^{rT} \\
&= \$1,000 \times e^{0.12 \times 5} \\
&= \mathbf{\$1,822.12}
\end{aligned}
$$

The future value is \$1,822.12.

b.
$$
\begin{aligned}
\text{FV} &= \$1,000 \times e^{0.10 \times 3} \\
&= \mathbf{\$1,349.86}
\end{aligned}
$$

The future value is \$1,349.86.

c.
$$
\begin{aligned}
\text{FV} &= \$1,000 \times e^{0.05 \times 10} \\
&= \mathbf{\$1,648.72}
\end{aligned}
$$

The future value is \$1,648.72.

d.
$$
\begin{aligned}
\text{FV} &= \$1,000 \times e^{0.07 \times 8} \\
&= \mathbf{\$1,750.67}
\end{aligned}
$$

The future value is \$1,750.67.

4.18   Convert the stated annual interest rate to the effective annual yield, EAY. The EAY is the appropriate discount rate because it captures the effect of compounding periods. Next, discount the cash flow at the EAY.

$$
\begin{aligned}
\text{EAY} &= [1+(r \,/\, m)]^m - 1 \\
&= [1+(0.10 \,/\, 4)]^4 - 1 \\
&= 0.10381
\end{aligned}
$$

Discount the cash flow back 12 periods.

$$
\begin{aligned}
\text{PV}(C_{12}) &= C_{12} \,/\, (1+\text{EAY})^{12} \\
&= \$5,000 \,/\, (1.10381)^{12} \\
&= \$1,528.36
\end{aligned}
$$

The problem could also have been solved in a single calculation:

$$PV(C_{12}) = C_T / [1+(r / m)]^{mT}$$
$$= \$5,000 / [1+(0.10 / 4)]^{4 \times 12}$$
$$= \mathbf{\$1,528.36}$$

The PV of the cash flow is \$1,528.36.

4.19   Deposit your money in the bank that offers the highest effective annual yield, EAY. The EAY is the rate of return you will receive after taking into account compounding. Convert each bank's stated annual interest rate into an EAY.

$$EAY(\text{Bank America}) \quad = [1+(r / m)]^m - 1$$
$$= [1+(0.041 / 4)]^4 - 1$$
$$= 0.0416 = \mathbf{4.16\%}$$

$$EAY(\text{Bank USA}) \quad = [1+(r / m)]^m - 1$$
$$= [1+(0.0405 / 12)]^{12} - 1$$
$$= 0.0413 = \mathbf{4.13\%}$$

You should deposit your money in Bank America since it offers a higher EAY (4.16%) than Bank USA offers (4.13%).

4.20   The price of any bond is the present value of its coupon payments. Since a consol pays the same coupon every year in perpetuity, apply the perpetuity formula to find the present value.

$$PV \quad = C_1 / r$$
$$= \$120 / 0.15$$
$$= \mathbf{\$800}$$

The price of the consol is \$800.

4.21   a.   Apply the perpetuity formula, discounted at 10 percent.

$$PV \quad = C_1 / r$$
$$= \$1,000 / 0.1$$
$$= \mathbf{\$10,000}$$

The PV is \$10,000.

    b.   Remember that the perpetuity formula yields the present value of a stream of cash flows one period before the initial payment. Therefore, applying the perpetuity formula to a stream of cash flows that begins two years from today will generate the present value of that perpetuity as of the end of year 1. Next, discount the PV as of the end of 1 year back one year, yielding the value today, year 0.

$$PV \quad = [C_2 / r] / (1+r)$$
$$= [\$500 / 0.1] / (1.1)$$
$$= \mathbf{\$4,545.45}$$

The PV is \$4,545.45.

    c.   Applying the perpetuity formula to a stream of cash flows that begins three years from today will generate the present value of that perpetuity as of the end of year 2. Thus, use the perpetuity formula to find the PV as of the end of year 2. Next, discount that value back two years to find the value today, year 0.

$$PV = [C_3 / r] / (1+r)^2$$
$$= [\$2,420 / 0.1] / (1.1)^2$$
$$= \$20,000$$

The PV is $20,000.

4.22   Applying the perpetuity formula to a stream of cash flows that starts at the end of year 9 will
generate the present value of that perpetuity as of the end of year 8.

$$PV_8 = [C_9 / r]$$
$$= [\$120 / 0.1]$$
$$= \$1,200$$

To find the PV of the cash flows as of the end of year 5, discount the PV of the perpetuity as of the
end of year 8 back three years.

$$PV_5 = PV_8 / (1+r)^3$$
$$= \$1,200 / (1.1)^3$$
$$= \$901.58$$

The PV as of the end of year 5 is $901.58.

4.23   Use the growing perpetuity formula. Since Harris Inc.'s last dividend was $3, the next dividend
(occurring one year from today) will be $3.15 (= $3 × 1.05). Do not take into account the
dividend paid yesterday.

$$PV = C_1 / (r - g)$$
$$= \$3.15 / (0.12 - 0.05)$$
$$= \$45$$

The price of the stock is $45.

4.24   Use the growing perpetuity formula to find the PV of the dividends. The PV is the maximum you
should be willing to pay for the stock.

$$PV = C_1 / (r - g)$$
$$= \$1 / (0.1 - 0.04)$$
$$= \$16.67$$

The maximum you should pay for the stock is $16.67.

4.25   The perpetuity formula yields the present value of a stream of cash flows one period before the
initial payment. Apply the growing perpetuity formula to the stream of cash flows beginning two
years from today to calculate the PV as of the end of year 1. To find the PV as of today, year 0,
discount the PV of the perpetuity as of the end of year 1 back one year.

$$PV = [C_2 / (r - g)] / (1+r)$$
$$= [\$200,000 / (0.1 - 0.05)] / (1.1)$$
$$= \$3,636,363.64$$

The PV of the technology is $3,636,363.64.

4.26 Barrett would be indifferent when the NPV of the project is equal to zero. Therefore, set the net present value of the project's cash flows equal to zero. Solve for the discount rate, r.

$$
\begin{aligned}
\text{NPV} &= \text{Initial Investment} + \text{Cash Flows} \\
0 &= -\$100,000 + \$50,000 / r \\
\mathbf{0.5} &= r
\end{aligned}
$$

The discount rate at which Barrett is indifferent to the project is 50%.

4.27 Because the cash flows occur quarterly, they must be discounted at the rate applicable for a quarter of a year. Since the stated annual interest rate is given in terms of quarterly periods, and the payments are given in terms of quarterly periods, simply divide the stated annual interest rate by four to calculate the quarterly interest rate.

$$
\begin{aligned}
\text{Quarterly Interest Rate} &= \text{Stated Annual Interest Rate} / \text{Number of Periods} \\
&= 0.12 / 4 \\
&= 0.03 = 3\%
\end{aligned}
$$

Use the perpetuity formula to find the PV of the security's cash flows.

$$
\begin{aligned}
\text{PV} &= C_1 / r \\
&= \$10 / 0.03 \\
&= \mathbf{\$333.33}
\end{aligned}
$$

The price of the security is $333.33.

4.28 The two steps involved in this problem are a) calculating the appropriate discount rate and b) calculating the PV of the perpetuity.

Since the payments occur quarterly, the cash flows must be discounted at the interest rate applicable for a quarter of a year.

$$
\begin{aligned}
\text{Quarterly Interest Rate} &= \text{Stated Annual Interest Rate} / \text{Number of Periods} \\
&= 0.15 / 4 \\
&= 0.0375 = 3.75\%
\end{aligned}
$$

Remember that the perpetuity formula provides the present value of a stream of cash flows one period before the initial payment. Therefore, applying the perpetuity formula to a stream of cash flows that begins 20 periods from today will generate the present value of that perpetuity as of the end of period 19. Next, discount that value back 19 periods, yielding the price today, year 0.

$$
\begin{aligned}
\text{PV} &= [C_{20} / r] / (1+r)^{19} \\
&= [\$1 / 0.0375] / (1.0375)^{19} \\
&= \mathbf{\$13.25}
\end{aligned}
$$

The price of the stock is $13.25.

4.29 Calculate the NPV of the asset. Since the cash inflows form an annuity, you can use the present value of an annuity factor. The annuity factor is referred to as A^T_r, where T is the number of payments and r is the interest rate.

$$
\text{PV(Investment)} = -\$6,200
$$

$$
\begin{aligned}
\text{PV(Cash Inflows)} &= C\, A^T_r \\
&= \$1,200\, A^8_{0.1} \\
&= \$6,401.91
\end{aligned}
$$

The NPV of the asset is the sum of the initial investment (-$6,200) and the PV of the cash inflows ($6,401.91).

$$
\begin{aligned}
\text{NPV} &= \text{-Initial Investment + Cash Flows} \\
&= \text{-\$6,200 + \$6,401.91} \\
&= \mathbf{\$201.91}
\end{aligned}
$$

Since the asset has a positive NPV, $201.91, you should buy it.

4.30   There are 20 payments for an annuity beginning in year 3 and ending in year 22. Apply the annuity formula to this stream of 20 annual payments.

$$
\begin{aligned}
\text{PV(End of Year 2)} &= C\,A^{T}_{r} \\
&= \$2,000\,A^{20}_{0.08} \\
&= \$19,636.29
\end{aligned}
$$

Since the first cash flow is received at the end of year 3, applying the annuity formula to the cash flows will yield the PV as of the end of year 2. To find the PV as of today, year 0, discount that amount back two years.

$$
\begin{aligned}
\text{PV(Year 0)} &= \text{PV(End of Year 2)} / (1+r)^{T} \\
&= \$19,636.29 / (1.08)^{2} \\
&= \mathbf{\$16,834.95}
\end{aligned}
$$

The PV of the cash flows is $16,834.95.

4.31   There are 15 payments for an annuity beginning in year 6 and ending in year 20. Apply the annuity formula to this stream of 15 annual payments.

$$
\begin{aligned}
\text{PV(End of Year 5)} &= C\,A^{T}_{r} \\
&= \$500\,A^{15}_{0.15} \\
&= \$2,923.69
\end{aligned}
$$

Since the first cash flow is received at the end of year 6, applying the annuity formula to the cash flows will yield the PV as of the end of year 5. To find the PV as of today, year 0, discount that amount back five years at 12 percent.

$$
\begin{aligned}
\text{PV(Year 0)} &= \text{PV(End of Year 5)} / (1.12)^{5} \\
&= \$2,923.69 / (1.12)^{5} \\
&= \mathbf{\$1,658.98}
\end{aligned}
$$

The PV of the annuity is $1,658.98.

4.32   Set the price of the note equal to the present value of the annuity of $2,000 per year.

$$
\begin{aligned}
\text{P} &= C\,A^{T}_{r} \\
\$12,800 &= \$2,000\,A^{10}_{r}
\end{aligned}
$$

The problem can be solved by using a calculator to find the appropriate discount rate.

$$
\begin{aligned}
6.4 &= A^{10}_{r} \\
\mathbf{0.090626} &= r
\end{aligned}
$$

The problem can also be solved by using table A.2 in the back of the textbook. In table A.2, scan across the row for 10-year annuity factors until one approximates 6.4. 6.4177, corresponding to a rate of 9%, is close to the above factor, 6.4. Thus, the rate received is slightly more than 9%.

The rate received is 9.0626%.

4.33   a.   To calculate the necessary annual payments, first find the PV of the $25,000 which you will need in five years.

$$PV = C_5 / (1+r)^5$$
$$= \$25,000 / (1.07)^5$$
$$= \$17,824.65$$

Next, compute the annuity that will yield the same PV as calculated above. Solve for the deposit you will make each year.

PV $= C\,A_r^T$
$17,824.65 $= C\,A_{0.07}^5$
$17,824.65 / A_{0.07}^5   **= $4,347.27**

Depositing $4,347.27 into the 7% account each year will provide $25,000 five years from today.

b.   The lump sum payment must be the present value of the $25,000 you will need five years from today.

$$PV = C_5 / (1+r)^5$$
$$= \$25,000 / (1.07)^5$$
$$= \mathbf{\$17,824.65}$$

You must deposit $17,824.65 as a lump sum to have $25,000 in the account at the end of five years.

4.34   First, determine the balance of the loan Nancy must pay.

$$\text{Balance} = \$120,000\,(0.85)$$
$$= \$102,000$$

Apply the annuity formula since Nancy will pay the balance of the loan in 20 equal, end-of-year, payments. Set the present value of the annuity equal to the balance of the loan. Solve for the annual payment, C.

Balance $= C\,A_r^T$
$102,000 $= C\,A_{0.1}^{20}$
$102,000 / A_{0.1}^{20}$ $= C$
$11,980.88 $= C$

The equal installments are $11,980.88.

4.35   a.   The cash flows form a 31-year annuity where the first payment is received today. Remember to use the after-tax cash flows. The first payment of a standard annuity is received one year from today. Therefore, value all after-tax cash flows except the first after-tax payment using the standard annuity formula. Then add back the first after-tax payment to obtain the value of the option. Since the first payment is treated separately from the other payments, the annuity has 30 periods instead of 31 periods.

$$PV = (1 - T_c) C_1 A^T_r + (1 - T_c) C_0$$
$$= (1 - 0.28) \$160{,}000\ A^{30}_{0.1} + (1 - 0.28) \$160{,}000$$
$$= \$1{,}201{,}180.55$$

b.　　This option pays \$446,000, after-tax, immediately. The remaining money is received as a 30-year annuity that pays \$101,055, annually before tax. Find the PV of the annuity, discounted at 10 percent. Remember to apply taxes to the annuity.

$$PV = (1 - T_c) C_1 A^T_r + C_0$$
$$= (1 - 0.28) \$101{,}055\ A^{30}_{0.1} + \$446{,}000$$
$$= \$1{,}131{,}898.53$$

Choose the first option with a PV of \$1,201,180.55 since it has a higher PV than the second option, \$1,131.898.53.

4.36　　First, use the standard annuity formula to compute the present value of all the payments you must make for each of your children's educations.

PV(Each Child's Education)　　$= C A^T_r$
　　　　　　　　　　　　　　　$= \$21{,}000\ A^4_{0.15}$
　　　　　　　　　　　　　　　$= \$59{,}954.55$

The annuity formula values any annuity as of one year before the first cash flow. Since the first payment for each child is made when the child enters college, the above value represents the cost of the older child's education 14 years from now and of the younger child's education 16 years from now. To find the PV of the children's education at year 0, discount the above PV back 14 years and 16 years for both the older and younger child, respectively.

PV(Older Child)　　$= $ PV(Education) $/ (1+r)^{14}$
　　　　　　　　　$= \$59{,}954.55 / (1.15)^{14}$
　　　　　　　　　$= \$8{,}473.30$

PV(Younger Child)　　$= \$59{,}954.55 / (1.15)^{16}$
　　　　　　　　　　$= \$6{,}407.03$

PV(Total Cost)　　$= $ PV(Older Child) $+ $ PV(Younger Child)
　　　　　　　　$= \$8{,}473.30 + \$6{,}407.03$
　　　　　　　　$= \$14{,}880.32$

You will make 15 payments, since your first payment is made one year from today and the last payment is made when your first child enters college, 15 years from now. To find the amount of each payment, set the total PV of the children's education costs equal to a 15-year annuity, discounted at 15 percent. Solve for the annual payment, C.

PV(Total Cost)　　　　　$= C A^T_r$
\$14,880.32　　　　　　$= C A^{15}_{0.15}$
\$14,880.32 $/ A^{15}_{0.15}$　$= C$
\$2,544.79　　　　　$= C$

The annual payment that will allow you to pay for the total cost of your children's college educations in 15 years is \$2,544.79.

4.37　　To determine whether or not the policy is worth buying, calculate the NPV of the policy. The parent's six payments are cash outflows and the insurance company's payment is a cash inflow. The PV of the parent's payments can be calculated by applying the annuity formula, discounted at six percent, to both the first three payments (each \$750) and the last three payments (each \$800).

$$PV(\text{First 3 Payments}) = C_1 A^T_r$$
$$= -\$750\, A^3_{0.06}$$
$$= -\$2,004.76$$

The annuity formula calculates the PV as of one period prior to the first cash flow. Since the first $800 payment occurs four years from today, the PV of the annuity of the last three payments must be discounted back three years.

$$PV(\text{Last 3 Payments}) = [C_4 A^T_r] / (1+r)^3$$
$$= [-\$800\, A^3_{0.06}] / (1.06)^3$$
$$= -\$1,795.45$$

Discount the insurance company's payment back 65 years. Take note that the discount rate is six percent for years 1 through 6 and seven percent for years 7 through 65.

$$PV(\text{Insurance Payment}) = C_{65} / [(1+r)^{\text{Year 1 - 6}} (1+r)^{\text{Year 7 - 65}}]$$
$$= \$250,000 / [(1.06)^6 (1.07)^{59}]$$
$$= \$3,254.33$$

$$NPV = PV(\text{First 3 Payments}) + PV(\text{Last 3 Payments}) + PV(\text{Insurance Payment})$$
$$= -\$2,004.76 + -\$1,795.45 + \$3,254.33$$
$$= -\$545.88$$

Since the NPV of the policy is negative, -$545.88, it is not worth buying.

4.38   Calculate the present value of the lease offer. An annuity in advance is a stream of cash flows beginning today. Since the annual lease payments form an annuity in advance, value all payments except the one made today using the standard annuity formula. Add back the payment made today. The immediate payment is not discounted because it occurs today, year 0. Because the first payment is treated separately, the annuity has nine periods instead of 10 periods.

$$PV(\text{Payments}) = C_0 + C_1 A^T_r$$
$$= -\$15,000 + -\$15,000\, A^9_{0.08}$$
$$= -\$108,703.32$$

$$PV(\text{Purchase Option}) = C_T / (1+r)^T$$
$$= -\$25,000 / (1.08)^{10}$$
$$= -\$11,579.84$$

$$PV(\text{Lease}) = PV(\text{Payments}) + PV(\text{Purchase Option})$$
$$= -\$108,703.32 - \$11,579.84$$
$$= -\$120,283.16$$

Since the PV of the lease offer is greater than $120,000, the cost of the machine, you should not accept the offer.

4.39   Remember that your salary grows by four percent each year, and you just received a $50,000 salary payment. Thus, your salary next year will be $52,000 (=$50,000 × 1.04). Two percent of next year's salary will be deposited into the account.

$$C = (\text{Last Year's Salary}) (1+g) (\text{Percent Deposited})$$
$$= (\$50,000) (1.04) (0.02)$$
$$= \$1,040.00$$

Since your salary will continue to grow at four percent annually, your deposits will also grow at this rate. Apply the growing annuity formula, discounted at eight percent, to calculate the PV of your retirement account.

$$
\begin{aligned}
PV \quad &= C \, GA^T_{r,g} \, * \\
&= \$1,040.00 \, GA^{40}_{0.08,\,0.04} \\
&= \$20,254.12
\end{aligned}
$$

To determine how much will be in the account at your retirement in 40 years, calculate the future value.

$$
\begin{aligned}
FV \quad &= PV \, (1+r)^T \\
&= \$20,254.12 \, (1.08)^{40} \\
&= \mathbf{\$440,011.02}
\end{aligned}
$$

At the time of your retirement, the account will have $440,011.02.

*The notation $GA^T_{r,\,g}$ represents a growing annuity consisting of T payments growing at a rate of g per payment, discounted at r.

4.40   Discount the individual cash flows to compute the NPV of the project. The cash flow, C_0, is the initial investment.

$$
\begin{aligned}
PV(C_0) &= -\$5,000 \\
PV(C_1) &= \$700 / (1.1) &= \$636.36 \\
PV(C_2) &= \$900 / (1.1)^2 &= \$743.80 \\
PV(C_3) &= \$1,000 / (1.1)^3 &= \$751.32 \\
PV(C_4) &= \$1,000 / (1.1)^4 &= \$683.01 \\
PV(C_5) &= \$1,000 / (1.1)^5 &= \$620.92 \\
PV(C_6) &= \$1,000 / (1.1)^6 &= \$564.47 \\
PV(C_7) &= \$1,250 / (1.1)^7 &= \$641.45 \\
PV(C_8) &= \$1,375 / (1.1)^8 &= \$641.45
\end{aligned}
$$

$$
\begin{aligned}
NPV \quad &= -\$5,000 + \$636.36 + \$743.80 + \$751.32 + \$683.01 + \$620.92 + \$564.47 + \\
&\quad\ \$641.45 + \$641.45 \\
&= \mathbf{\$282.78}
\end{aligned}
$$

Purchase the machine since it has a positive NPV.

4.41   a.   <u>Engineer</u>:

Apply the annuity formula, discounted at five percent, to calculate the PV of his undergraduate education.

$$
\begin{aligned}
PV(\text{Undergraduate}) \quad &= C \, A^T_r \\
&= -\$12,000 \, A^4_{0.05} \\
&= -\$42,551.41
\end{aligned}
$$

To find the PV of his practical experience in years 5 and 6, discount the two cash flows by five years and six years, respectively.

$$
\begin{aligned}
PV(\text{Experience}) \quad &= \$20,000 / (1.05)^5 + \$25,000 / (1.05)^6 \\
&= \$34,325.90
\end{aligned}
$$

Discount the corresponding two cash flows for the master's degree by seven years and eight years.

PV(Master)
$$= -\$15{,}000 / (1.05)^7 + -\$15{,}000 / (1.05)^8$$
$$= -\$20{,}812.81$$

After completion of his master's degree, your brother will earn \$40,000 per year for the next 25 years. Since the annuity formula calculates the PV as of one year before the first cash flow, applying the annuity formula to your brother's future earnings will generate the PV as of the end of year 8. Discount that PV back eight years to find the PV as of today, year 0.

PV(Earnings)
$$= C_9\, A^T_r / (1+r)^8$$
$$= \$40{,}000\, A^{25}_{0.05} / (1.05)^8$$
$$= \$381{,}573.46$$

Thus, the NPV of his decision to become an engineer is:

NPV(Engineer)
$$= \text{PV(Undergraduate)} + \text{PV(Experience)} + \text{PV(Master)} + \text{PV(Earnings)}$$
$$= -\$42{,}551.41 + \$34{,}325.90 - \$20{,}812.81 + \$381{,}573.46$$
$$= \mathbf{\$352{,}535.14}$$

Accountant:

Apply the annuity formula, discounted at five percent, to calculate the PV of the accounting undergraduate education.

PV(Undergraduate)
$$= -\$13{,}000\, A^4_{0.05}$$
$$= -\$46{,}097.36$$

Apply the annuity formula to calculate the PV of the future earnings. Since the annuity formula calculates the PV as of one year before the first cash flow, applying the annuity formula to your brother's future earnings will generate the PV as of the end of year 4. Discount that PV back four periods to find the PV as of today.

PV(Earnings)
$$= C_5\, A^T_r / (1+r)^4$$
$$= \$31{,}000\, A^{30}_{0.05} / (1.05)^4$$
$$= \$392{,}055.56$$

Thus, the NPV of his decision to become an accountant is:

NPV(Accountant)
$$= \text{PV(Undergraduate)} + \text{PV(Earnings)}$$
$$= -\$46{,}097.36 + \$392{,}055.56$$
$$= \mathbf{\$345{,}958.20}$$

Since the NPV of becoming an engineer, \$352,535.14, is higher than the NPV of becoming an accountant, \$345,958.20, your brother should study engineering.

b. After your brother announces that the appropriate discount rate is six percent, recalculate the NPVs the same way as above, using a six percent discount rate.

NPV(Engineer)
$$= \text{PV(Undergraduate)} + \text{PV(Experience)} + \text{PV(Master)} + \text{PV(Earnings)}$$
$$= -\$12{,}000\, A^4_{0.06} + \$20{,}000 / (1.06)^5 + \$25{,}000 / (1.06)^6 - \$15{,}000 / (1.06)^7 - \$15{,}000 / (1.06)^8 + \$40{,}000\, A^{25}_{0.06} / (1.06)^8$$
$$= \mathbf{\$292{,}418.30}$$

NPV(Accountant) $\quad$ = PV(Undergraduate) + PV(Earnings)
$$= -\$13{,}000 \ A^4_{0.06} + \$31{,}000 \ A^{30}_{0.06} / (1.06)^4$$
$$= \mathbf{\$292{,}947.73}$$

Your brother made a poor decision. At a six percent rate, the NPV of becoming an accountant, $292,947.73, is higher than the NPV of becoming an engineer, 292,418.30. Thus, he should have chosen to study accounting.

4.42　Use the growing annuity formula, discounted at 12 percent and growing at four percent, to find the PV of Tom's annual salary payments.

PV(Salary) $\quad$ $= C \ GA^T_{r,\,g}$ *
$$= \$35{,}000 \ GA^{25}_{0.12,\,0.04}$$
$$= \$368{,}894.18$$

* The notation $GA^T_{r,\,g}$ represents a growing annuity consisting of T payments growing at a rate of g per payment, discounted at r.

The yearly bonuses are equal to 10 percent of his salary. Since his salary grows at four percent, the annual bonus will also grow at four percent. Use the growing annuity formula, discounted at 12 percent and growing at four percent, to find the PV of Tom's annual bonus payments.

PV(Bonus) $\quad$ $= (0.1) \ (\$35{,}000) \ GA^{25}_{0.12,\,0.04}$
$$= \$36{,}889.42$$

Mr. Adams will also receive a signing bonus today.

PV(Signing) $\quad$ $= \$10{,}000$

PV(Offer) $\quad$ = PV(Salary) + PV(Bonus) + PV(Signing)
$$= \$368{,}894.18 + \$36{,}889.42 + \$10{,}000$$
$$= \mathbf{\$415{,}783.60}$$

The PV of the offer is $415,783.60.

4.43　Apply the growing annuity formula to find the PV of the cash flows.

PV(Cash Flows) $\quad$ $= C \ GA^T_{r,\,g}$ *
$$= \$10{,}000 \ GA^5_{0.1,\,0.07}$$
$$= \$43{,}041.91$$

Subtract the initial cost of $40,000 from the PV of the growing annuity to find the NPV of the revision.

PV(Cost) $\quad$ $= -\$40{,}000$

NPV $\quad$ = PV(Cash Flows) + PV(Cost)
$$= \$43{,}041.91 - \$40{,}000$$
$$= \mathbf{\$3{,}041.91}$$

Since the NPV of the revision is positive, $3,041.91, revise the textbook. The firm's return on the project will be greater than 10 percent since the NPV is positive.

* The notation $GA^T_{r,\,g}$ represents a growing annuity consisting of T payments growing at a rate of g per payment, discounted at r.

4.44   First, find the PV of Ian's retirement income and his cabin purchase. Since the first retirement payment is made at the end of year 31, applying the annuity formula to the cash flows will yield the PV as of the end of year 30. To find the PV as of today, year 0, discount that value back 30 periods.

$$PV(\text{Retirement}) = C_{31}\, A^T_r / (1+r)^{30}$$
$$= \$300{,}000\, A^{20}_{0.07} / (1.07)^{30}$$
$$= \$417{,}511.53$$

Since the cabin is purchased at the end of year 10, discount that cash flow back 10 periods to find the PV as of today, year 0.

$$PV(\text{Cabin}) = \$350{,}000 / (1.07)^{10}$$
$$= \$177{,}922.25$$

Next, find the PV of his annual savings from year 1 through year 10, using the annuity formula.

$$PV(\text{Savings}) = \$40{,}000\, A^{10}_{0.07}$$
$$= \$280{,}943.26$$

Find the difference between the PV of his savings from year 1 through year 10 and the total PV of Ian's two expenditures (retirement and cabin).

$$\text{Difference} = PV(\text{Savings}) - [PV(\text{Retirement}) + PV(\text{Cabin})]$$
$$= \$280{,}943.26 - (\$417{,}511.53 + \$177{,}922.25)$$
$$= -\$314{,}491.52$$

In present value terms, Ian must save an additional $314,491.52 in order to meet his objectives. To determine the amount he must save from year 11 through year 30, set the PV of his savings over this time period equal to the difference of $314,491.52. Since the annual savings will begin 11 years from today, discount the annuity back 10 periods. Solve for the amount Ian needs to save each year, C.

Difference	$= C\, A^T_r / (1+r)^{10}$
$314,491.52	$= C\, A^{20}_{0.07} / (1.07)^{10}$
$[\$314{,}491.52\,(1.07)^{10}] / A^{20}_{0.07}$	$= C$
$58,396.23	$= C$

Ian needs to save $58,396.23 annually from year 11 to year 30 in order to meet his objectives.

4.45   Since Jack's salary is paid monthly, the payments need to be discounted at the monthly interest rate.

$$\text{Monthly Interest Rate} = \text{Stated Annual Interest Rate / Number of Periods}$$
$$= 0.12 / 12$$
$$= 0.01$$

Next, calculate the PV of his monthly salary. Since he will receive 36 monthly payments (=12 payments per year × 3 years), the PV is:

$$PV(\text{Salary}) = C\, A^T_r$$
$$= \$5{,}000\, A^{36}_{0.01}$$
$$= \$150{,}537.53$$

Next, calculate the PV of his bonuses. The end-of-year bonuses must be discounted at the effective annual yield, EAY. The EAY is the appropriate discount rate because it captures the effect of compounding periods. Find the EAY and then apply the annuity formula, discounted at the EAY, to calculate the PV of the bonuses.

$$
\begin{aligned}
\text{EAY} &= [1+(r/m)]^m - 1 \\
&= [1+(0.12/12)]^{12} - 1 \\
&= 0.12683 = 12.683\%
\end{aligned}
$$

$$
\begin{aligned}
\text{PV(Bonus)} &= C\, A^T_r \\
&= \$10{,}000\, A^3_{0.12683} \\
&= \$23{,}739.20
\end{aligned}
$$

$$
\begin{aligned}
\text{PV(Contract)} &= \text{PV(Salary)} + \text{PV(Bonus)} \\
&= \$150{,}537.53 + \$23{,}739.20 \\
&= \mathbf{\$174{,}276.73}
\end{aligned}
$$

The PV of the contract is $174,276.73.

4.46 First, determine the balance of the loan.

$$
\begin{aligned}
\text{Balance} &= \$15{,}000\,(0.80) \\
&= \$12{,}000
\end{aligned}
$$

Convert the stated annual interest rate to a monthly interest rate since the payments are made monthly.

$$
\begin{aligned}
\text{Monthly Interest Rate} &= \text{Stated Annual Interest Rate / Number of Periods} \\
&= 0.08/12 \\
&= 0.0067
\end{aligned}
$$

Set the balance of the loan equal to the present value of the annuity of 48 monthly payments, discounted at 0.0067. Solve for the monthly payment, C.

Balance	$= C\, A^T_r$
$12,000	$= C\, A^{48}_{0.0067}$
$12,000 / $A^{48}_{0.0067}$	$= C$
$293.18	$= C$

The monthly installments will be $293.18.

4.47 The balance of the loan is:

$$
\begin{aligned}
\text{Balance} &= \$10{,}000 - \$1{,}000 \\
&= \$9{,}000
\end{aligned}
$$

Because the payments are made on a monthly basis, first calculate the monthly interest rate.

$$
\begin{aligned}
\text{Monthly Interest Rate} &= 0.096/12 \\
&= 0.008
\end{aligned}
$$

Next, to find Susan's monthly payments, set the balance of the loan equal to an annuity with 60 periods (=12 months × 5 years), discounted at the monthly interest rate.

$$\text{Balance} = C\, A^T_r$$
$$\$9{,}000 = C\, A^{60}_{0.008}$$
$$\$9{,}000 / A^{60}_{0.008} = C$$
$$\$189.46 = C$$

To find the balance of the loan that Susan will prepay, first find the number of remaining payments beginning with the November 1, 2002 payment. Since her first payment was made on October 1, 2000, her payment on October 1, 2002 was her 25th. Thus, she has 35 remaining payments, including the immediate November, 2002 payment.

Each of the remaining 35 payments is $189.46. To find the PV, value all payments except the impending November payment using the standard annuity formula. Then add back the November payment to obtain the PV of her repayment. Since the November payment is treated separately from the other payments, the annuity has 34 periods instead of 35 periods.

$$\text{PV(Loan)} = C_1\, A^T_r + C_0$$
$$= \$189.46\, A^{34}_{0.008} + 189.46$$
$$= \$5{,}809.81$$

Susan also incurs a 1% penalty. Thus, the total repayment is:

$$\text{Repayment} = \text{PV(Loan)}\,(1+\text{Penalty})$$
$$= \$5{,}809.81\,(1.01)$$
$$= \mathbf{\$5{,}867.91}$$

The total repayment is $5,867.91.

4.48   To find the PV of the flower purchases, you must first find the weekly interest rate and the weekly growth rate. Divide both the stated annual interest rate and the stated annual growth rate by 52 to calculate the weekly interest rate and weekly growth rate.

$$\text{Weekly Interest Rate} = 0.104 / 52$$
$$= 0.002$$

$$\text{Weekly Growth Rate} = 0.039 / 52$$
$$= 0.00075$$

Apply the growing annuity formula, discounted at 0.002 with payments growing at a rate of 0.00075 weekly, to find the PV of Joe's commitment. The growing annuity has 1,560 periods (=30 years × 52 weeks).

$$\text{PV} = C_1\, GA^T_{r,\,g}\,*$$
$$= \$5\, GA^{1{,}560}_{0.002,\,0.00075}$$
$$= \mathbf{\$3{,}429.38}$$

The PV of Joe DiMaggio's commitment is $3,429.38.

*The notation $GA^T_{r,\,g}$ represents a growing annuity consisting of T payments growing at a rate of g per payment, discounted at r.

4.49   Since Goose receives his first payment on July 1 and all later payments are made in one-year intervals on July 1, discount the cash flows to July 1 of year 0 using the annual discount rate of nine percent. Then use the six-month discount rate (0.044) to discount the cash flows back to January of year 0.

The PVs of the guaranteed payments over the first six years are:

$$PV(C_1) = \$875{,}000 / (1.044) = \$838{,}122.61$$
$$PV(C_2) = \$650{,}000 / [(1.09)(1.044)] = \$571{,}197.58$$
$$PV(C_3) = \$800{,}000 / [(1.09)^2 (1.044)] = \$644{,}965.51$$
$$PV(C_4) = \$1{,}000{,}000 / [(1.09)^3 (1.044)] = \$739{,}639.35$$
$$PV(C_5) = \$1{,}000{,}000 / [(1.09)^4 (1.044)] = \$678{,}568.21$$
$$PV(C_6) = \$300{,}000 / [(1.09)^5 (1.044)] = \$186{,}761.89$$

Apply the annuity formula, discounted at nine percent, to find the PV of the 17 deferred payments of \$240,000 from 1990 through 2006. The annuity formula will calculate the PV of the cash flows as of July 1, 1989. Discount that value back 5.5 periods to find the PV of the deferred payments as of January 1984.

$$PV(\text{Deferred Payments}) = C_7 A^T_r / [(1+\text{Six Month Rate})(1+\text{Annual Rate})^T]$$
$$= \$240{,}000\, A^{17}_{0.09} / [(1.044)(1.09)^5]$$
$$= \$1{,}276{,}499.81$$

Perform a similar calculation to find the PV of the 10 deferred payments of \$125,000 from 2007 through 2016. The annuity formula will calculate the PV of the cash flows as of July 1, 2006. Discount that value back 22.5 periods to find the PV of the deferred payments as of January 1984.

$$PV(\text{Deferred Payments 2}) = \$125{,}000\, A^{10}_{0.09} / [(1.044)(1.09)^{22}]$$
$$= \$115{,}399.28$$

$$NPV(\text{Contract}) = PV(C_1) + PV(C_2) + PV(C_3) + PV(C_4) + PV(C_5) + PV(C_6) +$$
$$PV(\text{Deferred Payments 1}) + PV(\text{Deferred Payments 2})$$
$$= \$838{,}122.61 + \$571{,}197.58 + \$644{,}965.51 + \$739{,}639.35 +$$
$$\$678{,}568.21 + \$186{,}761.89 + \$1{,}276{,}499.81 + \$115{,}399.28$$
$$= \mathbf{\$5{,}051{,}154.24}$$

The PV of the contract is \$5,051,154.24.

To find the equivalent annual salary from year 1984 through 1988, set the PV of the five-year annuity equal to the PV of the contract.

$$PV(\text{Contract}) = C\, A^T_r$$
$$\$5{,}051{,}154.24 = C\, A^5_{0.09}$$
$$\$5{,}051{,}154.24 / A^5_{0.09} = C$$
$$\mathbf{\$1{,}298{,}613.65} = C$$

The equivalent annual salary from year 1984 through 1988 is \$1,298,613.65.

4.50   First, calculate the monthly interest rate.

$$\text{Monthly Interest Rate} = 0.08 / 12$$
$$= 0.0067$$

Mike's balloon payment is the PV of the remaining mortgage payments as of the end of year 8. To calculate the PV of the remaining payments, first calculate Mike's monthly payment. Because he had to make a 20 percent down payment, Mike borrows \$320,000 (=\$400,000 × 0.8). Set this amount equal to a 360 period annuity (=30 years × 12 monthly payments), discounted at the monthly interest rate.

Loan	$= C \, A^{360}_{0.0067}$
$320,000	$= C \, A^{360}_{0.0067}$
$320,000 / A^{360}_{0.0067}$	$= C$
$2,356.98	$= C$

At the end of the eighth year, Mike will have made 96 payments (=8 years × 12 monthly payments). Thus, he will have 264 remaining payments (=360 – 96). His balloon payment is the PV of those remaining payments. Apply the annuity formula, discounted at 0.0067, to the 264 remaining monthly payments to find the PV of Mike's balloon payment, as of the end of year 8.

PV(Balloon)	$= \$2,356.98 \, A^{264}_{0.0067}$
	$= \$291,439.54$

The value of Mike's balloon payment at the end of year 8 will be $291,439.54.

4.51   First, calculate the monthly interest rate.

Monthly Interest Rate	= 0.12 / 12
	= 0.01

Then set the PV of the lease payments equal to $4,000, the retail price of the equipment. Since the first payment is due immediately, value all payments except the payment made today using the standard annuity formula. Because the first payment is treated separately from the others, the annuity has 23 periods instead of 24 periods. Add back the payment made immediately.

PV	$= C \, A^{T}_{r} + C$
$4,000	$= C \, A^{23}_{0.01} + C$
$4,000	$= C \, (A^{23}_{0.01} + 1)$
$4,000 / (A^{23}_{0.01} + 1)$	$= C$
$186.43	$= C$

The monthly lease payment will be $186.43.

4.52   The effective annual yield (EAY) is the appropriate discount rate because it captures the effect of compounding periods. First calculate the EAY.

EAY	$= [1+(r / m)]^{m} - 1$
	$= [1+(0.08 / 4)]^{4} - 1$
	$= 0.0824$

Next, discount the payments of the annuity. The first payment is made at the end of year 5. Since the standard annuity formula calculates the PV of the cash flows as of one year before the first payment, applying the formula will yield the PV as of the end of year 4. Discount that value back four years to find the PV of the annuity as of today.

PV	$= C_5 \, A^{T}_{r} / (1+r)^{4}$
	$= \$900 \, A^{10}_{0.0824} / (1.0824)^{4}$
	$= \$4,352.43$

The PV of the annuity is $4,352.43.

4.53   For the project to be an attractive investment, the NPV should be >0.

Initial Investment $= C_0 = -1,800$ (all numbers hereafter are in thousands)
Note: First year of production occurs in year 3
$C_1 = 0$
$C_2 = 0$
$C_3 = 60$
$C_4 = 60*1.04 = 62.4$
$C_5 = 62.4*1.04 = 64.9$
$C_6 = 64.9*1.04 = 67.5$
$C_7 = 67.5*1.04 = 70.2$
$C_8 = 70.2*1.04 = 73$

Starting year 8, cash flows form a perpetuity

Therefore, $-1,800 + 0/1.1^1 + 0/1.1^2 + 60/1.1^3 + 62.4/1.1^4 + 64.9/1.1^5 + 67.5/1.1^6 + 70.2/1.1^7 +$

$$\frac{\left(\dfrac{73}{0.10-g}\right)}{(1.1)^7} = 0 \text{ (in the limiting case, NPV is at least zero)}$$

Note: Using the formula for PV of perpetuity gives the PV for one year before the year of first cash flow of the perpetuity. In our problem, PV formula for the perpetuity gives the present value in year 7 which needs to be discounted back by 7 years

Solving we get, **g = 7.66%**

(Be wary of truncation or rounding errors)

4.54   In this problem, we need to calculate Paul's annual savings in the 5 years of operation of his health club and compute their future value in year 5.

Savings $(S) =$ Revenue $(R) -$ Cost (C)

Since both annual fee as well as membership are growing, we need to computed the effective growth rate (EGR) for revenues:

EGR $= (1 + 10\%)(1 + 3\%) - 1$
EGR $= 13.3\%$ $R_0 =$ 200,000.00

    $R_1 =$ 226,600.00
    $R_2 =$ 256,737.80
    $R_3 =$ 290,883.93
    $R_4 =$ 329,571.49
    $R_5 =$ 373,404.50

    $G =$ 2% $C_0 =$ 80,000.00

    $C1 =$ 81,600.00
    $C2 =$ 83,232.00
    $C3 =$ 84,896.64
    $C4 =$ 86,594.57
    $C5 =$ 88,326.46

$$S1 = \quad 145,000.00$$
$$S2 = \quad 173,505.80$$
$$S3 = \quad 205,987.29$$
$$S4 = \quad 242,976.92$$
$$S5 = \quad 285,078.03$$

Using Table A.3, we get future value of savings = $1,203,594.91

Paul buys a boat for $500,000. Therefore, at the end of year 5, Paul is left with $703,594.91

The annual amount that Paul can spend while on his world tour for a remaining life of 15 years is $82,200.61.

Appendix 4A: Net Present Value: First Principles of Finance

4A.1 $120,000 – ($150,000 – $100,000) (1.1) = $65,000

4A.2 $40,000 + ($50,000 – $20,000) (1.12) = $73,600

4A.3   Financial markets arise to facilitate borrowing and lending between individuals. By borrowing and lending, people can adjust their pattern of consumption over time to fit their particular preferences. This allows corporations to accept all positive NPV projects, regardless of the inter-temporal consumption preferences of the shareholders.

4A.4   a.   Since the PV of labor income is $60, and $60 = $40 + $22/(1 + r), r must be equal to 10%.
        b.   NPV = $75 – $60 = $15
        c.   Her wealth is $75. Letting C denote consumption, she wants $75 = C + C/(1 + r) where r = 0.10. Solve for C; C = $39.29.

4A.5   a. $90,000/$80,000 – 1 = 0.125 = 12.5%
        b.   Harry will invest $10,000 in financial assets and $30,000 in productive assets today.
        c.   NPV = –$30,000 + $56,250/1.125
              = $20,000

Chapter 5: How to Value Bonds and Stocks

5.1   The present value of any pure discount bond is its face value discounted back to the present.

    a.   PV $= F / (1+r)^{10}$
                     $= \$1,000 / (1.05)^{10}$
                     $= \$613.91$

    b.   PV $= \$1,000 / (1.10)^{10}$
                     $= \$385.54$

    c.   PV $= \$1,000 / (1.15)^{10}$
                     $= \$247.19$

5.2   First, find the amount of the semiannual coupon payment.

    Semiannual Coupon Payment   = Annual Coupon Payment / 2
                                       = $(0.08 \times \$1,000) / 2$
                                       = $\$40$

    a.   Since the stated annual interest rate is compounded semiannually, simply divide this rate by two in order to calculate the semiannual interest rate.

    Semiannual Interest Rate   = 0.08 / 2
                                = 0.04

The bond has 40 coupon payments (=20 years × 2 payments per year). Apply the annuity formula to calculate the PV of the 40 coupon payments. In addition, the $1,000 payment at maturity must be discounted back 40 periods.

    P $= C\ A^{T}_{r} + F / (1+r)^{40}$
          $= \$40\ A^{40}_{0.04} + \$1,000 / (1.04)^{40}$
          $= \$1,000$

The price of the bond is $1,000. Notice that whenever the coupon rate and the market rate are the same, the bond is priced at par. That is, its market value is equal to its face value.

    b.   Semiannual Interest Rate   = 0.10 / 2
                                = 0.05

    P $= \$40\ A^{40}_{0.05} + \$1,000 / (1.05)^{40}$
        $= \$828.41$

The price of the bond is $828.41. Notice that whenever the coupon rate is below the market rate, the bond is priced below par.

    c.   Semiannual Interest Rate   = 0.06 / 2
                                  = 0.03

    P $= \$40\ A^{40}_{0.03} + \$1,000 / (1.03)^{40}$
        $= \$1,231.15$

The price of the bond is $1,231.15. Notice that whenever the coupon rate is above the market rate, the bond is priced above par.

5.3   Since the payments occur semiannually, discount them at the semiannual interest rate. Convert the effective annual yield (EAY) to a semiannual interest rate.

$$\text{Semiannual Interest Rate} = (1+\text{EAY})^{1/T} - 1$$
$$= (1.12)^{1/2} - 1$$
$$= 0.0583$$

a.   Calculate the semiannual coupon payment.

$$\text{Semiannual Coupon Payment} = \text{Annual Coupon Payment} / 2$$
$$= (0.08 \times \$1,000) / 2$$
$$= \$40$$

Apply the annuity formula to calculate the PV of the 40 coupon payments (=20 years × 2 payments per year). In addition, the $1,000 payment at maturity must be discounted back 40 periods. The appropriate discount rate is the semiannual interest rate.

$$P = C\, A^{T}_{r} + F / (1+r)^{40}$$
$$= \$40\, A^{40}_{0.0583} + \$1,000 / (1.0583)^{40}$$
$$= \mathbf{\$718.65}$$

The price of the bond is $718.65.

b.   Calculate the semiannual coupon payment.

$$\text{Semiannual Coupon Payment} = (0.10 \times \$1,000) / 2$$
$$= \$50$$

Apply the annuity formula to calculate the PV of the 30 coupon payments (=15 years × 2 payments per year). In addition, the $1,000 payment at maturity must be discounted back 30 periods. The appropriate discount rate is the semiannual interest rate.

$$P = \$50\, A^{30}_{0.0583} + \$1,000 / (1.0583)^{30}$$
$$= \mathbf{\$883.64}$$

The price of the bond is $883.64.

5.4   First, calculate the semiannual interest rate.

$$\text{Semiannual Interest Rate} = (1+\text{EAY})^{1/T} - 1$$
$$= (1.10)^{1/2} - 1$$
$$= 0.04881$$

Next, find the semiannual coupon payment.

$$\text{Semiannual Coupon Payment} = (0.08 \times \$1,000) / 2$$
$$= \$40$$

The bond has 40 payments (=20 years × 2 payments per year). Apply the annuity formula to find the PV of the coupon payments. In addition, discount the $1,000 payment at maturity back 40 periods. The appropriate discount rate is the semiannual interest rate.

$$P = C \, A^T_r + F / (1+r)^{40}$$
$$= \$40 \, A^{40}_{0.04881} + \$1,000 / (1.04881)^{40}$$
$$= \mathbf{\$846.33}$$

The price of the bond is $846.33.

5.5   First, calculate the semiannual interest rate.

$$\text{Semiannual Interest Rate} = 0.10 / 2$$
$$= 0.05$$

Set the price of the bond equal to the sum of the PV of the 30 semiannual coupon payments (=15 years × 2 payments per year) and the PV of the payment at maturity. The PV of the semiannual coupon payments should be expressed as an annuity. Solve for C, the semiannual coupon payment.

P	$= C \, A^T_r + F / (1+r)^{30}$
$923.14	$= C \, A^{30}_{0.05} + \$1,000 / (1.05)^{30}$
$[\$923.14 - \$1,000 / (1.05)^{30}] / A^{30}_{0.05}$	$= C$
$45	$= C$

To find the coupon rate on the bond, set the semiannual coupon payment, $45, equal to the product of the coupon rate and face value of the bond, divided by two.

Semiannual Coupon Payment	= (Coupon Rate × Face Value) / 2
$45	= (Coupon Rate × $1,000) / 2
$90	= Coupon Rate × $1,000
$90 / $1,000	= Coupon Rate
0.09	= Coupon Rate

The annual coupon rate is 9 percent.

5.6   a.   The market interest rate and the coupon rate are equal because the bond is selling at par. Since the face value of the bond is $1,000 and the semiannual coupon payment is $60, the semiannual coupon rate is six percent (=$60 / $1,000). Thus, the semiannual interest rate is also six percent. Calculate the yield, expressed as an effective annual yield, by compounding the semiannual interest rate over two periods.

$$\text{Yield} = (1+r)^2 - 1$$
$$= (1.06)^2 - 1$$
$$= \mathbf{0.1236}$$

The yield is 0.1236.

b.   You are willing to pay a price equal to the PV of the bond's payments. To find the PV of the 12 coupon payments, apply the annuity formula, discounted at the semiannual rate of return. Also, discount the $1,000 payment made at maturity back to the present. The discount rate, r, is the same as calculated in part (a).

$$P = C \, A^T_r + F / (1+r)^{12}$$
$$= \$30 \, A^{12}_{0.06} + \$1,000 / (1.06)^{12}$$
$$= \mathbf{\$748.49}$$

The price of the bond is $748.49.

c. If the five-year bond pays $40 in semiannual payments and is priced at par, the semiannual rate of return will be different from that in part (a). Since the face value of the bond is $1,000 and the semiannual coupon payment is $40, the semiannual interest rate is four percent (=$40 / $1,000). To calculate the price of the bond, apply the annuity formula, discounted at the semiannual interest rate. In addition, discount the $1,000 payment made at maturity back 12 periods.

$$P = C\, A^T_r + F / (1+r)^{12}$$
$$= \$30\, A^{12}_{0.04} + \$1,000 / (1.04)^{12}$$
$$= \mathbf{\$906.15}$$

The price of the bond is $906.15.

5.7 a. Since the coupon rates of the bonds are equal to the market interest rate, the bonds are priced at face value. Both bonds have face values of $1,000.

$$P_A = \mathbf{\$1,000}$$

$$P_B = \mathbf{\$1,000}$$

b. Discount the cash flows of the bonds at 12 percent. Since the coupon rates of both bonds are less than the market interest rate, the bonds will be priced at a discount.

$$P_A = \$100\, A^{20}_{0.12} + \$1,000 / (1.12)^{20}$$
$$= \mathbf{\$850.61}$$

$$P_B = \$100\, A^{10}_{0.12} + \$1,000 / (1.12)^{10}$$
$$= \mathbf{\$887.00}$$

c. Discount the cash flows of the bonds at eight percent. Since the coupon rates of both bonds are greater than the market interest rate, the bonds will be priced at a premium.

$$P_A = \$100\, A^{20}_{0.08} + \$1,000 / (1.08)^{20}$$
$$= \mathbf{\$1,196.36}$$

$$P_B = \$100\, A^{10}_{0.08} + \$1,000 / (1.08)^{10}$$
$$= \mathbf{\$1,134.20}$$

5.8 a. The prices of long-term bonds should fall. The price of any bond is the PV of the cash flows associated with the bond. As the interest rate increases, the PV of those cash flows falls. This can be easily seen by looking at a one-year, pure discount bond.

$$P = \$1,000 / (1+i)$$

As i increases, the denominator, $(1 + i)$, rises, thus reducing the value of the numerator ($1,000). The price of the bond decreases.

b. The effect on stocks is not as clear-cut as the effect on bonds. The nominal interest rate is a function of both the real interest rate, r, and the inflation rate, i.e.,

$$(1+i) = (1+r)\,(1+\text{Inflation})$$

From this relationship it is easy to conclude that, as inflation rises, the nominal interest rate, *i*, rises. However, stock prices are a function of dividends and future prices as well as the interest rate. Those dividends and future prices are determined by the earning power of the firm. Inflation may increase or decrease firm earnings. Thus, a rise in interest rates has an uncertain effect on the general level of stock prices.

5.9 Set the price of the bond equal to the PV of its cash flows, discounted at the yield to maturity, *r*. Solve for *r*.

a.
$$P = C \, A^T_r + F / (1+r)^{20}$$
$$\$1,200 = \$80 \, A^{20}_r + \$1,000 / (1+r)^{20}$$
$$r = \mathbf{0.0622}$$

The yield to maturity is 6.22 percent.

b.
$$\$950 = \$80 \, A^{10}_r + \$1,000 / (1+r)^{10}$$
$$r = \mathbf{0.0877}$$

The yield to maturity is 8.77 percent.

5.10 The appropriate discount rate is the semiannual interest rate because the bond makes semiannual payments. Thus, calculate the appropriate semiannual interest rate for both bonds *A* and *B*.

$$\text{Semiannual Interest Rate} = 0.12 / 2$$
$$= 0.06$$

a. The price of Bond *A* is the sum of the PVs of each of its cash flow streams. Apply the delayed annuity formula to calculate the PV of the 16 payments of \$2,000 that begin in year 7 as well as to calculate the PV of the 12 payments of \$2,500 that begin in year 15. Because the payments are made semiannually, the delayed annuities begin in periods 13 and 29, respectively. Applying the annuity formula will yield the PV of a stream as of one period prior to its first payment. Thus, applying the annuity formula will yield the PV of the streams as of periods 12 and 28, respectively. To find the PV as of today (year 0) discount those streams back 12 and 28 periods, respectively. Also, discount the payment made at maturity back 40 periods.

$$P_A = C \, A^T_r / (1+r)^{12} + C \, A^T_r / (1+r)^{28} + F / (1+r)^{40}$$
$$= \$2,000 \, A^{16}_{0.06} / (1.06)^{12} + \$2,500 \, A^{12}_{0.06} / (1.06)^{28} + \$40,000 / (1.06)^{40}$$
$$= \mathbf{\$18,033.86}$$

The price of Bond *A* is \$18,033.86.

b. Discount Bond *B*'s face value back 40 periods at the semiannual interest rate.

$$P_B = \$40,000 / (1.06)^{40}$$
$$= \mathbf{\$3,888.89}$$

The price of Bond *B* is \$3,888.89.

5.11 a. **True.** The bond with the shortest maturity is the ATT 5 1/8, which matures in 2003. Its closing price is 100, or 100 percent of the \$1,000 face value.

b. **True.** The coupon rate of the bond maturing in 2018 is nine percent. The coupon payment is \$90 (=\$1,000 × 0.09).

c. **True.** The price of the bond on February 10, 2002 was 107 3/8. Since that price marked a 1/8 decline from the day before, the price on February 9, 2002 was 107 4/8, or $1,075.

d. **False.** The current yield is the annual coupon payment divided by the price of the bond. For the AT&T bond maturing in 2002, the current yield is 6.84 percent (=$71.25 / $1,041.25).

e. **True.** Since the bond is priced at a premium, the coupon rate must be higher than the current yield to maturity.

5.12 a. **True.** Since the bond is priced at a discount, the yield to maturity must be greater than the bond's coupon rate.

b. **False.** The closing price of the bond on Thursday, April 22, 2002 is 100 3/8, or $1,003.75. Since that price marked a 1/8 decline from the day before, the close on April 21, 2002 is 100 1/2, or $1,005.

c. **True.** The coupon rate is 7.5 percent. Thus, the annual coupon payment is $75 (=$1,000 × 0.075).

d. **True.** The current yield is the annual coupon payment divided by the price of the bond. The current yield is 0.0729 (=$75 / $1,028.85).

5.13 The price of a share of stock is the PV of its dividend payments. Since a dividend of $2 was paid yesterday, the next dividend payment, to be received one year from today, will be $2.16 (=$2 × 1.08). The dividend for each of the two successive years will also grow at eight percent.

$$
\begin{aligned}
\text{PV(Year } 1-3) &= \text{Div}_1 / (1+r) + \text{Div}_2 / (1+r)^2 + \text{Div}_3 / (1+r)^3 \\
&= \$2.16 / (1.12) + \$2.33 / (1.12)^2 + \$2.52 / (1.12)^3 \\
&= \$5.58
\end{aligned}
$$

The dividend at year 4 is $2.62 since the $2 dividend that occurred yesterday has grown three years at eight percent and one year at four percent [=$2 × (1.08)³ × 1.04]. Applying the perpetuity formula to the dividends that begin in year 4 will generate the PV as of the end of year 3. Discount that value back three periods to find the PV as of today, year 0.

$$
\begin{aligned}
\text{PV(Year } 4 - \infty) &= [\text{Div}_4 / (r - g)] / (1+r)^3 \\
&= [\$2.62 / (0.12 - 0.04)] / (1.12)^3 \\
&= \$23.31
\end{aligned}
$$

The price of the bond is the sum of the PVs of the first three dividend payments and the PV of the dividend payments thereafter.

$$
\begin{aligned}
P &= \text{Div}_1 / (1+r) + \text{Div}_2 / (1+r)^2 + \text{Div}_3 / (1+r)^3 + [\text{Div}_4 / (r - g)] / (1+r)^3 \\
&= \$2.16 / (1.12) + \$2.33 / (1.12)^2 + \$2.52 / (1.12)^3 + [\$2.62 / (0.12 - 0.04)] / (1.12)^3 \\
&= \mathbf{\$28.89}
\end{aligned}
$$

The price of the stock is $28.89.

5.14 a. **True.** The dividend yield is the dividend payment divided by the price of the stock.

$$
\begin{aligned}
\text{Dividend Yield} &= \text{Div}_1 / P_0 \\
&= \$1.8 / \$115 \\
&= \mathbf{0.0156}
\end{aligned}
$$

b.   **False.** On February 11, 2002, the stock closed at $115, marking a $1.25 decline from the previous day's close. Thus, on February 10, 2002, the stock's closing price was $116.25.

c.   **True.** The closing price of the stock was $115 on February 11, 2002.

d.   **True.** Set the price-earnings ratio (P/E) of 30 equal to the stock's price (P) divided by the earnings per share (EPS). Solve for earnings.

P/E $= P_0 / \text{EPS}$
30      $= \$115 / \text{EPS}$
EPS $= \$115 / 30$
EPS $= \mathbf{\$3.83}$

5.15   Use the growing perpetuity formula to price the stock. The first dividend payment is $1.39 ($=\$1.30 \times 1.07$). The dividend of $1.30 was paid yesterday, and thus, does not figure into today's stock price. Solve for the discount rate, r.

P $= \text{Div}_1 / (r - g)$
$98.13 $= \$1.39 / (r - .07)$
r $= \mathbf{0.084}$

The required return is 8.4 percent.

5.16   To find the number of shares you own, divide the total value of your shares ($100,000) by the price per share. The price of each share is the PV of its cash flows, which include after-tax dividend payments and capital gains. You will receive pre-tax dividend payments of $2 and $4 in years 1 and 2, respectively.

PV(Dividends) $= (1 - T) \text{Div}_1 / (1+r) + (1 - T) \text{Div}_2 / (1+r)^2$
                $= (0.72) \$2 / (1.15) + (0.72) \$4 / (1.15)^2$
                $= \$3.43$

At the end of year 3, you will sell the stock at $50.

PV(Cap. Gain) $= C / (1+r)^3$
                $= \$50 / (1.15)^3$
                $= \$32.88$

The price per share is the sum of the PV of the dividend payments and the PV of the capital gain.

P $= (1 - T_c) \text{Div}_1 / (1+r) + (1 - T_c) \text{Div}_2 / (1+r)^2 + C / (1+r)^3$
        $= (0.72) \$2 / (1.15) + (0.72) \$4 / (1.15)^2 + \$50 / (1.15)^3$
        $= \$36.31$

Divide the total value of your position by the price per share to find the number of shares held.

Shares = Total Value / Price Per Share
        $= \$100,000 / \$36.31$
        $= \mathbf{2,754}$

You own 2,754 shares.

5.17   a.   Apply the constant-dividend growth model to find the price of the stock.

$$P = Div_1 / (r - g)$$
$$= \$2 / (0.12 - 0.05)$$
$$= \$28.57$$

The price of the stock is $28.57.

b.   To determine the price of the stock 10 years from today, find the PV of the stock's dividends as of year 10. The first relevant dividend is paid at year 11. That payment is equal to the original $2 dividend compounded at five percent over 10 years, $3.26 $[=(1.05)^{10} \times \$2]$. Apply the growing perpetuity formula, discounted at 12 percent and growing at five percent. Remember that the growing perpetuity formula values the cash flows as of one year prior to the first cash flow. Therefore, the result is the PV of the dividend payments as of year 10, the year at which you are valuing the stock.

$$P_{10} = Div_{11} / (r - g)$$
$$= (1.05)^{10} \, \$2 / (0.12 - 0.05)$$
$$= \$46.54$$

The price of the stock in 10 years from today will be $46.54.

5.18   Find the PV of the dividend payments. Since the dividend of $1.15 was just paid yesterday, the dividend payment in year 1 is $1.36 (=$1.15 × 1.18). Remember to adjust the dividend payment each year for the appropriate growth rate.

Div_1	$= \$1.15 \times 1.18$	$= \$1.36$
Div_2	$= \$1.15 \times 1.18^2$	$= \$1.60$
Div_3	$= \$1.15 \times 1.18^2 \times 1.15$	$= \$1.84$
Div_4	$= \$1.15 \times 1.18^2 \times 1.15 \times 1.06$	$= \$1.95$

Apply the growing perpetuity formula to find the PV of the dividend payments starting in year 4 and growing at six percent forever. Since the perpetuity formula yields the PV of the cash flows as of year 3, discount the perpetuity back three periods to find its value as of today.

$$P = Div_1 / (1+r) + Div_2 / (1+r)^2 + Div_3 / (1+r)^3 + [Div_4 / (r-g)] / (1+r)^3$$
$$= \$1.36 / (1.12) + \$1.60 / (1.12)^2 + \$1.84 / (1.12)^3 + [\$1.95 / (0.12 - 0.06)] / (1.12)^3$$
$$= \$26.93$$

The price of the stock is $26.93.

5.19   Apply the growing perpetuity formula, discounted at 14 percent and declining at 10 percent per year, to find the PV of all the dividend payments beginning a year from now. The dividend payment a year from now is $4.50 $[=\$5 \times (1 - 0.10)]$. Add the dividend payment of $5 that is about to be paid. Since it occurs tomorrow, do not discount this payment. The PV of the dividend payments is the value of the firm's stock.

$$P = Div_1 / (r - g) + Div_0$$
$$= \$4.50 / [0.14 - (-0.10)] + \$5$$
$$= \$23.75$$

The value of the firm's stock is $23.75.

5.20 The dividend payments must be discounted at the quarterly interest rate.

$$\text{Quarterly Interest Rate} = 0.1 / 4$$
$$= 0.025$$

Apply the annuity formula, discounted at 0.025, to find the PV of the first 12 quarterly payments of $1.

$$PV_{1\text{-}12} = Div_1\, A^T_r$$
$$= \$1\, A^{12}_{0.025}$$
$$= \$10.26$$

Next, apply the perpetuity formula to find the PV of the dividend payments that start at quarter 13 and grow at 0.5 percent each quarter. The dividend payment at quarter 13 is $1.005 (=$1 × 1.005). Since the perpetuity formula calculates the PV of the payments as of quarter 12, discount that value back 12 quarters to find the value as of today.

$$PV_{13\text{-}\infty} = [Div_{13} / (r - g)] / (1+r)^{12}$$
$$= [\$1.005 / (0.025 - 0.005)] / (1.025)^{12}$$
$$= \$37.36$$

The price of the stock is the sum of the present values of the dividend payments.

$$P = Div_1\, A^T_r + [Div_{13} / (r - g)] / (1+r)^{12}$$
$$= \$1\, A^{12}_{0.025} + [\$1.005 / (0.025 - 0.005)] / (1.025)^{12}$$
$$= \mathbf{\$47.62}$$

The price of the stock is $47.62.

5.21 The price of the stock is the PV of the dividend payments. Apply the discounted-dividend model to find the price of a share of stock. Since the $1.40 dividend was just paid, the first dividend payment will be $1.47 (=$1.4 × 1.05). Apply the growing perpetuity formula, discounted at 10 percent and growing at five percent per year.

$$P = Div_1 / (r - g)$$
$$= \$1.47 / (0.1 - 0.05)$$
$$= \mathbf{\$29.40}$$

The share price is $29.40.

5.22 The price of the stock is the PV of the dividend payments. Discount the dividends paid in years 3 and 4 back to year 0. Next, apply the growing perpetuity formula to the dividend payments that start in year 5. Since the growing perpetuity formula values the dividend payment as of the end of year 4, discount that value back 4 years to calculate the PV of the dividend payment as of today, year 0. Remember that the dividend in year 5 is $2.12 (=$2 × 1.06).

$$P = Div_3 / (1+r)^3 + Div_4 / (1+r)^4 + [Div_5 / (r - g)] / (1+r)^4$$
$$= \$2.00 / (1.16)^3 + \$2.00 / (1.16)^4 + [\$2.12 / (0.16 - 0.06)] / (1.16)^4$$
$$= \mathbf{\$14.09}$$

The share price is $14.09.

5.23 Discount each future dividend payment. The dividend payment at the end of year 1 is $5.99 (=$5.25 × 1.14). The dividend at the end of year 2 is $6.64 (=$5.25 × 1.14 × 1.11), and so on. After the annual dividend growth rate reaches 5 percent, apply the growing perpetuity formula to find the PV of the future payments. Remember to discount the value of the growing perpetuity back four periods because it values the stream as of one year before the first payment at date 5.

$$
\begin{array}{lll}
Div_1 & = \$5.25 \times 1.14 & = \$5.99 \\
Div_2 & = \$5.25 \times 1.14 \times 1.11 & = \$6.64 \\
Div_3 & = \$5.25 \times 1.14 \times 1.11 \times 1.08 & = \$7.17 \\
Div_4 & = \$5.25 \times 1.14 \times 1.11 \times 1.08 \times 1.05 & = \$7.53 \\
Div_5 & = \$5.25 \times 1.14 \times 1.11 \times 1.08 \times 1.05 \times 1.05 & = \$7.91
\end{array}
$$

$$
\begin{aligned}
P &= Div_1 / (1+r)^1 + Div_2 / (1+r)^2 + Div_3 / (1+r)^3 + Div_4 / (1+r)^4 \\
&\quad + [Div_5 / (r-g)] / (1+r)^4 \\
&= (\$5.99) / (1.14) + (\$6.64) / (1.14)^2 + (\$7.17) / (1.14)^3 + (\$7.53) / (1.14)^4 + \\
&\quad [(\$7.91) / (0.14 - 0.05)] / (1.14)^4 \\
&= \mathbf{\$71.70}
\end{aligned}
$$

A share of Webster stock is $71.70.

5.24   Express the price of Allen's stock as the PV of the dividend payments.

The PV of the first two dividend payments can be expressed as follows.

$$
\begin{aligned}
PV &= Div / (1+r) + Div / (1+r)^2 \\
&= Div / (1.12) + Div / (1.12)^2
\end{aligned}
$$

Apply the growing perpetuity formula, discounted at 12 percent and growing at four percent, to find the PV of the dividend payments that begin in year 3. Remember that the dividend paid at year 3 is four percent greater than the previous year's dividend. Thus, the payment at year 3 is $(1.04) \times Div$. Since the growing perpetuity formula values a stream as of one year prior to the first cash flow, discount the value of the growing perpetuity back two years to find the PV as of today.

$$
\begin{aligned}
PV &= [(1+g) Div / (r-g)] / (1+r)^2 \\
&= [(1.04) Div / (0.12 - 0.04)] / (1.12)^2
\end{aligned}
$$

Set the current market price of the stock equal to the PV of all of the stock's future dividend payments. Solve for *Div*.

$$
\begin{aligned}
P &= Div / (1+r) + Div / (1+r)^2 + [(1+g) Div / (r-g)] / (1+r)^2 \\
\$30 &= Div / (1.12) + Div / (1.12)^2 + [(1.04) Div / (0.12 - 0.04)] / (1.12)^2 \\
Div &= \mathbf{\$2.49}
\end{aligned}
$$

The expected dividend payment next year is $2.49.

5.25   a.   The growth rate of a firm's earnings is equal to the retention ratio of the firm times the return on equity. Applying this formula, we find a growth rate of:

$$
\begin{aligned}
g &= \text{Retention Ratio} \times \text{Return on Equity} \\
&= (0.60)(0.14) \\
&= \mathbf{0.084} \\
&= \mathbf{8.4\%}
\end{aligned}
$$

The firm's growth rate is 8.4 percent.

b.   Multiply the firm's current earnings ($20,000,000) by the growth rate calculated in part (*a*) to find next year's earnings.

Next Year's Earnings $\quad$ = Current Earnings $\times (1+g)$
$\qquad\qquad\qquad\qquad\qquad$ = \$20,000,000 (1.084)
$\qquad\qquad\qquad\qquad\qquad$ = **\$21,680,000**

The firm's earnings next year will be \$21,680,000.

5.26 $\quad$ Express the rate of return in terms of the dividend yield and g, the growth rate of dividends. The dividend yield is the next dividend payment, Div_1, divided by the current stock price, P. The rate of return, r, is equal to the sum of the dividend yield and g.

$\qquad$ r $\qquad$ = $Div_1 / P + g$

To solve for the growth rate, g, apply the formula for the growth rate of a firm's earnings.

$\qquad$ g $\qquad$ = Retention Ratio $\times$ Return on Retained Earnings
$\qquad\qquad\qquad$ = (0.75) (0.12)
$\qquad\qquad\qquad$ = 0.09

Find the dividend payment per share made yesterday. Since the retention ratio is 75 percent, the firm pays out 25 percent of its \$10 million earnings as dividend payments. Thus, the total dividend payment made yesterday was \$2,500,000 [=\$10,000,000 $\times$ (1 – 0.75)]. To find the dividend paid per share, divide the total dividend payment by the total number of shares outstanding.

$\qquad$ Dividend per Share $\qquad$ = [Total Earnings $\times$ (1 – Retention Ratio)] / Number of Shares
$\qquad\qquad\qquad\qquad\qquad$ = [\$10,000,000 $\times$ (1 – 0.75)] / 1,250,000
$\qquad\qquad\qquad\qquad\qquad$ = \$2

Take note that the dividend payment *next* year is needed to solve for the rate of return, r. Next year, the firm's earnings and dividend will grow at the annual growth rate of nine percent, as calculated above. Thus, the dividend will be \$2.18 (=\$2 $\times$ 1.09). Solve for the discount rate, r.

$\qquad$ r $\qquad$ = $Div_1 / P_0 + g$
$\qquad\qquad\quad$ = \$2.18 / \$30 + 0.09
$\qquad\qquad\quad$ = **0.1627**

The rate of return on the stock is 16.27 percent.

5.27 $\quad$ First, determine the annual dividend growth rate over the past four years. The following equation relates the dividend paid yesterday to the dividend paid four years ago. Solve for the growth rate, g.

$\qquad$ Div_0 $\qquad\qquad$ = $Div_{-4} (1+g)^4$
$\qquad$ \$1.66 $\qquad\qquad$ = \$0.80 $(1+g)^4$
$\qquad$ g $\qquad\qquad\qquad$ = **0.2002**

For years 1 through 5, the dividend payment will grow at an annual rate of 20.02 percent. Dividends will grow at eight percent per year for the next two years.

$\qquad$ Div_7 $\quad$ = $Div_0 \times (1+g_{1-5})^5 \times (1+g_{6-7})^2$
$\qquad\qquad\quad$ = \$1.66 $\times (1.2002)^5 \times (1.08)^2$
$\qquad\qquad\quad$ = **\$4.82**

The dividend payment in year 7 is \$4.82.

5.28 a. The price of the stock is the net present value of the company's cash flows. Apply the growing perpetuity formula to find the total PV of the firm's revenues and expenses. Remember to multiply last year's revenues and costs by the growth rate since the revenues and costs given in the problem represent last year's cash flows.

PV(Revenues) $= C / (r - g)$
$= (\$3,000,000 \times 1.05) / (0.15 - 0.05)$
$= \$31,500,000$

PV (Costs) $= C / (r - g)$
$= (\$1,500,000 \times 1.05) / (0.15 - 0.05)$
$= \$15,750,000$

NPV $=$ PV(Revenues) $-$ PV(Costs)
$= C / (r - g) - C / (r - g)$
$= (\$3,000,000 \times 1.05) / (0.15 - 0.05) - (\$1,500,000 \times 1.05) / (0.15 - 0.05)$
$= \$15,750,000$

Divide the NPV by the number of shares to find the price per share.

P $=$ Value of Firm / Number of Shares
$= \$15,750,000 / 1,000,000$
$= \mathbf{\$15.75}$

The price of the stock is \$15.75.

b. The value of a company is the NPV of its current operations plus the NPV of its growth opportunities (NPVGO).

The second cash flow from the new project is discounted back one period. The perpetuity formula is used to find the PV of the cash inflows. Since the perpetuity formula values the cash flows as of the end of year 1, this PV must be discounted back one year.

PV $= C_0 + C_1 / (1+r) + [C_2 / r] / (1+r)$
$= -\$15,000,000 - \$5,000,000 / (1.15) + [\$6,000,000 / 0.15] / (1.15)$
$= \$15,434,782.61$

Divide the NPV by the number of shares to find the per-share effect of the new project.

Per Share Effect $= \$15,434,782.61 / 1,000,000$
$= \mathbf{\$15.43}$

The share price will increase by the per-share NPV of the growth opportunity.

Share Price $=$ PV(EPS) $+$ NPVGO
$= \mathbf{PV(EPS) + \$15.43}$

Since the NPVGO per share is \$15.43, the price per share will increase by \$15.43.

5.29 a. Value the firm as a "cash cow," ignoring future projects. Apply the perpetuity formula to calculate the PV of the firm's revenues. The price per share is the PV of the revenues divided by the number of shares outstanding.

PV $= C_1 / r$
$= \$100,000,000 / 0.15$
$= \$666,666,666.67$

Share Price   = \$666,666,666.67 / 20,000,000
                               = **\$33.33**

The share price, excluding future growth opportunities, is \$33.33.

b.   Calculate the NPV of the growth opportunity (NPVGO). The initial cash outlay occurs today and does not need to be discounted. Discount the cash outlay in the second year back to today (year 0). Apply the perpetuity formula to find the PV of the annual earnings as of the end of year 1. Discount that value back one year to find the PV of the annual earnings as of today.

$$\text{NPVGO} = C_0 + C_1 + [C_2 / r] / (1+r)^T$$
$$= -\$15,000,000 - \$5,000,000 / 1.15 + [\$10,000,000 / 0.15] / (1.15)$$
$$= \mathbf{\$38,623,188.41}$$

The value of the growth opportunity is \$38,623,188.41.

c.   Apply the NPVGO model to calculate the price of the stock. The share price is equal to the per-share value of the firm's existing operations, plus the per-share value of growth opportunities. The earnings per share of the firm's existing operations was calculated in part (*a*) and the NPV of the growth opportunity was calculated in part (*b*). Divide the NPVGO by the number of shares to find the per-share NPVGO.

Share Price   = Per-Share PV(Existing Operations) + NPVGO / (Number of Shares)
                               = \$33.33 + \$38,623,188.41 / 20,000,000
                               = **\$35.26**

The share price will be \$35.26 if the firm undertakes the investment.

5.30   a.   If Avalanche does not make the investment, the value of a share of stock will be the PV of its current dividend payments. Apply the perpetuity formula.

P   = Div / r
       = \$4 / 0.14
       = **\$28.57**

The price per share is \$28.57.

b.   First, calculate the growth rate of the investment return. The firm will retain 25 percent of its earnings, and will earn a 40 percent return on its investments.

g   = Retention Ratio × Return on Retained Earnings
       = (0.25) (0.4)
       = 0.1

Calculate the NPV of the investment. During year 3, twenty-five percent of the earnings will be reinvested. Therefore, \$1 is invested (=\$4 × .25). One year later, the shareholders receive a 40 percent return on the investment, in perpetuity. The perpetuity formula values that stream as of year 3. Since the investment opportunity will continue indefinitely and grows at 10 percent, apply the growing perpetuity formula to calculate the NPV of the investment as of year 2. Discount that value back two years to today.

NPVGO   = [(Investment + Return / r) / (r − g)] / (1+r)²
                   = [(-\$1 + \$0.40 / .14) / (0.14 − 0.1)] / (1.14)²
                   = **\$35.73**

The value of the stock is the PV of the firm without making the investment plus the NPV of the investment.

P   = PV(EPS) + NPVGO
         = $28.57 + $35.73
         = **$64.30**

After the announcement of the investment, the share price is $64.30.

5.31   a.   Apply the perpetuity formula to find the price of the firm, P. The firm currently earns $800,000 from its existing operations and will earn an additional $100,000 when it accepts the project.

P   = ($800,000 + $100,000) / 0.15
         = $6,000,000

To calculate the price to earnings ratio, divide the total price of the firm ($6,000,000) by its current earnings ($800,000).

P/E   = $6,000,000 / $800,000
         = **7.5**

The P/E ratio of Pacific Energy is 7.5.

     b.   Again, calculate the price of the firm. The price, P, of the firm is the PV of its current cash flows plus the PV of the cash flows from the project. Apply the perpetuity formula to the current cash flows as well as to the cash flows of the project.

P   = Current Earnings / r + Project Earnings / r
         = $800,000 / 0.15 + $200,000 / 0.15
         = $6,666,666.67

To calculate the price to earnings ratio, divide the total price of the firm ($6,666,666.67) by its current earnings ($800,000).

P/E   = $6,666,666.67 / $800,000
         = **8.33**

The P/E ratio of U.S. Bluechips is 8.33.

5.32   a.   Price = $4/0.14 = $28.57

     b.   Price $= 28.57 + \dfrac{\left(-1+0.40/0.14\right)/0.04}{\left(1.14\right)^3}$

         = 28.57 + 31.33
         = $59.90

     c.   The expected return of 14% less the dividend yield of 5% provides a capital gain yield of 9%. If there is no investment the yield is 14%.

     d. $3/$59.90 = .05 and $4/$28.57 = .14 without the investment.

5.33.   Using dividend model, price of a stock can be written as $P = D/(k - g)$
Or it can be written as $P = E*PO/(k - g)$ where PO is the dividend payout ratio and denotes multiplication
Rearranging terms we get, $P/E = PO/(k - g)$
Substituting values $12 = .4/(k - g)$
→ $1/(k - g) = 12/0.4$
→ $1/(k - g) = 30$

$P = E*PO/(k - g)$
Now substituting $P = \$32$, $PO = 40\%$, $1/(k - g) = 30$ we get
$32 = E*.4*30$
→ $E = 8/3$

If the dividend payout ratio were 60%
$P = E*PO/(k - g)$
$P = (8/3)*.6*30 = $ **$48**

5.34   In this problem growth is occurring from two different sources:
1.   The learning curve
2.   New project

We need to separately compute the value from the two difference sources

First compute the growth from *learning curve*

EPS = Earnings/total number of outstanding shares
EPS = $10 million/10 million
Therefore, EPS = $1

From the NPVGO model, $P = E/(k - g) + NPVGO$

→ $P = 1/(0.10 - 0.05) + NPVGO$
= $\$20 + NPVGO$

Compute the NPVGO of the new project to be launched two years from now
Earnings (per share) of the firm two years from now = $1*(1 + 0.05)^2 = 1.1025$
Therefore, Initial Investment = 20% of $1.1025
$I_0 = \$0.22$
Present value of investment made two years from now $= -0.22/(1.1)^2 = -0.18$ ← cash out
Earnings from the new project is a perpetuity of $0.5
Value of Earnings perpetuity = $0.5/(0.1)
= $5
Present value of Earnings perpetuity = $5/1.1^2
= $4.13

NPVGO (per share) $= -0.18 + 4.13 = \$3.95$ ← cash out

Plugging in the NPVGO model we get,
$P = 20 + 3.95 = $ **$23.95**

Appendix 5A: The Term Structure of Interest Rates, Spot Rates, and Yields to Maturity

5A.1   a.   The present value of any coupon bond is the present value of its coupon payments and face value. Match each cash flow with the appropriate spot rate. For the cash flow that occurs at the end of the first year, use the one-year spot rate. For the cash flow that occurs at the end of the second year, use the two-year spot rate.

$$
\begin{aligned}
P &= C_1 / (1+r_1) + (C_2+F) / (1+r_2)^2 \\
&= \$60 / (1.1) + (\$60 + \$1,000) / (1.11)^2 \\
&= \$54.55 + \$860.32 \\
&= \mathbf{\$914.87}
\end{aligned}
$$

The price of the bond is \$914.87.

b.   The yield to the maturity is the discount rate, y, which sets the cash flows equal to the price of the bond.

$$
\begin{aligned}
P &= C_1 / (1+y) + (C_2+F) / (1+y)^2 \\
\$914.87 &= \$60 / (1+y) + (\$60 + \$1,000) / (1+y)^2 \\
y &= .1097 = \mathbf{10.97\%}
\end{aligned}
$$

The yield to maturity is 10.97%.

5A.2   The present value of any coupon bond is the present value of its coupon payments and face value. Match each cash flow with the appropriate spot rate.

$$
\begin{aligned}
P &= C_1 / (1+r_1) + (C_2+F) / (1+r_2)^2 \\
&= \$50 / (1.10) + (\$50 + \$1,000) / (1.08)^2 \\
&= \$45.45 + \$900.21 \\
&= \mathbf{\$945.66}
\end{aligned}
$$

The price of the bond is \$945.66.

5A.3   Apply the forward rate formula to calculate the one-year rate over the second year.

$$
\begin{aligned}
(1+r_1) \times (1+f_2) &= (1+r_2)^2 \\
(1.09) \times (1+f_2) &= (1.10)^2 \\
f_2 &= .1101
\end{aligned}
$$

The one-year forward rate over the second year is 11.01%.

5A.4   Calculate the forward rate over each year.

a.   Apply the forward rate formula to calculate the one-year forward rate over the second year.

$$
\begin{aligned}
(1+r_1) \times (1+f_2) &= (1+r_2)^2 \\
(1.05) \times (1+f_2) &= (1.07)^2 \\
f_2 &= .0904 = \mathbf{9.04\%}
\end{aligned}
$$

The one-year forward rate over the second year is 9.04%.

b. Apply the forward rate formula to calculate the one-year forward rate over the third year.

$$(1+r_2)^2 \times (1+f_3) = (1+r_3)^3$$
$$(1.07) \times (1+f_3) = (1.10)^3$$
$$f_3 = .1625 = \mathbf{16.25\%}$$

The one-year forward rate over the third year is 16.25%.

5A.5 Spot rate for year 1 is same as forward rate for year 1.

Using $f_2 = (1 + r_2)^2/(1 + r_1) - 1$

Given $f_2 = 12\%$, $r_1 = 5\%$, we get $r_2 = 8.4\%$

5A.6 Based upon the expectation, hypotheses, strategy 1 and strategy 2 will be in equilibrium at
$(1 + f_1)*(1 + f_2) = (1 + r_2)^2$

That is, if the expected spot rate for 2 years is equal to the product of successive one year forward rates. If the spot rate in year 2 is higher than implied by f_2 then strategy 11 is best. If lower, strategy 1 is best.

Chapter 6: Some Alternative Investment Rules

6.1   a.   The payback period is the time that it takes for the cumulative undiscounted cash inflows to equal the initial investment.

Project A:

Cumulative Undiscounted Cash Flows Year 1	= $4,000	= $4,000
Cumulative Undiscounted Cash Flows Year 2	= $4,000 +$3,500	= **$7,500**

Payback period   = **2**

Project *A* has a payback period of two years.

Project B:

Cumulative Undiscounted Cash Flows Year 1	= $2,500	= $2,500
Cumulative Undiscounted Cash Flows Year 2	= $2,500+$1,200	= $3,700
Cumulative Undiscounted Cash Flows Year 3	= $2,500+$1,200+$3,000	= **$6,700**

Project *B*'s cumulative undiscounted cash flows exceed the initial investment of $5,000 by the end of year 3. Many companies analyze the payback period in whole years. The payback period for project *B* is 3 years.

Project *B* has a payback period of three years.

Companies can calculate a more precise value using fractional years. To calculate the fractional payback period, find the fraction of year 3's cash flows that is needed for the company to have cumulative undiscounted cash flows of $5,000. Divide the difference between the initial investment and the cumulative undiscounted cash flows as of year 2 by the undiscounted cash flow of year 3.

Payback period   = 2 + ($5,000 - $3,700) / $3,000
                    = **2.43**

Since project *A* has a shorter payback period than project *B* has, the company should choose project *A*.

   b.   Discount each project's cash flows at 15 percent. Choose the project with the highest NPV.

Project A   = -$7,500 + $4,000 / (1.15) + $3,500 / (1.15)^2 + $1,500 / (1.15)^3
                  = **-$388.96**

Project B   = -$5,000 + $2,500 / (1.15) + $1,200 / (1.15)^2 + $3,000 / (1.15)^3
                  = **$53.83**

The firm should choose Project *B* since it has a higher NPV than Project *A* has.

6.2   a.   Find the payback period for the project. Since the cash inflows are constant, divide the initial investment by the annual cash inflow to determine the payback period.

Payback Period   = Initial Investment / Annual Cash Inflow
                     = $1,000,000 / $150,000
                     = **6.67**

The payback period is 6.67 years. Since the payback period is shorter than the cutoff period of ten years, the project should be accepted.

b. Find the number of years needed for the discounted cash inflows to equal the initial investment of $1 million. Apply the annuity formula, discounted at 10 percent, to find the approximate discounted payback period. The approximate discounted payback period is the year *in which* the PV of the initial investment is surpassed.

Since the discounted payback period will always be greater than the undiscounted payback period when there are positive cash inflows, start the approximation at year 7.

Cumulative Discounted Cash Flows Year 7 $= \$150,000\ A^7_{0.1}$ $= \$730,262.82$
Cumulative Discounted Cash Flows Year 8 $= \$150,000\ A^8_{0.1}$ $= \$800,238.93$
Cumulative Discounted Cash Flows Year 9 $= \$150,000\ A^9_{0.1}$ $= \$863,853.57$
Cumulative Discounted Cash Flows Year 10 $= \$150,000\ A^{10}_{0.1}$ $= \$921,685.07$
Cumulative Discounted Cash Flows Year 11 $= \$150,000\ A^{11}_{0.1}$ $= \$974,259.15$
Cumulative Discounted Cash Flows Year 12 $= \mathbf{\$150,000\ A^{12}_{0.1}}$ $\mathbf{= \$1,022,053.77}$

The cumulative discounted cash flows exceed the initial investment of $1,000,000 by the end of year 12. Many companies analyze the payback period in whole years. The payback period for the project is 12 years.

The discounted payback period is 12 years.

c. Apply the perpetuity formula, discounted at 10 percent, to calculate the PV of the annual cash inflows.

NPV $= -\$1,000,000 + \$150,000\ /\ 0.1$
$= \mathbf{\$500,000}$

The NPV of the project is $500,000.

6.3 a. The *average accounting return* is the average project earnings after taxes, divided by the average book value, or average net investment, of the machine during its life. The book value of the machine is the gross investment minus the accumulated depreciation.

Average Book Value $= (\text{Book Value}_0 + \text{Book Value}_1 + \text{Book Value}_2 + \text{Book Value}_3$
$+ \text{Book Value}_4 + \text{Book Value}_5)\ /\ (\text{Economic Life})$
$= (\$16,000 + \$12,000 + \$8,000 + \$4,000 + \$0)\ /\ (5\ \text{years})$
$= \$8,000$

Average Project Earnings $= \$4,500$

Divide the average project earnings by the average book value of the machine to calculate the average accounting return.

Average Accounting Return $= \text{Average Project Earnings}\ /\ \text{Average Book Value}$
$= \$4,500\ /\ \$8,000$
$= 0.5625$
$= \mathbf{56.25\%}$

The average accounting return is 56.25%.

b. 1. The average accounting return uses accounting data rather than net cash flows.

2. The average accounting return uses an arbitrary firm standard as the decision rule. The firm standard is arbitrary because it does not necessarily relate to a market rate of return.

3. The average accounting return does not consider the timing of cash flows. Hence, it does not consider the time value of money.

6.4 Determine the average book value of the investment. The book value is the gross investment minus accumulated depreciation.

	Purchase	Year 1	Year 2	Year 3	Year 4	Year 0
Gross Investment	$2,000,000	$2,000,000	$2,000,000	$2,000,000	$2,000,000	$2,000,000
Less: Accumulated Depreciation	0	400,000	800,000	1,200,000	1,600,000	2,000,000
Net Investment	$2,000,000	$1,600,000	$1,200,000	$800,000	$400,000	$0

Average Book Value = ($2,000,000 + $1,600,000 + $1,200,000 + $800,000 + $400,000 + $0) / (6)
= $1,000,000

Next, calculate average annual net income.

Net Income Year 1	= $100,000	
Net Income Year 2	= $100,000 × (1.07)	= $107,000
Net Income Year 3	= $100,000 × (1.07)^2	= $114,490
Net Income Year 4	= $100,000 × (1.07)^3	= $122,504
Net Income Year 5	= $100,000 × (1.07)^4	= $131,080

Average Net Income = ($100,000+$107,000+$114,490+$122,504+$131,080) / 5
= $115,015

The average accounting return is the average net income divided by the average book value.

Average Accounting Return = Average Net Income / Average Book Value
= $115,015 / $1,000,000
= 0.115
= **11.5%**

Since the machine's average accounting return, 11.5%, is below the company's cutoff of 20%, the machine should not be purchased.

6.5 First determine the average book value of the project. The book value is the gross investment minus accumulated depreciation.

	Purchase Date	Year 1	Year 2	Year 3
Gross Investment	$8,000	$8,000	$8,000	$8,000
Less: Accumulated Depreciation	0	4,000	6,500	8,000
Net Investment	$8,000	$4,000	$1,500	$0

$$\text{Average Book Value} = (\$8,000 + \$4,000 + \$1,500 + \$0) / (4 \text{ years})$$
$$= \$3,375$$

Remember to use the after-tax average net income when calculating the average accounting return.

$$\text{Average After-tax Net Income} = (1 - T_c) \text{ Annual Pre-tax Net Income}$$
$$= (1 - 0.25) \$2,000$$
$$= \$1,500$$

The average accounting return is the average after-tax net income divided by the average book value.

$$\text{Average Accounting Return} = \$1,500 / \$3,375$$
$$= 0.44$$
$$= 44\%$$

The average accounting return of the machine is 44%.

6.6   The internal rate of return is the discount rate at which the NPV of the project's cash flows equals zero. Set the project's cash flows, discounted at the internal rate of return (IRR), equal to zero. Solve for the IRR.

$$\text{IRR(Project A)} = C_0 + C_1 / (1+\text{IRR}) + C_2 / (1+\text{IRR})^2$$
$$0 = -\$3,000 + \$2,500 / (1+\text{IRR}) + \$1,000 / (1+\text{IRR})^2$$
$$\text{IRR} = 0.1289$$

$$\text{IRR(Project B)} = C_0 + C_1 / (1+\text{IRR}) + C_2 / (1+\text{IRR})^2$$
$$0 = -\$6,000 + \$5,000 / (1+\text{IRR}) + \$1,000 / (1+\text{IRR})^2$$
$$\text{IRR} = 0.1289$$

Note that since Project B's cash flows are two times those of Project A, the IRR's of both projects are the same.

The IRR of both Project A and Project B is 12.89%.

6.7   a.   The internal rate of return is the discount rate at which the NPV of the project's cash flows equal zero. Set the project's cash flows, discounted at the internal rate of return (IRR), equal to zero. Solve for the IRR.

$$\text{IRR} = C_0 + C_1 / (1+\text{IRR}) + C_2 / (1+\text{IRR})^2 + C_3 / (1+\text{IRR})^3$$
$$0 = -\$8,000 + \$4,000 / (1+\text{IRR}) + \$3,000 / (1+\text{IRR})^2 + \$2,000 / (1+\text{IRR})^3$$
$$\text{IRR} = 0.0693$$

The IRR is 6.93%.

    b.   **No.** An investing-type project is one with a negative initial cash outflow and positive future cash inflows. One accepts a project when the IRR is greater than the discount rate. Similarly, one rejects the project when the IRR is less than the discount rate. The project should not be accepted because the IRR (6.93%) is less than the discount rate (8%).

6.8 Set the project's cash flows, discounted at the internal rate of return (IRR), equal to zero. Solve for the IRR.

$$\text{IRR(Project A)} = C_0 + C_1 / (1+\text{IRR}) + C_2 / (1+\text{IRR})^2 + C_3 / (1+\text{IRR})^3$$
$$0 = -\$2,000 + \$2,000 / (1+\text{IRR}) + \$8,000 / (1+\text{IRR})^2 + \$8,000 / (1+\text{IRR})^3$$
$$\text{IRR} = \mathbf{1.88}$$

$$\text{IRR(Project B)} = C_0 + C_1 / (1+\text{IRR}) + C_2 / (1+\text{IRR})^2 + C_3 / (1+\text{IRR})^3$$
$$0 = -\$1,500 + \$500 / (1+\text{IRR}) + \$1,000 / (1+\text{IRR})^2 + \$1,500 / (1+\text{IRR})^3$$
$$\text{IRR} = \mathbf{0.362}$$

The IRR for Project A is 188% and the IRR for Project B is 36.2%.

6.9   a.   Set the project's cash flows, discounted at the internal rate of return (IRR), equal to zero. Solve for the IRR.

$$\text{IRR} = C_0 + C_1 / (1+\text{IRR}) + C_2 / (1+\text{IRR})^2 + C_3 / (1+\text{IRR})^3 + C_4 / (1+\text{IRR})^4$$
$$0 = \$5,000 - \$2,500 / (1+\text{IRR}) - \$2,000 / (1+\text{IRR})^2 - \$1,000 / (1+\text{IRR})^3$$
$$- \$1,000 / (1+\text{IRR})^4$$
$$\text{IRR} = \mathbf{0.1399}$$

The IRR is 13.99%.

b.   This problem differs from previous ones because the initial cash flow is positive and all future cash flows are negative. In other words, this is a financing-type project while previous projects were investing-type projects. For financing situations, accept the project when the IRR is less than the discount rate. Reject the project when the IRR is greater than the discount rate.

IRR   = 13.99%
Discount Rate   = 10%

IRR > Discount Rate

Reject the offer when the discount rate is less than the IRR.

c.   IRR   = 13.99%
Discount Rate   = 20%

IRR < Discount Rate

Accept the offer when the discount rate is greater than the IRR.

d.   Calculate the NPV when the discount rate is 10 percent.

$$\text{NPV} = \$5,000 - \$2,500 / (1.1) - \$2,000 / (1.1)^2 - \$1,000 / (1.1)^3 - \$1,000 / (1.1)^4$$
$$= \mathbf{-\$359.95}$$

When the discount rate is 10 percent, the NPV of the offer is -$359.95. Reject the offer.

Calculate the NPV when the discount rate is 20 percent.

$$\text{NPV} = \$5,000 - \$2,500 / (1.2) - \$2,000 / (1.2)^2 - \$1,000 / (1.2)^3 - \$1,000 / (1.2)^4$$
$$= \mathbf{\$466.82}$$

When the discount rate is 20 percent, the NPV of the offer is $466.82. Accept the offer.

e. Yes, the decisions under the NPV rule are consistent with the choices made under the IRR rule since the signs of the cash flows change only once.

6.10 a. Set the project's cash flows, discounted at the internal rate of return (IRR), equal to zero. Solve for the IRR.

IRR(Project A) $= C_0 + C_1 / (1+IRR) + C_2 / (1+IRR)^2$
0 $= -\$5,000 + \$3,500 / (1+IRR) + \$3,500 / (1+IRR)^2$
IRR $= 0.2569$

The IRR of project A is 25.69%.

IRR(Project B) $= C_0 + C_1 / (1+IRR) + C_2 / (1+IRR)^2$
0 $= -\$100,000 + \$65,000 / (1+IRR) + \$65,000 / (1+IRR)^2$
IRR $= 0.1943$

The IRR of project B is 19.43%.

b. Choose project A because it has a higher IRR than project B.

c. The difference in scale was ignored. Project B has a substantially larger initial investment than project A has. Thus, the simple IRR calculation may not lead to the best decision.

d. Calculate the incremental IRR. The incremental IRR is the IRR on the incremental investment from choosing the larger project instead of the smaller project. The incremental cash flows are the differences between the cash flows of project B and those of project A. Always subtract the project with the smaller initial cash outflow from the project with the larger initial cash outflow. In this way, the initial incremental cash flow will be negative.

	Year 0	Year 1	Year 2
Project B Cash Flows	-$100,000	$65,000	$65,000
Project A Cash Flows	-5,000	3,500	3,500
B – A	-$95,000	$61,500	$61,500

Next, find the IRR of those incremental cash flows.

IRR(B – A) $= C_0 + C_1 / (1+IRR) + C_2 / (1+IRR)^2$
0 $= -\$95,000 + \$61,500 / (1+IRR) + \$61,500 / (1+IRR)^2$
IRR $= 0.191$

The incremental IRR is 19.1%.

e. For investing-type projects, accept the larger project when the incremental rate of return is greater than the discount rate. Therefore, choose project B since the incremental IRR (19.1%) is greater than the 15 percent discount rate.

f. Calculate the NPV of each project.

NPV(Project A) $= -\$5,000 + \$3,500 / (1.15) + \$3,500 / (1.15)^2$
$= \$689.98$

The NPV of project A is $689.98.

NPV(Project B) $= -\$100,000 + \$65,000 / (1.15) + \$65,000 / (1.15)^2$
$= \$5,671.08$

The NPV of project B is $5,671.08.

Since the NPV of project B, $5,671.08, is greater than the NPV of project A, $689.98, choose project B.

6.11 a. Apply the growing perpetuity formula to find the PV of stream A. The perpetuity formula values the stream as of one year before the first payment. Therefore, the growing perpetuity formula values the stream of cash flows as of year 2. Next, discount the PV as of the end of year 2 back two years to find the PV as of today, year 0.

PV(A) $= [C_3 / (r - g)] / (1+r)^2$
$= [\$5,000 / (0.12 - 0.04)] / (1.12)^2$
$= \$49,824.62$

The PV of stream A is $49,824.62.

Apply the perpetuity formula to find the PV of stream B. The perpetuity formula discounts the stream back to year 1, one period prior to the first cash flow. Discount the PV as of the end of year 1 back one year to find the PV as of today, year 0.

PV(B) $= [C_2 / (r)] / (1+r)$
$= [-\$6,000 / (0.12)] / (1.12)$
$= -\$44,642.86$

The PV of stream B is -$44,642.86.

b. Streams A and B are combined to form project C.

Project A $= [C_3 / (r - g)] / (1+r)^2$

Project B $= [C_2 / (r)] / (1+r)$

Project C $=$ Project A + Project B
$= [C_3 / (r - g)] / (1+r)^2 + [C_2 / (r)] / (1+r)$

Set the new project's cash flows, discounted at the internal rate of return (IRR), equal to zero. Solve for the IRR. Use a graphing calculator to perform the calculation.

IRR(Project C) $= [C_3 / (IRR - g)] / (1+IRR)^2 + [C_2 / (IRR)] / (1+IRR)$
0 $= [\$5,000 / (IRR - 0.04)] / (1+IRR)^2 + [-\$6,000 / (IRR)] / (1+IRR)$
IRR $= 0.1465$

The IRR for project C is 14.65%.

c.   The correct decision rule for an investing-type project is to accept the project if the discount rate is below the IRR. Since there is one IRR, a decision can be made. At a point in the future, the cash flows from stream A will be greater than those from stream B. Therefore, although there are many cash flows, there will be only one change in sign. When the sign of the cash flows change more than once over the life of the project, there may be multiple internal rates of return. In such cases, there is no correct decision rule for accepting and rejecting projects using the internal rate of return.

6.12   **False.** The statement is false. If the cash flows of project B occur early and the cash flows of project A occur late, then for a low discount rate the NPV of A can exceed the NPV of B. Observe the following example.

	C_0	C_1	C_2	IRR	NPV @ 0%
Project A	-$1,000,000	$0	$1,440,000	0.20	$440,000
Project B	-2,000,000	2,400,000	0	0.20	400,000

However, in one particular case, the statement is true for equally risky projects. If the lives of the two projects are equal and the cash flows of project B are twice the cash flows of project A in every time period, the NPV of project B will be twice the NPV of project A.

6.13   a.   The profitability index, PI, is the ratio of the present value of the future expected cash flows *after* the initial investment to the amount of the initial investment.

$$PI(A) = [C_1 / (1+r) + C_2 / (1+r)^2 + C_3 / (1+r)^3] / \text{(Initial Investment)}$$
$$= [\$300 / (1.1) + \$700 / (1.1)^2 + \$600 / (1.1)^3] / (\$500)$$
$$= 2.6$$

The profitability index for project A is 2.6.

$$PI(B) = [C_1 / (1+r) + C_2 / (1+r)^2 + C_3 / (1+r)^3] / \text{(Initial Investment)}$$
$$= [\$300 / (1.1) + \$1,800 / (1.1)^2 + \$1,700 / (1.1)^3] / (\$2,000)$$
$$= 1.5$$

The profitability index for project B is 1.5.

b.   Greenplain should accept both projects A and B. The NPV of a project is positive whenever the profitability index (PI) is greater than one.

6.14   Although the profitability index (PI) is higher for project B than for project A, project A should be chosen because it has the greater NPV. Confusion arises because project B requires a smaller investment than project A requires. Since the denominator of the PI ratio is lower for project B than for project A, B can have a higher PI yet have a lower NPV. Only in the case of capital rationing could Global Investments' decision have been incorrect.

6.15   a.   The profitability index, PI, is the ratio of the present value of the future expected cash flows *after* the initial investment to the amount of the initial investment.

$$PI(A) = [C_1 / (1+r) + C_2 / (1+r)^2] / \text{(Initial Investment)}$$
$$= [\$70,000 / (1.12) + \$70,000 / (1.12)^2] / (\$100,000)$$
$$= 1.183$$

The profitability index for project A is 1.183.

$$PI(B) = [C_1 / (1+r) + C_2 / (1+r)^2] / \text{(Initial Investment)}$$
$$= [\$130,000 / (1.12) + \$130,000 / (1.12)^2] / (\$200,000)$$
$$= \mathbf{1.099}$$

The profitability index for project B is 1.099.

$$PI(C) = [C_1 / (1+r) + C_2 / (1+r)^2] / \text{(Initial Investment)}$$
$$= [\$75,000 / (1.12) + \$60,000 / (1.12)^2] / (\$100,000)$$
$$= \mathbf{1.148}$$

The profitability index for project C is 1.148.

b.   NPV (A) $= -\$100,000 + \$70,000 / (1.12) + \$70,000 / (1.12)^2$
                     $= \mathbf{\$18,303.57}$

The NPV of project A is \$18,303.57.

NPV(B) $= -\$200,000 + \$130,000 / (1.12) + \$130,000 / (1.12)^2$
                $= \mathbf{\$19,706.63}$

The NPV of project B is \$19,706.63.

NPV(C) $= -\$100,000 + \$75,000 / (1.12) + \$60,000 / (1.12)^2$
                $= \mathbf{\$14,795.92}$

The NPV of project C is \$14,795.92.

c.   **Accept projects A, B, and C.** Since the projects are independent, accept all three projects because their respective profitability indices are greater than one.

d.   **Accept project B.** Since the projects are mutually exclusive, choose the project with the highest PI, while taking into account the scale of the project.
          Because projects A and C have the same initial investment, the problem of scale does not arise when comparing the profitability indices. Based on the profitability index rule, project C can be eliminated because its PI is less than the PI of project A.
          Because of the problem of scale, one cannot compare the PIs of projects A and B. However, one can calculate the PI of the incremental cash flows of the two projects.

Project	C_0	C_1	C_2	PI
$B - A$	-\$100,000	\$60,000	\$60,000	1.014

When calculating incremental cash flows, remember to subtract the cash flows of the project with the smaller initial cash outflow from those of the project with the larger initial cash outflow. This procedure insures that the incremental initial cash outflow will be negative.
          The PI calculation is:

$$PI(B - A) = [\$60,000 / (1.12) + \$60,000 / (1.12)^2] / (\$100,000)$$
$$= \mathbf{1.014}$$

Amaro should accept project B since the PI of the incremental cash flows is greater than one.

e.   Project B has the highest NPV. Project A has the next highest NPV. Therefore, accept projects B and A.

6.16   The PV of the cash inflows subsequent to the initial investment can be calculated using the seven-year annuity formula, discounted at 15 percent. Divide the PV of those cash flows by the initial investment to find the profitability index, PI. Bill should accept the project if the PI is greater than one.

$$PI = [C_1 A^T_r] / (\text{Initial Investment})$$
$$= [\$40,000 A^7_{0.15}] / (\$160,000)$$
$$= 1.04$$

Bill should accept the project since it has a profitability index greater than one.

6.17   a.   The payback period is the time it takes to recoup the initial investment of a project. Accept any project with a payback period equal to or shorter than the company's standard payback period. Reject all other projects.

       b.   The average accounting return (AAR) is defined as the average project earnings divided by the average book value of the investment. Accept projects for which the AAR is equal to or greater than the firm's standard average accounting return. Reject all other projects.

       c.   The internal rate of return (IRR) is the discount rate that makes the net present value (NPV) of a project equal to zero. The acceptance and rejection criteria are:

       If $C_0 < 0$ and all future cash flows are positive, accept the project if the internal rate of return is greater than or equal to the discount rate.
       If $C_0 < 0$ and all future cash flows are positive, reject the project if the internal rate of return is less than the discount rate.
       If $C_0 > 0$ and all future cash flows are negative, accept the project if the internal rate of return is less than or equal to the discount rate.
       If $C_0 > 0$ and all future cash flows are negative, reject the project if the internal rate of return is greater than the discount rate.

       If the project has cash flows with more than one change in sign, there is likely to be more than one positive IRR. In that situation, there is no valid IRR accept/reject rule.

       d.   The profitability index (PI) is the present value of the cash flows subsequent to the initial investment divided by the initial investment. Accept any project for which the profitability index is greater than or equal to one. Reject any project that has a PI less than one.

       e.   The net present value (NPV) is the sum of the present values of all project cash flows. Accept those projects with NPVs that are greater than or equal to zero. Reject projects with negative NPVs.

6.18   a.   <u>Payback period for the New Sunday Early Edition:</u>

       Use the payback period rule to calculate the number of years that it takes for the cumulative undiscounted cash inflows to equal the initial investment.

Initial Investment		= -$1,200
Year 1	= $600	= $600
Year 2	= $600 + $550	= $1,150
Year 3	**= $600 + $550 + $450**	**= $1,600**

The undiscounted cash flows exceed the initial investment of $1,200 by the end of year 3. Many companies analyze the payback period in whole years. The payback period for the project is 3 years.

The New Sunday Early Edition has a payback period of three years.

Companies can calculate a more precise value using fractional years. Calculate the fraction of year 3's cash flow that is needed for the company to have cumulative undiscounted cash flows of $1,200. Find the difference between the initial investment and the cumulative undiscounted cash flows as of year 2, divided by the undiscounted cash flow of year 3.

Payback Period = 2 + ($1,200 - $1,150) / $450
= **2.11**

Payback period for the New Saturday Late Edition:

Use the payback period rule to calculate the number of years that it takes for the cumulative undiscounted cash inflows to equal the initial investment.

Initial Investment		= -$2,100
Year 1	= $1,000	= $1,000
Year 2	= $1,000 + $900	= $1,900
Year 3	**= $1,000 + $900 + $800**	**= $2,700**

In year 3, the undiscounted cash flows exceed the initial investment of $2,100 by the end of year 3. Many companies analyze the payback period in whole years. The payback period for the project is 3 years.

The payback period for the New Saturday Late Edition is three years.

Companies can calculate a more precise value using fractional years. Calculate the fraction of year 3's cash flows that is needed for the company to have cumulative undiscounted cash flows of $2,100. Find the difference between the initial investment and the cumulative undiscounted cash flows as of year 2, divided by the undiscounted cash flow of year 3.

Payback Period = 2 + ($2,100 - $1,900) / $800
= **2.25**

Using the whole number payback period, the projects are equally attractive. Using the fractional payback period calculation, the New Sunday Early Edition is more attractive because it has a shorter payback period than does the New Saturday Early Edition.

b. New Sunday Early Edition IRR

The internal rate of return is the discount rate at which the NPV of the project's cash flows equals zero. Set the project's cash flows, discounted at the internal rate of return (IRR), equal to zero. Solve for the IRR.

IRR = $C_0 + C_1 / (1+IRR) + C_2 / (1+IRR)^2 + C_3 / (1+IRR)^3$
0 = $-\$1,200 + \$600 / (1+IRR) + \$550 / (1+IRR)^2 + \$450 / (1+IRR)^3$
IRR = **0.1676**

New Saturday Late Edition IRR

The internal rate of return is the discount rate at which the NPV of the project's cash flows equals zero. Set the project's cash flows, discounted at the internal rate of return (IRR), equal to zero. Solve for the IRR.

$$\text{IRR} = C_0 + C_1 / (1+\text{IRR}) + C_2 / (1+\text{IRR})^2 + C_3 / (1+\text{IRR})^3$$
$$0 = -\$2,100 + \$1,000 / (1+\text{IRR}) + \$900 / (1+\text{IRR})^2 + \$800 / (1+\text{IRR})^3$$
$$\text{IRR} = \mathbf{0.1429}$$

The New Sunday Early Edition has a greater IRR than the New Saturday Late Edition.

c. Find the IRR of the incremental cash flows. The incremental IRR is the IRR on the incremental investment from choosing the larger project instead of the smaller project. Incremental cash flows are defined as the New Saturday Late Edition's Cash Flows minus the New Sunday Early Edition's cash flows. Remember to subtract the cash flows of the project with the smaller initial investment from those of the project with the larger initial investment, so that the incremental initial investment is negative.

	Year 0	Year 1	Year 2	Year 3
Saturday Edition	-\$2,100	\$1,000	\$900	\$800
Sunday Edition	-1,200	600	550	450
Saturday – Sunday	-\$900	\$400	\$350	\$350

$$\text{IRR} = C_0 + C_1 / (1+\text{IRR}) + C_2 / (1+\text{IRR})^2 + C_3 / (1+\text{IRR})^3$$
$$0 = -\$900 + \$400 / (1+\text{IRR}) + \$350 / (1+\text{IRR})^2 + \$350 / (1+\text{IRR})^3$$
$$\text{IRR} = \mathbf{0.1102}$$

For investing-type projects, accept the larger project when the incremental rate of return is greater than the discount rate. Since the discount rate of 12% is greater than the incremental IRR of 11.02%, choose the new Sunday Edition.

d. Average Accounting Return for the New Sunday Early Edition:

First, determine the average book value of the project. The book value is the gross investment minus accumulated depreciation.

Annual Depreciation = \$1,200 / 3
= \$400

	Year 0	Year 1	Year 2	Year 3
Gross Investment	\$1,200	\$1,200	\$1,200	\$1,200
Accumulated Depreciation	\$0	\$400	\$800	\$1,200
Book Value	\$1,200	\$800	\$400	\$0

Average Investment = (\$1,200 + \$800 + \$400 + \$0) / (4)
= \$600

Calculate the average annual income of the project.

Average Income = (\$400 + \$350 + \$300) / 3
= \$350

Divide the average project earnings by the average book value of the machine to calculate the average accounting return.

Average Accounting Return = (Average Income) / (Average Investment)
                           = $350 / $600
                           = **0.583**

The average accounting return for the New Sunday Early Edition is 58.3%.

Average Accounting Return for the New Saturday Late Edition:

First, determine the average book value of the project. The book value is the gross investment minus accumulated depreciation.

Annual Depreciation = $2,100 / 3
                     = $700

	Year 0	Year 1	Year 2	Year 3
Gross Investment	$2,100	$2,100	$2,100	$2,100
Accumulated Depreciation	$0	$700	$1,400	$2,100
Book Value	$2,100	$1,400	$700	$0

Average Investment = ($2,100 + $1,400 + $700 + $0) / (4)
                    = $1,050

Calculate the average annual income of the project.

Average Income = ($800 + $700 + $600) / 3
                = $700

Divide the average project earnings by the average book value of the machine to calculate the average accounting return.

Average Accounting Return = (Average Income) / (Average Investment)
                           = $700 / $1,050
                           = **0.667**

The average accounting return for the New Saturday Late Edition is 66.7%.

6.19 a. Discounted Payback Period for Deepwater Fishing:

Find the number of years that it takes for the discounted cash inflows to equal the initial investment of $600,000. The approximate discounted payback period is the year *in which* the PV of the initial investment is surpassed.

Cumulative Discounted Cash Flows Year 1 = $270,000 / (1.15)   = $234,782.61
Cumulative Discounted Cash Flows Year 2 = $270,000 / (1.15) + $350,000 / (1.15)^2
                                                                      = $499,432.89
Cumulative Discounted Cash Flows Year 3 = **$270,000 / (1.15) + $350,000 / (1.15)^2 +
                                          $300,000 / (1.15)^3 = $696,687.76**

The cumulative discounted cash flows exceed the initial investment of $600,000 by the end of year 3. Many companies analyze the payback period in whole years. The payback period for the project is three years.

The discounted payback period for deepwater fishing is three years.

<u>Discounted Payback Period for New Submarine Ride:</u>

Find the number of years that it will take the discounted cash inflows to equal the initial investment of $1,800,000. The approximate discounted payback period is the year *in which* the PV of the initial investment is surpassed.

Cumulative Discounted Cash Flows Year 1 = $1,000,000 / (1.15)   = $869,565.22
Cumulative Discounted Cash Flows Year 2 = $1,000,000 / (1.15) + $700,000 / (1.15)^2
                                                                                = $1,398,865.78
Cumulative Discounted Cash Flows Year 3 = **$1,000,000 / (1.15) + $700,000 / (1.15)^2 +**
                                                                $900,000 / (1.15)^3 = $1,990,630.39

The cumulative discounted cash flows exceed the initial investment of $1,800,000 by the end of year 3. Many companies analyze the payback period in whole years. The payback period for the project is three years.

The discounted payback period for the submarine ride is three years.

According to the payback period rule, the projects are equally desirable.

b.   <u>Deepwater Fishing IRR:</u>

Set the project's cash flows, discounted at the internal rate of return (IRR), equal to zero. Solve for the IRR.

IRR $= C_0 + C_1 / (1+\text{IRR}) + C_2 / (1+\text{IRR})^2 + C_3 / (1+\text{IRR})^3$
0      $= -\$600,000 + \$270,000 / (1+\text{IRR}) + \$350,000 / (1+\text{IRR})^2 + \$300,000 / (1+\text{IRR})^3$
IRR   **= 0.243**

The IRR of the deepwater fishing project is 24.3%.

<u>Submarine Ride IRR:</u>

Set the project's cash flows, discounted at the internal rate of return (IRR), equal to zero. Solve for the IRR.

IRR $= C_0 + C_1 / (1+\text{IRR}) + C_2 / (1+\text{IRR})^2 + C_3 / (1+\text{IRR})^3$
0      $= -\$1,800,000 + \$1,000,000 / (1+\text{IRR}) + \$700,000 / (1+\text{IRR})^2 +$
        $\$900,000 / (1+\text{IRR})^3$
IRR   **= 0.2146**

The IRR of the submarine ride is 21.46%.

Based on the IRR rule, the deepwater fishing project should be chosen because it has the higher IRR.

c.   Calculate the IRR of the incremental cash flows, defined as the New Saturday Late Edition's Cash Flows minus the New Sunday Early Edition's cash flows. Then calculate the IRR of the incremental cash flows. Remember to subtract the cash flows of the project with the smaller initial investment from those of the project with the larger initial investment, so that the incremental initial investment is negative.

	Year 0	Year 1	Year 2	Year 3
Submarine Ride	-1,800,000	1,000,000	700,000	900,000
Deepwater Fishing	-600,000	270,000	350,000	300,000
Submarine - Fishing	-$1,200,000	$730,000	$350,000	$600,000

$$\text{IRR} = C_0 + C_1 / (1+\text{IRR}) + C_2 / (1+\text{IRR})^2 + C_3 / (1+\text{IRR})^3$$
$$0 = -\$1,200,000 + \$730,000 / (1+\text{IRR}) + \$350,000 / (1+\text{IRR})^2 +$$
$$\$600,000 / (1+\text{IRR})^3$$
$$\text{IRR} = \textbf{0.1992}$$

For investing-type projects, accept the larger project when the incremental IRR is greater than the discount rate. Since the incremental IRR, 19.92%, is greater than the required rate of return, 15%, choose the submarine ride project. Note that the choice in part (c) differs from the choice in part (b). The choice in part (b) is flawed because there is a scale problem. That is, the submarine ride has a greater initial investment than does the deepwater fishing project. This problem is corrected only by calculating the IRR of the incremental cash flows.

d. NPV(Deepwater Fishing) $= -\$600,000 + \$270,000 / (1.15) + \$350,000 / (1.15)^2 +$
$$\$300,000 / (1.15)^3$$
$$= \textbf{\$96,687.76}$$

The NPV of the deepwater fishing project is \$96,687.76.

NPV(Submarine Ride) $= -\$1,800,000 + \$1,000,000 / (1.15) + \$700,000 / (1.15)^2 +$
$$\$900,000 / (1.15)^3$$
$$= \textbf{\$190,630.39}$$

The NPV of the submarine ride project is \$190,630.39.

Since the NPV of the submarine ride project is greater than the NPV of the deepwater fishing project, choose the submarine ride project. The NPV rule is always consistent with the incremental IRR rule.

6.20   a.   The project involves three cash flows: the initial investment, the annual cash inflows, and the abandonment costs. The mine will generate cash inflows over its 11-year economic life. To express the PV of the annual cash inflows, apply the growing annuity formula, discounted at the IRR and growing at eight percent.

PV(Cash Inflows) $= C_1 \, \text{GA}^T_{\text{IRR}, \, g} *$
$$= \$100,000 \, \text{GA}^{11}_{\text{IRR}, \, 0.08}$$

* The notation $\text{GA}^T_{r, \, g}$ represents a growing annuity consisting of T payments growing at a rate of g per payment, discounted at r.

At the end of 11 years, the Utah Mining Corporate will abandon the mine, incurring a \$50,000 charge. Discount that charge back 11 years at the IRR to express its PV.

PV(Abandonment) $= C_{11} / (1+\text{IRR})^{11}$
$$= -\$50,000 / (1+\text{IRR})^{11}$$

Solve the expression that equates the cash flows, discounted at the IRR, with zero. Solve for the IRR. Use a graphing calculator.

IRR $= $ -Initial Investment + PV(Cash Inflows) – PV(Abandonment)
$$0 = C_0 + C_1 \, \text{GA}^T_{\text{IRR}, \, g} - C_{11} / (1+\text{IRR})^T$$
$$0 = -\$600,000 + \$100,000 \, \text{GA}^{11}_{\text{IRR}, \, 0.08} - \$50,000 / (1+\text{IRR})^{11}$$
IRR $= \textbf{0.185565}$

The IRR of the mining project is approximately 18.56%.

b. **Yes.** Since the mine's IRR exceeds the required return of 10%, the mine should be opened. The correct decision rule for an investment-type project is to accept the project if the discount rate is above the IRR. Anytime there is a second change in sign, there is a possibility for multiple IRRs. By using a graphing calculator, one can determine that in this problem, there is only one IRR. Therefore, a decision can be made.

6-21 a)

Period	0	1	2	3	4	5	NPV
Worst Case							
Cash Flow	$ (250,000)	0	0	0	0	250,000	
PV 12% (CF)	= CF (250,000)	= CF/1.12 0	= CF/(1.12)^2 0	= CF/(1.12)^3 0	= CF/(1.12)^4 0	= CF/(1.12)^5 141,857	($180,143)

The worst case NPV is –$108,143 and will occur when the project has no cash flows until year five, when it returns $250,000.

b) The best case NPV can be an infinite amount. This is because payback period only tells you when you recover your investment. However, the cash flows are not limited to five years and could go on forever.

6.22 a) Payback period for Project A is at year 3.25 and for Project B is at year 1.5.
Therefore, Totally Electric should select Project B because of the shorter payback period.

b)

	Avg Net Income	Avg Investment	AAR
Project A	$37,500	$75,000	.50000
Project B	$13,250	$40,000	.33125

Totally Electric should select Project A because it has the highest average accounting return.

c)

	Period	0	1	2	3	4	NPV
Project A	Cash Flow	$(150,000)	15,000	35,000	50,000	200,000	
	PV 10% (CF)	= CF (150,000)	= CF/1.1 13,636	= CF/(1.1)^2 28,926	= CF/(1.1)^3 37,566	= CF/(1.1)^4 136,603	$66,730
Project B	Cash Flow	$ (80,000)	60,000	40,000	20,000	13,000	
	PV 10% (CF)	= CF (80,000)	= CF/1.1 54,545	= CF/(1.1)^2 33,058	= CF/(1.1)^3 15,026	= CF/(1.1)^4 8,879	$31,509

NPV of Project A is $66,730 and of Project B is $31,509, so Totally Electric should select Project A because it has a higher NPV.

d)

		0	1	2	3	4		IRR
Project A	PV IRR (CF)	= CF (150,000)	= CF/IRR 12,206	= CF/(IRR)^2 23,174	= CF/(IRR)^3 26,939	= CF/(IRR)^4 87,681	$0	22.9%
Project B	PV IRR (CF)	= CF (80,000)	= CF/IRR 44,983	= CF/(IRR)^2 22,483	= CF/(IRR)^3 8,428	= CF/(IRR)^4 4,107	$0	33.4%

IRR of Project A is 22.9% and of Project B is 33.4%, so Totally Electric should select Project B because it has a higher IRR.

Period	0	1	2	3	Sum of Cash Flow	Profitability Index	NPV
HDTV							
Cash Flow	$(1,000)	1,000	600	300			
PV 10% (CF)	$=CF$ (1,000)	$=CF/1.1$ 909	$=CF/(1.1)^2$ 496	$=CF/(1.1)^3$ 225	$1,630	1.63	$630
Plasma							
Cash Flow	$(2,200)	700	1,100	2,200			
PV 10% (CF)	$=CF$ (2,200)	$=CF/1.1$ 636	$=CF/(1.1)^2$ 909	$=CF/(1.1)^3$ 1,653	$3,198	1.45	$998

a) HDTV has a PI of 1.63 and Plasma has a PI of 1.45, therefore, Pinnacle should invest in HDTV technology.
b) HDTV has a NPV of $630 and Plasma has a NPV of $998, therefore, Pinnacle should invest in Plasma technology.
c)

Incremental Period	0	1	2	3	Cash Flow	PI	NPV
Plasma-HDTV							
Cash Flow	$(1,200)	$(300)	$500	$1,900			
PV 10% (CF)	$=CF$ (1,200)	$=CF/1.1$ (273)	$=CF/(1.1)^2$ 413	$=CF/(1.1)^3$ 1,427	$1,568	1.31	$368

The profitability index, like the IRR, is a ratio and therefore limited by the problem of scale. Because these investments are mutually exclusive, the Plasma investment should be selected because it has a higher NPV and the incremental PI is greater than 1.

6.24 a) Payback period for Board game is in year 1 and for CD-Rom is at year 1.5, so Mario Brothers should select Board game.

b)

Period	0	1	2	3	NPV
Board game					
Cash Flow	$(300)	400	100	100	
PV 10% (CF)	$=CF$ (300)	$=CF/1.1$ 364	$=CF/(1.1)^2$ 83	$=CF/(1.1)^3$ 75	$221
CD-Rom					
Cash Flow	$(1,500)	1,100	800	400	
PV 10% (CF)	$=CF$ (1,500)	$=CF/1.1$ 1,000	$=CF/(1.1)^2$ 661	$=CF/(1.1)^3$ 301	$462

From the analysis, NPV of Board game is $221 and of CD-Rom is $462, so Mario Brothers should select CD-Rom.

c)

Board game							
PV IRR (CF)	$= CF$ (300)	$= CF/IRR$ 242	$= CF/(IRR)^2$ 36	$= CF/(IRR)^3$ 22	$0	IRR	65.6%
CD-Rom							
PV IRR (CF)	$= CF$ (1,500)	$= CF/IRR$ 846	$= CF/(IRR)^2$ 473	$= CF/(IRR)^3$ 182	$0	IRR	30.1%

From the analysis, IRR of Board game is 65.6% and of CD-Rom is 30.1%, so Mario Brothers should select Board game.

d)

CD-Rom							
Cash flow	$(1,200)	$700	$700	$300			
PV IRR (CF)	(1,200)	571	466	163	$0	IRR	22.6%

Because the incremental IRR is 22.6% (>20% required IRR), the CD-Rom project should be selected.

6.25

Period	0	1	2	3	Sum of Cash Flow	Profitability Index	NPV
CDMA							
Cash Flow	$(10)	25	15	5			
PV 10% (CF)	(10)	$=CF/1.1$ 23	$=CF/(1.1)^2$ 12	$=CF/(1.1)^3$ 4	$39	3.89	$29
G4							
Cash Flow	$(20)	20	50	40			
PV 10% (CF)	(20)	$=CF/1.1$ 18	$=CF/(1.1)^2$ 41	$=CF/(1.1)^3$ 30	$90	4.48	$70
Wi-Fi							
Cash Flow	$(30)	20	40	100			
PV 10% (CF)	(30)	$=CF/1.1$ 18	$=CF/(1.1)^2$ 33	$=CF/(1.1)^3$ 75	$126	4.21	$96

a) G4 has a PI of 4.48, Wi-Fi has a PI of 4.21 and CDMA has a PI of 3.89.

b) Wi-Fi has a NPV of $96, G4 has a NPV of $70 and CDMA has a NPV of $29.

c)

Combined

Period	0	1	2	3	Cash Flow	PI	NPV
CDMA + G4	Cash Flow	$(30)	$45	$65	$45			
	PV 10% (CF)	= CF (30)	= CF/1.1 41	= CF/(1.1)^2 54	= CF/(1.1)^3 34	$128	4.28	$98

Although the Wi-Fi investment has the single largest NPV, this is not the best investment for Hanmi group. Because these investments are independent, and not mutually exclusive, Hanmi can invest in both CDMA ($10 mil) and G4 ($20 mil) which has a combined NPV of $98 (>$96 for Wi-Fi) and still be within the $30 million investment budget.

6.26 a) Payback period for AZM is at year 1 and for AZF is at year 2, so project AZM should be taken.

b)

	Period	0	1	2	3	SUM
AZM	Cash Flow	($200,000)	200,000	150,000	150,000	
	PV 10% (CF)	= CF ($200,000)	= CF/1.1 181,818	= CF/(1.1)^2 123,967	= CF/(1.1)^3 112,697	$218,482
AZF	Cash Flow	($500,000)	200,000	300,000	300,000	
	PV 10% (CF)	= CF ($500,000)	= CF/1.1 181,818	= CF/(1.1)^2 247,934	= CF/(1.1)^3 225,394	$155,147

From the analysis, NPV of AZM is $218,482 and of AZF is $155,147, so project AZM should be taken.

c)

	PV IRR (CF)	0	1	2	3	IRR
AZM	PV IRR (CF)	= CF ($200,000)	= CF/IRR 117,616	= CF/(RR)^2 51,876	= CF/(IRR)^3 30,507	$0	70%
AZF	PV IRR (CF)	= CF ($500,000)	= CF/IRR 159,105	= CF/(IRR)^2 189,858	= CF/(IRR)^3 151,037	$0	26%

From the analysis, IRR of AZM is 70% and of AZF is 26%, so project AZM should be taken.

d) Since both NPV and IRR favors project AZM, and AZM is a smaller investment to start out with, it is not necessary to conduct Incremental IRR analysis.

6.27. a) Payback period for Dry Prepreg is at year 2 and for Solvent Prepreg is at year 1, so project Solvent Prepreg should be taken.

b)

Period	0	1	2	3	SUM
Dry Prepreg Cash Flow	($1,000,000)	600,000	400,000	1,000,000	
PV 10% (CF)	= CF ($1,000,0000)	= CF/1.10 545,455	= CF/(1.10)^2 330,579	= CF/(1.10)^3 751,315	$627,348
Solvent Prepreg Cash Flow	($500,000)	500,000	300,000	100,000	
PV 10% (CF)	= CF ($500,000)	= CF/1.10 454,545	= CF/(1.10)^2 247,934	= CF/(1.10)^3 75,131	$277,611

From the analysis, NPV of Dry Prepreg is $627,348 and of Solvent Prepreg is $277,611, so project Dry Prepreg should be taken.

c)

Period	0	1	2	3		IRR
Dry Prepreg PV IRR (CF)	= CF ($1,000,000)	= CF/IRR 429,218	= CF/(IRR)^2 204,698	= CF/(IRR)^3 366,084	$0	40%
Solvent Prepreg PV IRR (CF)	= CF ($500,000)	= CF/IRR 335,122	= CF/(IRR)^2 134,768	= CF/(IRR)^3 30,109	($0)	49%

From the analysis, IRR of Dry Prepreg is 40% and of Solvent Prepreg is 49%, so project Solvent Prepreg should be taken.

d) Since Solvent Prepreg has a higher IRR, but is relatively smaller in terms of investment and NPV, Incremental IRR analysis is required.

Period	0	1	2	3		IRR
Dry-Solvent Cash Flow	($500,000)	100,000	100,000	900,000		
PV IRR (CF)	($500,000)	74,377	55,319	370,304	$0	34%

Because the incremental IRR is 34% (>30% min IRR req.), the Dry Prepreg project should be considered.

6.28

Period	0	1	2	3	4	5	SUM	IRR/PI
NP-30								
Cash Flow	($100,000)	40,000	40,000	40,000	40,000	40,000		
PV 15% (CF)	($100,000)	34,783	30,246	26,301	22,870	19,887	$34,086	29%
PV IRR (CF)	–$100,000	31,092	24,168	18,786	14,603	11,351	$0	
PI								1.34
NX-20								
Cash Flow	($30,000)	20,000	23,000	26,450	30,418	34,980		
PV 15% (CF)	($30,000)	17,391	17,391	17,391	17,391	17,391	$56,957	73%
PV IRR (CF)	–$30,000	11,559	7,683	5,107	3,394	2,256	$0	
PI								2.90
Incremental NP30-NX20								
Cash Flow	($70,000)	20,000	17,000	13,550	9,583	5,020	($0)	–3%
PV IRR (CF)	($70,000)	20,594	18,026	14,795	10,774	5,812		

6.29

Period	0	1	2	3	4	5	SUM	IRR/PI
A								
Cash Flow	($100,000)	50,000	50,000	40,000	30,000	20,000		
PV 15% (CF)	($100,000)	43,478	37,807	26,301	17,153	9,944	$34,682	31%
PV IRR (CF)	–$100,000	38,085	29,010	17,678	10,099	5,128	$0	
PI								1.35
B								
Cash Flow	($200,000)	60,000	60,000	60,000	100,000	200,000		
PV 15% (CF)	($200,000)	52,174	45,369	39,451	57,175	99,435	$93,604	30%
PV IRR (CF)	–$200,000	46,316	35,754	27,600	35,509	54,821	$0	
PI								1.47
Incremental B-A								
Cash Flow	($100,000)	10,000	10,000	20,000	70,000	180,000	$0	29%
PV IRR (CF)	($100,000)	7,776	6,047	9,404	25,595	51,178		

Implications

NPV   Project B should be taken.
IRR   Project A should be taken.
Incremental IRR   Project B should be taken (29% > the minimum acceptable IRR of 25%)
PI   Project B should be taken.

6.30

Period		0	1	2	SUM	IRR/PI
B	Cash Flow	(\$200,000)	200,000	111,000		
	PV 20% (CF)	(\$200,000)	166,667	77,083	\$43,750	
	PV IRR (CF)	–\$200,000	143,142	56,858	(\$0)	40%
	PI					1.37
C	Cash Flow	(\$100,000)	100,000	100,000		
	PV 20% (CF)	(\$100,000)	83,333	69,444	\$52,778	
	PV IRR (CF)	–\$100,000	61,803	38,197	\$0	62%
	PI					1.74
Incremental	Cash Flow	(\$100,000)	100,000	11,000	\$0	
B-C	PV IRR (CF)	(\$100,000)	90,909	9,091		10%

Clearly, project A will not have a positive NPV and therefore is not a viable project. From the analysis, projects B and C will have the same payback period. However, project C will have a higher NPV and IRR, therefore it should be recommended.

Use 20% discount rate for projects B and C since their risk are greater than the typical core projects of 10%.

6.31   Using Incremental Cash Flows:

Year	Cash Flows for Project Billion – Project Million
0	$-I_o + 1{,}500$
1	300
2	300
3	500

PV @ 12% of Cash Flow subsequent to Initial investment = 862.9

For Project Billion to be more attractive, $862.9/(-I_o + 1{,}500) > 1$ (Profitability Index should be greater than 1)

Solving we get $637.1 < I_o < 1500$

6.32   a) Project A would have a higher IRR since initial investment for Project A is less than that of Project B, if the cash flows for the two projects are identical.

b) False.

c) Yes since **both** the cash flows as well as the initial investment are twice that of Project B.

Chapter 7: Net Present Value and Capital Budgeting

7.1   a.   **Yes**, the reduction in the sales of the company's other products, referred to as **erosion**, should be treated as an incremental cash flow. These lost sales are included because they are a cost (a revenue reduction) that the firm must bear if it chooses to produce the new product.

       b.   **Yes**, expenditures on plant and equipment should be treated as incremental cash flows. These are costs of the new product line. However, if these expenditures have already occurred, they are **sunk costs** and are not included as incremental cash flows.

       c.   **No**, the research and development costs should not be treated as incremental cash flows. The costs of research and development undertaken on the product during the past 3 years are **sunk costs** and should not be included in the evaluation of the project. Decisions made and costs incurred in the past cannot be changed. They should not affect the decision to accept or reject the project.

       d.   **Yes**, the annual depreciation expense should be treated as an incremental cash flow. Depreciation expense must be taken into account when calculating the cash flows related to a given project. While depreciation is not a cash expense that directly affects cash flow, it decreases a firm's net income and hence, lowers its tax bill for the year. Because of this **depreciation tax shield**, the firm has more cash on hand at the end of the year than it would have had without expensing depreciation.

       e.   **No**, dividend payments should not be treated as incremental cash flows. A firm's decision to pay or not pay dividends is independent of the decision to accept or reject any given investment project. For this reason, it is not an incremental cash flow to a given project. Dividend policy is discussed in more detail in later chapters.

       f.   **Yes**, the resale value of plant and equipment at the end of a project's life should be treated as an incremental cash flow. The price at which the firm sells the equipment is a cash inflow, and any difference between the book value of the equipment and its sale price will create gains or losses that result in either a tax credit or liability.

       g.   **Yes**, salary and medical costs for production employees hired for a project should be treated as incremental cash flows. The salaries of all personnel connected to the project must be included as costs of that project.

7.2   Item I is a relevant cost because the opportunity to sell the land is lost if the new golf club is produced. Item II is also relevant because the firm must take into account the erosion of sales of existing products when a new product is introduced. If the firm produces the new club, the earnings from the existing clubs will decrease, effectively creating a cost that must be included in the decision. Item III is not relevant because the costs of Research and Development are sunk costs. Decisions made in the past cannot be changed. They are not relevant to the production of the new clubs. **Choice *C* is the correct answer.**

7.3 Cash Flow Chart:

		Year 0	Year 1	Year 2	Year 3	Year 4
1.	Sales revenue	-	$7,000	$7,000	$7,000	$7,000
2.	Operating costs	-	2,000	2,000	2,000	2,000
3.	Depreciation	-	2,500	2,500	2,500	2,500
4.	Income before tax [1-(2+3)]	-	2,500	2,500	2,500	2,500
5.	Taxes at 34%	-	850	850	850	850
6.	Net income [4-5]	0	1,650	1,650	1,650	1,650
7.	Cash flow from operation [1-2-5]	0	4,150	4,150	4,150	4,150
8.	Initial Investment	-$10,000	-	-	-	-
9.	Changes in net working capital	-200	-50	-50	100	200
10.	Total cash flow from investment [9+10]	-10,200	-50	-50	100	200
11.	Total cash flow [7+10]	-$10,200	$4,100	$4,100	$4,250	$4,350

a. Incremental Net Income [from 6]:

Year 0	Year 1	Year 2	Year 3	Year 4
0	$1,650	$1,650	$1,650	$1,650

b. Incremental cash flow [from 11]:

Year 0	Year 1	Year 2	Year 3	Year 4
-$10,200	$4,100	$4,100	$4,250	$4,350

c. The present value of each cash flow is simply the amount of that cash flow discounted back from the date of payment to the present. For example, discount the cash flow in Year 1 by 1 period (1.12), and discount the cash flow that occurs in Year 2 by 2 periods $(1.12)^2$. Note that since the Year 0 cash flow occurs today, its present value does not need to be adjusted.

$PV(C_0)$ = -$10,200
$PV(C_1)$ = $4,100 / (1.12) = $3,661
$PV(C_2)$ = $4,100 / (1.12)^2 = $3,268
$PV(C_3)$ = $4,250 / (1.12)^3 = $3,025
$PV(C_4)$ = $4,350 / (1.12)^4 = $2,765

NPV = $PV(C_0) + PV(C_1) + PV(C_2) + PV(C_3) + PV(C_4)$ = **$2,519**

These calculations could also have been performed in a single step:

NPV = -$10,200 + $4,100 / (1.12) + $4,100 / (1.12)^2 + $4,250 / (1.12)^3 + $4,350 / (1.12)^4
= **$2,519**

The NPV of the project is $2,519.

7.4   The initial payment, which occurs today (year 0), does not need to be discounted:

$$PV = \$1,400,000$$

The expected value of his bonus payment is:

$$\text{Expected Value} = C_0 \text{ (Probability of Occurrence)} + C_1 \text{ (Probability of Nonoccurrence)}$$
$$= \$750,000 \, (0.60) + \$0 \, (0.40)$$
$$= \$450,000$$

The expected value of his salary, including the expected bonus payment, is $2,950,000 (=$2,500,000 + $450,000).

The present value of his three-year salary with bonuses is:

$$\text{PV Annuity} = C_1 A^T_r$$
$$= \$2,950,000 \, A^3_{0.1236}$$
$$= \$7,041,799$$

Remember that the annuity formula yields the present value of a stream of cash flows one period prior to the initial payment. Therefore, applying the annuity formula to a stream of cash flows that begins four years from today will generate the present value of that annuity as of the end of year three. Discount that result by three years to find the present value.

$$\text{PV Delayed Annuity} = (A^T_r) / (1+r)^{T-1}$$
$$= (\$1,250,000 \, A^{10}_{0.1236}) / (1.1236)^3$$
$$= \$4,906,457$$

Thus, the total PV of his three-year contract is:

$$PV = \$1,400,000 + \$2,950,000 \, A^3_{0.1236} + (\$1,250,000 \, A^{10}_{0.1236}) / (1.1236)^3$$
$$= \$1,400,000 + \$7,041,799 + \$4,906,457$$
$$= \mathbf{\$13,348,256}$$

The present value of the contract is $13,348,256.

7.5   Compute the NPV of both alternatives. If either of the projects has a positive NPV, that project is more favorable to Benson than simply continuing to rent the building. If both of the projects have positive net present values, recommend the one with the higher NPV. If neither of the projects has a positive NPV, the correct recommendation is to reject both projects and continue renting the building to the current occupants.

Note that the remaining fraction of the value of the building and depreciation are not incremental and should not be included in the analysis of the two alternatives. The $225,000 purchase price of the building is a sunk cost and should be ignored.

Product A:	t = 0	t = 1 - 14	t = 15	
Revenues		$105,000	$105,000	
-Foregone rent		12,000	12,000	
-Expenditures		60,000	63,750	**
-Depreciation*		12,000	12,000	
Earnings before taxes		$21,000	$17,250	
-Taxes (34%)		7,140	5,865	
Net income		$13,860	$11,385	
+Depreciation		12,000	12,000	
Capital investment	-$180,000			
A/T-NCF	-$180,000	$25,860	$23,385	

*Since the two assets, equipment and building modifications, are depreciated on a straight-line basis, the depreciation expense will be the same in each year. To compute the annual depreciation expense, determine the total initial cost of the two assets ($144,000 + $36,000 = $180,000) and divide this amount by 15, the economic life of each of the 2 assets. Annual depreciation expense for building modifications and equipment equals $12,000 (= $180,000 / 15).

**Cash expenditures ($60,000) + Restoration costs ($3,750)

The cash flows in years 1 - 14 (C_1 - C_{14}) could have been computed using the following simplification:

$$\text{After-Tax NCF} = \text{Revenue} (1 - T_C) - \text{Expenses} (1 - T_C) + \text{Depreciation} (T_C)$$
$$= \$105,000 (0.66) - \$72,000 (0.66) + \$12,000 (0.34)$$
$$= \$25,860$$

The cash flows for year 15 could have been computed by adjusting the annual after-tax net cash flows of the project (computed above) for the after-tax value of the restoration costs.

$$\text{After-Tax value of restoration costs} = \text{Restoration Costs} (1 - T_C)$$
$$= -\$3,750 (0.66)$$
$$= -\$2,475$$

$$\text{After-Tax NCF} = \$25,860 - \$2,475$$
$$= \$23,385$$

The present value of the initial outlay is simply the cost of the outlay since it occurs today (year 0).

$$PV(C_0) = -\$180,000$$

Since the cash flows in years 1-14 are identical, their present value can be found by determining the value of a 14-year annuity with payments of $25,860, discounted at 12 percent.

$$PV(C_{1-14}) = \$25,860 \, A^{14}_{0.12} = \$171,404$$

Because the last cash flow occurs 15 years from today, discount the amount of the cash flow back 15 years at 12 percent to determine its present value.

$$PV(C_{15}) = \$23,385 / (1.12)^{15}$$
$$= \$4,272$$

$$NPV_A = PV(C_0) + PV(C_{1-14}) + PV(C_{15})$$
$$= -\$4,324$$

These calculations could also have been performed in a single step:

$$NPV_A = -\$180,000 + \$25,860\ A^{14}_{0.12} + \$23,385 / (1.12)^{15}$$
$$= -\$180,000 + \$171,404 + \$4,272$$
$$= -\$4,324$$

Since the net present value of Project A is negative, Benson would rather rent the building to its current occupants than implement Project A.

Product B	t = 0	t = 1 - 14	t = 15	
Revenues		$127,500	$127,500	
-Foregone rent		12,000	12,000	
-Expenditures		75,000	103,125	**
-Depreciation*		14,400	14,400	
Earnings before taxes		$26,100	-$2,025	
-Taxes (34%)		8,874	-689	
Net income		$17,226	-$1,336	
+Depreciation		14,400	14,400	
Capital investment	-$216,000			
A/T-NCF	-$216,000	$31,626	$13,064	

* Since the two assets, equipment and building modifications, are depreciated on a straight-line basis, the depreciation expense will be the same in each year. To compute the annual depreciation expense, determine the total initial cost of the two assets ($162,000 + $54,000 = $216,000) and divide this amount by 15, the economic life of each of the two assets. Annual depreciation expense for building modifications and equipment is $14,400 (= $216,000/ 15).

**Cash expenditures ($75,000) + Restoration costs ($28,125)

The cash flows in years 1 - 14 ($C_1 - C_{14}$) could have been computed using the following simplification:

$$After\text{-}Tax\ NCF = Revenue\ (1 - T) - Expenses\ (1 - T) + Depreciation\ (T)$$
$$= \$127,500\ (0.66) - \$87,000\ (0.66) + \$14,400\ (0.34)$$
$$= \$31,626$$

The cash flows for year 15 could have been computed by adjusting the annual after-tax net cash flows of the project (computed above) for the after-tax value of the restoration costs.

$$After\text{-}tax\ value\ of\ restoration\ costs = Restoration\ Costs\ (1 - T_C)$$
$$= -\$28,125(0.66)$$
$$= -\$18,562$$

$$After\text{-}Tax\ NCF = \$31,626 - \$18,562$$
$$= \$13,064$$

The present value of the initial outlay is simply the cost of the outlay since it occurs today (year 0).

$$PV(C_0) = -\$216,000$$

Because the cash flows in years 1-14 are identical, their present value can be found by determining the value of a 14-year annuity with payments of $31,626, discounted at 12 percent.

$$PV(C_{1-14}) = \$31,626\ A^{14}_{0.12}$$
$$= \$209,622$$

Since the last cash flow occurs 15 years from today, discount the amount of the cash flow back 15 years at 12 percent to determine its present value.

$$PV(C_{15}) = \$13,064 / (1.12)^{15}$$
$$= \$2,387$$

$$NPV_B = PV(C_0) + PV(C_{1-14}) + PV(C_{15})$$
$$= -\$216,000 + \$209,622 + \$2,387$$
$$= \textbf{-\$3,991}$$

These calculations could also have been performed in a single step:

$$NPV_B = -\$216,000 + \$31,626\ A^{14}_{0.12} + \$13,064 / (1.12)^{15}$$
$$= -\$216,000 + \$209,622 + \$2,387$$
$$= \textbf{-\$3,991}$$

Since the net present value of Project B is negative, Benson would rather rent the building to its current occupants than implement Project B.

Since the net present values of both Project A and Project B are negative, Benson should continue to rent the building to its current occupants.

7.6

	Year 0	Year 1	Year 2	Year 3	Year 4	Year 5
1. Keyboards Produced		10,000	10,000	10,000	10,000	10,000
2. Price per Keyboard		40	40(1.05)	$40(1.05)^2$	$40(1.05)^3$	$40(1.05)^4$
3. Sales revenue [1*2]		400,000	420,000	441,000	463,050	486,203
4. Cost per Keyboard		20	20(1.10)	$20(1.10)^2$	$20(1.10)^3$	$20(1.10)^4$
5. Operating costs[1*4]		200,000	220,000	242,000	266,200	292,820
6. Gross Margin [3-5]		200,000	200,000	199,000	196,850	193,383
7. Depreciation		80,000	80,000	80,000	80,000	80,000
8. Pretax Income [6-7]		120,000	120,000	119,000	116,850	113,383
9. Taxes at 34%		40,800	40,800	40,460	39,729	38,549
10. Net income [8-9]		79,200	79,200	78,540	77,121	74,834
11. Cash flow from operations [10+7]		159,200	159,200	158,540	157,121	154,834
12. Investment	-400,000					
13. Total Cash Flow	-$400,000	$159,200	$159,200	$158,540	$157,121	$154,834

Since the initial investment occurs today (year 0), its present value does not need to be adjusted.

$$PV(C_0) = -\$400,000$$
$$PV(C_1) = \$159,200 / (1.15) = \$138,435$$
$$PV(C_2) = \$159,200 / (1.15)^2 = \$120,378$$
$$PV(C_3) = \$158,540 / (1.15)^3 = \$104,243$$
$$PV(C_4) = \$157,121 / (1.15)^4 = \$89,834$$
$$PV(C_5) = \$154,834 / (1.15)^5 = \$76,980$$

$$NPV = PV(C_0) + PV(C_1) + PV(C_2) + PV(C_3) + PV(C_4) + PV(C_5) = \textbf{\$129,870}$$

These calculations could also have been performed in a single step:

$$NPV = -\$400,000 + \$159,200 / (1.15) + \$159,200 / (1.15)^2 + \$158,540 / (1.15)^3$$
$$+ \$157,121 / (1.15)^4 + \$154,834 / (1.15)^5$$
$$= \$129,870$$

The NPV of the investment is \$129,870.

7.7

		Year 0	Year 1	Year 2	Year 3	Year 4	Year 5
1.	Annual Salary Savings		\$120,000	\$120,000	\$120,000	\$120,000	\$120,000
2.	Depreciation		100,000	100,000	100,000	100,000	100,000
3.	Taxable Income [1- 2]		20,000	20,000	20,000	20,000	20,000
4.	Taxes		6,800	6,800	6,800	6,800	6,800
5.	Operating Cash Flow [1-4]		113,200	113,200	113,200	113,200	113,200
6.	Δ Net working capital	\$100,000					-100,000
7.	Investment	-\$500,000					66,000*
8.	Total Cash Flow	-\$400,000	\$113,200	\$113,200	\$113,200	\$113,200	\$79,200

* When calculating the salvage value, remember that tax liabilities or credits are generated on the *difference* between the resale value and the book value of the asset. In this case, the computer has a book value of \$0 and a resale value of \$100,000 at the end of year 5. The total amount received in salvage value is the resale value minus the taxes paid on the difference between the resale value and the book value: \$66,000 = \$100,000 - 0.34 (\$100,000 - \$0).

$$PV(C_0) = -\$400,000$$
$$PV(C_1) = \$113,200 / (1.12) = \$101,071$$
$$PV(C_2) = \$113,200 / (1.12)^2 = \$90,242$$
$$PV(C_3) = \$113,200 / (1.12)^3 = \$80,574$$
$$PV(C_4) = \$113,200 / (1.12)^4 = \$71,941$$
$$PV(C_5) = \$79,200 / (1.12)^5 = \$44,940$$

$$NPV = PV(C_0) + PV(C_1) + PV(C_2) + PV(C_3) + PV(C_4) + PV(C_5) = -\$11,232$$

These calculations could also have been performed in a single step:

$$NPV = -\$400,000 + \$113,200 / (1.12) + \$113,200 / (1.12)^2 + \$113,200 / (1.12)^3 +$$
$$\$113,200 / (1.12)^4 + \$79,200 / (1.12)^5$$
$$= -\$11,232$$

Since the NPV of the computer is negative, it is not a worthwhile investment.

	t = 0	t = 1- 2	t = 3
1. Revenues		$600,000	$600,000
2. Expenses		150,000	150,000
3. Depreciation		150,000	150,000
4. Pretax Income [1-2-3]		$300,000	$300,000
5. Taxes (35%)		105,000	105,000
6. Net Income [4-5]		$195,000	$195,000
7. Net Working Capital	- 25,000		$25,000
8. CF from Operations [6+3+7]	- 25,000	$345,000	$370,000
9. Capital Investment	- $750,000		$40,000
10. Tax benefit from Capital Loss*			$91,000
11. A/T-NCF	- $775,000	$345,000	$501,000

* The capital loss arises because the resale value ($40,000) is less than the net book value ($300,000). The tax benefit from the capital loss is computed by multiplying the amount of the capital loss by the tax rate ($91,000 = 0.35 * $260,000). This represents the tax shield, i.e. the reduction in taxes from the capital loss.

The cash flows in years 1 and 2 could also have been computed using the following simplification:

$$\text{After-Tax NCF} = \text{Revenue} (1 - T_c) - \text{Expenses} (1 - T_c) + \text{Depreciation} (T_c)$$
$$= \$600,000 (0.65) - \$150,000 (0.65) + \$150,000(0.35)$$
$$= \$345,000$$

$PV(C_0) = -\$775,000$
$PV(C_1) = \$345,000/ (1.17) = \$294,872$
$PV(C_2) = \$345,000/ (1.17)^2 = \$252,027$
$PV(C_3) = \$501,000/(1.17)^3 = \$312,810$

$\text{NPV} = PV(C_0) + PV(C_1) + PV(C_2) + PV(C_3) = $ **$84,709**

These calculations could also have been performed in a single step:

$\text{NPV} = -\$775,000 + \$345,000/ (1.17) + \$345,000/ (1.17)^2 + \$501,000/(1.17)^3$
$= -\$775,000 + \$294,872 + \$252,027 + \$312,810$
$= $ **$84,709**

The NPV of the new software is $84,709.

7.9   The least amount of money that the firm should ask for the first-year lease payment is the amount that will make the net present value of the purchase of the building equal to zero. In other words, the least that the firm will charge for its initial lease payment is the amount that makes the present value of future cash flows just enough to compensate it for its $4,000,000 purchase. In order to determine this amount, set the net present value of the project equal to zero. Solve for the amount of the initial lease payment.

Since the purchase of the building will occur today (year 0), its present value does not need to be adjusted.

PV(Purchase of Building) = -$4,000,000

Since the initial lease payment also occurs today (year 0), its present value also does not need to be adjusted. However, since it will be recorded as revenue for the firm and will be taxed, the inflow must be adjusted to the corporate tax rate.

$$\text{PV(Initial Lease Payment)} = C_0(1 - 0.34)$$

Note that in this problem we are solving for C_0, which is not yet known.

The second lease payment represents the first cash flow of a growing annuity. Since lease payments increase by three percent each year, the amount of the second payment is the amount of the first payment multiplied by 1.03, adjusted for taxes, or $C_0(1 - 0.66)(1.03)$. Recall that the appropriate discount rate is 12 percent, the growth rate is three percent, and that the annuity consists of only 19 payments, since the first of the 20 payments was made at t=0.

$$\text{PV(Remainder of Lease Payments)} = C_0(1 - 0.34)(1.03)(GA^{19}_{0.12,\,0.03})*$$

* The notation $GA^T_{r,\,g}$ represents a growing annuity consisting of T payments growing at a rate of g per payment, discounted at r.

Annual depreciation, calculated by the straight-line method (Initial Investment / Economic Life of Investment), is $200,000 (= $4,000,000 / 20). Since net income will be lower by $200,000 per year due to this expense, the firm's tax bill will also be lower. The annual depreciation tax shield is found by multiplying the annual depreciation expense by the tax rate. The annual tax shield is $68,000 (= $200,000 * 0.34). Apply the standard annuity formula to calculate the present value of the annual depreciation tax shield.

$$\text{PV(Depreciation Tax Shield)} = \$68,000 A^{20}_{0.12}$$

Recall that the least that the firm will charge for its initial lease payment is the amount that makes the present value of future cash flows just enough to compensate it for its $4,000,000 purchase. This is represented in the equation below:

PV(Purchase)	= PV(Lease Payments) + PV(Depreciation Tax Shield)
$4,000,000	$= C_0(1 - 0.34) + C_0(1 - 0.34)(1.03)(GA^{19}_{0.12,\,0.03}) + \$68,000 A^{20}_{0.12}$
C_0	= $523,117

Therefore, the least that the firm should charge for its initial lease payment is $523,117.

7.10 The decision to accept or reject the project depends on whether the NPV of the project is positive or negative.

(in thousands)

		Year 0	Year 1	Year 2	Year 3	Year 4
1.	Sales revenue	-	$1,200	$1,200	$1,200	$1,200
2.	Operating costs	-	300	300	300	300
3.	Depreciation	-	400	400	400	400
4.	Income before tax [1-2-3]	-	500	500	500	500
5.	Taxes at 35%	-	175	175	175	175
6.	Net income [4-5]	0	325	325	325	325
7.	Cash flow from operation [1-2-5]	0	725	725	725	725
8.	Initial Investment	-2000	-	-	-	237.5*
9.	Changes in net working capital	-100	-	-	-	100
10.	Total cash flow from investment [8+9]	-2,100	-	-	-	337.5
11.	Total cash flow [7+10]	-2,100	725	725	725	1,062.5

* Remember that, when calculating the salvage value, tax liabilities or credits are generated on the *difference* between the resale value and the book value of the asset. Since the capital asset is depreciated over five years, yet sold in the year 4, the book value at the time of sale is $400,000 (= $2,000,000 – $1,600,000). Since the salvage value of $150,000 is below book value, the resulting capital loss creates a *tax credit*.

$$\text{After-Tax Resale Value} = \$150,000 - 0.35\,(\$150,000 - 400,000)$$
$$= \$237,500$$

Note that an increase in required net working capital is a negative cash flow whereas a decrease in required net working capital is a positive cash flow. Thus, in year 0, the firm realizes a $100,000 cash *outflow* while in year 4 the firm realizes a $100,000 cash *inflow*. Since year 0 is today, year 0 cash flows do not need to be discounted.

$$PV(C_0) = -\$2,100,000$$
$$PV(C_1) = \$725,000 / (1.1655) \qquad = \$622,051$$
$$PV(C_2) = \$725,000 / (1.1655)^2 \qquad = \$533,720$$
$$PV(C_3) = \$725,000 / (1.1655)^3 \qquad = \$457,932$$
$$PV(C_4) = \$1,062,500 / (1.1655)^4 \qquad = \$575,811$$

$$NPV = PV(C_0) + PV(C_1) + PV(C_2) + PV(C_3) + PV(C_4) = \mathbf{\$89,514}$$

These calculations could also have been performed in a single step:

$$NPV = -\$2,100,000 + \$725,000 / (1.1655) + \$725,000 / (1.1655)^2 + \$725,000 / (1.1655)^3 + \$1,062,500 / (1.1655)^4$$
$$= \mathbf{\$89,514}$$

Since the NPV of the project is positive, Royal Dutch should proceed with the project.

7.11 To determine the maximum price that MMC should be willing to pay for the equipment, calculate how high the price for the new equipment must be for the project to have an NPV of zero. Determine the cash flows pertaining to the sale of the existing equipment, the purchase of the new equipment, the future incremental benefits that the new equipment will provide to the firm, and the sale of the new equipment in eight years.

Sale of existing equipment
To find the after-tax resale value of the equipment, take into consideration the current market value and the accumulated depreciation. The difference is the amount subject to capital gains taxes.

Purchase Price	= $40,000
Depreciation per year	= $40,000 / 10 years = $4,000 per year
Accumulated Depreciation	= 5 years * $4,000 per year = $20,000
Net Book Value of existing equipment	= Purchase Price – Accumulated Depreciation = $40,000 - $20,000 = $20,000
PV(After-Tax Net Resale Value)	= Sale Price – T_c (Sale Price – Net Book Value) = $20,000 - 0.34 ($20,000 – $20,000) = $20,000

Purchase of new equipment
Let I equal the maximum price that MMC should be willing to pay for the equipment.

PV(New Equipment) = -$I

Lower operating costs
Before-tax operating costs are lower by $10,000 per year for eight years if the firm purchases the new equipment. Lower operating costs raise net income, implying a larger tax bill.

Increased annual taxes due to higher net income	= $10,000 * 0.34 = $3,400

If the firm purchases the new equipment, its net income will be $10,000 higher but it will also pay $3,400 more in taxes. Therefore, lower operating costs increase the firm's annual cash flow by $6,600.

PV(Operating Cost Savings)	= $6,600 $A^8_{0.08}$ = $37,928

Incremental depreciation tax shield
The firm will realize depreciation tax benefits on the new equipment. However, the firm also foregoes the depreciation tax shield on the old equipment.

Incremental depreciation per year due to new equipment =
Annual Depreciation on new equipment – Annual Depreciation on old equipment if it had been retained

Annual Depreciation on New Equipment	= (Purchase Price/ Economic Life) = ($I/5)
Annual Depreciation on Old Equipment	= $4,000

Incremental Depreciation per year due to new equipment = ($I/5) - $4,000

Incremental Depreciation tax shield per year = Incremental Depreciation per year * T_C
$$= [(\$I/5) - \$4,000] * 0.34$$

PV(Incremental Depreciation Tax Shield) = $0.34[(\$I/5) - \$4,000] \, A^5_{0.08}$

Note that since both old and new equipment will be fully depreciated after 5 years, no depreciation tax shield is applicable in years 6-8.

Sale of New Equipment

The new equipment will be sold at the end of year 8. Since it will have been fully depreciated by year 5, capital gains taxes must be paid on the entire resale price.

Sale Price of new equipment	= $5,000
Net Book Value of new equipment	= $0 (It had been fully depreciated as of year 5.)
After-Tax Net Cash Flow	= Sale Price – T_c (Sale Price – Net Book Value)
	= $5,000 - 0.34 ($5,000 – 0)
	= $3,300
PV(Resale Value)	= $3,300 / (1.08)^8
	= $1,783

The maximum price that MMC should be willing to pay for the new equipment is the price that makes the NPV of the investment equal to zero. In order to solve for the price, set the net present value of all incremental after-tax cash flows related to the new equipment equal to zero and solve for *I*.

$$0 = (\$20,000 – \$I) + \$6,600 \, A^8_{0.08} + [0.34][(\$I/5) - \$4,000] \, A^5_{0.08} + \$3,300/ (1.08)^8$$

I = **$74,510**

Therefore, the maximum price that MMC should be willing to pay for the equipment is $74,510.

7.12   Purchase of New Equipment = **-$28,000,000**

Since the old equipment is sold at a price that is greater than its book value, the firm will record a capital gain on the sale, and this sale will be subject to the corporate tax rate.

After-Tax Salvage Value	= Sale Price – T_C(Sale Price – Net Book Value)
After-Tax Value of Sale of Old Equipment	= $20,000,000 - 0.40($20,000,000-$12,000,000)
	= **$16,800,000**

After-Tax Operating Cost Savings due to New Equipment
Year 1	= (1-0.40)($17,500,000)	= **$10,500,000**
Year 2	= (1-0.40)($17,500,000)(1.12)	= **$11,760,000**
Year 3	= (1-0.40)($17,500,000)(1.12)^2	= **$13,171,200**
Year 4	= (1-0.40)($17,500,000)(1.12)^3	= **$14,751,744**

Depreciation of Old Equipment
Year 1 = ($12,000,000/4)		= $3,000,000
Year 2 = ($12,000,000/4)		= $3,000,000
Year 3 = ($12,000,000/4)		= $3,000,000
Year 4 = ($12,000,000/4)		= $3,000,000

Depreciation of New Equipment
Year 1 = ($28,000,000 * 0.333)   = $9,324,000
Year 2 = ($28,000,000*0.399)   = $11,172,000
Year 3 = ($28,000,000*0.148)   = $4,144,000
Year 4 = ($28,000,000*0.120)   = $3,360,000

Incremental Depreciation due to New Equipment
Year 1 = $9,324,000 - $3,000,000   = **$6,324,000**
Year 2 = $11,172,000- $3,000,000   = **$8,172,000**
Year 3 = $4,144,000- $3,000,000   = **$1,144,000**
Year 4 = $3,360,000- $3,000,000   = **$360,000**

Incremental Depreciation Tax Shield due to New Equipment
Year 1 = $6,324,000 * 0.40   = **$2,529,600**
Year 2 = $8,172,000 * 0.40   = **$3,268,800**
Year 3 = $1,144,000 * 0.40   = **$457,600**
Year 4 = $360,000 * 0.40   = **$144,000**

a. Net Investment   = - Purchase of New Equipment + After-Tax Proceeds from Sale of Old
                        Equipment + Increase in Net Working Capital
                      = -$28,000,000 + $16,800,000 - $5,000,000
                      = **-$16,200,000**

Therefore, the cash outflow at the end of year 0 is $16,200,000.

b.

	Year 0	Year 1	Year 2	Year 3	Year 4
Purchase of New Equipment	-28,000,000				
After-Tax Sale of Old Equipment	16,800,000				
Δ Net Working Capital	-5,000,000				5,000,000
After-Tax Operating Cost Savings		10,500,000	11,760,000	13,171,200	14,751,744
Incremental Depreciation Tax Shield		2,529,600	3,268,800	457,600	144,000
After-Tax Incremental Cash Flow	**-16,200,000**	**13,029,600**	**15,028,800**	**13,628,800**	**19,895,744**

c. IRR Calculation:

In order to determine the internal rate return (IRR) of the investment in new equipment, determine
the discount rate that makes the NPV of the project equal to zero.

$0 = -\$16,200,000 + \$13,029,600/(1+IRR) + \$15,028,800/(1+IRR)^2 + \$13,628,800/(1+IRR)^3 + \$19,895,744/(1+IRR)^4$

IRR   = 0.7948
      = **79.48%**

The internal rate of return of the investment in new equipment is 79.48%.

d. NPV Calculation:

NPV $= -\$16,200,000 + \$13,029,600/(1.14) + \$15,028,800/(1.14)^2 + \$13,628,800/(1.14)^3 + \$19,895,744/(1.14)^4$
      = **$27,772,577**

The net present value of the investment in new equipment is $27,772,577.

7.13 $12 million   =   New market share − Current Market Erosion
                       $20 million   − $4 million
                       $100*20%   − $80*10%*.5

Note:

The $10 million for running shoe R & D is a sunk cost and not considered.

The $1 million for walking shoe R & D is a capital expenditure, but does not affect revenues.

The $1 million for the warehouse extension is a capital expenditure, but does not affect revenues.

7.14   Amount in thousands

Period	0	1	2	3	4	5	NPV
Signing bonus	$5,000						
Salary		$2,000	$2,000	$2,000	$2,000	$2,000	
Annual bonus*		$1,000	$1,000	$1,000	$1,000	$1,000	
Total Cash Flow	$5,000	$3,000	$3,000	$3,000	$3,000	$3,000	
PV 12% (CF)	= CF	= CF/1.12	= CF/(1.12)^2	= CF/(1.12)^3	= CF/(1.12)^4	= CF/(1.12)^5	
	5,000	2,679	2,392	2,135	1,907	1,702	$15,814,329

*annual bonus = $1 mil ($2 mil x 50%)

NPV = $15,814,329.

7.15

	Year 0	Year 1	Year 2	Year 3	Year 4	Year 5	NPV
Investments:							
Capital equipment	(60,000)						
Change in NWC		(28,000)	(13,500)	(15,525)	(17,854)	(20,532)	
Total cash flow from investments	(60,000)	(28,000)	(13,500)	(15,525)	(17,854)	(20,532)	
Income:							
Units		5,000	5,750	6,613	7,604	8,745	
Sales		225,000	258,750	297,563	342,197	393,526	
Fixed Costs		75,000	75,000	75,000	75,000	75,000	
Variable Costs		100,000	115,000	132,250	152,088	174,901	
Depreciation		(12,000)	(12,000)	(12,000)	(12,000)	(12,000)	
Income before depreciation		62,000	80,750	102,313	127,109	155,626	
Taxes at 34%		15,500	20,188	25,578	31,777	38,906	
Net Income		46,500	60,563	76,734	95,332	116,719	
Cash flow from operations:							
Net Income		46,500	60,563	76,734	95,332	116,719	
Depreciation		12,000	12,000	12,000	12,000	12,000	
Operating cash flow		58,500	72,563	88,734	107,332	128,719	
Total cash flow from project	(60,000)	30,500	59,063	73,209	89,478	108,188	
PV 25% (CF)	(60,000)	24,400	37,800	37,483	36,650	35,451	$111,784

The project's NPV is $111,784.
Note: We are assuming that initial net working capital (NWC) is needed for year 1 production and starts in year 1.

7.16

	Year 0	Year 1	Year 2	Year 3	Year 4	Year 5	NPV
Investments:							
Touch screen system	$ (150,000)						
Annual maintenance		$ (5,000)	$ (5,000)	$ (5,000)	$ (5,000)	$ (5,000)	
Change in NWC		$ (5,000)				$ 5,000	
Wages saved		$30,000	$30,000	$30,000	$30,000	$30,000	
Total cash flow from investments	$ (150,000)	$20,000	$25,000	$25,000	$25,000	$30,000	
Income:							
Revenue		$15,000	$15,000	$15,000	$15,000	$15,000	
COGS		$ (3,750)	$ (3,750)	$ (3,750)	$ (3,750)	$ (3,750)	
Cash flow from operations		$11,250	$11,250	$11,250	$11,250	$11,250	
Total cash flow from project	$ (150,000)	$31,250	$36,250	$36,250	$36,250	$41,250	
PV 15% (CF)	$=CF$ (150,000)	$=CF/1.15$ 27,174	$=CF/(1.15)^2$ 27,410	$=CF/(1.15)^3$ 23,835	$=CF/(1.15)^4$ 20,726	$=CF/(1.15)^5$ 20,509	($30,346)

No, the big burrito should not make this investment because it has a negative NPV.

7.17

Year	0	1	2	3	4	
Signing	$500,000					
Salary		$800,000	800,000	800,000	800,000	
Deferred					523,919	$=100000/0.105*(1-(1/1.105)^8$
Bonus		82,500	82,500	82,500	82,500	$=150000*0.55$
SUM	$500,000	882,500	882,500	882,500	1,406,419	
PV	$500,000	798,643	722,753	654,075	943,334	
SUM (PV)	$3,618,806					

7.18

Investments:	Year 0	Year 1	Year 2	Year 3	Year 4	Year 5	NPV
Capital equipment	(1,500,000)						
Capital gains taxes						(106,420)	
Change in NWC		500,000				(500,000)	
Salary savings		300,000	300,000	300,000	300,000	300,000	
After-tax salary savings		198,000	198,000	198,000	198,000	198,000	
Depreciation tax shield		102,000	163,200	97,920	58,650	58,650	
Total cash flow from project	(1,500,000)	800,000	361,200	295,920	256,650	50,230	
PV 15% (CF)	(1,500,000)	695,652	273,119	194,572	146,740	24,973	$(164,943)

No, it is not worthwhile to purchase the automation machine since it has a negative NPV.
Note: We are assuming the reduction in net working capital (NWC) in one-time only.

7.19

Investments:	Year 0	Year 1	Year 2	Year 3	Year 4	Year 5	NPV
Capital equipment	(10,000)						
Change in NWC		(1,000)				1,000	
Profits		6,000	6,000	6,000	6,000	6,000	
After-tax profits		3,960	3,960	3,960	3,960	3,960	
Depreciation tax shield		680	680	680	680	680	
Total cash flow from project	(10,000)	3,640	4,640	4,640	4,640	5,640	
PV 17% (CF)	(10,000)	3,111	3,390	2,897	2,476	2,572	$4,446

Yes, it is worthwhile to purchase the machine since it has a NPV of $4,446.
Note: We are assuming the increase in net working capital (NWC) is one-time only and it is associated with the use of the machine in Year 1.

7.20

	Year 0	Year 1	Year 2	Year 3	Year 4	Year 5	NPV
Investments:							
Capital equipment	(1,000,000)						
Change in NWC		(10,000)				10,000	
Costs		329,220	329,220	329,220	329,220	329,220	
After-tax Costs		217,285	217,285	217,285	217,285	217,285	
Depreciation tax shield		68,000	68,000	68,000	68,000	68,000	
Total cash flow from project	(1,000,000)	275,285	285,285	285,285	285,285	295,285	
PV 13% (CF)	(1,000,000)	243,615	223,420	197,717	174,971	160,269	0

a. At 26 cents per bottle (rounding down from 26.46 cents), the NPV of the machine will be 0.

b. No, it is not worthwhile to make the investment at 25 cents per bottle.

Note: We are assuming the increase in net working capital (NWC) is one-time only and it is associated with the use of the machine in Year 1.

7.21 Nominal cash flows should be discounted at the nominal discount rate. Real cash flows should be discounted at the real discount rate. Project A's cash flows are presented in real terms. Therefore, one must compute the real discount rate before calculating the NPV of Project A. Since the cash flows of Project B are given in nominal terms, discount its cash flows by the nominal rate in order to calculate its NPV.

$$
\begin{array}{ll}
\text{Nominal Discount Rate} & = 0.15 \\
\text{Inflation Rate} & = 0.04 \\
\text{1 + Real Discount Rate} & = (1 + \text{Nominal Discount Rate}) / (1 + \text{Inflation Rate}) \\
\text{Real Discount Rate} & = 0.1058 = 10.58\%
\end{array}
$$

Project A's cash flows are expressed in real terms and therefore should be discounted at the real discount rate of 10.58%.

Project A:
$$
\begin{array}{l}
PV(C_0) = -\$40{,}000 \\
PV(C_1) = \$20{,}000 / (1.1058) = \$18{,}086 \\
PV(C_2) = \$15{,}000 / (1.1058)^2 = \$12{,}267 \\
PV(C_3) = \$15{,}000 / (1.1058)^3 = \$11{,}093
\end{array}
$$

$$
\begin{array}{ll}
NPV_A & = PV(C_0) + PV(C_1) + PV(C_2) + PV(C_3) \\
& = \mathbf{\$1{,}446}
\end{array}
$$

These calculations could also have been performed in a single step:

$$
\begin{array}{ll}
NPV_A & = -\$40{,}000 + \$20{,}000 / (1.1058) + \$15{,}000 / (1.1058)^2 + \$15{,}000 / (1.1058)^3 \\
& = \mathbf{\$1{,}446}
\end{array}
$$

Project B's cash flows are expressed in nominal terms and therefore should be discounted at the nominal discount rate of 15%.

Project B:
$$
\begin{array}{l}
PV(C_0) = -\$50{,}000 \\
PV(C_1) = \$10{,}000 / (1.15) = \$8{,}696 \\
PV(C_2) = \$20{,}000 / (1.15)^2 = \$15{,}123 \\
PV(C_3) = \$40{,}000 / (1.15)^3 = \$26{,}301
\end{array}
$$

$$
\begin{array}{ll}
NPV_B & = PV(C_0) + PV(C_1) + PV(C_2) + PV(C_3) \\
& = \mathbf{\$120}
\end{array}
$$

These calculations could also have been performed in a single step:

$$
\begin{array}{ll}
NPV_B & = -\$50{,}000 + \$10{,}000 / (1.15) + \$20{,}000 / (1.15)^2 + \$40{,}000 / (1.15)^3 \\
& = \mathbf{\$120}
\end{array}
$$

Since the NPV of Project A is greater than the NPV of Project B, choose Project A.

7.22 Notice that the problem provides the nominal values at the end of the first year, so to find the values for revenue and expenses at the end of year 5, compound the values by four years of inflation, e.g. $\$200{,}000 * (1.03)^4 = \$225{,}102$. Since the resale value is given in nominal terms as of the end of year 5, it does not need to be adjusted for inflation. Also, no inflation adjustment is needed for either the depreciation charge or the recovery of net working capital since these items are already expressed in nominal terms. Note that an increase in required net working capital is a negative cash flow whereas a decrease in required net working capital is a positive cash flow.

	Year 0	Year 1	Year 2	Year 3	Year 4	Year 5
1. Revenue		$200,000	$206,000	$212,180	$218,545	$225,102
2. Expenses		50,000	51,500	53,045	54,636	56,275
3. Depreciation		50,000	50,000	50,000	50,000	50,000
4. Taxable Income [1 –2 –3]		100,000	104,500	109,135	113,909	118,827
5. Taxes		34,000	35,530	37,106	38,729	40,401
6. Operating Cash Flow [1 – 2 – 5]		116,000	118,970	122,029	125,180	128,426
7. Δ Net working capital	-10,000					10,000
8. Investment	-250,000					19,800*
9. Total Cash Flow	-$260,000	$116,000	$118,970	$122,029	$125,180	**$158,226**

* When calculating the salvage value of the asset, remember that only the gain on the sale of the asset is taxed. This gain is calculated as the difference between the resale value and the net book value of the asset at the time of sale. It follows that the tax associated with the sale is T_C *(Resale Value – Net Book Value)*. Therefore, the after-tax salvage value of the asset is $19,800 [= \$30,000 – 0.34(\$30,000 – 0)]$.

The nominal cash flow at year 5 is $158,226.

7.23   Since the problem lists nominal cash flows and a real discount rate, one must determine the nominal discount rate before computing the net present value of the project.

$$1 + \text{Real Discount Rate} = (1 + \text{Nominal Discount Rate}) / (1 + \text{Inflation Rate})$$
$$1.14 = (1+ \text{Nominal Discount Rate}) / (1.05)$$
$$\text{Nominal Discount Rate} = 0.197$$

	Year 0	Year 1	Year 2	Year 3	Year 4	Year 5	Year 6	Year 7
1. Sales revenue	-	$50,000	$52,500	$55,125	$57,881	$60,775	$63,814	$67,005
2. Operating costs	-	20,000	21,400	22,898	24,501	26,216	28,051	30,015
3. Depreciation	-	17,143	17,143	17,143	17,143	17,143	17,143	17,143
4. Income before tax [1-2-3]	-	12,857	13,957	15,084	16,237	17,416	18,620	19,847
5. Taxes at 34%	-	4,371	4,745	5,129	5,521	5,921	6,331	6,748
6. Net income [4-5]	-	8,486	9,212	9,955	10,716	11,495	12,289	13,099
7. Cash flow from operation [1-2-5]	-	25,629	26,355	27,098	27,859	28,638	29,432	30,242
8. Initial Investment	-120,000	-	-	-	-	-	-	-
10. Total cash flow from investment [9+10]	-120,000	-	-	-	-	-	-	-
11. Total cash flow [7+10]	-120,000	25,629	26,355	27,098	27,859	28,638	29,432	30,242

$$PV(C_0) = -\$120,000$$
$$PV(C_1) = \$25,629 / (1.197) = \$21,411$$
$$PV(C_2) = \$26,355 / (1.197)^2 = \$18,394$$
$$PV(C_3) = \$27,098 / (1.197)^3 = \$15,800$$
$$PV(C_4) = \$27,859 / (1.197)^4 = \$13,570$$
$$PV(C_5) = \$28,638 / (1.197)^5 = \$11,654$$
$$PV(C_6) = \$29,432 / (1.197)^6 = \$10,006$$
$$PV(C_7) = \$30,242 / (1.197)^7 = \$8,589$$

$$NPV = PV(C_0) + PV(C_1) + PV(C_2) + PV(C_3) + PV(C_4) + PV(C_5) + PV(C_6) + PV(C_7)$$
$$= \textbf{-\$20,576}$$

These calculations could also have been performed in a single step:

$$NPV = -\$120,000 + \$25,629 / (1.197) + \$26,025 / (1.197)^2 + \$27,098 / (1.197)^3$$
$$+ \$27,859 / (1.197)^4 + \$28,638 / (1.197)^5 + \$29,432 / (1.197)^6$$
$$+ \$30,242 / (1.197)^7$$
$$= \textbf{-\$20,576}$$

To solve the problem using a string of annuities, find the present value of each cash flow.

The investment occurs today and therefore is not discounted:

$$PV(\text{Investment}) = -\$120,000$$

The PV of the revenues is found by using the *growing annuity* formula. Note that nominal cash flows must be discounted by nominal rates. The following solution treats revenues as a growing annuity discounted at 19.7 percent and growing at five percent annually over seven years:

$$PV(\text{Revenues}) = C_1 (1 - T_c) \, GA^T_{r,\,g}$$
$$PV(\text{Revenues}) = \$50,000 \, GA^7_{0.197,\,0.05} (1 - 0.34)*$$
$$= \$134,775$$

* The notation $GA^T_{r,\,g}$ represents a growing annuity consisting of T payments growing at a rate of g per payment, discounted at r.

The PV of the expenses is found using the same method that was used in finding the PV of the revenues. Again, the expenses are treated as a nominal growing annuity, discounted at 19.7 percent and growing at seven percent annually over seven years:

$$PV \text{ Expenses} = C_1 \, GA^T_{r,\,g} (1 - T_c)$$
$$PV \text{ Expenses} = \$20,000 \, GA^7_{0.197,\,0.07} (1 - 0.34)$$
$$= \$56,534$$

Since the firm has positive net income, the firm will benefit from the *depreciation tax shield*. Apply the annuity formula to the string of annual tax shields to find the present value of the taxes saved.

$$PV(\text{Depreciation Tax Shield}) = T_c (\text{Annual Depreciation}) \, A^T_r$$
$$PV(\text{Depreciation Tax Shield}) = 0.34 \, (\$120,000 / 7) \, A^7_{0.197}$$
$$= \$21,183$$

The present value of the project is the sum of the previous annuities:

PV Project   = -Investment + Revenue - Expenses + Depreciation Tax Shield
PV Project   = -$120,000 + $134,775 - $56,534 + $21,183
PV Project   = **-$20,576**

Since the project has a negative NPV, -$20,576, it should be rejected.

The nominal cash flow during year 5 is $157,926.

7.24   Apply the growing perpetuity formula to the payments that are declining at a constant rate. Because the payments are declining, they have a *negative* growth rate.

The initial cash flow of the perpetuity occurs one year from today and is expressed in real terms.

$C_1 = \$120,000$

The real discount rate is 11%.

$r = 0.11$

The real growth rate is -6%.

$g = -0.06$

$$
\begin{aligned}
PV \quad &= C_1 / (r\text{-}g) \text{ , where } r > g \\
&= \$120,000 / [\, 0.11 - (-0.06)] \\
&= \$120,000 / (0.11 + 0.06) \\
&= \$120,000 / 0.17 \\
&= \mathbf{\$705,882}
\end{aligned}
$$

The present value of Phillip's net cash flows is $705,882.

7.25   Notice that the discount rate is expressed in real terms and the cash flows are expressed in nominal terms. In order to solve the problem, convert all nominal cash flows to real cash flows and discount them using the real discount rate.

Year 1 Revenue in Real Terms	= $150,000 / 1.06	= $141,509
Year 1 Labor Costs in Real Terms	= $80,000 / 1.06	= $75,472
Year 1 Other Costs in Real Terms	= $40,000 / 1.06	= $37,736
Year 1 Lease Payment in Real Terms	= $20,000 / 1.06	= $18,868

Revenues and labor costs form growing perpetuities and other costs form a declining perpetuity.

PV (Revenue)	= ($141,509.43) / (0.10 - 0.05)	= $2,830,189
PV (Labor Costs)	= ($75,471.70) / (0.10 - 0.03)	= $1,078,167
PV (Other Costs)	= ($37,735.85) / [0.10 - (-0.01)]	= $343,053

Since the lease payments are constant in nominal terms, they are declining in real terms by the inflation rate. Therefore, the lease payments form a declining perpetuity.

PV(Lease Payments)   = ($18,868 / [0.10 – (-0.06)]   = $117,925

$$
\begin{aligned}
NPV &= PV(\text{Revenue}) - PV(\text{Labor Costs}) - PV(\text{Other Costs}) - PV(\text{Lease Payments}) \\
&= \$2,830,189 - \$1,078,167 - \$343,053 - \$117,925 \\
&= \$1,291,044
\end{aligned}
$$

The NPV of the proposed toad ranch is $1,291,044.

Alternatively, one could solve this problem by expressing everything in nominal terms. This approach yields the same answer as given above. However, in this case, the computation would have been *much* more difficult. When faced with two alternative approaches, where both are equally correct, always choose the simplest one.

7.26

	Year 1	Year 2	Year 3	Year 4
Revenues	$40,000,000	$80,000,000	$80,000,000	$60,000,000
Labor Costs	30,600,000	31,212,000	31,836,240	32,472,965
Energy Costs	1,030,000	1,060,900	1,092,727	1,125,509
Revenues-Costs	8,370,000	47,727,100	47,071,033	26,401,526
After-tax Revenues-Costs	5,524,200	31,499,886	31,066,882	17,425,007

Since revenues and costs are expressed in real terms, after-tax income will be discounted at the real discount rate of 8%.

Remember that the depreciation tax shield also affects a firm's after-tax cash flows. The present value of the depreciation tax shield must be added to the present value of a firm's revenues and expenses to find the present value of the cash flows related to the project. The depreciation the firm will recognize each year is:

$$\text{Depreciation} = \text{Investment / Economic Life}$$
$$= \$32,000,000 / 4$$
$$= \$8,000,000$$

Next, find the annual depreciation tax shield. Remember that this reduction in taxes is equal to the tax rate times the depreciation expense for the year.

$$\text{Annual Depreciation Tax Shield} = T_c \, (\text{Annual Depreciation Expense})$$
$$= 0.34 \, (\$8,000,000)$$
$$= \$2,720,000$$

Remember that depreciation is a nominal quantity, and thus must be discounted at the nominal rate. To find the nominal rate, use the following equation:

$$1+ \text{Real Discount Rate} = (1+\text{Nominal Discount Rate}) / (1+\text{Inflation Rate})$$
$$1.08 = (1+\text{Nominal Discount Rate}) / (1.05)$$
$$\text{Nominal Discount Rate} = 0.134$$

To find the present value of the depreciation tax shield, apply the four-year annuity formula to the annual tax savings:

$$\text{PV(Tax Shield)} = C_1 \, A^4_{0.134}$$
$$= \$2,720,000 \, A^4_{0.134}$$
$$= \$8,023,779$$

$\text{PV}(C_0) = -\$32,000,000$	$= -\$32,000,000$
$\text{PV}(C_1) = \$5,524,200 / (1.08)$	$= \$5,115,000$
$\text{PV}(C_2) = \$31,499,886 / (1.08)^2$	$= \$27,006,075$
$\text{PV}(C_3) = \$31,066,882 / (1.08)^3$	$= \$24,661,893$
$\text{PV}(C_4) = \$17,425,007 / (1.08)^4$	$= \$12,807,900$
PV(Depreciation Tax Shield)	$= \$8,023,779$

$$\text{NPV} = PV(C_0) + PV(C_1) + PV(C_2) + PV(C_3) + PV(C_4) + PV(\text{Depreciation Tax Shield})$$
$$= \$45{,}614{,}647$$

These calculations also could have been performed in a single step:

$$\text{NPV} = -\$32{,}000{,}000 + \$5{,}524{,}200 / (1.08) + \$31{,}499{,}886 / (1.08)^2 + \$31{,}066{,}882 / (1.08)^3$$
$$+ \$17{,}425{,}007 / (1.08)^4 + (0.34)(\$8{,}000{,}000) A^4{}_{0.134}$$
$$= \$45{,}614{,}647$$

The NPV of the project is \$45,614,647.

7.27   In order to determine how much Sparkling Water, Inc. is worth today, find the present value of its cash flows.

Sparkling will receive \$2.50 per bottle in revenues in real terms at the end of year 1.

$$\text{After-Tax Revenue in Year 1 in real terms} = (2{,}000{,}000 * \$2.50)(1-0.34)$$
$$= \$3{,}300{,}000$$

Sparkling's revenues will grow at seven percent per year in real terms forever. Apply the growing perpetuity formula.

$$\text{PV(Revenues)} = C_1 / (r-g) \text{ , where } r > g$$
$$= \$3{,}300{,}000 / (0.10 - 0.07)$$
$$= \$110{,}000{,}000$$

Per bottle costs will be \$0.70 in real terms at the end of year 1.

$$\text{After-Tax Costs in Year 1 in real terms} = (2{,}000{,}000 * \$0.70)(1-0.34) = \$924{,}000$$

Sparkling's costs will grow at 5% per year in real terms forever. This string of payments forms a growing perpetuity.

$$\text{PV(Costs)} = C_1 / (r-g) \text{ , where } r > g$$
$$= \$924{,}000 / (0.10 - 0.05)$$
$$= \$18{,}480{,}000$$

$$\text{Value of the firm} = \text{PV(Revenues)} - \text{PV(Costs)}$$
$$= \$110{,}000{,}000 - \$18{,}480{,}000$$
$$= \$91{,}520{,}000$$

Sparkling Water, Inc., is worth \$91,520,000 today.

7.28   Since all cash flows are stated in nominal terms and the growth rates of both the sales price and the variable cost are stated in real terms, these rates must be restated in nominal terms in order to solve the problem. Since the discount rate is expressed in nominal terms, it does not need to be adjusted. Alternatively, one could solve this problem by expressing everything in real terms. This approach yields the same answer.

Find the nominal growth rates:

$$1 + \text{Real Rate} = (1 + \text{Nominal Rate}) / (1 + \text{Inflation Rate})$$

$$1.05 = (1 + \text{Nominal Selling Price Growth Rate}) / (1.05)$$
$$0.1025 = \text{Nominal Selling Price Growth Rate}$$

| 1.02 | $= (1 + \text{Nominal Variable Cost Growth Rate}) / (1.05)$ |
| 0.071 | $= \text{Nominal Variable Cost Growth Rate}$ |

The revenue stream is a five-year growing annuity. Pre-tax revenue in year 1 is found by multiplying the selling price ($3.15) by the number of units produced (1,000,000). The cash flows are growing at the nominal rate of 0.1025 and are discounted at 0.20. In order to find the after-tax present value, multiply revenues by $(1-T_C)$.

$$PV \text{ (Revenues)} = (1 - T_c) \text{ (Year 1 Selling Price) (Year 1 Production) } GA^T_{r,g} *$$
$$PV \text{ (Revenues)} = (1 - 0.34) (\$3.15) (1,000,000) GA^5_{0.20, \, 0.1025}$$
$$= \$7,364,645$$

* The notation $GA^T_{r, g}$ represents a growing annuity consisting of T payments growing at a rate of g per payment, discounted at r.

The PV of the variable costs is also calculated using the five-year growing annuity formula. Pre-tax variable costs in year 1 are found by multiplying the variable cost ($0.2625) by the number of units (1,000,000). The cash flows are growing at the nominal rate of 0.071 and are discounted at 0.20. In order to find the after-tax present value, multiply variable costs by $(1-T_C)$.

$$PV \text{ (Variable Costs)} = (1 - T_c) \text{ (Year 1 Variable Costs) (Year 1 Production) } GA^T_{r,g}$$
$$PV \text{ (Variable Costs)} = (1 - 0.34) (\$0.2625) (1,000,000) GA^5_{0.20, \, 0.071}$$
$$= \$582,479$$

Since the firm is subject to corporate taxes, it will benefit from the depreciation tax shield. First, find the annual depreciation tax shield, which is the tax rate multiplied by the annual depreciation expense. Next, find the PV of all annual tax shields via the annuity formula, using the nominal discount rate of 0.20. Depreciation is a nominal quantity, and therefore must be discounted at the nominal rate.

$$\text{Annual Depreciation Expense} = (\text{Investment}) / (\text{Economic Life})$$
$$= \$6,000,000 / 5$$
$$= \$1,200,000$$

To find the annual depreciation tax shield, perform the following calculation:

$$\text{Annual Depreciation Tax Shield} = T_c \text{ (Annual Depreciation Expense)}$$
$$= 0.34 (\$1,200,000)$$
$$= \$408,000$$

Next, apply the annuity formula to calculate the PV of the annual depreciation tax shields.

$$PV \text{(Depreciation Tax Shield)} = \$408,000 \, A^5_{0.20}$$
$$= \$1,220,170$$

The last relevant cash flow is the salvage value of the factory. Since the resale value ($638,140.78) is higher than the book value ($0), the firm must pay capital gains taxes on the difference. Once the after-tax value is calculated, the value must be discounted back five years to the present (year 0). Remember that the salvage value is expressed in nominal terms, and thus must be discounted by the nominal discount rate, 0.20.

$$\text{After-Tax Salvage Value} = \text{Salvage Value} - T_c \text{ (Salvage Value} - \text{Book Value)}$$
$$= \$638,140.78 - 0.34 (\$638,140.78 - \$0)$$
$$= \$421,173$$

PV(After-Tax Salvage Value) $= C_5 / (1+r)^5$
$= \$421,173 / (1.20)^5$
$= \$169,260$

To compute the NPV of the project, consider the PVs of all the relevant after-tax cash flows.

NPV $=$ -Investment + PV(Revenues) - PV(Costs) + PV(Depreciation Tax Shield) + PV(Salvage Value)
$= -\$6,000,000 + \$7,364,645 - \$582,479 + \$1,220,170 + \$169,260$
$= \mathbf{\$2,171,596}$

These calculations could also have been performed in a single step:

NPV $= -\$6,000,000 + (1 - 0.34) (\$3.15) (1,000,000) A^5_{0.20,\, 0.1025} - (1 - 0.34) (\$.2625)$
$(1,000,000) A^5_{0.20,\, 0.071} + 0.34 (\$6,000,000 / 5) A^5_{0.20} +$
$[\$638,140.78 - 0.34 (\$638,140.78 - \$0)] / (1.20)^5$
$= \mathbf{\$2,171,596}$

The NPV of the project is \$2,171,596.

7.29 Since the problem asks which medicine the company should produce, solve for the NPV of both medicines and select the one with the higher NPV.

Headache-only medicine:
First, find the PV of the initial investment. Since the cash outlay occurs today, no discounting is necessary.

PV(Initial Investment) = -\$10,200,000

Find the PV of the revenues if the headache-only medicine were produced. The problem states that the selling price will be \$4 in real terms. Since the discount rate, 0.13, is also given in real terms, no adjustment is necessary and inflation can be ignored. The problem also indicates that 5 million packages will be sold in each of the next three years. The PV will be expressed as a three-year annuity discounted at 0.13. Remember to find the after-tax revenues by multiplying pre-tax revenues by $(1 - T_c)$.

Annual Revenues Headache-only $= \$4 * 5,000,000$
$= \$20,000,000$

PV(Headache-only revenues) $= (1 - T_c) C_1 A^T_r,$
$= (1 - 0.34) \$20,000,000 A^3_{0.13}$
$= \$31,167,214$

Annual costs per unit will be \$1.50 in real terms. The PV will be expressed as a three-year annuity discounted at the real discount rate of 0.13. Remember to find the after-tax costs by multiplying pre-tax costs by $(1 - T_c)$.

Annual Costs Headache-only $= -\$1.50 * 5,000,000$
$= -\$7,500,000$

PV(Headache-only costs) $= (1 - T_c) C_1 A^T_r,$
$= (1 - 0.34)(-\$7,500,000 A^3_{0.13})$
$= -\$11,687,705$

Since Pill, Inc. has positive pre-tax income, the firm will benefit from a depreciation tax shield. Remember, depreciation is a nominal quantity and therefore must be discounted at the nominal rate.

$$1 + \text{Real Rate} = (1 + \text{Nominal Rate}) / (1 + \text{Inflation Rate})$$
$$1.13 = (1 + \text{Nominal Rate}) / (1.05)$$
$$\text{Nominal Rate} = 0.1865$$

Annual depreciation, calculated by the straight-line method (Initial Investment / Economic Life of Investment), is $3,400,000 (= $10,200,000 / 3 Years). The string of annual tax shields forms an annuity. The present value of this annuity is:

$$\text{PV(Depreciation Tax Shield)} = T_c (\text{Annual Depreciation Expense}) A^T_r$$
$$\text{PV(Depreciation Tax Shield)} = 0.34 (\$3,400,000) A^3_{0.1865}$$
$$= \$2,487,521$$

Since the resale value of the headache-only equipment is $0, it has no effect the NPV of the project. To find the NPV of the project, find the sum of the present values of the initial investment, after-tax revenues, after-tax costs, and the depreciation tax shield.

$$\text{NPV} = -\text{ Initial Investment} + \text{PV(Revenues)} - \text{PV(Costs)} + \text{Depreciation Tax Shield}$$
$$= -\$10,200,000 + \$31,167,214 - \$11,687,705 + \$2,487,521$$
$$= \mathbf{\$11,767,030}$$

These calculations could also have been performed in a single step:

$$\text{NPV} = -\$10,200,000 + (1 - 0.34) \$20,000,000 A^3_{0.13} - (1 - 0.34) \$7,500,000 A^3_{0.13} +$$
$$0.34 (\$3,400,000) A^3_{0.1865}$$
$$= \mathbf{\$11,767,030}$$

Headache and Arthritis medicine:
First, find the PV of the initial investment. Since the cash outlay occurs today, no discounting is necessary.

$$\text{PV(Initial Investment)} = -\$12,000,000$$

Find the PV of the revenues if the headache and arthritis medicine were produced. The problem states that the selling price will be $4 in real terms. Since the discount rate, 0.13, is also given in real terms, no adjustment is necessary, and inflation can be ignored. The problem also indicates that 10 million packages will be sold in each of the next 3 years. The PV will be expressed as a three-year annuity discounted at 0.13. Remember to find the after-tax revenues by multiplying pre-tax revenues by $(1 - T_c)$.

$$\text{Annual Revenues Headache and Arthritis} = \$4 * 10,000,000$$
$$= \$40,000,000$$

$$\text{PV(Headache and Arthritis revenues)} = (1 - T_c) C_1 A^T_r,$$
$$= (1 - 0.34) \$40,000,000 A^3_{0.13}$$
$$= \$62,334,429$$

The annual costs will be calculated using the same method. The problem states that annual costs per unit will be $1.70. Again, since the costs and discount rate are given in real terms, inflation can be ignored. The PV will be expressed as a three-year annuity discounted at 0.13. Remember to find the after-tax costs by multiplying pre-tax costs by $(1 - T_c)$.

$$\text{Annual Costs Headache and Arthritis} = -\$1.70 * 10,000,000$$
$$= -\$17,000,000$$

PV(Headache and arthritis costs) $= (1 - T_c) C_1 A^T_r$
$= (1 - 0.34) -\$17,000,000 A^3_{0.13}$
$= -\$26,492,132$

Since Pill, Inc. has positive income, it will benefit from a depreciation tax shield. Remember, depreciation is a nominal quantity and therefore must be discounted using the nominal rate.

1 + Real Discount Rate   = (1 + Nominal Discount Rate) / (1 + Inflation Rate)
1.13   = (1 + Nominal Discount Rate) / (1.05)
Nominal Discount Rate   = 0.1865

Annual depreciation, calculated by the straight-line method (Initial Investment / Economic Life of Investment), is \$4,000,000 (= \$12,000,000 / 3 Years). The string of annual tax shields forms an annuity. The present value of this annuity is:

PV(Depreciation Tax Shield) $= T_c (\text{Annual Depreciation}) A^T_r$
PV(Depreciation Tax Shield) $= 0.34 (\$4,000,000) A^3_{0.1865}$
                                        $= \$2,926,496$

Unlike the Headache-only medicine equipment, the Headache and Arthritis medicine equipment has a resale value of \$1 million at the end of three years. Since the net book value of the equipment is \$0, Pill, Inc. must pay capital gains taxes on the total \$1 million resale value. Because the resale value is stated in real terms, it is discounted using the real discount rate.

After-Tax Salvage Value   = Salvage Value – T_c (Salvage Value – Book Value)
                               = \$1,000,000 – 0.34 (\$1,000,000 – \$0)
                               = \$660,000

The salvage value must then be discounted in order to find the PV.

PV(Salvage Value) $= C_3 / (1 + r)^3$
                       $= \$660,000 / (1.13)^3$
                       $= \$457,413$

To find the NPV of the project, find the sum of the present values of the initial investment, after-tax revenues, after-tax costs, the depreciation tax shield, and the resale.

NPV = - Initial Investment + PV(Revenues) – PV(Costs) + PV(Tax Shield) + PV(Resale Value)
     = -\$12,000,000 + \$62,334,429 – \$26,492,132 + \$2,926,496 + \$457,413
     = \$27,226,206

These calculations could also have been performed in a single step:

NPV = -\$12,000,000 + (1 - 0.34) \$40,000,000 $A^3_{0.13}$ – (1 - 0.34) \$17,000,000 $A^3_{0.13}$
     + 0.34 (\$4,000,000) $A^3_{0.1865}$ + [\$1,000,000 – 0.34 (\$1,000,000 – \$0)] / $(1.13)^3$
     = \$27,226,206

Pill, Inc. should produce the Headache and Arthritis medicine since it has the higher NPV.

7.30   A time line of the costs of operating a series of such machines in perpetuity is shown below:

t = 0	t = 1	t = 2	t = 3	t = 4	t = 5	t = 6	
$12,000	$6,000	$6,000	$6,000	$4,000			...
				$12,000	$6,000	$6,000	...

The present value of one cycle is:

$$PV = \$12,000 + \$6,000 \, A^3_{0.06} + \$4,000 / 1.06^4$$
$$= \$12,000 + \$6,000 \, (2.6730) + \$4,000 / 1.06^4$$
$$= \$31,206$$

In order to calculate the equivalent annual cost (EAC) of the machine, set the NPV equal to an annuity with the same economic life as the machine.

$$\$31,206 = EAC * A^4_{0.06}$$
$$EAC = \$9,006$$

Making a payment of $9,006 for four years is equivalent to making one cycle of payments, in present value terms.

Therefore, the present value of the costs of operating a series of such machines in perpetuity is equal to the present value of a perpetuity with yearly payments of $9,006.

$$PV = C_1 / r$$
$$= \$9,006 / 0.06$$
$$= \mathbf{\$150,100}$$

The present value of operating the machines in perpetuity is $150,100.

7.31   In order to find the equivalent annual cost, first find the net present value of all costs related to the investment, net of any benefits the investment may yield.

The initial investment is not discounted because it occurs today.

PV(Initial Investment) = -$60,000

Each year, the machine requires $5,000 of maintenance. Apply the three-year annuity formula, discounted at 0.14. Remember to adjust the maintenance cost for taxes.

$$PV(\text{Maintenance}) = (1 - T_c) \, C_1 \, A^T_r$$
$$= (1 - 0.34) \, (-\$5,000 \, A^3_{0.14})$$
$$= -\$7,661$$

Since the firm generates positive income and is subject to corporate taxes, the firm benefits from a depreciation tax shield.

Annual Depreciation Expense $= \$60,000 / 3 = \$20,000.$

Annual Depreciation Tax Shield $= (T_c) \,(\text{Annual Depreciation Expense})$
$$= (0.34)\,(\$20,000)$$
$$= \$6,800$$

To find the PV of the annual depreciation tax shields, apply the formula for a three-year annuity.

PV(Annual Depreciation Tax Shields)
$$= C_1 \, A^T_r$$
$$= \$6{,}800 \, A^3_{0.14}$$
$$= \$15{,}787$$

The NPV of the project is the combination of the above cash flows.

NPV = -Initial Investment − PV(Maintenance) + PV(Tax Shield)
= -$60,000 - $7,661 + $15,787
= **-$51,874**

In order to calculate the equivalent annual cost (EAC), set the NPV of the equipment equal to an annuity with the same economic life. Since the project has an economic life of three years and is discounted at 14 percent, set the NPV equal to a three-year annuity, discounted at 14 percent.

$$-\$51{,}874 = EAC * A^3_{0.14}$$
EAC $= $ **-$22,344**

The equivalent annual cost for the project is $22,344.

7.32   In order to find equivalent annual cost, first find the net present value of all costs related to the investment, net of any benefits the investment may yield.

PV(Initial Investment) = -$60,000

The new system will incur maintenance costs of $2,000 per year for five years. The cost is treated as a five-year annuity, discounted at 0.18. Remember to adjust the maintenance cost for taxes.

PV(Maintenance Costs) $= (1 - 0.35) \, (-\$2{,}000) \, A^5_{0.18}$
$= -\$4{,}065$

Since the firm generates positive income, it will benefit from a depreciation tax shield.

Annual Depreciation Expense
$$= \$60{,}000 \, / \, 5$$
$$= \$12{,}000$$

Annual Depreciation Tax Shield
$= (T_c) \, (\text{Annual Depreciation Expense})$
$= (0.35) \, (\$12{,}000)$
$= \$4{,}200$

To find the PV of the annual depreciation tax shields, use the formula for a five-year annuity.

PV(Annual Depreciation Tax Shields)
$$= C_1 \, A^T_r$$
$$= \$4{,}200 \, A^5_{0.18}$$
$$= \$13{,}134$$

The NPV of the equipment is the combination of the above cash flows.

NPV $= $ -Initial Investment − PV(Maintenance) + PV(Depreciation Tax Shield)
$= $ -$60,000 - $4,065 + $13,134
$= $ -$50,931

In order to calculate the equivalent annual cost (EAC), set the net present value of the project equal to a five-year annuity. Solve for the payment amount, which is the equivalent annual cost.

$$-\$50,931 = EAC * A^5_{0.18}$$
$$EAC = -\$16,286$$

Therefore, the equivalent annual cost of the new admitting system is $16,286.

7.33   In order to find equivalent annual cost, first find the net present value of all costs related to the investment, net of any benefits the investment may yield.

PV(Initial Investment) = -$45,000

The project requires annual maintenance of $5,000, beginning a year from now. The cost is treated as a three-year annuity, discounted at 0.12. Remember to adjust the maintenance cost for taxes.

$$PV(Maintenance) = (1 - T_c) C_1 A^T_r$$
$$= (1 - 0.34)(-\$5,000) A^3_{0.12}$$
$$= -\$7,926$$

Since the firm generates positive income, it benefits from the depreciation tax shield. The annual depreciation expense is $15,000 (= $45,000 / 3).

The annual depreciation tax shield is the annual depreciation expense multiplied by the tax rate.

$$\text{Annual Depreciation Tax Shield} = (T_c) \text{ (Annual Depreciation Expense)}$$
$$= (0.34) (\$15,000)$$
$$= \$5,100$$

The string of annual depreciation tax shields forms a three-year annuity, discounted at 12%.

$$PV(\text{Depreciation Tax Shield}) = C_1 A^T_r$$
$$= \$5,100 \ A^3_{0.12}$$
$$= \$12,249$$

At the end of its life, the equipment will have a $10,000 salvage value. Since the equipment has been fully depreciated, a gain on the sale equal to the salvage value must be recognized.

$$\text{After-Tax Salvage Value} = \text{Salvage Value} - T_c \text{ (Salvage Value} - \text{Book Value)}$$
$$= \$10,000 - 0.34 (\$10,000 - \$0)$$
$$= \$6,600$$

The after-tax salvage value must be discounted back three periods to find its present value.

$$PV(\text{After-Tax Salvage Value}) = \$6,600 / (1.12)^3$$
$$= \$4,698$$

The NPV of the equipment is the combination of the above cash flows.

$$NPV = -\text{Initial Investment} - PV(\text{Maintenance}) + PV(\text{Depreciation Tax Shield}) + PV(\text{Salvage})$$
$$= -\$45,000 - \$7,926 + \$12,249 + \$4,698$$
$$= \mathbf{-\$35,979}$$

In order to calculate the equivalent annual cost, set the NPV of the equipment equal to an annuity with the same economic life. Since the project has an economic life of three years and is discounted at 12 percent, set the NPV equal to a three-year annuity, discounted at 12 percent.

$$-\$35,979 = EAC * A^{3}_{0.12}$$
$$EAC = -\$14,980$$

The equivalent annual cost for the project is $14,980.

7.34   Since the cash flows are given in real terms, they must be discounted at the real discount rate.

1+ Real Discount Rate	= (1+ Nominal Discount Rate) / (1+ Inflation Rate)
Real Discount Rate	= [(1.14) / (1.05)] − 1
	= 0.0857

Find the equivalent annual cost (EAC) of each of the copiers. The firm will choose the model with the lower equivalent annual cost.

XX40
Find the present value of both the initial cash outlay and the maintenance expenses. Since the initial cash outlay occurs today (year 0), it does not need to be discounted. To find the present value of the maintenance expenses, use the annuity formula.

$$\text{PV of cash outflows from XX40} = \$700 + \$100\ A^{3}_{0.0857}$$
$$= \$955$$

$$\$955 = EAC * A^{3}_{0.0857}$$
$$EAC = \$374$$

The equivalent annual cost of model XX40 is $374.

RH45
Find the present value of both the initial cash outlay and the maintenance expenses. Since the initial cash outlay occurs today (year 0), it does not need to be discounted. To find the present value of the maintenance expenses, use the annuity formula.

$$\text{PV of cash outflows from RH45} = \$900 + \$110\ A^{5}_{0.0857}$$
$$= \$1,333$$

$$\$1,333 = EAC * A^{5}_{0.0857}$$
$$EAC = \$339$$

The equivalent annual cost of model RH45 is $339.

Since the equivalent annual cost of model RH45 is lower, the firm should choose model RH45.

7.35   Use the equivalent annual cost (EAC) method to determine which facility Plexi Glasses should purchase.

Facility 1:
The first step is to find the NPV of the project. The initial investment is not discounted because it occurs today (year 0).

$$PV(\text{Initial Investment}) = -\$2,100,000$$

Maintenance costs are $60,000 and are incurred at the end of the year. These costs form a seven-year annuity, discounted at 0.10. Remember to adjust the maintenance cost for taxes.

$$
\begin{aligned}
PV(\text{Maintenance Costs}) &= (1 - T_c)\, C_1\, A^T_r \\
&= (1 - 0.34)(-\$60,000)\, A^7_{0.10} \\
&= -\$192,789
\end{aligned}
$$

The annual depreciation expense is $300,000 (= $2,100,000 / 7).

The annual depreciation tax shield is the annual depreciation expense multiplied by the tax rate.

$$
\begin{aligned}
\text{Annual Depreciation Tax Shield} &= (T_c)\,(\text{Annual Depreciation Expense}) \\
&= (0.34)\,(\$300,000) \\
&= \$102,000
\end{aligned}
$$

The string of annual depreciation tax shields form a seven-year annuity, discounted at 0.10.

$$
\begin{aligned}
PV(\text{Depreciation Tax Shield}) &= C_1\, A^T_r \\
&= \$102,000\, A^7_{0.10} \\
&= \$496,579
\end{aligned}
$$

The NPV of the project is the combination of the above cash flows.

$$
\begin{aligned}
NPV &= -\text{Initial Investment} - PV(\text{Maintenance Costs}) + PV(\text{Depreciation Tax Shield}) \\
&= -\$2,100,000 - \$192,789 + \$496,579 \\
&= \mathbf{-\$1,796,210}
\end{aligned}
$$

In order to calculate the equivalent annual cost, set the NPV of the equipment equal to an annuity with the same economic life. Since the project has an economic life of seven years and is discounted at 10 percent, the NPV is equal to a seven-year annuity, discounted at 10 percent.

$$
\begin{aligned}
NPV &= EAC * A^T_r \\
-\$1,796,210 &= EAC * A^7_{0.10} \\
EAC &= \mathbf{-\$368,951}
\end{aligned}
$$

The equivalent annual cost for the project is $368,951.

Facility 2:
The first step is to find the NPV of the project. The initial investment is not discounted because it occurs today (year 0).

$$PV(\text{Initial Investment}) = -\$2,800,000$$

Maintenance costs are $100,000 and are incurred at the end of the year. These costs form a 10-year annuity, discounted at 0.10. Remember to adjust the maintenance cost for taxes.

$$
\begin{aligned}
\text{PV(Maintenance Costs)} &= (1 - T_c)\, C_1\, A^T_r \\
&= (1 - 0.34)(\text{-}\$100,000)\, A^{10}_{0.10} \\
&= \text{-}\$405,541
\end{aligned}
$$

The annual depreciation expense is $280,000 (= $2,800,000 / 10).

The annual depreciation tax shield is the annual depreciation expense multiplied by the tax rate.

$$
\begin{aligned}
\text{Annual Depreciation Tax Shield} &= (T_c)\,(\text{Annual Depreciation Expense}) \\
&= (0.34)\,(\$280,000) \\
&= \$95,200
\end{aligned}
$$

Apply the annuity formula to calculate the PV of the annual depreciation tax shields.

$$
\begin{aligned}
\text{PV(Depreciation Tax Shield)} &= C_1\, A^T_r \\
&= \$95,200\, A^{10}_{0.10} \\
&= \$584,963
\end{aligned}
$$

The NPV of the project is the combination of the above cash flows.

$$
\begin{aligned}
\text{NPV} &= \text{-Initial Investment} - \text{PV(Maintenance Costs)} + \text{PV(Depreciation Tax Shield)} \\
&= \text{-}\$2,800,000 - \$405,541.43 + \$584,963 \\
&= \mathbf{\text{-}\$2,620,578}
\end{aligned}
$$

In order to calculate the equivalent annual cost, set the NPV of the equipment equal to an annuity with the same economic life. Since the project has an economic life of 10 years and is discounted at 10 percent, the NPV is equal to a 10-year annuity, discounted at 10 percent.

$$
\begin{aligned}
\text{-}\$2,620,578 &= \text{EAC} * A^{10}_{0.10} \\
\text{EAC} &= \text{-}\$426,487
\end{aligned}
$$

The equivalent annual cost for the project is $426,487.

The firm should choose facility 1 since it has the lower EAC.

7.36   Find the net present value (NPV) of each option. The firm will choose the option with the higher NPV. Remember to take into account both the maintenance costs and depreciation tax shields associated with both the old and new machines. Note that the replacement machine will be bought in five years regardless of the option chosen and therefore is not incremental to this decision.

Option 1
Sell old machine and purchase new machine now.

To find the cash flow from selling the old machine, consider both the sales price and the net book value of the machine. Since the firm will be selling the old machine ($2,000,000) for more than its net book value ($1,000,000), the resultant capital gain will be subject to corporate taxes.

$$
\begin{aligned}
\text{After-Tax Salvage Value} &= \text{Sale Price} - T_C(\text{Sale Price} - \text{Net Book Value}) \\
&= \$2,000,000 - 0.34(\$2,000,000 - \$1,000,000) \\
&= \$1,660,000
\end{aligned}
$$

$$
\text{PV(Salvage Value)} = \$1,660,000
$$

The new machine is purchased today (year 0) and does not need to be discounted.

$$PV(\text{New Machine}) = -\$3,000,000$$

To find the present value of the new machine's maintenance costs, use a five-year annuity, discounted at 12 percent. Remember to account for taxes.

$$
\begin{aligned}
PV(\text{Maintenance Costs}) &= (1 - 0.34)(-\$500,000)A^5_{0.12} \\
&= -\$1,189,576
\end{aligned}
$$

The firm will also recognize a depreciation tax shield from the new machine. The annual depreciation expense is $600,000 (= $3,000,000 / 5 years).

$$
\begin{aligned}
\text{Annual Depreciation Tax Shield} &= T_C * \text{Depreciation per year} \\
&= 0.34 * \$600,000 \\
&= \$204,000
\end{aligned}
$$

The present value of the depreciation tax shields can be found by using a five-year annuity, discounted at 12 percent.

$$
\begin{aligned}
PV(\text{Depreciation Tax Shield}) &= C_1 A^T_r \\
&= \$204,000\ A^5_{0.12} \\
&= \$735,374
\end{aligned}
$$

The new machine will be sold at the end of its economic life. Since the resale price ($500,000) is higher than the net book value ($0), the sale of the machine is subject to capital gains taxes. Since the sale occurs at the end of year 5, discount the after-tax salvage value back 5 periods.

$$
\begin{aligned}
\text{After-Tax Salvage Value} &= \text{Sale Price} - T_C(\text{Sale Price} - \text{Net Book Value}) \\
&= \$500,000 - 0.34(\$500,000 - 0) \\
&= \$330,000
\end{aligned}
$$

$$
\begin{aligned}
PV(\text{Salvage Value}) &= \$330,000 / (1.12)^5 \\
&= \$187,251
\end{aligned}
$$

$$
\begin{aligned}
NPV(\text{Option 1}) &= \$1,660,000 - \$3,000,000 - \$1,189,576 + \$735,374 + \$187,251 \\
&= -\$1,606,950
\end{aligned}
$$

The net present value (NPV) of selling the old machine and purchasing the new machine now is -$1,606,950.

Option 2
Sell old machine in five years and purchase new machine in five years.

The company will have to make the scheduled maintenance costs for the old machine. Use a five-year annuity, discounted at 12 percent to find the present value of the costs. Remember to account for taxes.

$$
\begin{aligned}
PV(\text{Maintenance Costs}) &= (1 - 0.34)(-\$400,000)A^5_{0.12} \\
&= -\$951,661
\end{aligned}
$$

The firm will continue to recognize depreciation on the old machine. The annual depreciation expense is $200,000 per year, and the firm will recognize a depreciation tax shield. The present value of the tax shield is found by using a five-year annuity, discounted at 12 percent.

Annual Depreciation Tax Shield $= 0.34 * \$200,000$
$= \$68,000$

PV(Depreciation Tax Shield) $= \$68,000 \, A^5_{0.12}$
$= \$245,125$

The salvage value at the end of the old machine's economic life of five years will be $200,000. Since the machine will have been depreciated to $0, the firm must pay capital gains taxes on the sale. To find the present value, discount the after-tax salvage value by five periods.

After-Tax Salvage Value $=$ Sale Price $- T_C$(Sale Price $-$ Net Book Value)
$= \$200,000 - 0.34(\$200,000 - 0)$
$= \$132,000$

PV(Salvage Value) $= \$132,000 \, / \, (1.12)^5$
$= \$74,900$

NPV(Option 2) $= -\$951,661 + \$245,125 + \$74,900$
$= -631,636$

The net present value (NPV) of selling the old machine and purchasing the new machine in five years is -631,636.

Since the NPV of Option 2 is higher than the NPV of Option 1, the firm will choose to sell the old equipment and purchase new equipment in five years.

7.37 SAL 5000
The first step is to find the NPV of the costs associated with the SAL 5000. Find the NPV of *one* SAL 5000, and later, when finding the equivalent annual cost (EAC) of the decision, multiply the final answer by 10. The initial investment is not discounted because it occurs today (year 0).

PV(Initial Investment) $= -\$3,750$

Each year, the computer requires $500 of maintenance. Apply the eight-year annuity formula, discounted at 11 percent, to find the PV of the cost.

PV(Maintenance Costs) $= C_1 \, A^T_r$
$= -\$500 \, A^8_{0.11}$
$= -\$2,573$

At the end of the computer's economic life, it will have a resale value of $500. Since there are no capital gains taxes, the PV is just that cash flow, discounted by eight periods.

PV(Salvage Value) $= C_8 \, / \, (1 + r)^8$
$= \$500 \, / \, (1.11)^8$
$= \$217$

The NPV of the computer is the combination of the above cash flows.

NPV $= -$Initial Investment $-$ PV(Maintenance Costs) $+$ PV(Salvage Value)
$= -\$3,750 - \$2,573 + \$217$
$= -\$6,106$

In order to calculate the equivalent annual cost, set the NPV of the computer equal to an annuity with the same economic life. Since the computer has an economic life of eight years, set the NPV equal to an eight-year annuity, discounted at 11 percent.

$$-\$6,106 = EAC * A^8_{0.11}$$
$$EAC = \textbf{-\$1,187}$$

Since Gold Star Industries would have to buy 10 SAL 5000s, the EAC here would be:

Total EAC   = (Number of SAL 5000s purchased) (EAC of one SAL 5000)
                          = (10) (-\$1,187)
                          = **-\$11,870**

The equivalent annual cost (EAC) for the decision to buy the SAL 5000 is \$11,870.

<u>DET 1000</u>
The first step is to find the NPV of the costs associated with the DET 1000. Find the NPV of *one* DET 1000, and later, when finding the equivalent annual cost (EAC) of the decision, multiply the final answer by 8. The initial investment is not discounted because it occurs today (year 0).

PV(Initial Investment) = -\$5,250

Each year, the computer requires \$700 of maintenance. Apply the six-year annuity formula, discounted at 11 percent, to find the PV of the cost.

PV(Maintenance Costs) $= C_1 A^T_r$
                              $= -\$700\ A^6_{0.11}$
                              = -\$2,961

At the end of the computer's economic life, it will have a resale value of \$600. Since there are no capital gains taxes, the PV is just that cash flow, discounted by six periods.

PV (Salvage Value) $= C_6 / (1 + r)^6$
                          $= \$600 / (1.11)^6$
                          = \$321

The NPV of the computer is the combination of the above cash flows.

NPV = -Initial Investment – PV(Maintenance) + PV(Salvage)
         = -\$5,250 - \$2,961+ \$321
         = **-\$7,890**

In order to calculate the equivalent annual cost, set the NPV of the computer equal to an annuity with the same economic life. Since the computer has an economic life of six years, set the NPV equal to a six-year annuity, discounted at 11 percent.

$$-\$7,890 = EAC * A^6_{0.11}$$
$$EAC = \textbf{-\$1,865}$$

Since Gold Star Industries would have to buy eight DET 1000s, the EAC here would be:

Total EAC	= (Number of DET 1000s purchased) (EAC of one DET 1000)
	= (8) (-$1,865)
	= **-$14,920**

The equivalent annual cost for the decision to buy the DET 1000 is $14,920.

Gold Star should purchase the SAL 5000 since it has a lower equivalent annual cost (EAC).

7.38   To evaluate the word processors, compute their equivalent annual costs (EAC).

EVF
Find the net present value of the costs associated with this model of word processor.

The present value of purchasing the 10 EVF word processors is:

$$\text{PV(Purchase)} \qquad = 10 * -\$8,000 = -\$80,000$$

The present value of the maintenance costs is found by using a four-year annuity, discounted at 14 percent.

$$\text{PV(Maintenance Costs)} \quad = (-\$2,000*10) \, A^4_{0.14}$$
$$= -\$58,274$$

$$\text{NPV} \quad = -\$80,000 -\$58,274$$
$$= -\$138,274$$

In order to calculate the equivalent annual cost, set the NPV of the word processor equal to an annuity with the same economic life. Since the computer has an economic life of four years, set the NPV equal to a four-year annuity, discounted at 14 percent.

$$\$138,274 \qquad = EAC * A^4_{0.14}$$
$$EAC \qquad = \mathbf{\$47,456}$$

The equivalent annual cost of the EVF word processor is $47,456.

AEH
Find the net present value of the costs associated with the AEH model.

The present value of purchasing the 11 AEH word processors now is:

$$\text{PV(Purchase)} \quad = -\$5,000 * 11$$
$$= -\$55,000$$

The present value of the maintenance costs is found by applying the three-year annuity formula, discounted at 14 percent.

$$\text{PV(Maintenance Costs)} \quad = (-\$2,500*11) \, A^3_{0.14}$$
$$= -\$63,845$$

At the end of the computer's economic life, it will have a resale value of $500. Since there are no capital gains taxes, the PV is just that cash flow, discounted back three periods.

$$PV(Resale) = (11*500)/(1.14)^3$$
$$= \$3,712$$

$$NPV = -\$55,000 - \$63,845 + \$3,712$$
$$= -\$115,133$$

In order to calculate the equivalent annual cost, set the NPV of the word processor equal to an annuity with the same economic life and discount rate. Since the computer has an economic life of three years, set the NPV equal to a three-year annuity, discounted at 14 percent.

$$\$115,133 = EAC * A^3_{0.14}$$
$$EAC = \$49,591$$

The equivalent annual cost of the AEH word processor is $49,591.

Harwell should purchase the EVF word processors since their equivalent annual cost is lower.

7.39   Mixer X
The first step is to find the NPV of the savings associated with Mixer X. The initial investment is not discounted because it occurs today (year 0).

$$PV(Initial\ Investment) = -\$400,000$$

Each year, the mixer generates after-tax cash flow savings of $120,000. Apply the five-year annuity formula, discounted at 11 percent, to find the PV of the cash flow savings.

$$PV(Savings) = C_1 A^T_r$$
$$= \$120,000\ A^5_{0.11}$$
$$= \$443,507$$

The NPV of the mixer is the sum of the above cash flows.

$$NPV = -Initial\ Investment + PV(Savings)$$
$$= -\$400,000 + \$443,507$$
$$= \$43,507$$

In order to calculate the equivalent annual benefit (EAB) of the mixer, set the NPV of the mixer equal to an annuity with the same economic life. Since the mixer has an economic life of five years, set the NPV equal to a five-year annuity, discounted at 11 percent.

$$\$43,507 = EAB * A^5_{0.11}$$
$$EAB = \$11,772$$

The equivalent annual benefit of Mixer X is $11,772.

Mixer Y
The first step is to find the NPV of the savings associated with Mixer Y. The initial investment is not discounted because it occurs today (year 0).

$$PV(Initial\ Investment) = -\$600,000$$

Each year, the mixer generates after-tax cash flow savings of $130,000. Apply the eight-year annuity formula, discounted at 11 percent, to find the PV of the cash flow savings.

$$PV(Savings) = C_1 A_r^T$$
$$= \$130,000 \, A_{0.11}^8$$
$$= \$668,996$$

The NPV of the mixer is the sum of the above cash flows.

$$NPV = \text{-Initial Investment} + PV(Savings)$$
$$= \text{-}\$600,000 + \$668,996$$
$$= \textbf{\$68,996}$$

In order to calculate the equivalent annual benefit of the mixer, set the NPV of the mixer equal to an annuity with the same economic life. Since the mixer has an economic life of eight years, set the NPV equal to an eight-year annuity, discounted at 11 percent.

$$\$68,996 = EAC * A_{0.11}^8$$
$$EAC = \textbf{\$13,407}$$

The equivalent annual benefit of Mixer Y is $13,407.

DJ Party, Inc. should buy Mixer Y since it yields a higher equivalent annual benefit.

7.40   Tamper A

Tamper A is purchased today (year 0) and does not need to be discounted.

$$PV(Purchase) = \text{-}\$600,000$$

The present value of the maintenance costs is found by applying the five-year annuity formula, discounted at 12 percent.

$$PV(Maintenance\ Costs) = \text{-}\$110,000 \, A_{0.12}^5$$
$$= \text{-}\$396,525$$

$$NPV = \text{-}\$600,000 - \$396,525 = \text{-}\$996,525$$

In order to calculate the equivalent annual cost (EAC) of the tamper, set the NPV equal to an annuity with the same economic life. Since the tamper has an economic life of five years, set the NPV equal to a five-year annuity, discounted at 12 percent.

$$\text{-}\$996,525 = EAC * A_{0.12}^5$$
$$EAC = \textbf{-}\$276,446$$

Tamper A has an equivalent annual cost of $276,446.

Tamper B

Tamper B is purchased today (year 0) and does not need to be discounted.

$$PV(Purchase) = \text{-}\$750,000$$

The present value of the maintenance costs is found by applying the seven-year annuity formula, discounted at 12 percent.

$$\text{PV(Maintenance Costs)} = -\$90,000 \ A^7_{0.12}$$
$$= -\$410,738$$

$$\text{NPV} = -\$750,000 - \$410,738 = -\$1,160,738$$

In order to calculate the equivalent annual cost of the tamper, set the NPV equal to an annuity with the same economic life. Since the tamper has an economic life of seven years, set the NPV equal to a seven-year annuity, discounted at 12 percent.

$$-\$1,160,738 = \text{EAC} * A^7_{0.12}$$
$$\text{EAC} = -\$254,338$$

Tamper B has an equivalent annual cost of \$254,338.

KZD Construction should choose Tamper B since it has a lower equivalent annual cost.

7.41   Klious needs to compare the equivalent annual cost (EAC) of the new machine to the cost incurred by keeping the old autoclave one additional year. First, find the EAC of the new autoclave. Next, find the total one-year cost, including the opportunity cost of not selling the old autoclave at the beginning of that particular year. If the EAC of the new autoclave is higher than the one-year total cost of keeping the existing autoclave, then Klious should not replace the old machine. If the total one-year cost of the existing autoclave is higher than the EAC of the new machine, Klious should replace.

The first step of the problem is to calculate the NPV of the new machine. The initial investment is not discounted because it occurs today (year 0).

$$\text{PV(Initial Investment)} = -\$3,000$$

Each year, the autoclave generates \$20 of maintenance costs. Apply the five-year annuity formula, discounted at 0.10 to calculate the PV of the maintenance costs.

$$\text{PV(Maintenance Costs)} = C_1 \ A^T_r$$
$$= -\$20 \ A^5_{0.10}$$
$$= -\$76$$

The autoclave has a salvage value of \$1,200 at the end of its economic life. Remember that the cash flow occurs at the end of year 5, and therefore must be discounted back five years.

$$\text{PV(Salvage Value)} = C_5 / (1 + r)^5$$
$$= \$1,200 / (1.10)^5$$
$$= \$745$$

The NPV of the autoclave is the combination of the above cash flows.

$$\text{NPV} = -\text{Initial Investment} - \text{PV(Maintenance Costs)} + \text{PV(Salvage Value)}$$
$$= -\$3,000 - \$76 + \$745$$
$$= -\$2,331$$

In order to calculate the equivalent annual cost of the new autoclave, set the NPV equal to an annuity with the same economic life. Since the autoclave has an economic life of five years, set the NPV equal to a five-year annuity, discounted at 10 percent.

$$-\$2,331 = \text{EAC} * A^5_{0.10}$$
$$\text{EAC} = -\$615$$

The equivalent annual cost of the new autoclave is \$615.

To make its decision, Klious must compare the total yearly cost from keeping the old autoclave with the $615 yearly cost of the new autoclave. The matrix below illustrates the relevant costs of keeping the existing autoclave.

Replacement Date/Year	Year 0	Year 1	Year 2	Year 3	Year 4	Year 5
Keep through Year 1	-900	-200	-	-	-	-
		850				
Keep through Year 2	-	-	-275	-	-	-
		-850	775			
Keep through Year 3	-	-	-	-325	-	-
			-775	700		
Keep through Year 4	-	-	-	-	-450	-
				-700	600	
Keep through Year 5	-	-	-	-	-	-500
					-600	500

Compute the total end-of-year cost of the old autoclave for an additional year. Remember to state the costs in terms of end-of-year dollars. This is necessary because the EAC of the new machine is stated in terms of end-of-year dollars.

Keeping the old autoclave through Year 1:
The foregone resale value is already stated as of the beginning of the year, and therefore does not need further discounting.

$$PV(\text{Foregone Resale Value}) = -\$900$$

Both the maintenance cost and the realizable resale value must be discounted back one year since these cash flows occur at the end of the year.

$$PV(\text{Maintenance Costs}) = -\$200 / (1.10)^1$$
$$= -\$182$$

$$PV(\text{Resale Value}) = \$850 / (1.10)^1$$
$$= \$773$$

The NPV of keeping the old autoclave through the first year is the combination of the above cash flows.

$$NPV = -\$900 - \$182 + \$773$$
$$= -\$309$$

Because the EAC of the new machine is expressed in terms of end-of-year dollars, multiply the NPV of the old machine's costs by the discount rate in order to find its future value as of the end of year 1.

$$FV = (-\$309)(1.10)$$
$$= -\$340$$

The cost of the old autoclave in terms of end-of-year 1 dollars is $340.

Since it is cheaper to operate the old autoclave ($340) than to purchase the new one ($615), Klious should continue to operate the old machine in year 1.

<u>Keeping the old autoclave through Year 2:</u>
The foregone resale value is already stated as of the beginning of the year, and therefore does not need further discounting.

PV(Foregone Resale Value) = -$850

Both the maintenance cost and the realizable resale value must be discounted back one year since they occur at the end of the year.

PV(Maintenance Costs) $= -\$275 / (1.10)^1$
$= -\$250$

PV(Resale Value) $= \$775 / (1.10)^1$
$= \$705$

The NPV of keeping the old autoclave through the second year is the combination of the above cash flows.

NPV = -$850 – $250 + $705
= -$395

Because the EAC of the new machine is expressed in terms of end-of-year dollars, multiply the NPV of the old machine's costs by the discount rate in order to find its future value as of the end of year 2.

FV = (-$395) (1.10)
= **-$435**

The cost of the old autoclave in terms of end-of-year 2 dollars is $435.

Since it is cheaper to operate the old autoclave ($435) than to purchase the new one ($615), Klious should continue to operate the old machine in year 2.

<u>Keeping the old autoclave through Year 3:</u>
The foregone resale value is already stated as of the beginning of the year, and therefore does not need further discounting.

PV(Foregone Resale Value) = -$775

Both the maintenance cost and the realizable resale value must be discounted back one year since they occur at the end of the year.

PV(Maintenance Costs) $= -\$325 / (1.10)^1$
$= -\$295$

PV(Resale Value) $= \$700 / (1.10)^1$
$= \$636$

The NPV of keeping the old autoclave through the third year is the combination of the above cash flows.

NPV = -$775 – $295 + $636
= -$434

Because the EAC of the new machine is expressed in terms of end-of-year dollars, multiply the NPV of the old machine's costs by the discount rate in order to find its future value in terms of end-of-year 3 dollars.

FV = (-$434) (1.10)
= **-$477**

The cost of the old autoclave in terms of end-of-year 3 dollars is $477.

Since it is cheaper to operate the old autoclave ($477) than to purchase the new one ($615), Klious should continue to operate the old machine in year 3.

<u>Keeping the old autoclave through Year 4:</u>
The foregone resale value is already stated as of the beginning of the year, and therefore does not need further discounting.

$$PV(\text{Foregone Resale}) = -\$700$$

Both the maintenance cost and the realizable resale value must be discounted back one year since they occur at the end of the year.

$$PV(\text{Maintenance}) \quad = -\$450 / (1.10)^1$$
$$= -\$409$$

$$PV(\text{Resale Value}) \quad = \$600 / (1.10)^1$$
$$= \$545$$

The NPV of keeping the old autoclave through the fourth year is the combination of the above cash flows.

$$NPV = -\$700 - \$409 + \$545$$
$$= -\$564$$

Because the EAC of the new machine is expressed in terms of end-of-year dollars, multiply the NPV of the old machine's costs by the discount rate in order to find its future value as of the end of year 4.

$$FV = (-\$564)(1.10)$$
$$= -\$620$$

The cost of the old autoclave in terms of end-of-year 4 dollars is $620.

Since it is more expensive to operate the old autoclave ($620) than to purchase the new one ($615), Klious should purchase the new autoclave at the end of year 3.

Case Study: I.Q. Inc.

(Unit: $Million)	Year 0	Year 1	Year 2	Year 3	Year 4	Year 5	NPV
Investments:							
Capital equipment	(1.000)				0.300		
Capital Gains taxes					(0.034)		
Change in NWC	(1.000)				1.000		
Revenue		8.600	9.939	11.486	13.274		
Costs		0.550	0.636	0.735	0.849		
SG&A		$ 0.50	0.515	0.530	0.546		
Profits		7.550	8.788	10.221	11.878		
After-tax Profits		4.983	5.800	6.746	7.840		
Depreciation tax shield		0.068	0.068	0.068	0.068		
Total Cash flow from project	(2.000)	5.051	5.868	6.814	9.174		
PV 15% (CF)	(2.000)	4.392	4.437	4.480	5.245		16.555

The project should be undertaken since it has a positive NPV.

Case Study: Jimmy's Hot Dog Stands

	Year 0	Year 1	Year 2	Year 3	Year 4	Year 5	NPV
Investments:							
Real Estate	(400,000)						
Capital equipment	(65,000)						
Change in NWC		(20,000)					
Total cash flow from investments	(465,000)	(20,000)	–	–	–	–	
Income:							
Revenue		510,000	510,000	510,000	510,000	510,000	
Labor Costs		96,000	96,000	96,000	96,000	96,000	
Raw Materials		157,080	157,080	157,080	157,080	157,080	
Depreciation		13,000	13,000	13,000	13,000	13,000	
Income before Taxes		243,920	243,920	243,920	243,920	243,920	
Taxes		82,933	82,933	82,933	82,933	82,933	
Net Income		160,987	160,987	160,987	160,987	160,987	
Cash flow from operations:							
Net Income		160,987	160,987	160,987	160,987	160,987	
Depreciation		13,000	13,000	13,000	13,000	13,000	
Operating cash flow		173,987	173,987	173,987	173,987	173,987	
Total cash flow from project	(465,000)	153,987	173,987	173,987	173,987	173,987	
PV 10% (CF)	(465,000)	139,988	143,791	130,719	118,836	108,032	$176,367

The NPV of this investment is $176,367.

B-161

Chapter 8: Risk Analysis, Real Options, and Capital Budgeting

8.1 Calculate the NPV of the expected payoff for the option of going directly to market.

$$\text{NPV(Go Directly)} = C_{\text{Success}}\,(\text{Prob. of Success}) + C_{\text{Failure}}\,(\text{Prob. of Failure})$$
$$= \$20,000,000\,(0.50) + \$5,000,000\,(0.50)$$
$$= \$12,500,000$$

The expected payoff of going directly to market is $12,500,000.

The test marketing requires a $2 million cash outlay. Choosing the test marketing option will also delay the launch of the product by one year. Thus, the expected payoff is delayed by one year and must be discounted back to year 0.

$$\text{NPV(Test Market)} = -C_0 + [C_{\text{Success}}\,(\text{Prob. of Success})] / (1+r)^T +$$
$$[C_{\text{Failure}}\,(\text{Prob. of Failure})] / (1+r)^T$$
$$= -\$2,000,000 + [\$20,000,000\,(0.75)] / (1.15) +$$
$$[\$5,000,000\,(0.25)] / (1.15)$$
$$= \$12,130,434.78$$

The expected payoff of test marketing the product is $12,130,434.78.

Sony should go directly to market with the product since that option has the highest expected payoff.

8.2 Calculate the NPV of each option. The manager should pursue the option with the highest NPV.

$$\text{NPV(Go Directly)} = C_{\text{Success}}\,(\text{Prob. of Success})$$
$$= \$1,200,000\,(0.50)$$
$$= \$600,000$$

The NPV of going directly to market is $600,000.

$$\text{NPV(Focus Group)} = C_0 + C_{\text{Success}}\,(\text{Prob. of Success})$$
$$= -\$120,000 + \$1,200,000\,(0.70)$$
$$= \$720,000$$

The NPV when conducting a focus group is $720,000.

$$\text{NPV(Consulting Firm)} = C_0 + C_{\text{Success}}\,(\text{Prob. of Success})$$
$$= -\$400,000 + \$1,200,000\,(0.90)$$
$$= \$680,000$$

The NPV when hiring a consulting firm is $680,000.

The firm should conduct a focus group since that option has the highest NPV.

8.3   Recommend the strategy that has the highest NPV.

NPV(Lower Prices) $= C_{Success}$ (Prob. of Success) $+ C_{Failure}$ (Prob. of Failure)
                       $= -\$1,300,000\ (0.55) - \$1,850,000\ (0.45)$
                       $= \mathbf{-\$1,547,500}$

NPV(Lobbyist) $= C_0 + C_{Success}$ (Prob. of Success) $+ C_{Failure}$ (Prob. of Failure)
                       $= -\$800,000 - \$0\ (0.75) - \$2,000,000\ (0.25)$
                       $= \mathbf{-\$1,300,000}$

The CFO should hire the lobbyist since that option has the highest NPV.

8.4   Since the NPV of Research is greater than that of no research, based on expected outcomes, B&B should go directly to market.

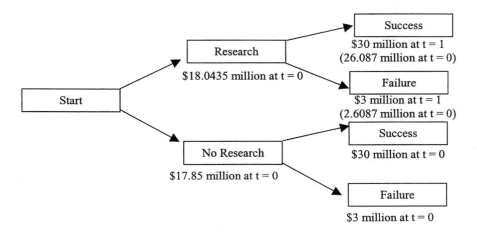

Note: Research $= -1$ million investment $+ 0.7 * (26.087)$ if successful $+ 0.3 * (2.6087)$ if unsuccessful
         No Research $= 0.55 * (30)$ if successful $+ 0.45 * (3)$ if unsuccessful

8.5   Carl should have taken the $5,000.
Expected return for 1% of movie profits is $3,000. Since only good scripts are made into movies and only a good movie would make a profit: (10% x 30% x $10 mil x 1%)

Movie studio decision tree:

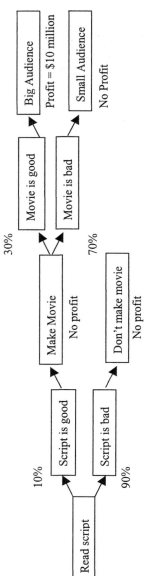

B-164

8.6   Apply the *accounting profit break-even point* (BEP) formula and solve for the sales price, x, that allows the firm to break even when producing 20,000 calculators. In order for the firm to break even, the revenues from the calculator sales (number of calculators sold × sales price per unit) must equal the total annual cost of producing the calculators. Remember to include taxes in the analysis.

Variable costs   = $15 per calculator

Fixed costs   = $900,000 per year

Depreciation   = (Initial Investment / Economic Life)
                       = ($600,000 / 5)
                       = $120,000 per year

Divide the after-tax sum of the depreciation expense and the fixed costs by the calculator's after-tax contribution margin (selling price, x, minus variable cost). The after-tax contribution margin is the amount that each additional calculator contributes to the firm's profit. Before the firm can realize a positive profit, it must have earned enough to cover its fixed costs and depreciation expense. Solve for x.

[(Fixed Costs + Depr.) $(1–T_c)$] / [(Sales Price – Variable Cost) $(1–T_c)$]   = BEP
[($900,000 + $120,000) $(1 – 0.30)$] / [$(x - \$150)$ $(1 – 0.30)$]   = 20,000
x = $66

The break-even sales price of the calculator is $66.

8.7   Apply the *accounting profit break-even point* formula. Divide the after-tax sum of the annual depreciation expense and the annual fixed costs by the television's after-tax contribution margin (selling price minus variable cost).

[(Fixed Costs + Depr.) $(1–T_c)$] / [(Sales Price - Variable Cost) $(1–T_c)$]   = BEP
[($120,000 + $20,000) $(1 -0.35)$] / [($1,500 - $1,100) $(1 - 0.35)$]   = **350**

The distributor must sell 350 televisions per year to break even.

8.8   a.   Apply the *accounting profit break-even point* formula. Divide the after-tax sum of the fixed costs and depreciation charge by the abalone's after-tax contribution margin (selling price minus variable cost). The number of abalones that the proprietor must sell in order for you to receive any profit is the break-even point (BEP).

[(Fixed Costs + Depr.) $(1–T_c)$] / [(Sales Price – Variable Cost) $(1-T_c)$]   = BEP

[($340,000 + $20,000) $(1 – 0.35)$] / [($2.00 - $0.72) $(1 – 0.35)$]
= **281,250**

The proprietor must sell at least 281,250 abalones per year in order for you to receive any profit.

     b.   To calculate the amount of profit you will receive if the proprietor sells 300,000 abalones, subtract the total cost incurred from the total revenue received. Remember to include taxes.

Total Revenue Per Year   = (Sales Price) (Number Sold) $(1 – T_c)$
                                    = ($2.00) (300,000) $(1 – 0.35)$
                                    = $390,000

Total Cost Per Year	$= [\text{Fixed Cost} + \text{Deprc.} + (\text{Variable Cost})(\text{Number Sold})](1\text{-}T_c)$
	$= [\$340,000 + \$20,000 + (\$0.72)(300,000)](1 - 0.35)$
	$= \$374,400$

Total Profit	$= \text{Total Revenue} - \text{Total Cost}$
	$= \$390,000 - \$374,400$
	$= \mathbf{\$15,600}$

You will receive $15,600 if the proprietor sells 300,000 abalones.

8.9   Played $2187.5 = \text{CEILING}\ ((1000 + 50)/(0.5\text{-}0.02),1)$

8.10   a) $\dfrac{(\text{Fixed Cost} + \text{Depreciation}) \times (1\text{-}Tc)}{(\text{Sales price} - \text{Variable cost}) \times (1\text{-}Tc)} = \dfrac{(0 + 2,000) \times (1 - .3)}{(10 - 8) \times (1 - .3)} = 1000 \ \ \text{T-shirts}$

      b) $\dfrac{(\text{EAC} + \text{Fixed cost}) \times (1 - Tc) + \text{Depreciation} \times (Tc)}{(\text{Sales price} - \text{Variable cost}) \times (1\text{-}Tc)} = \dfrac{(10,000 / 2.4018) + 0 + 0}{(10 - 8) \times (1 - .3)} = 2974 \ \ \text{T-shirts}$

8.11   When calculating the present value break-even point, express the initial investment of $140,000 as an equivalent annual cost (EAC). Divide the initial investment by the seven-year annuity factor, discounted at 15 percent. The EAC incorporates the opportunity cost of the investment.

EAC	$= \text{Initial Investment} / A^T_r$
	$= \$140,000 / A^7_{0.15}$
	$= \$33,650.45$

Calculate the annual depreciation expense.

| Depreciation | $= \$140,000 / 7$ |
| | $= \$20,000$ |

Calculate the present-value break-even point. The fixed costs are $340,000. Remember to incorporate taxes into the calculation. Remember to include the depreciation tax shield, which lowers the firm's tax bill.

$[\text{EAC} + (\text{Annual Fixed Costs})(1 - T_c) - (\text{Annual Depr.})(T_c)] / [(\text{Sales Price} - \text{Variable Cost})(1 - T_c)]$
$= \text{BEP}$

$[\$33,650.45 + \$340,000\,(0.65) - \$20,000\,(0.35)] / [(\$2 - \$0.72)(0.65)] = \mathbf{297,656.79}$
$\cong \mathbf{297,657 \ units}$

The present value break-even point is 297,657 abalones.

8.12   When calculating the present value break-even point, express the initial investment of $200,000 as an equivalent annual cost (EAC). Divide the initial investment by the five-year annuity factor, discounted at 12 percent.

equivalent Annual Cost

$$\text{EAC} = \text{Initial Investment} / A^T_r$$
$$= \$200,000 / A^5_{0.12}$$
$$= \$55,481.95$$

Calculate the annual depreciation expense.

$$\text{Depreciation} = \$200,000 / 5$$
$$= \$40,000$$

Calculate the present-value break-even point.

$$[\text{EAC}+(\text{Fixed Costs}) (1 - T_c) - (\text{Depr.}) (T_c)] / [(\text{Sales Price} - \text{Variable Cost}) (1 - T_c)] = \text{BEP}$$

$$[\$55,481.95 + (\$350,000) (0.75) - (\$40,000) (0.25)] / [(\$25 - \$5) (0.75)] = \textbf{20,532.13}$$

The present value break-even point is 20,532 units.

8.13   *The following represents a different approach to solving present-value break-even problems, unlike the EAC method used in problems 8.8 and 8.7. Both the EAC approach and this approach will yield the same answer.*

First, determine the cash flow from selling the old harvester. When calculating the salvage value, remember that tax liabilities or credits are generated on the *difference* between the resale value and the book value of the asset.

Use the original purchase price of the old harvester to determine annual depreciation.

$$\text{Depreciation Per Period} = \$45,000 / 15$$
$$= \$3,000$$

Since the machine is five years old, the firm has accumulated five annual depreciation charges, reducing the book value of the machine. The current book value of the machine is equal to the initial purchase price minus the accumulated depreciation.

$$\text{Book Value} = \text{Initial Purchase Price} - \text{Accumulated Depreciation}$$
$$= \$45,000 - (\$3,000 \times 5 \text{ years})$$
$$= \$30,000$$

Since the firm is able to resell the old harvester for $20,000, which is less than the $30,000 book value of the machine, the firm will generate a tax credit on the sale.

$$\text{PV(Resale Value)} = C - T_C (\text{Resale Value} - \text{Book Value})$$
$$= \$20,000 - 0.34 (\$20,000 - \$30,000)$$
$$= \$23,400$$

Calculate the incremental depreciation. Calculate the depreciation tax shield generated by the new harvester less the forgone depreciation tax shield from the old harvester. Let *P* be the break-even purchase price.

$$\text{Depreciation Tax Shield, New Harvester} = (\text{Initial Investment} / \text{Economic Life}) \times T_c$$
$$= (P / 10) (0.34)$$

Depreciation Tax Shield, Old Harvester $\quad = (\$45,000 / 15) (0.34)$
$\qquad\qquad\qquad\qquad\qquad\qquad\qquad\qquad\; = (\$3,000) (0.34)$

Incremental Depreciation Tax Shield $\qquad = (P / 10 - \$3,000) (0.34)$

Apply the 10-year annuity formula, discounted at 15 percent, to calculate the PV of the incremental depreciation tax shield.

PV(Depreciation Tax Shield) $\qquad\qquad\qquad = (P / 10 - \$3,000) (0.34) \; A^{10}_{0.15}$

The new harvester will generate year-end pre-tax cash flow savings of $10,000 per year for 10 years. Apply the 10-year annuity formula, discounted at 15 percent, to find the PV of those savings. Remember to include taxes.

PV(Savings) $\qquad\qquad\qquad\qquad\qquad = (1 - T_c) \, C_1 \, A^T_r$
$\qquad\qquad\qquad\qquad\qquad\qquad\qquad\quad = (1 - 0.34) \, \$10,000 \, A^{10}_{0.15}$
$\qquad\qquad\qquad\qquad\qquad\qquad\qquad\quad = \$33,123.87$

The break-even purchase price of the new harvester is the price, P, which makes the NPV of the machine equal to zero.

NPV $\quad = -P + $ PV(Resale Value) $+$ PV(Depreciation Tax Shield) $+$ PV(Savings)
$0 \qquad = -P + \$23,400 + (P / 10 - \$3,000) (0.34) \, A^{10}_{0.15} + \$33,123.87$
$P \qquad = \mathbf{\$61,981.06}$

The break-even purchase price is $61,981.06.

8.14	A 5,0.08	3.993
	EAC	75,136,936
	Depreciation	60,000
	PV	
	Break-Even	3,518

8.15　a.　Pessimistic:

Calculate the NPV of the pessimistic scenario. First, determine the yearly cash flow.

Cash Flow $\qquad = $ [Revenue - Variable Costs – Fixed Costs] $(1 – T_c) + $ Depr. Tax Shield
$\qquad\qquad\qquad = [(\$38 \times 23,000) – (\$21 \times 23,000) - \$320,000] (1- 0.35) +$
$\qquad\qquad\qquad\;\; (\$420,000 / 7) (0.35)$
$\qquad\qquad\qquad = \$67,150$

Apply the seven-year annuity formula to calculate the NPV of the machine. Subtract the initial investment.

NPV $\quad = C_0 + C_1 \, A^T_r$
$\qquad\quad = -\$420,000 + \$67,150 \, A^7_{0.13}$
$\qquad\quad = \mathbf{-\$123,021.71}$

The NPV of the pessimistic scenario is -$123,021.71.

Expected:

Calculate the NPV of the expected scenario. First, determine the yearly cash flow.

Cash Flow $= $ [Revenue - Variable Costs – Fixed Costs] $(1 – T_c)$ + Depr. Tax Shield
$= [(\$40 \times 25{,}000) – (\$20 \times 25{,}000) - \$300{,}000] (1- 0.35)$
$+ (\$420{,}000 / 7) (0.35)$
$= \$151{,}000$

Apply the seven-year annuity formula to calculate the NPV of the machine. Subtract the initial investment.

NPV $= C_0 + C_1 A^T_r$
$= -\$420{,}000 + \$151{,}000\ A^7_{0.13}$
$= \mathbf{\$247{,}814.18}$

The NPV of the expected scenario is $247,814.18.

Optimistic:

Calculate the NPV of the optimistic scenario. First, determine the yearly cash flow.

Cash Flow $= $ [Revenue – Variable Costs – Fixed Costs] $(1 – T_c)$
$+$ Depreciation Tax Shield
$= [(\$42 \times 27{,}000) – (\$19 \times 27{,}000) - \$280{,}000] (1- 0.35)$
$+ (\$420{,}000 / 7) (0.35)$
$= \$242{,}650$

Apply the seven-year annuity formula to calculate the NPV of the machine. Subtract the initial investment.

NPV $= C_0 + C_1 A^T_r$
$= -\$420{,}000 + \$242{,}650\ A^7_{0.13}$
$= \mathbf{\$653{,}146.42}$

The NPV of the optimistic scenario is $653,146.42.

b.   Calculate the expected NPV of the project to form your conclusion about the project. Remember that, since each scenario is equally likely, the expected NPV is the average of the three scenarios.

NPV $= $ [NPV(Pessimistic) + NPV(Expected) + NPV(Optimistic)] / (3)
$= [-\$123{,}021.71 + \$247{,}814.18 + \$653{,}146.42] / 3$
$= \mathbf{\$259{,}312.96}$

The expected NPV of the project is $259,312.96. You should conclude that the project is worthwhile.

8.16 <u>Pessimistic:</u>

Calculate the NPV of the pessimistic scenario. First, determine the yearly cash flow. To determine the number of rackets sold, multiply the market size by the market share.

Number of Rackets = Market Size × Market Share
= 110,000 × 0.22
= 24,200

Cash Flow = [Revenue – Variable Costs – Fixed Costs] $(1 - T_c)$
+ Depreciation Tax Shield
= [\$115 × 24,200 - \$72 × 24,200 - \$850,000] $(1 - 0.4)$
+ (\$1,500,000 / 5) (0.4)
= \$234,360

Apply the five-year an̄̄̄̄̄̄ to calculate the NPV of the racket project. Subtract the initial investment.

$A^5_{0.13}$

b.

Calcu̅ ̅ ̅ ̅ ̅ ̅ ̅ ̅ ̅ ̅ termine the yearly cash flow. To determine
the nun̄ the market share.

Nu̅ ̅ ̅ ̅ ̅ ̅ Share

Cash Flow – Fixed Costs] $(1 - T_c)$

̅0 × 30,000 - \$800,000] $(1 - 0.4)$
) (0.4)

Apply the five-year annuity formula to calculate the NPV of the racket project. Subtract the initial investment.

NPV $= C_0 + C_1 A^T_r$
= -\$1,500,000 + \$540,000 $A^5_{0.13}$
= **\$399,304.88**

<u>Optimistic:</u>

Calculate the NPV of the optimistic scenario. First, determine the yearly cash flow. To determine the number of rackets sold, multiply the market size by the market share.

$$\text{Number of Rackets} = \text{Market Size} \times \text{Market Share}$$
$$= 130{,}000 \times 0.27$$
$$= 35{,}100$$

$$\text{Cash Flow} = [\text{Revenue} - \text{Variable Costs} - \text{Fixed Costs}]\,(1 - T_c)$$
$$+ \text{Depreciation Tax Shield}$$
$$= [\$125 \times 35{,}100 - \$68 \times 35{,}100 - \$750{,}000]\,(1 - 0.4)$$
$$+ (\$1{,}500{,}000 / 5)\,(0.4)$$
$$= \$870{,}420$$

Apply the five-year annuity formula to calculate the NPV of the racket project. Subtract the initial investment.

$$\text{NPV} = C_0 + C_1\,A^T_r$$
$$= -\$1{,}500{,}000 + \$870{,}420\,A^5{}_{0.13}$$
$$= \mathbf{\$1{,}561{,}468.43}$$

Calculate the expected NPV of the project. Since each scenario is equally likely, the expected NPV is the average of the three scenarios.

$$\text{NPV} = [\text{NPV(Pessimistic)} + \text{NPV(Expected)} + \text{NPV(Optimistic)}] / (3)$$
$$= [-\$675{,}701.68 + \$399{,}304.88 + \$1{,}561{,}468.43] / (3)$$
$$= \mathbf{\$428{,}357.21}$$

The expected NPV of the project is $428,357.21. You should accept the project.

8.17 Holding all variables as expected, except a single sensitivity analysis variable that is held at pessimistic or optimistic.

NPV	Pessimistic	Optimistic
Market Size	$1,318,066	4,132,725
Market Share	$1,880,998	3,569,793
Price	$848,956	4,601,835
Variable Cost	$2,256,286	3,194,506
Fixed Cost	$2,600,300	2,850,492

NPV	
	Expected
	$2,725,396

Since under all scenarios NPVs come out positive, the project should be taken.

8.18

Expected

Investments:	Year 0	Year 1	Year 2	Year 3	Year 4	Year 5	NPV
Touch screen system	$ (150,000)						
Annual maintenance		$(5,000)	$(5,000)	$(5,000)	$(5,000)	$(5,000)	
Change in NWC		$(5,000)				$ 5,000	
Wages saved		$30,000	$30,000	$30,000	$30,000	$30,000	
Total cash flow from investments	$ (150,000)	$20,000	$25,000	$25,000	$25,000	$30,000	
Income:							
Revenue		$15,000	$15,000	$15,000	$15,000	$15,000	
COGS		$(3,750)	$(3,750)	$(3,750)	$(3,750)	$(3,750)	
Cash flow from operations		$11,250	$11,250	$11,250	$11,250	$11,250	
Total cash flow from project	$ (150,000)	$31,250	$36,250	$36,250	$36,250	$41,250	
PV 15% (CF)	$= CF$	$= CF/1.15$	$= CF/(1.15)^2$	$= CF/(1.15)^3$	$= CF/(1.15)^4$	$= CF/(1.15)^5$	
	(150,000)	27,174	27,410	23,835	20,726	20,509	($30,346)

Optimistic

Investments:	Year 0	Year 1	Year 2	Year 3	Year 4	Year 5	NPV
Touch screen system	$ (150,000)						
Annual maintenance		$(5,000)	$(5,000)	$(5,000)	$(5,000)	$(5,000)	
Change in NWC		$(5,000)				$ 5,000	
Wages saved		$30,000	$30,000	$30,000	$30,000	$30,000	
Total cash flow from investments	$ (150,000)	$20,000	$25,000	$25,000	$25,000	$30,000	
Income:							
Revenue		$20,000	$20,000	$20,000	$20,000	$20,000	
COGS		$(5,000)	$(5,000)	$(5,000)	$(5,000)	$(5,000)	
Cash flow from operations		$15,000	$15,000	$15,000	$15,000	$15,000	
Total cash flow from project	$ (150,000)	$35,000	$40,000	$40,000	$40,000	$45,000	
PV 15% (CF)	$= CF$	$= CF/1.15$	$= CF/(1.15)^2$	$= CF/(1.15)^3$	$= CF/(1.15)^4$	$= CF/(1.15)^5$	
	(150,000)	30,435	30,246	26,301	22,870	22,373	($17,776)

Since the NPV for all three scenarios is negative, they should not invest in this project.

8.19   a.   Apply the 10-year annuity formula, discounted at 10 percent, to calculate the NPV of the video game.

$$NPV = C_0 + C_1 A^T_r$$
$$= -\$4,000,000 + \$750,000 \ A^{10}_{0.1}$$
$$= \mathbf{\$608,425.33}$$

The NPV of the video game is \$608,425.33.

b.   Calculate the revised NPV of the project. The firm expects to receive net cash flow of \$750,000 at the end of the first year of operations. Discount that value back one period to year 0.

$$PV(\text{Year 1 Cash Flow}) = C_1 / (1+r)^T$$
$$= \$750,000 / (1.1)$$
$$= \$681,818.18$$

For the next nine years, the firm has a 50 percent chance of receiving annual cash flows of \$1,500,000 and a 50 percent chance of receiving annual cash flows of \$0. Should the firm receive cash flows of \$0, the firm should exercise the option of abandonment and receive the \$200,000 cash flow. The probability of exercising that option is 50 percent. Calculate the expected PV of the revised cash flows by applying the nine-year annuity formula. To calculate the expected PV as of year 0, discount that value back one period to year 0. The option is exercised in year 1 and must also be discounted back one period to year 0.

$$PV(\text{Revised}) = (\text{Prob.} \times C_2 \times A^T_r + \text{Prob.} \times \text{Salvage}) / (1+r)^T$$
$$= (0.5 \times \$1,500,000 \times A^9_{0.1} + 0.5 \times \$200,000) / (1.1)$$
$$= \$4,017,516.23$$

After including the initial investment, the revised NPV of the project is equal to the sum of the first year's cash flow, the PV of the expected cash flows for the next nine years, and the expected value of abandoning the project.

$$\text{Revised NPV} = C_0 + C_1 / (1+r)^T + [(\text{Prob.} \times C_2 \times A^T_r) + (\text{Prob.} \times C_2)] / (1+r)^T$$
$$= -\$4,000,000 + \$750,000 / (1.1) +$$
$$(0.5 \times \$1,500,000 \times A^9_{0.1} + 0.5 \times \$200,000) / (1.1)$$
$$= \mathbf{\$699,334.42}$$

The revised NPV is \$699,334.42.

c.   The market value of the project, M, is the NPV of the project without an option to abandon plus the value of the option, Opt. The NPV of the project without the option to abandon was calculated in part (a). The difference between the NPV as calculated in part (a) and the revised NPV is equal to the option value of abandonment, Opt.

M	$= NPV + Opt$
\$699,334.42	$= \$608,425.33 + Opt$
\$90,909.09	$= Opt$

The option value of abandonment is \$90,909.09.

8.20 a. Apply the 10-year annuity formula, discounted at 20 percent to calculate the NPV of the project. Total annual net cash flow is $200,000,000.

$$\begin{aligned}
\text{NPV} &= C_0 + C_1 A^T_r \\
&= -\$100,000,000 + \$200,000,000\, A^{10}_{0.2} \\
&= \mathbf{\$738,494,417.11}
\end{aligned}$$

The NPV of the project is $738,494,417.11.

  b. Allied Products should abandon the project if the PV of the revised cash flows for the next nine years is less than the project's scrap value. Since the option to abandon the project occurs in year 1, discount the revised cash flows to year 1 as well. To determine the level of expected cash flows below which Allied should abandon the project, calculate the equivalent annual cash flows the project must earn to equal the scrap value, $50 million. Set the scrap value equal to a nine-year annuity, discounted at 20 percent. Solve for C_1.

Scrap Value	$= C_1 A^T_r$
$50,000,000	$= C_1 A^9_{0.2}$
$50,000,000 / A^9_{0.2}$	$= C_1$
$12,403,973.08	$= C_1$

The firm should abandon the project after the first year if the revised expected annual cash flows are below $12,403,973.08. Below that level, the firm is better off abandoning the project and receiving the $50 million scrap value of the project.

8.21 a. NPV   (1.932) $= -10 + 10*0.3*(1/0.25 - 1/0.25*(1/1.25)^5)$

  b. Option Value 2.000 $= 0.5*9/1.25$

   New NPV 0.068 $= -10 + 10*0.3/1.25 + 0.5*15*0.3*(1/0.25 - 1/0.25*(1/1.25)^4)/(1.25) + 0.5*9/1.25$

8.22   a)

	0	1	2	3	4	5
Initial investment	$(3,000,000)	$ –	$ –	$ –	$ –	$ –
Cash flow from operations		$2,500,000	$2,500,000	$2,500,000	$2,500,000	$2,500,000
Total cash flow from project	$(3,000,000)	$2,500,000	$2,500,000	$2,500,000	$2,500,000	$2,500,000
PV 15% (CF)	= CF $(3,000,000)$	= CF/1.15 2,173,913	= CF/$(1.15)^2$ 1,890,359	= CF/$(1.15)^3$ 1,643,791	= CF/$(1.15)^4$ 1,429,383	= CF/$(1.15)^5$ 1,242,942

$5,380,388

b)

	0	1	2	3	4
Initial investment	$ –	$ –	$ –	$ –	$ –
Cash flow from operations		$500,000	$500,000	$500,000	$500,000
Total cash flow from project	$ –	$500,000	$500,000	$500,000	$500,000
PV 15% (CF)	= CF 0	= CF/1.15 434,783	= CF/$(1.15)^2$ 378,072	= CF/$(1.15)^3$ 328,758	= CF/$(1.15)^4$ 285,877

$1,427,489

Since this amount is less than $1.5 million, we would choose to abandon.

	0	1	2	3	4
Initial investment	$ –	$ –	$ –	$ –	$ –
Cash flow from operations		$4,000,000	$4,000,000	$4,000,000	$4,000,000
Total cash flow from project	$ –	$4,000,000	$4,000,000	$4,000,000	$4,000,000
PV 15% (CF)	= CF 0	= CF/1.15 3,478,261	= CF/$(1.15)^2$ 3,024,575	= CF/$(1.15)^3$ 2,630,065	= CF/$(1.15)^4$ 2,287,013

$11,419,913

If we abandon, then we receive $1,500,000. If it is a success, then we receive $11,419,913.
These outcomes are equally likely so ($1,500,000 + 11,419,913)/2 =   6,459,957
The present value is 6,459,957/1.15 =   5,617,354
Therefore, the option to abandon is 5,617,354 – 5,380,388 =   236,966

Chapter 9: Capital Market Theory: An Overview

9.1   a.   The capital gain is the appreciation of the stock price. Because the stock price increased from $37 per share to $38 per share, you earned a capital gain of $1 per share (=$38 - $37).

$$
\begin{aligned}
\text{Capital Gain} &= (P_{t+1} - P_t)\,(\text{Number of Shares}) \\
&= (\$38 - \$37)\,(500) \\
&= \mathbf{\$500}
\end{aligned}
$$

You earned $500 in capital gains.

      b.   The total dollar return is equal to the dividend income plus the capital gain. You received $1,000 in dividend income, as stated in the problem, and received $500 in capital gains, as found in part (*a*).

$$
\begin{aligned}
\text{Total Dollar Gain} &= \text{Dividend income} + \text{Capital gain} \\
&= \$1,000 + \$500 \\
&= \mathbf{\$1,500}
\end{aligned}
$$

Your total dollar gain is $1,500.

      c.   The percentage return is the total dollar gain on the investment as of the end of year 1 divided by the $18,500 initial investment (=$37 × 500).

$$
\begin{aligned}
R_{t+1} &= [\text{Div}_{t+1} + (P_{t+1} - P_t)] \,/\, P_t \\
&= [\$1,000 + \$500] \,/\, \$18,500 \\
&= \mathbf{0.0811}
\end{aligned}
$$

The percentage return on the investment is 8.11%.

      d.   **No.** You do not need to sell the shares to include the capital gains in the computation of your return. Since you could realize the gain if you choose, you should include it in your analysis.

9.2   a.   The capital gain is the appreciation of the stock price. Find the amount that Seth paid for the stock one year ago by dividing his total investment by the number of shares he purchased ($52.00 = $10,400 / 200). Because the price of the stock increased from $52.00 per share to $54.25 per share, he earned a capital gain of $2.25 per share (=$54.25 - $52.00).

$$
\begin{aligned}
\text{Capital Gain} &= (P_{t+1} - P_t)\,(\text{Number of Shares}) \\
&= (\$54.25 - \$52.00)\,(200) \\
&= \mathbf{\$450}
\end{aligned}
$$

Seth's capital gain is $450.

      b.   The total dollar return is equal to the dividend income plus the capital gain. He received $600 in dividend income, as stated in the problem, and received $450 in capital gains, as found in part (*a*).

$$
\begin{aligned}
\text{Total Dollar Gain} &= \text{Dividend income} + \text{Capital gain} \\
&= \$600 + \$450 \\
&= \mathbf{\$1,050}
\end{aligned}
$$

Seth's total dollar return is $1,050.

c.   The percentage return is the total dollar gain on the investment as of the end of year 1 divided by the initial investment of $10,400.

$$R_{t+1} = [Div_{t+1} + (P_{t+1} - P_t)] / P_t$$
$$= [\$600 + \$450] / \$10,400$$
$$= \mathbf{0.1010}$$

The percentage return is 10.10%.

e.   The dividend yield is equal to the dividend payment divided by the purchase price of the stock.

$$Dividend\ Yield = Div_1 / P_t$$
$$= \$600 / \$10,400$$
$$= \mathbf{0.0577}$$

The stock's dividend yield is 5.77%.

9.3   Apply the percentage return formula. Note that the stock price declined during the period. Since the stock price decline was greater than the dividend, your return was negative.

$$R_{t+1} = [Div_{t+1} + (P_{t+1} - P_t)] / P_t$$
$$= [\$2.40 + (\$31 - \$42)] / \$42$$
$$= \mathbf{-0.2048}$$

The percentage return is –20.48%.

9.4   Apply the holding period return formula. The expected holding period return is equal to the total dollar return on the stock divided by the initial investment.

$$R_{t+2} = [P_{t+2} - P_t] / P_t$$
$$= [\$54.75 - \$52] / \$52$$
$$= \mathbf{0.0529}$$

The expected holding period return is 5.29%.

9.5   Use the nominal returns, R, on each of the securities and the inflation rate, π, of 3.1% to calculate the real return, r.

$$r = [(1 + R) / (1 + \pi)] - 1$$

a.   The nominal return on large-company stocks is 12.2%. Apply the formula for the real return, r.

$$r = [(1 + R) / (1 + \pi)] - 1$$
$$= [(1 + 0.122) / (1 + 0.031)] - 1$$
$$= \mathbf{0.0883}$$

The real return on large-company stocks is 8.83%.

b.	The nominal return on long-term corporate bonds is 6.2%. Apply the formula for the real return, r.

$$r = [(1 + R) / (1 + \pi)] - 1$$
$$= [(1 + 0.062) / (1 + 0.031)] - 1$$
$$= \mathbf{0.03}$$

The real return on long-term corporate bonds is 3.0%.

c.	The nominal return on long-term government bonds is 5.8%. Apply the formula for the real return, r.

$$r = [(1 + R) / (1 + \pi)] - 1$$
$$= [(1 + 0.058) / (1 + 0.031)] - 1$$
$$= \mathbf{0.0262}$$

The real return on long-term government bonds is 2.62%.

d.	The nominal return on U.S. Treasury bills is 3.8%. Apply the formula for the real return, r.

$$r = [(1 + R) / (1 + \pi)] - 1$$
$$= [(1 + 0.038) / (1 + 0.031)] - 1$$
$$= \mathbf{0.00679}$$

The real return on U.S. Treasury bills is 0.679%.

9.6	The difference between risky returns on common stocks and risk-free returns on Treasury bills is called the *risk premium*. The average risk premium was 8.4 percent (= 0.122 – 0.038) over the period. The expected return on common stocks can be estimated as the current return on Treasury bills, 2 percent, plus the average risk premium, 8.4 percent.

Risk Premium	= Average common stock return – Average Treasury bill return
	= 0.122 – 0.038
	= 0.084

E(R)	= Treasury bill return + Average risk premium
	= 0.02 + 0.084
	= **0.104**

The expected return on common stocks is 10.4 percent.

9.7	Below is a diagram that depicts the stocks' price movements. Two years ago, each stock had the same price, P_0. Over the first year, General Materials' stock price increased by 10 percent, or $(1.1) \times P_0$. Standard Fixtures' stock price declined by 10 percent, or $(0.9) \times P_0$. Over the second year, General Materials' stock price decreased by 10 percent, or $(0.9)(1.1) \times P_0$, while Standard Fixtures' stock price increased by 10 percent, or $(1.1)(0.9) \times P_0$. Today, each of the stocks is worth 99% of its original value.

	2 years ago	1 year ago	Today	
General Materials	P_0	$(1.1) P_0$	$(1.1)(0.9) P_0$	= **$(0.99) P_0$**
Standard Fixtures	P_0	$(0.9) P_0$	$(0.9)(1.1) P_0$	= **$(0.99) P_0$**

9.8   Apply the five-year holding-period return formula to calculate the total return on the S&P 500 over the five-year period.

$$\text{Five-year holding-period return} = (1 +R_1) \times (1 +R_2) \times (1 +R_3) \times (1 +R_4) \times (1 +R_5) - 1$$
$$= (1 + -0.0491) \times (1 + 0.2141) \times (1 + 0.2251) \times$$
$$(1 + 0.0627) \times (1 + 0.3216) - 1$$
$$= \mathbf{0.9864}$$

The five-year holding-period return is 98.64 percent.

9.9   The historical risk premium is the difference between the average annual return on long-term corporate bonds and the average risk-free rate on Treasury bills. The average risk premium is 2.4 percent (= 0.062 − 0.038).

$$\text{Risk Premium} = \text{Average corporate bond return} - \text{Average Treasury bill return}$$
$$= 0.062 - 0.038$$
$$= \mathbf{0.024}$$

The expected return on long-term corporate bonds is equal to the current return on Treasury bills, 2 percent, plus the average risk premium, 2.4 percent.

$$E(R) = \text{Treasury bill return} + \text{Average risk premium}$$
$$= 0.02 + 0.024$$
$$= \mathbf{0.044}$$

The expected return on long-term corporate bonds is 4.4%.

9.10   a.   To calculate the expected return, multiply the return for each of the three scenarios by the respective probability of occurrence.

$$E(R_M) = R_{Recession} \times \text{Prob(Recession)} + R_{Normal} \times \text{Prob(Normal)} + R_{Boom} \times \text{Prob(Boom)}$$
$$= -0.082 \times 0.25 + 0.123 \times 0.50 + 0.258 \times 0.25$$
$$= \mathbf{0.1055}$$

The expected return on the market is 10.55 percent.

$$E(R_T) = R_{Recession} \times \text{Prob(Recession)} + R_{Normal} \times \text{Prob(Normal)} + R_{Boom} \times \text{Prob(Boom)}$$
$$= 0.035 \times 0.25 + 0.035 \times 0.50 + 0.035 \times 0.25$$
$$= \mathbf{0.035}$$

The expected return on Treasury bills is 3.5 percent.

       b.   The expected risk premium is the difference between the expected market return and the expected risk-free return.

$$\text{Risk Premium} = E(R_M) - E(R_T)$$
$$= 0.1055 - 0.035$$
$$= \mathbf{0.0705}$$

The expected risk premium is 7.05 percent.

9.11 a. Divide the sum of the returns by seven to calculate the average return over the seven-year period.

$$\overline{R} = (R_{t-7} + R_{t-6} + R_{t-5} + R_{t-4} + R_{t-3} + R_{t-2} + R_{t-1}) / (7)$$
$$= (-0.026 + -0.01 + 0.438 + 0.047 + 0.164 + 0.301 + 0.199) / (7)$$
$$= \mathbf{0.159}$$

The average return is 15.9 percent.

b. The variance, σ^2, of the portfolio is equal to the sum of the squared differences between each return and the mean return $[(R - \overline{R})^2]$, divided by six.

R	$R - \overline{R}$	$(R - \overline{R})^2$
-0.026	-0.185	0.03423
-0.01	-0.169	0.02856
0.438	0.279	0.07784
0.047	-0.112	0.01254
0.164	0.005	0.00003
0.301	0.142	0.02016
0.199	0.040	0.00160
	Total	0.17496

Because the data are historical, the appropriate denominator in the calculation of the variance is six ($=T-1$).

$$\sigma^2 = [\Sigma(R - \overline{R})^2] / (T-1)$$
$$= 0.17496 / (7-1)$$
$$= \mathbf{0.02916}$$

The variance of the portfolio is 0.02916.

The standard deviation is equal to the square root of the variance.

$$\sigma = (\sigma^2)^{1/2}$$
$$= (0.02916)^{1/2}$$
$$= \mathbf{0.1708}$$

The standard deviation of the portfolio is 0.1708.

9.12 a. Calculate the difference between the return on common stocks and the return on Treasury bills.

Year	Common Stocks	Treasury Bills	Realized Risk Premium
-7	32.4%	11.2%	**21.2%**
-6	-4.9	14.7	**-19.6**
-5	21.4	10.5	**10.9**
-4	22.5	8.8	**13.7**
-3	6.3	9.9	**-3.6**
-2	32.2	7.7	**24.5**
Last	18.5	6.2	**12.3**

b. The average realized risk premium is the sum of the premium of each of the seven years, divided by seven.

Average Risk Premium $= (0.212 + -0.196 + 0.109 + .137 + -0.036 + 0.245 + 0.123) / 7$
$= \mathbf{0.0849}$

The average risk premium is 8.49 percent.

c. **Yes.** It is possible for the observed risk premium to be negative. This can happen in any single year, as it did in years -6 and -3. The average risk premium over many years is likely positive.

9.13 a. To calculate the expected return, multiply the return for each of the three scenarios by the respective probability of that scenario occurring.

$E(R)$ $= R_{Recession} \times \text{Prob(Recession)} + R_{Moderate} \times \text{Prob(Moderate)} + R_{Rapid} \times \text{Prob(Rapid)}$
$= 0.05 \times 0.2 + 0.08 \times 0.6 + 0.15 \times 0.2$
$= \mathbf{0.088}$

The expected return is 8.8 percent.

b. The variance, σ^2, of the stock is equal to the sum of the weighted squared differences between each return and the mean return $[\text{Prob}(R) \times (R - \bar{R})^2]$. Use the mean return calculated in part (a).

R	$R - \bar{R}$	$(R - \bar{R})^2$	$\text{Prob}(R) \times (R - \bar{R})^2$
0.05	-0.038	0.001444	0.0002888
0.08	-0.008	0.000064	0.0000384
0.15	0.062	0.003844	0.0007688
		Variance	**0.0010960**

The standard deviation, σ, is the square root of the variance.

σ $= (\sigma^2)^{1/2}$
$= (0.0010960)^{1/2}$
$= \mathbf{0.03311}$

The standard deviation is 0.03311.

9.14 a. To calculate the expected return, multiply the market return for each of the five scenarios by the respective probability of occurrence.

$\bar{R}_M$ $= (0.23 \times 0.12) + (0.18 \times 0.4) + (0.15 \times 0.25) + (0.09 \times 0.15) + (0.03 \times 0.08)$
$= \mathbf{0.153}$

The expected return on the market is 15.3 percent.

b. To calculate the expected return, multiply the stock's return for each of the five scenarios by the respective probability of occurrence.

$\bar{R}$ $= (0.12 \times 0.12) + (0.09 \times 0.4) + (0.05 \times 0.25) + (0.01 \times 0.15) + (-0.02 \times 0.08)$
$= \mathbf{0.0628}$

The expected return on Tribli stock is 6.28 percent.

9.15   a.   Divide the sum of the returns by four to calculate the expected returns on Belinkie Enterprises and Overlake Company over the four-year period.

$$\overline{R}_{Belinkie} = (R_1 + R_2 + R_3 + R_4) / (4)$$
$$= (0.04 + 0.06 + 0.09 + 0.04) / 4$$
$$= \textbf{0.0575}$$

The expected return on Belinkie Enterprises stock is 5.75 percent.

$$\overline{R}_{Overlake} = (R_1 + R_2 + R_3 + R_4) / (4)$$
$$= (0.05 + 0.07 + 0.10 + 0.14) / (4)$$
$$= \textbf{0.09}$$

The expected return on Overlake Company stock is 9 percent.

   b.   The variance, σ^2, of each stock is equal to the sum of the weighted squared differences between each return and the mean return $[\text{Prob}(R) \times (R - \overline{R})^2]$. Use the mean return calculated in part (a). Each of the four states is equally likely.

Belinkie Enterprises:

R	$R - \overline{R}$	$(R - \overline{R})^2$	$\text{Prob}(R) \times (R - \overline{R})^2$
0.04	-0.0175	0.00031	0.000077
0.06	0.0025	0.00001	0.000003
0.09	0.0325	0.00106	0.000264
0.04	-0.0175	0.00031	0.000077
		Variance	**0.000421**

The variance of Belinkie Enterprises stock is 0.000421.

Overlake Company:

R	$R - \overline{R}$	$(R - \overline{R})^2$	$\text{Prob}(R) \times (R - \overline{R})^2$
0.05	-0.04	0.0016	0.0004
0.07	-0.02	0.0004	0.0001
0.10	0.01	0.0001	0.000025
0.14	0.05	0.0025	0.000625
		Variance	**0.00115**

The variance of Overlake Company stock is 0.00115.

9.16   a.   Divide the sum of the returns by five to calculate the average return over the five-year period.

$$\overline{R}_S = (R_1 + R_2 + R_3 + R_4 + R_5) / (5)$$
$$= (0.477 + 0.339 + -0.35 + 0.31 + -0.005) / (5)$$
$$= \textbf{0.1542}$$

The average return on small-company stocks is 15.42 percent.

$$\overline{R}_M = (R_1 + R_2 + R_3 + R_4 + R_5) / (5)$$
$$= (0.402 + 0.648 + -0.58 + 0.328 + 0.004) / (5)$$
$$= \textbf{0.1604}$$

The average return on the market index is 16.04 percent.

b.   The variance, σ^2, of each is equal to the sum of the squared differences between each return and the mean return $[(R - \overline{R})^2]$, divided by four. The standard deviation, σ, is the square root of the variance.

Small-company stocks:

R_S	$R_S - \overline{R}_S$	$(R_S - \overline{R}_S)^2$
0.477	0.3228	0.10419984
0.339	0.1848	0.03415104
-0.35	-0.5042	0.25421764
0.31	0.1558	0.02427364
-0.005	-0.1592	0.02534464
	Total	0.44218680

Because the data are historical, the appropriate denominator in the variance calculation is four $(=T-1)$.

$$\sigma^2{}_S = [\Sigma(R_S - \overline{R}_S)^2] / (T - 1)$$
$$= 0.44218680 / (5 - 1)$$
$$= \mathbf{0.1105467}$$

The variance of the small-company returns is 0.1105467.

The standard deviation is equal to the square root of the variance.

$$\sigma_S = (\sigma^2{}_S)^{1/2}$$
$$= (0.1105467)^{1/2}$$
$$= \mathbf{0.33249}$$

The standard deviation of the small-company returns is 0.33249.

Market Index of Common Stocks:

R_S	$R_S - \overline{R}_S$	$(R_S - \overline{R}_S)^2$
0.402	0.2416	0.05837056
0.648	0.4876	0.23775376
-0.58	-0.7404	0.54819216
0.328	0.1676	0.02808976
0.004	-0.1564	0.02446096
	Total	0.89686720

Because the data are historical, the appropriate denominator in the variance calculation is four ($=T-1$).

$$\sigma^2_S = [\Sigma(R_S - \overline{R}_S)^2] / (T-1)$$
$$= (0.89686720) / (5-1)$$
$$= \mathbf{0.2242168}$$

The variance of the market index of common stocks is 0.2242168.

The standard deviation is equal to the square root of the variance.

$$\sigma_S = (\sigma^2_S)^{1/2}$$
$$= (0.2242168)^{1/2}$$
$$= \mathbf{0.47352}$$

The standard deviation of the market index is 0.47352.

9.17   Common Stocks:

Divide the sum of the returns by seven to calculate the average return over the seven-year period.

$$\overline{R}_{CS} = (R_1 + R_2 + R_3 + R_4 + R_5 + R_6 + R_7) / (7)$$
$$= (0.3242 + -0.0491 + 0.2141 + 0.2251 + 0.0627 + 0.3216 + 0.1847) / (7)$$
$$= \mathbf{0.1833}$$

The average return on common stocks is 18.33 percent.

The variance, σ^2, is equal to the sum of the squared differences between each return and the mean return $[(R - \overline{R})^2]$, divided by six.

R_{CS}	$R_{CS} - \overline{R}_{CS}$	$(R_{CS} - \overline{R}_{CS})^2$
0.3242	0.1409	0.0198
-0.0491	-0.2324	0.0540
0.2141	0.0308	0.0009
0.2251	0.0418	0.0017
0.0627	-0.1206	0.0146
0.3216	0.1383	0.0191
0.1847	0.0014	0.0000
	Total	0.1102

Because the data are historical, the appropriate denominator in the variance calculation is six ($=T-1$).

$$\sigma^2_{CS} = [\Sigma(R_{CS} - \overline{R}_{CS})^2] / (T-1)$$
$$= (0.1102) / (7-1)$$
$$= \mathbf{0.018372}$$

The variance of the common stock returns is 0.018372.

Small Stocks:

Divide the sum of the returns by seven to calculate the average return over the seven-year period.

$$\overline{R}_{SS} = (R_1 + R_2 + R_3 + R_4 + R_5 + R_6 + R_7) / (7)$$
$$= (0.3988 + 0.1388 + 0.2801 + 0.3967 + -0.0667 + 0.2466 + 0.0685) / (7)$$
$$= \mathbf{0.2090}$$

The average return on small stocks is 20.90 percent.

The variance, σ^2, is equal to the sum of the squared differences between each return and the mean return $[(R - \overline{R})^2]$, divided by six.

R_{SS}	$R_{SS} - \overline{R}_{SS}$	$(R_{SS} - \overline{R}_{SS})^2$
0.3988	0.1898	0.0360
0.1388	-0.0702	0.0049
0.2801	0.0711	0.0051
0.3967	0.1877	0.0352
-0.0667	-0.2757	0.0760
0.2466	0.0376	0.0014
0.0685	-0.1405	0.0197
	Total	0.1784

Because the data are historical, the appropriate denominator in the calculation of the variance is six ($=T-1$).

$$\sigma^2_{SS} = [\Sigma(R_{SS} - \overline{R}_{SS})^2] / (T - 1)$$
$$= (0.1784) / (7 - 1)$$
$$= \mathbf{0.029734}$$

The variance of the small stock returns is 0.029734.

Long-Term Corporate Bonds:

Divide the sum of the returns by seven to calculate the average return over the seven-year period.

$$\overline{R}_{CB} = (R_1 + R_2 + R_3 + R_4 + R_5 + R_6 + R_7) / (7)$$
$$= (-0.0262 + -0.0096 + 0.4379 + 0.0470 + 0.1639 + 0.3090 + 0.1985) / (7)$$
$$= \mathbf{0.1601}$$

The average return on long-term corporate bonds is 16.01 percent.

The variance, σ^2, is equal to the sum of the squared differences between each return and the mean return $[(R - \overline{R})^2]$, divided by six.

R_{CB}	$R_{CB} - \overline{R}_{CB}$	$(R_{CB} - \overline{R}_{CB})^2$
-0.0262	-0.1863	0.0347
-0.0096	-0.1697	0.0288
0.4379	0.2778	0.0772
0.0470	-0.1131	0.0128
0.1639	0.0038	0.0000
0.3090	0.1489	0.0222
0.1985	0.0384	0.0015
	Total	0.1771

Because the data are historical, the appropriate denominator in the calculation of the variance is six $(=T-1)$.

$$
\begin{aligned}
\sigma^2_{CB} &= [\Sigma(R_{CB} - \overline{R}_{CB})^2] / (T-1) \\
&= (0.1771) / (7-1) \\
&= \mathbf{0.029522}
\end{aligned}
$$

The variance of the long-term corporate bond returns is 0.029522.

Long-Term Government Bonds:

Divide the sum of the returns by seven to calculate the average return over the seven-year period.

$$
\begin{aligned}
\overline{R}_{GB} &= (R_1 + R_2 + R_3 + R_4 + R_5 + R_6 + R_7) / (7) \\
&= (-0.0395 + -0.0185 + 0.4035 + 0.0068 + 0.1543 + 0.3097 + 0.2444) / (7) \\
&= \mathbf{0.1568}
\end{aligned}
$$

The average return on long-term government bonds is 15.68 percent.

The variance, σ^2, is equal to the sum of the squared differences between each return and the mean return $[(R - \overline{R})^2]$, divided by six.

R_{GB}	$R_{GB} - \overline{R}_{GB}$	$(R_{GB} - \overline{R}_{GB})^2$
-0.0395	-0.1963	0.0385
-0.0185	-0.1383	0.0191
0.4035	0.2467	0.0609
0.0068	-0.1500	0.0225
0.1543	-0.0025	0.0000
0.3097	0.1529	0.0234
0.2444	0.0876	0.0077
	Total	0.1721

Because the data are historical, the appropriate denominator in the calculation of the variance is six $(=T-1)$.

$$
\begin{aligned}
\sigma^2_{GB} &= [\Sigma(R_{GB} - \overline{R}_{GB})^2] / (T-1) \\
&= (0.1721) / (7-1) \\
&= \mathbf{0.02868}
\end{aligned}
$$

The variance of the long-term government bond returns is 0.02868.

U.S. Treasury Bills:

Divide the sum of the returns by seven to calculate the average return over the seven-year period.

$$\overline{R}_{TB} = (R_1 + R_2 + R_3 + R_4 + R_5 + R_6 + R_7) / (7)$$
$$= (0.1124 + 0.1471 + 0.1054 + 0.0880 + 0.0985 + 0.0772 + 0.0616) / (7)$$
$$= \mathbf{0.0986}$$

The average return on the Treasury bills is 9.86 percent.

The variance, σ^2, is equal to the sum of the squared differences between each return and the mean return $[(R - \overline{R})^2]$, divided by six.

R_{TB}	$R_{TB} - \overline{R}_{TB}$	$(R_{TB} - \overline{R}_{TB})^2$
0.1124	0.0138	0.0002
0.1471	0.0485	0.0024
0.1054	0.0068	0.0000
0.0880	-0.0106	0.0001
0.0985	-0.0001	0.0000
0.0772	-0.0214	0.0005
0.0616	-0.0370	0.0014
	Total	0.0045

Because the data are historical, the appropriate denominator in the calculation of the variance is six ($=T-1$).

$$\sigma^2_{TB} = [\Sigma(R_{TB} - \overline{R}_{TB})^2] / (T - 1)$$
$$= (0.0045) / (7 - 1)$$
$$= \mathbf{0.00075}$$

The variance of the Treasury bill returns is 0.00075.

9.18   a.   Divide the sum of the returns by six to calculate the average return over the six-year period.

$$\overline{R}_S = (R_1 + R_2 + R_3 + R_4 + R_5 + R_6 + R_7) / (6)$$
$$= (0.0685 + -0.0930 + 0.2287 + 0.1018 + -0.2156 + 0.4463) / (6)$$
$$= \mathbf{0.0895}$$

The average return on small-company stocks is 8.95 percent.

$$\overline{R}_T = (R_1 + R_2 + R_3 + R_4 + R_5 + R_6 + R_7) / (6)$$
$$= (0.0616 + 0.0547 + 0.0635 + 0.0837 + 0.0781 + 0.056) / (6)$$
$$= \mathbf{0.0663}$$

The average return on U.S. Treasury bills is 6.63 percent.

   b.   The variance, σ^2, of each security is equal to the sum of the squared differences between each return and the mean return $[(R - \overline{R})^2]$, divided by five. The standard deviation is equal to the square root of the variance.

Small-Company Stocks:

R_S	$R_S - \overline{R}_S$	$(R_S - \overline{R}_S)^2$
0.0685	-0.020950	0.000439
-0.0930	-0.182450	0.033288
0.2287	0.139250	0.019391
0.1018	0.012350	0.000153
-0.2156	-0.305050	0.093056
0.4463	0.356850	0.127342
	Total	0.273667

Because the data are historical, the appropriate denominator in the calculation of the variance is five ($=T-1$).

$$\sigma^2{}_S \quad = [\Sigma(R_S - \overline{R}_S)^2] / (T-1)$$
$$= (0.273667) / (6-1)$$
$$= \mathbf{0.054733}$$

The variance of small-company stocks is 0.0547.

The standard deviation is equal to the square root of the variance.

$$\sigma_S \quad = (\sigma^2{}_S)^{1/2}$$
$$= (0.054733)^{1/2}$$
$$= \mathbf{0.2340}$$

The standard deviation of small-company stocks is .2340.

U.S. Treasury bills:

R_T	$R_T - \overline{R}_T$	$(R_T - \overline{R}_T)^2$
0.0616	-0.004667	0.000022
0.0547	-0.011567	0.000134
0.0635	-0.002767	0.000008
0.0837	0.017433	0.000304
0.0781	0.011833	0.000140
0.0560	-0.010267	0.000105
	Total	0.000713

Because the data are historical, the appropriate denominator in the calculation of the variance is five ($=T-1$).

$$\sigma^2{}_T \quad = [\Sigma(R_T - \overline{R}_T)^2] / (T-1)$$
$$= (0.000713) / (6-1)$$
$$= \mathbf{0.000143}$$

The variance of small-company stocks is 0.000143.

The standard deviation is equal to the square root of the variance.

$$\sigma_T \quad = (\sigma^2{}_T)^{1/2}$$
$$= (0.000143)^{1/2}$$
$$= \mathbf{0.0119}$$

The standard deviation of small-company stocks is 0.0119.

c.   The average return on Treasury bills is lower than the average return on small-company stocks. However, the standard deviation of the returns on Treasury bills is also lower than the standard deviation of the small-company stock returns. There is a positive relationship between the risk of a security and the expected return on a security.

9.19   According to the normal distribution, there is a 95.44 percent probability that a return will be within two standard deviations of the mean. Thus, roughly 95 percent of International Trading's returns will fall within two standard deviations of the mean.

Range of Returns $= \overline{R} \pm (2 \times \sigma)$
$= 0.175 \pm (2 \times 0.085)$
$= \textbf{[0.005, 0.345]}$

The range in which 95 percent of the returns will fall is between 0.5 percent and 34.5 percent.

Chapter 10: Return and Risk: *The Capital-Asset-Pricing Model (CAPM)*

10.1   a.   Expected Return $= (0.1)(-0.045) + (.2)(0.044) + (0.5)(0.12) + (0.2)(0.207)$
$$= 0.1057$$
$$= \mathbf{10.57\%}$$

The expected return on Q-mart's stock is 10.57%.

        b.   Variance (σ^2) $= (0.1)(-0.045 - 0.1057)^2 + (0.2)(0.044 - 0.1057)^2 + (0.5)(0.12 - 0.1057)^2 +$
$\qquad\qquad\qquad (0.2)(0.207 - 0.1057)^2$
$$= 0.005187$$

Standard Deviation (σ) $= (0.005187)^{1/2}$
$$= 0.0720$$
$$= \mathbf{7.20\%}$$

The standard deviation of Q-mart's returns is 7.20%.

10.2   a.   Expected Return$_A$ $= (1/3)(0.063) + (1/3)(0.105) + (1/3)(0.156)$
$$= 0.1080$$
$$= \mathbf{10.80\%}$$

The expected return on Stock A is 10.80%.

            Expected Return$_B$ $= (1/3)(-0.037) + (1/3)(0.064) + (1/3)(0.253)$
$$= 0.933$$
$$= \mathbf{9.33\%}$$

The expected return on Stock B is 9.33%.

        b.   Variance$_A$ (σ_A^2) $= (1/3)(0.063 - 0.108)^2 + (1/3)(0.105 - 0.108)^2 + (1/3)(0.156 - 0.108)^2$
$$= 0.001446$$

Standard Deviation$_A$ (σ_A) $= (0.001446)^{1/2}$
$$= 0.0380$$
$$= \mathbf{3.80\%}$$

The standard deviation of Stock A's returns is 3.80%.

            Variance$_B$ (σ_B^2) $= (1/3)(-0.037 - 0.0933)^2 + (1/3)(0.064 - 0.0933)^2 + (1/3)(0.253 - 0.0933)^2$
$$= 0.014447$$

Standard Deviation$_B$ (σ_B) $= (0.014447)^{1/2}$
$$= 0.1202$$
$$= \mathbf{12.02\%}$$

The standard deviation of Stock B's returns is 12.02%.

        c.   Covariance$(R_A, R_B) = (1/3)(0.063 - 0.108)(-0.037 - 0.0933) + (1/3)(0.105 - 0.108)(0.064 - 0.933)$
$\qquad\qquad\qquad + (1/3)(0.156 - 0.108)(0.253 - 0.0933)$
$$= \mathbf{0.004539}$$

The covariance between the returns of Stock A and Stock B is 0.004539.

$\text{Correlation}(R_A, R_B) = \text{Covariance}(R_A, R_B) / (\sigma_A * \sigma_B)$
$= 0.004539 / (0.0380 * 0.1202)$
$= \mathbf{0.9937}$

The correlation between the returns on Stock A and Stock B is 0.9937.

10.3　a.　$\text{Expected Return}_{HB} = (0.25)(-0.02) + (0.60)(0.092) + (0.15)(0.154)$
$= 0.0733$
$= \mathbf{7.33\%}$

The expected return on Highbull's stock is 7.33%.

$\text{Expected Return}_{SB} = (0.25)(0.05) + (0.60)(0.062) + (0.15)(0.074)$
$= 0.0608$
$= \mathbf{6.08\%}$

The expected return on Slowbear's stock is 6.08%.

b.　$\text{Variance}_A (\sigma_{HB}^2) = (0.25)(-0.02 - 0.0733)^2 + (0.60)(0.092 - 0.0733)^2 + (0.15)(0.154 - 0.0733)^2$
$= 0.003363$

$\text{Standard Deviation}_A (\sigma_{HB}) = (0.003363)^{1/2}$
$= 0.0580$
$= \mathbf{5.80\%}$

The standard deviation of Highbear's stock returns is 5.80%.

$\text{Variance}_B (\sigma_{SB}^2) = (0.25)(0.05 - 0.0608)^2 + (0.60)(0.062 - 0.0608)^2 + (0.15)(0.074 - 0.0608)^2$
$= 0.000056$

$\text{Standard Deviation}_B (\sigma_B) = (0.000056)^{1/2}$
$= 0.0075$
$= \mathbf{0.75\%}$

The standard deviation of Slowbear's stock returns is 0.75%.

c.　$\text{Covariance}(R_{HB}, R_{SB}) = (0.25)(-0.02 - 0.0733)(0.05 - 0.0608) + (0.60)(0.092 - 0.0733)(0.062 - 0.0608) + (0.15)(0.154 - 0.0733)(0.074 - 0.0608)$
$= \mathbf{0.000425}$

The covariance between the returns on Highbull's stock and Slowbear's stock is 0.000425.

$\text{Correlation}(R_A, R_B) = \text{Covariance}(R_A, R_B) / (\sigma_A * \sigma_B)$
$= 0.000425 / (0.0580 * 0.0075)$
$= \mathbf{0.9770}$

The correlation between the returns on Highbull's stock and Slowbear's stock is 0.9770.

10.4   Value of Atlas stock in the portfolio   = (120 shares)($50 per share)
$$= \$6{,}000$$

Value of Babcock stock in the portfolio = (150 shares)($20 per share)
$$= \$3{,}000$$

Total Value in the portfolio   = $6,000 + $3000
$$= \$9{,}000$$

Weight of Atlas stock   = $6,000 / $9,000
$$= 2/3$$

The weight of Atlas stock in the portfolio is 2/3.

Weight of Babcock stock   = $3,000 / $9,000
$$= 1/3$$

The weight of Babcock stock in the portfolio is 1/3.

10.5   a.   The expected return on the portfolio equals:

$$E(R_P) = (W_F)[E(R_F)] + (W_G)[E(R_G)]$$

where $E(R_P)$ = the expected return on the portfolio
$E(R_F)$ = the expected return on Security F
$E(R_G)$ = the expected return on Security G
W_F = the weight of Security F in the portfolio
W_G = the weight of Security G in the portfolio

$$\begin{aligned} E(R_P) &= (W_F)[E(R_F)] + (W_G)[E(R_G)] \\ &= (0.30)(0.12) + (0.70)(0.18) \\ &= 0.1620 \\ &= 16.20\% \end{aligned}$$

The expected return on a portfolio composed of 30% of Security F and 70% of Security G is 16.20%.

b.   The variance of the portfolio equals:

$$\sigma^2_P = (W_F)^2(\sigma_F)^2 + (W_G)^2(\sigma_G)^2 + (2)(W_F)(W_G)(\sigma_F)(\sigma_G)[\text{Correlation}(R_F, R_G)]$$

where σ^2_P = the variance of the portfolio
W_F = the weight of Security F in the portfolio
W_G = the weight of Security G in portfolio
σ_F = the standard deviation of Security F
σ_G = the standard deviation of Security G
R_F = the return on Security F
R_G = the return on Security G

$$\begin{aligned} \sigma^2_P &= (W_F)^2(\sigma_F)^2 + (W_G)^2(\sigma_G)^2 + (2)(W_F)(W_G)(\sigma_F)(\sigma_G)[\text{Correlation}(R_F, R_G)] \\ &= (0.30)^2(0.09)^2 + (0.70)^2(0.25)^2 + (2)(0.30)(0.70)(0.09)(0.25)(0.2) \\ &= 0.033244 \end{aligned}$$

The standard deviation of the portfolio equals:

$$\sigma_P = (\sigma^2_P)^{1/2} \quad \text{SD}$$

where σ_P = the standard deviation of the portfolio
          σ^2_P = the variance of the portfolio

$$\sigma_P = (\sigma^2_P)^{1/2}$$
$$= (0.033244)^{1/2}$$
$$= 0.1823$$
$$= \mathbf{18.23\%}$$

If the correlation between the returns of Security F and Security G is 0.2, the standard deviation of the portfolio is 18.23%.

10.6   a.   The expected return on the portfolio equals:

$$E(R_P) = (W_A)[E(R_A)] + (W_B)[E(R_B)]$$

where $E(R_P)$ = the expected return on the portfolio
          $E(R_A)$ = the expected return on Stock A
          $E(R_B)$ = the expected return on Stock B
          W_A = the weight of Stock A in the portfolio
          W_B = the weight of Stock B in the portfolio

$$E(R_P) = (W_A)[E(R_A)] + (W_B)[E(R_B)]$$
$$= (0.40)(0.15) + (0.60)(0.25)$$
$$= 0.21$$
$$= \mathbf{21\%}$$

The expected return on a portfolio composed of 40% stock A and 60% stock B is 21%.

The variance of the portfolio equals:

$$\sigma^2_P = (W_A)^2(\sigma_A)^2 + (W_B)^2(\sigma_B)^2 + (2)(W_A)(W_B)(\sigma_A)(\sigma_B)[\text{Correlation}(R_A, R_B)]$$

where σ^2_P = the variance of the portfolio
          W_A = the weight of Stock A in the portfolio
          W_B = the weight of Stock B in the portfolio
          σ_A = the standard deviation of Stock A
          σ_B = the standard deviation of Stock B
          R_A = the return on Stock A
          R_B = the return on Stock B

$$\sigma^2_P = (W_A)^2(\sigma_A)^2 + (W_B)^2(\sigma_B)^2 + (2)(W_A)(W_B)(\sigma_A)(\sigma_B)[\text{Correlation}(R_A, R_B)]$$
$$= (0.40)^2(0.10)^2 + (0.60)^2(0.20)^2 + (2)(0.40)(0.60)(0.10)(0.20)(0.5)$$
$$= 0.0208$$

The standard deviation of the portfolio equals:

$$\sigma_P = (\sigma^2_P)^{1/2}$$

where σ_P = the standard deviation of the portfolio
                             σ^2_P = the variance of the portfolio

$$\sigma_P = (0.0208)^{1/2}$$
$$= 0.1442$$
$$\mathbf{=14.42\%}$$

If the correlation between the returns on Stock A and Stock B is 0.5, the standard deviation of the portfolio is 14.42%.

b. $\sigma^2_P = (W_A)^2(\sigma_A)^2 + (W_B)^2(\sigma_B)^2 + (2)(W_A)(W_B)(\sigma_A)(\sigma_B)[\text{Correlation}(R_A, R_B)]$
          $= (0.40)^2(0.10)^2 + (0.60)^2(0.20)^2 + (2)(0.40)(0.60)(0.10)(0.20)(-0.5)$
          $= 0.0112$

        $\sigma_P = (0.0112)^{1/2}$
            $= 0.1058$
            $\mathbf{=10.58\%}$

If the correlation between the returns on Stock A and Stock B is -0.5, the standard deviation of the portfolio is 10.58%.

c.   As Stock A and Stock B become more negatively correlated, the standard deviation of the portfolio decreases.

10.7   a.   Value of Macrosoft stock in the portfolio   = (100 shares)($80 per share)
                                                                           = $8,000

Value of Intelligence stock in the portfolio   = (300 shares)($40 per share)
                                                                           = $12,000

Total Value in the portfolio   = $8,000 + $12,000
                                          = $20,000

Weight of Macrosoft stock   = $8,000 / $20,000
                                     = 0.40

Weight of Intelligence stock = $12,000 / $20,000
                                     = 0.60

The expected return on the portfolio equals:

$$E(R_P) = (W_{MAC})[E(R_{MAC})] + (W_I)[E(R_I)]$$

where $E(R_P)$ = the expected return on the portfolio
                $E(R_{MAC})$ = the expected return on Macrosoft stock
                $E(R_I)$ = the expected return on Intelligence Stock
                W_{MAC} = the weight of Macrosoft stock in the portfolio
                W_I = the weight of Intelligence stock in the portfolio

$$E(R_P) = (W_{MAC})[E(R_{MAC})] + (W_I)[E(R_M)]$$
$$= (0.40)(0.15) + (0.60)(0.20)$$
$$= 0.18$$
$$= \mathbf{18\%}$$

The expected return on her portfolio is 18%.

The variance of the portfolio equals:

$$\sigma^2{}_P = (W_{MAC})^2(\sigma_{MAC})^2 + (W_I)^2(\sigma_I)^2 + (2)(W_{MAC})(W_I)(\sigma_{MAC})(\sigma_I)[\text{Correlation}(R_{MAC}, R_I)]$$

where $\sigma^2{}_P$ = the variance of the portfolio
W_{MAC} = the weight of Macrosoft stock in the portfolio
W_I = the weight of Intelligence stock in the portfolio
σ_{MAC} = the standard deviation of Macrosoft stock
σ_I = the standard deviation of Intelligence stock
R_{MAC} = the return on Macrosoft stock
R_I = the return on Intelligence stock

$$\begin{aligned}
\sigma^2{}_P &= (W_{MAC})^2(\sigma_{MAC})^2 + (W_I)^2(\sigma_I)^2 + (2)(W_{MAC})(W_I)(\sigma_{MAC})(\sigma_I)[\text{Correlation}(R_{MAC}, R_I)] \\
&= (0.40)^2(0.08)^2 + (0.60)^2(0.20)^2 + (2)(0.40)(0.60)(0.08)(0.20)(0.38) \\
&= 0.018342
\end{aligned}$$

The standard deviation of the portfolio equals:

$$\sigma_P = (\sigma^2{}_P)^{1/2}$$

where σ_P = the standard deviation of the portfolio
$\sigma^2{}_P$ = the variance of the portfolio

$$\begin{aligned}
\sigma_P &= (0.018342)^{1/2} \\
&= 0.1354 \\
&= \mathbf{13.54\%}
\end{aligned}$$

The standard deviation of her portfolio is 13.54%.

b.   Janet started with 300 shares of Intelligence stock. After selling 200 shares, she has 100 shares left.

Value of Macrosoft stock in the portfolio = (100 shares)($80 per share)
                                            = $8,000

Value of Intelligence stock in the portfolio = (100 shares)($40 per share)
                                               = $4,000

Total Value in the portfolio = $8,000 + $4,000
                              = $12,000

Weight of Macrosoft stock = $8,000 / $12,000
                           = 2/3

Weight of Intelligence stock = $4,000 / $12,000
                             = 1/3

$$\begin{aligned}
E(R_P) &= (W_{MAC})[E(R_{MAC})] + (W_I)[E(R_I)] \\
&= (2/3)(0.15) + (1/3)(0.20) \\
&= 0.1667 \\
&= \mathbf{16.67\%}
\end{aligned}$$

The expected return on her portfolio is 16.67%.

$$\sigma^2_P = (W_{MAC})^2(\sigma_{MAC})^2 + (W_I)^2(\sigma_I)^2 + (2)(W_{MAC})(W_I)(\sigma_{MAC})(\sigma_I)[\text{Correlation}(R_{MAC}, R_I)]$$
$$= (2/3)^2(0.08)^2 + (1/3)^2(0.20)^2 + (2)(2/3)(1/3)(0.08)(0.20)(0.38)$$
$$= 0.009991$$

$$\sigma_P = (0.009991)^{1/2}$$
$$= 0.1000$$
$$= \mathbf{10.00\%}$$

The standard deviation of her portfolio is 10.00%.

10.8   a.   Expected Return$_A$ $= (0.20)(0.07) + (0.50)(0.07) + (0.30)(0.07)$
$$= 0.07$$
$$= \mathbf{7\%}$$

The expected return on Stock A is 7%.

Variance$_A$ (σ_A^2) $= (0.20)(0.07 - 0.07)^2 + (0.50)(0.07 - 0.07)^2 + (0.30)(0.07 - 0.07)^2$
$$= 0$$

The variance of the returns on Stock A is 0.

Standard Deviation$_A$ (σ_A) $= (0)^{1/2}$
$$= 0.00$$
$$= \mathbf{0\%}$$

The standard deviation of the returns on Stock A is 0%.

Expected Return$_B$ $= (0.20)(-0.05) + (0.50)(0.10) + (0.30)(0.25)$
$$= 0.1150$$
$$= \mathbf{11.50\%}$$

The expected return on Stock B is 11.50%.

Variance$_B$ (σ_B^2) $= (0.20)(-0.05 - 0.1150)^2 + (0.50)(0.10 - 0.1150)^2 + (0.30)(0.25 - 0.1150)^2$
$$= \mathbf{0.011025}$$

The variance of the returns on Stock B is 0.011025.

Standard Deviation$_B$ (σ_B) $= (0.011025)^{1/2}$
$$= 0.1050$$
$$= \mathbf{10.50\%}$$

The standard deviation of the returns on Stock B is 10.50%.

b.   Covariance$(R_A, R_B) = (0.20)(0.07 - 0.07)(-0.05 - 0.1150) + (0.50)(0.07 - 0.07)(0.10 - 0.1150)$
$$(0.30)(0.07 - 0.07)(0.25 - 0.1150)$$
$$= \mathbf{0}$$

The covariance between the returns on Stock A and Stock B is 0.

Correlation$(R_A, R_B) = \text{Covariance}(R_A, R_B) / (\sigma_A * \sigma_B)$
$$= 0 / (0 * 0.1050)$$
$$= \mathbf{0}$$

The correlation between the returns on Stock A and Stock B is 0.

c.   The expected return on the portfolio equals:

$$E(R_P) = (W_A)[E(R_A)] + (W_B)[E(R_B)]$$

where $E(R_P)$ = the expected return on the portfolio
        $E(R_A)$ = the expected return on Stock A
        $E(R_B)$ = the expected return on Stock B
        W_A = the weight of Stock A in the portfolio
        W_B = the weight of Stock B in the portfolio

$$\begin{aligned} E(R_P) &= (W_A)[E(R_A)] + (W_B)[E(R_B)] \\ &= (1/2)(0.07) + (1/2)(0.115) \\ &= 0.0925 \\ &= \mathbf{9.25\%} \end{aligned}$$

The expected return of an equally weighted portfolio is 9.25%.

$$\sigma^2_P = (W_A)^2(\sigma_A)^2 + (W_B)^2(\sigma_B)^2 + (2)(W_A)(W_B)(\sigma_A)(\sigma_B)[\text{Correlation}(R_A, R_B)]$$

where σ^2_P = the variance of the portfolio
        W_A = the weight of Stock A in the portfolio
        W_B = the weight of Stock B in the portfolio
        σ_A = the standard deviation of Stock A
        σ_B = the standard deviation of Stock B
        R_A = the return on Stock A
        R_B = the return Stock B

$$\begin{aligned} \sigma^2_P &= (W_A)^2(\sigma_A)^2 + (W_B)^2(\sigma_B)^2 + (2)(W_A)(W_B)(\sigma_A)(\sigma_B)[\text{Correlation}(R_A, R_B)] \\ &= (1/2)^2(0)^2 + (1/2)^2(0.105)^2 + (2)(1/2)(1/2)(0)(0.105)(0) \\ &= 0.002756 \end{aligned}$$

The standard deviation of the portfolio equals:

$$\sigma_P = (\sigma^2_P)^{1/2}$$

where σ_P = the standard deviation of the portfolio
                 σ^2_P = the variance of the portfolio

$$\begin{aligned} \sigma_P &= (0.002756)^{1/2} \\ &= 0.0525 \\ &= \mathbf{5.25\%} \end{aligned}$$

The standard deviation of the returns on an equally weighted portfolio is 5.25%.

10.9   a.   The expected return on the portfolio equals:

$$E(R_P) = (W_A)[E(R_A)] + (W_B)[E(R_B)]$$

where $E(R_P)$ = the expected return on the portfolio
        $E(R_A)$ = the expected return on Stock A
        $E(R_B)$ = the expected return on Stock B
        W_A = the weight of Stock A in the portfolio
        W_B = the weight of Stock B in the portfolio

$$E(R_P) = (W_A)[E(R_A)] + (W_B)[E(R_B)]$$
$$= (0.30)(0.10) + (0.70)(0.20)$$
$$= 0.17$$
$$= 17\%$$

The expected return on the portfolio is 17%.

The variance of a portfolio equals:

$$\sigma^2_P = (W_A)^2(\sigma_A)^2 + (W_B)^2(\sigma_B)^2 + (2)(W_A)(W_B)(\sigma_A)(\sigma_B)[\text{Correlation}(R_A, R_B)]$$

where σ^2_P = the variance of the portfolio
    W_A = the weight of Stock A in the portfolio
    W_B = the weight of Stock B in the portfolio
    σ_A = the standard deviation of Stock A
    σ_B = the standard deviation of Stock B
    R_A = the return on Stock A
    R_B = the return on Stock B

$$\sigma^2_P = (W_A)^2(\sigma_A)^2 + (W_B)^2(\sigma_B)^2 + (2)(W_A)(W_B)(\sigma_A)(\sigma_B)[\text{Correlation}(R_A, R_B)]$$
$$= (0.30)^2(0.05)^2 + (0.70)^2(0.15)^2 + (2)(0.30)(0.70)(0.05)(0.15)(0)$$
$$= 0.01125$$

The standard deviation of the portfolio equals:

$$\sigma_P = (\sigma^2_P)^{1/2}$$

where σ_P = the standard deviation of the portfolio
      σ^2_P = the variance of the portfolio

$$\sigma_P = (0.01125)^{1/2}$$
$$= 0.1061$$
$$= 10.61\%$$

The standard deviation of the portfolio is 10.61%.

b. $$E(R_P) = (W_A)[E(R_A)] + (W_B)[E(R_B)]$$
$$= (0.90)(0.10) + (0.10)(0.20)$$
$$= 0.11$$
$$= 11\%$$

The expected return on the portfolio is 11%.

$$\sigma^2_P = (W_A)^2(\sigma_A)^2 + (W_B)^2(\sigma_B)^2 + (2)(W_A)(W_B)(\sigma_A)(\sigma_B)[\text{Correlation}(R_A, R_B)]$$
$$= (0.90)^2(0.05)^2 + (0.10)^2(0.15)^2 + (2)(0.90)(0.10)(0.05)(0.15)(0)$$
$$= 0.00225$$

$$\sigma_P = (0.00225)^{1/2}$$
$$= 0.0474$$
$$= 4.74\%$$

The standard deviation of the portfolio is 4.74%.

c.   No, you would not hold 100% of Stock A because the portfolio in part *b* has a higher expected return and lower standard deviation than Stock A.

You may or may not hold 100% of Stock B, depending on your risk preference. If you have a low level of risk-aversion, you may prefer to hold 100% Stock B because of its higher expected return. If you have a high level of risk-aversion, however, you may prefer to hold a portfolio containing both Stock A and Stock B since the portfolio will have a lower standard deviation, and hence, less risk, than holding Stock B alone.

10.10   The expected return on the portfolio must be less than or equal to the expected return on the asset with the highest expected return. It cannot be greater than this asset's expected return because all assets with lower expected returns will pull down the value of the weighted average expected return.

Similarly, the expected return on any portfolio must be greater than or equal to the expected return on the asset with the lowest expected return. The portfolio's expected return cannot be below the lowest expected return among all the assets in the portfolio because assets with higher expected returns will pull up the value of the weighted average expected return.

10.11   a.   Expected Return$_A$ $= (0.40)(0.03) + (0.60)(0.15)$
$= 0.1020$
$= \mathbf{10.20\%}$

The expected return on Security A is 10.20%.

Variance$_A$ (σ_A^2) $= (0.40)(0.03 - 0.102)^2 + (0.60)(0.15 - 0.102)^2$
$= 0.003456$

Standard Deviation$_A$ (σ_A) $= (0.003456)^{1/2}$
$= 0.0588$
$= \mathbf{5.88\%}$

The standard deviation of the returns on Security A is 5.88%.

Expected Return$_B$ $= (0.40)(0.065) + (0.60)(0.065)$
$= 0.0650$
$= \mathbf{6.50\%}$

The expected return on Security B is 6.50%.

Variance$_B$ (σ_B^2) $= (0.40)(0.065 - 0.065)^2 + (0.60)(0.065 - 0.065)^2$
$= 0$

Standard Deviation$_B$ (σ_B) $= (0)^{1/2}$
$= 0.00$
$= \mathbf{0\%}$

The standard deviation of the returns on Security B is 0%.

b.   Total Value of her portfolio $= \$2,500 + \$3,500$
$= \$6,000$

Weight of Security A $= \$2,500 / \$6,000$
$= 5/12$

Weight of Security B   = \$3,500 / \$6,000
                         = 7/12

$E(R_P) = (W_A)[E(R_A)] + (W_B)[E(R_B)]$

where $E(R_P)$ = the expected return on the portfolio
        $E(R_A)$ = the expected return on Security A
        $E(R_B)$ = the expected return on Security B
        W_A = the weight of Security A in the portfolio
        W_B = the weight of Security B in the portfolio

$E(R_P) = (W_A)[E(R_A)] + (W_B)[E(R_B)]$
$= (5/12)(0.102) + (7/12)(0.065)$
$= 0.0804$
$= 8.04\%$

The expected return of her portfolio is 8.04%.

The variance of a portfolio equals:

$\sigma^2_P = (W_A)^2(\sigma_A)^2 + (W_B)^2(\sigma_B)^2 + (2)(W_A)(W_B)(\sigma_A)(\sigma_B)[Correlation(R_A, R_B)]$

where σ^2_P = the variance of the portfolio
        W_A = the weight of Security A in the portfolio
        W_B = the weight of Security B in the portfolio
        σ_A = the standard deviation of Security A
        σ_B = the standard deviation of Security B
        R_A = the return on Security A
        R_B = the return on Security B

$\sigma^2_P = (W_A)^2(\sigma_A)^2 + (W_B)^2(\sigma_B)^2 + (2)(W_A)(W_B)(\sigma_A)(\sigma_B)[Correlation(R_A, R_B)]$
$= (5/12)^2(0.0588)^2 + (7/12)^2(0)^2 + (2)(5/12)(7/12)(0.0588)(0)(0)$
$= 0.000600$

The standard deviation of the portfolio equals:

$\sigma_P = (\sigma^2_P)^{1/2}$

where σ_P = the standard deviation of the portfolio
                σ^2_P = the variance of the portfolio

$\sigma_P = (0.00600)^{1/2}$
$= 0.0245$
$= 2.45\%$

The standard deviation of her portfolio is 2.45%.

10.12   The wide fluctuations in the price of oil stocks do not indicate that these stocks are a poor investment. If an oil stock is purchased as part of a well-diversified portfolio, only its contribution to the risk of the entire portfolio matters. This contribution is measured by systematic risk or beta. Since price fluctuations in oil stocks reflect diversifiable plus non-diversifiable risk, observing the standard deviation of price movements is not an adequate measure of the appropriateness of adding oil stocks to a portfolio.

10.13   a. $\text{Expected Return}_1 = (0.10)(0.25) + (0.40)(0.20) + (0.40)(0.15) + (0.10)(0.10)$

$$= 0.1750$$
$$= \mathbf{0.1750}$$

The expected return on Security 1 is 17.50%.

$\text{Variance}_1\ (\sigma_1{}^2) = (0.10)(0.25 - 0.175)^2 + (0.40)(0.20 - 0.175)^2 + (0.40)(0.15 - 0.175)^2$
$$+ (0.10)(0.10 - 0.175)^2$$
$$= 0.001625$$

$\text{Standard Deviation}_1\ (\sigma_1) = (0.001625)^{1/2}$
$$= 0.0403$$
$$= \mathbf{4.03\%}$$

The standard deviation of the returns on Security 1 is 4.03%.

$\text{Expected Return}_2 = (0.10)(0.25) + (0.40)(0.15) + (0.40)(0.20) + (0.10)(0.10)$
$$= 0.1750$$
$$= \mathbf{0.1750}$$

The expected return on Security 2 is 17.50%.

$\text{Variance}_2\ (\sigma_2{}^2) = (0.10)(0.25 - 0.175)^2 + (0.40)(0.15 - 0.175)^2 + (0.40)(0.20 - 0.175)^2$
$$+ (0.10)(0.10 - 0.175)^2$$
$$= 0.001625$$

$\text{Standard Deviation}_2\ (\sigma_2) = (0.001625)^{1/2}$
$$= 0.0403$$
$$= \mathbf{4.03\%}$$

The standard deviation of the returns on Security 2 is 4.03%.

$\text{Expected Return}_3 = (0.10)(0.10) + (0.40)(0.15) + (0.40)(0.20) + (0.10)(0.25)$
$$= 0.1750$$
$$= \mathbf{0.1750}$$

The expected return on Security 3 is 17.50%.

$\text{Variance}_3(\sigma_3{}^2) = (0.10)(0.10 - 0.175)^2 + (0.40)(0.15 - 0.175)^2 + (0.40)(0.20 - 0.175)^2$
$$+ (0.25)(0.10 - 0.175)^2$$
$$= 0.001625$$

$\text{Standard Deviation}_3\ (\sigma_3) = (0.001625)^{1/2}$
$$= 0.0403$$
$$= \mathbf{4.03\%}$$

The standard deviation of the returns on Security 3 is 4.03%.

      b. $\text{Covariance}(R_1, R_2) = (0.10)(0.25 - 0.175)(0.25 - 0.175) + (0.40)(0.20 - 0.175)(0.15 - 0.175) +$
$$+ (0.40)(0.15 - 0.175)(0.20 - 0.175) + (0.10)(0.10 - 0.175)(0.10 - 0.175)$$
$$= \mathbf{0.000625}$$

The covariance between the returns on Security 1 and Security 2 is 0.000625.

$$\text{Correlation}(R_1,R_2) = \text{Covariance}(R_1, R_2) / (\sigma_1 * \sigma_2)$$
$$= 0.000625 / (0.0403 * 0.0403)$$
$$= \mathbf{0.3848}$$

The correlation between the returns on Security 1 and Security 2 is 0.3848.

$$\text{Covariance}(R_1, R_3) = (0.10)(0.25 - 0.175)(0.10 - 0.175) + (0.40)(0.20 - 0.175)(0.15 - 0.175) +$$
$$+ (0.40)(0.15 - 0.175)(0.20 - 0.175) + (0.10)(0.10 - 0.175)(0.25 - 0.175)$$
$$= \mathbf{-0.001625}$$

The covariance between the returns on Security 1 and Security 3 is -0.001625.

$$\text{Correlation}(R_1,R_3) = \text{Covariance}(R_1, R_3) / (\sigma_1 * \sigma_3)$$
$$= -0.001625 / (0.0403 * 0.0403)$$
$$= \mathbf{-1}$$

The correlation between the returns on Security 1 and Security 3 is -1.

$$\text{Covariance}(R_2, R_3) = (0.10)(0.25 - 0.175)(0.10 - 0.175) + (0.40)(0.15 - 0.175)(0.15 - 0.175) +$$
$$+ (0.40)(0.20 - 0.175)(0.20 - 0.175) + (0.10)(0.10 - 0.175)(0.25 - 0.175)$$
$$= \mathbf{-0.000625}$$

The covariance between the returns on Security 2 and Security 3 is -0.000625.

$$\text{Correlation}(R_2,R_3) = \text{Covariance}(R_2, R_3) / (\sigma_2 * \sigma_3)$$
$$= -0.000625 / (0.0403 * 0.0403)$$
$$= \mathbf{-0.3848}$$

The correlation between the returns on Security 2 and Security 3 is –0.3848.

c. The expected return on the portfolio equals:

$$E(R_P) = (W_1)[E(R_1)] + (W_2)[E(R_2)]$$

where $E(R_P)$ = the expected return on the portfolio
           $E(R_1)$ = the expected return on Security 1
           $E(R_2)$ = the expected return on Security 2
           W_1 = the weight of Security 1 in the portfolio
           W_2 = the weight of Security 2 in the portfolio

$$E(R_P) = (W_1)[E(R_1)] + (W_2)[E(R_2)]$$
$$= (1/2)(0.175) + (1/2)(0.175)$$
$$= 0.175$$
$$= \mathbf{17.50\%}$$

The expected return of the portfolio is 17.50%.

The variance of a portfolio equals:

$$\sigma^2_P = (W_1)^2(\sigma_1)^2 + (W_2)^2(\sigma_2)^2 + (2)(W_1)(W_2)(\sigma_1)(\sigma_2)[\text{Correlation}(R_1, R_2)]$$

where σ^2_P = the variance of the portfolio
           W_1 = the weight of Security 1 in the portfolio
           W_2 = the weight of Security 2 in the portfolio
           σ_1 = the standard deviation of Security 1
           σ_2 = the standard deviation of Security 2
           R_1 = the return on Security 1
           R_2 = the return on Security 2

$$\begin{aligned}
\sigma^2_P &= (W_1)^2(\sigma_1)^2 + (W_2)^2(\sigma_2)^2 + (2)(W_1)(W_2)(\sigma_1)(\sigma_2)\ [\text{Correlation}(R_1, R_2)] \\
&= (1/2)^2(0.0403)^2 + (1/2)^2(0.0403)^2 + (2)(1/2)(1/2)(0.0403)(0.0403)(0.3848) \\
&= 0.001125
\end{aligned}$$

The standard deviation of the portfolio equals:

$$\sigma_P = (\sigma^2_P)^{1/2}$$

where σ_P = the standard deviation of the portfolio
                      σ^2_P = the variance of the portfolio

$$\begin{aligned}
\sigma_P &= (0.001125)^{1/2} \\
&= 0.0335 \\
&= \mathbf{3.35\%}
\end{aligned}$$

The standard deviation of the returns on the portfolio is 3.35%.

d. $$\begin{aligned}
E(R_P) &= (W_1)[E(R_1)] + (W_3)[E(R_3)] \\
&= (1/2)(0.175) + (1/2)(0.175) \\
&= 0.175 \\
&= \mathbf{17.50\%}
\end{aligned}$$

The expected return on the portfolio is 17.50%.

$$\begin{aligned}
\sigma^2_P &= (W_1)^2(\sigma_1)^2 + (W_3)^2(\sigma_3)^2 + (2)(W_1)(W_3)(\sigma_1)(\sigma_3)\ [\text{Correlation}(R_1, R_3)] \\
&= (1/2)^2(0.0403)^2 + (1/2)^2(0.0403)^2 + (2)(1/2)(1/2)(0.0403)(0.0403)(-1) \\
&= 0
\end{aligned}$$

$$\begin{aligned}
\sigma_P &= (0)^{1/2} \\
&= 0 \\
&= \mathbf{0\%}
\end{aligned}$$

The standard deviation of the returns on the portfolio is 0%.

e. $$\begin{aligned}
E(R_P) &= (W_2)[E(R_2)] + (W_2)[E(R_3)] \\
&= (1/2)(0.175) + (1/2)(0.175) \\
&= 0.175 \\
&= \mathbf{17.50\%}
\end{aligned}$$

The expected return of the portfolio is 17.50%.

$$\begin{aligned}
\sigma^2_P &= (W_2)^2(\sigma_2)^2 + (W_3)^2(\sigma_3)^2 + (2)(W_2)(W_3)(\sigma_2)(\sigma_3)\ [\text{Correlation}(R_2, R_3)] \\
&= (1/2)^2(0.0403)^2 + (1/2)^2(0.0403)^2 + (2)(1/2)(1/2)(0.0403)(0.0403)(-0.3848) \\
&= 0.000500
\end{aligned}$$

$$\sigma_P = (0.000500)^{1/2}$$
$$= 0.0224$$
$$= \textbf{2.24\%}$$

The standard deviation of the returns on the portfolio is 2.24%.

f. As long as the correlation between the returns on two securities is below 1, there is a benefit to diversification. A portfolio with negatively correlated stocks can achieve greater risk reduction than a portfolio with positively correlated stocks, holding the expected return on each stock constant. Applying proper weights on perfectly negatively correlated stocks can reduce portfolio variance to 0.

10.14 a.

State	Return on A	Return on B	Probability
1	15%	35%	(0.40)(0.50) = 0.2
2	15%	-5%	(0.40)(0.50) = 0.2
3	10%	35%	(0.60)(0.50) = 0.3
4	10%	-5%	(0.60)(0.50) = 0.3

b.
$$E(R_P) = (0.20)[(0.50)(0.15) + (0.50)(0.35)] + (0.20)[(0.50)(0.15) + (0.50)(-0.05)] +$$
$$(0.30)[(0.50)(0.10) + (0.50)(0.35)] + (0.30)[(0.50)(0.10) + (0.50)(-0.05)]$$
$$= 0.135$$
$$= \textbf{13.5\%}$$

The expected return on the portfolio is 13.5%.

10.15 a. The expected return on a portfolio equals:

$$E(R_P) = \Sigma\, E(R_i)\, /\, N$$

where $E(R_P)$ = the expected return on the portfolio
$E(R_i)$ = the expected return on Security i
N = the number of securities in the portfolio

$$E(R_P) = \Sigma\, E(R_i)\, /\, N$$
$$= [(0.10)(N)]\, /\, N$$
$$= 0.10$$
$$= \textbf{10\%}$$

The expected return on an equally weighted portfolio containing all N securities is 10%.

The variance of a portfolio equals:

$$\sigma_P^2 = \Sigma\,\Sigma\, [\text{Covariance}(R_i, R_j)\, /\, N^2] + \Sigma\, \sigma_i^2\, /\, N^2$$

where σ_P^2 = the variance of the portfolio
R_i = the returns on security i
R_j = the return on security j
N = the number of securities in the portfolio
σ_i^2 = the variance of security i

$$\sigma_P^2 = \Sigma\,\Sigma\, [\text{Covariance}(R_i, R_j)\, /\, N^2] + \Sigma\, \sigma_i^2\, /\, N^2$$

Since there are N securities, there are (N)(N-1) different pairs of covariances between the returns on these securities.

$$\sigma_P^2 = (N)(N-1)(0.0064) / N^2 + [N(0.0144)] / N^2$$
$$= (0.0064)(N-1) / N + (0.0144)/(N)$$

The variance of an equally weighted portfolio containing all N securities can be represented by the following expression:

(0.0064)(N-1) / N + (0.0144)/(N)

b. As N approaches infinity, the expression (N-1)/N approaches 1 and the expression (1/N) approaches 0. It follows that, as N approaches infinity, the variance of the portfolio approaches 0.0064 [= (0.0064)(1) + (0.0144)(0)], which equals the covariance between any two individual securities in the portfolio.

c. The covariance of the returns on the securities is the most important factor to consider when placing securities into a well-diversified portfolio.

10.16 The statement is false. Once the stock is part of a well-diversified portfolio, the important factor is the contribution of the stock to the variance of the portfolio. In a well-diversified portfolio, this contribution is the covariance of the stock with the rest of the portfolio.

10.17 The covariance is a more appropriate measure of a security's risk in a well-diversified portfolio because the covariance reflects the effect of the security on the variance of the portfolio. Investors are concerned with the variance of their portfolios and not the variance of the individual securities. Since covariance measures the impact of an individual security on the variance of the portfolio, covariance is the appropriate measure of risk.

10.18 If we assume that the market has not stayed constant during the past three years, then the lack in movement of Southern Co.'s stock price only indicates that the stock either has a standard deviation or a beta that is very near to zero. The large amount of movement in Texas Instrument' stock price does not imply that the firm's beta is high. Total volatility (the price fluctuation) is a function of both systematic and unsystematic risk. The beta only reflects the systematic risk. Observing the standard deviation of price movements does not indicate whether the price changes were due to systematic factors or firm specific factors. Thus, if you observe large stock price movements like that of TI, you cannot claim that the beta of the stock is high. All you know is that the total risk of TI is high.

10.19 Because a well-diversified portfolio has no unsystematic risk, this portfolio should like on the Capital Market Line (CML). The slope of the CML equals:

$$\text{Slope}_{CML} = [E(R_M) - r_f] / \sigma_M$$

where $E(R_M)$ = the expected return on the market portfolio
  r_f = the risk-free rate
  σ_M = the standard deviation of the market portfolio

$$\text{Slope}_{CML} = [E(R_M) - r_f] / \sigma_M$$
$$= (0.12 - 0.05) / 0.10$$
$$= 0.70$$

a. The expected return on the portfolio equals:

$$E(R_P) = r_f + \text{Slope}_{CML}(\sigma_P)$$

where $E(R_P)$ = the expected return on the portfolio
r_f = the risk-free rate
σ_P = the standard deviation of the portfolio

$$E(R_P) = r_f + Slope_{CML}(\sigma_P)$$
$$= 0.05 + (0.70)(0.07)$$
$$= 0.99$$
$$= \mathbf{9.9\%}$$

A portfolio with a standard deviation of 7% has an expected return of 9.9%.

b. $E(R_P) = r_f + Slope_{CML}(\sigma_P)$
$0.20 = 0.05 + (0.70)(\sigma_P)$

$\sigma_P = (0.20 - 0.05) / 0.70$
$= 0.2143$
$= \mathbf{21.43\%}$

A portfolio with an expected return of 20% has a standard deviation of 21.43%.

10.20 a. The slope of the Characteristic Line (CL) of Fuji equals:

$$Slope_{CL} = [E(R_{FUJI})_{BULL} - E(R_{FUJI})_{BEAR}] / [(R_M)_{BULL} - (R_M)_{BEAR}]$$

where $E(R_{FUJI})_{BULL}$ = the expected return on Fuji in a bull market
$E(R_{FUJI})_{BEAR}$ = the expected return on Fuji in a bear market
$(R_M)_{BULL}$ = the return on the market portfolio in a bull market
$(R_M)_{BEAR}$ = the return on the market portfolio in a bear market

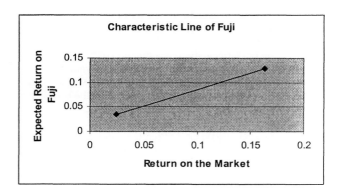

$$Slope_{CL} = [E(R_{FUJI})_{BULL} - E(R_{FUJI})_{BEAR}] / [(R_M)_{BULL} - (R_M)_{BEAR}]$$
$$= (0.128 - 0.034) / (0.163 - 0.025)$$
$$= \mathbf{0.68}$$

Beta, by definition, equals the slope of the characteristic line. Therefore, Fuji's beta is 0.68.

10.21 Polonius' portfolio will be the market portfolio. He will have no borrowing or lending in his portfolio.

10.22 a. $E(R_P) = (1/3)(0.10) + (1/3)(0.14) + (1/3)(0.20)$
$= 0.1467$
$= \mathbf{14.67\%}$

The expected return on an equally weighted portfolio is 14.67%.

b.   The beta of a portfolio equals the weighted average of the betas of the individual securities within the portfolio.

β_P = (1/3)(0.7) + (1/3)(1.2) + (1/3)(1.8)
   = **1.23**

The beta of an equally weighted portfolio is 1.23.

c.   If the Capital Asset Pricing Model holds, the three securities should be located on a straight line (the Security Market Line). For this to be true, the slopes between each of the points must be equal.

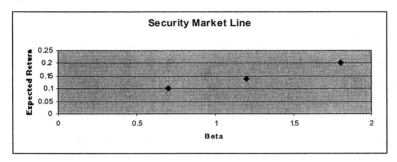

Slope between A and B = (0.14 – 0.10) / (1.2 – 0.7)
              = 0.08

Slope between A and C = (0.20 – 0.10) / (1.8 – 0.7)
              = 0.091

Slope between B and C = (0.20 – 0.14) / (1.8 – 1.2)
              = 0.10

Since the slopes between the three points are different, the securities are not correctly priced according to the Capital Asset Pricing Model.

10.23   According to the Capital Asset Pricing Model:

$E(r)$ = r_f + β(EMRP)

   where $E(r)$ = the expected return on the stock
        r_f = the risk-free rate
        β = the stock's beta
        EMRP = the expected market risk premium

In this problem:

        r_f = 0.06
        β = 1.2
        EMRP = 0.085

The expected return on Holup's stock is:

$$E(r) = r_f + \beta(EMRP)$$
$$= 0.06 + 1.2(0.085)$$
$$= \mathbf{0.162}$$

The expected return on Holup's stock is 16.2%.

10.24   According to the Capital Asset Pricing Model:

$$E(r) = r_f + \beta(EMRP)$$

where $E(r)$ = the expected return on the stock
        r_f = the risk-free rate
        β = the stock's beta
        EMRP = the expected market risk premium

In this problem:

$$r_f = 0.06$$
$$\beta = 0.80$$
$$EMRP = 0.085$$

The expected return on Stock A equals:

$$E(r) = r_f + \beta(EMRP)$$
$$= 0.06 + 0.80(0.085)$$
$$= \mathbf{0.128}$$

The expected return on Stock A is 12.8%.

10.25   According to the Capital Asset Pricing Model:

$$E(r) = r_f + \beta[E(r_m) - r_f]$$

where $E(r)$ = the expected return on the stock
        r_f = the risk-free rate
        β = the stock's beta
        $E(r_m)$ = the expected return on the market portfolio

In this problem:

$$r_f = 0.08$$
$$\beta = 1.5$$
$$E(r_m) = 0.15$$

The expected return on Stock B equals:

$$E(r) = r_f + \beta[E(r_m) - r_f]$$
$$= 0.08 + 1.5(0.15 - 0.08)$$
$$= \mathbf{0.185}$$

The expected return on Stock B is 18.5%.

10.26   According to the Capital Asset Pricing Model:

$E(r) = r_f + \beta(EMRP)$

where $E(r)$ = the expected return on the stock
         r_f = the risk-free rate
         β = the stock's beta
         $EMRP$ = the expected market risk premium

In this problem:

$E(r)$ = 0.142
r_f = 0.037
$EMRP$ = 0.075

$E(r) = r_f + \beta(EMRP)$
$0.142 = 0.037 + \beta(0.075)$

$\beta = (0.142 - 0.037) / 0.075$
$\quad = \mathbf{1.4}$

The beta of Tristar's stock is 1.4.

10.27   Because the Capital Asset Pricing Model holds, both securities must lie on the Security Market Line (SML). Given the betas and expected returns on the two stocks, solve for the slope of the SML.

Slope of SML = $[E(r_{MP}) - E(r_{PSD})] / (\beta_{MP} - \beta_{PSD})$

where $E(r_{MP})$ = the expected return on Murck Pharmaceutical
         $E(r_{PSD})$ = the expected return on Pizer Drug Corp
         β_{MP} = the beta of Murck Phamraceutical
         β_{PSD} = the beta of Pizer Drug Corp

Security Market Line

Slope of SML = $[E(r_{MP}) - E(r_{PSD})] / (\beta_{MP} - \beta_{PSD})$
             = $(0.25 - 0.14) / (1.4 - 0.7)$
             = 0.1571

A security with a beta of 0.7 has an expected return of 0.14. As you move along the SML from a beta of 0.7 to a beta of 1, beta increases by 0.3 (= 1 − 0.7). Since the slope of the security market line is 0.1571, as beta increases by 0.3, expected return increases by 0.0471 (= 0.3 * 0.1571). Therefore, the expected return on a security with a beta of one equals 18.71% (= 0.14 + 0.0471).

Since the market portfolio has a beta of one, the expected return on the market portfolio is 18.71%.

According to the Capital Asset Pricing Model:

$$E(r) = r_f + \beta[E(r_m) - r_f]$$

where
- $E(r)$ = the expected return on the security
- r_f = the risk-free rate
- β = the security's beta
- $E(r_m)$ = the expected return on the market portfolio

Since Murck Pharmaceutical has a beta of 1.4 and an expected return of 0.25, we know that:

$$0.25 = r_f + 1.4(0.1871 - r_f)$$

$$r_f = \mathbf{0.03}$$

The risk-free rate is 3%.

Thus, the entire SML looks like:

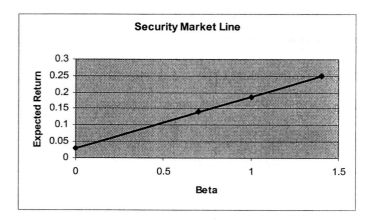

10.28   a. $E(r_A) = (0.25)(-0.10) + (0.50)(0.10) + (0.25)(0.20)$
                 $= \mathbf{0.075}$

        The expected return on Stock A is 7.5%.

        $E(r_B) = (0.25)(-0.30) + (0.50)(0.05) + (0.25)(0.40)$
                 $= \mathbf{0.05}$
        The expected return on Stock B is 5%.

    b.   From part *a*, we know that:

        $E(r_A) = 0.075$
        $E(r_B) = 0.05$

We also know that the beta of A is 0.25 greater than the beta of B. Therefore, as beta increases by 0.25, the expected return on a security increases by 0.025 (= 0.075 – 0.5). Consider the following graph:

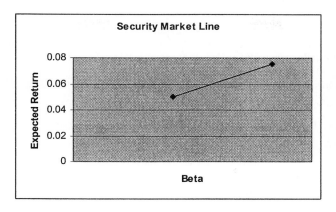

The slope of the security market line (SML) equals:

$$Slope_{SML} = Rise / Run$$
$$= Increase\ in\ Expected\ Return\ /\ Increase\ in\ Beta$$
$$= (0.075 – 0.05) / 0.25$$
$$= 0.10$$

The slope of the Security Market Line equals 10%.

The expected market risk premium is the difference between the expected return on the market and the risk-free rate. Since the market's beta is 1 and the risk-free rate has a beta of zero, the slope of the Security Market Line equals the expected market risk premium.

The expected market risk premium is 10%.

10.29   a.

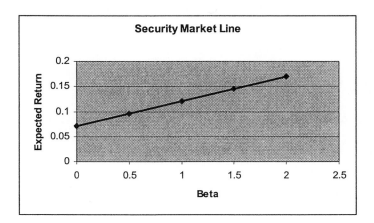

b.   According to the security market line drawn in part a, a security with a beta of 0.80 should have an expected return of:

$$E(r) = r_f + \beta(\text{EMRP})$$
$$= 0.07 + 0.8(0.05)$$
$$= 0.11$$
$$= 11\%$$

Since this asset has an expected return of only 9%, it lies below the security market line. Because the asset lies below the security market line, it is overpriced. Investors will sell the overpriced security until its price falls sufficiently so that its expected return rises to 11%.

c.   According to the security market line drawn in part *a*, a security with a beta of 3 should have an expected return of:

$$E(r) = r_f + \beta(\text{EMRP})$$
$$= 0.07 + 3(0.05)$$
$$= 0.22$$
$$= 22\%$$

Since this asset has an expected return of 25%, it lies above the security market line. Because the asset lies above the security market line, it is underpriced. Investors will buy the underpriced security until its price rises sufficiently so that its expected return falls to 22%.

10.30   According to the Capital Asset Pricing Model (CAPM), the expected return on the stock should be:

$$E(r) = r_f + \beta(\text{EMRP})$$

where $E(r)$ = the expected return on the stock
r_f = the risk-free rate
β = the stock's beta
EMRP   = the expected market risk premium

$$E(r) = r_f + \beta(\text{EMRP})$$
$$= 0.05 + 1.8(0.08)$$
$$= \mathbf{0.194}$$

According to the CAPM, the expected return on the stock should be 19.4%. However, the security analyst expects the return to be only 18%. Therefore, the analyst is pessimistic about this stock relative to the market's expectations.

10.31   a.   According to the Capital Asset Pricing Model:

$$E(r) = r_f + \beta[E(r_m) - r_f]$$

where $E(r)$ = the expected return on the stock
r_f = the risk-free rate
β = the stock's beta
$E(r_m)$ = the expected return on the market portfolio

In this problem:

r_f = 0.064
β = 1.2
$E(r_m)$ = 0.138

The expected return on Solomon's stock is:

$$E(r) = r_f + \beta[E(r_m) - r_f]$$
$$= 0.064 + 1.2(0.138 - 0.064)$$
$$= \mathbf{0.1528}$$

The expected return on Solomon's stock is 15.28%.

b. If the risk-free rate decreases to 3.5%, the expected return on Solomon's stock is:

$$E(r) = r_f + \beta[E(r_m) - r_f]$$
$$= 0.035 + 1.2(0.138 - 0.035)$$
$$= \mathbf{0.1586}$$

The expected return on Solomon's stock is 15.86%.

10.32   First, calculate the standard deviation of the market portfolio using the Capital Market Line (CML).

We know that the risk-free rate asset has a return of 5% and a standard deviation of zero and the portfolio has an expected return of 25% and a standard deviation of 4%. These two points must lie on the Capital Market Line.

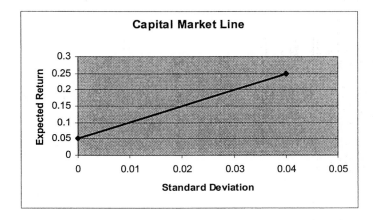

The slope of the Capital Market Line equals:

$Slope_{CML}$ = Rise / Run
= Increase in Expected Return / Increase in Standard Deviation
= (0.25– 0.05) / (0.04 - 0)
= 5

According to the Capital Market Line:

$$E(r_i) = r_f + Slope_{CML}(\sigma_i)$$

where $E(r)$ = the expected return on security i
r_f = the risk-free rate
$Slope_{CML}$ = the slope of the Capital Market Line
σ_i = the standard deviation of security i

Since we know the expected return on the market portfolio is 20%, the risk-free rate is 5%, and the slope of the Capital Market Line is 5, we can solve for the standard deviation of the market portfolio (σ_m).

$E(r_m)$ $= r_f + \text{Slope}_{CML}(\sigma_m)$
0.20 $= 0.05 + (5)(\sigma_m)$

σ_m $= (0.20 - 0.05) / 5$
$= 0.03$

The standard deviation of the market portfolio is 3%.

Next, use the standard deviation of the market portfolio to solve for the beta of a security that has a correlation with the market portfolio of 0.5 and a standard deviation of 2%.

$\beta_{Security}$ $= [\text{Correlation}(R_{Security}, R_{Market})*(\sigma_{Security})] / \sigma_{Market}$
$= (0.5*0.02) / 0.03$
$= 1/3$

The beta of the security equals 1/3.

According to the Capital Asset Pricing Model:

$E(r) = r_f + \beta[E(r_m) - r_f]$

	where	$E(r)$	= the expected return on the security
		r_f	= the risk-free rate
		β	= the security's beta
		$E(r_m)$	= the expected return on the market portfolio

In this problem:

r_f $= 0.05$
β $= 1/3$
$E(r_m)$ $= 0.20$

$E(r) = r_f + \beta[E(r_m) - r_f]$
$= 0.05 + 1/3(0.20 - 0.05)$
$= \mathbf{0.10}$

A security with a correlation of 0.5 with the market portfolio and a standard deviation of 2% has an expected return of 10%.

10.33 a. According to the Capital Asset Pricing Model:

$E(r) = r_f + \beta(EMRP)$

	where	$E(r)$	= the expected return on the stock
		r_f	= the risk-free rate
		β	= the stock's beta
		$EMRP$	= the expected market risk premium

In this problem:

$E(r)$ $= 0.167$
r_f $= 0.076$
β $= 1.7$

$E(r) = r_f + \beta(EMRP)$

$0.167 = 0.076 + 1.7(EMRP)$

$EMRP = (0.167 - 0.076) / 1.7$

$= \mathbf{0.0535}$

The expected market risk premium is 5.35%.

b. According to the Capital Asset Pricing Model:

$E(r) = r_f + \beta(EMRP)$

where $E(r)$ = the expected return on the stock
r_f = the risk-free rate
β = the stock's beta
$EMRP$ = the expected market risk premium

In this problem:

$r_f = 0.076$
$\beta = 0.8$
$EMRP = 0.0535$

$E(r) = r_f + \beta(EMRP)$

$= 0.076 + 0.8(0.0535)$

$= \mathbf{0.1188}$

The expected return on Magnolia stock is 11.88%.

c. The beta of a portfolio is the weighted average of the betas of the individual securities in the portfolio. The beta of Potpourri is 1.7, the beta of Magnolia is 0.8, and the beta of a portfolio consisting of both Potpourri and Magnolia is 1.07.

Therefore:

$1.07 = (W_P)(1.7) + (W_M)(0.8)$

where W_P = the weight of Potpourri stock in the portfolio
W_M = the weight of Magnolia stock in the portfolio

Because your total investment must equal 100%:

$W_P = 1 - W_M$

$1.07 = (1 - W_M)(1.7) + (W_M)(0.8)$

$1.07 = 1.7 - 1.7W_M + 0.8W_M$

$-0.63 = -0.90W_M$

$W_M = \mathbf{0.70}$

$W_P = 1 - W_M$

$= 1 - 0.70$

$= \mathbf{0.30}$

You have 70% of your portfolio ($7,000) invested in Magnolia stock and 30% of your portfolio ($3,000) invested in Potpourri stock.

$$E(r) \quad = (0.70)(0.1188) + (0.30)(0.167)$$
$$= \mathbf{0.1333}$$

The expected return of the portfolio is 13.33%.

10.34   According to the Capital Asset Pricing Model:

$$E(r_P) \quad = r_f + \beta_P[E(r_m) - r_f]$$

where $E(r_P)$ = the expected return on the portfolio
r_f = the risk-free rate
β_P = the beta of the portfolio
$E(r_m)$ = the expected return on the market portfolio

The beta of a portfolio equals:

$$\beta_P \quad = [Correlation(R_P, R_m) * \sigma_P] / \sigma_m$$

where R_P = the return on the portfolio
R_m = the return on the market portfolio
σ_P = the standard deviation of the portfolio
σ_m = the standard deviation of the market portfolio

Since the market portfolio has a variance of 0.0121, it has a standard deviation of 11% [$= (0.0121)^{1/2}$].
Since the portfolio has a variance of 0.0169, it has a standard deviation of 13% [$= (0.0169)^{1/2}$].

Therefore, the beta of the portfolio equals:

$$\beta_P \quad = [Correlation(R_P, R_m) * \sigma_P] / \sigma_m$$
$$= (0.45*0.13) / 0.11$$
$$= 0.5318$$

The beta of the portfolio is 0.5318.

The expected return on the portfolio is:

$$E(r_P) \quad = r_f + \beta_P[E(r_m) - r_f]$$
$$= 0.063 + 0.5318(0.148 - 0.063)$$
$$= \mathbf{0.1082}$$

The expected return on portfolio Z is 10.82%.

10.35   a.   The equation for the Security Market Line is:

$$E(r) = r_f + \beta(EMRP)$$

Since the risk-free rate equals 4.9% and the expected market risk premium is 9.4%, the CAPM implies:

$$E(r) = 0.049 + \beta(0.094)$$

b.   First, calculate the beta of Durham Company's stock.

$$\beta = Covariance(R_{Durham}, R_{Market}) / (\sigma_{Market})^2$$

= 0.0635 / 0.04326
= 1.467

Use the Capital Asset Pricing Model to determine the required return on Durham's stock.

According to the Capital Asset Pricing Model:

$$E(r) = r_f + \beta(EMRP)$$

where $E(r)$ = the expected return
         r_f = the risk-free rate
         β = the stock's beta
         EMRP   = the expected market risk premium

In this problem:
         r_f = 0.049
         β = 1.467
         EMRP   = 0.094

$E(r)$ $= r_f + \beta(EMRP)$
       $= 0.049 + 1.467(0.094)$
       $= \mathbf{0.1869}$

The required return on Durham's stock is 18.69%.

10.36   Because the Capital Asset Pricing Model holds, both securities must lie on the Security Market Line (SML). Given the betas and expected returns of the two stocks, solve for the slope of the SML.

Slope of SML $= [E(r_J) - E(r_W)] / (\beta_J - \beta_W)$

where $E(r_J)$ = the expected return on Johnson's stock
         $E(r_W)$ = the expected return on Williamson's Stock
         β_J = the beta of Johnson's stock
         β_W = the beta of Williamson's stock

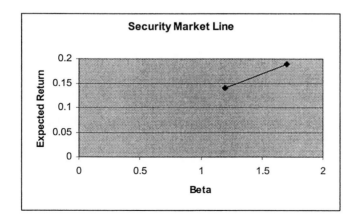

Slope of SML $= [E(r_J) - E(r_W)] / (\beta_J - \beta_W)$
             $= (0.19 - 0.14) / (1.7 - 1.2)$
             $= 0.10$

A security with a beta of 1.2 has an expected return of 0.14. As you move along the SML from a beta of 1.2 to a beta of 1, beta decreases by 0.2 (= 1.2 – 1). Since the slope of the security market line is 0.10, as beta decreases by 0.2, expected return decreases by 0.02 (= 0.2 * 0.10). Therefore, the expected return on a security with a beta of one equals 12% (= 0.14 - 0.02).

Since the market portfolio has a beta of one, the expected return on the market portfolio is 12%.

According to the Capital Asset Pricing Model:

$E(r) = r_f + \beta[E(r_m) – r_f]$

where $E(r)$ = the expected return on the security
           r_f = the risk-free rate
           β = the security's beta
           $E(r_m)$ = the expected return on the market portfolio

Since Williamson has a beta of 1.2 and an expected return of 0.14, we know that:

$0.14 = r_f + 1.2(0.12 – r_f)$

$r_f = 0.02$

The risk-free rate is 2%.

Thus, the entire SML looks like:

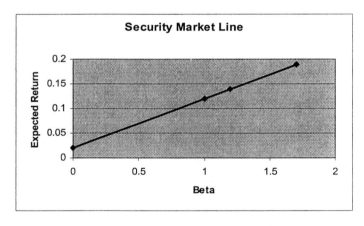

10.37   The statement is false. If a security has a negative beta, investors would want to hold the asset to reduce the variability of their portfolios. Those assets will have expected returns that are lower than the risk-free rate. To see this, examine the Capital Asset Pricing Model.

$E(r) = r_f + \beta[E(r_m) – r_f]$

where $E(r)$ = the expected return on a security
           r_f = the risk-free rate
           β = the security's beta
           $E(r_m)$ = the expected return on the market portfolio

If $\beta < 0$, $E(r) < r_f$

10.38   First, determine the beta of the portfolio.

Total Amount Invested   = $5,000 + $10,000 + $8,000 + $7,000
= $30,000

Weight of Stock A = $5,000 / $30,000 = 1/6
Weight of Stock B = $10,000 / $30,000 = 1/3
Weight of Stock C = $8,000 / $30,000 = 4/15
Weight of Stock D = $7,000 / $30,000 = 7/30

The beta of a portfolio is the weighted average of the betas of its individual securities.

$\beta_{Portfolio}$ = (1/6)(0.75) + (1/3)(1.1) + (4/15)(1.36) + (7/30)(1.88)
= 1.293

Use the Capital Asset Pricing Model (CAPM) to find the expected return on the portfolio.

According to the CAPM:

$E(r) = r_f + \beta[E(r_m) - r_f]$

where $E(r)$ = the expected return on the portfolio
r_f = the risk-free rate
β = the portfolio's beta
$E(r_m)$ = the expected return on the market portfolio

In this problem:

r_f = 0.04
β = 1.293
$E(r_m)$ = 0.15

$E(r) = r_f + \beta[E(r_m) - r_f]$
= 0.04 + 1.293(0.15 − 0.04)
= **0.1822**

The expected return on the portfolio is 18.22%.

10.39   a.   Let β_i = the beta of Security i
σ_i = the standard deviation of Security i
σ_m = the standard deviation of the market
$\rho_{i,m}$ = the correlation between returns on Security i and the market

(i) β_i $= (\rho_{i,m})(\sigma_i) / \sigma_m$
$0.9 = (\rho_{i,m})(0.12) / 0.10$

$\rho_{i,m} = \textbf{0.75}$

Beta = $\dfrac{(Corr)(SD)}{SD_{(M)}}$

(ii) β_i $= (\rho_{i,m})(\sigma_i) / \sigma_m$
$1.1 = (0.4)(\sigma_i) / 0.10$

σ_i = **0.275**

(iii) β_i $= (\rho_{i;m})(\sigma_i) / \sigma_m$
$= (0.75)(0.24) / 0.10$
$= \mathbf{1.8}$

(iv) The market has a correlation of 1 with itself.

(v) The beta of the market is 1.

(vi) The risk-free asset has 0 standard deviation.

(vii) The risk-free asset has 0 correlation with the market portfolio.

(viii) The beta of the risk-free asset is 0.

b. According to the Capital Asset Pricing Model:

$E(r) = r_f + \beta[E(r_m) - r_f]$

where $E(r)$ = the expected return on the stock
  r_f = the risk-free rate
  β = the stock's beta
  $E(r_m)$ = the expected return on the market portfolio

Firm A
r_f $= 0.05$
β $= 0.9$
$E(r_m)$ $= 0.15$

$E(r)$ $= r_f + \beta[E(r_m) - r_f]$
$= 0.05 + 0.9(0.15 - 0.05)$
$= \mathbf{0.14}$

According to the CAPM, the expected return on Firm A's stock should be 14%. However, the expected return on Firm A's stock given in the table is only13%. Therefore, Firm A's stock is overpriced, and you should sell it.

Firm B
r_f $= 0.05$
β $= 1.1$
$E(r_m)$ $= 0.15$

$E(r)$ $= r_f + \beta[E(r_m) - r_f]$
$= 0.05 + 1.1(0.15 - 0.05)$
$= \mathbf{0.16}$

According to the CAPM, the expected return on Firm B's stock should be 16%. The expected return on Firm B's stock given in the table is also 16%. Therefore, Firm A's stock is correctly priced.

Firm C

r_f = 0.05
β = 1.8
$E(r_m)$ = 0.15

$$E(r) = r_f + \beta[E(r_m) - r_f]$$
$$= 0.05 + 1.8(0.15 - 0.05)$$
$$= \mathbf{0.23}$$

According to the CAPM, the expected return on Firm C's stock should be 23%. However, the expected return on Firm C's stock given in the table is 25%. Therefore, Firm A's stock is underpriced, and you should buy it.

10.40   a.   A typical, risk-averse investor seeks high returns and low risks. For a risk-averse investor holding a well-diversified portfolio, beta is the appropriate measure of the risk of an individual security. To assess the two stocks, find the expected return and beta of each of the two securities.

Stock *A*

Since Stock *A* pays no dividends, the return on Stock *A* is simply $[(P_1 - P_0) - 1]$.

where P_0 = the price of the stock today
           P_1 = the price of the stock one period from today

$$E(r_A) = (0.10)(40/50 - 1) + (.80)(55/50 - 1) + (0.10)(60/50 - 1)$$
$$= (0.10)(-0.20) + (0.80)(0.10) + (0.10)(0.20)$$
$$= \mathbf{0.08}$$

$$\sigma_A^2 = (0.10)(-0.20 - 0.08)^2 + (0.80)(0.10 - 0.08)^2 + (0.10)(0.20 - 0.08)^2$$
$$= 0.0096$$

$$\sigma_A = (0.0096)^{1/2}$$
$$= 0.098$$

$$\beta_A = \text{Correlation}(R_A, R_M)(\sigma_A) / \sigma_M$$
$$= (0.8)(0.098) / 0.10$$
$$= \mathbf{0.784}$$

Stock *A* has an expected return of 8% and a beta of 0.784.

Stock *B*

$E(r) = \mathbf{0.09}$ (Given)

$$\beta_B = \text{Correlation}(R_B, R_M)(\sigma_B) / \sigma_M$$
$$= (0.2)(0.12) / 0.10$$
$$= \mathbf{0.24}$$

Stock *B* has an expected return of 9% and a beta of 0.24.

The expected return on Stock *B* is higher than the expected return on Stock *A*. The risk of Stock *B*, as measured by its beta, is lower than the risk of Stock *A*. Thus, a typical risk-averse investor holding a well-diversified portfolio will prefer Stock *B*.

b. $E(r_P) = (0.70)E(r_A) + (0.30)E(r_B)$
$= (0.70)(0.08) + (0.30)(0.09)$
$= \mathbf{0.083}$

The expected return on a portfolio consisting of 70% of Stock A and 30% of Stock B is 8.3%.

$\sigma_P^2 = (0.70)^2(0.098)^2 + (0.30)^2(0.12)^2 + 2(0.70)(0.30)(0.60)(0.098)(0.12)$
$= 0.008965$

$\sigma_P = (0.008965)^{1/2}$
$= \mathbf{0.0947}$

The standard deviation of a portfolio consisting of 70% of Stock A and 30% of Stock B is 9.47%.

c. The beta of a portfolio is the weighted average of the betas of its individual securities.

$\beta_P = (0.70)(0.784) + (0.30)(0.24)$
$= \mathbf{0.6208}$

The beta of a portfolio consisting of 70% of Stock A and 30% of Stock B is 0.6208.

10.41 a. The variance of a portfolio of two assets equals:

$\sigma_P^2 = (X_A)^2(\sigma_A)^2 + (X_B)^2(\sigma_B)^2 + 2(X_A)(X_B)\text{Covariance}(R_A, R_B)$

where X_A = the weight of Stock A in the portfolio
X_B = the weight of Stock B in the portfolio
σ_A = the standard deviation of Stock A
σ_B = the standard deviation of Stock B

Let $X_A = 1 - X_B$. Then,

$\sigma_P^2 = (1-X_B)^2(\sigma_A)^2 + (X_B)^2(\sigma_B)^2 + 2(1-X_B)(X_B)\text{Covariance}(R_A, R_B)$

From the problem, we know:

σ_A = 0.10
σ_B = 0.20
$\text{Covariance}(R_A, R_B)$ = 0.001

Therefore,

$\sigma_P^2 = (1-X_B)^2(0.10)^2 + (X_B)^2(0.20)^2 + 2(1-X_B)(X_B)(0.001)$
$= (0.01)(1-X_B)^2 + (0.04)(X_B)^2 + (0.002)(1-X_B)(X_B)$
$= (0.01)[1 - 2X_B + (X_B)^2] + (0.04)(X_B)^2 + (0.002)[X_B - (X_B)^2]$
$= 0.01 - 0.02X_B + 0.01(X_B)^2 + (0.04)(X_B)^2 + 0.002X_B - 0.002(X_B)^2$

Minimize this function (the portfolio variance). We do this by differentiating the function with respect to X_B.

$\delta(\sigma_P^2) / \delta(X_B) = -0.02 + 0.02X_B + 0.08X_B + 0.002 - 0.004X_B$
$= -0.018 + 0.096X_B$

Set this expression equal to zero. Then solve for X_B.

$0 = -0.018 + 0.096X_B$

$$X_B = (0.018) / (0.096)$$
$$= \mathbf{0.1875}$$

$$X_A = 1 - X_B$$
$$= 1 - 0.1875$$
$$= \mathbf{0.8125}$$

In order to minimize the variance of the portfolio, the weight of Stock A in the portfolio should be 81.25% and the weight of Stock B in the portfolio should be 18.75%.

b. Using the weights calculated in part a, determine the expected return of the portfolio.

$$E(r_P) = (X_A)[E(r_A)] + (X_B)[E(r_B)]$$
$$= (0.8125)(0.05) + (0.1875)(0.10)$$
$$= \mathbf{0.0594}$$

The expected return on the minimum variance portfolio is 5.94%.

c. From the problem, we know:

$$\sigma_A = 0.10$$
$$\sigma_B = 0.20$$
$$\text{Covariance}(R_A, R_B) = -0.02$$

Therefore,

$$\sigma_P{}^2 = (1-X_B)^2(0.10)^2 + (X_B)^2(0.20)^2 + 2(1-X_B)(X_B)(-0.02)$$
$$= (0.01)(1-X_B)^2 + (0.04)(X_B)^2 + (-0.04)(1-X_B)(X_B)$$
$$= (0.01)[1 - 2X_B + (X_B)^2] + (0.04)(X_B)^2 + (-0.04)[X_B - (X_B)^2]$$
$$= 0.01 - 0.02X_B + 0.01(X_B)^2 + (0.04)(X_B)^2 - 0.04X_B + 0.04(X_B)^2$$

Differentiate this function with respect to X_B.

$$\delta(\sigma_P{}^2) / \delta(X_B) = -0.02 + 0.02X_B + 0.08X_B - 0.04 + 0.08X_B)$$
$$= -0.06 + 0.18X_B$$

Set this expression equal to zero. Then solve for X_B.

$0 = -0.06 + 0.18X_B$

$$X_B = (0.06) / (0.18)$$
$$= \mathbf{1/3}$$

$$X_A = 1 - X_B$$
$$= 1 - (1/3)$$
$$= \mathbf{2/3}$$

In order to minimize the variance of the portfolio, the weight of Stock A in the portfolio should be 1/3 and the weight of Stock B in the portfolio should be 2/3.

d.   The variance of a portfolio of two assets equals:

$$\sigma_P^2 = (X_A)^2(\sigma_A)^2 + (X_B)^2(\sigma_B)^2 + 2(X_A)(X_B)\text{Covariance}(R_A, R_B)$$

where X_A = the weight of Stock A in the portfolio
         X_B = the weight of Stock B in the portfolio
         σ_A = the standard deviation of Stock A
         σ_B = the standard deviation of Stock B

In this problem:

X_A $= 1/3$
X_B $= 2/3$
σ_A $= 0.10$
σ_B $= 0.20$
$\text{Covariance}(R_A, R_B) = -0.02$

Therefore, the variance of the portfolio is:

$$
\begin{aligned}
\sigma_P^2 &= (X_A)^2(\sigma_A)^2 + (X_B)^2(\sigma_B)^2 + 2(X_A)(X_B)\text{Covariance}(R_A, R_B) \\
&= (1/3)^2(0.10)^2 + (2/3)^2(0.20)^2 + (2)(1/3)(2/3)(-0.02) \\
&= \mathbf{0.01}
\end{aligned}
$$

The variance of the portfolio is 0.01.

Chapter 11: An Alternative View of Risk and Return:
The Arbitrage Pricing Theory

11.1   **Real GNP** was higher than anticipated. Since returns are positively related to the level of GNP, returns should rise based on this factor.

Inflation was exactly the amount anticipated. Since there was no surprise in this announcement, it will not affect Lewis-Striden returns.

Interest Rates are lower than anticipated. Since returns are negatively related to interest rates, the lower than expected rate is good news. Returns should rise due to interest rates.

The President's death is bad news. Although the president was expected to retire, his retirement would not be effective for six months. During that period he would still contribute to the firm. His untimely death mean that those contributions would not be made. Since he was generally considered an asset to   the firm, his death will cause returns to fall.

The poor research results are also bad news. Since Lewis-Striden must continue to test the drug, it will not go into production as early as expected. The delay will affect expected future earnings, and thus it will dampen returns now.

The research breakthrough is positive news for Lewis Striden. Since it was unexpected, it will cause returns to rise.

The competitor's announcement is also unexpected, but it is not a welcome surprise. This announcement will lower the returns on Lewis-Striden.

Systematic risk is risk that cannot be diversified away through formation of a portfolio. Generally, systematic risk factors are those factors that affect a large number of firms in the market, however, those factors will not necessarily affect all firms equally. The systematic factors in the list are real GNP, inflation and interest rates.

Unsystematic risk is the type of risk that can be diversified away through portfolio formation. Unsystematic risk factors are specific to the firm or industry. Surprises in these factors will affect the returns of the firm in which you are interested, but they will have no effect on the returns of firms in a different industry and perhaps little effect on other firms in the same industry. For Lewis-Striden, the unsystematic risk factors are the president's ability to contribute to the firm, the research results and the competitor.

11.2   a.   Let m = systematic risk portion of return:

$$m = \beta_1 \Delta F_1 + \beta_2 \Delta F_2 + \beta_3 \Delta F_3$$
$$= 0.042(4,480 - 4,416) - 1.4(4.3\% - 3.1\%) - 0.67(11.8\% - 9.5\%)$$
$$= 0.53\%$$

b.   Let ε = the unsystematic portion of risk, since the news was only about this firm:

$$\varepsilon = -2.6\%$$

c. Total Return = Expected return, plus 2 the components of unexpected return: the systematic risk portion of return and the unsystematic portion:

$$R = \bar{R} + m + \varepsilon$$
$$= 9.5\% - .53\% - 2.6\%$$
$$= 6.37\%$$

11.3 a. Let m = systematic risk portion of return:

$$m = 2.04(4.8\% - 3.5\%) - 1.4(15.2\% - 14.0\%)$$
$$= 0.372\%$$

b. Let ε = the unsystematic portion of risk:

$$\varepsilon = 0.36\%(27 - 23)$$
$$= 1.44\%$$

c. Total Return:

$$R = \bar{R} + m + \varepsilon$$
$$= 10.0\% + 0.37\% + 1.44\%$$
$$= 11.81\%$$

11.4 a. The market model is specified by :

$$R = \bar{R} + \beta \left(R_m - \bar{R}_m\right) + \varepsilon$$

so applying that to each Stock:

Stock A:

$$R_A = \bar{R}_A + \beta_A \left(R_m - \bar{R}_m\right) + \varepsilon_A$$
$$= 10.5\% + 1.2\left(R_m - 14.2\%\right) + \varepsilon_A$$

Stock B:

$$R_B = \bar{R}_B + \beta\left(R_m - \bar{R}_m\right) + \varepsilon_B$$
$$= 13.0\% + 0.98\left(R_m - 14.2\%\right) + \varepsilon_B$$

Stock C:

$$R_C = \bar{R}_C + \beta_C\left(R_m - \bar{R}_m\right) + \varepsilon_C$$
$$= 15.7\% + 1.37(R_m - 14.2\%) + \varepsilon_C$$

11.4 (continued)

b. Since we don't have the actual market return or unsystematic risk, we will get a formula with those values as unknowns:

$$R_P = 0.30R_A + 0.45R_B + 0.25R_C$$
$$= 0.30\left[10.5\% + 1.2(R_m - 14.2\%) + \varepsilon_A\right]$$
$$+0.45\left[13.0\% + 0.98(R_m - 14.2\%) + \varepsilon_B\right]$$
$$+0.25\left[15.7\% + 1.37(R_m - 14.2\%) + \varepsilon_c\right]$$

$$= 0.30(10.5\%) + 0.45(13\%) + 0.25(15.7\%)$$
$$+\left\{0.30(1.2) + 0.45(0.98) + 0.25(1.37)\right\}(R_m - 14.2\%)$$
$$+0.30\varepsilon_A + 0.45\varepsilon_B + 0.25\varepsilon_c$$

$$= 12.925\% + 1.1435(R_m - 14.2\%) + 0.30\varepsilon_A + 0.45\varepsilon_B + 0.25\varepsilon_C$$

c. Now, continuing with the Market Model (as in part a), when $R_m = 15\%$, and all $\varepsilon_i = 0$:

i. returns of individual stocks:

$$R_A = 10.5\% + 1.2(15\% - 14.2\%)$$
$$= 11.46\%$$
$$R_B = 13\% + 0.98(15\% - 14.2\%)$$
$$= 13.78\%$$
$$R_C = 15.7\% + 1.37(15\% - 14.2\%)$$
$$= 16.8\%$$

ii. return of the portfolio:

$$R_p = 12.925\% + 1.1435(15\% - 14.2\%)$$
$$= 13.84\%$$

Alternate Solution for return on portfolio, where X_i is the weight in the portfolio of stock i:

$$R_p = X_a R_a + X_b R_b + X_c R_c$$
$$= .3(11.46) + .45(13.78) + .25(16.8)$$
$$= 13.84$$

11.5 a. Since five stocks have the same expected returns and the same betas, the portfolio also has the same expected return and beta. However, the unsystematic risks might be different:

$$\overline{R}_p = 11.0 + 0.84F_1 + 1.69F_2 + \frac{1}{5}\left(\varepsilon_1 + \varepsilon_2 + \varepsilon_3 + \varepsilon_4 + \varepsilon_5\right)$$

b.

$$\overline{R}_p = 11.0 + 0.84F_1 + 1.69F_2 + \frac{1}{5}\left(\varepsilon_1 + \varepsilon_2 + \varepsilon_3 + \varepsilon_4 + \varepsilon_5\right)$$

As $N \to \infty$, $\frac{1}{N} \to 0$, but $\varepsilon_j s$ are finite, so $\frac{1}{N}\left(\varepsilon_1 + \varepsilon_2 + \varepsilon_3 + \varepsilon_4 + \varepsilon_5\right) \to 0$

Thus, $\overline{R}_p = 11.0 + 0.84F_1 + 1.69F_2$

11.6 To determine which investment investor would prefer, you must compute the variance of portfolios created by many stocks from either market. Note, because you know that diversification is good, it is reasonable to assume that once an investor chose the market in which he or she will invest, he or she will buy many stocks in that market.

Known:

$$E_F = 0 \text{ and } \sigma = 0.1$$
$$E_\varepsilon = 0 \text{ and } \sigma_{\varepsilon_i} = 0.2 \text{ for all i.}$$

Assume:

The weight of each stock is 1/N;

that is, $X_i = 1/N$ for all i.

If a portfolio is composed of N stocks each forming 1/N proportion of the portfolio, the return on the portfolio is 1/N times the sum of the returns on the N stocks.

To find the variance of the respective portfolios in the 2 markets, we need to use the definition of variance from Statistics:

$$Var(x) = E\left[x - E(x)\right]^2$$

In our case:

$$Var(R_p) = E\left[R_p - E(R_p)\right]^2$$

11.6 (continued)

Note however, to use this, first we must find R_p and $E(R_p)$. So, using the assumption about equal weights and then substituting in the known equation for R_i:

$$R_P = \frac{1}{N}\sum R_i$$

$$= \frac{1}{N}\sum(0.1 + \beta F + \varepsilon_i)$$

$$= 0.1 + \beta F + \frac{1}{N}\sum \varepsilon_i$$

Also, recall from Statistics a property of Expected Value:

if: $\tilde{Z} = a\tilde{X} + \tilde{Y}$

where a is a constant, and $\tilde{Z}, \tilde{X},$ and $\tilde{Y}$ are random variables, then

$$E(\tilde{Z}) = E(a)E(\tilde{X}) + E(\tilde{Y})$$

and

$$E(a) = a.$$

Now use the above to find $E(R_p)$:

$$E(R_P) = E\left[0.1 + \beta F + \frac{1}{N}\Sigma\varepsilon_i\right]$$

$$= 0.1 + \beta E(F) + \frac{1}{N}\sum E(\varepsilon_i)$$

$$= 0.1 + \beta(0) + \frac{1}{N}\sum 0$$

$$= 0.1$$

Next, substitute both of these results into the original equation for variance:

$$Var(R_P) = E\left[R_P - E(R_P)\right]^2$$

$$= E\left[0.1 + \beta F + \frac{.01}{N}\sum \varepsilon_i - 0.1\right]^2$$

$$= E\left[\beta F + \frac{1}{N}\sum \varepsilon\right]^2$$

$$= E\left[\beta^2 F^2 + 2\beta F \frac{1}{N}\sum \varepsilon + \frac{1}{N^2}(\Sigma \varepsilon)^2\right]$$

$$= \beta^2 s^2 + \frac{1}{N}s^2 \varepsilon_i + \left(1 - \frac{1}{N}\right)Cov(\varepsilon_i, \varepsilon_j)$$

Finally, since we can have as many stocks in each market as we want,
in the limit, as $N \to \infty$, $\frac{1}{N} \to 0$,
so we get:

$$Var(R_p) = \beta^2 s^2 + Cov(\varepsilon_i, \varepsilon_j)$$

and since $Cov(\varepsilon_i, \varepsilon_j) = \sigma_i \sigma_j Corr(\varepsilon_i, \varepsilon_j)$, and the problem states that $\sigma_1 = \sigma_2 = .1$

$$Var(R_p) = \beta^2 s^2 + \sigma_1 \sigma_2 Corr(\varepsilon_i, \varepsilon_j)$$

$$= \beta^2 (0.01) + 0.04 Corr(\varepsilon_i, \varepsilon_j)$$

So now, summarize what we have so far:

$$R_{1i} = 0.10 + 1.5F + \varepsilon_{1i}$$

$$R_{2i} = 0.10 + 0.5F + \varepsilon_{2i}$$

$$E(R_{1p}) = E(R_{2P}) = 0.1$$

$$Var(R_{1p}) = 0.0225 + 0.04 Corr(\varepsilon_{1i}, \varepsilon_{1j})$$

$$Var(R_{2P}) = 0.0025 + 0.04 Corr(\varepsilon_{2i}, \varepsilon_{2j})$$

and finally we can begin answering the questions a, b, & c for various values of the correlations:

a.   Substitute $Corr\left(\varepsilon_{1i},\varepsilon_{1j}\right)=Corr\left(\varepsilon_{2i},\varepsilon_{2j}\right)=0$ into the respective variance formulas:

$$Var\left(R_{1p}\right)=0.0225$$
$$Var\left(R_{2p}\right)=0.00225$$

Since $Var\left(R_{1p}\right)>Var\left(R_{2p}\right)$, (and expected returns are equal) a risk averse investor will prefer to invest in the second market.

b. $Corr\left(\varepsilon_{1i},\varepsilon_{1j}\right)=0.9$ and $Corr\left(\varepsilon_{2i},\varepsilon_{2j}\right)=0$

$$Var\left(R_{1p}\right)=0.0225+0.04(0.9)$$
$$Var\left(R_{1p}\right)=0.0585$$
$$Var\left(R_{2p}\right)=0.0025+0.04(0)$$
$$Var\left(R_{2p}\right)=0.0025$$

Since $Var\left(R_{1p}\right)>Var\left(R_{2p}\right)$, a risk averse investor will prefer to invest in the second market.

c. $Corr\left(\varepsilon_{1i},\varepsilon_{1j}\right)=0$ and $Corr\left(\varepsilon_{2i},\varepsilon_{2j}\right)=0.5$

$$Var\left(R_{1p}\right)=0.0225+0.04(0)$$
$$Var\left(R_{1p}\right)=0.0225$$
$$Var\left(R_{2p}\right)=0.0025+0.04(0.5)$$
$$Var\left(R_{2p}\right)=0.0225$$

Since $Var\left(R_{1p}\right)=Var\left(R_{2p}\right)$, a risk averse investor will be indifferent between investing in the two markets.

d.   Since the expected returns are equal, indifference implies that the variances of the portfolios in the two markets are also equal. So, set the variance equations equal, and solve for the correlation of one market in terms of the other:

$$Var\left(R_{1p}\right)=Var\left(R_{2p}\right)$$
$$0.0225+0.04Corr\left(\varepsilon_{1i},\varepsilon_{1j}\right)=0.0025+0.04Corr\left(\varepsilon_{2i},\varepsilon_{2j}\right)$$
$$Corr\left(\varepsilon_{2i},\varepsilon_{2j}\right)=Corr\left(\varepsilon_{1i},\varepsilon_{1j}\right)+0.5$$

Therefore, for any set of correlations that have this relationship (as found in part c), a risk averse investor will be indifferent between the two markets.

11.7   a.   In order to find standard deviation (notated here, s), you must first find the Variance, since $s = \sqrt{Var}$. Recall from Statistics a property of Variance:

if: $\tilde{Z} = a\tilde{X} + \tilde{Y}$

where a is a constant, and $\tilde{Z}, \tilde{X}$, and $\tilde{Y}$ are random variables, then

$$Var(\tilde{Z}) = a^2 Var(\tilde{X}) + Var(\tilde{Y})$$

and

$$Var(a) = 0.$$

The problem states that return-generation can be described by:

$$R_{i,t} = \alpha_i + \beta_i(R_m) + \varepsilon_{i,t}$$

Realize that $R_{i,t}$, R_m, and $\varepsilon_{i,t}$ are random variables, and α_i and β_i are constants. Then, apply the above properties to this model, and you get:

$$Var(R_j) = \beta_i^2 Var(R_m) + Var(\varepsilon_i)$$

and now find s for each asset (percents have been converted here to decimal*):

$$s_A^2 = 0.7^2(0.0121) + 0.01 = 0.015929$$
$$s_A = \sqrt{0.015929} = .1262 = 12.62\%$$

$$s_B^2 = 1.2^2(0.0121) + 0.0144 = 0.031824$$
$$s_B = \sqrt{0.031824} = 0.1784 = 17.84\%$$

$$s_C^2 = 1.5^2(0.0121) + 0.0225 = 0.049725$$
$$s_C = \sqrt{0.049725} = 0.2230 = 22.30\%$$

*Note that because of taking the square root, there is potential here for getting confused about the percent. Keep in mind that "percent" is only for the convenience of presentation. It is always a good idea to convert to decimal before doing calculations, and do your work in decimals. Then you can convert back to percent for the final answer.

11.7   (continued)

b.i: From above formula for variance, note that as $N \to \infty$, $\frac{\mathrm{Var}(\varepsilon_i)}{N} \to 0$, so you get:

$$\mathrm{Var}(R_i) = \beta_i^2 \mathrm{Var}(R_m)$$

So, the variances for the assets are (no confusion about % here, so you can just stay in %):

$$s_A^2 = 0.7^2 (1.21) = 0.5929\%$$
$$s_B^2 = 1.2^2 (1.21) = 1.7424\%$$
$$s_C^2 = 1.5^2 (1.21) = 2.7225\%$$

b.ii.   Use the model : $\bar{R}_i = R_F + (\bar{R}_m - R_F)\beta_i$, which is the CAPM (or APT Model when there is one factor and that factor is the Market).

$$\bar{R}_A = 3.3 + (10.6 - 3.3)(0.7) = 8.41\%$$
$$\bar{R}_B = 3.3 + (10.6 - 3.3)(1.2) = 12.06\%$$
$$\bar{R}_C = 3.3 + (10.6 - 3.3)(1.5) = 14.25\%$$

Compare these results for expected asset returns as per CAPM or APT with the expected returns given in the table. This shows that assets A & B are accurately priced, but asset C is overpriced (the model shows the return *should* be higher). Thus, rational investors will not hold asset C.

b.iii. If short selling is allowed, rational investors will sell short asset C, causing the price of asset C to decrease until no arbitrage opportunity exists. In other words, the price of asset C should decrease until the return becomes 14.25%.

11.8   a.   Let $X_1 =$ the proportion of Security 1 in the portfolio and
                         $X_2 =$ the proportion of Security 2 in the portfolio

and note that since the weights must sum to 1.0,

$$X_1 = (1 - X_2).$$

Recall from Chapter 10 that the beta for a portfolio (or in this case the beta for a factor) is the weighted average of the security betas, so

$$\beta_{p1} = X_1\beta_{11} + X_2\beta_{21}$$
$$= X_1\beta_{11} + (1 - X_1)\beta_{21}$$

Now, apply the condition given in the hint that the return of the portfolio does not depend on F_1. This means that the portfolio beta for that factor will be 0:

$$\beta_{p1} = 0 = X_1\beta_{11} + (1 - X_1)\beta_{21}$$
$$0 = X_1(1.0) + (1 - X_1)(0.5)$$

and solving for X_1 and X_2:

$$X_1 = -1$$
$$X_2 = 2$$

Thus, sell short Security 1 and buy Security 2.

To find the expected return on that portfolio, use

$$R_p = X_1R_1 + X_2R_2$$

so applying the above:

$$E(R_p) = (-1)20\% + 2(20\%) = 20\%$$
$$\beta_{p2} = (-1)(1.5) + 2(2) = 2.5$$

11.8   (continued)

b.   Following the same logic as in part a, we have

$$\beta_{p1} = 0 = X_3\beta_{31} + (1 - X_3)\beta_{41}$$
$$0 = X_3(1.0) + (1 - X_3)(1.5)$$

and

$$X_3 = 3$$
$$X_4 = -2$$

Thus, sell short Security 4 and buy Security 3. Then,

$$E(R_p) = 3(10\%) + (-2)(10\%) = 10\%$$
$$\beta_{p2} = 3(0.5) - 2(0.75) = 0$$

Note that since both β_{p1} and β_{p2} are 0, this is a risk free portfolio!

c.   The portfolio in part b provides a risk free return of 10%, which is higher than the 5% return provided by the risk free security. To take advantage of this opportunity, borrow at the risk free rate of 5% and invest the funds in a portfolio built by selling short security four and buying security three with weights (3,-2) as in part b.

d.   First assume that the risk free security will not change. The price of security four (that everyone is trying to sell short) will decrease, and the price of security three (that everyone is trying to buy) will increase. Hence the return of security four will increase and the return of security three will decrease.

The alternative is that the prices of securities three and four will remain the same, and the price of the risk-free security drops until its return is 10%.

Finally, a combined movement of all security prices is also possible. The prices of security four and the risk-free security will decrease and the price of security three will increase until the opportunity disappears.

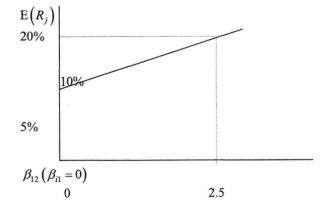

Chapter 12: Risk, Cost of Capital, and Capital Budgeting

12.1   The discount rate for the project is equal to the expected return for the security, R_S, since the project has the same risk as the firm as a whole. Apply the CAPM to express the firm's required return, R_S, in terms of the firm's beta, β, the risk-free rate, R_F, and the expected market return, $\overline{R}_M$.

$$
\begin{aligned}
R_S &= R_F + \beta \times (\overline{R}_M - R_F) \\
&= 0.05 + 0.95\,(0.09) \\
&= 0.1355
\end{aligned}
$$

Subtract the initial investment at year 0. To calculate the PV of the cash inflows, apply the annuity formula, discounted at 0.1355.

$$
\begin{aligned}
\text{NPV} &= C_0 + C_1\,A^T_r \\
&= -\$1,200,000 + \$340,000\,A^5_{0.1355} \\
&= -\$20,016.52
\end{aligned}
$$

Do not undertake the project since the NPV is negative.

12.2   a.   Calculate the average return for Douglas stock and the market.

$$
\begin{aligned}
\overline{R}_D &= (\text{Sum of Yearly Returns}) / (\text{Number of Years}) \\
&= (-0.05 + 0.05 + 0.08 + 0.15 + 0.10) / (5) \\
&= \mathbf{0.066}
\end{aligned}
$$

$$
\begin{aligned}
\overline{R}_M &= (-0.12 + 0.01 + 0.06 + 0.10 + 0.05) / (5) \\
&= \mathbf{0.020}
\end{aligned}
$$

To calculate the beta of Douglas stock, calculate the variance of the market, $(R_M - \overline{R}_M)^2$, and the covariance of Douglas stock's return with the market's return, $(R_D - \overline{R}_D) \times (R_M - \overline{R}_M)$. The beta of Douglas stock is equal to the covariance of Douglas stock's return and the market's return divided by the variance of the market. Remember to divide both the covariance of Douglas stock's return and the market's return and the variance of the market by 4. Because the data are historical, the appropriate denominator in the calculation of the variance is 4 ($=T-1$).

$R_D - \overline{R}_D$	$R_M - \overline{R}_M$	$(R_M - \overline{R}_M)^2$	$(R_D - \overline{R}_D)(R_M - \overline{R}_M)$
-0.116	-0.14	0.0196	0.01624
-0.016	-0.01	0.0001	0.00016
0.014	0.04	0.0016	0.00056
0.084	0.08	0.0064	0.00672
0.034	0.03	0.0009	0.00102
		0.0286	0.02470

$$
\begin{aligned}
\beta_D &= [\text{Cov}\,(R_D, R_M) / (T-1)] / [\text{Var}\,(R_M) / (T-1)] \\
&= (0.02470 / 4) / (0.0286 / 4) \\
&= \mathbf{0.864}
\end{aligned}
$$

The beta of Douglas stock is 0.864.

12.3 Calculate the square root of the stock's variance and the market's variance to find the standard deviation, σ, of each.

$$\sigma_C = (\sigma^2{}_C)^{1/2}$$
$$= (0.004225)^{1/2}$$
$$= 0.065$$

$$\sigma_M = (\sigma^2{}_M)^{1/2}$$
$$= (0.001467)^{1/2}$$
$$= 0.0383$$

Use the formula for beta:

$$\beta_C = [\text{Corr}\ (R_C, R_M) \times \sigma_C]\ /\ \sigma_M$$
$$= [(0.675)\ (0.065)]\ /\ (0.0383)$$
$$= \mathbf{1.146}$$

The beta of Ceramics Craftsman is 1.146.

12.4   a.   To compute the beta of Mercantile's stock, divide the covariance of the stock's return with the market's return by the market variance. Since those two values are provided in the problem, the 13 quarterly returns of Mercantile's stock and the market are not needed for the calculation.

$$\beta_D = \text{Cov}\ (R_D, R_M)\ /\ \sigma^2{}_M$$
$$= (0.038711)\ /\ (0.038588)$$
$$= \mathbf{1.0032}$$

The beta of Mercantile Banking Corporation is 1.0032.

   b.   The beta of the average stock is one. Since Mercantile's beta is close to one, its stock has approximately the same risk as the overall market.

12.5   a. R_L can have three values, 0.16, 0.18, or 0.20. The probability that R_L takes one of these values is the sum of the joint probabilities of the return pair, Prob(R_L, R_J), that includes the particular value of R_L. For example, if R_L is equal to 0.16, R_J will be either 0.16, 0.18, or 0.22. The probability that R_L is 0.16 and R_J is 0.16 is 0.10. The probability that R_L is 0.16 and R_J is 0.18 is 0.06. The probability that R_L is 0.16 and R_J is 0.22 is 0.04. Thus, the probability that R_L assumes a value 0.16 is 0.20 (=0.10 + 0.06 + 0.04). The same procedure is used to calculate the probability that R_L is 0.18 and the probability that R_L is 0.20.

R_L	Probability
0.16	0.20
0.18	0.60
0.20	0.20

   b.   i.   The expected return on asset L is calculated by weighting each possible return by its probability. Multiply each possible return, R_L, by its probability, as found in part (a).

$$\overline{R}_L = \Sigma[R_L \times \text{Prob}(R_L)]$$
$$= (0.16)(0.20) + (0.18)(0.60) + (0.20)\ (0.20)$$
$$= \mathbf{0.18}$$

The expected return on asset L is 18%.

ii. The variance of asset L is the weighted sum of the squared differences between the possible values of R_L and the expected return on R_L found in part (i). Weight the squared differences by the probabilities of each value found in part (a).

$$
\begin{aligned}
\sigma^2{}_L &= \Sigma[(R_L - \overline{R}_L)^2 \times \text{Prob}(R_L)] \\
&= (0.16 - 0.18)^2\,(0.20) + (0.18 - 0.18)^2\,(0.60) + (0.20 - 0.18)^2\,(0.20) \\
&= \mathbf{0.00016}
\end{aligned}
$$

The variance of asset L is 0.00016.

iii. The standard deviation of asset L is the square root of the variance calculated in part (ii).

$$
\begin{aligned}
\sigma_L &= (\sigma^2{}_L)^{1/2} \\
&= (0.00016)^{1/2} \\
&= \mathbf{0.01265}
\end{aligned}
$$

The standard deviation of asset L is 0.01265.

c. Repeat the procedure used in part (a) to calculate the probability of each value of R_J.

R_J	Probability
0.16	0.10
0.18	0.20
0.20	0.40
0.22	0.20
0.24	0.10

d. i. The expected return on asset J is the weighted probability of each possible return. Multiply each possible return, R_J, by the probability of each return found in part (c).

$$
\begin{aligned}
\overline{R}_J &= \Sigma[R_J \times \text{Prob}(R_J)] \\
&= (0.16)(0.10) + (0.18)(0.20) + (0.20)(0.40) + (0.22)(0.20) + \\
&\quad (0.24)(0.10) \\
&= \mathbf{0.20}
\end{aligned}
$$

The expected return on asset J is 20%.

ii. The variance of asset J is the weighted sum of the squared differences between the possible values of R_J and the expected return on R_J found in part (i). Weight the squared differences by the probabilities of each value found in part (c).

$$
\begin{aligned}
\sigma^2{}_J &= \Sigma[(R_J - \overline{R}_J)^2 \times \text{Prob}(R_J)] \\
&= (0.16 - 0.20)^2\,(0.10) + (0.18 - 0.20)^2\,(0.20) + (0.20 - 0.20)^2\,(0.40) + \\
&\quad (0.22 - 0.20)^2\,(0.20) + (0.24 - 0.20)^2\,(0.10) \\
&= \mathbf{0.00048}
\end{aligned}
$$

The variance of asset J is 0.00048.

iii. The standard deviation of asset J is the square root of the variance calculated in part (ii).

$$\sigma_J = (\sigma^2_J)^{1/2}$$
$$= (0.00048)^{1/2}$$
$$= 0.02191$$

The standard deviation of asset J is 0.02191.

d. The covariance is the expected value of $[(R_L - \overline{R}_L)(R_J - \overline{R}_J)]$.

$$\text{Cov } (R_L, R_J) = \Sigma \ [(R_L - \overline{R}_L) \times (R_J - \overline{R}_J) \times \text{Prob } (R_L, R_J)]$$
$$= (0.16 - 0.18)(0.16 - 0.20)(0.10) + (0.16 - 0.18)(0.18 - 0.20)(0.06)$$
$$+ (0.16 - 0.18)(0.22 - 0.20)(0.04) + (0.18 - 0.18)(0.18 - 0.20)(0.12)$$
$$+ (0.18 - 0.18)(0.20 - 0.20)(0.36) + (0.18 - 0.18)(0.22 - 0.20)(0.12)$$
$$+ (0.20 - 0.18)(0.18 - 0.20)(0.02) + (0.20 - 0.18)(0.20 - 0.20)(0.04)$$
$$+ (0.20 - 0.18)(0.22 - 0.20)(0.04) + (0.20 - 0.18)(0.24 - 0.20)(0.10)$$
$$= 0.000176$$

The covariance of asset L's return with asset J's return is 0.000176.

The correlation coefficient of R_L and R_J is the covariance divided by the standard deviation of assets L and J.

$$\text{Corr } (R_L, R_J) = \text{Cov } (R_L, R_J) \ / \ (\sigma_L \sigma_J)$$
$$= 0.000176 \ / \ (0.01265 \times 0.02191)$$
$$= 0.635$$

The correlation coefficient of asset L and J is 0.635.

e. Divide the product of the correlation coefficient and the standard deviation of asset J by the standard deviation of the market, asset L, to calculate the beta for asset J.

$$\beta_J = [\text{Corr } (R_L, R_J) \times \sigma_J] \ / \ \sigma_L$$
$$= [(0.635)(0.02191)] \ / \ (0.01265)$$
$$= 1.10$$

The beta of asset J is 1.10.

12.6 You are assuming that the new project's risk is the same as the risk of the firm as a whole, and that the firm is financed entirely with equity.

12.7 a. Jang Cosmetics should use its stock beta in the evaluation of the project only if the risk of the perfume project is the same as the risk of Jang Cosmetics as a whole.

b. If the risk of the project is the same as the risk of the firm, use the firm's stock beta. Otherwise, Jang should use the beta of an all-equity firm that has similar risks as the perfume project. An effective way to estimate the beta of the perfume project is to average the betas of several all-equity, perfume-producing firms.

12.8 First, calculate the expected return on Compton's stock.

$$\overline{R}_S = \Sigma [R_S \times \text{Prob}(R_S)]$$
$$= (0.03)(0.1) + (0.08)(0.3) + (0.20)(0.4) + (0.15)(0.2)$$
$$= 0.137$$

Calculate the expected return on Compton's debt.

$$\overline{R}_B = \Sigma[R_B \times \text{Prob}(R_B)]$$
$$= (0.08)\,(0.1) + (0.08)\,(0.3) + (0.1)\,(0.4) + (0.1)\,(0.2)$$
$$= 0.092$$

Calculate the expected return on the market.

$$\overline{R}_M = \Sigma[R_M \times \text{Prob}(R_M)]$$
$$= (0.05)\,(0.1) + (0.1)\,(0.3) + (0.15)\,(0.4) + (0.2)\,(0.2)$$
$$= 0.135$$

Calculate the covariance of the stock's return with the market's return.

$$\text{Cov}\,(R_S, R_M) = \Sigma\,[(R_S - \overline{R}_S) \times (R_M - \overline{R}_M) \times \text{Prob}]$$
$$= (0.03 - 0.137)\,(0.05 - 0.135)\,(0.1) + (0.08 - 0.137)\,(0.1 - 0.135)$$
$$(0.3) + (0.2 - 0.137)\,(0.15 - 0.135)\,(0.4) + (0.15 - 0.137)\,(0.2 - 0.135)$$
$$(0.2)$$
$$= 0.002055$$

Calculate the covariance of the debt's return with the market's return.

$$\text{Cov}\,(R_B, R_M) = \Sigma\,[(R_B - \overline{R}_B) \times (R_M - \overline{R}_M) \times \text{Prob}]$$
$$= (0.08 - 0.092)\,(0.05 - 0.135)\,(0.1) + (0.08 - 0.092)\,(0.1 - 0.135)$$
$$(0.3) + (0.1 - 0.092)\,(0.15 - 0.135)\,(0.4) + (0.1 - 0.092)\,(0.2 - 0.135)$$
$$(0.2)$$
$$= 0.00038$$

Calculate the market variance.

$$\sigma^2_M = \Sigma[(R_M - \overline{R}_M)^2 \times \text{Prob}(R_M)]$$
$$= (0.05 - 0.135)^2\,(0.1) + (0.1 - 0.135)^2\,(0.3) + (0.15 - 0.135)^2\,(0.4) +$$
$$(0.2 - 0.135)^2\,(0.2)$$
$$= 0.002025$$

a. Calculate the beta of Compton Technology's debt by dividing the covariance of the debt's return with the market's return by the variance of the market.

$$\beta_B = \text{Cov}\,(R_B, R_M) / \sigma^2_M$$
$$= (0.00038) / (0.002025)$$
$$= \mathbf{0.188}$$

The beta of Compton Technology debt is 0.188.

b. Calculate the beta of Compton Technology's stock by dividing the covariance of the stock's return with the market's return by the variance of the market.

$$\beta_S = \text{Cov}\,(R_S, R_M) / \sigma^2_M$$
$$= (0.002055) / (0.002025)$$
$$= \mathbf{1.015}$$

The beta of Compton Technology stock is 1.015.

c. Calculate the equity to value ratio [S / (S+B)] and the debt to value ratio [B / (S+B)] by substitution.

B / S = 0.5
B = 0.5 S

$$[S / (S+B)] = [S / (S + 0.5 \times S)]$$
$$= [S / (1.5 \times S)]$$
$$= 1 / 1.5$$
$$= 0.667$$

$$[B / (S+B)] = [0.5 \times S / (S + 0.5 \times S)]$$
$$= [(0.5 \times S) / (1.5 \times S)]$$
$$= 1 / 3$$
$$= 0.333$$

When there are no taxes, the asset beta is equal to the weighted average of the stock beta and the debt beta.

$$\beta_{Asset} = [S / (S+B)] \times \beta_S + [B / (S+B)] \times \beta_B$$
$$= (0.667) (1.015) + (0.333) (0.188)$$
$$= \mathbf{0.740}$$

The asset beta of Compton Technology is 0.740.

12.9   The discount rate for the projects should be lower that the rate implied by the security market line. The security market line is used to calculate the cost of equity. The appropriate discount rate for projects is the firm's weighted average cost of capital. Since the firm's cost of debt is generally less that the firm's cost of equity, the rate implied by the security market line will be too high.

12.10 Beta measures the responsiveness of a security's returns to movements in the market. Beta is determined by the cyclicality of a firm's revenues. This cyclicality is magnified by the firm's operating and financial leverage.

a. **Revenues.** The cyclicality of a firm's sales is an important factor in determining beta. In general, stock prices will rise when the economy expands and will fall when the economy contracts. As we said above, beta measures the responsiveness of a security's returns to movements in the market. Therefore, firms whose revenues are more responsive to movements in the economy will generally have higher betas than firms with less-cyclical revenues.

b. **Operating leverage.** Operating leverage is the percentage change in earnings before interest and taxes (EBIT) for a percentage change in sales. A firm with high operating leverage will have greater fluctuations in EBIT for a change in sales than a firm with low operating leverage. In this way, operating leverage magnifies the cyclicality of a firm's revenues, leading to a high beta.

c. **Financial leverage.** Financial leverage arises from the use of debt in the firm's capital structure. A levered firm must make fixed interest payments regardless of its revenues. The effect of financial leverage on beta is analogous to the effect of operating leverage on beta. Fixed interest payments cause the percentage change in net income to be greater than the percentage change in EBIT, magnifying the cyclicality of a firm's revenues. Thus, returns on highly-levered stocks should be more responsive to movements in the market than the returns on stocks with little or no debt in their capital structure.

12.11   a.   Apply the CAPM to calculate the cost of equity.

$$r_S = R_F + \beta_S \times (\overline{R}_M - R_F)$$
$$= 0.06 + 1.15\,(0.1)$$
$$= \mathbf{0.175}$$

The cost of equity is 17.5%.

     b.   To calculate the weighted average cost of capital for the project, r_{WACC}, first determine the cost of debt, r_B. Use the cost of equity, r_S, calculated in part (*a*).

$$r_B = R_F + \beta_B \times (\overline{R}_M - R_F)$$
$$= 0.06 + 0.3\,(0.1)$$
$$= 0.09$$

$$r_S = 0.175$$

Next, calculate the weighted average cost of capital. To determine the proper weights, express the firm's proportion of debt in terms of the firm's proportion of equity. Solve for the equity to value ratio [S / (S+B)] and the debt to value ratio [B / (S+B)].

B / S   = 0.25
B   = 0.25 S

$$[S / (S+B)] = [S / (S + 0.25 \times S)]$$
$$= [S / (1.25 \times S)]$$
$$= 1 / 1.25$$
$$= 0.80$$

$$[B / (S+B)] = [0.25 \times S / (S + 0.25 \times S)]$$
$$= [(0.25 \times S) / (1.25 \times S)]$$
$$= 1 / 5$$
$$= 0.20$$

Interest on debt is tax deductible at the corporate level, which leads to tax benefits for the firm. Multiply the cost of debt, r_B, by $(1 - T_C)$, to include the tax benefit created by the interest tax shield. The tax benefit of debt will lower the firm's overall cost of capital.

$$r_{WACC} = [S / (S+B)] \times r_S + [B / (S+B)] \times r_B \times (1 - T_C)$$
$$= (0.80)\,(0.175) + (0.20)\,(0.09)\,(0.65)$$
$$= \mathbf{0.1517}$$

The weighted average cost of capital is 15.17%.

12.12   a.   Apply the CAPM to estimate Adobe Online's cost of equity, R_S. The following equation expresses the firm's required return, R_S, in terms of the firm's beta, β_S, the risk-free rate, R_F, and the market return, $\overline{R}_M$.

$$R_S = R_F + \beta \times (\overline{R}_M - R_F)$$
$$= 0.07 + 1.29\,(0.13 - 0.07)$$
$$= \mathbf{0.1474}$$

Adobe Online's cost of equity is 14.74%.

b. Use the debt-to-equity ratio to determine the weighted average cost of capital. Calculate the equity to value ratio [S / (S+B)] and the debt to value ratio [B / (S+B)] by substitution.

B / S   = 1.0
B   = S

[S / (S+B)]   = [S / (S + S)]
                = [S / (2 × S)]
                = 1 / 2
                = 0.5

[B / (S+B]   = [1.0 × S / (S + 1.0 × S)]
                = [(S) / (2 × S)]
                = 1 / 2
                = 0.5

Remember that interest on debt is tax deductible at the corporate level, which will lower the firm's overall cost of capital. Multiply the cost of debt, r_B, by $(1 - T_C)$ to include the interest tax shield in the weighted average cost of capital.

r_{WACC} $= [S / (S+B)] \times r_S + [B / (S+B)] \times r_B \times (1 - T_C)$
            $= (0.5) (0.1474) + (0.5) (0.07) (1 - 0.35)$
            $= \mathbf{0.09645}$

The weighted average cost of capital is 9.645%.

12.13   Use the market value of debt to compute the weighted average cost of capital. To calculate the market value of the debt, multiply the book value of Luxury's debt by 120 percent.

B $= \$60,000,000 \times 1.2$
        $= \$72,000,000$

The market value of Luxury's stock is equal to the number of shares outstanding multiplied by the market price per share.

S $= 5,000,000 \times \$20$
        $= \$100,000,000$

The value of the firm is the market value of Luxury's debt plus the market value of Luxury's stock.

V $= B + S$
        $= \$72,000,000 + \$100,000,000$
        $= \$172,000,000$

Calculate the debt-to-value and equity-to-value ratios. These ratios will be used to compute the weighted average cost of capital.

B / (S + B) $= \$72,000,000 / \$172,000,000$
                $= 0.4186$

S / (S + B) $= \$100,000,000 / \$172,000,000$
                $= 0.5814$

Use the cost of debt and cost of equity, 12 percent and 18 percent, respectively, and the weights calculated above, to determine the weighted average cost of capital. Remember that interest on debt is tax deductible at the corporate level, which will lower the firm's overall cost of capital. Multiply the cost of debt, r_B, by $(1 - T_C)$ to include the interest tax shield in the weighted average cost of capital.

$$
\begin{aligned}
r_{WACC} &= [S / (S+B)] \times r_S + [B / (S+B)] \times r_B \times (1 - T_C) \\
&= (0.5814)(0.18) + (0.4186)(0.12)(0.75) \\
&= \mathbf{0.1423}
\end{aligned}
$$

The weighted average cost of capital for Luxury Porcelain Company is 14.23%.

12.14   Use the market value of debt to calculate the weighted average cost of capital. To compute the market value of the debt, multiply the book value of First Data's debt by 95 percent.

$$
\begin{aligned}
B &= \$180,000,000 \times 0.95 \\
&= \$171,000,000
\end{aligned}
$$

The market value of First Data Co.'s stock is equal to the number of shares outstanding multiplied by the market price per share.

$$
\begin{aligned}
S &= 20,000,000 \times \$25 \\
&= \$500,000,000
\end{aligned}
$$

The value of the firm is the market value of First Data Co.'s debt plus the market value of the stock.

$$
\begin{aligned}
V &= B + S \\
&= \$171,000,000 + \$500,000,000 \\
&= \$671,000,000
\end{aligned}
$$

Calculate the debt-to-value and equity-to-value ratios. These ratios will be used to compute the weighted average cost of capital.

$$
\begin{aligned}
B / (S + B) &= \$171,000,000 / \$671,000,000 \\
&= 0.2548
\end{aligned}
$$

$$
\begin{aligned}
S / (S + B) &= \$500,000,000 / \$671,000,000 \\
&= 0.7452
\end{aligned}
$$

Apply the weighted average cost of capital formula, using the cost of debt and cost of equity given in the problem, 10 percent and 20 percent, respectively. Remember that interest on debt is tax deductible at the corporate level, which will lower the firm's overall cost of capital. Multiply the cost of debt, r_B, by $(1 - T_C)$ to include the interest tax shield in the weighted average cost of capital.

$$
\begin{aligned}
r_{WACC} &= [S / (S+B)] \times r_S + [B / (S+B)] \times r_B \times (1 - T_C) \\
&= (0.7452)(0.20) + (0.2548)(0.10)(0.60) \\
&= \mathbf{0.1643}
\end{aligned}
$$

The weighted average cost of capital for First Data Co. is 16.43%.

12.15   The appropriate discount rate for the project is the weighted average cost of capital. Use the debt-to-equity ratio to calculate the weighted average cost of capital. Determine the equity to value ratio $[S / (S+B)]$ and the debt to value ratio $[B / (S+B)]$ by substitution.

$$B / S = 0.75$$
$$B = 0.75 \times S$$

$$
\begin{aligned}
[S / (S+B)] &= [S / (S + 0.75 \times S)] \\
&= [S / (1.75 \times S)] \\
&= 1 / 1.75 \\
&= 0.5714
\end{aligned}
$$

$$
\begin{aligned}
[B / (S+B)] &= [(0.75 \times S) / (S + 0.75 \times S)] \\
&= [(0.75 \times S) / (1.75 \times S)] \\
&= 0.75 / 1.75 \\
&= 0.4286
\end{aligned}
$$

Remember that interest on debt is tax deductible at the corporate level, which will lower the firm's overall cost of capital. Multiply the cost of debt, r_B, by $(1 - T_C)$ to include the interest tax shield in the weighted average cost of capital.

$$
\begin{aligned}
r_{WACC} &= [S / (S+B)] \times r_S + [B / (S+B)] \times r_B \times (1 - T_C) \\
&= (0.5714)(0.15) + (0.4286)(0.09)(0.65) \\
&= \mathbf{0.1108}
\end{aligned}
$$

To calculate the NPV of the project, subtract the initial (year 0) outlay. Next, apply the annuity formula, discounted at the weighted average cost of capital, to calculate the PV of the cash inflows.

$$
\begin{aligned}
NPV &= C_0 + C_1 A^T_r \\
&= -\$25,000,000 + \$7,000,000\, A^5_{0.1108} \\
&= \mathbf{\$819,299.04}
\end{aligned}
$$

Since the project has a positive NPV, $819,299.04, the company should accept the project.

12.16   The correct discount rate for the project is the weighted average cost of capital. Since the debt-to-equity ratio is equal to one, the debt-to-value and equity-to-value ratios will be equal to 0.5.

Remember that interest on debt is tax deductible at the corporate level, which will lower the firm's overall cost of capital. Multiply the cost of debt, r_B, by $(1 - T_C)$ to include the interest tax shield in the weighted average cost of capital.

$$
\begin{aligned}
r_{WACC} &= [S / (S+B)] \times r_S + [B / (S+B)] \times r_B \times (1 - T_C) \\
&= (0.5)(0.28) + (0.5)(0.1)(0.65) \\
&= 0.1725
\end{aligned}
$$

To calculate the NPV of the project, subtract the initial (year 0) outlay. Next, apply the annuity formula, discounted at the weighted average cost of capital, to calculate the PV of the cash inflows. Remember to adjust the pre-tax annual earnings of $600,000 for taxes.

$$
\begin{aligned}
NPV &= C_0 + (1 - T_c)\, C_1 A^T_r \\
&= -\$1,000,000 + (0.65)\,\$600,000\, A^5_{0.1725} \\
&= \mathbf{\$240,608.65}
\end{aligned}
$$

The NPV of the project is $240,608.65. The firm should accept the project.

Chapter 13: Corporate-Financing Decisions and Efficient Capital Markets

13.1   a.   Firms should accept financing proposals with positive net present values (NPVs).

        b.   Firms can create valuable financing opportunities in three ways:

           Fool investors. A firm can issue a complex security to receive more than the fair market value. Financial managers attempt to package securities to receive the greatest value.

           Reduce costs or increase subsidies. A firm can package securities to reduce taxes. Such a security will increase the value of the firm. In addition, financing techniques involve many costs, such as accountants, lawyers, and investment bankers. Packaging securities in a way to reduce these costs will also increase the value of the firm.

           Create a new security. A previously unsatisfied investor may pay extra for a specialized security catering to his or her needs. Corporations gain from developing unique securities by issuing these securities at premium prices.

13.2   **Weak form.** Market prices reflect information contained in historical prices. Investors are unable to earn abnormal returns using historical prices to predict future price movements.

        Semi-strong form. In addition to historical data, market prices reflect all publicly-available information. Investors with insider, or private information, are able to earn abnormal returns.

        Strong form. Market prices reflect all information, public or private. Investors are unable to earn abnormal returns using insider information or historical prices to predict future price movements.

13.3   a.   **False.** Market efficiency implies that prices reflect all available information, but it does not imply certain knowledge. Many pieces of information that are available and reflected in prices are fairly uncertain. Efficiency of markets does not eliminate that uncertainty and therefore does not imply perfect forecasting ability.

        b.   **True.** Market efficiency exists when prices reflect all available information. To be efficient in the weak form, the market must incorporate all historical data into prices. Under the semi-strong form of the hypothesis, the market incorporates all publicly-available information in addition to the historical data. In strong form efficient markets, prices reflect all publicly and privately available information.

        c.   **False.** Market efficiency implies that market participants are rational. Rational people will immediately act upon new information and will bid prices up or down to reflect that information.

        d.   **False.** In efficient markets, prices reflect all available information. Thus, prices will fluctuate whenever new information becomes available.

        e.   **True.** Competition among investors results in the rapid transmission of new market information. In efficient markets, prices immediately reflect new information as investors bid the stock price up or down.

13.4   a.   Aerotech's stock price should rise immediately after the announcement of the positive news.

        b.   Only scenario (*ii*) indicates market efficiency. In that case, the price of the stock rises immediately to the level that reflects the new information, eliminating all possibility of abnormal returns. In the other two scenarios, there are periods of time during which an investor could trade on the information and earn abnormal returns.

13.5   **False.** The stock price would have adjusted before the founder's death only if investors had perfect forecasting ability. The 12.5% increase in the stock price after the founder's death indicates that either the market did not anticipate the death or that the market had anticipated it imperfectly. However, the market reacted immediately to the new information, implying efficiency. It is interesting that the stock price rose after the announcement of the founder's death. This price behavior indicates that the market felt he was a liability to the firm.

13.6   The announcement should not deter investors from buying UPC's stock. If the market is semi-strong form efficient, the stock price will have already reflected the present value of the payments that UPC must make. The expected return after the announcement should still be equal to the expected return before the announcement. UPC's current stockholders bear the burden of the loss, since the stock price falls on the announcement. After the announcement, the expected return moves back to its original level.

13.7   The market is generally considered to be efficient up to the semi-strong form. Therefore, no systematic profit can be made by trading on publicly-available information. Although illegal, the lead engineer of the device can profit from purchasing the firm's stock *before* the news release on the implementation of the new technology. The price should immediately and fully adjust to the new information in the article. Thus, no abnormal return can be expected from purchasing after the publication of the article.

13.8   Under the semi-strong form of market efficiency, the stock price should stay the same. The accounting system changes are publicly available information. Investors would identify no changes in either the firm's current or its future cash flows. Thus, the stock price will not change after the announcement of increased earnings.

13.9   No, Alex cannot make money by investing in firms with prior price run-ups. The market's expectations of the firms' current and future cash flows would already have been reflected in the current stock prices before the stock issuance. Positive cumulative abnormal returns prior to an event can easily occur in an efficient capital market. The price run-ups are due to good news, and firms typically issue new stock after good news. Thus, price increases prior to new stock issuances are neither consistent nor inconsistent with the efficient markets hypothesis.

13.10   Because the number of subscribers has increased dramatically, the time it takes for information in the newsletter to be reflected in prices has shortened. With shorter adjustment periods, it becomes impossible to earn abnormal returns with the information provided by Durkin.

        If Durkin is using only publicly-available information in its newsletter, its ability to pick stocks is inconsistent with the efficient markets hypothesis. Under the semi-strong form of market efficiency, all publicly-available information should be reflected in stock prices. The use of private information for trading purposes is illegal.

13.11   You should not agree with your broker. The performance ratings of the small manufacturing firms were published and became public information. Prices should adjust immediately to the information, thus preventing future abnormal returns.

13.12   Stock prices should immediately and fully rise to reflect the announcement. Thus, one cannot expect abnormal returns following the announcements.

13.13   Systematic profit from historical price patterns is not consistent with the efficient markets hypothesis. The weak form of market efficiency is violated if investors can systematically profit from trading rules based on patterns in historical stock prices.

13.14   a.   **No.** Earnings information is in the public domain and reflected in the current stock price.

      b.   **Possibly.** If the rumors were publicly disseminated, the prices would have already adjusted for the possibility of a merger. If the rumor is information that you received from an insider, you could earn excess returns, although trading on that information is illegal.

      c.   **No.** The information is already public, and thus, already reflected in the stock price.

13.15   Serial correlation occurs when the current value of a variable is related to the future value of the variable. If the market is efficient, the information about the serial correlation in the macroeconomic variable and its relationship to net earnings should already be reflected in the stock price. In other words, although there is serial correlation in the variable, there will not be serial correlation in stock returns. Therefore, knowledge of the correlation in the macroeconomic variable will not lead to abnormal returns for investors.

13.16   The statement is false because every investor has a different risk preference. Although the expected return from every well-diversified portfolio is the same after adjusting for risk, investors still need to choose funds that are consistent with their particular risk level.

13.17   **Choice (c).** Choice (c) correctly describes the price movement of the stock. At the time of the announcement, the price of the stock should immediately decrease to reflect the negative information. Choice (a) violates the efficient markets hypothesis (EMH) because the share price should adjust immediately. A price adjustment over an extended period of time would allow investors to realize abnormal returns. Such a possibility violates the EMH. The same holds for choice (b). If the price of the stock were temporarily depressed below fair value, investors would have the opportunity to earn abnormal returns. Choice (d) is incorrect because there is enough information to predict the stock price movement.

13.18   In an efficient market, the cumulative abnormal return (CAR) for Prospectors would rise substantially at the announcement of a new discovery. The CAR falls slightly on any day when no discovery is announced. There is a small positive probability that there will be a discovery on any given day. If there is no discovery on a particular day, the price should fall slightly because the good event did not occur. The substantial price increases on the rare days of discovery should balance the small declines on the other days, leaving CARs that are horizontal over time. The substantial price increases on the rare days of discovery should balance the small declines on all the other days, leavings CARs that are horizontal over time.

13.19   Behavioral finance attempts to explain both the 1987 stock market crash and the Internet bubble by changes in investor sentiment and psychology. These changes can lead to non-random price behavior.

13.20   Chart the abnormal returns for each of the three airlines for the days preceding and following the announcement. The abnormal return is calculated by subtracting the market return from a stock's return on a particular day, $R_i - R_M$. Group the returns by the number of days before or after the announcement for each respective airline. Calculate the cumulative average abnormal return by adding each abnormal return to the previous day's abnormal return.

Abnormal returns $(R_i - R_M)$

Days from announcement	Delta	United	American	Sum	Average abnormal return	Cumulative average residual
-4	-0.2	-0.2	-0.2	-0.6	-0.2	-0.2
-3	0.2	-0.1	0.2	0.3	0.1	-0.1
-2	0.2	-0.2	0.0	0.0	0.0	-0.1
-1	0.2	0.2	-0.4	0.0	0.0	-0.1
0	3.3	0.2	1.9	5.4	1.8	1.7
1	0.2	0.1	0.0	0.3	0.1	1.8
2	-0.1	0.0	0.1	0.0	0.0	1.8
3	-0.2	0.1	-0.2	-0.3	-0.1	1.7
4	-0.1	-0.1	-0.1	-0.3	-0.1	1.6

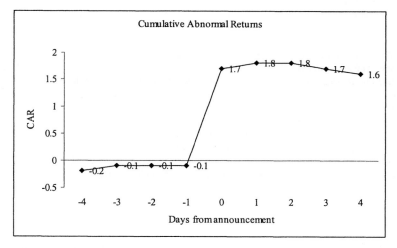

The market reacts favorably to the announcements. Moreover, the market reacts only on the day of the announcement. Before and after the event, the cumulative abnormal returns are relatively flat. This behavior is consistent with market efficiency.

13.21   The diagram does not support the efficient markets hypothesis. The CAR should remain relatively flat following the announcements. The diagram reveals that the CAR rose in the first month, only to drift down to lower levels during later months. Such movement violates the semi-strong form of the efficient markets hypothesis because an investor could earn abnormal profits while the stock price gradually decreased.

13.22 a. **Supports.** The CAR remained constant after the event at time 0. This result is consistent with market efficiency, because prices adjust immediately to reflect the new information.

Drops in CAR prior to an event can easily occur in an efficient capital market. For example, consider a sample of forced removals of the CEO. Since any CEO is more likely to be fired following bad rather than good stock performance, CARs are likely to be negative prior to removal. Because the firing of the CEO is announced at time 0, one cannot use this information to trade profitably *before* the announcement. Thus, price drops prior to an event are neither consistent nor inconsistent with the efficient markets hypothesis.

b. **Rejects.** Because the CAR increases after the event date, one can profit by buying after the event. This possibility is inconsistent with the efficient markets hypothesis.

c. **Supports.** The CAR does not fluctuate after the announcement at time 0. While the CAR was rising before the event, insider information would be needed for profitable trading. Thus, the graph is consistent with the semi-strong form of efficient markets.

d. **Supports.** The diagram indicates that the information announced at time 0 was of no value.

13.23 There appears to be a slight drop in the CAR prior to the event day. For the reason stated in problem 13.22, part (*a*), such movement is neither consistent nor inconsistent with the efficient markets hypothesis (EMH).

Movements at the event date are neither consistent nor inconsistent with the efficient markets hypothesis.

Once the verdict is reached, the diagram shows that the CAR continues to decline after the court decision, allowing investors to earn abnormal returns. The CAR should remain constant on average, even if an appeal is in progress, because no new information about the company is being revealed. Thus, the diagram is not consistent with the efficient markets hypothesis (EMH).

Chapter 14: Long-Term Financing: *An Introduction*

14.1   a.   Since the "common stock" entry in the balance sheet represents the total par value of the stock, simply divide that by the par per share:

$$\frac{\text{Common Stock}}{\text{Par Value}} = \frac{\$135{,}430}{\$2} = 67{,}715 \text{ shares}$$

      b.   Capital surplus is the amount received over par, so capital surplus minus par gives you the total dollars received.

In aggregate, the solution is:

Net capital from the sale of shares   = Common Stock + Capital Surplus
                                                         = \$135,430 + \$203,145
                                                         = \$338,575

Therefore, the average price is $338,575 / 67,715 = $5 per share

Alternatively, you can do this per share:

Average price   = Par value + Average capital surplus
                       = \$2 + \$203,145 / 67,715
                       = \$5 per share

      c.   Book value   = Assets - Liabilities = Equity
                           = Common stock + Capital surplus + Retained earnings
                           = \$2,708,600

Therefore, book value per share is $2,708,600 / 67,715= $40.

14.2   a.   Common stock = (Shares outstanding) x (Par value)
                               = 500 x \$1
                               = \$500

Total = 500 + 50,000 + 100,000 = $150,500

      b.   After issuing 1000 new shares, the firm will have 1500 shares outstanding, and the Capital surplus is found as:

Capital Surplus = Surplus last year + Surplus on sale
                            = \$50,000 + (\$30 - \$1)1,000
                            = \$79,000

That gives us:

Common stock	$1,500
Capital surplus	79,000
Retained earnings	100,000
Total	$180,500

14.3 a. In order to create the equity statement (following the example in the previous question or the text), first find the components:

Common stock = 325,000 shares outstanding x $5 par
= $1,625,000

Capital Surplus = (Avg price - par) (#shares)
= ($5(1.12) - $5) (325,000)
= $195,000

Retained earnings = previous retained earnings + Net income - Dividends
= $3,545,000 + $260,000 - ($260,000)(0.04)
= 3,794,600

Now, putting it all together:

Shareholders' equity

Common stock	$1,625,000
Capital in excess of par	195,000
Retained earnings	3,794,600
Total	$5,614,600

b. Common stock = (325,000 outstanding + 25,000 new shares) x $5 par
= $1,750,000

Capital Surplus = previous capital surplus, plus surplus from sale of new issues
= $195,000 + (Avg price - par) (# new shares)
= $195,000 + ($4 - $5) (25,000)
                [note the "surplus" is negative!]
= $170,000

Retained earnings = previous retained earnings + Net income - Dividends
= $3,545,000 + $260,000 - ($260,000)(0.04)
= 3,794,600

Shareholders' equity

Common stock	$1,750,000
Capital in excess of par*	170,000
Retained earnings	3,794,600
Total	$5,714,600

14.4   a.   Under straight voting, one share equals one vote. Thus, to ensure the election of one director you must hold a majority of the shares. Since two million shares are outstanding, you must hold more than 1,000,000 shares to have a majority of votes.

b.   Cumulative voting is often more easily understood through a story. Remember that your goal is to elect one board member of the seven who will be chosen today. Suppose the firm has 28 shares outstanding. You own 4 of the shares and one other person owns the remaining 24 shares. Under cumulative voting, the total number of votes equals the number of shares times the number of directors being elected, $(28)(7) = 196$. Therefore, you have 28 votes and the other stockholder has 168 votes.

Also, suppose the other shareholder does not wish to have your favorite candidate on the board. If that is true, the best you can do to try to ensure electing one member is to place all of your votes on your favorite candidate. To keep your candidate off the board, the other shareholder must have enough votes to elect all seven members who will be chosen. If the other shareholder splits her votes evenly across her seven favorite candidates, then eight people, your one favorite and her seven favorites, will all have the same number of votes. There will be a tie! If she does not split her votes evenly (for example 29 28 28 28 28 28 27) then your candidate will win a seat. To avoid a tie and assure your candidate of victory, you must have 29 votes which means you must own more than 4 shares.

Notice what happened. If seven board members will be elected and you want to be certain that one of your favorite candidates will win, you must have more than one-eighth of the shares.

That is, if the percentage of the shares you must have to win is N, then:

$$N > \frac{1}{(number\ of\ members\ being\ elected + number\ you\ want\ to\ select)}.$$

Also notice that the number of shares you need does not change if more than one person owns the remaining shares. If several people owned the remaining 168 shares they could form a coalition and vote together.

Thus, in the Unicorn election, you will need more than $1/(7+1) = 12.5\%$ of the shares to elect one board member. You will need more than $(2,000,000)(0.125) = 250,000$ shares.

14.4 (continued)

To view cumulative voting more rigorously:

1) let V = the *Total Number* of votes
   = the number of shares times the number of directors being elected
   = 2,000,000 x 7
   = 14,000,000

2) Let N be the number of shares you need. The number of shares necessary is

$$7N > \frac{V - 7N}{7}$$
$$7N > \frac{14,000,000 - 7N}{7}$$
$$N > 250,000$$

3) You will need more than 250,000 shares.

14.5 She can be certain to have one of her candidate friends elected under the cumulative voting rule. Modifying the equations in the previous question for percentages, let N be the percentage of shares needed, and V = 6 x 100%. Then,

$$6N > \frac{600\% - 6N}{6}$$
$$N > 14.28\%$$

Alternatively, you can find this as : the lowest percentage of shares she needs to own to elect at least one out of 6 candidates is higher than $1/7$ = 14.3%.
Either way, her current ownership of 17.3% is more than enough to ensure one seat.

If the voting rule is staggered as described in the question, she would need to own more than $1/4$=25% of the shares to elect one out of the three candidates for certain. In this case, she would not have enough shares.

14.6 a. You currently own 120 shares or 28.57% of the outstanding shares. You need to control 1/3 of the votes, which requires 140 shares. You need just over 20 additional shares to elect yourself to the board.

b. You need just over 25% of the shares, which is 250,000 shares. At $5 a share it will cost you $2,500,000 to guarantee yourself a seat on the board.

14.7   The differences between preferred stock and debt are:

a.   The dividends of preferred stock cannot be deducted as interest expenses when determining taxable corporate income. From the individual investor's point of view, preferred dividends are ordinary income for tax purposes. From corporate investors, 70% of the amount they receive as dividends from preferred stock are exempt from income taxes.

b.   In case of liquidation (at bankruptcy), preferred stock is junior to debt and senior to common stock.

c.   There is no legal obligation for firms to pay out preferred dividends as opposed to the obligated payment of interest on bonds. Therefore, firms cannot be forced into default if a preferred stock dividend is not paid in a given year. Preferred dividends can be cumulative or non-cumulative, and they can also be deferred indefinitely (of course, indefinitely deferring the dividends might have an undesirable effect on the market value of the stock).

14.8   Some firms can benefit from issuing preferred stock. The reasons can be:

a.   Public utilities can pass the tax disadvantage of issuing preferred stock on to their customers, so there is substantial amount of straight preferred stock issued by utilities.

b.   Firms reporting losses to the IRS already don't have positive income for tax deduction, so they are not affected by the tax disadvantage of dividend vs. interest payment. They may be willing to issue preferred stock.

c.   Firms that issue preferred stock can avoid the threat of bankruptcy that exists with debt financing because preferred dividends are not legal obligation as interest payment on corporate debt.

14.9   a.   The return on non-convertible preferred stock is lower than the return on corporate bond for two reasons:

i.   Corporate investors receive 70% tax deductibility on dividends if they hold the stock. Therefore, they are willing to pay more for the stock; that lowers its return.

ii.   Issuing corporations are willing and able to offer higher returns on debt since the interest on the debt reduces their tax liabilities. Preferred dividends are paid out of net income, hence they provide no tax shield.

b.   Corporate investors are the primary holders of preferred stock since, unlike individual investors, they can deduct 70% of the dividend when computing their tax liability. Therefore, they are willing to accept the lower return which the stock generates.

14.10   The following table summarizes the main difference between debt and equity:

	Debt	Equity
Repayment is an obligation of the firm	Yes	No
Grants ownership of the firm	No	Yes
Provides a tax shield	Yes	No
Liquidation will result if not paid	Yes	No

Companies often issue hybrid securities because of the potential tax shield and the bankruptcy advantage. If the IRS accepts the security as debt, the firm can use it as a tax shield. If the security maintains the bankruptcy and ownership advantages of equity, the firm has the best of both worlds.

14.11   The trends in long-term financing in the United States were presented in the text. If Cable Company follows the trends, it will probably use 80% internal financing, net income of the project plus depreciation less dividends, and 20% external financing, long term debt and equity.

Chapter 15: Capital Structure: *Basic Concepts*

15.1   a.   Since Alpha Corporation is an all-equity firm, its value is equal to the market value of its outstanding shares. Alpha has 5,000 shares of common stock outstanding, worth $20 per share.

Therefore, the value of Alpha Corporation is $100,000 (= 5,000 shares * $20 per share).

    b.   Modigliani-Miller Proposition I states that in the absence of taxes, the value of a levered firm equals the value of an otherwise identical unlevered firm. Since Beta Corporation is identical to Alpha Corporation in every way except its capital structure and neither firm pays taxes, the value of the two firms should be equal.

Modigliani-Miller Proposition I (No Taxes): $V_L = V_U$

Alpha Corporation, an unlevered firm, is worth $100,000 ($V_U$).

Therefore, the value of Beta Corporation (V_L) is $100,000.

    c.   The value of a levered firm equals the market value of its debt plus the market value of its equity.

$$V_L = B + S$$

The value of Beta Corporation is $100,000 ($V_L$), and the market value of the firm's debt is $25,000 (B).

The value of Beta's equity is: $\begin{aligned} S \ &= V_L - B \\ &= \$100,000 - \$25,000 \\ &= \$75,000 \end{aligned}$

Therefore, the market value of Beta Corporation's equity (S) is $75,000.

    d.   Since the market value of Alpha Corporation's equity is $100,000, it will cost **$20,000** (= 0.20 * $100,000) to purchase 20% of the firm's equity.

Since the market value of Beta Corporation's equity is $75,000, it will cost **$15,000** (= 0.20 * $75,000) to purchase 20% of the firm's equity.

    e.   Since Alpha Corporation expects to earn $350,000 this year and owes no interest payments, the dollar return to an investor who owns 20% of the firm's equity is expected to be **$70,000** (= 0.20 * $350,000) over the next year.

While Beta Corporation also expects to earn $350,000 before interest this year, it must pay 12% interest on its debt. Since the market value of Beta's debt at the beginning of the year is $25,000, Beta must pay $3,000 (= 0.12 * $25,000) in interest at the end of the year. Therefore, the amount of the firm's earnings available to equity holders is $347,000 (= $350,000 - $3,000). The dollar return to an investor who owns 20% of the firm's equity is **$69,400** (= 0.20 * $347,000).

    f.   The initial cost of purchasing 20% of Alpha Corporation's equity is $20,000, but the cost to an investor of purchasing 20% of Beta Corporation's equity is only $15,000 (see part *d*).

In order to purchase $20,000 worth of Alpha's equity using only $15,000 of his own money, the investor must borrow $5,000 to cover the difference. The investor must pay 12% interest on his borrowings at the end of the year.

Since the investor now owns 20% of Alpha's equity, the dollar return on his equity investment at the end of the year is $70,000 (= 0.20 * $350,000). However, since he borrowed $5,000 at 12% per annum, he must pay $600 (= 0.12 * $5,000) at the end of the year.

Therefore, the cash flow to the investor at the end of the year is $69,400 (= $70,000 - $600).

Notice that this amount exactly matches the dollar return to an investor who purchases 20% of Beta's equity.

Strategy Summary:
1. Borrow $5,000 at 12%.
2. Purchase 20% of Alpha's stock for a net cost of $15,000 (= $20,000 - $5,000 borrowed).

g. The equity of Beta Corporation is riskier. Beta must pay off its debt holders before its equity holders receive any of the firm's earnings. If the firm does not do particularly well, all of the firm's earnings may be needed to repay its debt holders, and equity holders will receive nothing.

15.2 a. A firm's debt-equity ratio is the market value of the firm's debt divided by the market value of a firm's equity.

The market value of Acetate's debt $10 million, and the market value of Acetate's equity is $20 million.

Debt-Equity Ratio = Market Value of Debt / Market Value of Equity
$$= \$10 \text{ million} / \$20 \text{ million}$$
$$= \tfrac{1}{2}$$

Therefore, Acetate's Debt-Equity Ratio is ½.

b. In the absence of taxes, a firm's weighted average cost of capital (r_{wacc}) is equal to:

$$r_{wacc} = \{B / (B+S)\}\, r_B + \{S / (B+S)\} r_S$$

where B = the market value of the firm's debt
S = the market value of the firm's equity
r_B = the pre-tax cost of a firm's debt
r_S = the cost of a firm's equity.

In this problem: $B = \$10,000,000$
$S = \$20,000,000$
$r_B = 14\%$

The Capital Asset Pricing Model (CAPM) must be used to calculate the cost of Acetate's equity (r_S)

According to the CAPM: $r_S = r_f + \beta_S\{E(r_m) - r_f\}$

where r_f = the risk-free rate of interest
$E(r_m)$ = the expected rate of return on the market portfolio
β_S = the beta of a firm's equity

In this problem: r_f = 8%
$E(r_m)$ = 18%
β_S = 0.9

Therefore, the cost of Acetate's equity is:

$$r_S = r_f + \beta_S\{E(r_m) - r_f\}$$
$$= 0.08 + 0.9(\ 0.18 - 0.08)$$
$$= \mathbf{0.17}$$

The cost of Acetate's equity (r_S) is 17%.

Acetate's weighted average cost of capital equals:

$$r_{wacc} = \{B / (B+S)\}\ r_B + \{S / (B+S)\}r_S$$
$$= (\$10\ \text{million} / \$30\ \text{million})(0.14) + (\$20\ \text{million} / \$30\ \text{million})(0.17)$$
$$= (1/3)(0.14) + (2/3)(0.17)$$
$$= \mathbf{0.16}$$

Therefore, Acetate's weighted average cost of capital is 16%.

c. According to Modigliani-Miller Proposition II (No Taxes):

$$r_S = r_0 + (B/S)(r_0 - r_B)$$

where r_0 = the cost of capital for an all-equity firm
r_S = the cost of equity for a levered firm
r_B = the pre-tax cost of debt

In this problem: $r_S = 0.17$
$r_B = 0.14$
$B = \$10{,}000{,}000$
$S = \$20{,}000{,}000$

Thus: $0.17 = r_0 + (1/2)(r_0 - 0.14)$

Solving for r_0: $\mathbf{r_0 = 0.16}$

Therefore, the cost of capital for an otherwise identical all-equity firm is 16%.

This is consistent with Modigliani-Miller's proposition that, in the absence of taxes, the cost of capital for an all-equity firm is equal to the weighted average cost of capital of an otherwise identical levered firm.

15.3 Since Unlevered is an all-equity firm, its value is equal to the market value of its outstanding shares. Unlevered has 10 million shares of common stock outstanding, worth $80 per share.

Therefore, the value of Unlevered is $800 million (= 10 million shares * $80 per share).

Modigliani-Miller Proposition I states that, in the absence of taxes, the value of a levered firm equals the value of an otherwise identical unlevered firm. Since Levered is identical to Unlevered in every way except its capital structure and neither firm pays taxes, the value of the two firms should be equal.

Modigliani-Miller Proposition I (No Taxes): $V_L = V_U$

Therefore, the market value of Levered, Inc., *should be* $800 million also.

Since Levered has 4.5 million outstanding shares, worth $100 per share, the market value of Levered's equity is $450 million. The market value of Levered's debt is $275 million.

The value of a levered firm equals the market value of its debt plus the market value of its equity.

Therefore, the current market value of Levered, Inc. is:

$$V_L = B + S$$
$$= \$275 \text{ million} + \$450 \text{ million}$$
$$= \textbf{\$725 million}$$

The market value of Levered's equity needs to be $525 million, $75 million higher than its current market value of $450 million, for MM Proposition I to hold.

Since Levered's market value is less than Unlevered's market value, Levered is relatively underpriced and an investor should buy shares of the firm's stock.

15.4   a.   Since the market value of Knight's equity is $1,714,000, 5% of the firm's equity costs $85,700 (= 0.05 * $1,714,000).

Since the market value of Veblen's equity is $2,400,000, 5% of the firm's equity costs $120,000 (= 0.05 * $2,400,000). In order to compare dollar returns, the initial net cost of both positions should be the same. Therefore, the investor will borrow $34,300 (= $120,000 - $87,500) at 6% per annum when purchasing $120,000 of Veblen's equity for a net cost of $85,700 (= $120,000 - $34,300).

An investor who owns 5% of Knight's equity will be entitled to 5% of the firm's earnings available to common stock holders at the end of each year. While Knight's expected operating income is $300,000, it must pay $60,000 to debt holders before distributing any of its earnings to stockholders. Knight's expected earnings available to stockholders is $240,000 (= $300,000 -$60,000).

Therefore, an investor who owns 5% of Knight's stock expects to receive a dollar return of $12,000 (= 0.05 * $240,000) at the end of each year based on an initial net cost of $85,700.

An investor who owns 5% of Veblen's equity will be entitled to 5% of the firm's earnings at the end of each year. Since Veblen is an all-equity firm, it owes none of its money to debt holders and can distribute all $300,000 of its earnings to stockholders. An investor who owns 5% of Veblen's equity will expect to receive a dollar return of $15,000 at the end of each year. However, since this investor borrowed $34,300 at 6% per annum in order to fund his equity purchase, he owes $2,058 (= 0.06 * $34,300) in interest payments at the end of each year. This reduces his expected net dollar return to $12,942 (= $15,000 - $2,058).

Therefore, an investor who borrows $34,300 at 6% per anunm in order to purchase 5% of Veblen's stock will expect to receive a dollar return of $12,942 at the end of the year for an initial net cost of $85,700.

For a net cost of $85,700, purchasing 5% of Veblen's equity yields a higher expected dollar return than purchasing 5% of Knight's equity.

   b.   Both of the above two strategies cost $85,700. Since the dollar return to the investment in Veblen is *higher*, all investors will choose to invest in Veblen over Knight.

The process of investors purchasing Veblen's equity rather than Knight's will cause the market value of Veblen's equity to rise and the market value of Knight's equity to fall. Any differences in the dollar returns to the two strategies will be eliminated, and the process will cease when the total market values of the two firms are equal.

15.5   Before the restructuring the market value of Grimsley's equity was $5,000,000 (= 100,000 shares * $50 per share). Since Grimsley issues $1,000,000 worth of debt and uses the proceeds to repurchase shares, the market value of the firm's equity after the restructuring is $4,000,000 (= $5,000,000 - $1,000,000). Because the firm used the $1,000,000 to repurchase 20,000 shares, the firm has 80,000 (100,000 – 20,000) shares outstanding after the restructuring. Note that the market value of Grimsley's stock remains at $50 per share (= $4,000,000 / 80,000 shares). This is consistent with Modigliani and Miller's theory.

Since Ms. Hannon owned $10,000 worth of the firm's stock, she owned 0.2% (= $10,000 / $5,000,000) of Grimsley's equity before the restructuring. Ms. Hannon also borrowed $2,000 at 20% per annum, resulting in $400 (= 0.20 * $2,000) of interest payments at the end of the year.

Let Y equal Grimsley's earnings over the next year. Before the restructuring, Ms. Hannon's payout, net of personal interest payments, at the end of the year was:

(0.002)($Y) - $400

After the restructuring, the firm must pay $200,000 (= 0.20 * $1,000,000) in interest to debt holders at the end of the year before it can distribute any of its earnings to equity holders. Also, since the market value of Grimsley's equity dropped from $5,000,000 to $4,000,000, Ms. Hannon's $10,000 holding of stock now represents 0.25% (= $10,000 / $4,000,000) of the firm's equity. For these two reasons, Ms. Hannon's payout at the end of the year will change.

After the restructuring, Ms. Hannon's payout at the end of the year will be:

 (0.0025)($Y - $200,000) - $400

which simplifies to:

(0.0025)($Y) - $900

In order for the payout from her post-restructuring portfolio to match the payout from her pre-restructuring portfolio, Ms. Hannon will need to sell 0.05% (= 0.0025 – 0.002) of Grimsley's equity. She will then receive 0.2% of the firm's earnings, just as she did before the restructuring. Ignoring any personal borrowing or lending, this will change Ms. Hannon's payout at the end of the year to:

(0.002)($Y - $200,000)

which simplifies to:

(0.002)($Y) - $400

Therefore, Ms. Hannon must sell $2,000 (= 0.0005 * $4,000,000) of Grimsley's stock and eliminate any personal borrowing in order to rebalance her portfolio. Her new financial positions are:

	Value of Grimsley Shares	Total Borrowing	Total Lending
Ms. Hannon	$ 8,000	$ -	$ -

Since Ms. Finney owned $50,000 worth of the firm's stock, she owned 1% (= $50,000 / $5,000,000) of Grimsley's equity before the restructuring. Ms. Finney also lent $6,000 at 20% per annum, resulting in the receipt of $1,200 (= 0.20 * $6,000) in interest payments at the end of the year.

Therefore, before the restructuring, Ms.Finney's payout, net of personal interest payments, at the end of the year was:

(0.01)($Y) + $1,200

After the restructuring, the firm must pay $200,000 (= 0.20 * $1,000,000) in interest to debt holders at the end of the year before it can distribute any of its earnings to equity holders. Also, since the market value of Grimsley's equity dropped from $5,000,000 to $4,000,000, Ms. Finney's $50,000 holding of stock now represents 1.25% (= $50,000 / $4,000,000) of the firm's equity. For these two reasons, Ms. Finney's payout at the end of the year will change.

After the restructuring, Ms. Finney's payout at the end of the year will be:

(0.0125)($Y - $200,000) + $1,200

which simplifies to:

(0.0125)($Y) - $1,300

In order for the payout from her post-restructuring portfolio to match the payout from her pre-restructuring portfolio, Ms. Finney will need to sell 0.25% (= 0.0125 – 0.01) of Grimsley's equity. She will then receive 1% of the firm's earnings, just as she did before the restructuring. Ignoring any personal borrowing or lending, this will change Ms. Finney's payout at the end of the year to:

(0.01)($Y - $200,000)

which simplifies to:

(0.01)($Y) - $2,000

In order to receive a net cash inflow of $1,200 at the end of the year in addition to her 1% claim on Grimsley's earnings, Ms. Finney will need to receive $3,200 {= $1,200 – (-$2,000)} in personal interest payments at the end of the year. Since Ms. Finney can lend at an interest rate of 20% per annum, she will need to lend $16,000 (= $3,200 / 0.20) in order to receive an interest payment of $3,200 at the end of the year. After lending $16,000 at 20% per annum, Ms. Finney's new payout at the end of the year is:

(0.01)($Y - $200,000) + $3,200

which simplifies to:

(0.01)($Y) + $1,200

Therefore, Ms. Finney must sell $10,000 (= 0.0025 * $4,000,000) of Grimsley's stock and add $10,000 more to her lending position in order to rebalance her portfolio. Her new financial positions are:

	Value of Grimsley Shares	Total Borrowing	Total Lending
Ms. Finney	$ 40,000	$ -	$ 16,000

Since Ms. Grace owned $20,000 worth of the firm's stock, she owned 0.4% (= $20,000 / $5,000,000) of Grimsley's equity before the restructuring. Ms. Grace had no personal position in lending or borrowing.

Therefore, before the restructuring, Ms. Grace's payout at the end of the year was:

(0.004)($Y)

After the restructuring, the firm must pay $200,000 (= 0.20 * $1,000,000) in interest to debt holders at the end of the year before it can distribute any of its earnings to equity holders. Also, since the market value of Grimsley's equity dropped from $5,000,000 to $4,000,000, Ms. Grace's $20,000 holding of stock now represents 0.5% (= $20,000 / $4,000,000) of the firm's equity. For these two reasons, Ms. Grace's payout at the end of the year will change.

After the restructuring, Ms. Grace's payout at the end of the year will be:

(0.005)($Y - $200,000)

which simplifies to:

(0.005)($Y) - $1,000

In order for the payout from her post-restructuring portfolio to match the payout from her pre-restructuring portfolio, Ms. Grace will need to sell 0.1% (= 0.005 – 0.004) of Grimsley's equity. She will then receive 0.4% of the firm's earnings, just as she did before the restructuring. This will change Ms. Grace's payout at the end of the year to:

(0.004)($Y - $200,000)

which simplifies to:

(0.004)($Y) - $800

In order to receive no net cash flow at the end of the year other than her 0.4% claim on Grimsley's earnings, Ms. Grace will need to receive $800 {= $0 – (-$800)} in interest payments at the end of the year. Since Ms. Grace can lend at an interest rate of 20% per annum, she will need to lend $4,000 (= $800 / 0.20) in order to receive an interest payment of $800 at the end of the year. After lending $4,000 at 20% per annum, Ms.Grace's new payout at the end of the year is:

(0.004)($Y - $200,000) + $800

which simplifies to:

(0.004)($Y)

Therefore, Ms. Grace must sell $4,000 (= 0.001 * $4,000,000) of Grimsley's stock and lend $4,000 in order to rebalance her portfolio. Her new financial positions are:

	Value of Grimsley Shares	Total Borrowing	Total Lending
Ms.Grace	$ 16,000	$ -	$ 4,000

15.6 a.   According to Modigliani-Miller the weighted average cost of capital (r_{wacc}) for a levered firm is equal to the cost of equity for an unlevered firm in a world with no taxes. Since Rayburn pays no taxes, its weighted average cost of capital after the restructuring will equal the cost of the firm's equity before the restructuring.

Therefore, Rayburn's weighted average cost of capital will be 18% after the restructuring.

b.   According to Modigliani-Miller Proposition II (No Taxes):

$r_S = r_0 + (B/S)(r_0 - r_B)$

where r_0 = the cost of capital for an all-equity firm
         r_S = the cost of equity for a levered firm
         r_B = the pre-tax cost of debt

In this problem: $r_0 = 0.18$
                    $r_B = 0.10$
                    $B = \$400,000$
                    $S = \$1,600,000$

The cost of Rayburn's equity after the restructuring is:

r_S $= r_0 + (B/S)(r_0 - r_B)$
         $= 0.18 + (\$400,000 / \$1,600,000)(0.18 - 0.10)$
         $= 0.18 + (1/4)(0.18 - 0.10)$
         $= \mathbf{0.20}$

Therefore, Rayburn's cost of equity after the restructuring will be 20%.

In accordance with Modigliani-Miller Proposition II (No Taxes), the cost of Rayburn's equity will rise as the firm adds debt to its capital structure since the risk to equity holders increases with leverage.

c.   In the absence of taxes, a firm's weighted average cost of capital (r_{wacc}) is equal to:

r_{wacc} $= \{B / (B+S)\}\, r_B + \{S / (B+S)\}r_S$

where B = the market value of the firm's debt
         S = the market value of the firm's equity
         r_B = the pre-tax cost of the firm's debt
         r_S = the cost of the firm's equity.

In this problem: $B = \$400,000$
                    $S = \$1,600,000$
                    $r_B = 10\%$
                    $r_S = 20\%$

Rayburn's weighted average cost of capital after the restructuring will be:

r_{wacc} $= \{B / (B+S)\}\, r_B + \{S / (B+S)\}r_S$
              $= (\$400,000 / \$2,000,000)(0.10) + (\$1,600,000 / \$2,000,000)(0.20)$
              $= (1/5)(0.10) + (4/5)(0.20)$
              $= \mathbf{0.18}$

Consistent with part *a*, Rayburn's weighted average cost of capital after the restructuring remains at 18%.

15.7   a.   Strom is an all-equity firm with 250,000 shares of common stock outstanding, where each share is worth $20.

Therefore, the market value of Strom's equity before the buyout is $5,000,000 (= 250,000 shares * $20 per share).

Since the firm expects to earn $750,000 per year in perpetuity and the appropriate discount rate to its unlevered equity holders is 15%, the market value of Strom's assets is equal to a perpetuity of $750,000 per year, discounted at 15%.

Therefore, the market value of Strom's assets before the buyout is $5,000,000 (= $750,000 / 0.15).

Strom's market-value balance sheet prior to the announcement of the buyout is:

Strom, Inc.

Assets =	$ 5,000,000	Debt =	$ -
		Equity =	$ 5,000,000
Total Assets =	$ 5,000,000	Total D + E =	$ 5,000,000

b.   i.   According to the efficient-market hypothesis, Strom's stock price will change immediately to reflect the NPV of the project. Since the buyout will cost Strom $300,000 but increase the firm's annual earnings by $120,000 into perpetuity, the NPV of the buyout can be calculated as follows:

$$NPV_{BUYOUT} = -\$300,000 + (\$120,000 / 0.15)$$
$$= \$500,000$$

Remember that the required return on the acquired firm's earnings is also 15% per annum.

The market value of Strom's equity will increase immediately after the announcement to $5,500,000 (= $5,000,000 + $500,000).

Since Strom has 250,000 shares of common stock outstanding and the market value of the firm's equity is $5,500,000, Strom's new stock price will immediately rise to $22 per share (= $5,500,000 / 250,000 shares) after the announcement of the buyout.

According to the efficient-market hypothesis, Strom's stock price will immediately rise to $22 per share after the announcement of the buyout.

ii.   After the announcement, Strom has 250,000 shares of common stock outstanding, worth $22 per share.

Therefore, the market value of Strom's equity immediately after the announcement is $5,500,000 (= 250,000 shares * $22 per share).

The NPV of the buyout is $500,000.

Strom's market-value balance sheet after the announcement of the buyout is:

Strom, Inc.

Old Assets =	$ 5,000,000	Debt =	$ -
NPV$_{BUYOUT}$ =	$ 500,000	Equity =	$ 5,500,000
Total Assets =	$ 5,500,000	Total D + E =	$ 5,500,000

iii. Strom needs to issue $300,000 worth of equity in order to fund the buyout. The market value of the firm's stock is $22 per share after the announcement.

Therefore, Strom will need to issue 13,636.3636 shares (= $300,000 / $22 per share) in order to fund the buyout.

iv. Strom will receive $300,000 (= 13,636.3636 shares * $22 per share) in cash after the equity issue. This will increase the firm's assets by $300,000. Since the firm now has 263,636.3636 (= 250,000 + 13,636.3636) shares outstanding, where each is worth $22, the market value of the firm's equity increases to $5,800,000 (=263,636.3636 shares * $22 per share).

Strom's market-value balance sheet after the equity issue will be:

Strom, Inc.

Old Assets =	$ 5,000,000	Debt =	$	-
Cash =	$ 300,000	Equity =	$ 5,800,000	
NPV_{BUYOUT} =	$ 500,000			
Total Assets =	$ 5,800,000	Total D + E =	$ 5,800,000	

v. When Strom makes the purchase, it will pay $300,000 in cash and receive the present value of its competitor's facilities. Since these facilities will generate $120,000 of earnings forever, their present value is equal to a perpetuity of $120,000 per year, discounted at 15%.

$$PV_{NEW\ FACILITIES} = \$120,000 / 0.15$$
$$= \$800,000$$

Strom's market-value balance sheet after the buyout is:

Strom, Inc.

Old Assets =	$ 5,000,000	Debt =	$	-
$PV_{NEW\ FACILITIES}$ =	$ 800,000	Equity =	$ 5,800,000	
Total Assets =	$ 5,800,000	Total D + E =	$ 5,800,000	

vi. The expected return to equity holders is the ratio of annual earnings to the market value of the firm's equity.

Strom's old assets generate $750,000 of earnings per year, and the new facilities generate $120,000 of earnings per year. Therefore, Strom's expected earnings will be $870,000 per year. Since the firm has no debt in its capital structure, all of these earnings are available to equity holders. The market value of Strom's equity is $5,800,000.

The expected return to Strom's equity holders is 15% (= $870,000 / $5,800,000).

Therefore, adding more equity to the firm's capital structure does not alter the required return on the firm's equity.

vii. In the absence of taxes, a firm's weighted average cost of capital (r_{wacc}) is equal to:

$$r_{wacc} = \{B / (B+S)\}\ r_B + \{S / (B+S)\}r_S$$

where B = the market value of the firm's debt
      S = the market value of the firm's equity
      r_B = the pre-tax cost of the firm's debt
      r_S = the cost of the firm's equity.

In this problem: B = $0
               S = $5,800,000
               r_B = 0%
               r_S = 15%

Strom's weighted average cost of capital after the buyout is:

$$r_{wacc} = \{B / (B+S)\}\, r_B + \{S / (B+S)\} r_S$$
$$= (\$0 / \$5,800,000)(0) + (\$5,800,000 / \$5,800,000)(0.15)$$
$$= (1)(0.15)$$

$$= \mathbf{0.15}$$

Therefore, Strom's weighted average cost of capital after the buyout is 15% if Strom issues equity to fund the purchase.

c.   i.   After the announcement, the value of Strom's assets will increase by the $500,000, the net present value of the new facilities. Under the efficient-market hypothesis, the market value of Strom's equity will immediately rise to reflect the NPV of the new facilities.

Therefore, the market value of Strom's equity will be $5,500,000 (= $5,000,000 + $500,000) after the announcement. Since the firm has 250,000 shares of common stock outstanding, Strom's new stock price will be $22 per share (= $5,500,000 / 250,000).

Strom's market-value balance sheet after the announcement is:

Strom, Inc.

Old Assets =	$ 5,000,000	Debt =	$ -
NPV_{BUYOUT} =	$ 500,000	Equity =	$ 5,500,000
Total Assets =	$ 5,500,000	Total D + E =	$ 5,500,000

ii.   Strom will receive $300,000 in cash after the debt issue. The market value of the firm's debt will be $300,000.

Strom's market-value balance sheet after the debt issue will be:

Strom, Inc.

Old Assets =	$ 5,000,000	Debt =	$ 300,000
Cash =	$ 300,000	Equity =	$ 5,500,000
NPV_{BUYOUT} =	$ 500,000		
Total Assets =	$ 5,800,000	Total D + E =	$ 5,800,000

iii.   Strom will pay $300,000 in cash for the facilities. Since these facilities will generate $120,000 of earnings forever, their present value is equal to a perpetuity of $120,000 per year, discounted at 15%.

$$PV_{NEW\ FACILITIES} = \$120,000 / 0.15$$
$$= \$800,000$$

Strom's market-value balance sheet after the buyout will be:

Strom, Inc.				
Old Assets =	$ 5,000,000	Debt =	$	300,000
PV$_{NEW\ FACILITIES}$ =	$ 800,000	Equity =	$	5,500,000
Total Assets =	$ 5,800,000	Total D + E =	$	5,800,000

iv. The expected return to equity holders is the ratio of annual earnings to the market value of the firm's equity.

Strom's old assets generate $750,000 of earnings per year, and the new facilities generate $120,000 of earnings per year. Therefore, Strom's earnings will be $870,000 per year. Since the firm has $300,000 worth of 10% debt in its capital structure, the firm must make $30,000 (= 0.10 * $300,000) in interest payments. Therefore, Strom's net earnings are only $840,000 (= $870,000 - $30,000). The market value of Strom's equity is $5,500,000.

The expected return to Strom's equity holders is 15.27% (= $840,000 / $5,500,000).

Therefore, adding more debt to the firm's capital structure increases the required return on the firm's equity. This is in accordance with Modigliani-Miller Proposition II.

v. In the absence of taxes, a firm's weighted average cost of capital (r_{wacc}) is equal to:

$$r_{wacc} = \{B / (B+S)\}\ r_B + \{S / (B+S)\}r_S$$

where B = the market value of the firm's debt
S = the market value of the firm's equity
r_B = the pre-tax cost of the firm's debt
r_S = the cost of the firm's equity.

In this problem: B = $300,000
S = $5,500,000
r_B = 10%
r_S = 15.27%

Strom's weighted average cost of capital after the buyout will be:

$$
\begin{aligned}
r_{wacc} &= \{B / (B+S)\}\ r_B + \{S / (B+S)\}r_S \\
&= (\$300,000 / \$5,800,000)(0.10) + (\$5,500,000 / \$5,800,000)(0.1527) \\
&= (3/58)(0.10) + (55/58)(0.1527)
\end{aligned}
$$

$$= 0.15$$

Therefore, Strom's weighted average cost of capital after the buyout will be 15% regardless of whether the firm issues debt or equity.

15.8 a. Without the power plant, the Gulf expects to earn $27 million per year into perpetuity. Since Gulf is an all-equity firm and the required rate of return on the firm's equity is 10%, the market value of Gulf's assets is equal to the present value of a perpetuity of $27,000,000 per year, discounted at 10%.

$$
\begin{aligned}
PV(Perpetuity) &= C / r \\
&= \$27,000,000 / 0.10 \\
&= \textbf{\$270,000,000}
\end{aligned}
$$

Therefore, the market value of Gulf's assets before the firm announces that it will build a new power plant is $270,000,000. Since Gulf is an all-equity firm, the market value of Gulf's equity is also $270,000,000.

Gulf's market-value balance sheet before the announcement of the buyout is made is:

Gulf Power

Assets =	$ 270,000,000	Debt =	$ -
		Equity =	$ 270,000,000
Total Assets =	$ 270,000,000	Total D + E =	$ 270,000,000

Since the market value of Gulf's equity is $270 million and the firm has 10 million shares outstanding, Gulf's stock price before the announcement to build the new power plant is $27 per share (= $270 million / 10 million shares).

b.   i.   According to the efficient-market hypothesis, the market value of Gulf's equity will change immediately to reflect the net present value of the project. Since the new power plant will cost Gulf $20 million but will increase the firm's annual earnings by $3 million in perpetuity, the NPV of the new power plant can be calculated as follows:

$$NPV_{NEW\ POWER\ PLANT} = -\$20\ million + (\$3\ million/\ 0.10)$$
$$= \$10\ million$$

Remember that the required return on the firm's equity is 10% per annum.

Therefore, the market value of Gulf's equity will increase to $280 million (= $270 million + $10 million) immediately after the announcement.

Gulf's market-value balance sheet after the announcement will be:

Gulf Power

Old Assets =	$ 270,000,000	Debt =	$ -
$NPV_{POWER\ PLANT}$ =	$ 10,000,000	Equity =	$ 280,000,000
Total Assets =	$ 280,000,000	Total D + E =	$ 280,000,000

Since Gulf has 10 million shares of common stock outstanding and the total market value of the firm's equity is $280 million , Gulf's new stock price will immediately rise to $28 per share (= $280 million / 10 million shares) after the firm's announcement.

ii.   Gulf needs to issue $20 million worth of equity in order to fund the construction of the power plant. The market value of the firm's stock will be $28 per share after the announcement.

Therefore, Gulf will need to issue 714,285.71 shares (= $20 million / $28 per share) in order to fund the construction of the power plant.

iii.   Gulf will receive $20 million (= 714,285.71 shares * $28 per share) in cash after the equity issue. Since the firm now has 10,714,285.71 (= 10 million + 714,285.71) shares outstanding, where each share is worth $28, the market value of the firm's equity increases to $300,000,000 (=10,714,285.71 shares * $28 per share).

Gulf's market-value balance sheet after the equity issue will be:

Gulf Power

Old Assets =	$ 270,000,000	Debt =	$ -
Cash =	$ 20,000,000	Equity =	$ 300,000,000
$NPV_{POWER\ PLANT}$ =	$ 10,000,000		
Total Assets =	$ 300,000,000	Total D + E =	$ 300,000,000

iv. Gulf will pay $20,000,000 in cash for the power plant. Since the plant will generate $3 million in annual earnings forever, its present value is equal to a perpetuity of $3 million per year, discounted at 10%.

$$PV_{NEW\ POWER\ PLANT} = \$3\ million\ /\ 0.10$$
$$= \$30\ million$$

Gulf's market-value balance sheet after the construction of the power plant will be:

Gulf Power

Old Assets =	$ 270,000,000	Debt =	$	-
PV$_{POWER\ PLANT}$ =	$ 30,000,000	Equity =	$ 300,000,000	
Total Assets =	$ 300,000,000	Total D + E =	$ 300,000,000	

v. Since Gulf is an all-equity firm, its value will equal the market value of its equity.

Therefore, the value of Gulf Power will be $300 million if the firm issues equity to finance the construction of the power plant.

c. i. Under the efficient-market hypothesis, the market value of the firm's equity will immediately rise by $10 million following the announcement to reflect the NPV of the power plant.

Therefore, the total market value of Gulf's equity will be $280 million (= $270 million + $10 million) after the firm's announcement.

Gulf's market-value balance sheet after the announcement will be:

Gulf Power

Old Assets =	$ 270,000,000	Debt =	$	-
NPV$_{POWER\ PLANT}$ =	$ 10,000,000	Equity =	$ 280,000,000	
Total Assets =	$ 280,000,000	Total D + E =	$ 280,000,000	

Since the firm has 10 million shares of common stock outstanding, Gulf's new stock price will be $28 per share (= $280 million / 10 million shares).

ii. Gulf will receive $20 million in cash after the debt issue. The market value of the firm's debt will be $20 million.

Gulf's market-value balance sheet after the debt issue will be:

Gulf Power

Old Assets =	$ 270,000,000	Debt =	$ 20,000,000
Cash =	$ 20,000,000	Equity =	$ 280,000,000
NPV$_{POWER\ PLANT}$ =	$ 10,000,000		
Total Assets =	$ 300,000,000	Total D + E =	$ 300,000,000

iii. Gulf will pay $20 million in cash for the power plant. Since the plant will generate $3 million of earnings forever, its present value is equal to a perpetuity of $3 million per year, discounted at 10%.

$$PV_{POWER\ PLANT} = \$3\ million\ /\ 0.10$$
$$= \$30\ million$$

Gulf's market-value balance sheet after it builds the new power plant is:

Gulf Power

Old Assets =	$	270,000,000	Debt =	$	20,000,000
PV$_{POWER\ PLANT}$ =	$	30,000,000	Equity =	$	280,000,000
Total Assets =	$	300,000,000	Total D + E =	$	300,000,000

iv. The value of a levered firm is the sum of the market values of the firm's debt and equity. Since the market value of Gulf's debt will be $20 million and the market value of Gulf's equity will be $280 million, the value of Gulf Power will be $300 million if the firm decides to issue debt in order to fund the outlay for the power plant.

Therefore, the value of Gulf Power will be $300 million regardless of whether the firm issues debt or equity to fund the construction of the new power plant.

v. According to Modigliani-Miller Proposition II (No Taxes):

$$r_S = r_0 + (B/S)(r_0 - r_B)$$

where r_0 = the required return on an unlevered firm's equity
r_S = the required return on a firm's equity
r_B = the required return on a firm's debt

In this problem: $r_0 = 0.10$
$r_B = 0.08$
$B = \$20$ million
$S = \$280$ million

The required return on Gulf's levered equity is:

r_S $= r_0 + (B/S)(r_0 - r_B)$
$= 0.10 + (\$20$ million $/ \$280$ million$)(0.10 - 0.08)$
$= 0.10 + (1/14)(0.10 - 0.08)$
$= \mathbf{10.14\%}$

Therefore, the required return on Gulf's levered equity is 10.14%.

vi. In the absence of taxes, a firm's weighted average cost of capital (r_{wacc}) is equal to:

r_{wacc} $= \{B / (B+S)\}\ r_B + \{S / (B+S)\}r_S$

where B = the market value of the firm's debt
S = the market value of the firm's equity
r_B = the required return on the firm's debt
r_S = the required return on the firm's equity.

In this problem: B = $20 million
S = $280 million
$r_B = 8\%$
$r_S = 10.14\%$

Gulf's weighted average cost of capital after the construction of the new power plant is:

$$r_{wacc} = \{B / (B+S)\} r_B + \{S / (B+S)\} r_S$$
$$= (\$20 \text{ million} / \$300 \text{ million})(0.08) + (\$280 \text{ million} / \$300 \text{ million})(0.1014)$$
$$= (1/15)(0.08) + (14/15)(0.1014)$$
$$= \mathbf{0.10}$$

Therefore, Gulf's weighted average cost of capital will be 10% following either debt or equity financing.

15.9   a.   False. A reduction in leverage will decrease both the risk of the stock and its expected return. Modigliani and Miller state that, in the absence of taxes, these two effects exactly cancel each other out and leave the price of the stock and the overall value of the firm unchanged.

b.   False. Modigliani-Miller Proposition II (No Taxes) states that the required return on a firm's equity is positively related to the firm's debt-equity ratio $[r_S = r_0 + (B/S)(r_0 - r_B)]$. Therefore, any increase in the amount of debt in a firm's capital structure will increase the required return on the firm's equity.

15.10   Assumptions of the Modigliani-Miller theory in a world without taxes:

1.   Individuals can borrow at the same interest rate at which the firm borrows.

Since investors can purchase securities on margin, an individual's effective interest rate is probably no higher than that for a firm. Therefore, this assumption is reasonable when applying MM's theory to the real world. If a firm were able to borrow at a rate lower than individuals, the firm's value would increase through corporate leverage. As MM Proposition I states, this is not the case in a world with no taxes.

2.   There are no taxes.

In the real world, firms do pay taxes. In the presence of corporate taxes, the value of a firm is positively related to its debt level. Since interest payments are deductible, increasing debt reduces taxes and raises the value of the firm.

3.   There are no costs of financial distress.

In the real world, costs of financial distress can be substantial. Since stockholders eventually bear these costs, there are incentives for a firm to lower the amount of debt in its capital structure. This topic will be discussed in more detail in later chapters.

15.11   a.   Since Digital has 1 million shares of common stock outstanding, with each share worth $10, the value of the firm's equity is $10 million (= 1 million shares * $10 per share). Therefore, 1% of the firm's equity costs $100,000 (= 0.01 * $10 million).

If Michael borrows 20% of the cost, it will cost him $80,000, net of debt, to purchase 1% of Digital's equity.

If Michael borrows 40% of the cost, it will cost him $60,000, net of debt, to purchase 1% of Digital's equity.

If Michael borrows 60% of the cost, it will cost him $40,000, net of debt, to purchase 1% of Digital's equity.

b. Since Michael purchased 1% of the Digital's equity, he has a right to 1% of the firm's annual earnings. Since the firm is expected to generate $1,500,000 of earnings per year, Michael will receive a cash inflow of $15,000.

If Michael wishes to borrow 20% of the purchase price of his investment, he will need to borrow $20,000 (= 0.20 * $100,000) and fund $80,000 of the purchase on his own. Since the interest rate on this debt is 10% per annum, Michael will owe $2,000 (= 0.10 * $20,000) in interest payments at the end of the year.

Therefore, if Michael borrows 20% of the purchase price, the expected return on his investment will be 16.25% [= ($15,000 - $2,000) / $80,000].

If Michael wishes to borrow 40% of the purchase price of his investment, he will need to borrow $40,000 (= 0.40 * $100,000) and fund $60,000 of the purchase on his own. Since the interest rate on this debt is 10% per annum, Michael will owe $4,000 (= 0.10 * $40,000) in interest payments at the end of the year.

Therefore, if Michael borrows 40% of the purchase price, the expected return on his investment will be 18.33% [= ($15,000 - $4,000) / $60,000].

If Michael wishes to borrow 60% of the purchase price of his investment, he will need to borrow $60,000 (= 0.60 * $100,000) and fund $40,000 of the purchase on his own. Since the interest rate on this debt is 10% per annum, Michael will owe $6,000 (= 0.10 * $60,000) in interest payments at the end of the year.

Therefore, if Michael borrows 60% of the purchase price, the expected return on his investment will be 22.50% [= ($15,000 - $6,000) / $40,000].

15.12 a. Before the announcement of the stock repurchase plan, the market value of the Locomotive's outstanding debt is $7.5 million. The ratio of the market value of the firm's debt to the market value of the firm's equity is 40%.

The market value of Locomotive's equity can be calculated as follows:

Since B = $7.5 million and B/S = 40%:

($7.5 million / S) = 0.40

S = $18.75 million

The market value of the firm's equity prior to the announcement is $18.75 million.

The value of a levered firm is equal to the sum of the market value of the firm's debt and the market value of the firm's equity.

The market value of Locomotive Corporation, a levered firm, is:

$$V_L = B + S$$
$$= \$7.5 \text{ million} + \$18.75 \text{ million}$$
$$= \textbf{\$26.25 million}$$

Therefore, the market value of Locomotive Corporation is $26.25 million prior to the stock repurchase announcement.

According to MM Proposition I (No Taxes), changes in a firm's capital structure have no effect on the overall value of the firm. Therefore, the value of the firm will not change after the announcement of the stock repurchase plan

The market value of Locomotive Corporation will remain at $26.25 million after the stock repurchase announcement.

b.   The expected return on a firm's equity is the ratio of annual earnings to the market value of the firm's equity.

Locomotive expects to generate $3.75 million in earnings per year.

Before the restructuring, Locomotive has $7.5 million of 10% debt outstanding. The firm was scheduled to pay $750,000 (= $7.5 million * 0.10) in interest at the end of each year.

Therefore, annual earnings before the stock repurchase announcement are $3,000,000 (= $3,750,000 - $750,000).

Since the market value of the firm's equity before the announcement is $18.75 million, the expected return on the firm's levered equity (r_S) before the announcement is 0.16 (= $3 million / $18.75 million).

The expected return on Locomotive's levered equity is 16% before the stock repurchase plan is announced.

c.   According to Modigliani-Miller Proposition II (No Taxes):

$r_S = r_0 + (B/S)(r_0 - r_B)$

where r_0 = the expected return on the assets of an all-equity firm
         r_S = the expected return on the equity of a levered firm
         r_B = the pre-tax cost of debt

In this problem: $r_S = 0.16$
                    $r_B = 0.10$
                    $B = \$7.5$ million
                    $S = \$18.75$ million

Thus: $0.16 = r_0 + (\$7.5 \text{ million} / \$18.75 \text{ million})(r_0 - 0.10)$
         $0.16 = r_0 + (0.40)(r_0 - 0.10)$

Solving for r_0: $r_0 = 0.1429$

Therefore, the expected return on the equity of an otherwise identical all-equity firm is 14.29%.

This problem can also be solved in the following way:

r_0 = Earnings Before Interest / V_U

Locomotive generates $3,750,000 of earnings before interest. According to Modigliani-Miller Proposition I, in a world with no taxes, the value of a levered firm equals the value of an otherwise-identical unlevered firm. Since the value of Locomotive as a levered firm is $26.25 million (= $7.5 + $18.75) and since the firm pays no taxes, the value of Locomotive as an unlevered firm (V_U) is also $26.25 million.

$r_0 = \$3.75 \text{ million} / \$26.25 \text{ million}$
$\qquad = 0.1429$
$\qquad = 14.29\%$

   d.   According to Modigliani-Miller Proposition II (No Taxes):

$$r_S = r_0 + (B/S)(r_0 - r_B)$$

where r_0 = the expected return on the assets of an all-equity firm
            r_S = the expected return on the equity of a levered firm
            r_B = the pre-tax cost of debt for a levered firm

Notice that the term (B/S) represents the firm's debt-to-equity ratio. After the stock repurchase announcement, the firm's expected debt-to-equity ratio changes from 40% to 50%. As shown in part c, the expected return on the equity of an otherwise identical all-equity firm is 14.29%.

To determine the expected return on Locomotive's equity after the stock repurchase announcement, the appropriate variables are:

$r_0 \quad = 0.1429$
$r_B \quad = 0.10$
$B/S = 0.50$

The expected return on Locomotive's levered equity after the stock repurchase announcement is:

$r_S \qquad = r_0 + (B/S)(r_0 - r_B)$
$\qquad = 0.1429 + (0.50)(0.1429 - 0.10)$
$\qquad = \mathbf{0.1644}$

Therefore, the expected return on Locomotive's equity is 16.44% after the stock repurchase announcement.

15.13   a.   Modigliani-Miller Proposition I states that in a world with corporate taxes:

$$V_L = V_U + T_C B$$

where V_L = the value of a levered firm
        V_U = the value of an unlevered firm
        T_C = the corporate tax rate
        B = the value of debt in a firm's capital structure

In this problem:

$\qquad V_L \quad = \$1,700,000$
$\qquad B \quad = \$500,000$
$\qquad T_C \quad = 0.34$

If the firm were financed entirely by equity, the value of the firm would be:

$V_U \quad = V_L - T_C B$
$\qquad = \$1,700,000 - (0.34)(\$500,000)$
$\qquad = \mathbf{\$1,530,000}$

Therefore, the value of this firm would be $1,530,000 if it were financed entirely by equity.

b. While the firm generates $306,000 of annual earnings before interest and taxes, it must make interest payments of $50,000 (= $500,000 * 0.10). Interest payments reduce the firm's taxable income.

Therefore, the firm's pre-tax earnings are $256,000 (= $306,000 - $50,000).

Since the firm is in the 34% tax bracket, it must pay taxes of $87,040 (= 0.34 * $256,000) at the end of each year.

Therefore, the amount of the firm's annual after-tax earnings is $168,960 (= $256,000 – $87,040). These earnings are available to the stockholders.

The following table summarizes this solution:

EBIT	$306,000
Interest	50,000
Pre-Tax Earnings	256,000
Taxes at 34%	87,040
After-Tax Earnings	168,960

15.14 Modigliani-Miller Proposition I states that in a world with corporate taxes:

$$V_L = V_U + T_C B$$

where V_L = the value of a levered firm
V_U = the value of an unlevered firm
T_C = the corporate tax rate
B = the value of debt in a firm's capital structure

Since the firm is an all-equity firm with 175,000 shares of common stock outstanding, currently worth $20 per share, the market value of this unlevered firm (V_U) is $3,500,000 (= 175,000 shares * $20 per share).

The firm plans to issue $1,000,000 debt and is subject to a corporate tax rate of 30%.

In this problem: V_U = $3,500,000
T_C = 0.30
B = $1,000,000

The market value of a levered firm is:

V_L = $V_U + T_C B$
   = $3,500,000 + (0.30)($1,000,000)
   = $3,800,000

The value of a levered firm is equal to the sum of the market value of its debt and the market value of its equity.

That is, the value of a levered firm is:

V_L = S + B

Rearranging this equation, the market value of the firm's levered equity, S, is:

$$
\begin{aligned}
S \quad &= V_L - B \\
&= \$3,800,000 - \$1,000,000 \\
&= \mathbf{\$2,800,000}
\end{aligned}
$$

Therefore, the market value of the firm's equity is $2,800,000 after the firm announces the stock repurchase plan.

15.15   a.   The value of an all-equity firm is the present value of its after-tax expected earnings:

$$V_U = [(EBIT)(1-T_C)] / r_0$$

where V_U = the value of an unlevered firm
    $EBIT$ = the firm's expected annual earnings before interest and taxes
    T_C = the corporate tax rate
    r_0 = the after-tax required rate of return on an all-equity firm

In this problem:

$$
\begin{aligned}
EBIT &= \$2,500,000 \\
T_C &= 0.34 \\
r_0 &= 0.20
\end{aligned}
$$

The value of Strider Publishing is:

$$
\begin{aligned}
V_U \quad &= [(EBIT)(1-T_C)] / r_0 \\
&= [(\$2,500,000)(1 - 0.34)] / 0.20 \\
&= \mathbf{\$8,250,000}
\end{aligned}
$$

Therefore, the value of Strider Publishing as an all-equity firm is $8,250,000.

b.   Modigliani-Miller Proposition I states that in a world with corporate taxes:

$$V_L = V_U + T_C B$$

where V_L = the value of a levered firm
    V_U = the value of an unlevered firm
    T_C = the corporate tax rate
    B = the value of debt in a firm's capital structure

In this problem:

$$
\begin{aligned}
V_U &= \$8,250,000 \\
T_C &= 0.34 \\
B &= \$600,000
\end{aligned}
$$

The value of Strider Publishing will be:

$$
\begin{aligned}
V_L \quad &= V_U + T_C B \\
&= \$8,250,000 + (0.34)(\$600,000) \\
&= \mathbf{\$8,454,000}
\end{aligned}
$$

Therefore, the value of Strider Publishing Company will be $8,454,000 if it issues $600,000 of debt and repurchases stock.

c. Since interest payments are tax deductible, debt lowers the firm's taxable income and creates a tax shield for the firm. This tax shield increases the value of the firm.

d. The Modigliani-Miller assumptions in a world with corporate taxes are:
1. There are no personal taxes.
2. There are no costs of financial distress.
3. The debt level of a firm is constant through time.

Both personal taxes and costs of financial distress will be covered in more detail in a later chapter.

15.16 a. Modigliani-Miller Proposition I states that in a world with corporate taxes:

$$V_L = V_U + T_C B$$

where
V_L = the value of a levered firm
V_U = the value of an unlevered firm
T_C = the corporate tax rate
B = the value of debt in a firm's capital structure

The value of an unlevered firm is the present value of its after-tax earnings:

$$V_U = [(EBIT)(1-T_C)] / r_0$$

where
V_U = the value of an unlevered firm
$EBIT$ = the firm's expected annual earnings before interest and taxes
T_C = the corporate tax rate
r_0 = the after-tax required rate of return on an all-equity firm

In this problem:

$EBIT$ = \$1,200,000
T_C = 0.35
r_0 = 0.12

The value of Gibson as an unlevered firm:

V_U = [(EBIT)(1-T_C)] / r_0
= [(\$1,200,000)(1 - 0.35)] / 0.12
= **\$6,500,000**

The value of Gibson if it were an all-equity firm is \$6,500,000.

Since Gibson's pre-tax cost of debt is 8% per annum and the firm makes interest payments of \$200,000 per year, the value of the firm's debt must be \$2,500,000 (= \$200,000 / 0.08). As a check, notice that 8% annual interest on \$2,500,000 of debt yields \$200,000 (= 0.08 * \$2,500,000) of interest payments per year.

The current value of Gibson's debt is \$2,500,000.

Thus:
V_U = \$6,500,000
T_C = 0.35
B = \$2,500,000

The total market value of Gibson is:

$$V_L = V_U + T_C B$$
$$= \$6,500,000 + (0.35)(\$2,500,000)$$
$$= \mathbf{\$7,375,000}$$

Therefore, the total market value of Gibson is $7,375,000.

b. If there are no costs of financial distress or bankruptcy, increasing the level of debt in a firm's capital structure will always increase the value of a firm. This implies that every firm will want to be financed entirely (100%) by debt if it wishes to maximize its value.

c. This conclusion is not applicable in the real world since it does not consider costs of financial distress, bankruptcy, or other agency costs that might offset the benefit of increased leverage. These costs will be discussed in further detail in later chapters.

15.17 a. The expected return on a firm's equity is the ratio of annual after-tax earnings to the market value of the firm's equity.

Green expects $1,500,000 of pre-tax earnings per year. Because the firm is subject to a corporate tax rate of 40%, it must pay $600,000 worth of taxes every year. Since the firm has no debt in its capital structure and makes no interest payments, Green's annual after-tax expected earnings are $900,000 (= $1,500,000 - $600,000).

The market value of Green's equity is $10,000,000.

Therefore, the expected return on Green's unlevered equity is 9% (= $900,000 / $10,000,000).

Notice that perpetual annual earnings of $900,000, discounted at 9%, yields a market value of the firm's equity of $10,000,000 (= $900,000 / 0.09).

b. Green is an all-equity firm. The present value of the firm's after-tax earnings is $10,000,000 {= ($1,500,000 - $600,000) / 0.09}.

Green's market-value balance sheet before the announcement of the debt issue is:

Green Manufacturing

Assets =	$ 10,000,000	Debt =	$ -
		Equity =	$ 10,000,000
Total Assets =	$ 10,000,000	Total D + E =	$ 10,000,000

Since the market value of Green's equity is $10,000,000 and the firm has 500,000 shares of common stock outstanding, the price of Green's stock is $20 per share (= $10,000,000 / 500,000 shares) before the announcement of the debt issue.

c. Modigliani-Miller Proposition I states that in a world with corporate taxes:

$$V_L = V_U + T_C B$$

where V_L = the value of a levered firm
V_U = the value of an unlevered firm
T_C = the corporate tax rate
B = the value of debt in a firm's capital structure

When Green announces the debt issue, the value of the firm will increase by the present value of the tax shield on the debt. Since Green plans to issue $2,000,000 of debt and the firm is subject to a corporate tax rate of 40%, the present value of the firm's tax shield is:

$$PV(\text{Tax Shield}) = T_C B$$
$$= (0.40)(\$2,000,000)$$
$$= \$800,000$$

Therefore, the value of Green Manufacturing will increase by $800,000 as a result of the debt issue.

The value of Green Manufacturing after the repurchase announcement is:

$$V_L = V_U + T_C B$$
$$= \$10,000,000 + (0.40)(\$2,000,000)$$
$$= \$10,800,000$$

Since the firm has not yet issued any debt, Green's equity is also worth $10,800,000.

Green's market-value balance sheet after the announcement of the debt issue is:

Green Manufacturing

Old Assets =	$ 10,000,000	Debt =	$ -
PV(Tax Shield) =	$ 800,000	Equity =	$ 10,800,000
Total Assets =	$ 10,800,000	Total D + E =	$ 10,800,000

d. Since the market value of Green's equity after the announcement of the debt issue is $10,800,000 and the firm has 500,000 shares of common stock outstanding, the price of Green's stock is $21.60 per share (= $10,800,000 / 500,000 shares) after the announcement of the debt issue.

Therefore, immediately after the repurchase announcement, Green's stock price will rise to $21.60 per share.

e. Green will issue $2,000,000 worth of debt and use the proceeds to repurchase shares of common stock. Since the price of Green's stock after the announcement will be $21.60 per share, Green can repurchase 92,592.59 shares (= $2,000,000 / $21.60 per share) as a result of the debt issue.

Green will repurchase 92,592.59 shares with the proceeds from the debt issue.

Since Green had 500,000 shares of common stock outstanding and repurchased 92,592.59 as a result of the debt issue, the firm will have 407,407.41(= 500,000 – 92,592.59) shares of common stock outstanding after the repurchase.

Green will have 407,407.41 shares of common stock outstanding after the repurchase.

f. After the restructuring has taken place, Green will have $2,000,000 worth of debt in its capital structure. The value of Green after the restructuring is $10,800,000.

The value of a levered firm is equal to the sum of the market value of its debt and the market value of its equity.

That is, the value of a levered firm is:

$$V_L = S + B$$

Rearranging this equation, the market value of the Green's levered equity after the announcement of the debt issue is:

$$S = V_L - B$$
$$= \$10,800,000 - \$2,000,000$$
$$= \$8,800,000$$

Green's market-value balance sheet after the restructuring is:

Green Manufacturing

Old Assets =	$ 10,000,000	Debt =	$ 2,000,000
PV(Tax Shield) =	$ 800,000	Equity =	$ 8,800,000
Total Assets =	$ 10,800,000	Total D + E =	$ 10,800,000

Since the market value of Green's equity after the restructuring is $8,800,000 and the firm has 407,407.41 shares of common stock outstanding, the price of Green's stock will be $21.60 per share (= $8,800,000 / 407,407.41 shares) after the restructuring.

Therefore, Green's stock price will remain at $21.60 per share after the restructuring has taken place.

g. According to Modigliani-Miller Proposition II with corporate taxes

$$r_S = r_0 + (B/S)(r_0 - r_B)(1 - T_C)$$

where
- r_0 = the required return on the equity of an unlevered firm
- r_S = the required return on the equity of a levered firm
- r_B = the pre-tax cost of debt for a levered firm
- T_C = the corporate tax rate
- B = the market value of the firm's debt
- S = the market value of the firm's equity

In this problem:

- r_0 = 0.09 (see part *a*)
- r_B = 0.06
- T_C = 0.40
- B = $2,000,000
- S = $8,800,000

The required return on Green's levered equity after the restructuring is:

$$r_S = r_0 + (B/S)(r_0 - r_B)(1 - T_C)$$
$$= 0.09 + (\$2,000,000 / \$8,800,000)(0.09 - 0.06)(1 - 0.40)$$
$$= 0.09 + (5/22)(0.09 - 0.06)(1 - 0.40)$$
$$= \mathbf{0.941}$$

Therefore, the required return on Green's levered equity after the restructuring is 9.41%.

15.18 a. Modigliani-Miller Proposition I states that in a world with corporate taxes:

$$V_L = V_U + T_C B$$

where V_L = the value of a levered firm
V_U = the value of an unlevered firm
T_C = the corporate tax rate
B = the value of debt in a firm's capital structure

The value of an unlevered firm is the present value of its after-tax earnings:

$V_U = [(EBIT)(1-T_C)] / r_0$

where V_U = the value of an unlevered firm
EBIT = the firm's expected annual earnings before interest and taxes
T_C = the corporate tax rate
r_0 = the after-tax required rate of return on an all-equity firm

In this problem:

EBIT = \$4,000,000
T_C = 0.35
r_0 = 0.15

The value of Holland if it were unlevered is:

$$V_U = [(EBIT)(1-T_C)] / r_0$$
$$= [(\$4,000,000)(1 - 0.35)] / 0.15$$
$$= \$17,333,333$$

The value of Holland if it were an all-equity firm is \$17,333,333.

Holland currently has \$10,000,000 of debt in its capital structure and is subject to a corporate tax rate of 35%.

Thus: V_U = \$17,333,333
T_C = 0.35
B = \$10,000,000

The value of Holland is:

$$V_L = V_U + T_C B$$
$$= \$17,333,333 + (0.35)(\$10,000,000)$$
$$= \$20,833,333$$

Therefore, the value of Holland is \$20,833,333.

b. According to Modigliani-Miller Proposition II with corporate taxes:

$r_S = r_0 + (B/S)(r_0 - r_B)(1 - T_C)$

where r_0 = the required return on the equity of an unlevered firm
r_S = the required return on the equity of a levered firm
r_B = the pre-tax cost of debt
T_C = the corporate tax rate
B = the market value of the firm's debt
S = the market value of the firm's equity

In this problem:

$$
\begin{aligned}
r_0 &= 0.15 \\
r_B &= 0.10 \\
T_C &= 0.35 \\
B &= \$10,000,000 \\
S &= \$10,833,833
\end{aligned}
$$

The required return on Holland's levered equity is:

$$
\begin{aligned}
r_S &= r_0 + (B/S)(r_0 - r_B)(1 - T_C) \\
&= 0.15 + (\$10,000,000 / \$10,833,833)(0.15 - 0.10)(1 - 0.35) \\
&= 0.15 + (0.9230)(0.15\text{-}0.10)(1 - 0.30) \\
&= \mathbf{0.18}
\end{aligned}
$$

Therefore, the cost of Holland's levered equity is 18%.

c.   In a world with corporate taxes, a firm's weighted average cost of capital (r_{wacc}) is equal to:

$$
r_{wacc} = \{B / (B+S)\}(1 - T_C)\, r_B + \{S / (B+S)\}\, r_S
$$

where B = the market value of the firm's debt
S = the market value of the firm's equity
r_B = the required return on the firm's debt
r_S = the required return on the firm's equity.
T_C = the corporate tax rate

The value of Holland's debt is \$10,000,000. Since the value of the firm (\$20,833,833) is the sum of the value of the firm's debt and the value of the firm's equity, the market value of the firm's equity is \$10,833,833 (= \$20,833,833 - \$10,000,000).

Thus:
$$
\begin{aligned}
B &= \$10,000,000 \\
S &= \$10,833,833 \\
r_B &= 0.10 \\
r_S &= 0.18 \\
T_C &= 0.35
\end{aligned}
$$

Holland's weighted average cost of capital is:

$$
\begin{aligned}
r_{wacc} &= \{B / (B+S)\}(1 - T_C)\, r_B + \{S / (B+S)\}\, r_S \\
&= (\$10,000,000 / \$20,833,833)(1 - 0.35)(0.10) + (\$10,833,833 / \$20,833,833)(0.18) \\
&= (0.48)(1 - 0.35)(0.10) + (0.52)(0.18) \\
&= \mathbf{0.1248}
\end{aligned}
$$

Therefore, Holland's weighted average cost of capital is 12.48%.

15.19   a.   In a world with corporate taxes, a firm's weighted average cost of capital (r_{wacc}) is equal to:

$$
r_{wacc} = \{B / (B+S)\}(1 - T_C)\, r_B + \{S / (B+S)\}\, r_S
$$

where B / (B+S) = the firm's debt-to-value ratio
S / (B+S) = the firm's equity-to-value ratio
r_B = the pre-tax cost of debt
r_S = the cost of equity for a levered firm.
T_C = the corporate tax rate

While the problem does not list Williamson's debt-to-value ratio or Williamson's equity-to-value ratio, it does say that the firm's debt-to-equity ratio is 2.5.

If Williamson's debt-to-equity ratio is 2.5:

$B / S = 2.5$

Solving for B:

$B = (2.5 * S)$

The above formula for r_{wacc} uses the following ratio: $B / (B+S)$

Since $B = (2.5 * S)$:

$$
\begin{aligned}
B/(B+S) \quad &= (2.5 * S) / \{ (2.5 * S) + S\} \\
&= (2.5 * S) / (3.5 * S) \\
&= (2.5 / 3.5) \\
&= 0.7143
\end{aligned}
$$

Williamson's debt-to-value ratio is 71.43%

The above formula for r_{wacc} also uses the following ratio: $S / (B+S)$

Since $B = (2.5 * S)$:

$$
\begin{aligned}
\text{Williamson's equity-to-value ratio} \quad &= S / \{(2.5*S) + S\} \\
&= S / (3.5 * S) \\
&= (1 / 3.5) \\
&= 0.2857
\end{aligned}
$$

Williamson's equity-to-value ratio is 28.57%.

In order to solve for the cost of Williamson's equity capital (r_S), set up the following equation:

$$
\begin{aligned}
r_{wacc} \quad &= \{B / (B+S)\}(1 - T_C)\, r_B + \{S / (B+S)\}r_S \\
0.15 &= (0.7143)(1 - 0.35)(0.10) + (0.2857)(r_S)
\end{aligned}
$$

$r_S \quad = \mathbf{0.3625}$

Therefore, the cost of Williamson's equity capital is 36.25%.

b. According to Modigliani-Miller Proposition II with corporate taxes:

$r_S = r_0 + (B/S)(r_0 - r_B)(1 - T_C)$

where
$\quad r_0 \quad$ = the cost of equity for an unlevered firm
$\quad r_S \quad$ = the cost of equity for a levered firm
$\quad r_B \quad$ = the pre-tax cost of debt
$\quad T_C \quad$ = the corporate tax rate
$\quad B/S$ = the firm's debt-to-equity ratio

In this problem:

$$r_S = 0.3625$$
$$r_B = 0.10$$
$$T_C = 0.35$$
$$B/S = 2.5$$

In order to solve for the cost of Williamson's unlevered equity (r_0), set up the following equation:

$$r_S = r_0 + (B/S)(r_0 - r_B)(1 - T_C)$$

$$0.3625 = r_0 + (2.5)(r_0 - 0.10)(1 - 0.35)$$

$$r_0 = \mathbf{0.20}$$

Therefore, Williamson's unlevered cost of equity is 20%.

c. If Williamson's debt-to-equity ratio is 0.75, the cost of the firm's equity capital (r_S) will be:

$$
\begin{aligned}
r_S &= r_0 + (B/S)(r_0 - r_B)(1 - T_C)\\
&= 0.20 + (0.75)(0.20 - 0.10)(1 - 0.35)\\
&= 0.2488
\end{aligned}
$$

If Williamson's debt-to-equity ratio is 0.75:

$$B / S = 0.75$$

Solving for B:

$$B = (0.75 * S)$$

A firm's debt-to-value ratio is: $B / (B+S)$

Since $B = (0.75 * S)$:

$$
\begin{aligned}
\text{Williamson's debt-to-value ratio} &= (0.75 * S) / \{ (0.75 * S) + S\}\\
&= (0.75 * S) / (1.75 * S)\\
&= (0.75 / 1.75)\\
&= 0.4286
\end{aligned}
$$

Williamson's debt-to-value ratio is 42.86%

A firm's equity-to-value ratio is: $S / (B+S)$

Since $B = (0.75 * S)$:

$$
\begin{aligned}
\text{Williamson's equity-to-value ratio} &= S / \{(0.75*S) + S\}\\
&= S / (1.75 * S)\\
&= (1 / 1.75)\\
&= 0.5714
\end{aligned}
$$

Williamson's equity-to-value ratio is 57.14%.

Williamson's weighted average cost of capital (r_{wacc}) is:

$$r_{wacc} = \{B / (B+S)\}(1 - T_C)\, r_B + \{S / (B+S)\}r_S$$
$$= (0.4286)(1 - 0.35)(0.10) + (0.5714)(0.2488)$$
$$= 0.17$$

Therefore, Williamson's weighted average cost of capital (r_{wacc}) is 17% if the firm's debt-to-equity ratio is 0.75.

If Williamson's debt-to-equity ratio is 1.5, then the cost of the firm's equity capital (r_S) will be:

$$r_S = r_0 + (B/S)(r_0 - r_B)(1 - T_C)$$
$$= 0.20 + (1.5)(0.20 - 0.10)(1 - 0.35)$$
$$= 0.2975$$

If Williamson's debt-equity ratio is 1.5:

$$B / S = 1.5$$

Solving for B:

$$B = (1.5 * S)$$

A firm's debt-to-value ratio is: $B / (B+S)$

Since $B = (1.5 * S)$:

$$\text{Williamson's debt-to-value ratio} = (1.5 * S) / \{ (1.5 * S) + S\}$$
$$= (1.5 * S) / (2.5 * S)$$
$$= (1.5 / 2.5)$$
$$= 0.60$$

Williamson's debt-to-value ratio is 60%

A firm's equity-to-value ratio is: $S / (B+S)$

Since $B = (1.5 * S)$:

$$\text{Williamson's equity-to-value ratio} = S / \{(1.5*S) + S\}$$
$$= S / (2.5 * S)$$
$$= (1 / 2.5)$$
$$= 0.40$$

Williamson's equity-to-value ratio is 40%.

Williamson's weighted average cost of capital (r_{wacc}) is:

$$r_{wacc} = \{B / (B+S)\}(1 - T_C)\, r_B + \{S / (B+S)\}r_S$$
$$= (0.60)(1 - 0.35)(0.10) + (0.40)(0.2975)$$
$$= 0.158$$

Therefore, Williamson's weighted average cost of capital (r_{wacc}) is 15.8% if the firm's debt-to-equity ratio is 1.5.

15.20   a.   The value of an unlevered firm is the present value of its after-tax earnings:

$$V_U = [(EBIT)(1-T_C)] / r_0$$

where V_U = the value of an unlevered firm
        EBIT = the firm's expected annual earnings before interest and taxes
        T_C = the corporate tax rate
        r_0 = the after-tax required rate of return on an all-equity firm

In this problem:

EBIT = $100,000
T_C = 0.40
r_0 = 0.25

The value of General Tools (GT) as an unlevered firm is:

$$V_U = [(EBIT)(1-T_C)] / r_0$$
$$= [(\$100,000)(1 - 0.40)] / 0.25$$
$$= \$240,000$$

The value of General Tools is $240,000 as an all-equity firm.

b.   Modigliani-Miller Proposition I states that in a world with corporate taxes:

$$V_L = V_U + T_C B$$

where V_L = the value of a levered firm
        V_U = the value of an unlevered firm
        T_C = the corporate tax rate
        B   = the value of debt in a firm's capital structure

In this problem:

V_U = $240,000
T_C = 0.40
B   = $100,000

If GT borrows $100,000 and uses the proceeds to purchase shares, the firm's value will be:

$$V_L = V_U + T_C B$$
$$= \$240,000 + (0.40)(\$100,000)$$
$$= \$280,000$$

Therefore, the value of General Tools will be $280,000 if the firm adds $100,000 of debt to its capital structure.

15.21   a.   If Stephenson wishes to maximize the overall value of the firm, it should use debt to finance the $100 million purchase. Since interest payments are tax deductible, debt in the firm's capital structure will decrease the firm's taxable income, creating a tax shield that will increase the overall value of the firm.

b.   Since Stephenson is an all-equity firm with 15 million shares of common stock outstanding, worth $32.50 per share, the market value of the firm is $487.5 million (= 15 million shares * $32.50 per share).

Stephenson's market-value balance sheet before the announcement of the land purchase is:

Stephenson Real Estate

Assets =	$	487,500,000	Debt =	$	-
			Equity =	$	487,500,000
Total Assets =	$	487,500,000	Total D + E =	$	487,500,000

c. i. As a result of the purchase, the firm's pre-tax earnings will increase by $25 million per year in perpetuity. These earnings are taxed at a rate of 40%. Therefore, after taxes, the purchase increases the annual expected earnings of the firm by $15 million {($25 million)(1 - 0.40)}.

Since Stephenson is an all-equity firm, the appropriate discount rate is the firm's unlevered cost of equity capital (r_0), which is 12.5%.

$$
\begin{aligned}
\text{NPV(Purchase)} &= -\$100,000,000 + \{(\$25,000,000)(1 - 0.40) / 0.125\} \\
&= -\$100,000,000 + (\$15 \text{ million} / 0.125) \\
&= \$20,000,000
\end{aligned}
$$

Therefore, the net present value of the land purchase is $20 million.

ii. After the announcement, the value of Stephenson will increase by $20 million, the net present value of the purchase. Under the efficient-market hypothesis, the market value of the firm's equity will immediately rise to reflect the NPV of the project.

Therefore, the market value of Stephenson's equity will be $507.5 million (= $487.5 million + $20 million) after the firm's announcement.

Stephenson s market-value balance sheet after the announcement is:

Stephenson Real Estate

Old Assets =	$	487,500,000	Debt =	$	-
$\text{NPV}_{\text{PROJECT}}$ =	$	20,000,000	Equity =	$	507,500,000
Total Assets =	$	507,500,000	Total D + E =	$	507,500,000

Since the market value of the firm's equity is $507.5 million and the firm has 15 million shares of common stock outstanding, Stephenson's stock price after the announcement will be $33.83 per share (= $507.5 million / 15 million shares).

Stephenson's stock price after the announcement is $33.83 per share.

Since Stephenson must raise $100 million to finance the purchase and the firm's stock is worth $33.83 per share, Stephenson must issue 2,955,956 shares (= $100 million / $33.83 per share) in order to finance the purchase.

Stephenson must issue 2,955,956 shares in order to finance the initial outlay for the purchase.

iii. Stephenson will receive $100 million (= 2,955,956 shares * $33.83 per share) in cash as a result of the equity issue. This will increase the firm's assets and equity by $100 million.

Stephenson's market-value balance sheet after the equity issue is:

Stephenson Real Estate

Old Assets =	$	487,500,000	Debt =	$	-
Cash =	$	100,000,000	Equity =	$	607,500,000
$NPV_{PROJECT}$ =	$	20,000,000			
Total Assets =	$	607,500,000	Total D + E =	$	607,500,000

Since Stephenson issued 2,955,956 shares in order to finance the purchase, the firm now has 17,955,956 (= 15,000,000 + 2,955,956) shares outstanding.

Stephenson will have 17,955,956 shares of common stock outstanding after the equity issue.

Since the market value of the firm's equity is $607.5 million and the firm has 17,955,956 shares of common stock outstanding, Stephenson's stock price after the equity issue will be $33.83 per share (= $607.5 million / 17,955,956 million shares).

Stephenson's stock price after the equity issue remains at $33.83 per share.

iv. The project will generate $25 million of additional annual pre-tax earnings forever. These earnings will be taxed at a rate of 40%. Therefore, after taxes, the project increases the annual earnings of the firm by $15 million {=($25 million)(1 - 0.40)}. The present value of these cash flows is equal to a perpetuity making annual payments of $15 million, discounted at 12.5%.

$PV_{PROJECT}$ = $15 million / 0.125
                      = $120 million

Stephenson's market-value balance sheet after the purchase has been made is:

Stephenson Real Estate

Old Assets =	$	487,500,000	Debt =	$	-
$PV_{PROJECT}$ =	$	120,000,000	Equity =	$	607,500,000
Total Assets =	$	607,500,000	Total D + E =	$	607,500,000

d.   i.   Modigliani-Miller Proposition I states that in a world with corporate taxes:

$V_L = V_U + T_C B$

where V_L = the value of a levered firm
           V_U = the value of an unlevered firm
           T_C = the corporate tax rate
           B   = the value of debt in a firm's capital structure

As was shown in part c, Stephenson will be worth $607.5 million if it finances the purchase with equity. If it were to finance the initial outlay of the project with debt, the firm would have $100 million worth of 8% debt outstanding.

Thus: V_U = $607.5 million
        T_C = 0.40
        B   = $100 million

If Stephenson chooses to finance the purchase using debt, the firm's market value will be:

$$V_L = V_U + T_C B$$
$$= \$607.5 \text{ million} + (0.40)(\$100 \text{ million})$$
$$= \mathbf{\$647.5 \text{ million}}$$

Therefore, Stephenson will be worth $647.5 million if it chooses to finance the purchase with debt.

ii. After the announcement, the value of Stephenson will immediately rise by the PV of the project. Since the market value of the firm's debt is $100 million and the value of the firm is $647.5 million, the market value of Stephenson's equity must be $547.5 million (= $647.5 million - $100 million).

Stephenson's market-value balance sheet after the debt issue is:

Stephenson Real Estate				
$V_U =$	$ 607,500,000	Debt =	$	100,000,000
$T_C{*}B =$	$ 40,000,000	Equity =	$	547,500,000
Total Assets =	$ 647,500,000	Total D + E =	$	647,500,000

Since the market value of the Stephenson's equity is $547.5 million and the firm has 15 million shares of common stock outstanding, Stephenson's stock price after the debt issue will be $36.50 per share (= $547.5 million / 15 million shares).

Stephenson's stock price after the debt issue will be $36.50 per share.

e. If Stephenson uses equity in order to finance the project, the firm's stock price will remain at $33.83 per share. If the firm uses debt in order to finance the project, the firm's stock price will rise to $36.50 per share.

Therefore, debt financing maximizes the per share stock price of a firm's equity.

Chapter 16: Capital Structure: *Limits to the Use of Debt*

16.1   a.   The value of a firm's equity is the discounted expected cash flow to the firm's stockholders.

If there is a boom, Good Time will generate cash flow of $250 million. Since Good Time owes its bondholders $150 million, the firm's stockholders will receive $100 million (= $250 million - $150 million) if there is a boom.

If there is a recession, Good Time will generate a cash flow of $100 million. Since the bondholder's have the right to the first $150 million that the firm generates, Good Time' stockholders will receive $0 if there is a recession.

The probability of a boom is 60%. The probability of a recession is 40%. The appropriate discount rate is 12%.

The value of Good Time's equity is:

{(0.60)($100 million) + (0.40)($0)} / 1.12 = **$53.57 million**

The value of Good Time's equity is $53.57 million.

      b.   Promised Return = (Face Value of Debt / Market Value of Debt) – 1

Since the debt holders have been promised $150 million at the end of the year, the face value of Good Time's debt is $150 million. The market value of Good Time's debt is $108.93 million.

The promised return on Good Time's debt is:

Promised Return = (Face Value of Bond / Market Value of Bond) – 1
                  = ($150 million / $108.93 million) – 1
                  = 0.3770

The promised return on Good Time's debt is 37.70%.

      c.   The value of a firm is the sum of the market value of the firm's debt and equity. The value of Good Time's debt is $108.93 million. As shown in part *a*, the value of Good Time's equity is $53.57 million.

The value of Good Time is:

V_L = B + S
      = $108.93 million + $53.57 million
      = $162.5 million

The value of Good Time Company is $162.5 million.

      d.   The market value of a firm's debt is the discounted expected cash flow to the firm's debt holders.

If there is a boom, Good Time will generate cash flow of $250 million. Since Good Time owes its debt holders $150 million, the firm's bondholders will receive $150 million if there is a boom.

While the firm's debt holders are owed $150 million, Good Time will only generate $100 million of cash flow if there is a recession. The firm's debt holders cannot receive more than the firm can afford to pay them. Therefore, Good Time's debt holders will only receive $100 million if there is a recession.

The probability of a boom is 60%. The probability of a recession is 40%. The appropriate discount rate is 12%.

If no bankruptcy costs are priced into the debt, the value of Good Time's debt is:

{(0.60)($150 million) + (0.40)($100)} / 1.12 = **$116.07 million**

Therefore, in a world with no bankruptcy costs, Good Time's debt would be worth $116.07 million.

e. The market value of a firm's debt is the discounted expected cash flow to the firm's debt holders. We know that the debt holders will receive $150 million in a boom and that the market value of the debt is $108.93 million.

Let X be the amount that bondholders expect to receive in the event of a recession:

$108.93 million = {(0.60)($150 million) + (0.40)(X)} / 1.12

X = **$80 million**

Therefore, the market value of Good Time's debt indicates that the firm's bondholders expect to receive $80 million in the event of a recession.

f. Since the firm will generate $100 million of cash flow in the event of a recession but the firm's bondholders only expect to receive a payment of $80 million, Good Time's cost of bankruptcy is expected to be $20 million (= $100 million - $80 million), should bankruptcy occur at the end of the year.

Good Time expects bankruptcy costs of $20 million, should bankruptcy occur at the end of the year.

16.2 a. The total value of a firm's equity is the discounted expected cash flow to the firm's stockholders.

If the expansion continues, each firm will generate earnings before interest and taxes of $2 million. If there is a recession each firm will generate earnings before interest and taxes of only $800,000.

Since Steinberg owes its bondholders $750,000 at the end of the year, its stockholders will receive $1.25 million (= $2 million - $750,000) if the expansion continues. If there is a recession, its stockholders will only receive $50,000 (= $800,000 - $750,000).

The market value of Steinberg's equity is:

{(0.80)($1,250,000) + (0.20)($50,000)} / 1.15 = **$878,261**

The value of Steinberg's equity is $878,261.

Steinberg's bondholders will receive $750,000 regardless of whether there is a recession or a continuation of the expansion.

The market value of Steinberg's debt is:
{(0.80)($750,000) + (0.20)($750,000)} / 1.15 = **$652,174**

The value of Steinberg's debt is $652,174.

Since Dietrich owes its bondholders $1 million at the end of the year, its stockholders will receive $1 million (= $2 million - $1 million) if the expansion continues. If there is a recession, its stockholders will receive nothing since the firm's bondholders have a more senior claim on all $800,000 of the firm's earnings.

The market value of Dietrich's equity is:

$$\{(0.80)(\$1,000,000) + (0.20)(\$0)\} / 1.15 = \mathbf{\$695,652}$$

The value of Dietrich's equity is $695,652.

Dietrich's bondholders will receive $1 million if the expansion continues and $800,000 if there is a recession.

The market value of Dietrich's debt is:

$$\{(0.80)(\$1,000,000) + (0.20)(\$800,000)\} / 1.15 = \mathbf{\$834,783}$$

The value of Dietrich's debt is $834,783.

b. The value of Steinberg is the sum of the value of the firm's debt and equity.

The value of Steinberg is:

$$
\begin{aligned}
V_L &= B + S \\
&= \$652,174 + \$878,261 \\
&= \mathbf{\$1,530,435}
\end{aligned}
$$

The value of Steinberg is $1,530,435.

The value of Dietrich is the sum of the value of the firm's debt and equity.

The value of Dietrich is:

$$
\begin{aligned}
V_L &= B + S \\
&= \$834,783 + 695,652 \\
&= \mathbf{\$1,530,435}
\end{aligned}
$$

The value of Dietrich is also $1,530,435.

c. You should disagree with the CEO's statement. The risk of bankruptcy *per se* does not affect a firm's value. It is the actual costs of bankruptcy that decrease the value of a firm. Note that this problem assumes that there are no bankruptcy costs.

16.3 Direct Costs:

Legal and administrative costs:
    Costs associated with the litigation arising from a liquidation or bankruptcy. These costs include lawyer's fees, courtroom costs, and expert witness fees.

Indirect Costs:

Impaired ability to conduct business:
    Firms may suffer a loss of sales due to a decrease in consumer confidence and loss of reliable supplies due to a lack of confidence by suppliers.

Incentive to take large risks:

> When faced with projects of different risk levels, managers acting in the stockholders' interest have an incentive to undertake high-risk projects. Imagine a firm with only one project, which pays $100 in an expansion and $60 in a recession. If debt payments are $60, the stockholders receive $40 (= $100 - $60) in the expansion but nothing in the recession. The bondholders receive $60 for certain.
>
> Now, alternatively imagine that the project pays $110 in an expansion but $50 in a recession. Here, the stockholders receive $50 (= $110 - $60) in the expansion but nothing in the recession. The bondholders receive only $50 in the recession because there is no more money in the firm. That is, the firm simply declares bankruptcy, leaving the bondholders "holding the bag."
>
> Thus, an increase in risk can benefit the stockholders. The key here is that the bondholders are hurt by risk, since the stockholders have limited liability. If the firm declares bankruptcy, the stockholders are not responsible for the bondholders' shortfall.

Incentive to under-invest:

> If a company is near bankruptcy, stockholders may well be hurt if they contribute equity to a new project, even if the project has a positive NPV. The reason is that some (or all) of the cash flows will go to the bondholders. Suppose a real estate developer owns a building that is likely to go bankrupt, with the bondholders receiving the property and the developer receiving nothing. Should the developer take $1 million out of his own pocket to add a new wing to a building? Perhaps not, even if the new wing will generate cash flows with a present value greater than $1 million. Since the bondholders are likely to end up with the property anyway, the developer will pay the additional $1 million and likely end up with nothing to show for it.

Milking the property:

> In the event of bankruptcy, bondholders have the first claim to the assets of the firm. When faced with a possible bankruptcy, the stockholders have strong incentives to vote for increased dividends or other distributions. This will ensure them of getting some of the assets of the firm before the bondholders can lay claim to them.

16.4   You should disagree with the statement.

If a firm has debt, it *might* be advantageous to stockholders for the firm to undertake risky projects, even those with negative net present values. This incentive results from the fact that most of the risk of failure is borne by bondholders. Therefore, value is transferred from the bondholders to the shareholders by undertaking risky projects, even if the projects have negative NPVs. This incentive is even stronger when the probability and costs of bankruptcy are high. A numerical example illustrating this concept is included in the solution to question 16.3 under the heading "Incentive to take large risks".

16.5   You should recommend that the firm issue equity in order to finance the project.

The tax-loss carry-forwards make the firm's effective tax rate zero. Therefore, the company will not benefit from the tax shield that debt provides. Moreover, since the firm already has a moderate amount of debt in its capital structure, additional debt will likely increase the probability that the firm will face financial distress or bankruptcy. As long as there are bankruptcy costs, the firm should issue equity in order to finance the project.

16.6   a.   If the low-risk project is undertaken, the firm will be worth $500 if the economy is bad and $700 if the economy is good. Since each of these two scenarios is equally probable, the expected value of the firm is $600 {= (0.50)($500) + (0.50)($700)}.

If the high-risk project is undertaken, the firm will be worth $100 if the economy is bad and $800 if the economy is good. Since each of these two scenarios is equally probable, the expected value of the firm is $450 {= (0.50)($100) + (0.50)($800)}.

The low-risk project maximizes the expected value of the firm.

b. If the low-risk project is undertaken, the firm's equity will be worth $0 if the economy is bad and $200 if the economy is good. Since each of these two scenarios is equally probable, the expected value of the firm's equity is $100 {= (0.50)($0) + (0.50)($100)}.

If the high-risk project is undertaken, the firm's equity will be worth $0 if the economy is bad and $300 if the economy is good. Since each of these two scenarios is equally probable, the expected value of the firm's equity is $150 {= (0.50)($0) + (0.50)($300)}.

c. Risk-neutral investors prefer the strategy with the highest expected value. Fountain's stockholders prefer the high-risk project since it maximizes the expected value of the firm's equity.

d. In order to make stockholders indifferent between the low-risk project and the high-risk project, the bondholders will need to raise their required debt payment so that the expected value of equity if the high-risk project is undertaken is equal to the expected value of equity if the low risk project is undertaken.

As shown in part *a*, the expected value of equity if the low-risk project is undertaken is $100.

If the high-risk project is undertaken, the value of the firm will be $100 if the economy is bad and $800 if the economy is good. If the economy is bad, the entire $100 will go to the firm's bondholders and Fountain's stockholders will receive nothing. If the economy is good, Fountain's stockholders will receive the difference between $800, the total value of the firm, and the required debt payment.

Let X be the debt payment that bondholders will require if the high-risk project is undertaken:

Expected Value of Equity = (0.50)($0) + (0.50)($800 – X)

In order for stockholders to be indifferent between the two projects, the expected value of equity if the high-risk project is undertaken must be equal to $100.

$100 = (0.50)($0) + (0.50)($800-X)

X   = $600

Therefore, the bondholders should promise to raise the required debt payment by $100 (= $600 - $500) if the high-risk project is undertaken in order to make Fountain's stockholders indifferent between the two projects.

16.7   Stockholders can undertake the following measures in order to minimize the costs of debt:

1.   Use Protective Covenants:
      Firms can enter into agreements with the bondholders that are designed to decrease the cost of debt.

      There are two types of Protective Covenants:
      i.   Negative Covenants prohibit the company from taking actions that would expose the bondholders to potential losses. An example would be prohibiting the payment of dividends in excess of earnings.
      ii.   Positive Covenants specify an action that the company agrees to take or a condition the company must abide by. An example would be agreeing to maintain its working capital at a minimum level.

2.   Repurchase Debt:
      A firm can eliminate the costs of bankruptcy by eliminating debt from its capital structure.

3.   Consolidate Debt:
      If a firm decreases the number of debt holders, it may be able to decrease the direct costs of bankruptcy should the firm become insolvent.

16.8   Modigliani and Miller's theory with corporate taxes indicates that, since there is a positive tax advantage of debt, the firm should maximize the amount of debt in its capital structure. In reality, however, no firm adopts an all-debt financing strategy. MM's theory ignores both the financial distress and agency costs of debt. The marginal costs of debt continue to increase with the amount of debt in the firm's capital structure so that, at some point, the marginal costs of additional debt will outweigh its marginal tax benefits. Therefore, there is an optimal level of debt for every firm at the point where the marginal tax benefits of the debt equal the marginal increase in financial distress and agency costs.

16.9   There are two major sources of the agency costs of equity:

1.   Shirking
      Managers with small equity holdings have a tendency to reduce their work effort, thereby hurting both the debt holders and outside equity holders.

2.   More Perquisites
      Since management receives all the benefits of increased perquisites but only shoulder a fraction of the cost, managers have an incentive to overspend on luxury items at the expense of debt holders and outside equity holders.

16.10 a. i. If Fortune remains an all-equity firm, its value will equal V_U, the value of Fortune as an unlevered firm.

The general expression for the value of a levered firm in a world with both corporate and personal taxes is:

$$V_L = V_U + [\, 1 - \{(1 - T_C)(1 - T_S) / (1 - T_B)\}\,] * B$$

where V_L = the value of a levered firm
         V_U = the value of an unlevered firm
         B = the market value of the firm's debt
         T_C = the tax rate on corporate income
         T_S = the personal tax rate on equity distributions
         T_B = the personal tax rate on interest income

In this problem:

         B = \$13,500,000
         T_C = 0.40
         T_S = 0.30
         T_B = 0.30

The value of Fortune as a levered firm is:

$$
\begin{aligned}
V_L &= V_U + [\, 1 - \{(1 - T_C)(1 - T_S) / (1 - T_B)\}\,] * B \\
    &= V_U + [\, 1 - \{1 - 0.40)(1 - 0.30) / (1 - 0.30)\}\,] * \$13,500,000 \\
    &= V_U + (0.40)(\$13,500,000) \\
    &= \mathbf{V_U + \$5,400,000}
\end{aligned}
$$

As was stated in Chapter 15, stockholders prefer a policy that maximizes the value of the firm.

Equity holders will prefer Fortune to become a levered firm since the debt will increase the firm's value by $5.4 million.

ii. The IRS will prefer the plan that generates the highest amount of tax revenue. The IRS taxes corporate income at 40%, interest income at 30%, and equity distributions at 30%.

Under the unlevered plan:

The IRS generates $1,200,000 (= 0.40 * $3,000,000) of corporate tax revenue on the firm's earnings and $540,000 (= 0.30 * $1,800,000) of personal tax revenue on Fortune's equity distributions. Since the firm has no debt, no interest payments are made, and the IRS will not generate any tax revenue on interest.

The IRS generates $1,740,000 (= $1,200,000 + $540,000) of tax revenue under the unlevered plan.

Under the levered plan:

The IRS generates $660,000 (= 0.40 * $1,650,000) of corporate tax revenue on the firm's earnings, $297,000 (= 0.30 * $990,000) of personal tax revenue on Fortune's equity distributions, and $405,000 (= 0.30 * $1,350,000) of personal tax revenue on the firm's interest payments.

The IRS generates $1,362,000 (= $660,000 + $297,000 + $405,000) of tax revenue under the levered plan.

Since the all-equity plan generates higher tax revenues, the IRS will prefer an unlevered capital structure.

iii. As an unlevered firm, Fortune would generate $1,800,000 of net income every year into perpetuity. Since the firm distributes all earnings to equity holders, this amount will be taxed at a rate of 30%, providing a $1,260,000 {= $1,800,000 * (1 – 0.30)} annual after-tax cash flow to the firm's equity holders. Since stockholders demand a 20% return after taxes, the value of Fortune if it were an unlevered firm is equal to a perpetuity of $1,260,000 per year, discounted at 20%.

V_U = $1,260,000 / 0.20
    = **$6,300,000**

The value of Fortune as an unlevered firm is $6.3 million.

The general expression for the value of a levered firm in a world with both corporate and personal taxes is:

$$V_L = V_U + [\ 1 - \{(1 - T_C)(1 - T_S) / (1 - T_B)\}\ ] * B$$

where V_L = the value of a levered firm
       V_U = the value of an unlevered firm
       B = the market value of the firm's debt
       T_C = the tax rate on corporate income
       T_S = the personal tax rate on equity distributions
       T_B = the personal tax rate on interest income

In this problem:

$$V_U = \$6{,}300{,}000$$
$$B = \$13{,}500{,}000$$
$$T_C = 0.40$$
$$T_S = 0.30$$
$$T_B = 0.30$$

The value of Fortune as a levered firm is:

$$
\begin{aligned}
V_L &= V_U + [\,1 - \{(1 - T_C)(1 - T_S) / (1 - T_B)\}\,] * B \\
&= \$6{,}300{,}000 + [\,1 - \{1 - 0.40)(1 - 0.30) / (1 - 0.30)\}\,] * \$13{,}500{,}000 \\
&= \$6{,}300{,}000 + (0.40)(\$13{,}500{,}000) \\
&= \mathbf{\$11{,}700{,}000}
\end{aligned}
$$

The value of Fortune as a levered firm is $11.7 million.

b. i.   Under the unlevered plan, the firm's earnings available to equity holders is $1,800,000. Since equity distributions are taxed at a rate of 20%, the annual after-tax cash flow to Fortune's equity holders is $1,440,000 {= $1,800,000 * (1 – 0.20)}.

The annual after-tax cash flow to equity holders under the unlevered plan is $1,440,000.

Under the levered plan, the firm's earnings available to equity holders is $990,000. Since equity distributions are taxed at a rate of 20%, the annual after-tax cash flow to Fortune's equity holders is $792,000 {= $990,000 * (1 – 0.20)}.

The annual after-tax cash flow to equity holders under the levered plan is $792,000.

   ii.   Under the unlevered plan, Fortune will have no debt.

The annual after-tax cash flow to debt holders under the unlevered plan is $0.

Under the levered plan, the firm will make annual interest payments of $1,350,000 to debt holders. Since interest income is taxed at a rate of 55%, the annual after-tax cash flow to Fortune's debt holders is $607,500 {= $1,350,000 * (1 – 0.55)}.

The annual after-tax cash flow to debt holder under the levered plan is $607,500

16.11   a.   In their no tax model, MM assume that T_C, T_B, and C(B) are all zero. Under these assumptions, $V_L = V_U$, signifying that the capital structure of a firm has no effect on its value. There is no optimal debt-equity ratio.

   b.   In their model with corporate taxes, MM assume that $T_C > 0$ and both T_B and C(B) are equal to zero. Under these assumptions, $V_L = V_U + T_C B$, implying that raising the amount of debt in a firm's capital structure will increase the overall value of the firm. This model implies that the debt-equity ratio of every firm should be infinite.

   c.   If $T_S = 0$ and the costs of financial distress are zero, the general expression for the value of a levered firm equals:

$$V_L = V_U + [\,1 - \{(1 - T_C) / (1 - T_B)\}\,] * B - C(B)$$

where	V_L	= the value of a levered firm
	V_U	= the value of an unlevered firm
	B	= the market value of a firm's debt
	T_C	= the tax rate on corporate income
	T_B	= the personal tax rate on interest income

Therefore, the change in the value of an all-equity firm that issues debt and uses the proceeds to repurchase equity is:

Change in Value = [1 – {(1 – T_C) / (1 - T_B)}] * B

In this problem:

$$T_C = 0.34$$
$$T_B = 0.20$$
$$B = \$1,000,000$$
$$C(B) = 0$$

The change in the value of the firm is:

Change in Value = [1 – {(1 – 0.34) / (1 – 0.20)}] * $1,000,000
= **$175,000**

The value of the firm will increase by $175,000 if it issues $1 million of debt and uses the proceeds to repurchase equity.

d.   If $T_S = 0$ and the costs of financial distress are zero, the general expression for the value of a levered firm equals:

$V_L = V_U$ + [1 – {(1 – T_C) / (1 - T_B)}] * B

where	V_L	= the value of a levered firm
	V_U	= the value of an unlevered firm
	B	= the market value of a firm's debt
	T_C	= the tax rate on corporate income
	T_B	= the personal tax rate on interest income

Therefore, the change in the value of an all-equity firm that issues $1 of perpetual debt instead of $1 of perpetual equity is:

Change in Value = [1 – {(1 – T_C) / (1 - T_B)}] * ($1)

If the firm is not able to benefit from interest deductions, the firm's taxable income will remain the same regardless of the amount of debt in its capital structure, and no tax shield will be created by issuing debt. Therefore, the firm will receive no tax benefit as a result of issuing debt in place of equity. In other words, the *effective* corporate tax rate when considering the *change* in the value of the firm is zero. Debt will have no effect on the value of the firm since interest payments will not be tax deductible.

In this problem:

$$T_C = 0$$
$$T_B = 0.20$$

The change in the value of the firm is:

$$\text{Change in Value} = [1 - \{(1 - T_C) / (1 - T_B)\}] * (\$1)$$
$$= [1 - \{(1 - 0) / (1 - 0.20)\}] * (\$1)$$
$$= -\$0.25$$

The value of the firm will decrease by \$0.25 if it adds \$1 of perpetual debt rather than \$1 of equity.

16.12   a.   If OPC decides to retire all of its debt, it will become an unlevered firm. The value of an all-equity firm is the present value of the firm's after-tax cash flow to equity holders.

$$V_U = \{(EBIT)(1 - T_C)(1 - T_S)\} / r_0$$

where V_U = the value of an unlevered firm
        EBIT = the firm's annual earnings before interest and taxes
        T_C = the tax rate on corporate income
        T_S = the tax rate on equity distributions
        r_0 = the required rate of return on the firm's unlevered equity

In this problem:

EBIT = \$1,100,000
T_C = 0.35
T_S = 0.10
r_0 = 0.20

The value of OPC as an all-equity firm is:

$$V_U = \{(EBIT)(1 - T_C)(1 - T_S)\} / r_0$$
$$= \{(\$1,100,000)(1 - 0.35)(1 - 0.10)\} / 0.20$$
$$= \mathbf{\$3,217,500}$$

The value of OPC will be \$3,217,500 if it decides to retire its debt and become an all-equity firm.

b.   The general expression for the value of a levered firm in a world with both corporate and personal taxes is:

$$V_L = V_U + [1 - \{(1 - T_C)(1 - T_S) / (1 - T_B)\}] * B$$

where V_L = the value of a levered firm
        V_U = the value of an unlevered firm
        B   = the market value of a firm's debt
        T_C = the tax rate on corporate income
        T_S = the personal tax rate on equity distributions
        T_B = the personal tax rate on interest income

In this problem:

V_U = \$3,217,500
B   = \$2,000,000
T_C = 0.35
T_S = 0.10
T_B = 0.25

The value of OPC as a levered firm is:

$$V_L = V_U + [\ 1 - \{(1 - T_C)(1 - T_S) / (1 - T_B)\}\ ] * B$$
$$= \$3,217,500 + [\ 1 - \{(1 - 0.35)(1 - 0.10) / (1 - 0.25)\}\ ] * \$2,000,000$$
$$= \mathbf{\$3,657,500}$$

The value of OPC will be \$3,657,500 if it remains a levered firm.

16.13   a.   The value of an all-equity firm is the present value of the firm's expected cash flows to equity holders.

$$V_U = \text{Expected (Operating Income)} / r_0$$

The estimates of Frodo's annual operating income and their respective probabilities are listed below:

Operating Income	Probability
$1,000	0.1
$2,000	0.4
$4,200	0.5

The expected value of Frodo's operating income is the probability-weighted average of its earnings estimates:

$$\text{Expected Value} = (\$1,000)(0.10) + (\$2,000)(0.40) + (\$4,200)(0.50)$$
$$= \mathbf{\$3,000}$$

Frodo's expected operating income every year is \$3,000.

Since Frodo's expected operating income will remain unchanged into perpetuity and the required return on the firm's unlevered equity is 20%, the value of Frodo in a world without taxes is:

$$V_U = \text{Expected (Operating Income)} / r_0$$
$$= \$3,000 / 0.20$$
$$= \mathbf{\$15,000}$$

The value of Frodo in a world without taxes is \$15,000.

b.   i.   Modigliani-Miller Proposition I states that in a world without corporate taxes:

$$V_L = V_U$$

where V_L = the value of a levered firm
           V_U = the value of an unlevered firm

Changes in capital structure have no effect on the value of a firm in a world without taxes.

Therefore, if Frodo issues $7,500 of 10% debt and uses the proceeds to repurchase equity, the value of the firm will remain at $15,000 in a world without taxes.

In a world without taxes, the value of Frodo will remain at \$15,000.

ii.   The value of a levered firm equals the market value of its debt plus the market value of its equity.

$$V_L = B + S$$

The total value of Frodo (V_L) is $15,000, and the market value of the firm's debt (B) is $7,500.

Therefore, the value of Frodo's equity is:

$S = V_L - B$
$= \$15{,}000 - \$7{,}500$
$= \mathbf{\$7{,}500}$

The market value of Frodo's equity equals \$7,500 in a world without taxes.

iii. According to Modigliani-Miller Proposition II (No Taxes):

$r_S = r_0 + (B/S)(r_0 - r_B)$

where r_0 = the required rate of return on the equity of an unlevered firm
r_S = the required rate of return on the equity of a levered firm
r_B = the cost of debt

In this problem: $r_0 = 0.20$
$r_B = 0.10$
$B = \$7{,}500$
$S = \$7{,}500$

The required rate of return on Frodo's levered equity is:
$r_S \quad = r_0 + (B/S)(r_0 - r_B)$
$= 0.20 + (\$7{,}500 \,/\, \$7{,}500)(0.20 - 0.10)$
$= 0.20 + (1)(0.20\text{-}0.10)$
$= \mathbf{0.30}$

The required rate of return on Frodo's levered equity is 30%.

iv. In the absence of taxes, a firm's weighted average cost of capital (r_{wacc}) equals:

$r_{wacc} \quad = \quad \{B \,/\, (B+S)\}\, r_B + \{S \,/\, (B+S)\} r_S$

where B = the market value of the firm's debt
S = the market value of the firm's equity
r_B = the cost of debt
r_S = the required return on a firm's equity.

In this problem: $B = \$7{,}500$
$S = \$7{,}500$
$r_B = 0.10$
$r_S = 0.30$

Frodo's weighted average cost of capital is:

$r_{wacc} \quad = \quad \{B \,/\, (B+S)\}\, r_B + \{S \,/\, (B+S)\} r_S$
$= \quad \{\$7{,}500 \,/\, (\$7{,}500 + \$7{,}500)\}(0.10) + \{\$7{,}500 \,/\, (\$7{,}500 + \$7{,}500)\}(0.30)$
$= \quad (1/2)(0.10) + (1/2)(0.30)$
$= \quad \mathbf{0.20}$

Frodo's weighted average cost of capital is 20%.

c. i. Taxes will decrease the value of the firm because the government becomes a claimant on the firm's assets. Recall that the size of the pie does not change, but now less is available for the firm's stockholders and bondholders.

ii. Modigliani-Miller Proposition I states that in a world with corporate taxes:

$$V_L = V_U + T_C B$$

where V_L = the value of a levered firm
        V_U = the value of an unlevered firm
        T_C = the corporate tax rate
        B   = the value of debt in a firm's capital structure

The value of an all-equity firm is the present value of the firm's after-tax cash flow to equity holders.

V_U = Expected (Operating Income)*$(1 - T_C) / r_0$
     = {$3,000*(1 - .40)} / 0.20
     = $9,000

Thus: V_U = $9,000
        T_C = 0.40
        B   = $7,500

The value of Frodo in a world with corporate taxes is:

V_L = $V_U + T_C B$
     = $9,000 + (0.40)($7,500)
     = **$12,000**

The value of Frodo is $12,000 if corporate income is taxed at a rate of 40%.

d.   The general expression for the value of a levered firm in a world with both corporate and personal taxes is:

$$V_L = V_U + [1 - \{(1 - T_C)(1 - T_S) / (1 - T_B)\}] * B$$

Where V_L = the value of a levered firm
        V_U = the value of an unlevered firm
        B   = the market value of a firm's debt
        T_C = the tax rate on corporate income
        T_S = the personal tax rate on equity distributions
        T_B = the personal tax rate on interest income

The value of an all-equity firm (V_U) is the present value of the firm's expected after-tax cash flows to equity holders.

V_U = {Expected (Operating Income)*$(1 - T_C)(1 - T_S)$} / r_0

where V_U = the value of an unlevered firm
        T_C = the tax rate on corporate income
        T_S = the tax rate on equity distributions
        r_0 = the required rate of return on the firm's unlevered equity

In this problem:

        E(OI) = $3,000
        T_C = 0.40
        T_S = 0.15
        r_0 = 0.20

The value of Frodo as an all-equity firm in a world with both corporate and personal taxes is:

V_U = {Expected (Operating Income)*$(1 - T_C)(1 - T_S)$} / r_0
= {($3,000)(1 - 0.40)(1 - 0.15)$} / 0.20
= $7,650

Thus: V_U = $7,650
         B   = $7,500
         T_C = 0.40
         T_S = 0.15
         T_B = 0.35

The value of Frodo as a levered firm in a world with both corporate and personal taxes is:

V_L = V_U + [1 - {$(1 - T_C)(1 - T_S)$ / $(1 - T_B)$}] * B
= $7,650 + [1 - {$(1 - 0.40)(1 - 0.15)$ / $(1 - 0.35)$}]*$7,500
= **$9,265**

The value of Frodo as a levered firm is $9,265 in a world with both corporate and personal taxes.

16.14   a.   The president is incorrect when he claims that common stock is the cheapest form of financing. While 9.5% is the lowest pre-tax rate that Mueller can obtain, the lowest after-tax rate that the firm can obtain is 11.05% [$= (1 - 0.35)(0.17)$] on the pollution-control bonds.

Mr. Daniels is also incorrect. If there are personal taxes, the increase in the value of the firm is not simply $T_C B$; rather, the increase in firm value would be [1 - {$(1 - T_C)(1 - T_S)$ / $(1 - T_B)$}] * B.

Ms. Henderson is also incorrect. Consider the following expression for the increase in firm value due to debt:

ΔV = [1 - {$(1 - T_C)(1 - T_S)$ / $(1 - T_B)$}] * B

If the corporate bonds are issued:

   T_C = 0.35
   T_S = 0
   T_B = 0.15
   B   = $100 million

ΔV = [1 - {$(1 - T_C)(1 - T_S)$ / $(1 - T_B)$}] * B
= [1 - {$(1 - 0.35)(1 - 0)$ / $(1 - 0.15)$}] * $100 million
= $23.53 million

If the corporate bonds are issued, the value of the firm will increase by $23.53 million.

If the pollution-control bonds are issued:

   T_C = 0.35
   T_S = 0
   T_B = 0
   B   = $100 million

$$\Delta V = [1 - \{(1 - T_C)(1 - T_S) / (1 - T_B)\}] * B$$
$$= [1 - \{(1 - 0.35)(1 - 0) / (1 - 0)\}] * \$100 \text{ million}$$
$$= \$35 \text{ million}$$

If the pollution-control bonds are issued, the value of the firm will increase by $35 million.

Therefore, Ms. Henderson's claim that the debt choice does not matter is also incorrect.

b. Mueller should not be indifferent about which financing plan it chooses. Issuing equity adds no value to the firm, and the two debt alternatives add different amounts to the value of the firm.

Ranking the alternatives:

Type of Financing	Value Added
1. Pollution Control Bonds	$35 million
2. Corporate Bonds	$23.53 million
3. Common Stock	$0

Note that this analysis only implies that debt adds value *relative* to equity. The absolute value of this firm is likely to fall with any of the three financing choices since pollution-control equipment represents a cash outflow.

16.15   a. The general expression for the value of a levered firm in a world with both corporate and personal taxes is:

$$V_L = V_U + [\, 1 - \{(1 - T_C)(1 - T_S) / (1 - T_B)\}] * B - C(B)$$

where
V_L = the value of a levered firm
V_U = the value of an unlevered firm
B = the market value of the firm's debt
T_C = the tax rate on corporate income
T_B = the personal tax rate on interest income
$C(B)$ = the present value of the costs of financial distress and agency costs

The value of an all-equity firm (V_U) is the present value of the firm's after-tax cash flows to equity holders.

$$V_U = \{(EBIT)(1 - T_C)(1 - T_S)\} / r_0$$

where V_U = the value of an unlevered firm
$EBIT$ = the firm's earnings before interest and taxes
T_C = the tax rate on corporate income
T_S = the tax rate on equity distributions
r_0 = the required rate of return on the firm's unlevered equity

In this problem:

$EBIT = \$800,000$
$T_C = 0.35$
$T_S = 0$
$r_0 = 0.10$

The value of Weinberg as an all-equity firm in a world with both corporate and personal taxes is:

$$V_U = \{(EBIT)(1 - T_C)(1 - T_S)\} / r_0$$
$$= \{(\$800,000)(1 - 0.35)(1 - 0)\} / 0.10$$
$$= \$5,200,000$$

Thus:
	V_U	= $5,200,000
	B	= $1,200,000
	T_C	= 0.35
	T_S	= 0
	T_B	= 0.15
	C(B)	= $60,000 (= 0.05 * $1,200,000)

The value of Weinberg as a levered firm in a world with both corporate and personal taxes is:

$$V_L = V_U + [\ 1 - \{(1 - T_C)(1 - T_S) / (1 - T_B)\}] * B - C(B)$$
$$= \$5,200,000 + [\ 1 - \{(1 - 0.35)(1 - 0) / (1 - 0.15)\}]*\$1,200,000 - \$60,000$$
$$= \mathbf{\$5,422,353}$$

The value of Weinberg as a levered firm is \$5,422,353 in a world with both corporate and personal taxes.

b. Since the value of Weinberg is \$5,200,000 as an unlevered firm and \$5,422,353 as a levered firm, the added value of including debt in the firm's capital structure is \$222,353 (= \$5,422,353 - \$5,200,000).

The added value of the firm's debt is \$222,353.

16.16 a. Since NETC is an all-equity firm, its cost of capital is equal to the required return on its equity. Use the Capital Asset Pricing Model (CAPM) to determine the required return on NETC's unlevered equity.

According to CAPM: $r_S = r_f + \beta_S\{E(r_m) - r_f\}$

where
r_S = the required return on a firm's equity
r_f = the expected return on a risk-free asset
$E(r_m)$ = the expected rate of return on the market portfolio
β_S = the beta of a firm's equity

The beta of a firm's equity is equal to:

β_S $= Cov(x, m) / \sigma^2_m$

where $Cov(x, m)$ = the covariance between the return on the firm's common stock and the return on the market portfolio
σ^2_m = the variance of returns on the market portfolio

In this problem:

$$Cov(x, m) = 0.048$$
$$\sigma^2_m = 0.04$$

The beta of NETC's equity is:

β_S $= Cov(x, m) / \sigma^2_m$
$= 0.048 / 0.04$
$= 1.2$

Thus: r_f $= 0.10$
$E(r_m) = 0.20$
β_S $= 1.2$

The required return on NETC's capital is:

r_S $= r_f + \beta_S\{E(r_m) - r_f\}$
$= 0.10 + 1.2(0.20 - 0.10)$
$= \mathbf{0.22}$

NETC's overall cost of capital is 22%.

b. NETC should purchase the machine with the higher net present value (NPV). Remember that the firm will need a machine for the next four years.

Since the economic life of the Heavy-Duty Model is four years, the firm will only need to purchase the machine once.

$NPV_{HEAVY\ DUTY}$ = -Price + PV(Annual Cost Savings) + PV(Depreciation Tax Shield)

The Heavy-Duty Model will generate $640 of cost savings every year for four years. This is equivalent to the firm generating $640 of additional earnings each year for four years. Because these earnings are subject to a corporate income tax of 34%, the annual after-tax cash flow created by the firm's additional savings is $422.40 {= $640(1 − 0.34). Since the required return on NETC's equity is 22%, the firm's after-tax annual cost savings can be valued as an annuity with four annual payments of $422.40, discounted at 22%.

PV(Annual Cost Savings) $= \$422.40 A^4_{0.22}$
$= \$1,053.31$

NETC uses straight-line depreciation. Since the economic life of the Heavy-Duty Model is four years, NETC will recognize an annual depreciation expense of $250 (= $1,000 / 4 years). The annual tax shield provided by this added expense is $85 (= $250*0.34). The depreciation tax shield is valued as a four-year annuity with annual payments of $85, discounted at 22%.

PV(Depreciation Tax Shield) $= \$85 A^4_{0.22}$
$= \$211.96$

The NPV of the Heavy-Duty Model is:

$NPV_{HEAVY\ DUTY}$ = -Price + PV(Annual Cost Savings) + PV(Depreciation Tax Shield)
$= -\$1,000 + \$1,053.31 + \$211.96$
$= \$265.27$

The NPV of the Heavy-Duty Model is $265.27.

Since the economic life of the Light-Weight Model is only 2 years, the firm will need to buy one machine now and one in two years. The cash flows associated with the second purchase must be discounted by two years.

$NPV_{LIGHT\ WEIGHT}$ = -Price + PV(Annual Cost Savings) + PV(Depreciation Tax Shield) +
$\{(-$ Price + PV(Annual Cost Savings) + PV(Depreciation Tax Shield)$\}\ /\ (1.22)^2$

The Light-Weight Model will generate annual cost savings of $616 for two years. This is equivalent to the firm generating $616 of additional earnings each year for two years. Since these earnings are subject to a corporate income tax of 34%, the annual after-tax cash flow created by the firm's additional savings is $406.56 {= $616(1 − 0.34). Since the required return on NETC's equity is 22%, the firm's after-tax annual cost savings can be valued as a two-year annuity with annual payments of $406.56, discounted at 22%.

$$\text{PV(Annual Cost Savings)} = \$406.56 A^2_{0.22}$$
$$= \$606.40$$

NETC uses straight-line depreciation. Since the economic life of the Light-Weight Model is two years, NETC will recognize an annual depreciation expense of $250 (= $500 / 2 years). The annual tax shield provided by this added expense is $85 (= $250*0.34). This depreciation tax shield is valued as a two-year annuity with annual payments of $85, discounted at 22%.

$$\text{PV(Depreciation Tax Shield)} = \$85 A^2_{0.22}$$
$$= \$126.78$$

The NPV of the Light-Weight Model is:

$$\text{NPV}_{\text{LIGHT WEIGHT}} = \text{-Price} + \text{PV(Annual Cost Savings)} + \text{PV(Depreciation Tax Shield)} +$$
$$\{(\text{- Price} + \text{PV(Annual Cost Savings)} + \text{PV(Depreciation Tax Shield)}\} / (1.22)^2$$

$$= \text{-}\$500 + \$606.40 + \$126.78 + \{(\text{-}\$500 + \$606.40 + \$126.78)\} / (1.22)^2$$
$$= \mathbf{\$389.84}$$

The NPV of the Light-Weight Model is $389.84.

Since its NPV is higher, NETC should purchase the Light-Weight Model.

c. i. Modigliani-Miller Proposition I states that in a world with corporate taxes:

$$V_L = V_U + T_C B$$

where
V_L = the value of a levered firm
V_U = the value of an unlevered firm
T_C = the corporate tax rate
B = the value of debt in a firm's capital structure

In this problem:

V_U = $10 million
B = $2 million
T_C = 0.34

The new value of NETC will be:

$$V_L = V_U + T_C B$$
$$= \$10,000,000 + (0.34)(\$2,000,000)$$
$$= \mathbf{\$10,680,000}$$

The value of the NETC will be $10,680,000 if the CFO's plan adopted.

ii.   The value of a levered firm is the sum of the market value of the firm's debt and the market value of the firm's equity.

$$V_L = B + S$$

In this problem:

$$V_L = \$10,680,000$$
$$B = \$2,000,000$$

Therefore, the value of NETC's levered equity must be:

$$
\begin{aligned}
S &= V_L - B \\
&= \$10,680,000 - \$2,000,000 \\
&= \mathbf{\$8,680,000}
\end{aligned}
$$

The value of NETC's levered equity is \$8,680,000.

d.   Since the value of NETC as a levered firm is \$10,680,000 and costs of financial distress are 2% of this value, the NETC's costs of financial distress total \$213,600 (= 0.02 * \$10,680,000). This reduces the firm's value to \$10,466,400. Since this amount is greater than \$10 million, the value of NETC as an unlevered firm, adding debt to the firm's capital structure increases the firm's value. NETC should not remain an unlevered firm.

Appendix: 16B: The Miller Model and the Graduated Income Tax

16.17   a.   According to the Miller Model, in equilibrium:

$$r_B (1 - T_C) = r_S$$

where r_B = the pre-tax cost of debt (the interest rate)
        T_C = the corporate tax rate
        r_S = the required return on a firm's equity

In this problem:

$$T_C = 0.35$$
$$r_S = 0.11$$

Therefore, in order for there to be equilibrium:

$$r_B (1 - T_C) = r_S$$
$$r_B (1 - 0.35) = 0.11$$
$$r_B = 0.11 / (1 - 0.35)$$
$$= 0.1692$$

The equilibrium interest rate is 16.92%.

b.   In order to determine whether each group would prefer to hold debt or equity, it is necessary to compare the after-personal tax interest rate to the required return on unlevered equity for each of the three groups of investors. A group of investors will prefer to hold the security that offers them the highest rate of return.

The required rate of return to equity holders is 11%. Since the effective personal tax rate on equity distributions is zero, personal taxes do not change the required return to equity holders.

The market interest rate is 16.92%.

The after-personal tax interest rate for investors who face a 10% tax on interest income is 15.23% {= 0.1692 * (1 - 0.10)}. Since the after-personal tax interest rate (15.23%) is greater than the required return on equity (11%), this group is better off holding debt.

Investors whose interest income is taxed at 10% will buy debt.

The after-personal tax interest rate for investors who face a 20% tax on interest income is 13.54% {= 0.1692 * (1 - 0.20)}. Since the after-tax interest rate (13.54%) is greater than the required return on equity (11%), this group is also better off holding debt.

Investors whose interest income is taxed at 20% will buy debt.

The after-personal tax rate interest rate for investors who face a 40% tax on interest income is 10.15% {= 0.1692 * (1 - 0.40)}. Since the after-tax interest rate (10.15%) is less than the required return on equity (11%), this group is also better off holding equity.

Investors whose interest income is taxed at 40% will buy equity.

c. According to the Miller Model, firm value does not vary with capital structure in equilibrium. Therefore, Firm A's value would be equal to an all-equity financed firm with EBIT of $1 million in perpetuity.

$$V_A = [(EBIT)(1 - T_C)] / r_S$$
$$= [(\$1,000,000)(1 - 0.35)] / 0.11$$
$$= \$5,909,091$$

The value of Firm A is $5.91 million.

16.18   a.   According to the Miller Model, in equilibrium:

$$r_B (1 - T_C) = r_S$$

where r_B = the pre-tax cost of debt (the interest rate)
T_C = the corporate tax rate
r_S = the required return on a firm's equity

In this problem:

$$T_C = 0.35$$
$$r_S = 0.081$$

Therefore:

$$r_B (1 - T_C) = r_S$$
$$r_B (1 - 0.35) = 0.081$$
$$r_B = 0.081 / (1 - 0.35)$$
$$= 0.1246$$

The equilibrium market rate of interest is 12.46%.

b. In order to determine whether each group would prefer to hold debt or equity, compare the after-personal tax interest rate on debt to the required return on unlevered equity for each of the three groups of investors. A group of investors will prefer to hold the security that offers them the highest rate of return.

The required rate of return to equity holders is 8.1%. Since the effective personal tax rate on equity distributions is zero, personal taxes do not change the required return to equity holders.

The market interest rate is 12.46%.

Group A faces a 50% tax on interest income. The after-personal tax interest rate for investors in Group A is 6.23% {= 0.1246 * (1 - 0.50)}. Since the after-personal tax interest rate (6.23%) is less than the required return on equity (8.1%), Group A will buy equity.

Group A will buy equity.

Group B faces a 32.5% tax on interest income. The after-personal tax interest rate for investors in Group B is 8.41% {= 0.1246 * (1 - 0.325)}. Since the after-personal tax interest rate (8.41%) is greater than the required return on equity (8.1%), Group B will buy debt.

Group B will buy debt.

Group C faces a 10% tax on interest income. The after-personal tax rate interest rate for investors in Group C is 11.21% {= 0.1121 * (1 - 0.10)}. Since the after-personal tax interest rate (11.21%) is greater than the required return on equity (8.1%), Group C will buy debt.

Group C will buy debt.

d.   The total market value of all companies is the sum of the market value of debt and the market value of equity for each firm. From part *b*, we know that investors in Group B and Group C will invest in debt. Therefore, their investable funds comprise the total market value of debt in the economy. The market value of debt is $325 million (= $220 million + $105 million). Since there are $85 million of corporate earnings in perpetuity and the all-equity discount rate is 8.1%, the market value of equity in the economy is:

$$\text{Equity Value} = (EBIT - \{r_B * B\})(1 - T_C) / r_S$$
$$= (\$85 \text{ million} - \{0.1246 * \$325 \text{ million}\})(1 - 0.35) / 0.081$$
$$= \$357.1 \text{ million}$$

The market value of equity is $357.1 million.

It is no coincidence that the value of equity is exactly equal to Group A's investable funds. The required return on equity is determined in equilibrium by the amount of available funds from investors who wish to buy equity. Had there been more (less) funds available for equity investment, the required return on equity would be lower (higher).

Therefore, the market value of all companies is:

$$V_L = B + S$$
$$= \$325 \text{ million} + \$357.1 \text{ million}$$
$$= \textbf{\$682.1 million}$$

The market value of all companies is $682.1 million.

c.   The total tax bill is the sum of the taxes paid by corporations and individuals.

Corporate Taxes:

$$\text{Corporate Taxes} = T_C * \text{Earnings After Interest}$$
$$= T_C * (EBIT - \{r_B * B\})$$
$$= 0.35 * (\$85 \text{ million} - \{0.1246 * \$325 \text{ million}\})$$
$$= \$15,576,750$$

Personal Taxes:

There are no taxes on equity distributions:

Interest Income:

Group A holds no debt and therefore earns no interest income.

Group B holds $220 million of debt and is subject to a personal tax rate on interest income of 32.5%.

$$\text{Group B's Personal Taxes} = T_B * (B * r_B)$$
$$= 0.325 * (\$220 \text{ million} * 0.1246)$$
$$= \$8,908,900$$

Group C holds $105 million of debt and is subject to a personal tax rate on interest income of 10%.

Group C's Personal Taxes $= T_B * (B * r_B)$
$$= 0.10 * (\$105 \text{ million} * 0.1246)$$
$$= \$1,308,300$$

The total amount of personal taxes is $10,217,200 (= $8,908,900 + $1,308,300).

Total Tax Bill $=$ Corporate Taxes + Personal Taxes
$$= \$15,576,750 + \$10,217,200$$
$$= \mathbf{\$25,793,950}$$

The total tax bill is $25,793,950.

16.19 a. According to the Miller Model, in equilibrium:

$r_B (1 - T_C) = r_S$

where r_B = the pre-tax cost of debt (the interest rate)
$\quad\quad\quad T_C$ = the corporate tax rate
$\quad\quad\quad r_S$ = the required return on a firm's equity

Therefore, the equilibrium interest rate paid by corporations is:

$r_B (1 - T_C) = r_S$
$r_B (1 - 0.40) = 0.06$
$r_B \quad = 0.06 / (1 - 0.4)$
$\quad\quad = 0.10$

Corporations pay an interest rate of 10%.

In order to determine whether each group would prefer to hold debt or equity, compare the after-personal tax interest rate on debt to the required return on unlevered equity for each of the four groups. A group will prefer to hold the security that offers them the highest rate of return.

The required rate of return to equity holders is 6%. Since equity income is untaxed at the personal level, personal taxes do not change the required return to equity holders.

The market interest rate is 10%.

Group L faces a 50% tax on interest income. The after-personal tax interest rate for investors in Group L is 5% {= 0.10 * (1 - 0.50)}. Since the after-personal tax interest rate (5%) is less than the required return on equity (6%), Group L will buy equity.

Group L will buy equity with its $700 million of wealth.

Group M faces a 40% tax on interest income. The after-personal tax interest rate for investors in Group M is 6% {= 0.10 * (1 - 0.40)}. Since the after-personal tax interest rate (6%) equals the required return on equity (6%), Group M is indifferent between holding debt and equity.

Group M is indifferent between buying debt or equity with its $300 million of wealth.

Group N faces a 20% tax on interest income. The after-personal tax rate interest rate for investors in Group N is 8% {= 0.10 * (1 - 0.20)}. Since the after-personal tax interest rate (8%) is greater than the required return on equity (6%), Group N will buy debt.

Group N will buy debt with its $200 million of wealth.

Group O pays no tax on interest income. The after-personal tax rate interest rate for investors in Group O is 10% {= 0.10 * (1 - 0)}. Since the after-personal tax interest rate (10%) is greater than the required return on equity (6%), Group O will buy debt.

Group O will buy debt with its $500 million of wealth.

Therefore, if Group M chooses to buy all debt, there will be $1 billion (= $300 million + $200 million + $500 million) of debt in the economy. If Group M chooses to buy all equity, there will be only $700 million (= $200 million + $500 million) of debt in the economy.

The value of equity in the economy can be computed using the following expression:

Equity Value $= (EBIT - r_B B)(1 - T_C) / r_S$

If Group M chooses to buy all debt, the value of equity in the economy is:

Equity Value $= (\$150 \text{ million} - \{0.10 * \$1 \text{ billion}\})(1 - 0.40)) / 0.06$
$= \$500 \text{ million}$

It is no coincidence that the value of equity is exactly equal to Group L's investable funds. The required return on equity is determined in equilibrium by the amount of available funds from investors who wish to buy equity. Had there been more (less) funds available for equity investment, the required return on equity would be lower (higher).

If Group M chooses to buy all equity, the value of equity in the economy is:

Equity Value $= (\$150 \text{ million} - \{0.10 * \$700 \text{ million}\})(1 - 0.40)) / 0.06$
$= \$800 \text{ million}$

Therefore, if Group M chooses to buy all debt, the aggregate debt-equity ratio in the economy will be 2 (= $1 billion / $500 million). However, if Group M chooses to buy all equity, the aggregate debt-equity ratio in the economy will be 0.875 (= $700 million / $800 million).

The debt-equity ratio in the economy can range from 0.875 to 2.

b. According to the Miller Model, in equilibrium:

$r_B (1 - T_C) = r_S$

where r_B = the pre-tax cost of debt (the interest rate)
T_C = the corporate tax rate
r_S = the required return on a firm's equity

Therefore, the equilibrium interest rate paid by corporations is:

$r_B (1 - T_C) = r_S$
$r_B (1 - 0.30) = 0.06$
$r_B = 0.06 / (1 - 0.30)$
$= 0.0857$

Corporations pay an interest rate of 8.57%.

In order to determine whether each group would prefer to hold debt or equity, compare the after-personal tax interest rate on debt to the required return on unlevered equity for each of the four groups. A group will prefer to hold the security that offers them the highest rate of return.

The required rate of return to equity holders is 6%. Since equity income is untaxed at the personal level, personal taxes do not change the required return to equity holders.

The market interest rate is 8.57%.

Group L faces a 50% tax on interest income. The after-personal tax interest rate for investors in Group L is 4.29% {= 0.0857 * (1 - 0.50)}. Since the after-personal tax interest rate (4.29%) is less than the required return on equity (6%), Group L will buy equity.

Group L will buy equity with its $500 million of wealth.

Group M faces a 40% tax on interest income. The after-personal tax interest rate for investors in Group M is 5.14% {= 0.0857 * (1 - 0.40)}. Since the after-personal tax interest rate (5.14%) is less than the required return on equity (6%), Group M will buy equity.

Group M will buy equity with its $300 million of wealth.

Group N faces a 20% tax on interest income. The after-personal tax rate interest rate for investors in Group N is 6.86% {= 0.0857 * (1 - 0.20)}. Since the after-personal tax interest rate (6.86%) is greater than the required return on equity (6%), Group N will buy debt.

Group N will buy debt with its $200 million of wealth.

Group O pays no tax on interest income. The after-personal tax rate interest rate for investors in Group O is 8.57% {= 0.0857 * (1 - 0)}. Since the after-personal tax interest rate (8.57%) is greater than the required return on equity (6%), Group O will buy debt.

Group O will buy debt with its $500 million of wealth.

Therefore, the value of debt in the economy is $700 million (= $200 million + $500 million).

The value of equity in the economy can be computed using the following expression:

Equity Value $= (EBIT - r_B B)(1 - T_C) / r_S$
Equity Value $= (\$150 \text{ million} - \{0.0857 * \$700 \text{ million}\})(1 - 0.30)) / 0.06$
$\qquad\quad = \$1{,}050 \text{ million}$

The debt-equity ratio in the economy is 2/3 (= $700 million / $1,050 million).

Chapter 17: Valuation and Capital Budgeting for the Levered Firm

17.1   a.   The maximum price that Hertz should be willing to pay for the fleet of cars with all-equity funding is the price that makes the NPV of the transaction equal to zero.

NPV   = -Purchase Price + PV[(1- T_C)(Earnings Before Taxes and Depreciation)] + PV(Depreciation Tax Shield)

Let P equal the purchase price of the fleet.

NPV   = $-P + (1-0.34)(\$100,000)A^5_{0.10} + (0.34)(P/5)A^5_{0.10}$

Set the NPV equal to zero.

$$0 = -P + (1-0.34)(\$100,000)A^5_{0.10} + (0.34)(P/5)A^5_{0.10}$$
$$P = \$250,191.93 + (P)(0.34/5)A^5_{0.10}$$
$$P = \$250,191.93 + 0.2578P$$
$$0.7422P = \$250,191.93$$
$$P = \$337,095$$

Therefore, the most that Hertz should be willing to pay for the fleet of cars with all-equity funding is $337,095.

b.   The adjusted present value (APV) of a project equals the net present value of the project if it were funded completely by equity plus the net present value of any financing side effects. In Hertz's case, the NPV of financing side effects equals the after-tax present value of the cash flows resulting from the firm's debt.

APV = NPV(All-Equity) + NPV(Financing Side Effects)

<u>NPV(All-Equity)</u>

NPV   = -Purchase Price + PV[(1- T_C)(Earnings Before Taxes and Depreciation)] + PV(Depreciation Tax Shield)

Hertz paid $325,000 for the fleet of cars. Because this fleet will be fully depreciated over five years using the straight-line method, annual depreciation expense equals $65,000 (= $325,000/5).

NPV   = $-\$325,000 + (1-0.34)(\$100,000)A^5_{0.10} + (0.34)(\$65,000)A^5_{0.10}$
     = $8,968

<u>NPV(Financing Side Effects)</u>

The net present value of financing side effects equals the after-tax present value of cash flows resulting from the firm's debt.

NPV(Financing Side Effects)   = Proceeds – After-Tax PV(Interest Payments) – PV(Principal Payments)

Given a known level of debt, debt cash flows should be discounted at the pre-tax cost of debt (r_B), 8%.

NPV(Financing Side Effects)   = $\$200,000 – (1 – 0.34)(0.08)(\$200,000)A^5_{0.08} – [\$200,000/(1.08)^5]$
     = $21,720

APV

$$\begin{aligned} \text{APV} \; &= \text{NPV(All-Equity)} + \text{NPV(Financing Side Effects)} \\ &= \$8,968 + \$21,720 \\ &= \mathbf{\$30,688} \end{aligned}$$

Therefore, if Hertz uses \$200,000 of five-year, 8% debt to fund the \$325,000 purchase, the Adjusted Present Value (APV) of the project is \$30,688.

17.2   The adjusted present value of a project equals the net present value of the project under all-equity financing plus the net present value of any financing side effects. In Gemini's case, the NPV of financing side effects equals the after-tax present value of the cash flows resulting from the firm's debt.

APV = NPV(All-Equity) + NPV(Financing Side Effects)

NPV(All-Equity)

$$\begin{aligned} \text{NPV} \; &= \text{-Initial Investment} + \text{PV}[(1\text{-}T_C)(\text{Earnings Before Taxes and Depreciation})] + \\ &\quad \text{PV(Depreciation Tax Shield)} \end{aligned}$$

Since the initial investment of \$2.1 million will be fully depreciated over three years using the straight-line method, annual depreciation expense equals \$700,000 (= \$2,100,000 / 3).

$$\begin{aligned} \text{NPV} \; &= \text{-}\$2,100,000 + (1\text{-}0.30)(\$900,000)A^3_{0.18} + (0.30)(\$700,000)A^3_{0.18} \\ &= \text{-}\$273,611 \end{aligned}$$

NPV(Financing Side Effects)

The net present value of financing side effects equals the after-tax present value of cash flows resulting from the firm's debt.

NPV(Financing Side Effects)   = Proceeds, net of flotation costs – After-Tax PV(Interest Payments) – PV(Principal Payments) + PV(Flotation Cost Tax Shield)

Given a known level of debt, debt cash flows should be discounted at the pre-tax cost of debt (r_B), 12.5%. Since \$21,000 in flotation costs will be amortized over the three-year life of the loan, \$7,000 = (\$21,000 / 3) of flotation costs will be expensed per year.

$$\begin{aligned} \text{NPV(Financing Side Effects)} \; &= (\$2,100,000 - \$21,000) - (1 - 0.30)(0.125)(\$2,100,000)A^3_{0.125} - \\ &\quad [\$2,100,000/(1.125)^3] + (0.30)(\$7,000)A^3_{0.125} \\ &= \$171,532 \end{aligned}$$

APV

$$\begin{aligned} \text{APV} \; &= \text{NPV(All-Equity)} + \text{NPV(Financing Side Effects)} \\ &= \text{-}\$273,611 + \$171,532 \\ &= \mathbf{\text{-}\$102,079} \end{aligned}$$

Since the adjusted present value (APV) of the project is negative, Gemini should not undertake the project.

17.3   The adjusted present value of a project equals the net present value of the project under all-equity financing plus the net present value of any financing side effects.

According to Modigliani-Miller Proposition II with corporate taxes:

$$r_S = r_0 + (B/S)(r_0 - r_B)(1 - T_C)$$

where
- r_0 = the required return on the equity of an unlevered firm
- r_S = the required return on the equity of a levered firm
- r_B = the pre-tax cost of debt
- T_C = the corporate tax rate
- B/S = the firm's debt-to-equity ratio

In this problem:

$$r_S = 0.18$$
$$r_B = 0.10$$
$$T_C = 0.40$$
$$B/S = 0.25$$

Solve for MVP's unlevered cost of capital (r_0):

$$r_S = r_0 + (B/S)(r_0 - r_b)(1 - T_C)$$
$$0.18 = r_0 + (0.25)(r_0 - 0.10)(1 - 0.40)$$

$$r_0 = 0.17$$

The cost of MVP's unlevered equity is 17%.

APV = NPV(All-Equity) + NPV(Financing Side Effects)

NPV(All-Equity)

NPV = PV(Unlevered Cash Flows)
= $-\$15,000,000 + \$4,000,000/1.17 + \$8,000,000/(1.17)^2 + \$9,000,000/(1.17)^3$
= -$117,753

NPV(Financing Side Effects)

The net present value of financing side effects equals the after-tax present value of cash flows resulting from the firm's debt.

NPV(Financing Side Effects) = Proceeds– After-Tax PV(Interest Payments) – PV(Principal Payments)

Year	1	2	3	4+
Outstanding Debt at the Start of the Year (B)	$6,000,000	$4,000,000	$2,000,000	$0
Debt Repayment at the End of the Year	$2,000,000	$2,000,000	$2,000,000	$0

Given a known level of debt, debt cash flows should be discounted at the pre-tax cost of debt (r_B), 10%.

NPV(Financing Side Effects) = $\$6,000,000 - (1 - 0.40)(0.10)(\$6,000,000) / (1.10) -$
$\$2,000,000/(1.10) - (1 - 0.40)(0.10)(\$4,000,000)/(1.10)^2 -$
$\$2,000,000/(1.10)^2 - (1 - 0.40)(0.10)(\$2,000,000)/(1.10)^3 -$
$\$2,000,000/(1.10)^3$
= $410,518

APV

$$APV = NPV(\text{All-Equity}) + NPV(\text{Financing Side Effects})$$
$$= -\$117,753 + \$410,518$$
$$= \mathbf{\$292,765}$$

Since the adjusted present value (APV) of the project is positive, MVP should proceed with the expansion.

17.4   The adjusted present value of a project equals the net present value of the project under all-equity financing plus the net present value of any financing side effects. In the joint venture's case, the NPV of financing side effects equals the after-tax present value of cash flows resulting from the firms' debt.

$$APV = NPV(\text{All-Equity}) + NPV(\text{Financing Side Effects})$$

NPV(All-Equity)

$$NPV = -\text{Initial Investment} + PV[(1 - T_C)(\text{Earnings Before Interest, Taxes, and Depreciation})] + PV(\text{Depreciation Tax Shield})$$

Since the initial investment of $20 million will be fully depreciated over five years using the straight-line method, annual depreciation expense equals $4,000,000 (= $20,000,000/5).

$$NPV = -\$20,000,000 + [(1-0.25)(\$3,000,000)A^{20}_{0.12}] + (0.25)(\$4,000,000)A^{5}_{0.12}$$
$$= \$411,024$$

NPV(Financing Side Effects)

The NPV of financing side effects equals the after-tax present value of cash flows resulting from the firms' debt.

Given a known level of debt, debt cash flows should be discounted at the pre-tax cost of debt (r_B), 10%.

$$NPV(\text{Financing Side Effects}) = \text{Proceeds} - \text{After-tax } PV(\text{Interest Payments}) - PV(\text{Principal Repayments})$$
$$= \$10,000,000 - (1 - 0.25)(0.05)(\$10,000,000)A^{15}_{0.09} - [\$10,000,000/((1.09)^{15}]$$
$$= \$4,231,861$$

APV

$$APV = NPV(\text{All-Equity}) + NPV(\text{Financing Side Effects})$$
$$= \$411,024 + \$4,231,861$$
$$= \mathbf{\$4,642,885}$$

The Adjusted Present Value (APV) of the project is $4,642,885.

17.5 a. In order to value a firm's equity using the Flow-to-Equity approach, discount the cash flows available to equity holders at the cost of the firm's levered equity (r_S).

	One Restaurant	Milano Pizza Club
Sales	$1,000,000	$3,000,000
Cost of Goods Sold	($400,000)	($1,200,000)
General and Administrative Costs	($300,000)	($900,000)
Interest Expense	($25,650)	($76,950)
Pre-Tax Income	$274,350	$823,050
Taxes at 40%	($109,740)	($329,220)
Cash Flow Available to Equity Holders	$164,610	$493,830

Since this cash flow will remain the same forever, the present value of cash flows available to the firm's equity holders is a perpetuity of $493,830, discounted at 21%.

PV(Flows-to-Equity) = $493,830 / 0.21
= $2,351,571

The value of Milano Pizza Club's equity is $2,351,571.

b. The value of a firm is equal to the sum of the market values of its debt and equity.

$V_L = B + S$

The market value of Milano Pizza Club's equity (S) is $2,351,571 (see part *a*).

The problem states that the firm has a debt-to-equity ratio of 30%, which can be written algebraically as:

$B / S = 0.30$

Since S = $2,351,571:

$B / \$2,351,571 = 0.30$

$B = \$705,471$

The market value of Milano Pizza Club's debt is $705,471, and the value of the firm is $3,057,042 (= $705,471 + $2,351,571).

The value of Milano Pizza Club is $3,057,042.

17.6 a. In order to determine the cost of the firm's debt (r_B), solve for the discount rate that makes the present value of the bond's future cash flows equal to the bond's current price.

Since WWI's one-year, $1,000 par value bonds carry a 7% coupon, bond holders will receive a payment of $1,070 =[$1,000 + (0.07)($1,000)] in one year.

$972.73 = \$1,070 / (1 + r_B)$
$r_B = 0.10$

Therefore, the cost of WWI's debt is 10%.

b.　Use the Capital Asset Pricing Model to find the return on WWI's unlevered equity (r_0).

According to the Capital Asset Pricing Model:

$$r_0 = r_f + \beta_{Unlevered}(r_m - r_f)$$

where　r_0　= the cost of a firm's unlevered equity
r_f　= the risk-free rate
r_m　= the expected return on the market portfolio
$\beta_{Unlevered}$ = the firm's beta under all-equity financing

In this problem:

r_f　= 0.08
r_m　= 0.16
$\beta_{Unlevered}$ = 0.9

$$
\begin{aligned}
r_0 &= r_f + \beta_{Unlevered}(r_m - r_f) \\
&= 0.08 + 0.9(0.16\text{-}0.08) \\
&= 0.152
\end{aligned}
$$

The cost of WWI's unlevered equity is 15.2%.

Next, find the cost of WWI's levered equity.

According to Modigliani-Miller Proposition II with corporate taxes

$$r_S = r_0 + (B/S)(r_0 - r_B)(1 - T_C)$$

where　r_0　= the cost of a firm's unlevered equity
r_S　= the cost of a firm's levered equity
r_B　= the pre-tax cost of debt
T_C　= the corporate tax rate
B/S = the firm's target debt-to-equity ratio

In this problem:

r_0　= 0.152
r_B　= 0.10
T_C　= 0.34
B/S = 0.50

The cost of WWI's levered equity is:

$$
\begin{aligned}
r_S &= r_0 + (B/S)(r_0 - r_B)(1 - T_C) \\
&= 0.152 + (0.50)(0.152\text{-}0.10)(1 - 0.34) \\
&= \mathbf{0.1692}
\end{aligned}
$$

The cost of WWI's levered equity is 16.92%.

c. In a world with corporate taxes, a firm's weighted average cost of capital (r_{wacc}) is equal to:

$$r_{wacc} = \{B / (B+S)\}(1 - T_C) \, r_B + \{S / (B+S)\}r_S$$

where $B / (B+S)$ = the firm's debt-to-value ratio
                    $S / (B+S)$ = the firm's equity-to-value ratio
                    r_B = the pre-tax cost of debt
                    r_S = the cost of equity
                    T_C = the corporate tax rate

The problem does not provide either WWI's debt-to-value ratio or WWI's equity-to-value ratio. However, the firm's debt-to-equity ratio of 0.50 is given, which can be written algebraically as:

$B / S = 0.50$

Solving for B:

$B = (0.5 * S)$

A firm's debt-to-value ratio is: $B / (B+S)$

Since $B = (0.5 * S)$:

WWI's debt-to-value ratio $= (0.5 * S) / \{ (0.5 * S) + S\}$
                                      $= (0.5 * S) / (1.5 * S)$
                                      $= 0.5 / 1.5$
                                      $= 1/3$

WWI's debt-to-value ratio is 1/3.

A firm's equity-to-value ratio is: $S / (B+S)$

Since $B = (0.5 * S)$:

WWI's equity-to-value ratio $= S / \{(0.5*S) + S\}$
                                       $= S / (1.5 * S)$
                                       $= (1 / 1.5)$
                                       $= 2/3$

WWI's equity-to-value ratio is 2/3.

Thus, in this problem:

$B / (B+S)$	= 1/3
$S / (B+S)$	= 2/3
r_B	= 0.10
r_S	= 0.1692
T_C	= 0.34

r_{wacc} $= \{B / (B+S)\}(1 - T_C) \, r_B + \{S / (B+S)\}r_S$
                   $= (1/3)(1 - 0.34)(0.10) + (2/3)(0.1692)$
                   $= 0.1348$

WWI's weighted average cost of capital is 13.48%.

17.7 a. Bolero has a capital structure with three parts: long-term debt, short-term debt, and equity.

  i. Book Value Weights:

Type of Financing	Book Value	Weight	Cost
Long-term debt	$5,000,000	25%	10%
Short-term debt	$5,000,000	25%	8%
Common Stock	$10,000,000	50%	15%
Total	$20,000,000	100%	

Since interest payments on both long-term and short-term debt are tax-deductible, multiply the pre-tax costs by $(1-T_C)$ to determine the after-tax costs to be used in the weighted average cost of capital calculation.

$$r_{wacc} = (Weight_{LTD})(Cost_{LTD})(1-T_C) + (Weight_{STD})(Cost_{STD})(1-T_C) + (Weight_{Equity})(Cost_{Equity})$$
$$= (0.25)(0.10)(1-0.34) + (0.25)(0.08)(1-0.34) + (0.50)(0.15)$$
$$= 0.1047$$

If Bolero uses book value weights, the firm's weighted average cost of capital would be 10.47%.

  ii. Market Value Weights:

Type of Financing	Market Value	Weight	Cost
Long-term debt	$2,000,000	10%	10%
Short-term debt	$5,000,000	25%	8%
Common Stock	$13,000,000	65%	15%
Total	$20,000,000	100%	

Since interest payments on both long-term and short-term debt are tax-deductible, multiply the pre-tax costs by $(1-T_C)$ to determine the after-tax costs to be used in the weighted average cost of capital calculation.

$$r_{wacc} = (Weight_{LTD})(Cost_{LTD})(1-T_C) + (Weight_{STD})(Cost_{STD})(1-T_C) + (Weight_{Equity})(Cost_{Equity})$$
$$= (0.10)(0.10)(1-0.34) + (0.25)(0.08)(1-0.34) + (0.65)(0.15)$$
$$= 0.1173$$

If Bolero uses market value weights, the firm's weighted average cost of capital would be 11.73%.

  iii. Target Weights:

If Bolero has a target debt-to-equity ratio of 100%, then both the target equity-to-value and target debt-to-value ratios must be 50%. Since the target values of long-term and short-term debt are equal, the 50% of the capital structure targeted for debt would be split evenly between long-term and short-term debt (25% each).

Type of Financing	Target Weight	Cost
Long-term debt	25%	10%
Short-term debt	25%	8%
Common Stock	50%	15%
Total	100%	

Since interest payments on both long-term and short-term debt are tax-deductible, multiply the pre-tax costs by $(1-T_C)$ to determine the after-tax costs to be used in the weighted average cost of capital calculation.

$$
\begin{aligned}
r_{wacc} &= (Weight_{LTD})(Cost_{LTD})(1-T_C) + (Weight_{STD})(Cost_{STD})(1-T_C) + (Weight_{Equity})(Cost_{Equity}) \\
&= (0.25)(0.10)(1-0.34) + (0.25)(0.08)(1-0.34) + (0.50)(0.15) \\
&= 0.1047
\end{aligned}
$$

If Bolero uses target weights, the firm's weighted average cost of capital would be 10.47%.

b. The differences in the WACCs are due to the different weighting schemes. The firm's WACC will most closely resemble the WACC calculated using target weights since future projects will be financed at the target ratio. Therefore, the WACC computed with target weights should be used for project evaluation.

17.8 a. In a world with corporate taxes, a firm's weighted average cost of capital (r_{wacc}) equals:

$$
r_{wacc} = \{B / (B+S)\}(1 - T_C) \, r_B + \{S / (B+S)\} r_S
$$

where $B / (B+S)$ = the firm's debt-to-value ratio
     $S / (B+S)$ = the firm's equity-to-value ratio
     r_B = the pre-tax cost of debt
     r_S = the cost of equity
     T_C = the corporate tax rate

The market value of Neon's debt is \$24 million, and the market value of the firm's equity is \$60 million (= 4 million shares * \$15 per share).

Therefore, Neon's current debt-to-value ratio is 28.57% [= \$24 / (\$24 + \$60)], and the firm's current equity-to-value ratio is 71.43% [= \$60 / (\$24 + \$60)].

Since Neon's CEO believes its current capital structure is optimal, these values can be used as the target weights in the firm's weighted average cost of capital calculation.

Neon's bonds yield 11% per annum. Since the yield on a firm's bonds is equal to its pre-tax cost of debt, r_B equals 11%.

Use the Capital Asset Pricing Model to determine Neon's cost of equity.

According to the Capital Asset Pricing Model:

$$
r_S = r_f + \beta_{Equity}(r_m - r_f)
$$

where r_S = the cost of a firm's equity
    r_f = the risk-free rate
    $r_m - r_f$ = the expected market risk premium
    β_{Equity} = the firm's equity beta

β_{Equity} = [Covariance(Stock Returns, Market Returns)] / Variance(Market Returns)

The covariance between Neon's stock returns and returns on the market portfolio is 0.031. The standard deviation of market returns is 0.16.

The variance of returns is equal to the standard deviation of those returns squared. The variance of the returns on the market portfolio is 0.0256 [= $(0.16)^2$].

Neon's equity beta is 1.21 $(= 0.031 / 0.0256)$.

The inputs to the CAPM in this problem are:

$r_f = 0.07$
$r_m - r_f = 0.085$
$\beta_{Equity} = 1.21$

$r_S = r_f + \beta_{Equity}(r_m - r_f)$
$\quad = 0.07 + 1.21(0.085)$
$\quad = 0.1729$

The cost of Neon's equity (r_S) is 17.29%.

The inputs for the weighted average cost of capital calculation are:

$B / (B+S)$	$= 0.2857$
$S / (B+S)$	$= 0.7143$
r_B	$= 0.11$
r_S	$= 0.1729$
T_C	$= 0.34$

$r_{wacc} = \{B / (B+S)\}(1 - T_C) r_B + \{S / (B+S)\}r_S$
$\quad = (0.2857)(1 - 0.34)(0.11) + (0.7143)(0.1729)$
$\quad = 0.1442$

Neon's weighted average cost of capital is 14.42%,

Use the weighted average cost of capital to discount Neon's expected unlevered cash flows.

$NPV = -\$27,500,000 + \$9,000,000 A^5_{0.1442}$
$\quad\quad = \mathbf{\$3,088,379}$

Since the NPV of the equipment is positive, Neon should make the purchase.

b.　　The weighted average cost of capital used in part *a* will not change if the firm chooses to fund the project entirely with debt. It will remain 14.42%. The weighted average cost of capital is based on *target* capital structure weights. Since the current capital structure is optimal, all-debt funding for the project simply implies that the firm will have to use more equity in the future to bring the capital structure back towards the target.

17.9　　a.　　In a world with corporate taxes, a firm's weighted average cost of capital (r_{wacc}) equals:

$r_{wacc} = \{B / (B+S)\}(1 - T_C) r_B + \{S / (B+S)\}r_S$

where		
	$B / (B+S)$	$=$ the firm's debt-to-value ratio
	$S / (B+S)$	$=$ the firm's equity-to-value ratio
	r_B	$=$ the pre-tax cost of debt
	r_S	$=$ the cost of equity
	T_C	$=$ the corporate tax rate

Since the firm's target debt-to-equity ratio is 200%, the firm's target debt-to-value ratio is 2/3, and the firm's target equity-to-value ratio is 1/3.

The inputs to the WACC calculation in this problem are:

$B / (B+S)$ = 2/3
$S / (B+S)$ = 1/3
r_B = 0.10
r_S = 0.20
T_C = 0.34

r_{wacc} = $\{B / (B+S)\}(1 - T_C) r_B + \{S / (B+S)\}r_S$
= $(2/3)(1 - 0.34)(0.10) + (1/3)(0.20)$
= **0.1107**

NEC's weighted average cost of capital is 11.07%.

Use the weighted average cost of capital to discount NEC's unlevered cash flows.

NPV = -$20,000,000 + $8,000,000 / 0.1107
= **$52,267,389**

Since the NPV of the project is positive, NEC should proceed with the expansion.

17.10   a.   ABC was an all-equity firm prior to its recapitalization. The value of ABC as an all-equity firm equals the present value of after-tax cash flows, discounted at the cost of the firm's unlevered equity of 18%.

V_U = $[(\text{Pre-Tax Earnings})(1 - T_C)] / r_0$
= $[(\$30,000,000)(1 - 0.34)] / 0.18$
= **$110,000,000**

The value of ABC before the recapitalization is announced is $110 million.

Since ABC is an all-equity firm, the value of ABC's equity before the announcement is also $110 million.

ABC has 1 million shares of common stock outstanding. The price per share before the announcement is $110 (= $110 million / 1 million shares)

b.   The adjusted present value of a firm equals it value under all-equity financing (V_U) plus the net present value of any financing side effects. In ABC's case, the NPV of financing side effects equals the after-tax present value of cash flows resulting from the firm's debt.

APV = V_U + NPV(Financing Side Effects)

From part *a*:

V_U = $110,000,000

NPV(Financing Side Effects)

The NPV of financing side effects equals the after-tax present value of cash flows resulting from the firms' debt.

Given a known level of debt, debt cash flows should be discounted at the pre-tax cost of debt (r_B), 10%.

NPV(Financing Side Effects) = Proceeds − After-tax PV(Interest Payments)
$$= \$50,000,000 - (1 - 0.34)(0.10)(\$50,000,000)/0.10$$
$$= \$17,000,000$$

APV

$$\text{APV} = V_U + \text{NPV(Financing Side Effects)}$$
$$= \$110,000,000 + \$17,000,000$$
$$= \mathbf{\$127,000,000}$$

The value of ABC after the recapitalization plan is announced is $127 million.

Since ABC has not yet issued the debt, the value of ABC's equity after the announcement is also $127 million.

ABC has 1 million shares of common stock outstanding. The price per share after the announcement is $127 (= $127 million / 1 million shares).

c.   ABC will receive $50 million in cash as a result of the debt issue. Since the firm's stock is worth $127 per share, ABC will repurchase 393,701 shares (= $50,000,000 / $127 per share). After the repurchase, the firm will have 606,299 (= 1,000,000 − 393,701) shares of common stock outstanding.

Since the value of ABC is $127 million and the firm has $50 million of debt, the value of ABC's equity after the recapitalization is $77 million (= $127 million - $50 million).

ABC has 606,299 shares of common stock outstanding after the recapitalization. The price per share after the repurchase is $127 (= $77 million / 606,299 shares).

d.   In order to value a firm's equity using the Flow-to-Equity approach, discount the cash flows available to equity holders at the cost of the firm's levered equity (r_S).

According to Modigliani-Miller Proposition II with corporate taxes

$$r_S = r_0 + (B/S)(r_0 - r_B)(1 - T_C)$$

where r_0 = the required return on the equity of an unlevered firm
        r_S = the required return on the equity of a levered firm
        r_B = the pre-tax cost of debt
        T_C = the corporate tax rate
        B   = the market value of the firm's debt
        S   = the market value of the firm's equity

In this problem:

        r_0 = 0.18
        r_B = 0.10
        T_C = 0.34
        B   = $50,000,000
        S   = $77,000,000

The required return on ABC's levered equity after the recapitalization is:

$$r_S = r_0 + (B/S)(r_0 - r_B)(1 - T_C)$$
$$= 0.18 + (\$50,000,000 / \$77,000,000)(0.18 - 0.10)(1 - 0.34)$$
$$= \mathbf{0.2143}$$

The required return on ABC's levered equity after the recapitalization is 21.43%.

Since ABC has $50,000,000 of 10% debt, the firm will make interest payments of $5,000,000 (= $50,000,000 * 0.10) at the end of each year.

Cash Flows to Equity	
EBIT	$30,000,000
Interest	5,000,000
Pre-Tax Earnings	25,000,000
Taxes at 34%	8,500,000
After-Tax Earnings	16,500,000

Since the firm pays all of its after-tax earnings out as dividends at the end of each year, equity holders will receive $16,500,000 of cash flow per year in perpetuity.

S = Cash Flows Available to Equity Holders / r_S
= $16,500,000 / 0.2143
= **$77 million**

Note: the unrounded cost of equity of 21.42857143% must be used to calculate the exact answer.

The value of ABC's equity after the recapitalization is $77 million.

17.11   a.   If Mojito were financed entirely by equity, the value of the firm would be equal to the present value of its unlevered after-tax earnings, discounted at its unlevered cost of capital of 16%.

Mojito Mint Company	
Sales Revenue	$19,740,000
Variable Costs	11,844,000
EBIT	7,896,000
Taxes at 40%	3,158,400
Unlevered After-Tax Earnings	4,737,600

V_U = $4,737,600 / 0.16
= **$29,610,000**

Therefore, Mojito Mint Company would be worth $29,610,000 as an unlevered firm.

b.   According to Modigliani-Miller Proposition II with corporate taxes:

$$r_S = r_0 + (B/S)(r_0 - r_B)(1 - T_C)$$

where r_0 = the required return on the equity of an unlevered firm
r_S = the required return on the equity of a levered firm
r_B = the pre-tax cost of debt
T_C = the corporate tax rate
B/S = the firm's debt-to-equity ratio

In this problem:

$$r_0 = 0.16$$
$$r_B = 0.10$$
$$T_C = 0.40$$
$$B/S = 2/3$$

The required return on Mojito's levered equity is:

$$
\begin{aligned}
r_S &= r_0 + (B/S)(r_0 - r_B)(1 - T_C) \\
&= 0.16 + (2/3)(0.16 - 0.10)(1 - 0.40) \\
&= \mathbf{0.184}
\end{aligned}
$$

The required return on Mojito's levered equity (r_S) is 18.4%.

c.   In a world with corporate taxes, a firm's weighted average cost of capital (r_{wacc}) equals:

$$r_{wacc} = \{B / (B+S)\}(1 - T_C)\, r_B + \{S / (B+S)\}r_S$$

where
- $B / (B+S)$ = the firm's debt-to-value ratio
- $S / (B+S)$ = the firm's equity-to-value ratio
- r_B = the pre-tax cost of debt
- r_S = the cost of equity
- T_C = the corporate tax rate

The problem does not provide either Mojito's debt-to-value ratio or Mojito's equity-to-value ratio. However, the firm's debt-to-equity ratio of 2/3 is given, which can be written algebraically as:

$B / S = 2/3$

Solving for B:

$B = (2/3)(S)$

A firm's debt-to-value ratio is: $B / (B+S)$

Since $B = (2/3)(S)$:

$$
\begin{aligned}
\text{Mojito's debt-to-value ratio} &= (2/3)(S) / \{ (2/3)(S) + S\} \\
&= (2/3)(S) / (5/3)(S) \\
&= (2/3)/(5/3) \\
&= 2/5
\end{aligned}
$$

Mojito's debt-to-value ratio is 2/5.

A firm's equity-to-value ratio is: $S / (B+S)$

Since $B = (2/3)(S)$:

$$
\begin{aligned}
\text{Mojito's equity-to-value ratio} &= S / \{(2/3)(S) + S\} \\
&= S / (5/3)(S) \\
&= (1 / (5/3)) \\
&= 3/5
\end{aligned}
$$

Mojito's equity-to-value ratio is 3/5.

The inputs to the WACC calculation are:

$$
\begin{aligned}
B / (B+S) &= 2/5 \\
S / (B+S) &= 3/5 \\
r_B &= 0.10 \\
r_S &= 0.184 \\
T_C &= 0.40
\end{aligned}
$$

$$
\begin{aligned}
r_{wacc} &= \{B / (B+S)\}(1 - T_C)\, r_B + \{S / (B+S)\}r_S \\
&= (2/5)(1 - 0.40)(0.10) + (3/5)(0.184) \\
&= \mathbf{0.1344}
\end{aligned}
$$

Mojito's weighted average cost of capital is 13.44%.

Use the weighted average cost of capital to discount the firm's unlevered after-tax earnings.

$$
\begin{aligned}
V_L &= \$4,737,600 / 0.1344 \\
&= \mathbf{\$35,250,000}
\end{aligned}
$$

Therefore, the value of Mojito Mint Company is $35,250,000.

Since the firm's equity-to-value ratio is 3/5, the value of Mojito's equity is $21,150,000 {= (3/5)($35,250,000)}.

Since the firm's debt-to-value ratio is 2/5, the value of Mojito's debt is $14,100,000 {= (2/5)($35,250,000)}.

d. In order to value a firm's equity using the Flow-to-Equity approach, discount the cash flows available to equity holders at the cost of the firm's levered equity (r_S).

Since the pre-tax cost of the firm's debt is 10%, and the firm has $14,100,000 of debt outstanding, Mojito must pay $1,410,000 (= 0.10 * $14,100,000) in interest at the end of each year.

Mojito Mint Company	
Sales Revenue	19,740,000
Variable Costs	11,844,000
EBIT	7,896,000
Interest	1,410,000
Pre-Tax Earnings	6,486,000
Taxes at 40%	2,594,400
After-Tax Earnings	3,891,600

Since the firm pays all of its after-tax earnings out as dividends at the end of each year, equity holders will receive $3,891,600 of cash flow per year in perpetuity.

$$
\begin{aligned}
S &= \text{Cash Flows Available to Equity Holders} / r_S \\
&= \$3,891,600 / 0.184 \\
&= \mathbf{\$21,150,000}
\end{aligned}
$$

The value of Mojito's equity is $21,150,000.

17.12 a. Since Lone Star is currently an all-equity firm, its value equals the present value of its unlevered after-tax earnings, discounted at its unlevered cost of capital of 20%.

Lone Star Industries	
EBIT	$152.00
Taxes at 40%	$60.80
Unlevered After-Tax Earnings	$91.20

$V_U = \$91.20 / 0.20$
$= \$456$

Lone Star Industries is worth $456 as an unlevered firm.

b. The adjusted present value of a firm equals its value under all-equity financing (V_U) plus the net present value of any financing side effects. In ABC's case, the NPV of financing side effects equals the after-tax present value of cash flows resulting from debt.

$APV = V_U + NPV(\text{Financing Side Effects})$

From part *a*:

$V_U = \$456$

NPV(Financing Side Effects)

The NPV of financing side effects equals the after-tax present value of cash flows resulting from the firms' debt.

Given a known level of debt, debt cash flows should be discounted at the pre-tax cost of debt (r_B), 10%.

NPV(Financing Side Effects) $= \text{Proceeds} - \text{After-tax PV(Interest Payments)}$
$= \$500 - (1 - 0.40)(0.10)(\$500)/0.10$
$= \$200$

APV

$APV = V_U + NPV(\text{Financing Side Effects})$
$= \$456 + \$200$
$= \$656$

The value of Lone Star Industries is $656 with leverage.

Since Lone Star has $500 of debt, the value of the firm's equity is $156 = ($656 - $500).

c. According to Modigliani-Miller Proposition II with corporate taxes

$r_S = r_0 + (B/S)(r_0 - r_B)(1 - T_C)$

where r_0 = the required return on the equity of an unlevered firm
   r_S = the required return on the equity of a levered firm
   r_B = the pre-tax cost of debt
   T_C = the corporate tax rate
   B = the market value of the firm's debt
   S = the market value of the firm's equity

In this problem:

$$
\begin{aligned}
r_0 &= 0.20 \\
r_B &= 0.10 \\
T_C &= 0.40 \\
B &= \$500 \\
S &= \$156
\end{aligned}
$$

The required return on Lone Star's levered equity is:

$$
\begin{aligned}
r_S &= r_0 + (B/S)(r_0 - r_B)(1 - T_C) \\
&= 0.20 + (\$500/\$156)(0.20 - 0.10)(1 - 0.40) \\
&= \mathbf{0.3923}
\end{aligned}
$$

Therefore, the required return on Lone Star's levered equity (r_S) is 39.23%.

d.   In order to value a firm's equity using the Flow-to-Equity approach, discount the cash flows available to equity holders at the cost of the firm's levered equity (r_S).

Since the pre-tax cost of debt is 10% and the firm has $500 of debt outstanding, Lone Star must pay $50 (= 0.10 * $500) in interest at the end of each year.

Lone Star Industries	
EBIT	$152.00
Interest	$50.00
Pre-Tax Earnings	$102.00
Taxes at 40%	$40.80
After-Tax Earnings	$61.20

$$
\begin{aligned}
S &= \text{Cash Flows Available to Equity Holders} / r_S \\
&= \text{After-Tax Earnings} / r_S \\
&= \$61.20 / 0.3923 \\
&= \mathbf{\$156}
\end{aligned}
$$

The value of Lone Star's equity is $156.

17.13   Use the Capital Asset Pricing Model to find the average cost of levered equity (r_S) in the holiday gift industry.

According to the Capital Asset Pricing Model:

$$
r_S = r_f + \beta_{Equity}(r_m - r_f)
$$

where r_S = the cost of a firm's levered equity
r_f = the risk-free rate
r_m = the expected return on the market portfolio
β_{Equity} = the firm's equity beta

In this problem:

$$r_f = 0.09$$
$$r_m = 0.17$$
$$\beta_{Equity} = 1.5$$

$$r_S = r_f + \beta_{Equity}(r_m - r_f)$$
$$= 0.09 + 1.5\,(0.17\text{-}0.09)$$
$$= 0.21$$

The average cost of levered equity in the holiday gift industry is 21%.

Next, find the average cost of unlevered equity (r_0) in the holiday gift industry.

According to Modigliani-Miller Proposition II with corporate taxes

$$r_S = r_0 + (B/S)(r_0 - r_B)(1 - T_C)$$

where r_0 = the cost of unlevered equity
r_S = the cost of levered equity
r_B = the pre-tax cost of debt
T_C = the corporate tax rate
B/S = the firm's target debt-to-equity ratio

In this problem:

$$r_S = 0.21$$
$$r_B = 0.10$$
$$T_C = 0.40$$
$$B/S = 0.30$$

The average cost of unlevered equity in the holiday gift industry is:

$$r_S = r_0 + (B/S)(r_0 - r_B)(1 - T_C)$$
$$0.21 = r_0 + (.30)(r_0 - 0.10)(1 - 0.40)$$

$$r_0 = 0.1932$$

The average cost of unlevered equity in the holiday gift industry is 19.32%.

Next, use the average cost of unlevered equity in the holiday gift industry to find the cost of Blue Angel's levered equity.

According to Modigliani-Miller Proposition II with corporate taxes

$$r_S = r_0 + (B/S)(r_0 - r_B)(1 - T_C)$$

where r_0 = the cost of unlevered equity
r_S = the cost of levered equity
r_B = the pre-tax cost of debt
T_C = the corporate tax rate
B/S = the firm's target debt-to-equity ratio

In this problem:

$$r_0 = 0.1932$$
$$r_B = 0.10$$
$$T_C = 0.40$$
$$B/S = 0.35$$

The cost of Blue Angel's levered equity is:

r_S $= r_0 + (B/S)(r_0 - r_B)(1 - T_C)$
$= 0.1932 + (0.35)(0.1932 - 0.10)(1 - 0.40)$
$= 0.2128$

The cost of Blue Angel's levered equity is 21.28%.

Since the project is financed at the firm's target debt-equity ratio, it must be discounted at the Blue Angel's weighted average cost of capital.

In a world with corporate taxes, a firm's weighted average cost of capital (r_{wacc}) equals:

r_{wacc} $= \{B / (B+S)\}(1 - T_C) r_B + \{S / (B+S)\}r_S$

where | $B / (B+S)$ | = the firm's debt-to-value ratio
| $S / (B+S)$ | = the firm's equity-to-value ratio
| r_B | = the pre-tax cost of debt
| r_S | = the cost of levered equity
| T_C | = the corporate tax rate

The problem does not provide either Blue Angel's debt-to-value ratio or Blue Angel's equity-to-value ratio. However, the firm's debt-to-equity ratio of 0.35 is given, which can be written algebraically as:

$B / S = 0.35$

Solving for B:

$B = (0.35)(S)$

A firm's debt-to-value ratio is: $B / (B+S)$

Since $B = (0.35)(S)$:

Blue Angel's debt-to-value ratio $= (0.35)(S) / \{ (0.35)(S) + S\}$
$= (0.35)(S) / (1.35)(S)$
$= (0.35)/(1.35)$
$= 0.2593$

Blue Angel's debt-to-value ratio is 0.2593.

A firm's equity-to-value ratio is: $S / (B+S)$

Since $B = (0.35)(S)$:

Blue Angel's equity-to-value ratio $= S / \{(0.35)(S) + S\}$
$$= S / (1.35S)$$
$$= (1 / 1.35)$$
$$= 0.7407$$

Blue Angel's equity-to-value ratio is 0.7407.

The inputs to the WACC calculation are:

$B / (B+S)$	$= 0.2593$
$S / (B+S)$	$= 0.7407$
r_B	$= 0.10$
r_S	$= 0.2128$
T_C	$= 0.40$

r_{wacc} $= \{B / (B+S)\}(1 - T_C)\, r_B + \{S / (B+S)\}r_S$
$$= (0.2593)(1 - 0.40)(0.10) + (0.7407)(0.2128)$$
$$= 0.1732$$

Blue Angel's weighted average cost of capital is 17.32%.

Use the weighted average cost of capital to discount the project's cash flows.

$NPV_{PROJECT}$ $= -\$325,000 + \$55,000 * GA^5{}_{.1732,\ .05} + [\$55,000(1.05)^5 / .1732] / (1.1732)^5$
$$= \$47,424$$

Since the NPV of the project is positive, Blue Angel should undertake the project.

17.14   a.   If flotation costs are not taken into account, the net present value of a loan equals:

NPV_{Loan} = Gross Proceeds – After-tax present value of interest and principal payments

Proceeds net of flotation costs

The gross proceeds of the loan are \$4,250,000.

After-tax present value of interest and principal payments

Interest is paid off the gross proceeds of \$4,250,000. Since the loan carries an interest rate of 9%, Kendrick will make interest payments of \$382,500 $[= (0.09)(\$4,250,000)]$ at the end of each year. However, since these payments are tax deductible, the after-tax cost of these payments is only \$229,500 $\{= (1-.40)(\$382,500)\}$ per year. At the end of ten years, Kendrick must repay the \$4,250,000 in gross proceeds.

Since the level of debt is known, the appropriate discount rate to use is Kendrick's pre-tax cost of debt, 9%.

After-Tax PV of Payments $= \$229,500 A^{10}{}_{0.09} + \$4,250,000 / (1.09)^{10}$
$$= \$3,268,098$$

The after-tax present value of interest and principal payments is \$3,268,098.

NPV_{Loan} = Gross Proceeds – After-tax present value of interest and principal payments
$$= \$4,250,000 - \$3,268,098$$
$$= \$981,902$$

The NPV of the loan excluding flotation costs is $981,902.

b. If flotation costs are taken into account, the net present value of a loan equals:

NPV_{Loan} = (Proceeds net of flotation costs) – (After-tax present value of interest and principal payments) + (Present value of the flotation cost tax shield)

Proceeds net of flotation costs

The gross proceeds of the loan are $4,250,000. Flotation costs will be $53,125 (= 0.0125 * $4,250,000).

Proceeds net of flotation costs are $4,196,875 (= $4,250,000 - $53,125).

After-tax present value of interest and principal payments

Interest is paid off the gross proceeds of $4,250,000. Since the loan carries an interest rate of 9%, Kendrick will make interest payments of $382,500 [= (0.09)($4,250,000)] at the end of each year. However, since these payments are tax deductible, the after-tax cost of these payments is only $229,500 {= (1-.40)($382,500)} per year. At the end of ten years, Kendrick must repay the $4,250,000 in gross proceeds.

Since the level of debt is known, the appropriate discount rate to use is Kendrick's pre-tax cost of debt, 9%.

After-Tax PV of Payments = $229,500A$^{10}_{0.09}$ + $4,250,000 / (1.09)^{10}$
= $3,268,098

The after-tax present value of interest and principal payments is $3,268,098.

Present Value of the flotation cost tax shield

Flotation costs will be amortized over the 10-year life of the loan, generating tax shields for Kendrick.

Total flotation costs are $53,125 [= (0.0125)($4,250,000)]. Straight-line amortization of these costs over ten years yields annual flotation costs of $5,312.50 (= $53,125/10).

The annual tax shield relating to these costs is:

Annual Tax Shield = (T_C)(Annual Flotation Expense)
= (0.40)($5,312.50)
= $2,125

PV(Flotation Cost Tax Shield) = $2,125A$^{10}_{0.09}$
= $13,638

The present value of the flotation cost tax shield is $13,638.

$$NPV_{Loan} = \text{(Proceeds net of flotation costs)} - \text{(After-tax present value of interest and principal payments)} + \text{(Present value of the flotation cost tax shield)}$$

$$= \$4,196,875 - \$3,268,098 + \$13,638$$
$$= \mathbf{\$942,415}$$

The NPV of the loan including flotation costs is $942,415.

17.15 a. The equity beta of a firm financed entirely by equity is equal to its unlevered beta.

Find each of the firm's equity betas, given an unlevered beta of 1.2.

<u>North Pole</u>

$$\beta_{Equity} = [1 + (1-T_C)(B/S)]\beta_{Unlevered}$$

where

β_{Equity}	= the equity beta
$\beta_{Unlevered}$	= the unlevered beta
T_C	= the corporate tax rate
B	= the value of the firm's debt
S	= the value of the firm's equity

In this problem:

$\beta_{Unlevered}$	= 1.2
T_C	= 0.35
B	= \$1,000,000
S	= \$1,500,000

$$\begin{aligned}\beta_{Equity} &= [1 + (1-T_C)(B/S)]\beta_{Unlevered}\\ &= [1 + (1-0.35)(\$1,000,000/\$1,500,000)][1.2]\\ &= \mathbf{1.72}\end{aligned}$$

North Pole's equity beta is 1.72.

<u>South Pole</u>

$$\beta_{Equity} = [1 + (1-T_C)(B/S)]\beta_{Unlevered}$$

where

β_{Equity}	= the equity beta
$\beta_{Unlevered}$	= the unlevered beta
T_C	= the corporate tax rate
B	= the value of the firm's debt
S	= the value of the firm's equity

In this problem:

$\beta_{Unlevered}$	= 1.2
T_C	= 0.35
B	= \$1,500,000
S	= \$1,000,000

$$\beta_{Equity} = [1 + (1-T_C)(B/S)]\beta_{Unlevered}$$
$$= [1 + (1-0.35)(\$1,500,000/\$1,000,000)][1.2]$$
$$= \mathbf{2.37}$$

South Pole's equity beta is 2.37.

b. According to the Capital Asset Pricing Model:

$$r_S = r_f + \beta_{Equity}(r_m - r_f)$$

where r_S = the required rate of return on a firm's equity
                      r_f = the risk-free rate
                      r_m = the expected return on the market portfolio
                      β_{Equity} = the equity beta

North Pole:

$$r_f = 0.0425$$
$$r_m = 0.1275$$
$$\beta_{Equity} = 1.72$$

$$r_S = r_f + \beta_{Equity}(r_m - r_f)$$
$$= 0.0425 + 1.72(0.1275-0.0425)$$
$$= \mathbf{0.1887}$$

The required return on North Pole's equity is 18.87%.

North Pole:

$$r_f = 0.0425$$
$$r_m = 0.1275$$
$$\beta_{Equity} = 2.37$$

$$r_S = r_f + \beta_{Equity}(r_m - r_f)$$
$$= 0.0425 + 2.37(0.1275-0.0425)$$
$$= \mathbf{0.2440}$$

The required return on South Pole's equity is 24.40%.

Chapter 18: Dividends and Other Payouts

18.1   February 16: Declaration date - the board of directors declares a dividend payment that will be made on March 14.
February 24: Ex-dividend date - the shares trade ex dividend on and after this date. Sellers before this date receive the dividend. Purchasers on or after this date do not receive the dividend.
February 26: Record date - the declared dividends are distributable to shareholders of record on this date.
March 14: Payable date - the checks are mailed.

18.2   Based on Miller and Modigliani reasoning, the stock will sell for $8.75. This is the same price you paid for the stock, and you are selling *before* the ex-dividend date. When the stock goes ex-dividend, the price is expected to fall $0.75 a share.

18.3   a.   If the dividend is declared, the price of the stock will drop on the ex-dividend date by the value of the dividend, $5. It will then trade for $95.

        b.   If it is not declared, the price will remain at $100.

        c.   Mann's outflows for investments are $2,000,000. These outflows occur immediately. One year from now, the firm will realize $1,000,000 in net income and it will pay $500,000 in dividends, but the need for financing is immediate. Mann must finance $2,000,000 through the sale of shares worth $100. It must sell $2,000,000 / $100 = 20,000 shares.

        d.   The MM model is not realistic since it does not account for taxes, brokerage fees, uncertainty over future cash flows, investors' preferences, signaling effects, and agency costs.

18.4   a.   The ex-dividend date is Feb. 27, which is two business days before the record date.

        b.   The stock price should drop by $1.25 on the ex-dividend date.

18.5   Knowing that share price can be expressed as the present value of expected future dividends does not make dividend policy relevant. Under the growing perpetuity model, if overall corporate cash flows are unchanged, then a change in dividend policy only changes the timing of the dividends. The PV of those dividends is the same. This is true because, given that future earnings are held constant, dividend policy simply represents a transfer between current and future stockholders.

        In a more realistic context and assuming a finite holding period, the value of the shares should represent the future stock price as well as the dividends. Any cash flow not paid as a dividend will be reflected in the future stock price. As such the PV of the flows will not change with shifts in dividend policy; dividend policy is still irrelevant.

18.6   a.   The price is the PV of the dividends, and there are only 2 more cash flows associated with this stock: $D_1 = \$2$ and $D_2 = \$17.5375$. Find the present value of this cash flow series:

$$PV = \frac{\$2}{1.15} + \frac{\$17.5375}{1.15^2}$$
$$= \$15$$

       b.   The current value of your shares is ($15)(500) = $7,500. since you want equal payments, you want an annuity, which solves:

$$\$7,500 = \frac{X}{1.15} + \frac{X}{1.15^2}$$

Solving for X, the cash flows are $4,613.3721 each year, However, you will receive $1,000 in dividends in the first year, so you must sell shares to make up the difference,

At the end of the first year, you must sell just enough shares to generate $3,613.3721. In order to do that, first you must determine the stock price. At that time, the price will be the PV of the liquidating dividend:

$$\frac{\$17.5375}{1.15} = \$15.25$$

and

$$\frac{\$3,613.3721}{\$15.25} = 236.942 \text{ shares}$$

So you must sell 236.942 shares.

At the end of the 2nd year, the remaining shares will each earn the liquidating dividend. To check your work, note that you will receive $4,613.38 [(500 - 236.942) x $17.5375]. (Rounding causes the discrepancy).

18.7   a.   Assume that the dividend has yet to be paid. Since the firm has a 100% payout policy, the entire net income, $32,000 will be paid as a dividend. Then, the current value of the firm is the discounted value from 1 year hence, plus the current income:

$$\text{Value} = \$32,000 + \frac{\$1,545,600}{1.12}$$
$$= \$1,412,000$$

       b.   The current price of $141.20 per share will fall by the value of the dividend to $138:

$$\text{Price} = \$141.20 - \frac{\$32,000 \text{ net income}}{10,000 \text{ shares outstanding}}$$
$$= \$141.20 - \$3.20$$
$$= \$138.00$$

c.

i.   According to MM, it cannot be true that the low dividend is depressing the price. Since dividend policy is irrelevant, the level of the dividend should not matter. Any funds not distributed as dividends add to the value of the firm hence the stock price. These directors merely want to change the timing of the dividends (more now, less in the future). As the calculations below indicate, the value of the firm is unchanged by their proposal. Therefore, share price will be unchanged.

To show this, consider what would happen if the dividend was increased to $4.25. Since only the existing shareholders will get the dividend, the required dollar amount is $4.25 x 10,000 shares = $42,500. Then, the dollars to be raised are:

$42,500 required funds
- $32,000 net income
$10,500 dollars to be raised with sale of new shares

Since those new shareholders must also earn 12%, their share of the firm one year from now is 10,500 x 1.12 = $11,760, meaning that the old shareholders' interest falls to $1,545,600 - $11,760 = $1,533,840. Under this scenario, the current value of the firm is

$$\text{Value} = \$42,500 + \frac{\$1,533,840}{1.12}$$
$$= \$1,412,000$$

Since the firm value is the same as under a), the change in dividend policy had no effect.

ii.   The new shareholders are not entitled to receive the current dividend. They will receive only the value of the equity one year hence. The PV of those flows is

$$\frac{\$1,533,840}{1.12} = \$1,369,500$$

so the share price will be

$$\frac{\$1,369,500}{10,000} = \$136.95$$

and shares sold will be

$$\frac{\$10,500}{\$136.95} = 76.67$$

18.8   a.   Expected price is the PV of future cashflows. Since the $1.2 million is current period, and the $15 million is already PV, we don't have to discount. Therefore, price per share is total dollars scaled by total shares

$$Price = \frac{\$1,200,000 + \$15,000,000}{1,000,000} = \$16.2$$

    b.   He can invest the dividends into the Gibson stock.

$$Dividends\ that\ he\ gets = \frac{\$1.2\ million\ x\ 50\%\ x\ 1,000}{1,000,000} = \$600$$

$$Expected\ share\ price\ after\ dividend = \frac{0.6 + 15}{1} = \$15.6$$

Number of shares that Jeff needs to buy = 600 / 15.6 = 38

18.9   For either alternative, assume the $2,000,000 cash is after corporate tax.

Alternative 1:
Firm invests cash, either in T-bills or in preferred stock, and then pays out as special dividend in 3 years

If the firm invests in T-Bills:

after corporate tax yield = 7(1 - .35) = 4.55

$$FV = 2,000,000(1 + .0455)^3$$
$$= 2,285,609.89$$

After personal tax cash flow to the stock holders:

$$ATCF = 2,285,609.89(1 - .31)$$
$$= 1,577,070.82$$

If the firm invests in preferred stock (assume dividends will be re-invested in the same preferred stock):

after corporate tax dividend:

preferred dividends: 11% (2,000,000)   = $220,000
Since 70% of preferred dvds are excluded from tax:
Taxable dvds   = 220,000 x .3 = 66,000
Tax   = 66,000 x .35 = 23,100

after corporate tax dividend   = 220,000 - 23,100
            = 196,900

Therefore,

18.9 (continued)

$$\text{after corp tax yield on pref stock} = \frac{196{,}900}{2{,}000{,}000} = .09845$$

$$FV = 2{,}000{,}000(1.09845)^3$$
$$= 2{,}650{,}762.85$$

After personal tax cash flow to the stock holders:

$$ATCF = 2{,}650{,}762.82(1-.31)$$
$$= 1{,}829{,}026.37$$

Alternative 2:
Firm pays out dividend now, and individuals invest in T-bills:

After personal tax cash to be invested
$$= 2{,}000{,}000(1-.31)$$
$$= 1{,}380{,}000$$

After personal tax yield on T-bills
$$= .07 (1-.31)$$
$$= .0483$$

After personal tax cash flow to the stock holders:

$$ATCF = FV = 1{,}380{,}000(1.0483)^3$$
$$= 1{,}589{,}775.66$$

The after-tax cash flow for the shareholders is maximized when the firm invests the cash in the preferred stocks.

18.10 You should not expect to find either low dividend, high growth stocks or tax-free municipal bonds in the University of Pennsylvania's portfolio. Since the university does not pay taxes on investment income, it will want to invest in securities, which provide the highest pre-tax return. Since tax-free municipal bonds generally provide lower returns than taxable securities, there is no reason for the university to hold municipal bonds.

The Litzenberger-Ramaswamy research (discussed in the section on empirical evidence) found that high dividend stocks pay higher pre-tax returns than risk comparable low dividend stocks because of the taxes on dividend income. Since the University of Pennsylvania does not pay taxes, it would be wise to invest in high dividend stocks rather than low dividend stocks in the same risk class.

18.11 a.   If $T_C = T_0 = 0$, then

$$P_e - P_b = D$$

$$\frac{P_e - P_b}{D} = 1$$

So, the stock price will fall by the amount of the dividend.

b.   If $T_C = 0$ and $T_0 \neq 0$ then

$$\frac{P_e - P_b}{D} = 1 - T_0$$

So, the stock price will fall by the after-tax proceeds from the dividend.

c.   In a, there was no tax disadvantage to dividends. Thus, investors are indifferent between buying the stock at P_b and receiving the dividend or waiting, buying the stock at P_e and receiving a subsequent capital gain. When only the dividend is taxed, after-tax proceeds must be equated for investors to be indifferent. Since the after-tax proceeds from the dividend are $D (1 - T_0)$, the price will fall by that amount.

d.   No, Elton and Gruber's paper is not a prescription for dividend policy. In a world with taxes, a firm should never issue stock to pay a dividend, but the presence of taxes does not imply that firms should not pay dividends from excess cash. The prudent firm, when faced with other financial considerations and legal constraints may choose to pay dividends.

18.12 a.   Let x be the ordinary income tax rate. The individual receives an after-tax dividend of $1,000(1-x) which she invests in Treasury bonds. The T-bond will generate after-tax cash flows to the investor of $1,000 (1 - x)[1+0.08(1-x)].

If the firm invests the money, its proceeds are $1,000 [1 + 0.08 (1-0.35)].

To be indifferent, the investor's proceeds must be the same whether she invests the after-tax dividend or receives the proceeds from the firm's investment and pays taxes on that amount.

Set the 2 equations equal and solve for x:

$$1,000(1-x)\left[1+0.08(1-x)\right] = (1-x)\left\{1,000\left[1+0.08(1-0.35)\right]\right\}$$

$$x = 0.35$$

Note: This argument does not depend upon the length of time the investment is held.

b.   Yes, this is a reasonable answer. She is only indifferent if the after-tax proceeds from the $1,000 investment in identical securities are identical; that occurs only when the tax rates are identical.

c. Since both investors will receive the same pre-tax return, you would expect the same answer as in part a. Yet, because Carlson enjoys a tax benefit from investing in stock (70% of income from stock is exempt from corporate taxes), the tax rate on ordinary income which induces indifference, is much lower. Again, set the 2 equations equal and solve for x:

$$1,000(1-x)\left[1+0.12(1-x)\right]=\left(1-x\left\{1,000\left[1+.12\left(1-\left[(0.30)(.35)\right]\right)\right]\right\}\right)$$

$$x=10.5\%$$

d. It is a compelling argument, but there are legal constraints, which deter firms from investing large sums in stock of other companies.

18.13   The bird-in-the-hand argument is based upon the erroneous assumption that increased dividends make a firm less risky. If capital spending and investment spending are unchanged, the firm's overall cash flows are not affected by the dividend policy.

18.14   This argument is theoretically correct. In the real world with transaction costs of security trading, home-made dividends can be more expensive than dividends directly paid out by the firms. However, the existence of financial intermediaries such as mutual funds reduces the transaction costs for individuals greatly. Thus, as a whole, the desire for current income shouldn't be a major factor favoring high-current-dividend policy.

18.15   To minimize her tax burden, your aunt should divest herself of high dividend yield stocks and invest in low dividend yield stock. Or, if possible, she should keep her high dividend stocks, borrow an equivalent amount of money and invest that money in a tax deferred account.

18.16   This is not evidence on investor preferences. A rise in stock price when the current dividend is increased may reflect expectations that future earnings, cash flows, etc. will rise. The better performance of the 115 companies, which raised their payouts, may also reflect a signal by management through the dividends that the firms were expected to do well in the future.

18.17   Virginia Power's investors probably were not aware of the cash flow crunch. Thus, the price drop was due to the negative information about the cost overruns. Even if they were suspicious that there were overruns, the announcement would still cause a drop in price because it removed all uncertainty about overruns and indicated their magnitude.

18.18   As the firm has been paying out regular dividends for more than 10 years, the current severe cut in dividends can cause the shareholders to lower their expectations on current and future cash flows of the firm. It then results in the drop in the stock price.

18.19 a.   Cap's past behavior suggests a preference for capital gains while Widow Jones exhibits a preference for current income.

b.   Cap could show the widow how to construct homemade dividends through the sale of stock. Of course, Cap will also have to convince her that she lives in an MM world. Remember that homemade dividends can only be constructed under the MM assumptions.

c.   Widow Jones may still not invest in Neotech because of the transaction costs involved in constructing homemade dividends. Also the Widow may desire the uncertainty resolution which comes with high dividend stocks.

18.20   The capital investment needs of small, growing companies are very high. Therefore, payment of dividends could curtail their investment opportunities. Their other option is to issue stock to pay the dividend thereby incurring issuance costs. In either case, the companies and thus their investors are better off with a zero dividend policy during the firms' rapid growth phases. This fact makes these firms attractive only to low dividend clienteles.

This example demonstrates that dividend policy is relevant when there are issuance costs. Indeed, it may be relevant whenever the assumptions behind the MM model are not met.

18.21   Unless there is an unsatisfied high dividend clientele, a firm cannot improve its share price by switching policies. If the market is in equilibrium, the number of people who desire high dividend payout stocks should exactly equal the number of such stocks available. The supplies and demands of each clientele will be exactly met in equilibrium. If the market is not in equilibrium, the supply of high dividend payout stocks may be less than the demand. Only in such a situation could a firm benefit from a policy shift.

18.22 a.   Using the formula from the text:
$$Div_1 = Div_0 + s\,(t\,EPS_1 - Div_0)$$
$$= 1.25 + 0.3\,(0.4 \times 4.5 - 1.25)$$
$$= 1.415$$

b.   same as in part a, except adjustment rate, s, is 0.6:
$$Div_1 = Div_0 + s\,(t\,EPS_1 - Div_0)$$
$$= 1.25 + 0.6\,(0.4 \times 4.5 - 1.25)$$
$$= 1.58$$

Note: Part "a" is more conservative since the adjustment rate is lower.

18.23   This finding implies that firms use initial dividends to "signal" their potential growth and positive NPV prospects to the stock market. The initiation of regular cash dividends also serves to convince the market that their high current earnings are not temporary.

Chapter 19: Issuing Securities to the Public

19.1   a.   A general cash offer is a public issue of a security that is sold to all interested investors. A general cash offer is not restricted to current stockholders.

       b.   A rights offer is an issuance that gives the current stockholders the opportunity to maintain a proportionate ownership of the company. The shares are offered to the current shareholders before they are offered to the general public.

       c.   A registration statement is the filing with the SEC, which discloses all pertinent information concerning the corporation that wants to make a public offering.

       d.   A prospectus is the legal document that must be given to every investor who contemplates purchasing registered securities in a public offering. The prospectus describes the details of the company and the particular issue.

       e.   An initial public offering (IPO) is the original sale of a company's securities to the public. An IPO is also called an unseasoned issue.

       f.   A seasoned new issue is a new issue of stock after the company's securities have previously been publicly traded.

       g.   Shelf registration is an SEC procedure, which allows a firm to file a master registration statement summarizing the planned financing for a two year period. The firm files short forms whenever it wishes to sell any of the approved master registration securities during the two year period.

19.2   a.   The Securities Exchange Act of 1933 regulates the trading of new, unseasoned securities.

       b.   The Securities Exchange Act of 1934 regulates the trading of seasoned securities. This act regulates trading in what is called the secondary market.

19.3   Competitive offer and negotiated offer are two methods to select investment bankers for underwriting. Under the competitive offers, the issuing firm can award its securities to the underwriter with the highest bid, which in turn implies the lowest cost. On the other hand, in negotiated deals, the underwriter gains much information about the issuing firm through negotiation, which helps increase the possibility of a successful offering.

19.4   a.   Firm commitment underwriting is an underwriting in which an investment banking firm commits to buy the entire issue. It will then sell the shares to the public. The investment banking firm assumes all financial responsibility for any unsold shares.

       b.   A syndicate is a group of investment banking companies that agree to cooperate in a joint venture to underwrite an offering of securities.

c. The spread is the difference between the underwriter's buying price and the offering price. The spread is a fee for the services of the underwriting syndicate.

d. Best efforts underwriting is an offering in which the underwriter agrees to distribute as much of the offering as possible. Any unsold portions of the offering are returned to the issuing firm.

19.5 a. The risk in a firm commitment underwriting is borne by the underwriter(s). The syndicate agrees to purchase all of an offering. Then they sell as much of it as possible. Any unsold shares remain the responsibility of the underwriter(s). The risk that the security's price may become unfavorable also lies with the underwriter(s).

b. The issuing firm bears the risk in a best efforts underwriting. The underwriter(s) agrees to make its best effort to sell the securities for the firm. Any unsold securities are the responsibility of the firm.

19.6 In general, the new price per share after the offering is:

$$P = \frac{market\ value\ +\ proceeds\ from\ offering}{total\ number\ of\ shares}$$

i. At $40: $P = \dfrac{\$400,000\ +\ (\$40 \times 5,000)}{15,000} = \$40$

Note that the new value is unchanged, because the new shares were offered at the current value.

ii. At $20: $P = \dfrac{\$400,000\ +\ (\$20 \times 5,000)}{15,000} = \$33.33$

iii. At $10: $P = \dfrac{\$400,000\ +\ (\$10 \times 5,000)}{15,000} = \$30$

19.7 The poor performance result should not surprise the professor. Since he subscribed to every initial public offering, he was bound to get fewer superior performers and more poor performers. Financial analysts studied the companies and separated the bad prospects from the good ones. The analysts invested in only the good prospects. These issues became oversubscribed. Since these good prospects were oversubscribed, the professor received a limited amount of stock from them. The poor prospects were probably under-subscribed, so he received as much of their stock as he desired. The result was that his performance was below average because the weight on the poor performers in his portfolio was greater than the weight on the superior performers. This result is called the winner's curse. The professor "won" the shares, but his bane was that the shares he "won" were poor performers.

19.8   There are two possible reasons for stock price drops on the announcement of a new equity issue:

    i.   Management may attempt to issue new shares of stock when the stock is over-valued, that is, the intrinsic value is lower than the market price. The price drop is the result of the downward adjustment of the overvaluation.

    ii.   When there is an increase in the possibility of financial distress, a firm is more likely to raise capital through equity than debt. The market price drops because the market interprets the equity issue announcement as bad news.

19.9   The costs of new issues include underwriter's spread, direct and indirect expenses, negative abnormal returns associated with the equity offer announcement, under-pricing, and green-shoe option.

19.10   a.   To determine the required number of new shares, use the formula in the text:

$$\text{Number of New Shares} = \frac{\text{Funds to be raised}}{\text{Subscription price}}$$
$$= \frac{\$12,000,000}{\$15}$$
$$= 800,000$$

    b.   To get the number of rights needed to purchase 1 share of stock, use the formula in the text:

$$\text{Number of Rights} = \frac{\text{"old" shares}}{\text{"new" shares}}$$
$$= \frac{2,400,000}{800,000}$$
$$= 3$$

    c.   The shareholders must remit $15 and three rights for each share of new stock they wish to purchase.

19.11   a.   In general, the ex-rights price is

$$P_{Ex-Rights} = \frac{\text{Market value} + \text{Proceeds from offering}}{\text{Total number of shares}}$$

so, in our case:

$$P_{Ex-Rights} = \frac{\$25 \times 100,000 + \$20 \times 10,000}{100,000 + 10,000}$$
$$= 24.55$$

b. The value of a right is the difference between the rights-on price of the stock and the ex-rights price of the stock.

Value of right = rights-on stock price - ex-rights stock price

$$= \$25 - \$24.55$$
$$= \$0.45$$

Alternative solution:
The value of a right can also be computed as:

$$\text{Value of right} = \frac{\text{Ex-rights price - Subscription price}}{\text{Number of rights required to buy a share of stock}}$$

$$= \frac{\$24.55 - \$20}{10}$$

$$= \$0.45$$

c. The market value of the firm after the issue is the number of shares times the ex-rights price.

Value = 110,000 x $24.55 ≈ $2,700,000
(Note that the exact ex-rights price is $24.5454.)

d. The most important reason to offer rights is to reduce issuance costs. Also, rights offerings do not dilute ownership and they provide shareholders with more flexibility. Shareholders can either exercise or sell their rights.

19.12 The value of a right = $50 - $45 = $5
The number of new shares = $5,000,000 / $25 = 200,000
The number of rights / share = ($45 - $25) / $5 = 4
The number of old shares = 200,000 x 4 = 800,000

19.13 a. Assume you hold three shares of the company's stock. The value of your holdings before you exercise your rights is 3 x $45 = $135. When you exercise, you must remit the three rights you receive for owning three shares, and ten dollars. You have increased your equity investment by $10.
The value of your holdings is $135 + $10 = $145. After exercise, you own four shares of stock. Thus, the price per share of your stock is $145 / 4 = $36.25.

b. The value of a right is the difference between the rights-on price of the stock and the ex-rights price of the stock:

Value of right = rights-on stock price - ex-rights stock price

$$= \$45 - \$36.25$$
$$= \$8.75$$

c. The price drop will occur on the ex-rights date, even though the ex-rights date is neither the expiration date nor the date on which the rights are first exercisable. If you purchase the stock before the ex-rights date, you will receive the rights. If you purchase the stock on or after the ex-rights date, you will not receive the rights. Since rights have value, the stockholder receiving the rights must pay for them. The stock price drop on the ex-rights day is similar to the stock price drop on an ex-dividend day.

19.14   Recall from question 19.11

$$P_{Ex-Rights} = \frac{\text{Market value} + \text{Proceeds from offering}}{\text{Total number of shares}}$$

Value of right = rights-on stock price - ex-rights stock price

or

$$\text{Value of right} = \frac{\text{Ex-rights price - Subscription price}}{\text{Number of rights required to buy a share of stock}}$$

and

$$\text{Number of New Shares} = \frac{\text{Funds to be raised}}{\text{Subscription price}}$$

From the last equation, we can find the Subscription price:

$$\text{Subscription price} = \frac{\text{Funds to be raised}}{\text{Number of New Shares}}$$

From the problem, we can also see that Number of New Shares is going to be a function of the required rights. From Problem 19.10, we had

$$\text{Number of Rights Required} = \frac{\text{"old" shares}}{\text{"new" shares}}$$

which we can rewrite as:

$$\text{"new" shares} = \frac{\text{"old" shares}}{\text{Number of Rights}}$$

a.   First, find the value of each of the components:

Market Value   = $13/share x 1,000,000 shares
Proceeds   = $2,000,000
New Shares   = (1,000,000 / 2) = 500,000
Total Shares   = current shares + new shares
                              = 1,000,000 + 500,000
                              = 1,500,000

$$P_{Ex-Rights} = \frac{13,000,000 + 2,000,000}{1,500,000} = 10$$

$$\text{Subscription price} = \frac{\$2,000,000}{500,000} = \$4$$

$$\text{Value of right} = \frac{\$10 - \$4}{2} = \$3$$

b.   Following the same procedure, just changing the required number of rights:

Market Value   = $13/share x 1,000,000 shares
Proceeds   = $2,000,000
New Shares   = (1,000,000 / 4) = 250,000
Total Shares   = current shares + new shares
                              = 1,000,000 + 250,000
                              = 1,500,000

$$P_{Ex-Rights} = \frac{13,000,000 + 2,000,000}{1,250,000} = 12$$

$$\text{Subscription price} = \frac{\$2,000,000}{250,000} = \$8$$

$$\text{Value of right} = \frac{\$12 - \$8}{4} = \$1$$

c.   Since rights issues are constructed so that existing shareholders' proportionate share will remain unchanged, we know that the stockholders' wealth should be the same between the two arrangements. However, a numerical example makes this more clear.

Assume that an investor holds 4 shares, and will exercise under either a) or b). Prior to exercise, the investor's portfolio value is #shares x stock price; equals 4(13) = $52. After exercise, the value of the portfolio will be the new number of shares x the Ex-rights price, less the subscription price paid.

Under a) the investor gets 2 new shares, so portfolio value will be
      6 x 10 - 2 x 4 = $52.

Under b) the investor gets 1 new share, so portfolio value will be
      5 x 12 - 1 x 8 = $52.

So, the shareholder's wealth position is unchanged either by the rights issue itself, or the choice of which right's issue the firm chooses.

19.15   If the interest of management is to increase the wealth of the current shareholders, a rights offering may be preferable because issuing costs as a percentage of capital raised is lower for rights offerings. Management does not have to worry about underpricing because shareholders get the rights, which are worth something. Rights offerings also prevent existing shareholders from losing proportionate ownership control. Finally, whether the shareholders exercise or sell their rights, they are the only beneficiaries.

19.16   Reasons for shelf registration include:

i.   Flexibility in raising money only when necessary without incurring additional issuance costs.

ii.   As Bhagat, Marr and Thompson showed, shelf registration is less costly than conventional underwritten issues.

iii.   Issuance of securities is greatly simplified.

19.17   Suppliers of venture capital can include:

i.   Wealthy families / individuals.

ii.   Investment funds provided by a number of private partnerships and corporations.

iii.   Venture capital subsidiaries established by large industrial or financial corporations.

iv.   "Angels" in an informal venture capital market.

19.18   The proceeds from IPO are used to:

i.   exchange inside equity ownership for outside equity ownership

ii.   finance the present and future operations of the IPO firms.

19.19   Basic empirical regularities in IPOs include:

i.   underpricing of the offer price,

ii.   best-efforts offerings are generally used for small IPOs and firm-commitment offerings are generally used for large IPOs,

iii.   the underwriter price stabilization of the after market and,

iv.   that issuing costs are higher in negotiated deals than in competitive ones.

Chapter 20: Long-Term Debt

20.1   When you purchase a bond on a day other than a coupon payment date, there will be an adjustment in the actual price paid. Since coupons are paid in arrears, you can think of them as earned monthly, but paid at the end of each 6-month period. Therefore, if you buy a bond *during* any 6-month period, at the end of that period you will receive a coupon for some months you did not "earn." Those months of coupon must be paid to the one who earned them -- the seller, and you make that payment at the time you buy the bond.

In each of the following, the rate is 10%, so the monthly interest is 10% / 12 = 0.83333%. Since the bonds are trading at 100 (or 100% of par), you will pay

$$Price = 100\% + N(.8333\%)$$

where N is the number of months since the last coupon payment.

a.   If you purchase the bond on March 1, you owe the seller two months of interest. Therefore, N=2, and the price is:

$$Price = 100\% + 2(.8333\%) = 101.667\%$$

If the face value of the bonds is $1,000, then you will pay $1,000 + $1,000 (0.016667) = $1,016.67.

b.   If you purchase the bond on October 1, you owe the seller three months of interest. Therefore, N=3, and the price is

$$Price = 100\% + 3(.8333\%) = 102.5\%$$

If the face value of the bonds is $1,000, then you will pay $1,000 + $1,000 (0.025) = $1,025.

c.   Since July 1 is an interest payment date, there is no accrued interest on the Raeo bonds. If today is July 1, you will pay 100% of the face value for the bond. If the face value of the bonds is $1,000, then you will pay $1,000.

d.   If you purchase the bond on August 15, you owe the seller six weeks (1 1/2 months) of interest. Therefore, N=1.50, and the price is

$$Price = 100\% + 1.5(.8333\%) = 101.25\%$$

If the face value of the bonds is $1,000, then you will pay $1,000 + $1,000 (0.0125) = $1,012.50.

20.2   a.   A protective covenant is the part of an indenture or loan agreement that limits the actions of the borrowing company.

b.   A negative covenant prohibits actions that the company may want to take. Examples include limits on dividends, inability to pledge assets, prohibition of mergers and prohibitions on additional issue of long-term debt.

c.   A positive covenant specifies actions that the firm is obliged to take. Examples include maintaining a minimum level of working capital and furnishing additional financial statements to the lender.

d.   A sinking fund is an account managed by a bond trustee for the purpose of repaying bonds.

20.3   Sinking funds provide additional security to bonds. If a firm is experiencing financial difficulty, it is likely to have trouble making its sinking fund payments. Thus, the sinking fund provides an early warning system to the bondholders about the quality of the bonds.
A drawback to sinking funds is that they give the firm an option that the bondholders may find distasteful. If bond prices are low, the firm may satisfy its sinking fund by buying bonds in the open market. If bond prices are high though, the firm may satisfy its sinking fund by purchasing bonds at face value. Those bonds being repurchased are chosen through a lottery.

20.4   Open-end mortgage is riskier because the firm can issue additional bonds on its property. The additional bonds will cause an increase in interest payments; this increases the risk to the existing bonds.

20.5   The difference between the call price and the face value is the call premium. The first few years during which a company is prohibited from calling its bonds is the call-protected period (or the grace period).

20.6   a.   If KIC's bonds are non-callable, the price today is the PV of the coupon which will be received at the end of the next year, plus the expected value of the bond one year hence. The price of the bond one year from now will depend upon the interest rate which prevails in the market.
[Note: the problem has been simplifed for you by making these bonds perpetuities. For bonds with more common maturities (say, 20 or 30 years), you could use the pricing formulas you learned in Chapter 5]

The first step is to find the value of the bonds under each of the interest rate assumptions. Since the bonds to be issued will be perpetuities, the price is found as

$$Price = \frac{Coupon}{r}$$

20.6 (continued)

So, at 14%

$$\text{Price} = \frac{120}{.14} = 857.14$$

and at 7%

$$\text{Price} = \frac{120}{.07} = 1,714.29$$

From the formula in the text:

$$\text{Value}_{\text{Non-Callable Bond}} = \frac{1^{st} \text{ yr coupon} + \text{E(price at end of year)}}{1+r}$$

$$= \frac{120 + [.5(P_{14\%}) + .5(P_{7\%})]}{1+r}$$

$$= \frac{120 + [.5(857.14) + .5(1,714.29)]}{1.11}$$

$$= 1,266.41$$

[Note for students who have studied term structure: the assumption of risk-neutrality implies that the forward rate is equal to the expected future spot rate.]

b.   If the KIC bond is callable, then the bond value will be less than the amount computed in part a. If the bond price rises above $1,450, KIC will call it. Therefore, bondholders will not pay as much for a callable bond.

20.7   If interest rates rise to 15%, the price of the Bowdeen bonds will fall. If the price of the firm's bonds is low, Bowdeen will not call them. The firm would be foolish to pay the call price for something worth less than the call price. In this case, the bondholders will receive the coupon payment, C. They will still be holding a bond worth C / 0.15. Their total holding will be C + C / 0.15.

If interest rates fall to 8%, it is highly likely that the price of the bonds will rise above the call price. If this happens, Bowdeen will call the bonds. In this case, the bondholders will receive the call price, $1,250, plus the coupon payment, C.

The selling price today of the bonds is the PV of the expected payoffs to the bondholders.

Following the procedure in the book:

Step 1: determine end-of-yr payoff if rates drop to 8%
        = call price plus coupon
        = 1250 + C

20.7   (continued)

Step 2: determine end-of-yr payoff if rates rise to 15%
  = bondholders' position at year end
  = C/0.15 + C

Step 3: Set desired issue price equal to PV of Expected Value of end of year payoffs, and solve for C:

Expected Value of end of year payoffs = E(payoffs)
= (Prob of rate drop)(payoff if rate drops) + (Prob of rate rise)(payoff if rate rises)

$$\text{Issue price} = \frac{E(payoffs)}{1 + \text{discount rate}}$$

$$\$1,000 = \frac{(.40)\left[1250 + C\right] + (.60)\left[\dfrac{C}{0.15} + C\right]}{1.12}$$

$$C = 124.00$$

Therefore, the required coupon rate is

$$\frac{124}{1000} = .124 = 12.4\%$$

20.8   a.   This problem is very similar to 20.6, part a); this time we can combine the steps.

$$\text{Value}_{\text{Non-Callable Bond}} = \frac{1^{st} \text{ yr coupon} + \left[\text{Pr(rate rise)(Price if rate rise)} + \text{Pr(rate drop)(Price if rate drop)}\right]}{1 + r}$$

$$= \frac{80 + \left[.65\left(\dfrac{80}{.06}\right) + .35\left(\dfrac{80}{.09}\right)\right]}{1.08}$$

$$= 1,164.61$$

b.   Follow the procedure used in problem 20.7, except now the call premium is not fixed, but is a function of the coupon, which you must find.

Let C=coupon.

Payoff if rates drop to 6%	= call price + coupon
	= (1000 + C) + C
	= 1,000 + 2C

| Payoff if rates rise to 9% | = bondholders' position at year end |
| | = C/.09 + C |

20.8 (continued)

Set desired issue price equal to PV of Expected Value of end of year payoffs and solve for C:

Expected Value of end of year payoffs = E(payoffs)
= (Prob of rate drop)(payoff if rate drops) + (Prob of rate rise)(payoff if rate rises)

$$\text{Issue price} = \$1,000 = \frac{E(\text{payoffs})}{1 + \text{discount rate}}$$

$$\$1,000 = \frac{(.65)[1000 + 2C] + (.35)\left[\dfrac{C}{0.09} + C\right]}{1.08}$$

$$C = 77.63$$

c.   To the company, the value of the call provision will be given by the difference between the value of an outstanding, non-callable bond and the call provision.

Non-callable bond value = $77.63 / 0.06 = $1,293.83

Value to the company of the call provision:

$$\text{Value} = \frac{(1-.35)(\$1,293.83 - \$1,077.63)}{1.08}$$

$$= 130.12$$

20.9   To find next year's bond price if it is non-callable, notice from the solutions for 20.7 and 20.8, the equations to find the required coupon for a callable fond can be re-written for the value of a callable bond:

$$\text{Value}_{\text{Callable Bond}} = \frac{E(\text{payoffs 1 yr from now})}{1 + \text{discount rate}}$$

and

$$E(\text{payoff}) = \left[\text{Prob(rate rise)(Payoff if rate rise)} + \text{Prob(rate drop)(Payoff if rate drop)}\right]$$

where now it is the Value that is unknown, rather than C.
So, for this problem:

$$\text{Value} = \frac{(.60)[1150 + 90] + (.40)\left[\dfrac{90}{0.12} + 90\right]}{1.10}$$

$$= \frac{744 + 336}{1.10}$$

$$= 981.82$$

20.10   The NPV of the refunding is the difference between the gain from refunding and the refunding costs.

Let:
r_1 = the coupon rate of the old bonds and
r_2 = the coupon rate of the new bonds.
C = the call premium
F = the face value
B = the par value of the old bonds
K = the issuing costs

$$Gain = \frac{B(r_1 - r_2)}{r_2}$$
$$= \frac{\$500,000,000(.09 - .07)}{.07}$$
$$= \$142,857,143$$

$$Cost = \frac{C * B}{F + K}$$
$$= \frac{90(500,000,000)}{1,000 + 80,000,000}$$
$$= \$125,000,000$$

And then find the difference:

$$\begin{aligned} NPV &= \$142,857,143 - \$125,000,000 \\ &= \$17,857,143 \end{aligned}$$

20.11   Recall from your study of Capital Budgeting that incremental NPV = 0 implies indifference between 2 projects or alternatives. In this case

$$NPV = PV(Gain) - PV(Cost)$$

$$Gain = \frac{250(.08 - r_2)}{r_2}$$

$$\begin{aligned} Cost_{after\text{-}tax} &= 250(.12)(1 - .35) \\ &= 19.50 \end{aligned}$$

Since these are already in terms of PV and we want NPV = 0:

$$0 = \frac{250(.08 - r_2)}{r_2} - 19.50$$

$$\frac{-250(.08 - r_2)}{r_2} = 19.50$$

$$r_2 = .0742$$

Refinancing is a wise option if borrowing costs are below 7.42%.

20.12   As in the 2 previous problems, the solution requires finding the NPV. In this case, find the NPV of each alternative and choose the option with the highest NPV. Recall this is the procedure you learned in Capital Budgeting.

8% perpetual bond:

$$\text{Gain} = \frac{\$75 \text{ million}(.08-.07)}{.07}$$
$$= \$10,714,286$$

$$\text{Cost} = (\$75 \text{ million})(.085) + \$10 \text{ million}$$
$$= \$16,375,000$$

$$\text{NPV} = \text{Gain} - \text{Cost}$$
$$= -\$5,660,714$$

9% perpetual bond:

$$\text{Gain} = \frac{\$87.5 \text{ million}(.09-.0725)}{.0725}$$
$$= \$21,120,690$$

$$\text{Cost} = (\$87.5 \text{ million})(.095) + \$12 \text{ million}$$
$$= \$20,312,500$$

$$\text{NPV} = \text{Gain} - \text{Cost}$$
$$= \$808,190$$

So Ms. Kimberly should recommend the re-financing of the 9% perpetual bond, since that NPV is greater than $\text{NPV}_{8\%}$, <u>and</u> it is greater than $0.

20.13   Bonds with an S&P's rating of BB and below or a Moody's rating of Ba and below are called junk bonds (or below-investment grade bonds). The recent controversies of junk bonds are:

i.   Junk bonds increase the firm's interest deduction.

ii.   Junk bonds increase the possibility of high leverage, which may lead to wholesale default in economic downturns.

iii.   The recent wave of mergers financed by junk bonds has frequently resulted in dislocations and loss of jobs.

20.14 a. For a floating rate bond, the coupon payments are adjustable. The adjustments are usually tied to an interest rate index.

b. Deep discount bonds are also called pure discount bonds or zero coupon bonds. As the latter name implies, these bonds do not pay a coupon. To generate a return, these bonds are sold at prices well below par, since the price is the PV of the lump sum maturity value.

c. Income bonds are similar to conventional bonds, except their coupon payments are tied to the firm's income. The bondholders are paid only if the firm generates enough income to do so. These bonds are attractive for firms to issue because if the firm cannot make an interest payment, it is not in default.

20.15

Characteristic	Public Issues	Direct Financing
a. Require SEC registration	Yes	No
b. Higher interest cost	No	Yes
c. Higher fixed cost	Yes	No
d. Quicker access to funds	No	Yes
e. Active secondary market	Yes	No
f. Easily renegotiated	No	Yes
g. Lower floatation costs	No	Yes
h. Require regular amortization	Yes	No
i Ease of repurchase at favorable prices	Yes	No
j. High total cost to small borrowers	Yes	No
k. Flexible terms	No	Yes
l. Require less intensive investigation	Yes	No

20.16 a. Yes. The statement is true. In an efficient market, the callable bonds will be sold at a lower price than that of the non-callable bonds, other things being equal. This is because the holder of callable bonds effectively sold a call option to the bond issuer. Since the issuer holds the right to call the bonds, the price of the bonds will reflect the disadvantage to the bondholders and the advantage to the bond issuer (i.e., the bondholder has the obligation to surrender their bonds when the call option is exercised by the bond issuer.)
As interest rate falls, the call option of the callable bonds are more likely to be exercised by the bond issuer. Since the non-callable bonds do not have such a drawback, the value of the bond will go up to reflect the decrease in the market rate of interest. Thus, the price of non-callable bonds will move higher than that of the callable bonds.

Chapter 21: Leasing

21.1 a. Leasing can reduce uncertainty regarding the resale value of the asset that is leased.

b. Leasing does not provide 100% financing although it may look as though it does. Since firms must try to maintain their optimal debt ratio, the use of lease simply displaces debt. Thus, leasing does not provide 100% financing.

c. Although it is true that leasing displaces debt, empirical studies show that the companies that do a large amount of leasing also have a high debt-to-equity ratios.

d. If the tax advantages of leasing were eliminated, leasing would probably disappear. The main reason for the existence of long-term leasing is the differential in the tax rates paid by the lessee and the lessor.

21.2 The reservation payment is found by setting the NPV of the lease to $0, and then solving for the lease payment.

a. For Quartz Corp, the lessee:
Since Quartz's effective tax rate is 0, the after tax discount rate is 8%.

Set the NPV = 0, and solve for L:

$$\text{NPV (lease)} = \text{Cost - after tax PV(lease payments)}$$
$$0 = \$250,000 - L\,(A^5_{0.08})$$
$$= \$250,000 - L\,(3.9927)$$
$$L = \$62,614.11$$

The lease payment is Quartz's reservation price.
i.e. for L > 62,614.11, Quartz will have NPV<0.

b. For New Leasing, the lessor:

$$\text{NPV} = \text{Cost + after tax PV(Lease payments) + PV(Depr tax shield)}$$

$$\text{Depreciation} = \$250,000 / 5$$
$$= \$50,000 \text{ per annum}$$

$$\text{Depreciation tax shield} = \$50,000 \times 0.35$$
$$= \$17,500$$

$$\text{After-tax discount rate} = 0.08\,(1 - 0.35)$$
$$= 0.052$$

As in part a., set NPV = 0, and solve for L:

$$\text{NPV (lease)} = 0 = -\$250,000 + L\,(1 - 0.35)\,A^5_{0.052} + \$17,500\,A^5_{0.052}$$
$$L = \$62,405.09$$

This lease payment is New Leasing Co's reservation price.
i.e. for L < 62,405.09, New Leasing will have NPV<0.

c. A lease payment less than $62,405.09 will give New Leasing a negative NPV. A payment higher than $62,614.11 will give Quartz a negative NPV. In either case, no deal will be struck. Therefore, these represent the lower and upper bounds of possible lease prices during negotiations.

21.3 Use the method of Incremental NPV as demonstrated in Table 21.3 in text.

First, find the deprecation benefit (which will be lost if lease rather than purchase)
$$= 350,000 / 5 \ (.35)$$
$$= \$24,500$$

Second, find after tax discount rate
$$= .11 \ (1-.35)$$
$$= .0715$$

Now, put it together for the incremental cash flows from leasing instead of purchasing:

Lease minus Buy	Year 0	Year 1 - 5
Lease		
Lease payment		-$94,200
Tax benefit of lease payment		$32,970
Buy		
Cost of machine	-$350,000	
Lost depreciation tax benefit		$24,500
Lease – Buy	$350,000	-$85,730

Now find the NPV to make the lease/buy decision.

$$\text{NPV} = \$350,000 - \$85,730 \ A^5_{0.0715}$$
$$= -\$102.66 < \$0$$

Since the NPV of leasing rather than buying is negative, the firm should buy the machine.

21.4 The reservation payment is found by setting the NPV of the lease to $0, and then solving for the lease payment.

Maxwell's (the lessee) reservation price is:

Set the NPV = 0, and solve for L:

$$\text{NPV (lease)} = \text{Cost - after tax PV(lease payments)}$$
$$0 = \$200,000 - L \ (A^5_{0.10})$$
$$= \$200,000 - L \ (3.7908)$$
$$L = \$52,759.50$$

21.4 (continued)

Mercer's (the lessor) reservation price is:

$$NPV = Cost + \text{after tax PV(Lease payments)} + PV(\text{Depr tax shield})$$

$$\begin{aligned} \text{Depreciation} &= \$200,000 \,/\, 5 \\ &= \$40,000 \text{ per annum} \end{aligned}$$

$$\begin{aligned} \text{Depreciation tax shield} &= \$40,000 \times 0.35 \\ &= \$14,000 \end{aligned}$$

$$\begin{aligned} \text{After-tax discount rate} &= 0.10\,(1 - 0.35) \\ &= 0.065 \end{aligned}$$

Set the NPV = 0, and solve for L:

$$\begin{aligned} NPV \text{ (lease)} \quad = 0 \quad &= -\$200,000 + L\,(1 - 0.35)\,A^5_{0.065} + \$14,000\,A^5_{0.065} \\ L \quad &= \$52,502.94 \end{aligned}$$

Therefore, the negotiation range is from \$52,502.94 to \$52,759.50.

21.5 Similar problem as previous 2, except now both firms have a non-zero tax rate.

For Raymond Corp, the lessee:

After-tax discount rate = $.08(1-.25) = .06$

Set the NPV = 0, and solve for L:

$$\begin{aligned} NPV \text{ (lease)} \quad &= Cost - \text{after tax PV(lease payments)} \\ 0 \quad &= \$100,000 - (1-.25)L\,(A^5_{0.06}) \\ &= \$100,000 - (1-.25)L\,(4.21236) \\ L \quad &= \$31,652.85 \end{aligned}$$

The lease payment is Raymond's reservation price.
i.e. for L > 31,652.85, Raymond will have NPV<0.

For Liberty, the lessor:

$$NPV = Cost + \text{after tax PV(Lease payments)} + PV(\text{Depr tax shield})$$
$$\text{Depreciation} = \$100,000 \,/\, 5 = \$20,000 \text{ per annum}$$
$$\text{Depreciation tax shield} = \$20,000 \times 0.35 = \$7,000$$
$$\text{After-tax discount rate} = 0.08\,(1 - 0.35) = 0.052$$

Set NPV = 0, and solve for L:

$$\begin{aligned} NPV \text{ (lease)} \quad = 0 \quad &= -\$100,000 + L\,(1 - 0.35)\,A^5_{0.052} + \$7,000\,A^5_{0.052} \\ L \quad &= \$24,962.04 \end{aligned}$$

This lease payment is Liberty Co's reservation price.
i.e. for L < 24,962.04, Liberty will have NPV<0.

Therefore, the negotiation range is from \$24,962.04 to \$31,652.85.

21.6   a.   The lease payment which makes both parties equally well off is the payment which equates the NPVs for the firms. Since the tax rates of the two firms are equal, the perspective of the lessor is the opposite of the perspective of the lessee (i.e. the cash flows will be exactly opposite). Finding the lease payment that gives NPV = 0 for one will be the answer for both:

For the lessor:

NPV = Cost + after tax PV(Lease payments) + PV(Depr tax shield)

After tax discount rate = 10%(1-.34)
$$= 6.6\%$$

Depreciation = $86.87 / 2 = $43.435

Depreciation tax shield = $43.435 × 0.34
$$= \$14.768$$

Set NPV = 0, and solve for L:
$$NPV = 0 = -\$86.87 + 0.66\, L\; A^2_{0.066} + \$14.768\; A^2_{0.066}$$

L = $50.02

b.   Generalize the result from part a.

Let T_1 denote the lessor's tax rate.
Let T_2 denote the lessee's tax rate.
Let P denote the purchase price of the asset.
Let Dep equal the annual depreciation expense.
Let N denote the length of the lease in years.

$$Value_{lessor} = -P + \sum_{t=1}^{N} \frac{L(1-T_1) + Dep(T_1)}{[1+r(1-T_1)]^t}$$

$$Value_{lessee} = P - \sum_{t=1}^{N} \frac{L(1-T_2) + Dep(T_2)}{[1+r(1-T_2)]^t}$$

Since all the values in both equations above are the same except T_1 and T_2, we can see that the values of the lease to its two parties will be opposite in sign only if $T_1 = T_2$.

21.6   (continued)

c.   Since the lessor's tax bracket is unchanged, the "zero NPV" lease payment for the lessor is $50.02 as in part a.

If the lessee pays no taxes, the NPV is found as before; set NPV=0 and solve for L:

$$\text{NPV (lease)} = \text{Cost} - \text{after tax PV(lease payments)}$$
$$0 = -86.87 + L\ A^2_{0.10}$$
$$L = \$50.05$$

Both parties have positive NPV for $50.02 < L < $50.05.

21.7   a.   Assume that 10% is the market-wide interest rate. The decision to buy or lease is made by looking at the incremental cash flows. Find the after tax cash flows for each alternative.

Cash flows from leasing:

After tax savings on operations
$$= \$6,000\ (1 - .34)$$
$$= \$3,960$$
Tax benefit
$$= \$2,100 \times 0.34$$
$$= \$714$$

Year	0	1	2	3	4	5
A/T savings		$3,960	$3,960	$3,960	$3,960	$3,960
Lease payment		-2,100	-2,100	-2,100	-2,100	-2,100
Tax benefit		714	714	714	714	714
Net cash flows		2,574	2,574	2,574	2,574	2,574

Cash flows from purchasing:

After tax savings on operations
$$= \$9,000\ (1 - .34)$$
$$= \$5,940$$
Depreciation $= \$15,000 / 5 = \$3,000$ per annum
Depreciation tax shield
$$= \$3,000 \times 0.34$$
$$= \$1,020$$

Year	0	1	2	3	4	5
A/T savings		$5,940	$5,940	$5,940	$5,940	$5,940
Purchase	-15,000					
Dep tax shield		1,020	1,020	1,020	1,020	1,020
Net cash flows	-15,000	6,960	6,960	6,960	6,960	6,960

21.7   (continued)

Incremental cash flows from leasing instead of purchasing:

Year	0	1	2	3	4	5
Lease		$2,574	$2,574	$2,574	$2,574	$2,574
Purchase	-15,000	6,960	6,960	6,960	6,960	6,960
L – P	15,000	-4,386	-4,386	-4,386	-4,386	-4,386

NPV of the incremental cash flows:

The cash flows must be discounted at the after tax rate of 10% (1 - .34) = 6.6%.

$$NPV = \$15,000 - \$4,386 \; A^5_{0.066}$$
$$= \$15,000 - \$4,386 \, (4.1445)$$
$$= -\$3,177.78 < 0$$

Since the NPV of the lease-vs.-buy incremental cash flows is negative, Farmer should buy, not lease the equipment.

b.   As long as the company maintains its target debt-equity ratio, the answer does not depend upon the form of financing used for the direct purchase. A financial lease will displace debt regardless of the form of financing.

c.   The amount of displaced debt is the PV of the incremental cash flows from year one through five.

$$PV = \$4,386 \; A^5_{0.066}$$
$$= \$4,386 \, (4.1445)$$
$$= \$18,177.78$$

21.8   This problem is essentially the same as 21.2 and 21.4, <u>except</u> that the lease payments are beginning of year (note that this is probably a more realistic assumption). Since the depreciation tax shield is realized at end of year, there is a difference in timing of the cash flows that must be considered. This is easiest to see by mapping the cash flows into a time line.

Redwood:

	Year 0	Years 1 - 6	Year 7
Cost of machine	$420,000	$0	$0
Lease payment	-L	-L	$0
Net Cash Flow	$420,000-L	-L	0

Set NPV = 0, and solve for L:

NPV   =   0 $= 420,000 - L - A^6_{0.06} L$

L   = $70,978.03

For values of L > $70,978.03, Redwood will have NPV < 0.

American:

After tax discount rate $= .06 (1 - .35) = .039$
Depreciation $= 420000/7 = 60,000$
Depr Tax Shield $= 60,000 \times .35 = 21,000$

	Year 0	Years 1 - 6	Year 7
Cost of machine	-$420,000	$0	$0
Depr tax shield	0	$21,000	$21,000
A/T lease payment	(1-.35) L	(1-.35) L	$0
Net Cash Flow	.65L - 420,000	21,000 + .65L	21,000

Value of lease

$0 = -\$420,000 + (.65) L + (.65) L \ A^6_{0.039} + \$21,000 \ A^7_{0.039}$
$= -\$420,000 + \$21,000 (6.0243) + 4.0685 L$

L = $72,137

For values of L < $72,137, American has NPV < 0.

There is no room for negotiation, since at any value of L, one of the firms will have NPV < 0, therefore no agreement can be made.

21.9   The decision to buy or lease is made by looking at the incremental cash flows.

The loan that Sur Bank is offering merely helps you to establish the appropriate discount rate. Since the deal they are offering is the same as the market-wide rate, you can ignore the offer and simply use 12% as the before-tax discount rate. Recall from you Capital Budgeting section, you did not consider the financing which was to be applied to a specific project. The only exception would be if a specific and special financing deal were tied to a specific project (like a lower-than-market interest rate loan if you buy a particular car).

a.   **Cash flow from leasing:**

Tax benefit of lease payment = $1,200,000 x .35 = $420,000

Year	0	1	2	3
Lease payment		-$1,200,000	-$1,200,000	-$1,200,000
Tax benefit		420,000	420,000	420,000
Net cash flow		-$780,000	-$780,000	-$780,000

Cash flow from purchasing:

Depreciation tax shield = [$3,000,000 / 3] x 35% = $350,000

Year	0	1	2	3
Purchase cost	-$3,000,000			
Dep tax shield*		$350,000	$350,000	$350,000
Net cash flow	-3,000,000	350,000	350,000	350,000

Incremental cash flows from leasing instead of purchasing:

Year	0	1	2	3
Lease		-$780,000	-$780,000	-$780,000
Purchase	-$3,000,000	350,000	350,000	350,000
Lease - Purchase	$3,000,000	-1,130,000	-1,130,000	-1,130,000

After-tax discount rate = $0.12 \ (1 - .35)$
= 0.078

NPV of incremental cash flows = $\$3,000,000 - \$1,130,000 \ A_{0.078}^{3}$
= $\$3,000,000 - \$1,130,000 \ (2.5864)$
= $\$77,339.09 > 0$

Therefore, Wolfson should lease the machine.

21.9   (continued)

b.   Wolfson is indifferent at the lease payment which makes the NPV of the incremental cash flows zero.

Note that you can re-write the NPV equation in part a. as:

$$NPV = \text{Cash flows from leasing } - \text{ Cash flows from purchasing}$$

$$77,339.09 = 0 - (-3,000,000) + \sum_{t=1}^{3} \frac{1,200,000(1-.35) - 350,000}{(1.078)^t}$$

Using this relationship, set NPV = 0 (i.e. Wolfson is indifferent), and substitute the now unknown variable, L, for 1,200,000 and then solve for L:

$$0 = 3,000,0000 + \sum_{t=1}^{3} \frac{L(1-.35) - 350,000}{(1.078)^t}$$

$$= \$3,000,000 - (0.65\,L + \$350,000)\ A_{0.078}^{3}$$
$$= \$3,000,000 - (0.65\,L + \$350,000)\ (2.5864)$$

L $= \$1,246,002.96$

At a lease payment of $1,246,002.96, Wolfson will be indifferent between leasing and purchasing.

Chapter 22: Options and Corporate Finance: *Basic Concepts*

22.1

    a. An **option** is a contract giving its owner the right to buy or sell an asset at a fixed price on or before a given date.

    b. **Exercise** is the act of buying or selling the underlying asset under the terms of the option contract.

    c. The **strike price** is the fixed price in the option contract at which the holder can buy or sell the underlying asset. The strike price is also called the exercise price.

    d. The **expiration date** is the maturity date of the option. It is the last date on which an American option can be exercised and the only date on which a European option can be exercised.

    e. A **call option** gives the owner the right to buy an asset at a fixed price during a particular time period.

    f. A **put option** gives the owner the right to sell an asset at a fixed price during a particular time period.

22.2   An American option can be exercised on any date up to and including the expiration date. A European option can only be exercised on the expiration date. Since an American option gives its owner the right to exercise on any date up to and including the expiration date, it must be worth at least as much as a European option, if not more.

22.3   The put is not correctly priced. An American put option must always be worth more than the value of immediate exercise. The value of immediate exercise for a put option equals the strike price minus the current stock price. In this problem, the value of immediate exercise is $5 (= $40 - $35). Since the option is currently selling for $4.50, less than the value of immediate exercise, the option is underpriced. Consider the following investment strategy designed to take advantage of the mispricing:

Strategy	Cash Flow
1. Buy put option	-$4.50
2. Buy stock	-$35.00
3. Exercise put option	+$40.00
Arbitrage Profit	+$0.50

Therefore, Mr. Nash should buy the option for $4.50, buy the stock for $35, and immediately exercise the put option to receive its strike price of $40. This strategy yields a riskless, arbitrage profit of $0.50 (=$5 - $4.50).

22.4

    a. If the option is American, it can be exercised on any date up to and including its expiration on February 25.

    b. If the option is European, it can only be exercised on its expiration date, February 25.

    c. The option is not worthless. There is a chance that the stock price of Futura Corporation will rise above $45 sometime before the option's expiration on February 25. In this case, a call option with a strike price of $45 would be valuable at expiration. The probability of such an event happening is built into the current price of the option.

22.5

    a. The payoff to the owner of a call option at expiration is the maximum of zero and the current stock price minus the strike price. The payoff to the owner of a call option on Stock A on December 21 is:

$$\max[0, S_T - K] = \max[0, 55-50] = \mathbf{\$5}$$

        where S_T = the price of the underlying asset at expiration
                    K = the strike price

b. The payoff to the seller of a call option at expiration is the minimum of zero and the strike price minus the current stock price. The payoff to the seller of a call option on Stock A on December 21 is:

min[0, K- S_T] = min[0, 50-55] = **-$5**

In other words, the seller must *pay* $5.

c. The payoff to the owner of a call option at expiration is the maximum of zero and the current stock price minus the strike price. The payoff to the owner of a call option on Stock A on December 21 is:

max[0, S_T - K] = max[0, 45-50] = **$0**

d. The payoff to the seller of a call option at expiration is the minimum of zero and the strike price minus the current stock price. The payoff to the seller of a call option on Stock A on December 21 is:

min[0, K- S_T] = min[0, 50-45] = **$0**

e.

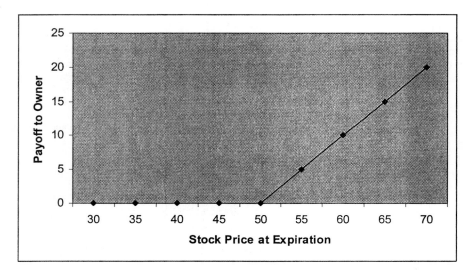

f.

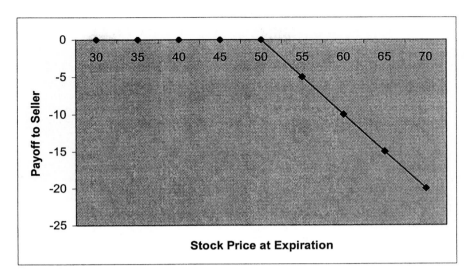

Stock Price at Expiration

g. The seller of a call option receives a premium, the price of the option, at the time of sale. At expiration, if the buyer chooses not to exercise, the premium becomes pure profit for the seller. Therefore, an individual will write (sell) a call option if he does not believe the stock price will rise above the strike price before expiration.

22.6 a. The payoff to the owner of a put option at expiration is the maximum of zero and the strike price minus the current stock price. The payoff to the owner of a put option on Stock A on December 21 is:

$$\max[0, K - S_T] = \max[0, 50\text{-}55] = \mathbf{\$0}$$

where S_T = the price of the underlying asset at expiration
K = the strike price

b. The payoff to the seller of a put option at expiration is the minimum of zero and the current stock price minus the strike price. The payoff to the seller of a call option on Stock A on December 21 is:

$$\min[0, S_T - K] = \min[0, 55\text{-}50] = \mathbf{\$0}$$

c. The payoff to the owner of a put option at expiration is the maximum of zero and the strike price minus the current stock price. The payoff to the owner of a put option on Stock A on December 21 is:

$$\max[0, K - S_T] = \max[0, 50\text{-}45] = \mathbf{\$5}$$

d. The payoff to the seller of a put option at expiration is the minimum of zero and the current stock price minus the strike price. The payoff to the seller of a call option on Stock A on December 21 is:

$$\min[0, S_T - K] = \min[0, 45\text{-}50] = \mathbf{-\$5}$$

In other words, the seller must *pay* $5.

e.

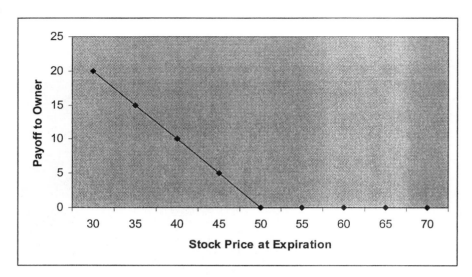

f.

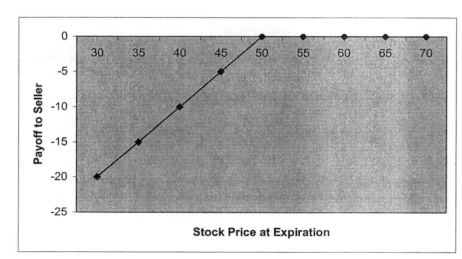

22.7 Let S_T = the stock price at expiration
K = the strike price

Payoffs to Mr. Eisner's Portfolio

	Expiration	
	If $S_T < \$80$	If $S_T > \$80$
Sell 10 Puts (K=$80)	$10(S_T - \$80)$	0
Buy 5 Calls (K=$80)	0	$5(S_T - \$80)$
Total	$10S_T - \$800$	$5S_T - \$400$

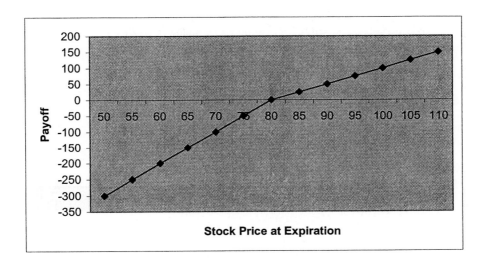

22.8 a. If the stock price is $65 at expiration:

The payoff to the owner of a call option at expiration is the maximum of zero and the current stock price minus the strike price. The payoff to each of Mr. Chang's call options is:

$$\max[0, S_T - K] = \max[0, 65-70] = \$0$$

where S_T = the price of the underlying asset at expiration
K = the strike price

Since Mr. Chang bought 2 call contracts and each contract is for 100 options, the payoff to Mr. Chang's position in call options is:

call contracts * # options per call contract * payoff per call option = 2 * 100 * $0 = **$0**

The payoff to the owner of a put option at expiration is the maximum of zero and the strike price minus the current stock price. The payoff to each of Mr. Chang's put options is:

$$\max[0, K - S_T] = \max[0, 75-65] = \$10$$

Since Mr. Chang bought 1 put contract and each contract is for 100 options, the payoff to Mr. Chang's position in put options is:

put contracts * # options per put contract * payoff per put option = 1 * 100 * $10 = **$1,000**

The total payoff of Mr. Chang's position is the sum of the payoffs of his positions in call and put options.

Total Payoff if the stock price is $65 at expiration = $0 + $1000 = $1,000

If the stock price is $72 at expiration:

The payoff to each call option is: $\max[0, S_T - K] = \max[0, 72-70] = \$2$
The payoff to each put option is: $\max[0, K - S_T] = \max[0, 75-72] = \$3$

The payoff to the position in calls is: 2 * 100 * $2 = **$400**
The payoff to the position in puts is: 1 * 100 * $3 = **$300**

Total Payoff if the stock price is $72 at expiration = $400 + $300 = $700

If the stock price is $80 at expiration:

The payoff to each call option is: $\max[0, S_T - K] = \max[0, 80-70] = \$10$
The payoff to each put option is: $\max[0, K - S_T] = \max[0, 75-80] = \$0$

The payoff to the position in calls is: 2 * 100 * $10 = **$2,000**
The payoff to the position in puts is: 1 * 100 * $0 = **$0**

Total Payoff if the stock price is $80 at expiration = $2,000 + $0 = $2,000

b.

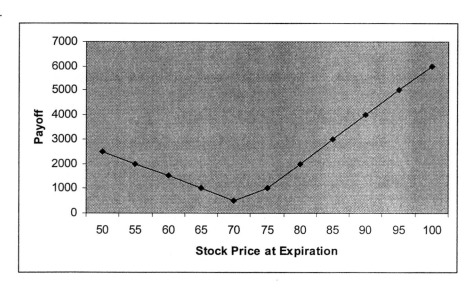

22.9   a.   If the stock is selling for $130, Louis will immediately exercise since the stock price is greater than the $100 strike price of the call options. If he then sells the stock at the market price of $130, his immediate cash flow is $30 (= $130 - $100) per option. Since Louis owns 1 contract and each contract is for 100 options, his cash flow at expiration is **$3,000** (= $30 * 100).

       b.   If the stock is selling for $90, Louis will choose not to exercise his options since exercising would require him to pay $100 (the strike price) for a stock that is only worth $90.

22.10   a.   Yes, there is an arbitrage opportunity. You should buy the American call option for $8, exercise the option (buy the underlying stock for the option's strike price of $50), and sell the stock at the market price of $60. This strategy yields a riskless arbitrage profit of $2 (= $60 - $50 - $8).

       b.   Arbitrage opportunities such as this imply that the lower bound on the price of an American call option is the value of immediate exercise, which is equal to the current stock price minus the strike price of the option $(S - K)$.

       c.   An upper bound on the price of an American call option is the current price of the underlying asset. A call option, which gives its owner the right to buy an underlying asset, cannot cost more than the underlying asset. If it did, selling the option, using the proceeds to purchase the underlying asset, and pocketing the difference would yield an arbitrage profit. Suppose Stock A is trading for $8 and a call option on Stock A with a strike price of $6 is selling for $10. Consider the following investment strategy designed to take advantage of the mispricing:

Strategy	Cash Flow
1. Sell call option	+$10.00
2. Buy stock	-$8.00
Arbitrage Profit	+$2.00

If the buyer of the call option decides to exercise, the seller will exchange the stock for the option's strike price of $6. Since the seller already owns the stock (and therefore does not need to purchase it), this results in an additional cash inflow of $6 for the seller, regardless of the price of the stock at the time of exercise. If the buyer decides not to exercise, the seller keeps both the stock and the $2 arbitrage profit. In either case, it is impossible for the seller of the call option to lose money.

22.11   1)   The **price of the underlying asset**. Holding all else equal, a rise in the price of the underlying asset will increase the value of an American call option since, for a fixed strike price, the owner will receive a more valuable asset.

       2)   The **strike price** of the option. Holding all else equal, an increase in the strike price will decrease the value of an American call option since the owner must pay more to receive the underlying asset.

       3)   The **time to expiration** of the option. Holding all else equal, an increase in the time to expiration will increase the value of an American call option. A longer period until expiration gives the owner more time to decide whether or not he should exercise the option. Also, upon exercise, the holder of the option must pay the strike price. When the time to expiration of an option is more distant, the present value of this payment falls.

       4)   The **volatility of the underlying asset**. Holding all else equal, an increase in the volatility of the underlying asset will increase the value of an American call option. An increase in the volatility of the underlying asset increases the value of exercise should the option end up in-the-money, allowing the option's owner to receive a larger positive payoff.

       5)   The **interest rate**. Holding all else equal, an increase in the interest rate will increase the value of an American call option. Upon exercise, the holder of the option must pay the strike price. When the interest rate rises, the present value of this future payment falls.

22.12   1)   The **price of the underlying asset**. Holding all else equal, a rise in the price of the underlying asset will decrease the value of an American put option since the owner is giving away a more valuable asset for a fixed strike price at expiration.

2)   The **strike price** of the option. Holding all else equal, an increase in the strike price will increase the value of an American put option since the owner receives more in exchange for the underlying asset at expiration.

3)   The **time to expiration** of the option. Holding all else equal, an increase in the time to expiration will increase the value of an American put option. A longer period until expiration gives the owner more time to decide whether or not he should exercise the option.

4)   The **volatility of the underlying asset**. Holding all else equal, an increase in the volatility of the underlying asset will increase the value of an American put option. An increase in the volatility of the underlying asset increases the value of exercise should the option end up in-the-money, allowing the option's owner to exercise and receive a larger positive payoff.

5)   The **interest rate**. Holding all else equal, an increase in the interest rate will decrease the value of an American put option. The owner of a put option will receive the strike price at expiration if he chooses to exercise. A higher interest rate decreases the present value of the strike price the owner hopes to receive.

22.13   According to Put-Call Parity, for two options with the same strike price and time to expiration, the cost of a call must equal the cost of a put plus the cost of the stock minus the present value of the strike price:

According to Put-Call Parity:

$C = P + S - PV(K)$

where   C   = the cost of a call option
         P   = the cost of a put option
         S   = the current price of the underlying asset
         PV(K)   = the present value of the strike price

Solving for the stock price, this equation shows that the stock price must equal the cost of a call minus the cost of a put plus the present value of the strike price:

Put-Call Parity: $S = C - P + PV(K)$

The cost of a call with a strike of $40 written on General Eclectic Stock is $8.
The cost of a put with a strike of $40 written on General Eclectic Stock is $2.
The present value of the strike price is $36.36 (= $40 / 1.10).

$S = C - P + PV(K)$
  $= \$8 - \$2 + \$36.36$
  $= \mathbf{\$42.36}$

The price of General Eclectic stock must be $42.36 per share in order to prevent arbitrage.

22.14   a.   While the market value of the put ($2) is less than the value of immediate exercise of $5 (= $140 - $135), there is no arbitrage opportunity since the option is European and cannot be exercised immediately. If this were an American option, one could buy the put for $2 and immediately exercise it for $5, yielding a riskless profit of $3. However, since this is a European option, the buyer must wait until the expiration date to exercise the put. If the stock price rises above $140 in one year, a put option with a strike of $140 will have no value at expiration.

b. Yes, there is a way for Kevin to create a synthetic call option. A payoff structure identical to a call option can be created by purchasing a put option, purchasing a share of stock, and borrowing the present value of the strike price.

In order to create a synthetic call option with a strike price of $140 and one year until expiration, Kevin should:

Buy a put option with a strike price of $140 and one year until expiration for $2.
Buy one share of Gimpellian Software's stock for $135.
Borrow $112 (= $140 / 1.25), which equals the present value of the strike price.

This synthetic call position costs **$25** (= 2 + 135 − 112).

In order to verify that this is in fact a synthetic call option, draw the payoff diagram and check that it looks exactly like the payoff diagram of a call option. This is done in part *c*.

c.

	Expiration	
	if $S_T < \$140$	if $S_T > \$140$
Buy 1 Put(K=$140)	$140 - S_T	0
Buy 1 Share	$+S_T$	$+S_T$
Borrow PV($140)	-$140	-$140
Total	0	S_T - $140

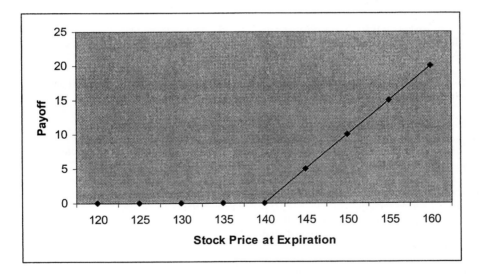

22.15 a. In order to solve a problem using the two-state option model, first draw a stock price tree containing both the current stock price and the stock's possible values at the time of the option's expiration. Next, draw a similar tree for the option, designating what its value will be at expiration given either of the 2 possible stock price movements.

Northwestern's stock price today is $100. It will either increase to $125 or decrease to $80 in one year. If the stock price rises to $125, Ken will exercise his call option for $110 and receive a payoff of $15 at expiration. If the stock price falls to $80, Ken will not exercise his call option, and he will receive no payoff at expiration.

Northwestern's Stock Price		Ken's European Call Option with a Strike of 110	
Today	1 Year	Today	1 Year

```
        125                      15      = max(0, 125 -110)
   100<                      ?<
        80                       0       = max(0, 80 -110)
```

If Northwestern's stock price rises, its return over the period is 25% [= (125/100) – 1]. If Northwestern's stock price falls, its return over the period is –20% [= (80/100) –1]. Use the following expression to determine the *risk-neutral* probability of a rise in the price of Northwestern's stock:

$$\text{Risk-Free Rate} = (\text{Probability}_{\text{Rise}})(\text{Return}_{\text{Rise}}) + (\text{Probability}_{\text{Fall}})(\text{Return}_{\text{Fall}})$$
$$= (\text{Probability}_{\text{Rise}})(\text{Return}_{\text{Rise}}) + (1 - \text{Probability}_{\text{Rise}})(\text{Return}_{\text{Fall}})$$

$$0.025 = (\text{Probability}_{\text{Rise}})(0.25) + (1 - \text{Probability}_{\text{Rise}})(-0.20)$$

$$\text{Probability}_{\text{Rise}} = 0.50$$

$$\text{Probability}_{\text{Fall}} = 1 - \text{Probability}_{\text{Rise}}$$
$$= 1 - 0.50$$
$$= 0.50$$

The risk-neutral probability of a rise in Northwestern's stock is 50%, and the risk-neutral probability of a fall in Northwestern's stock is 50%.

Using these risk-neutral probabilities, determine the expected payoff to Ken's call option at expiration.

Expected Payoff at Expiration = (.50)($15) + (.50)($0) = $7.50

Since this payoff occurs 1 year from now, it must be discounted at the risk-free rate of 2.5% in order to find its present value:

PV(Expected Payoff at Expiration) = ($7.50 / 1.025) = **$7.32**

Therefore, given the information Ken has about Northwestern's stock price movements over the next year, **a European call option with a strike price of $110 and one year until expiration is worth $7.32 today.**

b. Yes, there is a way for Ken to create a synthetic call option with identical payoffs to the call option described above. In order to do this, Ken will need to buy shares of Northwestern's stock and borrow at the risk-free rate.

The number of shares that Ken should buy is based on the delta of the option, where delta is defined as:

Delta = (Swing of option) / (Swing of stock)

Since the call option will be worth $15 if Northwestern's stock price rises and $0 if it falls, the swing of the call option is 15 (= 15 – 0).

Since the stock price will either be $125 or $80 at the time of the option's expiration, the swing of the stock is 45 (= 125 - 80).

Given this information:

Delta　　　= (Swing of option) / (Swing of stock)
　　　　　= (15 / 45)
　　　　　= 1/3

Therefore, Ken's first step in creating a synthetic call option is to buy 1/3 of a share of Northwestern's stock. Since Northwestern's stock is currently trading at $100 per share, this will cost him $33.33 [= (1/3)($100)].

In order to determine the amount that Ken should borrow, compare the payoff of the actual call option to the payoff of delta shares at expiration.

Call Option
If the stock price rises to $125:　payoff = $15
If the stock price falls to $80:　payoff = $0

Delta Shares
If the stock price rises to $125: payoff = (1/3)($125) = $41.66
If the stock price falls to $80:　payoff = (1/3)($80) = $26.66

Ken would like the payoff of his synthetic call position to be identical to the payoff of an actual call option. However, owning 1/3 of a share leaves him exactly $26.66 above the payoff at expiration, regardless of whether the stock price rises or falls. In order to reduce his payoff at expiration by $26.66, Ken should borrow the present value of $26.66 now. In one year, his obligation to pay $26.66 will reduce his payoffs so that they exactly match those of an actual call option.

Ken should purchase 1/3 of a share of Northwestern's stock and borrow $26.01 (= $26.66 / 1.025) in order to create a synthetic call option with a strike price of $110 and 1 year until expiration.

c.　Since Ken pays $33.33 to purchase 1/3 of a share and borrows $26.01, the total cost of the synthetic call option is $7.32 (= $33.33 - $26.01). This is exactly the same price that Ken would pay for an actual call option. Since an actual call option and a synthetic call option provide Ken with identical payoff structures, he should not expect to pay more for one than the other.

22.16 a.　In order to solve a problem using the two-state option model, first draw a stock price tree containing both the current stock price and the stock's possible values at the time of the option's expiration. Next, draw a similar tree for the option, designating what its value will be at expiration given either of the 2 possible stock price movements.

Biolab's stock price today is $30. It will either decrease to $15 or increase to $60 in six months. If the stock price falls to $15, Rob will exercise his put option for $40 and receive a payoff of $25 at expiration. If the stock price rises to $60, Rob will not exercise his put option, and he will receive no payoff at expiration.

BioLab's Stock Price   Rob's European Put Option with a Strike of 40

Today   6 months   Today   6 months

                    60   0   = max(0, 40-60)
30 <   ? <
                    15   25   = max(0, 40-15)

If Biolab's stock price rises, its return over the period is 100% [= (60/30) – 1]. If Biolab's stock price falls, its return over the period is –50% [= (15/30) –1]. Use the following expression to determine the *risk-neutral* probability of a rise in the price of Biolab's stock:

Risk-Free Rate $= (\text{Probability}_{Rise})(\text{Return}_{Rise}) + (\text{Probability}_{Fall})(\text{Return}_{Fall})$
$= (\text{Probability}_{Rise})(\text{Return}_{Rise}) + (1 - \text{Probability}_{Rise})(\text{Return}_{Fall})$

The risk-free rate over the next six months must be used in the order to match the timing of the expected stock price change. Since the risk-free rate per annum is 21%, the risk-free rate over the next six months is 10% [$= (1.21)^{1/2} -1$].

$0.10 \qquad = (\text{Probability}_{Rise})(1) + (1 – \text{Probability}_{Rise})(-0.50)$

$\text{Probability}_{Rise} = 0.40$

$\text{Probability}_{Fall} = 1 - \text{Probability}_{Rise}$
$= 1 – 0.40$
$= 0.60$

The risk-neutral probability of a rise in Biolab's stock is 40%, and the risk-neutral probability of a fall in Biolab's stock is 60%.

Using these risk-neutral probabilities, determine the expected payoff to Rob's put option at expiration.

Expected Payoff at Expiration = (.40)($0) + (.60)($25) = $15.00

Since this payoff occurs 6 months from now, it must be discounted at the risk-free rate of 21% per annum in order to find its present value:

PV(Expected Payoff at Expiration) = [$15.00 / $(1.21)^{1/2}$] = **$13.64**

Therefore, given the information Rob has about BioLab's stock price movements over the next six months, **a European put option with a strike price of $40 and six months until expiration is worth $13.64 today.**

b.   Yes, there is a way for Rob to create a synthetic put option with identical payoffs to the put option described above. In order to do this, Rob will need to short shares of BioLab's stock and lend at the risk-free rate.

The number of shares that Rob should sell is based on the delta of the option, where delta is defined as:

Delta = (Swing of option) / (Swing of stock)

Since the put option will be worth $0 if BioLab's stock price rises and $25 if it falls, the swing of the call option is -25 (= 0 – 25).

Since the stock price will either be $60 or $15 at the time of the option's expiration, the swing of the stock is 45 (= 60 - 15).

Given this information:

Delta   = (Swing of option) / (Swing of stock)
             = (-25 / 45)
             = -5/9

Therefore, Rob's first step in creating a synthetic put option is to short 5/9 of a share of BioLab's stock. Since BioLab's stock is currently trading at $30 per share, Rob receives $16.66 (= 5/9 * $30) as a result of his short sale.

In order to determine the amount that Rob should lend, compare the payoff of the actual put option to the payoff of delta shares at expiration.

Put Option
If the stock price rises to $60:   payoff = $0
If the stock price falls to $15:   payoff = $25

Delta Shares
If the stock price rises to $60:   payoff = (-5/9)($60) = -$33.33
If the stock price falls to $80:   payoff = (-5/9)($15) = -$8.33

Rob would like the payoff of his synthetic put position to be identical to the payoff of an actual put option. However, shorting 5/9 of a share leaves him exactly $33.33 below the payoff at expiration, regardless of whether the stock price rises or falls. In order to increase his payoff at expiration by $33.33, Rob should lend the present value of $33.33 now. In six months, he will receive $33.33, which will increase his payoffs so that they exactly match those of an actual put option.

Rob should short 5/9 of a share of Biolab's stock and lend $30.30 [= $33.33 / $(1.21)^{1/2}$] in order to create a synthetic put option with a strike price of $40 and 6 months until expiration.

c.   Since Rob receives $16.66 as a result of the short sale and lends $30.30, the total cost of the synthetic put option is $13.64 (= $30.30 – 16.66). This is exactly the same price that Rob would pay for an actual put option. Since an actual put option and a synthetic put option provide Rob with identical payoff structures, he should not expect to pay more for one than the other.

22.17 a.   Maverick would be interested in purchasing a call option on the price of gold with a strike price of $375 per ounce and 3 months until expiration. This option will compensate Maverick for any increases in the price of gold above the strike price and places a cap on the amount the firm must pay for gold at $375 per ounce.

b.   In order to solve a problem using the two-state option model, first draw a price tree containing both the current price of the underlying asset and the underlying asset's possible values at the time of the option's expiration. Next, draw a similar tree for the option, designating what its value will be at expiration given either of the 2 possible stock price movements.

The price of gold is \$350 per ounce today. If the price rises to \$400, Maverick will exercise its call option for \$375 and receive a payoff of \$25 at expiration. If the price of gold falls to \$325, Maverick will not exercise its call option, and the firm will receive no payoff at expiration.

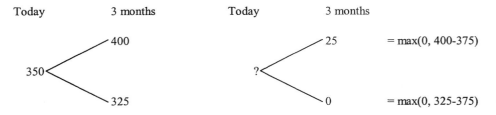

Price of Gold (per ounce)   Maverick's Call Option with a Strike of 375

Today   3 months   Today   3 months

350 — 400   ? — 25   = max(0, 400-375)

350 — 325   ? — 0   = max(0, 325-375)

If the price of gold rises, its return over the period is 14.29% [= (400/350) − 1]. If the price of gold falls, its return over the period is -7.14% [= (325/350) −1]. Use the following expression to determine the *risk-neutral* probability of a rise in the price of gold:

Risk-Free Rate = $(\text{Probability}_{\text{Rise}})(\text{Return}_{\text{Rise}}) + (\text{Probability}_{\text{Fall}})(\text{Return}_{\text{Fall}})$
                = $(\text{Probability}_{\text{Rise}})(\text{Return}_{\text{Rise}}) + (1 - \text{Probability}_{\text{Rise}})(\text{Return}_{\text{Fall}})$

The risk-free rate over the next three months must be used in the order to match the timing of the expected price change. Since the risk-free rate per annum is 16.99%, the risk-free rate over the next three months is 4% [= $(1.1699)^{1/4} - 1$].

0.04   = $(\text{Probability}_{\text{Rise}})(0.1429) + (1 - \text{Probability}_{\text{Rise}})(-0.0714)$

$\text{Probability}_{\text{Rise}}$ = 0.5198

$\text{Probability}_{\text{Fall}}$ = 1 - $\text{Probability}_{\text{Rise}}$
                = 1 − 0.5198
                = 0.4802

The risk-neutral probability of a rise in the price of gold is 51.98%, and the risk-neutral probability of a fall in the price of gold is 48.02%.

Using these risk-neutral probabilities, determine the expected payoff to Maverick's call option at expiration.

Expected Payoff at Expiration = (.5198)(\$25) + (.4802)(\$0) = \$13.00

Since this payoff occurs 3 months from now, it must be discounted at the risk-free rate of 16.99% per annum in order to find its present value:

PV(Expected Payoff at Expiration) = [\$13.00 / $(1.1699)^{1/4}$] = **\$12.50**

Therefore, given the information Maverick has about gold's price movements over the next three months, **a European call option with a strike price of \$375 and three months until expiration is worth \$12.50 today.**

c. Yes, there is a way for Maverick to create a synthetic call option with identical payoffs to the call option described above. In order to do this, Maverick will need to buy gold and borrow at the risk-free rate.

The amount of gold that Maverick should buy is based on the delta of the option, where delta is defined as:

Delta = (Swing of option) / (Swing of price of gold)

Since the call option will be worth $25 if the price of gold rises and $0 if it falls, the swing of the call option is 25 (= 25 – 0).

Since the price of gold will either be $400 or $325 at the time of the option's expiration, the swing of the price of gold is 75 (= 400 - 325).

Given this information:

Delta   = (Swing of option) / (Swing of price of gold)
          = (25 / 75)
          = 1/3

Therefore, Maverick's first step in creating a synthetic call option is to buy 1/3 of an ounce of gold. Since gold currently sells for $350 per ounce, Maverick must pay $116.67 (= 1/3 * $350) to purchase 1/3 of an ounce of gold.

In order to determine the amount that Maverick should borrow, compare the payoff of the actual call option to the payoff of delta shares at expiration.

<u>Call Option</u>
If the price of gold rises to $400:   payoff = $25
If the price of gold falls to $325:   payoff = $0

<u>Delta Shares</u>
If the price of gold rises to $400:   payoff = (1/3)($400) = $133.33
If the price of gold falls to $325:   payoff = (1/3)($325) = $108.33

Maverick would like the payoff of his synthetic call position to be identical to the payoff of an actual call option. However, buying 1/3 of a share leaves him exactly $108.33 above the payoff at expiration, regardless of whether the price of gold rises or falls. In order to decrease the firm's payoff at expiration by $108.33, Maverick should borrow the present value of $108.33 now. In three months, the firm must pay $108.33, which will decrease its payoffs so that they exactly match those of an actual call option.

Maverick should buy 1/3 of an ounce of gold and borrow $104.17 [= $108.33 / (1.1699)$^{1/4}$] in order to create a synthetic call option with a strike price of $375 and 3 months until expiration.

d.   Since Maverick pays $116.67 in order to purchase gold and borrows $104.17, the total cost of the synthetic call option is $12.50 (= $116.67 – $104.17). This is exactly the same price that Maverick would pay for an actual call option. Since an actual call option and a synthetic call option provide Maverick with identical payoff structures, the firm should not expect to pay more for one than the other.

22.18 a.   Mark would be interested in purchasing a put option on the index fund with a strike price of $1,300 and 1 year until expiration. This option will compensate Mark for any decreases in value of the index fund below the strike price and places a floor of $1,300 on the net worth of his position.

b.   In order to solve a problem using the two-state option model, first draw a stock price tree containing both the current stock price and the stock's possible values at the time of the option's expiration.

Next, draw a similar tree for the option, designating what its value will be at expiration given either of the 2 possible stock price movements.

The index fund is trading today at $1,400 per share. It will either increase by 25% or decrease by 20% in one year. If the fund increases by 25%, its value will be $1,750 (= $1,400 * 1.25) per share. If it decreases by 20%, its value will be $1,120 (= $1,400 * 0.80) per share. If the fund falls to $1,120, Mark will exercise his put option for $1,300 and receive a payoff of $180 at expiration. If the fund rises to $1,750, Mark will not exercise his put option, and he will receive no payoff at expiration.

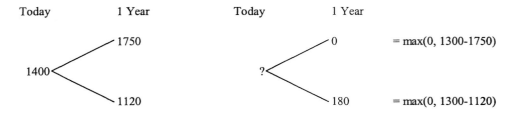

Index Fund's Value Today   Mark's Put Option with a Strike of 1300

If the price of the index fund rises, its return over the period is 25% [= (1750/1400) – 1]. If the price falls, its return over the period is –20% [= (1120/1400) –1]. Use the following expression to determine the *risk-neutral* probability of a rise in the index fund:

Risk-Free Rate = $(\text{Probability}_{\text{Rise}})(\text{Return}_{\text{Rise}}) + (\text{Probability}_{\text{Fall}})(\text{Return}_{\text{Fall}})$
            = $(\text{Probability}_{\text{Rise}})(\text{Return}_{\text{Rise}}) + (1 - \text{Probability}_{\text{Rise}})(\text{Return}_{\text{Fall}})$

0.07   = $(\text{Probability}_{\text{Rise}})(0.25) + (1 - \text{Probability}_{\text{Rise}})(-0.20)$

$\text{Probability}_{\text{Rise}}$ = 0.60

$\text{Probability}_{\text{Fall}}$ = 1 - $\text{Probability}_{\text{Rise}}$
            = 1 – 0.60
            = 0.40

The risk-neutral probability of a rise in the index fund is 60%, and the risk-neutral probability of a fall in the index fund is 40%.

Using these risk-neutral probabilities, determine the expected payoff to Mark's put option at expiration.

Expected Payoff at Expiration = (.60)($0) + (.40)($180) = $72.00

Since this payoff occurs 1 year from now, it must be discounted at the risk-free rate of 7% per annum in order to find its present value:

PV(Expected Payoff at Expiration) = ($72.00 / 1.07) = **$67.29**

Therefore, given the information Mark has about the index fund's price movements over the next year, **a put option with a strike price of $1,300 and 1 year until expiration is worth $67.29 today.**

d. Yes, there is a way for Mark to create a synthetic put option with identical payoffs to the put option described above. In order to do this, Mark will need to short shares of the index fund and lend at the risk-free rate.

The number of shares that Mark should sell is based on the delta of the option, where delta is defined as:

Delta = (Swing of option) / (Swing of stock)

Since the put option will be worth $0 if the index fund rises and $180 if it falls, the swing of the put option is -180 (= 0 − 180).

Since the index fund will either be worth $1,750 or $1,120 at the time of the option's expiration, the swing of the stock is 630 (= 1,750 − 1,120).

Given this information:

Delta = (Swing of option) / (Swing of stock)
       = (-180/630)
       = -2/7

Therefore, Mark's first step in creating a synthetic put option is to short 2/7 of a share of the index fund. Since the fund is currently trading at $1,400 per share, Mark receives $400 (= 2/7 * $1,400) as a result of his short sale.

In order to determine the amount that Mark should lend, compare the payoff of the actual put option to the payoff of delta shares at expiration.

Put Option
If the index fund rises to $1,750:   payoff = $0
If the index fund falls to $1,120:   payoff = $180

Delta Shares
If the index fund rises to $1,750:   payoff = (-2/7)($1,750) = -$500
If the index fund falls to $1,120:   payoff = (-2/7)($1,120) = -$320

Mark would like the payoff of his synthetic put position to be identical to the payoff of an actual put option. However, shorting 2/7 of a share of the index fund leaves him exactly $500 below the payoff at expiration, regardless of whether the fund rises or falls. In order to increase his payoff at expiration by $500, Mark should lend the present value of $500 now. In one year, he will receive $500, which will increase his payoffs so that they exactly match those of an actual put option.

Mark should short 2/7 of a share of the index fund and lend $467.29 (= $500 / 1.07) in order to create a synthetic put option with a strike price of $1,300 and 1 year until expiration.

d. Since Mark receives $400 as a result of the short sale and lends $467.29, the total cost of the synthetic put option is $67.29 (= $467.29 - $400). This is exactly the same price that Mark would pay for an actual put option. Since an actual put option and a synthetic put option provide Mark with identical payoff structures, he should not expect to pay more for one than the other.

22.19   The inputs to the Black-Scholes model are the current price of the underlying asset (S), the strike price of the option (K), the time to expiration of the option in fractions of a year (t), the variance of the underlying asset (σ^2), and the continuously-compounded risk-free interest rate (r).

In this problem, the inputs are:
$$S = \$55 \qquad \sigma^2 = 0.0625$$
$$K = \$50 \qquad r = 0.10$$
$$t = 1$$

After identifying the inputs, solve for d_1 and d_2:

d_1 $= [\ln(S/K) + (r + \tfrac{1}{2}\sigma^2)(t)] / (\sigma^2 t)^{1/2}$
$= [\ln(55/50) + \{0.10 + \tfrac{1}{2}(0.0625)\}(1)] / (0.0625*1)^{1/2}$
$= 0.9062$

d_2 $= d_1 - (\sigma^2 t)^{1/2}$
$= 0.9062 - (0.0625*1)^{1/2}$
$= 0.6562$

Find $N(d_1)$ and $N(d_2)$, the area under the normal curve from negative infinity to d_1 and negative infinity to d_2, respectively.

$N(d_1) = N(0.9062) = 0.8176$

$N(d_2) = N(0.6562) = 0.7442$

According to the Black-Scholes formula, the price of a European call option (C) on a non-dividend paying common stock is:

C $= SN(d_1) - Ke^{-rt}N(d_2)$
$= (55)(0.8176) - (50)e^{-(.10)(1)}(0.7442)$
$= \mathbf{\$11.30}$

The Black-Scholes Price of the call option is $11.30.

22.20   The inputs to the Black-Scholes model are the current price of the underlying asset (S), the strike price of the option (K), the time to expiration of the option in fractions of a year (t), the variance of the underlying asset (σ^2), and the continuously-compounded risk-free interest rate (r).

In this problem, the inputs are:
$$S = \$15 \qquad \sigma^2 = 0.25$$
$$K = \$25 \qquad r = 0.08$$
$$t = 0.50$$

After identifying the inputs, solve for d_1 and d_2:

d_1 $= [\ln(S/K) + (r + \tfrac{1}{2}\sigma^2)(t)] / (\sigma^2 t)^{1/2}$
$= [\ln(15/25) + \{0.08 + \tfrac{1}{2}(0.25)\}(0.50)] / (0.25*.50)^{1/2}$
$= -1.1549$

d_2 $= d_1 - (\sigma^2 t)^{1/2}$
$= -1.1549 - (0.25*.50)^{1/2}$
$= -1.5085$

Find $N(d_1)$ and $N(d_2)$, the area under the normal curve from negative infinity to d_1 and negative infinity to d_2, respectively.

$N(d_1) = N(-1.1549) = 0.1241$

$N(d_2) = N(-1.5085) = 0.0657$

According to the Black-Scholes formula, the price of a European call option (C) on a non-dividend paying common stock is:

$$
\begin{aligned}
C &= SN(d_1) - Ke^{-rt}N(d_2) \\
&= (15)(0.1241) - (25)e^{-(0.08)(0.50)}(0.0657) \\
&= \mathbf{\$0.28}
\end{aligned}
$$

The Black-Scholes Price of the call option is $0.28.

22.21 a. The inputs to the Black-Scholes model are the current price of the underlying asset (S), the strike price of the option (K), the time to expiration of the option in fractions of a year (t), the variance of the underlying asset (σ^2), and the continuously-compounded risk-free interest rate (r).

In this problem, the inputs are:
$$
\begin{array}{ll}
S = \$100 & \sigma^2 = 0.04 \\
K = \$100 & r = 0.05 \\
t = 2 &
\end{array}
$$

After identifying the inputs, solve for d_1 and d_2:

$$
\begin{aligned}
d_1 &= [\ln(S/K) + (r + \tfrac{1}{2}\sigma^2)(t)\,] / (\sigma^2 t)^{1/2} \\
&= [\ln(100/100) + \{0.05 + \tfrac{1}{2}(0.04)\}(2)\,] / (0.04*2)^{1/2} \\
&= 0.4950
\end{aligned}
$$

$$
\begin{aligned}
d_2 &= d_1 - (\sigma^2 t)^{1/2} \\
&= 0.4950 - (0.04*2)^{1/2} \\
&= 0.2122
\end{aligned}
$$

Find $N(d_1)$ and $N(d_2)$, the area under the normal curve from negative infinity to d_1 and negative infinity to d_2, respectively.

$N(d_1) = N(0.4950) = 0.6897$

$N(d_2) = N(0.2122) = 0.5840$

According to the Black-Scholes formula, the price of a European call option (C) on a non-dividend paying common stock is:

$$
\begin{aligned}
C &= SN(d_1) - Ke^{-rt}N(d_2) \\
&= (100)(0.6897) - (100)e^{-(0.05)(2)}(0.5840) \\
&= \mathbf{\$16.13}
\end{aligned}
$$

The Black-Scholes Price of the call option is $16.13.

b. Put-Call Parity implies that the cost of a European call option (C) must equal the cost of a European put option with the same strike price and time to expiration (P) plus the current stock price (S) minus the present value of the strike price [PV(K)].

In this problem:
$$
\begin{aligned}
C &= \$16.13 \\
S &= \$100 \\
PV(K) &= \$100 / e^{(.05*2)} = \$90.48
\end{aligned}
$$

Rearranging the Put-Call Parity formula:

$$P = C - S + PV(K)$$
$$= \$16.13 - \$100 + \$90.48$$
$$= \mathbf{\$6.61}$$

Therefore, Put-Call Parity implies that the Black-Scholes price of a European put option with a strike price of \$100 and 2 years until expiration should be \$6.61.

22.22 a. The inputs to the Black-Scholes model are the current price of the underlying asset (S), the strike price of the option (K), the time to expiration of the option in fractions of a year (t), the variance of the underlying asset (σ^2), and the continuously-compounded risk-free interest rate (r).

In this problem, the inputs are:

S = \$60	$\sigma^2 = 0.36$
K = \$30	r = 0.03
t = 0.25	

After identifying the inputs, solve for d_1 and d_2:

$$d_1 = [\ln(S/K) + (r + \tfrac{1}{2}\sigma^2)(t)] / (\sigma^2 t)^{1/2}$$
$$= [\ln(60/30) + \{0.03 + \tfrac{1}{2}(0.36)\}(0.25)] / (0.36*0.25)^{1/2}$$
$$= 2.4855$$

$$d_2 = d_1 - (\sigma^2 t)^{1/2}$$
$$= 2.4855 - (0.36*.25)^{1/2}$$
$$= 2.1855$$

Find $N(d_1)$ and $N(d_2)$, the area under the normal curve from negative infinity to d_1 and negative infinity to d_2, respectively.

$$N(d_1) = N(2.4855) = 0.9935$$

$$N(d_2) = N(2.1855) = 0.9856$$

According to the Black-Scholes formula, the price of a European call option (C) on a non-dividend paying common stock is:

$$C = SN(d_1) - Ke^{-rt}N(d_2)$$
$$= (60)(0.9935) - (30)e^{-(0.03)(0.25)}(0.9856)$$
$$= \mathbf{\$30.26}$$

The Black-Scholes Price of the call option is \$30.26.

b. Put-Call Parity implies that the cost of a European call option (C) must equal the cost of a European put option with the same strike price and time to expiration (P) plus the current stock price (S) minus the present value of the strike price [PV(K)].

In this problem:

C = \$30.26	
S = \$60	
PV(K) = \$30 / $e^{(.03*0.25)}$ = \$29.78	

Rearranging the Put-Call Parity formula:

$$P = C - S + PV(K)$$
$$= \$30.26 - \$60 + \$29.78$$
$$= \mathbf{\$0.04}$$

Therefore, Put-Call Parity implies that the Black-Scholes price of a European put option with a strike price of $30 and 3 months until expiration should be $0.04.

22.23 a.   The inputs to the Black-Scholes model are the current price of the underlying asset (S), the strike price of the option (K), the time to expiration of the option in fractions of a year (t), the variance of the underlying asset (σ^2), and the continuously-compounded risk-free interest rate (r).

In this problem, the inputs are: $S = \$37$ $\sigma^2 = 0.0225$
   $K = \$35$ $r = 0.07$
   $t = 1$

After identifying the inputs, solve for d_1 and d_2:

d_1 = $[\ln(S/K) + (r + \frac{1}{2}\sigma^2)(t)] / (\sigma^2 t)^{1/2}$
= $[\ln(37/35) + \{0.07 + \frac{1}{2}(0.0225)\}(1)] / (0.0225*1)^{1/2}$
= 0.9121

d_2 = $d_1 - (\sigma^2 t)^{1/2}$
= $0.9121 - (0.0225*1)^{1/2}$
= 0.7621

Find $N(d_1)$ and $N(d_2)$, the area under the normal curve from negative infinity to d_1 and negative infinity to d_2, respectively.

$N(d_1) = N(0.9121) = 0.8191$

$N(d_2) = N(0.7621) = 0.7770$

According to the Black-Scholes formula, the price of a European call option (C) on a non-dividend paying common stock is:

C   = $SN(d_1) - Ke^{-rt}N(d_2)$
= $(37)(0.8191) - (35)e^{-(0.07)(1)}(0.7770)$
= **$4.95**

The Black-Scholes Price of the call option is $4.95.

b.   The inputs to the Black-Scholes formula are: $S = \$37$ $\sigma^2 = 0.09$
   $K = \$35$ $r = 0.07$
   $t = 1$

After identifying the inputs, solve for d_1 and d_2:

d_1 = $[\ln(S/K) + (r + \frac{1}{2}\sigma^2)(t)] / (\sigma^2 t)^{1/2}$
= $[\ln(37/35) + \{0.07 + \frac{1}{2}(0.09)\}(1)] / (0.09*1)^{1/2}$
= 0.5686

d_2 = $d_1 - (\sigma^2 t)^{1/2}$
= $0.9121 - (0.09*1)^{1/2}$
= 0.2686

Find $N(d_1)$ and $N(d_2)$, the area under the normal curve from negative infinity to d_1 and negative infinity to d_2, respectively.

$N(d_1) = N(0.5686) = 0.7152$

$N(d_2) = N(0.2686) = 0.6059$

According to the Black-Scholes formula, the price of a European call option (C) on a non-dividend paying common stock is:

$$
\begin{aligned}
C &= SN(d_1) - Ke^{-rt}N(d_2) \\
&= (37)(0.7152) - (35)e^{-(0.07)(1)}(0.6059) \\
&= \mathbf{\$6.69}
\end{aligned}
$$

The Black-Scholes Price of the call option is $6.69.

c. An increase in the volatility (variance) of the underlying asset increases the Black-Scholes price of a call option. An increase in variance increases the value of exercise should the option end up in-the-money. In this example, an otherwise identical European call option increases in price from $4.95 to $6.69 when Steve's estimate of the variance of Scuba's stock returns changes from 0.0225 to 0.09.

d. The inputs to the Black-Scholes formula are:

S = $20	$\sigma^2 = 0.09$
K = $35	r = 0.07
t = 1	

After identifying the inputs, solve for d_1 and d_2:

$$
\begin{aligned}
d_1 &= [\ln(S/K) + (r + \tfrac{1}{2}\sigma^2)(t)] / (\sigma^2 t)^{1/2} \\
&= [\ln(20/35) + \{0.07 + \tfrac{1}{2}(0.09)\}(1)] / (0.09*1)^{1/2} \\
&= -1.4821
\end{aligned}
$$

$$
\begin{aligned}
d_2 &= d_1 - (\sigma^2 t)^{1/2} \\
&= -1.4821 - (0.09*1)^{1/2} \\
&= -1.7821
\end{aligned}
$$

Find $N(d_1)$ and $N(d_2)$, the area under the normal curve from negative infinity to d_1 and negative infinity to d_2, respectively.

$N(d_1) = N(-1.4821) = 0.0692$

$N(d_2) = N(-1.7821) = 0.0374$

According to the Black-Scholes formula, the price of a European call option (C) on a non-dividend paying common stock is:

$$
\begin{aligned}
C &= SN(d_1) - Ke^{-rt}N(d_2) \\
&= (20)(0.0692) - (35)e^{-(0.07)(1)}(0.0374) \\
&= \mathbf{\$0.16}
\end{aligned}
$$

The Black-Scholes Price of the call option is $0.16.

22.24   To calculate the total cost of the position, consider what Marie must do in order to obtain a collar:
  a. Purchase one share of Hollywood's stock
  b. Sell a call option on Hollywood's stock with a strike price of $120 and 6 months until expiration
  c. Purchase a put option on Hollywood's stock with a strike price of $50 and 6 months until expiration

a. To purchase one share of Hollywood's stock, Marie must pay the current market price of $80 per share.

b. Use the Black-Scholes model to calculate the proceeds that Marie will receive from the sale of a call option with a strike price of $120 and 6 months until expiration.

The inputs to the Black-Scholes formula are:

$$S = \$80 \qquad \sigma^2 = 0.25$$
$$K = \$120 \qquad r = 0.10$$
$$t = .50$$

After identifying the inputs, solve for d_1 and d_2:

$d_1 = [\ln(S/K) + (r + \tfrac{1}{2}\sigma^2)(t)] / (\sigma^2 t)^{1/2}$

$\quad = [\ln(80/120) + \{0.10 + \tfrac{1}{2}(0.25)\}(0.50)] / (0.25*0.50)^{1/2}$

$\quad = -0.8286$

$d_2 = d_1 - (\sigma^2 t)^{1/2}$

$\quad = -0.8286 - (0.25*0.50)^{1/2}$

$\quad = -1.1822$

Find $N(d_1)$ and $N(d_2)$, the area under the normal curve from negative infinity to d_1 and negative infinity to d_2, respectively.

$N(d_1) = N(-0.8286) = 0.2037$

$N(d_2) = N(-1.1822) = 0.1186$

According to the Black-Scholes formula, the price of a European call option (C) on a non-dividend paying common stock is:

$C = SN(d_1) - Ke^{-rt}N(d_2)$

$\quad = (80)(0.2037) - (120)e^{-(0.10)(0.50)}(0.1186)$

$\quad = \mathbf{\$2.76}$

The Black-Scholes Price of the call option is $2.76.

Marie will receive $2.76 as a result of selling a call option on Hollywood's stock with a strike price of $120 and 6 months until expiration.

c. Use the Black-Scholes model to calculate the price that Marie will pay to purchase a put option with a strike price of $50 and 6 months until expiration. In order to this, calculate the cost of a call option with a strike price of $50 and 6 months until expiration. Then use Put-Call Parity to find the cost of an otherwise identical put.

The inputs to the Black-Scholes formula are:

$$S = \$80 \qquad \sigma^2 = 0.25$$
$$K = \$50 \qquad r = 0.10$$
$$t = 0.50$$

After identifying the inputs, solve for d_1 and d_2:

$d_1 = [\ln(S/K) + (r + \tfrac{1}{2}\sigma^2)(t)] / (\sigma^2 t)^{1/2}$

$\quad = [\ln(80/50) + \{0.10 + \tfrac{1}{2}(0.25)\}(0.50)] / (0.25*0.50)^{1/2}$

$\quad = 1.6476$

$$d_2 = d_1 - (\sigma^2 t)^{1/2}$$
$$= 1.6476 - (0.25*0.50)^{1/2}$$
$$= 1.2940$$

Find $N(d_1)$ and $N(d_2)$, the area under the normal curve from negative infinity to d_1 and negative infinity to d_2, respectively.

$$N(d_1) = N(1.6476) = 0.9503$$

$$N(d_2) = N(1.2940) = 0.9022$$

According to the Black-Scholes formula, the price of a European call option (C) on a non-dividend paying common stock is:

$$C = SN(d_1) - Ke^{-rt}N(d_2)$$
$$= (80)(0.9503) - (50)e^{-(0.10)(0.50)}(0.9022)$$
$$= \$33.11$$

The Black-Scholes Price of the call option is $33.11.

According to Put-Call Parity: $C = P + S - PV(K)$

In this problem:
C   = \$33.11
S   = \$80
PV(K)   = $[\$50 / e^{(0.10*0.50)}] = \$47.56$

Rearranging the Put-Call Parity equation:

$$P = C - S + PV(K)$$
$$= \$33.11 - \$80 + \$47.56$$
$$= \mathbf{\$0.67}$$

Marie must pay $0.67 in order to purchase a put option on Hollywood's stock with a strike price of $50 and 6 months until expiration.

Total cost of collar   = Price of Stock + Price of Put – Price of Call
= $80 + $0.67 - $2.76
= **$77.91**

Therefore, Marie must pay $77.91 in order to purchase a collar with the characteristics described above on Hollywood's stock.

22.25   The equityholders of a firm financed partially with debt can be thought as holding a call option on the assets of the firm with a strike price equal to the debt's face value and a time to expiration equal to the debt's time to maturity. If the value of the firm exceeds the face value of the debt when it matures, the firm will pay off the debtholders in full, leaving the equityholders with the firm's remaining assets. However, if the value of the firm is less than the face value of debt when it matures, the firm must liquidate all of its assets in order to pay off the debtholders, and the equityholders receive nothing.

Let V_L = the value of a firm financed with both debt and equity
FV(Debt) = the face value of the firm's outstanding debt at maturity

	If V_L < FV(Debt)	If V_L > FV(Debt)
Payoff to Debtholders	V_L	FV(Debt)
Payoff to Equityholders	0	V_L - FV(Debt)
Total	V_L	V_L

Notice that the payoff to equityholders is identical to a call option of the form $\max(0, S_T - K)$, where the stock price at expiration (S_T) is equal to the value of the firm at the time of the debt's maturity and the strike price (K) is equal to the face value of outstanding debt.

22.26 a. Since the equityholders of a firm financed partially with debt can be thought of as holding a call option on the assets of the firm with a strike price equal to the debt's face value and a time to expiration equal to the debt's time to maturity, the value of Strudler's equity equals a call option with a strike price of $380 million and 1 year until expiration.

In order to value this option using the two-state option model, first draw a tree containing both the current value of the firm and the firm's possible values at the time of the option's expiration. Next, draw a similar tree for the option, designating what its value will be at expiration given either of the 2 possible changes in the firm's value.

The value of Strudler today is $400 million. It will either increase to $500 million or decrease to $320 million in one year as a result of its new project. If the firm's value increases to $500 million, the equityholders will exercise their call option, and they will receive a payoff of $120 million at expiration. However, if the firm's value decreases to $320 million, the equityholders will not exercise their call option, and they will receive no payoff at expiration.

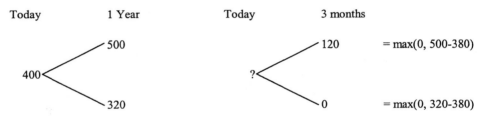

Value of Strudler, Inc. (in millions)   The Equityholders' Call Option with a Strike of $380 (in millions)

If the project is successful and Strudler's value rises, the return on Strudler over the period is 25% [= (500/400) – 1]. If the project is unsuccessful and Strudler's value falls, the return on Strudler over the period is –20% [= (320/400) –1]. Use the following expression to determine the risk-neutral probability of a rise in the value of Strudler:

Risk-Free Rate = (Probability$_{Rise}$)(Return$_{Rise}$) + (Probability$_{Fall}$)(Return$_{Fall}$)
$\qquad\qquad$ = (Probability$_{Rise}$)(Return$_{Rise}$) + (1 - Probability$_{Rise}$)(Return$_{Fall}$)

0.07 $\qquad$ = (Probability$_{Rise}$)(0.25) + (1 – Probability$_{Rise}$)(-0.20)

Probability$_{Rise}$ = 0.60

Probability$_{Fall}$ = 1 - Probability$_{Rise}$
$\qquad\qquad$ = 1 – 0.60
$\qquad\qquad$ = 0.40

The risk-neutral probability of a rise in the value of Strudler is 60%, and the risk-neutral probability of a fall in the value of Strudler is 40%.

Using these risk-neutral probabilities, determine the expected payoff to the equityholders' call option at expiration.

Expected Payoff at Expiration = (.60)($120,000,000) + (.40)($0) = $72,000,000

Since this payoff occurs 1 year from now, it must be discounted at the risk-free rate of 7% in order to find its present value:

PV(Expected Payoff at Expiration) = ($72,000,000 / 1.07) = **$67,289,720**

A call option with a strike price of $380 million and one year until expiration is worth $67,289,720 today.

Therefore, the current value of the firm's equity is $67,289,720.

The current value of the firm ($400 million) is equal to the value of its equity plus the value of its debt. In order to find the value of Strudler's debt, subtract the value of the firm's equity from the total value of the firm:

V_L = Debt + Equity
$400,000,000 = Debt + $67,289,720
Debt = **$332,710, 280**

Therefore, the current value of the firm's debt is $332,710,280.

b. Since the firm's equity is worth $67,289,720 and there are 500,000 shares outstanding, each share is worth:

Price Per Share = Equity Value / # shares outstanding
= $67,289, 720 / 500,000
= **$134.58**

Therefore, the price of Strudler's equity is $134.58 per share.

c. The market value of the firm's debt is $332,710,280. The present value of the same face amount of riskless debt is $355,140,187 (= $380,000,000 / 1.07). The firm's debt is worth less than the present value of riskless debt since there is a risk that it will not be repaid in full. In other words, the market value of the debt takes into account the risk of default. The value of riskless debt is $355,140,187. Since there is a chance that Strudler might not repay its debtholders in full, the debt is worth less than $355,140,187.

d. The value of Strudler today is $400 million. It will either increase to $800 million or decrease to $200 million in one year as a result of the new project. If the firm's value increases to $800 million, the equityholders will exercise their call option, and they will receive a payoff of $420 million at expiration. However, if the firm's value decreases to $200 million, the equityholders will not exercise their call option, and they will receive no payoff at expiration.

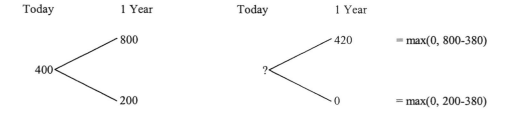

Value of Strudler, Inc. (in millions)   The Equityholders' call Option with a Strike of $380 (in millions)

If the project is successful and Strudler's value rises, the return on Strudler over the period is 100% [= (800/400) − 1]. If the project is unsuccessful and Strudler's value falls, the return on Strudler over the period is −50% [= (200/400) −1]. Use the following expression to determine the risk-neutral probability of a rise in the value of Strudler:

$$\text{Risk-Free Rate} = (\text{Probability}_{Rise})(\text{Return}_{Rise}) + (\text{Probability}_{Fall})(\text{Return}_{Fall})$$
$$= (\text{Probability}_{Rise})(\text{Return}_{Rise}) + (1 - \text{Probability}_{Rise})(\text{Return}_{Fall})$$

$$0.07 \qquad = (\text{Probability}_{Rise})(1) + (1 - \text{Probability}_{Rise})(-0.50)$$

$$\text{Probability}_{Rise} = 0.38$$

$$\begin{aligned}\text{Probability}_{Fall} &= 1 - \text{Probability}_{Rise}\\ &= 1 - 0.38\\ &= 0.62\end{aligned}$$

The risk-neutral probability of a rise in the value of Strudler is 38%, and the risk-neutral probability of a fall in the value of Strudler is 62%.

Using these risk-neutral probabilities, determine the expected payoff to the equityholders' call option at expiration.

$$\text{Expected Payoff at Expiration} = (.38)(\$420,000,000) + (.62)(\$0) = \$159,600,000$$

Since this payoff occurs 1 year from now, it must be discounted at the risk-free rate of 7% in order to find its present value:

$$\text{PV(Expected Payoff at Expiration)} = (\$159,600,000 / 1.07) = \mathbf{\$149,158,879}$$

A call option with a strike price of $380 million and one year until expiration is worth $149,158,879 today.

Therefore, the current value of the firm's equity is $149,158,879.

The current value of the firm ($400 million) is equal to the value of its equity plus the value of its debt. In order to find the value of Strudler's debt, subtract the value of the firm's equity from the total value of the firm:

$$V_L = \text{Debt} + \text{Equity}$$
$$\$400,000,000 = \text{Debt} + \$149,158,879$$
$$\text{Debt} = \mathbf{\$250,841,121}$$

Therefore, the current value of the firm's debt is $250,841,121.

The riskier project increases the value of the firm's equity and decreases the value of the firm's debt. If Strudler takes on the riskier project, the firm is less likely to be able to pay off its bondholders. Since the risk of default increases if the new project is undertaken, the value of the firm's debt decreases. Bondholders would prefer Strudler to undertake the more conservative project.

22.27   Since the firm has 700 bonds outstanding, each with a face value of $1,000, the total face value of the firm's outstanding debt is $700,000 (= 700 * $1,000). Given that the equityholders of a levered firm can be thought as holding a call option on the assets of the firm with a strike price equal to the debt's face value and a time to expiration equal to the debt's time to maturity, the value of this firm's equity equals a call option with a strike price of $700,000 and six months until expiration. Use the Black-Scholes formula to calculate the price of this call option.

The inputs to the Black-Scholes formula are:

$S = \$1,000,000$ $\sigma^2 = 0.16$
$K = \$700,000$ $r = 0.08$
$t = 0.50$

After identifying the inputs, solve for d_1 and d_2:

d_1 $= [\ln(S/K) + (r + \tfrac{1}{2}\sigma^2)(t)\,] / (\sigma^2 t)^{1/2}$

$= [\ln(1,000,000 / 700,000) + \{0.08 + \tfrac{1}{2}(0.16)\}(0.50)\,] / (0.16*0.50)^{1/2}$
$= 1.5439$

d_2 $= d_1 - (\sigma^2 t)^{1/2}$
$= 1.5439 - (0.16*0.50)^{1/2}$
$= 1.2610$

Find $N(d_1)$ and $N(d_2)$, the area under the normal curve from negative infinity to d_1 and negative infinity to d_2, respectively.

$N(d_1) = N(1.5439) = 0.9387$

$N(d_2) = N(1.2610) = 0.8963$

According to the Black-Scholes formula, the price of a European call option (C) on a non-dividend paying common stock is:

C $= SN(d_1) - Ke^{-rt}N(d_2)$
$= (1,000,000)(0.9387) - (700,000)e^{-(0.08)(0.50)} (0.8963)$
$= \mathbf{\$335,891}$

The Black-Scholes Price of the call option is $335,891.

Therefore, the current value of the firm's equity is $335,891.

The current value of the firm ($1 million) is equal to the value of its equity plus the value of its debt. In order to find the value of the firm's debt, subtract the value of the firm's equity from the total value of the firm:

$V_L = \text{Debt} + \text{Equity}$
$\$1,000,000 = \text{Debt} + \$335,891$
$\text{Debt} = \mathbf{\$664,109}$

Therefore, the current value of the firm's debt is $664,109.

Chapter 23: Options and Corporate Finance: *Extensions and Applications*

23.1 a. The inputs to the Black-Scholes model are the current price of the underlying asset (S), the strike price of the option (K), the time to expiration of the option in fractions of a year (t), the variance of the underlying asset (σ^2), and the continuously-compounded risk-free interest rate (r).

Mr. Levin has been granted 20,000 European call options on Mountainbrook's stock with 4 years until expiration. Since these options were granted at-the-money, the strike price of each option is equal to the current value of one share, or $50.

Therefore, the Black-Scholes inputs are:
$$S = \$50 \qquad \sigma^2 = 0.25$$
$$K = \$50 \qquad r = 0.06$$
$$t = 4$$

After identifying the inputs, solve for d_1 and d_2:

$$d_1 = [\ln(S/K) + (r + \tfrac{1}{2}\sigma^2)(t)\,] / (\sigma^2 t)^{1/2}$$
$$= [\ln(50/50) + \{0.06 + \tfrac{1}{2}(0.25)\}(4)\,] / (0.25*4)^{1/2}$$
$$= 0.7400$$

$$d_2 = d_1 - (\sigma^2 t)^{1/2}$$
$$= 0.7400 - (0.25*4)^{1/2}$$
$$= -0.2600$$

Find $N(d_1)$ and $N(d_2)$, the area under the normal curve from negative infinity to d_1 and negative infinity to d_2, respectively.

$$N(d_1) = N(0.7400) = 0.7704$$

$$N(d_2) = N(-0.2600) = 0.3974$$

According to the Black-Scholes formula, the price of a European call option (C) on a non-dividend paying common stock is:

$$C = SN(d_1) - Ke^{-rt}N(d_2)$$
$$= (50)(0.7704) - (50)e^{-(0.06)(4)}(0.3974)$$
$$= \$22.89$$

The Black-Scholes Price of one call option is $22.89.

Since Mr. Levin was granted 20,000 options, the current value of his options package is $457,794 (= 20,000 * $22.89).

b. Because Mr. Levin is risk-neutral, you should recommend the alternative with the highest net present value. Since the expected value of the stock option package is worth more than $450,000, Mr. Levin would prefer to be compensated with the options rather than with the immediate bonus.

c. If Mr. Levin is risk-averse, he may or may not prefer the stock option package to the immediate bonus. Even though the stock option package has a higher net present value, he may not prefer it because it is undiversified. The fact that he cannot sell his options prematurely makes it much more risky than the immediate bonus. Therefore, we cannot say which alternative he would prefer.

23.2   Jared's total compensation package consists of an annual salary of $500,000 for 3 years in addition to 10,000 at-the-money stock options.

First, find the present value of the salary payments. Since the payments occur at the end of the year, the payments can be valued as a three-year annuity, discounted at 10%.

PV(Annual Salary Payments) $= \$500,000 \, A^3_{0.10}$
                              $= \$1,243,426$

The present value of Jared's three annual salary payments is $1,243,426.

Next, use the Black-Scholes model to determine the value of the stock options. Jared was granted 10,000 call options on Blubell's stock. Blubell's current stock price is $30 per share. Since these options were granted at-the-money, the strike price of each option is also $30.

Therefore, the Black-Scholes inputs are: $S = \$30$ $\sigma^2 = 0.1225$
                                            $K = \$30$ $r = 0.05$
                                            $t = 3$

After identifying the inputs, solve for d_1 and d_2:

d_1 $= [\ln(S/K) + (r + \tfrac{1}{2}\sigma^2)(t)\,] / (\sigma^2 t)^{1/2}$
      $= [\ln(30/30) + \{0.05 + \tfrac{1}{2}(0.1225)\}(3)\,] / (0.1225*3)^{1/2}$
      $= 0.5505$

d_2 $= d_1 - (\sigma^2 t)^{1/2}$
      $= 0.5505 - (0.1225*3)^{1/2}$
      $= -0.0557$

Find $N(d_1)$ and $N(d_2)$, the area under the normal curve from negative infinity to d_1 and negative infinity to d_2, respectively.

$N(d_1) = N(0.5505) = 0.7090$

$N(d_2) = N(-0.0557) = 0.4778$

According to the Black-Scholes formula, the price of a European call option (C) on a non-dividend paying common stock is:

C $= SN(d_1) - Ke^{-rt}N(d_2)$
    $= (30)(0.7090) - (30)e^{-(0.05)(3)}(0.4778)$
    $= \$8.93$

The Black-Scholes Price of the call option is $8.93

Since Jared was granted 10,000 of these options, his stock option package is worth $89,300 (= 10,000 * $8.93).

Jared's total compensation package is equal to the sum of the values of his salary payments and the stock option package.

Therefore, the total value of Jared's compensation package at the date the contract is signed is $1,332,726 (= $1,243,426 + $89,300).

23.3   When solving a question dealing with real options, begin by identifying the option-like features of the situation. First, since Webber will exercise its option to build if the value of an office building rises, the right to build the office building is similar to a call option. Second, an office building in downtown Sacramento would be worth $10 million today. This amount can be viewed as the current price of the underlying asset (S). Third, it will cost Webber $10.5 million to construct such an office building. This amount can be viewed as the strike price of a call option (K), since it is the amount that the firm must pay in order to 'exercise' its right to erect an office building. Finally, since the firm's right to build on the land lasts only 1 year, the time to expiration (t) of the real option is one year. The Webber Company can use a Two-State model to value its option to build on the land.

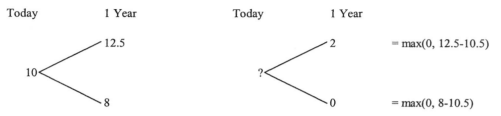

Value of an Office Building (in millions)   Webber's Real Call Option with a Strike of $10.5 (in millions)

If demand increases and the value of the building rises, the return on the value of the building over the period is 25% [= (12.5/10) − 1]. If demand decreases and the value of the building falls, the return on the value of the building over the period is −20% [= (8/10) −1]. Use the following expression to determine the risk-neutral probability of a rise in the value of the building:

Risk-Free Rate = (Probability$_{Rise}$)(Return$_{Rise}$) + (Probability$_{Fall}$)(Return$_{Fall}$)
                       = (Probability$_{Rise}$)(Return$_{Rise}$) + (1 - Probability$_{Rise}$)(Return$_{Fall}$)

0.025   = (Probability$_{Rise}$)(0.25) + (1 − Probability$_{Rise}$)(-0.20)

Probability$_{Rise}$ = 0.50

Probability$_{Fall}$ = 1 - Probability$_{Rise}$
                       = 1 − 0.50
                       = 0.50

The risk-neutral probability of a rise in the value of the building is 50%, and the risk-neutral probability of a fall in the value of the building is 50%.

Using these risk-neutral probabilities, determine the expected payoff of Webber's real option at expiration.

Expected Payoff at Expiration = (.50)($2,000,000) + (.50)($0) = $1,000,000

Since this payoff will occur 1 year from now, it must be discounted at the risk-free rate of 2.5% in order to find its present value:

PV(Expected Payoff at Expiration) = ($1,000,000 / 1.025) = **$975,610**

A call option with a strike price of $10.5 million and 1 year until expiration is worth $975,610.

Therefore, the right to build on office building in downtown Sacramento over the next year is worth $975,610 today.

Since $750,000 is less than the value of the real option to build, Webber should not accept the offer from his competitor. Instead, Webber should retain the right to erect an office building on the land.

23.4   When solving a question dealing with real options, begin by identifying the option-like features of the situation. First, since Jet Black will only choose to drill and excavate if the price of oil rises, the right to drill on the land can be viewed as a call option. Second, since the land contains 60,000 barrels of oil and the current price of oil is $25 per barrel, the current price of the underlying asset (S) to be used in the Black-Scholes model is $1,500,000 (= 60,000 barrels * $25 per barrel). Third, since Jet Black will not drill unless the price of oil in one year will compensate its excavation costs, $1.75 million can be viewed as the real option's strike price (K). Finally, since the winner of the auction has the right to drill for oil in one year, the real option can be viewed as having a time to expiration (t) of one year.

Therefore, the inputs to the Black-Scholes formula are: $S = \$1,500,000$ $\sigma^2 = 0.36$
$K = \$1,750,000$ $r = 0.10$
$t = 1$

After identifying the inputs, solve for d_1 and d_2:

d_1 $= [\ln(S/K) + (r + \tfrac{1}{2}\sigma^2)(t)] / (\sigma^2 t)^{1/2}$

  $= [\ln(1,500,000/1,750,000) + \{0.10 + \tfrac{1}{2}(0.36)\}(1)] / (0.36*1)^{1/2}$
  $= 0.2907$

d_2 $= d_1 - (\sigma^2 t)^{1/2}$
  $= 0.2907 - (0.36*1)^{1/2}$
  $= -0.3903$

Find $N(d_1)$ and $N(d_2)$, the area under the normal curve from negative infinity to d_1 and negative infinity to d_2, respectively.

$N(d_1) = N(0.2907) = 0.6144$

$N(d_2) = N(-0.3903) = 0.3482$

According to the Black-Scholes formula, the price of a European call option (C) on a non-dividend paying common stock is:

C $= SN(d_1) - Ke^{-rt}N(d_2)$
  $= (1,500,000)(0.6144) - (1,750,000)e^{-(0.10)(1)} (0.3482)$
  $= \$370,237$

The Black-Scholes Price of the call option is $370,237

Therefore, the maximum bid that Jet Black should be willing to make at the auction is $370,237.

23.5   When solving a question dealing with real options, begin by identifying the option-like features of the situation. First, since Sardano will only choose to manufacture the steel rods if the price of steel falls, the lease, which gives the firm the ability to manufacture steel, can be viewed as a put option. Second, since the firm will receive a fixed amount of money if it chooses to manufacture the rods, $1,000,000 (= 5,000 steel rods * {$300-$100}) can be viewed as the put option's strike price (K). Third, since the project requires Sardano to purchase 400 tons of steel and the current price of steel is $3,000 per ton, the current price of the underlying asset (S) to be used in the Black-Scholes formula is $1,200,000 (= 400 tons * $3,000 per ton). Finally, since Sardano must decide whether to purchase the steel or not in six months, the firm's real option to manufacture steel rods can be viewed as having a time to expiration (t) of six months.

In order to calculate the value of this real put option, use the Black-Scholes model to determine the value of an otherwise identical call option then infer the value of the put using Put-Call Parity.

Therefore, the inputs to the Black-Scholes formula are: S= $1,200,000 $\sigma^2 = 0.3025$

K =$1,000,000   r = 0.03

t = 0.50

After identifying the inputs, solve for d_1 and d_2:

d_1 $= [\ln(S/K) + (r + \frac{1}{2}\sigma^2)(t)] / (\sigma^2 t)^{1/2}$

$= [\ln(1,200,000/1,000,000) + \{0.03 + \frac{1}{2}(0.3025)\}(0.50)] / (0.3025*0.50)^{1/2}$
$= 0.7018$

d_2 $= d_1 - (\sigma^2 t)^{1/2}$
$=0.7018 - (0.3025*0.50)^{1/2}$
$= 0.3129$

Find $N(d_1)$ and $N(d_2)$, the area under the normal curve from negative infinity to d_1 and negative infinity to d_2, respectively.

$N(d_1) = N(0.7018) = 0.7586$

$N(d_2) = N(0.3129) = 0.6228$

According to the Black-Scholes formula, the price of a European call option (C) on a non-dividend paying common stock is:

C $= SN(d_1) - Ke^{-rt}N(d_2)$
$= (1,200,000)(0.7586) - (1,000,000)e^{-(0.03)(0.50)} (0.6228)$
$= \textbf{\$296,792}$

The Black-Scholes Price of the call option is $296,792.

According to Put-Call Parity: $C = P + S - PV(K)$

where   C   = the cost of a call option
P   = the cost of a put option
S   = the price of the underlying asset
PV(K)   = the present value of the strike price

In this problem: C   = $296,792
S   = $1,200,000
PV(K) $= [\$1,000,000 / e^{(0.03*0.50)}] = \$985,112$

Rearranging the Put-Call Parity equation:

$P = C - S + PV(K)$
$= \$296,792 - \$1,200,000 + \$985,112$
$= \textbf{\$81,904}$

According to Put-Call Parity, the Black-Scholes price of a put option with the characteristics described above is $81,904.

Therefore, the maximum amount that Sardano and Sons should be willing to pay for the lease of the warehouse is $81,904.

Chapter 24: Warrants and Convertibles

24.1   a.   A **warrant** is a security that gives its holder the right, but not the obligation, to buy shares of common stock directly from a company at a fixed price for a given period of time. Each warrant specifies the number of shares of stock that the holder can buy, the exercise price, and the expiration date.

          b.   A **convertible bond** is a bond that may be converted into another form of security, typically common stock, at the option of the holder at a specified price for a specified period of time.

24.2   a.   If the stock price is less than the exercise price of the warrant at expiration, the warrant is worthless. Prior to expiration, however, the warrant will have value as long as there is some probability that the stock price will rise above the exercise price in the time remaining until expiration. Therefore, if the stock price is below the exercise price of the warrant, the lower bound on the price of the warrant is zero.

          b.   If the stock price is above the exercise price of the warrant, the warrant must be worth at least the difference between these two prices. If warrants were selling for less than the difference between the current stock price and the exercise price, an investor could earn an arbitrage profit (i.e. an immediate cash inflow) by purchasing warrants, exercising them immediately, and selling the stock.

          c.   If the warrant is selling for more than the stock, it would be cheaper to purchase the stock than to purchase the warrant, which gives its owner the right to buy the stock. Therefore, an upper bound on the price of any warrant is the firm's current stock price.

24.3   a.   The primary difference between warrants and call options is that, when warrants are exercised, the firm issues new shares. Both the purchase price and the exercise price of a warrant are received by the firm and increase the value of its assets. Unless a firm is selling calls on its own shares, this does not hold true for options.

          b.   When call options are exercised, the number of shares the firm has outstanding remains unchanged. Shares of the company's stock are simply transferred from one individual to another. When warrants are exercised, however, the number of shares outstanding increases. This results in the value of the firm being spread out over a larger number of shares, often leading to a decrease in value of each individual share. The decrease in the per-share price of a company's stock due to a greater number of shares outstanding is known as **dilution**.

24.4   a.   Before the warrant was issued, Survivor's assets were worth $3,500 (= 7 oz of platinum * $500 per oz). Since there are only two shares of common stock outstanding, each share is worth **$1,750** (= $3,500 / 2 shares).

          b.   When the warrant was issued, the firm received $500 from Tina, increasing the total value of the firm's assets to $4,000 (= $3,500 + $500). If the two shares of common stock were the only outstanding claims on the firm's assets, each share would be worth $2,000 (= $4,000 / 2 shares). However, since the warrant gives Tina a claim on the firm's assets worth $500, the value of the firm's assets available to stockholders is only $3,500 (= $4,000 - $500). Since there are two shares outstanding, Survivor's value per share remains at **$1,750** (= $3,500 / 2 shares) after the warrant issue. Note that the firm uses Tina's $500 to purchase one more ounce of platinum.

          c.   If the price of platinum is $520 per ounce, the total value of the firm's assets is $4,160 (= 8 oz of platinum * $520 per oz). If Tina does not exercise her warrant, the value of the firm's assets would remain at $4,160 and there would be two shares of common stock outstanding. If Tina exercises her warrant, the firm would receive the warrant's $1,800 striking price and issue Tina one share. The total value of the firm's assets would increase to $5,960 (= $4,160 + $1,800). Since there would now be 3 shares outstanding and no warrants, Survivor's price per share would be $1,986.67 (= $5,960 / 3 shares). Since the $1,986.67 value of the share that she will receive is greater than the $1,800 exercise price of the warrant, investors will expect Tina to exercise. The firm's stock price will reflect this information and rise to **$1,986.67** per share on the warrant's expiration date.

24.5   a.   Since the stock price is currently below the exercise price of the warrant, the lower bound on the price of the warrant is zero. If there is only a small probability that the firm's stock price will rise above the exercise price of the warrant, the warrant has little value. An upper bound on the price of the warrant is $8, the current price of General Modem's common stock. One would never pay more than $8 to receive the right to purchase a share of the company's stock if the firm's stock were only worth $8.

b. If General Modem's stock is trading for $12 per share, the lower bound on the price of the warrant is $2, the difference between the current stock price and the warrant's exercise price. If warrants were selling for less than this amount, an investor could earn an arbitrage profit by purchasing warrants, exercising them immediately, and selling the stock. As always, the upper bound on the price of a warrant is the current stock price. In this case, one would never pay more than $12 for the right to buy a single share of General Modem's stock when he could purchase a share outright for $12.

24.6   Ricketti currently has 10 million shares of common stock outstanding that sell for $17 per share and 1 million warrants outstanding worth $3 each. Therefore, the value of the firm's assets before the warrants are exercised is $173 million [= (10 million shares * $17 per share) + (1 million warrants * $3 per warrant)]. Once the warrants are exercised, the total value of the firm's assets increases by $15 million (= 1 million warrants * $15 per warrant). Since each warrant gives its owner the right to receive one share, the number of shares of common stock outstanding increases by 1,000,000.

Therefore, once the warrants have been exercised, the value of Ricketti's assets is $188 million (= $173 million + $15 million) and there are 11 million (= 10 million + 1 million) shares of common stock outstanding.

The price per share of Ricketti's common stock after the warrants have been exercised is $17.09 (= $188 million / 11 million shares).

Note that since the warrants were exercised when the price per warrant ($3) was above the exercise value of each warrant ($2 = $17 - $15), the stockholders gain and the warrant holders lose.

24.7   No, the market price of the warrant will not equal zero. Since there is a chance that the market price of the stock will rise above the $21 per share exercise price before expiration, the warrant still has some value. Its market price will be greater than zero. (As a practical matter, warrants that are way out-of-the-money may sell at 0, due to transaction costs.)

24.8   Since Warrant X gives its owner the right to purchase 3 shares for $20 each, the total exercise price of each warrant is $60 (= 3 * $20). Each share of Firm Y is currently selling for $25 per share. The value of three shares of the firm is $75 (= 3 * $25). Therefore, Warrant X effectively gives its owner the right to buy $90 worth of stock for $75. It follows that the minimum value of Warrant X is $15 (= $90 - $75), the difference between the exercise price of the warrant and the value of the stock received from the warrant exercise. If Warrant X were selling for less than $15, an investor could earn an arbitrage profit by purchasing the warrant, exercising it immediately, and selling the stock. Here, the warrant holder pays less than $15 while receiving the $15 difference between the price of 3 shares and the exercise price.

24.9   The value of a single warrant (W) equals:

$$W = [\# / (\# + \#_W)] * Call\{S = (V/ \#), K = K_W\}$$

where $\#$ = the number of shares of common stock outstanding
        $\#_W$ = the number of warrants outstanding
        $Call\{S, K\}$ = a call option on an underlying asset worth S with a strike price K
        V = the firm's value net of debt
        K_W = the strike price of each warrant

In this problem:

        $\#$ = 4,000,000
        $\#_W$ = 500,000
        V = $88,000,000
        K_W = $20

Therefore, the value of a single warrant (W) equals:

$$W = [\# / (\# + \#_W)] * \text{Call}\{S = (V/ \#), K = K_W\}$$
$$= [4,000,000 / (4,000,000 + 500,000) * \text{Call}\{S = (\$88,000,000 / 4,000,000), K = \$20\}$$
$$= (8/9)*\text{Call}(S = \$22, K = \$20)$$

In order to value the call option, use the Black-Scholes formula.

The inputs to the Black-Scholes formula are:

$$S = \$22 \qquad \sigma^2 = 0.04$$
$$K = \$20 \qquad r = 0.07$$
$$t = 1$$

After identifying the inputs, solve for d_1 and d_2:

$$d_1 = [\ln(S/K) + (r + \tfrac{1}{2}\sigma^2)(t)\,] / (\sigma^2 t)^{1/2}$$
$$= [\ln(22/20) + \{0.07 + \tfrac{1}{2}(0.04)\}(1)\,] / (0.04*1)^{1/2}$$
$$= 0.9266$$

$$d_2 = d_1 - (\sigma^2 t)^{1/2}$$
$$= 0.9266 - (0.04*1)^{1/2}$$
$$= 0.7266$$

Find $N(d_1)$ and $N(d_2)$, the area under the normal curve from negative infinity to d_1 and negative infinity to d_2, respectively.

$$N(d_1) = N(0.9266) = 0.8229$$

$$N(d_2) = N(0.7266) = 0.7663$$

According to the Black-Scholes formula, the price of a European call option (C) on a non-dividend paying common stock is:

$$C = SN(d_1) - Ke^{-rt}N(d_2)$$
$$= (22)(0.8229) - (20)e^{-(0.07)(1)} (0.7663)$$
$$= \$3.81$$

The Black-Scholes Price of the call option is $3.81.

Therefore, the price of a single warrant (W) equals:

$$W = (8/9)*\text{Call}(S = \$22, K = \$20)$$
$$= (8/9)(\$3.81)$$
$$= \mathbf{\$3.39}$$

Therefore, the value of each of Superior Clamp's warrants is $3.39.

24.10   To calculate the number of warrants that Omega should issue in order to pay off $10 million in six months, use the Black-Scholes model to find the price of a single warrant, then divide this amount into the present value of $10 million to find the number of warrants to be issued.

Since Omega owes $10 million in 6 months and the current yield on Treasury bills that mature in six months is 10% per annum (continuously-compounded), Omega must raise $9,512,294 [= $10,000,000 / $(e^{(0.10*0.5)})$] from the warrant issue today in order to meet its debt obligation of $10 million in six months.

Since the value of Omega's assets is $150 million after the announcement, the value of the firm's assets will rise to $159.5 million (= $150 million + $9.5 million in proceeds) after the warrants are issued. Since the cash inflow from the warrants offsets the firm's $9.5 million in debt, the value of the warrants will be exactly the same as if the cash from the warrants were used to immediately pay off the debt. In this case, the value of the firm's assets after the warrant issue would be $150 million (= $159.5 million - $9.5 million cash to pay off debt). Use $150 million as the firm's value net of debt (V) in the Black-Scholes formula.

The firm has 1.5 million shares of common stock outstanding and wishes to issue warrants with a strike price of $95.

The value of a single warrant (W) equals:

$$W = [\# / (\# + \#_w)] * \text{Call}\{S = (V/ \#), K = K_w\}$$

where
  $\#$ = the number of shares of common stock outstanding
  $\#_w$ = the number of warrants outstanding
  Call$\{S, K\}$ = a call option on an underlying asset worth S with a strike price K
  V = the firm's value net of debt
  K_w = the strike price of each warrant

In this problem:

    $\#$ = 1,500,000
    V = $150,000,000
    K_w = $95

Therefore, the value of a single warrant (W) equals:

$$
\begin{aligned}
W \ &= [\# / (\# + \#_w)] * \text{Call}\{S = (V/ \#), K = K_w\} \\
&= [1,500,000 / (1,500,000 + \#_w)] * \text{Call}\{S = (\$150,000,000/ 1,500,000), K = \$95\} \\
&= [1,500,000 / (1,500,000 + \#_w)] * \text{Call}(S = \$100, K = \$95)
\end{aligned}
$$

Since the firm must raise $9,512,294 as a result of the warrant issue, we know $\#_w * W$ must equal $9,512,294.

Therefore, it can be stated that:

$$\$9,512,294 \ = (\#_w)(W)$$
$$\$9,512,294 \ = (\#_w)([1,500,000 / (1,500,000 + \#_w)] * \text{Call}(S = \$100, K = \$95)$$

In order to value the call option, use the Black-Scholes formula.

The inputs to the Black-Scholes formula are: $S = \$100$ $\sigma^2 = 0.5625$
                 $K = \$95$ $r = 0.10$
                 $t = 0.5$

After identifying the inputs, solve for d_1 and d_2:

d_1 $= [\ln(S/K) + (r + \tfrac{1}{2}\sigma^2)(t)] / (\sigma^2 t)^{1/2}$

   $= [\ln(100/95) + \{0.10 + \tfrac{1}{2}(0.5625)\}(0.50)] / (0.5625*0.50)^{1/2}$
   $= 0.4562$

d_2 = $d_1 - (\sigma^2 t)^{1/2}$
= $0.4562 - (0.5625*0.50)^{1/2}$
= -0.0742

Find $N(d_1)$ and $N(d_2)$, the area under the normal curve from negative infinity to d_1 and negative infinity to d_2, respectively.

$N(d_1)$ = $N(0.4562) = 0.6759$

$N(d_2)$ = $N(-0.0742) = 0.4704$

According to the Black-Scholes formula, the price of a European call option (C) on a non-dividend paying common stock is:

C = $SN(d_1) - Ke^{-rt}N(d_2)$
= $(100)(0.6759) - (95)e^{-(0.10)(0.50)} (0.4704)$
= $25.08

The Black-Scholes price of the call option is $25.08.

Inserting this value into the equation above:

$9,512,294 = (\#_w) [1,500,000 / (1,500,000 + \#_w)] *Call(S = \$100, K = \$95)$
$9,512,294 = (\#_w) [1,500,000 / (1,500,000 + \#_w)]*(\$25.08)$

$\#_w = \mathbf{507{,}634}$

Therefore, in order to pay off $10 million worth of debt in 6 months, Omega should issue 507,634 warrants today.

24.11   Since a convertible bond gives its holder the right to a fixed payment plus the right to convert, it must be worth at least as much as its straight value. Therefore, if the market value of a convertible bond is less than its straight value, there is an opportunity to make an arbitrage profit by purchasing the bond and holding it until expiration.

In Scenario A, the market value of the convertible bond is $1,000. Since this amount is greater than the convertible's straight value ($900), Scenario A is feasible.

In Scenario B, the market value of the convertible bond is $900. Since this amount is less than the convertible's straight value ($950), Scenario B is not feasible.

Scenario A is more likely.

24.12   a.   The conversion price indicates that for each $25 of face value of the bond, the convertible bondholder can receive 1 share. Since the $25 conversion price divides into the $1,000 face value of the bond 40 times (= $1,000 / $25), each convertible bond can be exchanged for 40 shares of Sportime's stock. Since each share is currently trading for $24, the value of immediate conversion of a single convertible bond is $960 (= $24 per share * 40 shares).

Therefore, the minimum value that each convertible bond should sell for is $960.

b. A convertible bond gives its owner the right to convert his bond into a fixed number of shares. The market price of a convertible bond includes a premium over the value of immediate conversion that accounts for the possibility of increases in the price of the firm's stock before the maturity of the bond. If the stock price rises, a convertible bondholder will convert and receive valuable shares of equity. If the stock price decreases, the convertible bondholder holds the bond and retains his right to a fixed interest and principal payments.

24.13 a. Rob Stevens currently owns 500,000 of Isner's 4,000,000 shares. Therefore, he owns **12.5%** (= 500,000 / 4,000,000) of the firm's common stock.

b. The conversion price indicates that for every $20 of face value of convertible bonds outstanding, Isner will be obligated to issue a new share upon conversion. Since there is currently $20 million worth of convertible bonds (face value) outstanding, Isner will issue 1,000,000 (= $20,000,000 / $20) new shares when it calls the convertible bonds and forces conversion. This increases the number of Isner's outstanding shares to 5,000,000 (= 4,000,000 + 1,000,000). After conversion, Rob Stevens will only own **10%** (= 500,000 / 5,000,000) of the firm's common stock.

24.14 a. The conversion ratio is defined as the number of shares that will be issued upon conversion. Since each bond is convertible into 28 shares of Hannon's common stock, the conversion ratio of the convertible bonds is **28**.

b. The conversion price is defined as the face amount of a convertible bond that the holder must surrender in order to receive a single share. Since the conversion ratio indicates that each bond is convertible into 28 shares and each convertible bond has a face value of $1,000, one must surrender **$35.71** (= $1,000 face value per bond / 28 shares per bond) in order to receive one share of Hannon's common stock.

c. The conversion premium is defined as the percentage difference between the conversion price of the convertible bonds and the current stock price. Since Hannon's common stock is trading for $31.25 per share and the conversion price of each of its convertible bonds is $35.71, the conversion premium is **14.27%** [= ($35.71 / $31.25) – 1].

d. The conversion value is defined as the amount that each convertible bond would be worth if it were immediately converted into common stock. Since each convertible bond gives its owner the right to 28 shares of Hannon's common stock, currently worth $31.25 per share, the conversion value of the each bond is **$875** (= 28 shares * $31.25 per share).

e. If Hannon's common stock price increases by $2, the new conversion value of the bonds will be **$931** (= 28 shares * 33.25 per share).

24.15 a. The straight value of a convertible bond is the bond's value if it were not convertible into common stock. Since the bond will pay $1,000 in 10 years and the appropriate discount rate is 10%, the present value of $1,000, discounted at 10% per annum, equals the straight value of this convertible bond.

Straight Value = $1,000 / (1.10)^{10}$
                = **$385.54**

Therefore, the straight value of the convertible bond is $385.54.

b. The conversion value is defined as the amount that the convertible bond would be worth if it were immediately converted into common stock. Since the convertible bond gives its owner the right to 25 shares of MGH's common stock, currently worth $12 per share, the conversion value of the bond is **$300** (= 25 shares * $12 per share).

Therefore, the conversion value of the convertible bond is $300.

c. The option value of a convertible bond is defined as the difference between the market value of the bond and the maximum of its straight value and conversion value. In this problem, the bond's market value is $400, its straight value is $385.54, and its conversion value is $300.

Option Value = Market Value - max[Straight Value, Conversion Value]
= $400 – max[$385.54, $300]
= $400 - $385.54
= **$14.46**

Therefore, the option value of the convertible bond is $14.46.

24.16 The conversion price is defined as the face amount of a convertible bond that the holder must surrender in order to receive a single share of stock. In this problem, the conversion price is $180. Since the bond has a face value of $1,000, it is convertible into 5.56 (= $1,000 / $180) shares.

The conversion value is defined as the amount that the convertible bond would be worth if it were immediately converted into common stock. Since the convertible bond gives its owner the right to 5.56 shares of common stock, currently worth $60 per share, the conversion value of the bond is **$333.33** (= 5.56 shares * $60 per share).

Therefore, the conversion value of this convertible bond is $333.33.

24.17 a. The straight value of a convertible bond is the bond's value if it were not convertible into common stock. The bond makes annual coupon payments of $60 (= 0.06 * $1,000) at the end of each year for 30 years. In addition, the owner will receive the bond's face value of $1,000 when the bond matures in 30 years. The straight value of the bond equals the present value of its cash flows.

Since the bond makes annual coupon payments of $60 (= 0.06 * $1,000) for 30 years, the present value of the coupon payments can be found by calculating the present value of an annuity that makes payments of $60 for 30 years, discounted at 12%.

PV(Coupon Payments) = $60A$^{30}_{0.12}$ = $483.31

Since the repayment of principal occurs in 30 years, the present value of the principal payment can be found by discounting the $1,000 face value of the bond by 12% for 30 years.

PV(Principal Payment) = $1,000 / $(1.12)^{30}$ = $33.38

Straight Value = PV(Coupon Payments) + PV(Principal Payment)
= $483.31 + $33.38
= **$516.69**

Therefore, the straight value of the convertible bond is $516.69.

b. The conversion price is defined as the face amount of a convertible bond that the holder must surrender in order to receive a single share. In this problem, the conversion price is $125. Since the bond has a face value of $1,000, it is convertible into 8 (= $1,000 / $125) shares.

The conversion value is defined as the amount that the convertible bond would be worth if it were immediately converted into common stock. Since the convertible bond gives its owner the right to 8 shares of common stock, currently worth $35 per share, the conversion value of the bond is **$280** (= 8 shares * $35 per share).

Therefore, the conversion value of this convertible bond is $280.

c. If Firm A's stock price were growing by 15% per year forever, each share of its stock would be worth approximately $35(1.15)^t$ after t years. Since each bond is convertible into 8 shares, the conversion value of the bond equals $(\$35*8)(1.15)^t$ after t years. In order to calculate the number of years that it will take for the conversion value to equal $1,100, set up the following equation:

$(\$35*8)(1.15)^t = \$1,100$

$t = \textbf{9.79}$

Therefore, it will take 9.79 years for the conversion value of the convertible bond to exceed $1,100.

Chapter 25: Derivatives and Hedging Risk

25.1   a.   A **forward contract** is an arrangement calling for the future delivery of an asset at an agreed-upon price.

b.   A **futures contract** obliges traders to purchase or sell an asset at an agreed-upon price on a specified future date. The long position is held by the trader who commits to purchase. The short position is held by the trader who commits to sell. Futures differ from forward contracts in their standardization, exchange trading, margin requirements, and daily settling (marking to market).

25.2   1.   Futures contracts are standardized and traded on exchanges, while forward contracts are tailor-made to suit the specific needs of two counterparties. The standardization of contracts increases the liquidity of futures markets in comparison to forward markets and also allows traders to enter into their positions with a certain degree of anonymity.

2.   The holder of a futures contract is insulated from default risk due to clearing corporations and margin requirements. The owner of a forward contract has no guarantee that his counterparty will not default, and therefore forward holders must carefully evaluate each others' credit risk before entering into a contract.

3.   Since futures positions are marked-to-market at the close of trading, gains and losses on futures positions are realized daily, while gains or losses on a forward contract are not realized until the delivery of the asset.

25.3   a.   i.   Since the futures price of wheat is $5.10 per bushel at the end of trading on March 18, the delivery price on that date is **$5.10 per bushel**.

ii.   On the delivery date, the long and short positions in a futures contract transact with the clearing corporation at the current futures price. Therefore, you will pay the current futures price of **$5.10 per barrel** in order to receive the wheat. The difference between the price that you pay at delivery and the price at which you entered into the contract is reconciled by daily marked-to-market gains and losses.

iii.   On March 15, you entered into a long futures position in wheat at a price of $5.00 per bushel. Since the closing futures price is $5.03 per bushel, your account receives a **cash inflow of $0.03** at the end of the day. Your position in wheat futures increases to $5.03 per bushel (= $5.00 + $0.03).

On March 16, your opening long position in wheat futures is $5.03 per bushel. Since the closing futures price is $5.08 per bushel, your account receives a **cash inflow of $0.05** at the end of the day. Your position in wheat futures increases to $5.08 per bushel (= $5.00 + $0.03 + $0.05).

On March 17, your opening long position in wheat futures is $5.08 per bushel. Since the closing futures price is $5.12 per bushel, your account receives a **cash inflow of $0.04** at the end of the day. Your position in wheat futures increases to $5.12 per bushel (= $5.00 + $0.03 + $0.05 + $0.04).

On March 18, your opening long position in wheat futures is $5.12 per bushel. Since the closing futures price is $5.10 per bushel, your account experiences a **cash outflow of $0.02** at the end of the day. Your position in wheat futures decreases to $5.10 per bushel (= $5.00 + $0.03 + $0.05 + $0.04 - $0.02). Since you receive a notice of delivery on this date, you will **pay the $5.10 futures price** and receive 1 bushel of wheat.

iv. The following is a summary of your futures position:

		Event	Cash Flow
March	15	Enter into Long Futures Positon at $5.00 per bushel	None
March	15	Futures Price Increases to $5.03 per bushel	$0.03
March	16	Futures Price Increases to $5.08 per bushel	$0.05
March	17	Futures Price Increases to $5.12 per bushel	$0.04
March	18	Futures Price Decreases to $5.10 per bushel	-$0.02
March	18	Pay Futures Price of $5.10 at Delivery	-$5.10
		Total Net Cash Flow	-$5.00

Therefore, the net amount that you pay for one bushel of wheat is $5.00 per bushel.

b. i. Since the futures price wheat is $4.98 per bushel at the end of trading on March 18, the delivery price on that date is **$4.98 per bushel**.

ii. On the delivery date, the long and short positions in a futures contract transact with the clearing corporation at the current futures price. Therefore, you will pay the current futures price of **$4.98 per barrel** in order to receive the wheat. The difference between the price that you pay at delivery and the price at which you entered into the contract is reconciled by daily marked-to-market gains and losses.

iii. On March 15, you entered into a long futures position in wheat at a price of $5.00 per bushel. Since the closing futures price is $5.03 per bushel, your account receives a **cash inflow of $0.03** at the end of the day. Your position in wheat futures increases to $5.03 per bushel (= $5.00 + $0.03).

On March 16, your opening long position in wheat futures is $5.03 per bushel. Since the closing futures price is $5.08 per bushel, your account receives a **cash inflow of $0.05** at the end of the day. Your position in wheat futures increases to $5.08 per bushel (= $5.00 + $0.03 + $0.05).

On March 17, your opening long position in wheat futures is $5.08 per bushel. Since the closing futures price is $5.12 per bushel, your account receives a **cash inflow of $0.04** at the end of the day. Your position in wheat futures increases to $5.12 per bushel (= $5.00 + $0.03 + $0.05 + $0.04).

On March 18, your opening long position in wheat futures is $5.12 per bushel. Since the closing futures price is $5.10 per bushel, your account experiences a **cash outflow of $0.02** at the end of the day. Your position in wheat futures decreases to $5.10 per bushel (= $5.00 + $0.03 + $0.05 + $0.04 - $0.02).

On March 19, your opening long position in wheat futures was $5.10 per bushel. Since the closing futures price is $4.98 per bushel, you will experience a **cash outflow of $0.12** at the end of the day. Your position in wheat futures decreases to $4.98 per bushel (= $5.00 + $0.03 + $0.05 + $0.04 - $0.02 - $0.12). Since you will receive a notice of delivery on this date, you will **pay the $4.98 futures price** and receive 1 bushel of wheat. Notice that even though you only paid $4.98 for the delivery of wheat, the net amount that you paid for it out of your pocket is $5.00 per bushel, the futures price at which you originally entered into the position.

iv. The following is a summary of your futures position:

		Event	Cash Flow
March	15	Enter into Long Futures Positon at $5.00 per bushel	None
March	15	Futures Price Increases to $5.03 per bushel	$0.03
March	16	Futures Price Increases to $5.08 per bushel	$0.05
March	17	Futures Price Increases to $5.12 per bushel	$0.04
March	18	Futures Price Decreases to $5.10 per bushel	-$0.02
March	19	Futures Price Decreases to $4.98 per bushel	-$0.12
March	19	Pay Futures Price of $4.98 at Delivery	-$4.98
		Total Net Cash Flow	-$5.00

Therefore, the net amount that you pay for one bushel of wheat is $5.00 per bushel.

25.4   a.   The forward price of an asset with no carrying costs or convenience value is:

Forward Price $= S_0(1 + r)$

where S_0 = the current price of the underlying asset
         r = the interest rate between the initiation of the forward contract and the delivery date

Since you will receive the bond's face value of $1,000 in 11 years and the 11-year spot interest rate is currently 8% per annum, the current price of the bond is $428.88 [= \$1,000 / (1.08)^{11}]$.

Since the forward contract defers delivery of the bond for one year, the appropriate interest rate to use in the forward pricing equation is the one-year spot interest rate of 3%:

Forward Price $= \$428.88(1.03) =$ **$441.75**

Therefore, the forward price of your contract is $441.75.

b.   If both the 1-year and 11-year spot interest rates unexpectedly shift downward by 2%, the appropriate interest rates to use when pricing the bond is 6% per annum (EAY), and the appropriate interest rate to use in the forward pricing equation is 1% per annum (EAY).

Given these changes, the current price of the bond increases to $526.79 [= \$1,000 / (1.06)^{11}]$.

The new forward price of the contract is:

Forward Price $= \$526.79(1.01) =$ **$532.06**

Therefore, the forward price of an otherwise identical contract will increase to $532.06 given the unexpected change in the 1-year and 11-year spot interest rates.

25.5   a.   You would create a short position by selling futures contracts.

b.   A short position reduces your overall risk if you are hurt by decreases in the price of the underlying asset. For example, if you are selling oil in one year at the spot price, you will make less money if the price of oil falls over the next year. In order to hedge this risk, you should sell oil futures contracts that expire in approximately one year.

c.   You would create a long position by purchasing futures contracts.

d. A long position reduces your overall risk if you are hurt by increases in the price of the underlying asset. For example, if you are planning to purchase oil in one year at the spot price, you will have to pay more for the oil if the spot price increases over the next year. In order to hedge this risk, you should buy oil futures contracts that expire in approximately one year.

25.6   If Mark Fisher believes that the futures price of silver will fall over the next month, he should take on a short position in silver futures contracts with approximately one month until expiration. By selling futures contracts now, he will be locking in a sales price that is higher than what he believes he will be able to purchase silver futures for in one month's time.

25.7   William Santiago is a little naïve about the capabilities of hedging. While hedging can significantly reduce the risk of changes in foreign exchange markets, it cannot completely eliminate it. Basis risk is the primary reason that hedging cannot reduce 100% of any firm's exposure to price fluctuations. Basis risk arises when the price movements of the hedging instrument do not perfectly match the price movements of the asset being hedged.

25.8   a. The forward price of an asset with no carrying costs or convenience value is:

Forward Price $= S_0(1+ r)$

where S_0 = the current price of the underlying asset
           r = the interest rate between the initiation of the forward contract and the delivery date

Since you will receive the bond's face value of $1,000 in 18 months and the 18-month spot interest rate is currently 10.67% (EAY), the current price of the bond is $858.92 [= $1,000 / (1.1067)^{3/2}$].

Since the forward contract defers delivery of the bond for six months, the appropriate interest rate to use in the forward pricing equation is the six-month spot interest rate of 9.83% (EAY).

Forward Price $= \$858.92(1.0983)^{1/2} = \mathbf{\$900.15}$

Therefore, the forward price of your contract is $900.15.

b. It is important to remember that 100 basis points equals 1% and one basis point equals 0.01%. Therefore, if all rates increase by 30 basis points, each rate increases by 0.003. The new 18-month spot rate (EAY) is 0.1097 (= 0.1067 + 0.003), and the new 6-month spot rate (EAY) is 0.1013 (= 0.0983 + 0.003).

Since the owner of a forward contract will receive the bond's face value of $1,000 in 18 months and the 18-month spot interest rate is currently 10.97% (EAY) the current price of the bond is $855.44 [= $1,000 / (1.1097)^{3/2}$].

Since the forward contract defers delivery of the bond for six months, the appropriate interest rate to use in the forward pricing equation is the six-month spot interest rate of 10.13% (EAY).

Forward Price $= \$855.44(1.1013)^{1/2} = \mathbf{\$897.72}$

Therefore, the forward price of an otherwise identical contract is $897.72 given the 30 basis point increase in all semiannual rates.

25.9   Let r equal the interest rate between the initiation of the contract and the delivery of the asset.

Cash Flows From Strategy 1

	Today	1 Year
Purchase Silver	$-S_0$	--
Borrow	$+S_0$	$-S_0(1+r)$
Total Cash Flow	0	$-S_0(1+r)$

Cash Flows from Strategy 2

	Today	1 Year
Purchase Silver Forward	--	$-f$
Total Cash Flow	0	$-f$

Notice that each strategy results in the ownership of silver in one year for no cash outflow today. Since the payoffs from both the strategies are identical, the two strategies must cost the same in order to preclude arbitrage.

The forward price (f) of a contract on an asset with no carrying costs or convenience value equals the current spot price of the asset (S_0) multiplied by 1 plus the appropriate interest rate between the initiation of the contract and the delivery date of the asset.

Therefore, f must equal $S_0(1+r)$.

25.10   Kevin will be hurt if the yen loses value relative to the dollar over the next eight months. Depreciation in the yen relative to the dollar results in a decrease in the yen / dollar exchange rate. Since Kevin is hurt by a decrease in the exchange rate, he should take on a **short position in yen per dollar futures contracts** in order to hedge his risk.

25.11   a.   Your former roommate's annual mortgage payments form a 20-year annuity, discounted at the long-term interest rate of 10%. Solve for the payment amount so that the present value of the annuity equals $300,000, the amount of principal that your former roommate plans to borrow.

$300,000 = C * A^{20}_{0.10}$

C = **$35,238**

Therefore, your former roommate's annual mortgage payment will be $35,238.

     b.   The most significant risk that you face is interest rate risk. If the current market rate of interest rises between today and the date that you meet with the president of MAX, the fair value of the mortgage will decrease, and the president will only be willing to purchase the mortgage from you for a price less than $300,000. If this is the case, you will not be able to loan your former roommate the full $300,000 that you promised her.

     c.   Treasury bond prices have an inverse relationship with interest rates. As interest rates rise, Treasury bonds become less valuable; as interest rates fall, Treasury bonds become more valuable. Since you are hurt when interest rates rise, you are also hurt when Treasury bonds decrease in value. In order to protect yourself from decreases in the price of Treasury bonds, you should take a short position in Treasury bond futures to hedge his interest rate risk. Since three-month Treasury bond futures contracts are available and each contract is for $100,000 of T-bonds, you would take a short position in three 3-month Treasury bond futures contracts in order to hedge your $300,000 exposure to changes in the market interest rate over the next three months

d. i. If the market interest rate is 12% on the date that you meet with the president of MAX, the fair value of the mortgage equals an annuity that makes annual payments of $35,238 for 20 years, discounted at 12%.

$$\text{Mortgage Value} = \$35,238 A^{20}{}_{0.12}$$
$$= \mathbf{\$263,208}$$

Therefore, MAX's president will be willing to pay you $263,208 for the mortgage if the market interest rate is 12% on the date of your meeting.

ii. An increase in the interest rate will cause the value of the T-bond futures contracts to decrease.

iii. You will make money on your short position in the T-bond futures contracts if interest rates rise.

e. i. If the market interest rate is 9% on the date that you meet with the president of MAX, the fair value of the mortgage equals an annuity that makes annual payments of $35,238 for 20 years, discounted at 9%.

$$\text{Mortgage Value} = \$35,238 A^{20}{}_{0.09}$$
$$= \mathbf{\$321,672}$$

Therefore, MAX's president will be willing to pay you $321,672 for the mortgage if the market interest rate is 9% on the date of your meeting.

ii. A decrease in the interest rate will cause the value of the T-bond futures contracts to increase.

iii. You will lose money on your short position in the T-bond futures contracts if interest rates fall.

25.12   a. The price of a bond equals the present value of its cash flows.

Price of Bond A $= \$1,000 / (1.11)$ $= \mathbf{\$900.90}$
Price of Bond B $= \$1,000 / (1.11)^5$ $= \mathbf{\$593.45}$
Price of Bond C $= \$1,000 / (1.11)^{10}$ $= \mathbf{\$352.18}$

b. If the market rate of interest increases to 14% per annum, the price of each bond will be:

Price of Bond A $= \$1,000 / (1.14)$ $= \mathbf{\$877.19}$
Price of Bond B $= \$1,000 / (1.14)^5$ $= \mathbf{\$519.37}$
Price of Bond C $= \$1,000 / (1.14)^{10}$ $= \mathbf{\$269.74}$

c. The percentage change in the price of each bond is calculated as follows:

Percentage Change in Bond Price $= (\text{New Price} / \text{Old Price}) - 1$

Percentage Change in Bond A $= (\$877.19 / \$900.90) - 1$
$= \mathbf{-2.63\%}$

Percentage Change in Bond B $= (\$519.37 / \$593.45) - 1$
$= \mathbf{-12.48\%}$

Percentage Change in Bond C $= (\$269.74 / \$352.18) - 1$
$= \mathbf{-23.41\%}$

Therefore, Bond C experienced the greatest percentage change in price.

25.13   a.   The price of a bond equals the present value of its cash flows.

Since Bond A pays an annual coupon of 7%, the bond's owner will receive $70 (= 0.07 * $1,000) at the end of each year in addition to the bond's $1,000 face value when the bond matures at the end of year 4..

Price of Bond A $= \$70 / 1.10 + \$70 / (1.10)^2 + \$70 / (1.10)^3 + \$1,070 / (1.10)^4$
$= \$904.90$

The price of Bond A is $904.90.

Since Bond B pays an annual coupon of 11%, the bond's owner will receive $110 (= 0.11 * $1,000) at the end of each year in addition to the bond's $1,000 face value when the bond matures at the end of year 4.

Price of Bond B $= \$110 / 1.10 + \$110 / (1.10)^2 + \$110 / (1.10)^3 + \$1,110 / (1.10)^4$
$= \$1,031.70$

The price of Bond B is $1,031.70.

The duration of a bond is the average time to payment of the bond's cash flows, weighted by the ratio of the present value of each payment to the price of the bond.

The relative value of each payment is the present value of the payment divided by the price of the bond. The contribution of each payment to the duration of the bond is the relative value of the payment multiplied by the amount of time (in years) until the payment occurs.

Bond A

Payment	PV of Payment	Relative Value	Time to Payment (in years)	Duration
$70	$63.64	0.0703	1	0.0703
$70	$57.85	0.0639	2	0.1279
$70	$52.59	0.0581	3	0.1744
$1,070	$730.82	0.8076	4	3.2305
				3.6031

The duration of Bond A is 3.6031 years.

Bond B

Payment	PV of Payment	Relative Value	Time to Payment (in years)	Duration
$110	$100.00	0.0969	1	0.0969
$110	$90.91	0.0881	2	0.1762
$110	$82.64	0.0801	3	0.2403
$1,110	$758.14	0.7349	4	2.9394
				3.4529

The duration of Bond B is 3.4529 years.

b. If the market interest rate decreases to 7% per annum:

Price of Bond A $= \$70 / 1.07 + \$70 / (1.07)^2 + \$70 / (1.07)^3 + \$1,070 / (1.07)^4$
= **\$1,000**

Price of Bond B $= \$110 / 1.07 + \$110 / (1.07)^2 + \$110 / (1.07)^3 + \$1,110 / (1.07)^4$
= **\$1,135.49**

c. Bond A should experience a greater percentage change in its price. Bond A has a higher duration than Bond B since a larger proportion of its payments occur in later years. Bonds with higher durations will experience greater percentage changes in price for a given movement in the interest rate.

d. The percentage change in the price of each bond is:

Percentage Change in Bond Price $= \text{(New Price / Old Price)} - 1$

Percentage Change in Bond A $= (\$1,000 / \$904.90) - 1$
= **10.51%**

Percentage Change in Bond B $= (\$1,135.49 / \$1,031.70) - 1$
= **10.06%**

25.14   The duration of a bond is the average time to payment of the bond's cash flows, weighted by the ratio of the present value of each payment to the price of the bond.

Since the bond is selling at par, the market interest rate must equal 9%, the annual coupon rate on the bond. The price of a bond selling at par is equal to its face value. Therefore, the price of this bond is $1,000.

The relative value of each payment is the present value of the payment divided by the price of the bond. The contribution of each payment to the duration of the bond is the relative value of the payment multiplied by the amount of time (in years) until the payment occurs.

Payment	PV of Payment	Relative Value	Time to Payment (in years)	Duration
$90	$82.57	0.0826	1	0.0826
$90	$75.75	0.0758	2	0.1515
$1,090	$841.68	0.8417	3	2.5250
				2.7591

Therefore, the duration of the bond is 2.7591 years.

25.15   The duration of a bond is the average time to payment of the bond's cash flows, weighted by the ratio of the present value of each payment to the price of the bond.

Since the bond is selling at par, the market interest rate must equal 9%, the annual coupon rate on the bond. The price of a bond selling at par is equal to its face value. Therefore, the price of this bond is $1,000.

The relative value of each payment is the present value of the payment divided by the price of the bond. The contribution of each payment to the duration of the bond is the relative value of the payment multiplied by the amount of time (in years) until the payment occurs.

Payment	PV of Payment	Relative Value	Time to Payment (in years)	Duration
$90	$82.57	0.0826	1	0.0826
$90	$75.75	0.0758	2	0.1515
$90	$69.50	0.0695	3	0.2085
$1,090	$772.18	0.7722	4	3.0887
				3.5313

Therefore, the duration of the bond is 3.5313 years.

25.16   The duration of a bond is the average timing of the bond's cash flows, weighted by the ratio of the present value of each payment to the price of the bond.

In order to determine the duration of a bond, first calculate the bond's price.

Since this bond pays an annual coupon of 5%, the bond's owner will receive $50 (= 0.05 * $1,000) at the end of each year in addition to the bond's $1,000 face value at the end of year 4. Use the market interest rate of 9% per annum to discount the bond's cash flows.

Price of Bond $= \$50 / 1.09 + \$50 / (1.09)^2 + \$50 / (1.09)^3 + \$1,050 / (1.09)^4$
$\quad\quad\quad\quad\quad = \mathbf{\$870.41}$

Next, set up the following table to calculate the bond's duration. The relative value of each payment is the present value of the payment divided by the price of the bond. The contribution of each payment to the duration of the bond is the relative value of the payment multiplied by the amount of time (in years) until the payment occurs.

Payment	PV of Payment	Relative Value	Time to Payment (in years)	Duration
$50	$45.87	0.0527	1	0.0527
$50	$42.08	0.0483	2	0.0967
$50	$38.61	0.0444	3	0.1331
$1,050	$743.85	0.8546	4	3.4184
				3.7008

Therefore, the duration of the bond is 3.7008 years.

25.17   The duration of a liability is the average time to payment of the cash flows required to retire the liability, weighted by the ratio of the present value of each payment to the present value of all payments related to the liability.

In order to determine the duration of a liability, first calculate the present value of all the payments required to retire it. Since the Hansels plan to pay $20,000 at the beginning of each year for four years, the present value of these payments can be calculated using the annuity formula. Use the market interest rate of 15% to discount these payments.

PV(College Payments two years from today)	=	$20,000A$^4_{0.15}$
	=	**$57,100**

The annuity formula yields the present value of the college payments one year prior to the initial payment. Since the first payment will occur three years from today, discount this amount must by two years in order to find its present value.

$$\text{PV(College Payments)} = \$57,100 / (1.15)^2$$
$$= \mathbf{\$43,176}$$

Therefore, the present value of the Hansels' college payments is $43,176.

Next, set up the following table to calculate the liability's duration. The relative value of each payment is the present value of the payment divided by the present value of the entire liability. The contribution of each payment to the duration of the entire liability is the relative value of the payment multiplied by the amount of time (in years) until the payment occurs.

Payment	PV of Payment	Relative Value	Time to Payment (in years)	Duration
$20,000	$13,150.32	0.3046	3	0.9137
$20,000	$11,435.06	0.2648	4	1.0594
$20,000	$9,943.53	0.2303	5	1.1515
$20,000	$8,646.55	0.2003	6	1.2016
				4.3262

Therefore, the duration of the Hansels' liability is 4.3262 years.

25.18   The duration of a portfolio of assets or liabilities is the weighted average of the duration of the portfolio's individual items, weighted by their relative market values.

a.   The total market value of Blue Steel's assets is $1,255 million (= $43 + $615 + $345 + $55 + $197). The relative market value and duration of each asset is listed below. The relative value of each asset is the market value of the asset divided by the market value of all the bank's assets.

	Relative Value	Duration (in years)
Federal Funds Deposits	0.0343	0
Accounts Receivable	0.4900	0.33
Short-Term Loans	0.2749	0.75
Long-Term Loans	0.0438	5
Mortagages	0.1570	15

Since the duration of a group of assets is the weighted average of the durations of each individual asset in the group, the duration of Blue Steel's assets is:

$$\text{Duration of Assets} = (0.0343)(0) + (0.4900)(0.33) + (0.2749)(0.75) + (0.0438)(5) + (0.1570)(15)$$
$$= \mathbf{2.94}$$

Therefore, the duration of Blue Steel's assets is 2.94 years.

b.   The total market value of Blue Steel's liabilities is $1,110 million (= $490 + $370 + $250). The relative market value and duration of each liability is listed below. The relative value of each liability is the market value of the liability divided by the market value of all the bank's liabilities.

	Relative Value	Duration (in years)
Checking and Savings Deposits	0.4414	0
Certificates of Deposit	0.3333	1.5
Long-Term Financing	0.2252	10

Since the duration of a group of liabilities is the weighted average of the durations of each individual liability in the group, the duration of Blue Steel's liabilities is:

Duration of Liabilities = (0.4414)(0) + (0.3333)(1.5) + (0.2252)(10)
                          = **2.75**

Therefore, the duration of Blue Steel's liabilities is 2.75 years.

c.   Since the duration of Blue Steel's assets does not equal the duration of its liabilities, the bank is not immune from interest rate risk.

25.19 The duration of a portfolio of assets or liabilities is the weighted average of the duration of the portfolio's individual items, weighted by their relative market values.

a.   The total market value of Magnum's assets is $1,800 million (= $100 + $500 + $1,200). The relative market value and duration of each asset is listed below. The relative value of each asset is the market value of the asset divided by the market value of all the bank's assets.

	Relative Value	Duration (in years)
Overnight Money	0.0556	0
Loans	0.2778	1
Mortgages	0.6667	12

Since the duration of a group of assets is the weighted average of the durations of each individual asset in the group, the duration of Magnum's assets is:

Duration of Assets = (0.0556)(0) + (0.2778)(1) + (0.6667)(12)
                    = **8.28**

Therefore, the duration of Magnum's assets is 8.28 years.

b.   The total market value of Magnum's liabilities is $1,200 million (= $300 + $400 + $500). The relative market value and duration of each liability is listed below. The relative value of each liability is the market value of the liability divided by the market value of all the bank's liabilities.

	Relative Value	Duration (in years)
Checking and Savings Accounts	0.2500	0
Certificates of Deposit	0.3333	1.1
Long-Term Debt	0.4167	19

Since the duration of a group of liabilities is the weighted average of the durations of each individual liability in the group, the duration of Magnum's liabilities is:

Duration of Liabilities = (0.2500)(0) + (0.3333)(1.1) + (0.4167)(19)
                          = **8.28**

Therefore, the duration of Magnum's liabilities is 8.28 years.

c.   The duration of Magnum's assets equals the duration of its liabilities. However, the bank is still not immune from interest rate risk since the value of its assets is greater than the value of its liabilities. Duration matching only eliminates risk if the value of the firm's assets equals the value of the firm's liabilities.

25.20   a.   Yes, there is an opportunity for the Miller Company and the Edwards Company to benefit from a swap. Miller wishes to borrow at a floating rate but has a comparative advantage in the fixed rate market, while Edwards would like to borrow at a fixed rate but has a comparative advantage in the floating rate market.

	Fixed Rate	Floating Rate
Miller	10%	LIBOR + 3%
Edwards	15%	LIBOR + 2%

b.   Since Miller would prefer to borrow at the lowest floating rate available and Edwards would like to borrow at the lowest fixed rate available, the following swap would benefit both parties:

1.   Miller borrows at the fixed rate of 10%.
2.   Edwards borrows at the floating rate of LIBOR + 2%.
3.   The two companies enter into a interest-rate swap in which Edwards agrees to make Miller's fixed rate payments and Miller agrees to make Edward's floating rate payments.

Chapter 26: Short-Term Finance and Planning

26.1   Start with the basic balance sheet equation, and substitute known definitions:

$$\text{Assets} = \text{Liabilities} + \text{Equity}$$

$$\text{Current Assets} + \text{Fixed Assets} = \text{Current Liabilities} + \text{Long-Term Debt} + \text{Equity}$$

Since Net Working Capital = Current Assets - Current Liabilities,
subtract Current Liabilities from both sides and substitute NWC:

$$\text{Net Working Capital} + \text{Fixed Assets} = \text{Long-Term Debt} + \text{Equity}$$

and we know that Current Assets = Cash + Other Current Assets, so we can substitute as:

$$\text{Cash} + \text{Other Current Assets} - \text{Current Liabilities}$$
$$= \text{Long-Term Debt} + \text{Equity} - \text{Fixed Assets}$$

Then finally write in terms of cash:

$$\text{Cash} =$$
$$\text{Long-Term Debt} + \text{Equity} - \text{Net Working Capital (excluding cash)} - \text{Fixed Assets}$$

26.2
a. Decrease
b. Decrease
c. No change
d. Increase
e. No change
f. No change
g. Increase
h. No change
i. Increase
j. Decrease
k. Increase
l. No change
m. No change
n. No change
o. Decrease
p. Decrease
q. No change
r. Decrease

26.3

Sources and Uses of Cash
20X6

Sources of cash:

Cash from operations	
Net income	$68,600
Depreciation	5,225
Decrease in net working capital	
Increase in accounts payable	5,500
New stock	3,000
Total sources of cash	$82,325

Uses of cash:

Increase in fixed assets	$12,725
Dividends	30,800
Increase in net working capital	
Investment in inventory	3,750
Increase in accounts receivable	9,750
Decrease in accrued expenses	3.300
Decrease in long-term debt	15,000
Total uses of cash	$75,325

Change in cash balance $7,000

26.4   Following example in Tables 26.1 & 26.2:

Sources and Uses of Cash
20X6

Sources of cash:

Cash from operations	
Net income	$83,000
Depreciation	50,000
Total cash flow from operations	133,000
Decrease in net working capital	
Decrease in inventory	114,000
Increase in accounts payable	23,000
Increase in loans payable	376,000
Total sources of cash	$646,000

Uses of cash:

Increase in fixed assets	$139,000
Dividends	100,000
Increase in net working capital	
Increase in accounts receivable	251,000
Decrease in taxes payable	132,000
Decrease in accrued expenses	11,000
Total uses of cash	$633,000

Change in cash balance $13,000

26.5   First find the applicable component ratios:

$$\text{Inventory turnover ratio} = \frac{\text{Costs of Good Sold}}{\text{Average Inventory}} = \frac{200}{(40+60)/2} = 4$$

$$\text{Receivable turnover ratio} = \frac{\text{Credit Sales}}{\text{Average Receivables}} = \frac{240}{(30+50)/2} = 6$$

$$\text{Accounts payable turnover ratio} = \frac{200}{(10+30)/2} = 10$$

$$\text{Days in inventory} = \frac{\text{days per year}}{\text{inventory turnover}} = \frac{365}{4}$$

$$\text{Days in receivables} = \frac{\text{days per year}}{\text{receivables turnover}} = \frac{365}{6}$$

$$\text{Days in payables} = \frac{\text{days per year}}{\text{accounts payables turnover}} = \frac{365}{10}$$

a. $$\text{Operating cycle} = \frac{\text{Days in}}{\text{Inventory}} + \frac{\text{Days in}}{\text{Receivables}} = \frac{365}{4} + \frac{365}{6} = 152.1 \text{ days}$$

b. $$\text{Cash cycle} = \text{operating cycle} - \frac{\text{Days in}}{\text{Payables}} = 152.1 - \frac{365}{10} = 115.6 \text{ days}$$

26.6   a.   The operating cycle begins when inventory stock arrives at a firm and ends when cash is collected from receivables. The operating cycle is also the sum of the cash cycle and the accounts payable period.

   b.   The cash cycle begins when cash is paid for materials and ends when cash is collected from receivables. The cash cycle is the time between cash disbursement and cash collection.

   c.   The accounts payable period is the length of time the firm is able to delay payment on the purchase of manufacturing resources.

26.7		**Cash cycle**	**Operating cycle**
	a.	Decrease	No change
	b.	No change	Decrease
	c.	Increase	No change
	d.	Decrease	Decrease
	e.	Increase	Increase
	f.	Decrease	Decrease

26.8   a.   A flexible short-term financing policy maintains a high ratio of current assets to sales. The policy includes limited use of short-term debt and heavy reliance on long-term debt.

       b.   A restrictive short-term financing policy entails a low ratio of current assets to sales. This policy relies upon the use of short-term liabilities.

       c.   If carrying costs are low and/or shortage costs are high, a flexible short-term financing policy is optimal.

       d.   If carrying costs are high and/or shortage costs are low, a restrictive short-term financing policy is optimal.

26.9   Shortage costs are those costs incurred by a firm when its investment in current assets is low. These costs are of two types.

       i.   Trading or order costs. Order costs are the costs of placing an order for more cash or more inventory.

       ii.   Costs related to safety reserves. These costs include lost sales, lost customer goodwill and disruption of production schedules.

26.10   a.   The current assets of Cleveland Compressor are financed largely by retained earnings. From 20X1 to 20X2, total current assets grew by $7,212. Only $2,126 of this increase was financed by the growth of current liabilities. Pnew York Pneumatic's current assets are largely financed by current liabilities. Bank loans are the most important of these current liabilities. They grew $3,077 to finance an increase in current assets of $8,333.

       b.   Cleveland Compressor holds the larger investment in current assets. It has current assets of $92,616 while Pnew York Pneumatic has $78,434 in current assets. The main reason for the difference is the larger sales of Cleveland Compressor.

26.10   (continued)

    c.   Cleveland Compressor is more likely to incur shortage costs because the ratio of current assets to sales is 0.57. That ratio for Pnew York Pneumatic is 0.86. Similarly, Pnew York Pneumatic is incurring more carrying costs for the same reason, a higher ratio of current assets to sales.

26.11   A long-term growth trend in sales will require some permanent investment in current assets. Thus, in the real world, net working capital is not zero. Also, the variation across time for assets means that net working capital is unlikely to be zero at any point in time.

26.12   a.   To solve this problem you must assume that all sales are on credit and the remaining 30% of credit sales (100% - 30% - 40%) are never collected. They are bad debts that are written off the books.

Let S be the sales in December. 30% of S will be collected in December and 40% of S will be collected in January. You are told that the balance of Account Receivables at the end of December is $36,000, and $30,000 of that amount is uncollected December sales.

Since 30% of December sales are collected in December, that $30,000 must be 70% of December sales:

$$0.7S = \$30,000$$
$$S = \$42,857$$

    b.

	December	January	February	March
Credit sales	$42,875	$90,000	$100,000	$120,000
Collections of current month	.3(42875) =12,875	.3(90000) =27,000	.3(100000) =30,000	.3(120000) =36,000
Collections of previous month		.4(42875) =17,143	.4(90000) =36,000	.4(100000) =40,000

January: $27,000 + $17,143 = $44,143
February: $30,000 + $36,000 = $66,000
March: $36,000 + $40,000 = $76,000

26.13

Quarter	1	2	3	4
Sales (basic trend), millions	100	120	144	172.8
Seasonal adjustments	0	-10	-5	15
Sales projections	100	110	139	187.8
Collection within month	30	33	41.7	56.34
30% of current month adj sales				
Collection next month		50	55	69.5
50% of previous month adj sales				
Cash Collection from Sales		83	96.7	125.84

26.14 First find the total collections of each month of the quarter:

Credit sales and Collections
Second Quarter, 20X5

	March	April	May	June
Credit sales	$180,000	$160,000	$140,000	$192,000
Collections of current month 50% of current sales		80,000	70,000	96,000
Collections of previous month 40% of previous sales		72,000	64,000	56,000
Total Collections		$152,000	$134,000	$152,000

Now, apply those data with those provided in the problem to complete the cash budget:

Cash Budget
Second Quarter, 20X5

	April	May	June
Beginning cash balance	$200,000	$226,000	$282,000
Cash receipts:			
Collections	152,000	134,000	152,000
Total cash available	$352,000	$360,000	$434,000
Cash disbursements:			
Pay credit purchases	$65,000	$68,000	$64,000
Wages, taxes, expenses	8,000	7,000	8,400
Interest	3,000	3,000	3,000
Equipment purchases	50,000	0	4,000
Total cash disbursed	$126,000	$78,000	$79,400
Ending cash balance	$226,000	$282,000	$354,600

26.15   The considerations in determining the most appropriate amount of short-term borrowing are:

i.   Cash reserves. Flexible financing strategy can reduce financial distress possibility, but it may reduce the return on equity.

ii.   Maturity hedging. Financing long-term assets with short-term borrowing is inherently risky as the short-term interest rate is more volatile.

iii.   Term structure. On average, long-term borrowing is more costly than short-term borrowing.

26.16   Short-term external financing options include:

i.   unsecured loans that can be either committed or uncommitted lines of credit.

ii.   secured loans that include blanket inventory lien, trust receipt, field-warehouse financing etc.

iii.   other sources like banker's acceptances, commercial paper, ..., etc.

Chapter 27: Cash Management

27.1   Firms need to hold cash to:

   a.   Satisfy the transaction needs. For example, cash is collected from sales and new financing and disbursed as wages, salaries, trade debts, taxes and dividends.

   b.   Maintain compensating balances. A minimum required compensating balance at banks providing credit service to the firm may impose a lower limit on the level of cash a firm holds.

27.2   a.   Decrease. Examine the Baumol model. As the interest rate (k) increases, the optimal cash balance must also decrease.

   b.   Increase. Examine the Baumol model. As brokerage costs (F, the per transaction costs) rise, the optimal balance increases.

   c.   Decrease. Clearly, if the bank lowers its compensating balance requirement, a firm will not be required to hold as much of its assets as cash (assuming that the firm's cash need for the transaction motive is below the compensating balance requirement).

   d.   Decrease. If the cost of borrowing falls, a firm need not hold as much of its assets as cash because the cost of running short (borrowing to fill cash needs) is lower.

   e.   Increase. As a firm's credit rating falls, its cost to borrow increases. Thus, the firm cannot as easily afford to run short of cash and its cash balance must be higher.

   f.   Increase. Introduction of direct banking fees would increase the fixed costs associated with holding cash. As fixed costs rise, the optimal balance must also rise.

27.3   In order to determine weekly earnings (sometimes the word "return" is used to mean dollar amounts) on the cash balances, first find the weekly interest rate

$$r = \frac{.12}{52} = .002308$$

and apply this to each of the weekly amounts:

Week	Avg Cash Balance	$ Earned
1	24,000	55.39
2	34,000	78.47
3	10,000	23.08
4	15,000	34.62
Avg monthly	83,000	191.56

Average annual earnings = 191.56 x 12 = $2,298.72

Note: this assumes interest is not compounded. The question does not specify what compounding assumptions should be made.

27.4   **a.**   The total amount of cash that will be disbursed during the year is:

$$\$345,000 * 12 = \$4,140,000$$

Using the optimal cash balance formula from the Baumol model,

$$C^* = \sqrt{\frac{2FT}{K}} = \sqrt{\frac{2(\$500)(4,140,000)}{0.07}} = \$243,193$$

$243,193 should be kept as cash. The balance, $556,807 (=$800,000-$243,193), should be invested in marketable securities.

b.   The number of times marketable securities will be sold during the next twelve months is $4,140,000 / $243,193 = 17 times

27.5   Start with the Baumol model and solve for Total Costs, T:

$$C^* = \sqrt{\frac{2FT}{K}}$$

$$\left(C^*\right)^2 = \frac{2FT}{K}$$

$$T = \frac{KC^{*2}}{2F}$$

$$= \frac{.075 \times (20 \text{ million})^2}{2 \times 5,000}$$

$$= \$3,000 \text{ million}$$

$$\text{Average weekly disbursement} = \frac{3,000 \text{ million}}{52}$$

$$= \$57.69 \text{ million}$$

27.6   Use the Miller-Orr formula.

The target cash balance = $Z^* = \sqrt[3]{\frac{3F\sigma^2}{4K}} + L$

The upper limit = H*=3Z*-2L

The daily opportunity cost = $K = \sqrt[365]{1.08} - 1 = 0.000211$

$$Z^* = \sqrt[3]{\frac{3(\$600)(\$1,440,000)}{4(0.000211)}} + \$20,000$$

$$= \$34,536$$

$$H^* = 3(34,536) - 2(20,000)$$

$$= 63,608$$

The target cash level is $34,536, and the upper limit is $63,608.

27.7 a. Since the upper limit, H*, is set by the firms, use that to find Z*:

$$H^* = 3Z^* - 2L$$

$$Z^* = \frac{H^* - 2L}{3}$$

Then,

$$Z_{Gold}^* = \frac{H_g + 2L_g}{3} = \frac{200,000 + 2 \times 100,000}{3} = \$133,333$$

$$Z_{Silver}^* = \frac{H_s + 2L_s}{3} = \frac{300,000 + 2 \times 150,000}{3} = \$200,000$$

b. Use the Miller/Orr equation for Z*, and solve for variance, σ^2:

$$Z^* = \sqrt[3]{\frac{3F\sigma^2}{4K}} + L$$

$$(Z^*)^3 = \frac{3F\sigma^2}{4K} + L^3$$

$$(Z^* - L)^3 = \frac{3F\sigma^2}{4K}$$

$$\sigma^2 = \frac{(Z^* - L)^3 \, 4K}{3F}$$

Now, find the variance for Gold Star:

$$K_G = \sqrt[365]{1.10} - 1 = 0.000261$$

$$\sigma_G^2 = (Z_G^* - L_G)^3 \, 4K_G/3F_G = \frac{(133,333 - 100,000)^3 \times 4 \times 0.000261}{3 \times 2,000} \approx 6,444,251$$

and Silver Star:

$$K_S = \sqrt[365]{1.09} - 1 = 0.000236$$

$$\sigma_S^2 = (Z_S^* - L_S)^3 \, 4K_S/3F_S = \frac{(200,000 - 150,000)^3 \times 4 \times 0.000236}{3 \times 2,000} \approx 15,733,333$$

So, Silver Star Co. has a more volatile daily cash flow.

27.8 Compare the cost and benefit of a lockbox:

Benefit of Lockbox:

Garden Groves daily float = 150 payments per day x $15,000 avg payment
= $2,250,000

27.8   (continued)

Increase in collected cash balance if a 3 day lockbox is installed
$$= 3 \ \times \ \$2,250,000$$
$$= \$6,750,000$$

Since this is a sustained increase in the cash balance, find the annual earnings from this increase if invested in money-market securities:

Annual earnings $= \$6,750,000 \times 0.075$
                      $= \$506,250$

Cost of Lockbox:

Variable cost $\$ 0.5 \times 150 \times 365 = \$27,375$
Fixed cost $= \underline{\ \ 80,000}$
Total cost $= \$107,375$

Net benefit of the lockbox $=$ Benefit - Cost
                                 $= \$506,250 \ - \ \$107,375$
                                 $= \$398,875$

The lockbox system should be installed.

27.9   To make the system profitable, the net earnings of installing the lockbox system must be non-negative. The lower limit for acceptability is zero profits.

Let N = number of customers per day, and write the benefit and cost of the lock box in terms of N:

Earnings = ($\$4,500$) (N) (2) (0.06) = $\$540 \times N$

Costs: Total Cost $=$ Variable Cost $+$ Fixed Cost

        Variable cost $=$ N (365) ($\$0.25$) $= \$91.25 \times N$
        Fixed cost $= \$15,000$
        Total cost $= 91.25 \ N \ + \ 15,000$

Then, set Earnings $=$ Total Cost, and solve for N:

   540 N $= \ 15,000 \ + 91.25 \ N$

      $N = 33.43$

Salisbury Stakes needs at least 34 customers per day for the lockbox system to be profitable.

27.10   Disbursement float   = avg daily pymts x avg days to clear
                              = $12,000 x 5
                              = $60,000

         Collection float   = avg pymt x availability time
                              = -$15,000 x 3
                              = -$45,000

         Net float   = disbursement float - collection float
                              = $60,000 - $45,000
                              = $15,000

If funds are collected in four days rather than three, disbursement float will not change. Collection float would change to -15,000 x 4 = -$60,000. This change would make the net float equal to zero.

27.11   a.   Reduction in outstanding cash balances = $100,000 x 3 days = $300,000

         b.   Return on savings = $300,000 (0.12) = $36,000

         c.   Maximum monthly charge = $36,000 / 12 = $3,000

27.12   The cash savings are the earnings from the interest bearing account that otherwise would not have been received.

         The $ Return on the delayed payment is (ignoring compounding)

         $$\$R = 200,000\left[.0004(3)\right]$$
         $$= \$240$$

         Since the disbursements occur every 2 weeks:

         Annual savings   = 240 x 26
                           = $6,240

         The Walter Company will save $6,240 per year.

27.13   If the Miller Company divides the eastern region, collections will be accelerated by one day freeing up $4 million per day. Compensating balances will be increased by $100,000 [=2($300,000)-$500,000]. The net effect is to have $3,900,000 to invest.

         If T-bills pay 7% per year, the annual net savings from the division of the eastern region is

         $3,900,000 x 0.07 = $273,000.

         Therefore, Miller should divide the Eastern Region.

27.14   **Lockbox Benefit**

daily float   = 7,500 x 250
                  = $1,875,000

increased cash = 1.5 days x $1,875,000
                  = $2,812,500

daily Interest   = 2,812,500 x .0003
                  = $843.75

annual interest = 843.75 x 365
                  = $307,968.75

Lockbox Cost: = 30,000 + .3 x 250 pymts x 365 days
                         = $57,375

Net Benefit of Lockbox = Benefit - Cost
                         = 307,986.75 - 57,375
                         = $250,593.75

Concentration Banking:

daily float   = 1,875,000

increased cash = 1 day x $1,875,000 = $1,875,000

daily interest   = 1,875,000 x .0003 = 562.50

annual interest = 562.50 x 365 = $205,312.50

Since there is no other additional cost for Concentration Banking, compare:

205,312.50: net benefit of concentration
250,593.75: net benefit of lockbox

So the lockbox system is recommended.

27.15   The important characteristics of short-term marketable securities are:

i.   maturity

ii.   default risk

iii.   marketability

iv.   taxability

Chapter 28: Credit Management

28.1   North County Publishing Company should adopt the new credit policy if its PV, PV (New), is greater than the PV of the current policy, PV (Old).

Note that we can write the general formula as:

$$PV(policy) = \frac{(avg\ sales)(1 - credit\ policy\ discount)}{1+\left\{(corporate\ discount\ rate)\left(\dfrac{avg\ days\ to\ pay}{days\ in\ year}\right)\right\}}$$

First, find the PV of the current (old) policy:

$$PV(Old) = \frac{\$10,000,000/365}{1+0.1(60/365)} = \$26,954.18$$

Now, find the PV(New):

Under the new policy, we expect 2 groups of customers -- a) those that take the discount and pay early, and b) those that do not take the discount and pay "late" (we will ignore those customers who take the discount and still pay late).

Since we are only given the average collection for *all* customers, we need to find the average collection period for each group. For those who take the discount, we will assume they pay on day 10.

Let T = the average number of days until payment for those customers who do not take the discount, and using the information given in the problem:

$$0.5\ (10\ days) + 0.5\ (T) = 30\ days$$
$$T = 50\ days$$

Now apply this to our general formula for PV, allowing for the fact that we have two kinds of customers:

$$PV(New) = PV(from\ customers\ who\ take\ the\ discount) + PV(those\ who\ don't)$$

$$=\left\{\frac{0.5\left(\dfrac{\$10,000,000}{365}\right)(0.98)}{1+0.1\left(\dfrac{10}{365}\right)}\right\} + \left\{\frac{0.5\left(\dfrac{\$10,000,000}{365}\right)}{1+0.1\left(\dfrac{50}{365}\right)}\right\}$$

$$= \$26,901.49$$

Because PV(Old) > PV(New), North County Publishing should not adopt the new policy.

28.1 (continued)

Notice that the decision is independent of the level of credit sales, since you can factor out the level of sales:.

$$PV(Old) = \left(\frac{\$10,000,000}{365}\right)\left\{\frac{1}{1+0.1\left(\frac{60}{365}\right)}\right\}$$

$$PV(New) = \left(\frac{\$10,000,000}{365}\right)\left\{\frac{0.5(0.98)}{1+0.1\left(\frac{10}{365}\right)} + \frac{0.5}{1+0.1\left(\frac{50}{365}\right)}\right\}$$

Since we are only interested in the *comparative value* of these PVs and we have the same constant as the first term in both equations, we can remove it and rewrite them as:

$$PV(Old) = \frac{1}{1+0.1\left(\frac{60}{365}\right)} = 0.9836$$

$$PV(New) = \frac{0.5(0.98)}{1+0.1\left(\frac{10}{365}\right)} + \frac{0.5}{1+0.1\left(\frac{50}{365}\right)} = .9819$$

Although the PV numbers are different, we still have PV(Old) > PV(New) and we get the same decision -- choose the Old policy.

28.2 If the credit terms are net 45 and accounts are 45 days past due on average, the average collection period is 90 days. Accounts receivable are

$$\frac{90 \text{ days}}{365 \text{ days}}(\$5,000,000) = \$1,232,876.71$$

28.3　The Tropeland Company should adopt the new credit policy if its PV, PV (New), is greater than the PV of the current policy, PV (Old).

Note that we can write the general formula as:

$$PV(\text{policy}) = \frac{(\text{avg sales})(1 - \text{credit policy discount})}{1 + \left\{(\text{corporate discount rate})\left(\dfrac{\text{avg days to pay}}{\text{days in year}}\right)\right\}}$$

First, find the PV of the current (old) policy:

$$PV(\text{Old}) = \frac{\$30{,}000{,}000/365}{1 + 0.12(60/365)} = \$80{,}601.83$$

Now, find the PV(New):

Under the new policy, we expect 2 groups of customers -- a) those that take the discount and pay early, and b) those that do not take the discount and pay "late" (we will ignore those customers who take the discount and still pay late).

Since we are only given the average collection for *all* customers, we need to find the average collection period for each group. For those who take the discount, we will assume they pay on day 10.

Let T = the average number of days until payment for those customers who do not take the discount, and using the information given in the problem:

$$0.5\,(10 \text{ days}) + 0.5\,(T) = 30 \text{ days}$$
$$T = 50 \text{ days}$$

Now apply this to our general formula for PV, allowing for the fact that we have two kinds of customers:

$$PV(\text{New}) = PV(\text{from customers who take the discount}) + PV(\text{those who don't})$$

$$= \left\{\frac{0.5\left(\dfrac{\$30{,}000{,}000}{365}\right)(0.96)}{1 + 0.12\left(\dfrac{10}{365}\right)}\right\} + \left\{\frac{0.5\left(\dfrac{\$30{,}000{,}000}{365}\right)}{1 + 0.12\left(\dfrac{50}{365}\right)}\right\}$$

$$= \$79{,}754.04$$

Because PV(Old) > PV(New), Tropeland should not adopt the new policy.

28.3 (continued)

Notice that the decision is independent of the level of credit sales, since you can factor out the level of sales:.

$$PV(Old) = \left(\frac{\$30,000,000}{365}\right)\left\{\frac{1}{1+0.12\left(\frac{60}{365}\right)}\right\}$$

$$PV(New) = \left(\frac{\$30,000,000}{365}\right)\left\{\frac{0.5(0.98)}{1+0.12\left(\frac{10}{365}\right)} + \frac{0.5}{1+0.12\left(\frac{50}{365}\right)}\right\}$$

Since we are only interested in the *comparative value* of these PVs and we have the same constant as the first term in both equations, we can remove it and rewrite them as:

$$PV(Old) = \frac{1}{1+0.12\left(\frac{60}{365}\right)} = 0.9804$$

$$PV(New) = \frac{0.5(0.98)}{1+0.12\left(\frac{10}{365}\right)} + \frac{0.5}{1+0.12\left(\frac{50}{365}\right)} = .9703$$

Although the PV numbers are different, we still have PV(Old) > PV(New) and we get the same decision -- choose the Old policy.

28.4 a. A firm should offer credit if the NPV of offering credit is greater than the NPV of the firm's current, no-credit policy.

Under the no-credit policy:

$$NPV = NCF_0 = (P_0 - C_0)\, Q_0$$

NPV(Current policy) = ($35 - $25)(2,000) = $20,000

Under the credit policy:

Let h = Probability of payment under the credit policy

NPV = PV(pymts received) - cost(units produced)

$$= \frac{h(P_0)(Q_0)}{1+r} - C_0 Q_0$$

28.4   (continued)

$$\text{NPV(Credit policy)} = \frac{(0.85)(\$40)(3,000)}{1.03} - (\$32)(3,000) = \$3,029.13$$

Since NPV(current) > NPV(credit policy), Berkshire should not offer credit to its customers.

b.   Berkshire will be indifferent if the NPV of the current policy equals the NPV of the credit policy. Set the equations in part (a) equal. Then solve for h (probability of payment under the credit policy):

$$\$20,000 = \frac{(h)(\$40)(3,000)}{1.03} - (\$32)(3,000)$$

$$h = 0.9957 = 99.57\%$$

Berkshire should offer its customers a credit plan if the probability that they will pay is greater than 99.57%.

28.5   Offering a credit policy is attractive if the NPV of the credit policy is greater than the NPV of the current, no-credit policy.

Under the no-credit policy:

$$NPV = NCF_0 = (P_0 - C_0)\, Q_0$$

$$\text{NPV(Current policy)} = (\$48 - \$43)(750) = \$3,750$$

Under the credit policy:

Let P = Price that would make Theodore Bruin Company indifferent.

$$NPV = PV(\text{pymts received}) - cost(\text{units produced})$$

$$= \frac{h(P_0)(Q_0)}{1+r} - C_0 Q_0$$

$$\text{NPV(Credit policy)} = \frac{(0.92)(P)(1,000)}{1.027} - (\$45)(1,000)$$

Set the NPVs equal, and solve for P:

$$\$3,750 = \frac{(0.92)(P)(1,000)}{1.027} - (\$45)(1,000)$$

$$P = \$54.42$$

The new price per unit must be greater than $54.42. Thus, the price must increase at least $6.42 (=$54.42-$48).

28.6   Fast Typing should offer credit if the NPV of offering credit is greater than the NPV of the firm's current, no-credit policy.

Under the no-credit policy:

$$NPV = NCF_0 = (P_0 - C_0)\, Q_0$$

NPV(Current policy) = ($900 - $600)(5,000) = $1,500,000

Under the credit policy:

Let h = Probability of payment under the credit policy

NPV = PV(pymts received) - cost(units produced)

$$= \frac{h(P_0)(Q_0)}{1+r} - C_0 Q_0$$

$$NPV(\text{Credit policy}) = \frac{h(\$900)(9,000)}{1.015} - (\$650)(9,000)$$

Set the NPVs equal, and solve for h:

$$\$1,500,000 = \frac{h(\$900)(9,000)}{1.015} - (\$650)(9,000)$$

$$h = .9210$$

If the probability of payment is greater than 92.10%, Fast Typing should offer credit.

28.7   If the cost of subscribing to the credit agency is less than the savings from collection of the bad debts, Silver Spokes Bicycle Shop should subscribe.

Cost of the subscription = $500 + $4(300) = $1,700

Savings from not selling to bad credit risks = ($240)(300)(0.05) = $3,600

Silver Spokes should subscribe to the collection agency.
The shop's net savings are $1,900 (= $3,600 - $1,700).

28.8   In principle, the optimal credit policy occurs at the minimum total-credit-cost point. Total credit cost is the sum of carrying costs (the costs associated with granting credit and making an investment in receivables), and the opportunity costs (the lost sales from refusing to offer credit). In perfect financial market, there's no optimal credit policy. In imperfect financial markets, taxes, bankruptcy costs and agency costs are factors that can influence the optimal credit policy.

28.9   The information commonly used to assess credit-worthiness include:
        i.   financial statements
        ii. credit reports on customers' payment history with other firms
        iii. banks
        iv. the customers' payment history with the firm.

28.10   The average collection period is the weighted average of collection period for
        customers who take the discount, and those customers who do not:

$$\text{Average collection period} = 0.4(15) + 0.6(40) = 30 \text{ days}$$

$$\text{Average daily sales} = 85,000 \times \$55 \, / \, 365 = \$12,808.22$$

Then, total accounts receivables is 30 days' worth of daily sales:

$$\text{Accounts receivable} = 30 \times \$12,808.22 = \$384.247$$

The new credit terms will increase the number of customers who take the discount.
As a result, the average collection period will decrease. The drop in the collection
period will cause the investment in account receivable to decrease.

28.11   If $600,000 is the average monthly sales, the average investment in account
        receivable is

$$\frac{\$600,000 \times 90}{30} = \$1,800,000$$

28.12   Because of the fixed cost of $400,000, we must first find the profit per unit:

$$PV(\text{Gross Revenue}) = \frac{1,500 \times (1 - .02)}{1 + .10\left(\dfrac{30}{365}\right)}$$

$$= \$1458.02$$

$$\text{Cost} = 1,500 \, (1 - .04)$$
$$= \$1440$$

$$\text{Per unit revenue} = \text{Gross Revenue - Cost}$$
$$= 1458 - 1440$$
$$= \$18$$

$$\text{Gross profit} = (100,000 \times \$18) - 400,000$$
$$= \$1,400,000$$

Chapter 29: Mergers and Acquisitions

29.1   The salient point here is that both firms are shown at market value. Therefore, Lager is paying 300,000 for an asset valued at 200,000 (the total value of Philadelphia Pretzel shown on the balance sheet). The merger creates $100,000 of goodwill (300,000 - 200,000).

Balance Sheet
Lager Brewing
(in $ thousands)

Current assets	$480	Current liabilities	$200
Other assets	140	Long-term debt	400
Net fixed assets	580	Equity	700
Goodwill	100		
Total assets	$1,300	Total liabilities	$1,300

29.2   In this problem, Lager is paying 300,000 for an asset worth 240,000. Since the balance sheet for Philadelphia Pretzel shows assets at book value instead of market value, the goodwill will be only $60,000 (=$300,000 - $240,000). Thus, the net fixed assets are $620,000 (=$1,300,000 - $480,000 - $140,000 - $60,000).

Balance Sheet
Lager Brewing
(in $ thousands)

Current assets	$480	Current liabilities	$200
Other assets	140	Long-term debt	400
Net fixed assets	620	Equity	700
Goodwill	60		
Total assets	$1,300	Total liabilities	$1,300

29.3   Now, they will use the pooling-of-interests method, so the assets are carried at the pre-merger levels, and the aggregate value of the two firms is unchanged by the merger.

Balance Sheet
Lager Brewing
(in $ thousands)

Current assets	$480	Current liabilities	$280
Other assets	140	Long-term debt	100
Net fixed assets	580	Equity	820
Total assets	$1,200	Total liabilities	$1,200

29.4   a.   False. Although the reasoning seems correct, the Stillman-Eckbo data do not support the monopoly power theory.

b.   True. When managers act in their own interest, acquisitions are an important control device for shareholders. It appears that some acquisitions and takeovers are the consequence of underlying conflicts between managers and shareholders.

c.   False. Even if markets are efficient, the presence of synergy will make the value of the combined firm different from the sum of the values of the separate firms. Incremental cash flows provide the positive NPV of the transaction.

d.   False. In an efficient market, traders will value takeovers based on "Fundamental factors" regardless of the time horizon. Recall that the evidence as a whole suggests efficiency in the markets. Mergers should be no different.

e.   False. The tax effect of an acquisition depends on whether the merger is taxable or non-taxable. In a taxable merger, there are two opposing factors to consider, the capital gains effect and the write-up effect. The net effect is the sum of these two effects.

f.   True. Because of the coinsurance effect, wealth might be transferred from the stockholders to the bondholders. Acquisition analysis usually disregards this effect and considers only the total value.

29.5   Recall that the PV of a perpetuity is found as

$$PV = \frac{CF}{i}$$

where CF is the cash flow received yearly and i is the annual discount rate.

So, for Small Fry, the value is found as

$$\text{Value} = \frac{8}{.16} = 50$$

When the rate is the unknown, solve for i. So, for the Benefits from acquisition:

$$42.5 = \frac{5}{i}$$

$$i = \frac{5}{42.5} = .1176$$

Similar for all but the last entry.

29.5   (continued)

For the final entry, first sum the component values, then use that to solve for the rate:

$$\text{Value}_{\text{Whale-Fry}} = \text{Value}_{\text{SmallFry}} + \text{Value}_{\text{Whale}} + \text{Value}_{\text{Benefits from Acquisition}}$$
$$= 50 + 250 + 42.5$$
$$= 292.5$$

$$292.5 = \frac{33}{i}$$
$$i = .1128$$

Now, apply the same techniques to fill-in the remaining numbers:

(in $ millions)	Net Cash Flow Per Year (Perpetual)	Discount Rate (%)	Value
Small Fry	8	16%	50
Whale	20	10%	200
Benefits from Acquisition:	5	11.76%	42.5
Revenue Enhancement	2.5	20%	12.5
Cost Reduction	2	10%	20
Tax Shelters	0.5	5%	10
Whale-Fry	$33	11.28%	$292.5

Per share price = ($292.5-100)/5 = $38.5

29.6   a.   To find the distribution of joint values, we first must find the joint probabilities.

First, find the joint probabilities for each possible combination of weather in the two towns. The weather conditions are independent, therefore, the joint probabilities are the products of the individual probabilities.

Possible states	Joint probability
Rain Rain	0.1 x 0.1=0.01
Rain Warm	0.1 x 0.4=0.04
Rain Hot	0.1 x 0.5=0.05
Warm Rain	0.4 x 0.1=0.04
Warm Warm	0.4 x 0.4=0.16
Warm Hot	0.4 x 0.5=0.20
Hot Rain	0.5 x 0.1=0.05
Hot Warm	0.5 x 0.4=0.20
Hot Hot	0.5 x 0.5=0.25

Next, note that the revenue when rainy is the same regardless of which town. So, since the state "Rain - Warm" has the same outcome (revenue) as "Warm - Rain", their probabilities can be added. The same is true of "Rain - Hot" / "Hot - Rain" and "Warm - Hot" / "Hot - Warm". Thus the joint probabilities are

29.6 (continued)

Possible states	Joint probability
Rain Rain	0.01
Rain Warm	0.08
Rain Hot	0.10
Warm Warm	0.16
Warm Hot	0.40
Hot Hot	0.25

Finally, the joint values are the sums of the values of the two companies for the particular state.

Possible states		Joint value
Rain Rain	100,000 + 100,000	$200,000
Rain Warm	100,000 + 200,000	300,000
Warm Warm	200,000 + 200,000	400,000
Rain Hot	100,000 + 400,000	500,000
Warm Hot	200,000 + 400,000	600,000
Hot Hot	400,000 + 400,000	800,000

b. Recall, if a firm cannot service its debt, the bondholders receive the value of the assets. Thus, the value of the debt is the value of the company if the face value of the debt is greater than the value of the company. If the value of the company is greater than the value of the debt, the value of the debt is its face value. Here the value of the common stock is always the residual value of the firm over the value of the debt.

Joint Prob.	Joint Value	Debt Value	Stock Value
0.01	$200,000	$200,000	$0
0.08	300,000	300,000	0
0.16	400,000	400,000	0
0.10	500,000	400,000	100,000
0.40	600,000	400,000	200,000
0.25	800,000	400,000	400,000

c. To show that the value of the combined firm is the sum of the individual values, you must show that the expected joint value is equal to the sum of the separate expected values.

$$\text{Expected joint value} = 0.01(\$200,000) + 0.08(\$300,000) + 0.16(\$400,000) +$$
$$0.10(\$500,000) + 0.40(\$600,000) + 0.25(\$800,000)$$
$$= \$580,000$$

29.6   (continued)

Since the firms are identical, the sum of the expected values should be twice the expected value of either.

Expected individual value $= 0.1(\$100,000) + 0.4(\$200,000) + 0.5(\$400,000)$
$$= \$290,000$$

Expected combined value $= 2\ (\$290,000) = \$580,000$
which is the same as the expected joint value

d.   The bondholders are better off if the value of the debt after the merger is greater than the value of the debt before the merger.

Value of the debt before the merger:

debt value, either company $= 0.1(\$100,000) + 0.4(\$200,000) + 0.5(\$200,000)$
$$= \$190,000$$

Total debt value, pre-merger $= 2(\$190,000)$
$$= \$380,000$$

To get the expected debt value, post-merger, find the weighted average of the debt values under the 6 possible states:

debt value, post-merger $= 0.01(\$200,000) + 0.08(\$300,000) + 0.16(\$400,000)$
$$+ 0.10(\$400,000) + 0.40(\$400,000) + 0.25(\$400,000)$$
$$= \$390,000$$

The bondholders are $10,000 better off after the merger.

29.7   The decision hinges upon the risk of surviving. That is, consider the wealth transfer from bondholders to stockholders when risky projects are undertaken. High-risk projects will reduce the expected value of the bondholders' claims on the firm. The telecommunications business is riskier than the utilities business.

If the total value of the firm does not change, the increase in risk should favor the stockholder. Hence, management should approve this transaction.

If the total value of the firm drops because of the transaction, and the wealth effect is lower than the reduction in total value, management should reject the project.

29.8   If the market is "smart," the P/E ratio will not be constant.

a.   Value = $2,500 + $1,000 = $3,500

b.   EPS   = Post-merger earnings / Total number of shares
               =($100 + $100)/200 =$1

c.   Price per share = Value/Total number of shares
                          =$3,500/200 =$17.50

d.   If the market is "fooled," the P/E ratio will be constant at 25.

    EPS   = Post-merger earnings / Total number of shares

                 = $200/200 = $1.00

    Price   = P/E * EPS = 25 * $1 = $25

    Value   = Post-merger Price * Total number of shares

                 = $25 * 200 = $5,000

29.9   a.   After the merger, Arcadia Financial will have 130,000 [=10,000 + (50,000)(6/10)] shares outstanding. The earnings of the combined firm will be $325,000. The earnings per share of the combined firm will be $2.50 (=$325,000/130,000). The acquisition will increase the EPS for the stockholders from $2.25 to $2.50.

b.   There will be no effect on the original Arcadia stockholders. No synergies exist in this merger since Arcadia is buying Coldran at its market price. Examining the relative values of the two firms demonstrates this.

First, find the pre-merger stock prices:

$$\text{Share price of Arcadia} = \frac{(16 * \$225,000)}{100,000}$$

$$= \$36$$

$$\text{Share price of Coldran} = \frac{(10.8 * \$100,000)}{50,000}$$

$$= \$21.60$$

Now, compare the relative value of these prices: $21.6/$36 = 0.6.

Since the problem states that Coldran's shareholders receive 0.6 shares of Arcadia for every share of Coldran, no synergies exist.

29.10 a. The synergy will be the present value of the incremental cash flows of the proposed purchase. Since the cash flows are perpetual, this amount is

$$\frac{\$600,000}{0.08} = \$7,500,000$$

b. The value of Flash-in-the-Pan to Fly-by-Night is the synergy plus the current market value of Flash-in-the-Pan.

$$V = \$7,500,000 + \$20,000,000$$
$$= \$27,500,000$$

c. The value of each alternative is:

Cash alternative $= \$15,000,000$

Stock alternative $= 0.25\ (\$27,500,000 + \$35,000,000)$
$$= \$15,625,000$$

d. Since these values are already in PV terms, the NPVs are simply Value - Cost:

NPV of cash alternative $= \$27,500,000\ -\ \$15,000,000$
$$= \$12,500,000$$

NPV of stock alternative $= \$27,500,000\ -\ \$15,625,000$
$$= \$11,875,000$$

e. Use the cash alternative, because its NPV is greater.

29.11 a. The value of Portland Industries before the merger is $9,000,000 (=750,000x12).

Recall that the discounted value of CF's growing at a constant rate is given by

$$PV = \frac{CF(1+g)}{r\text{-}g}$$

where r is the risk-adjusted discount, and g is the growth rate.
We can use this to determine the effect of the changed growth rate, but first we must find the value of r for Portland:

Since the value of Portland is also the value of the expected future dividends, we can write using the above :

$$\$9,000,000 = \frac{\$1.80*250,000*1.05}{(r-0.05)}$$

and solving for r, find r = 0.1025

Then, applying the new growth rate, find the value of Portland Industries after the merger is

29.11   (continued)

$$Value = \frac{(\$1.80 * 250,000)1.07}{(0.1025 - 0.07)}$$
$$= \$14,815,385$$

This is the value of Portland Industries to Freeport.

b.   NPV   = Gain - Cost
         = Value of Portland - (Price * #shares)
         = $14,815,385 - ($40 * 250, 000)
         = $ 4,815,385

c.   If Freeport offers stock, the value of Portland Industries to Freeport is the same, but the cost differs:

Value of the combined firm =

(Value of Freeport before merger) + (Value of Portland to Freeport)

= $15 * 1,000,000 + $14,815,385
= $29,815,385

Cost = (Fraction of combined firm owned by Portland's stockholders)

* (Value of the combined firm)

$$Fraction\ of\ ownership = \frac{600,000}{1,000,000 + 600,000}$$
$$= 0.375$$

Cost = 0.375 * $29,815,385
       = $11,180,769
NPV = $14,815,385 - $11,180,769
       = $3,634,616

d.   From parts b & c, we have:

NPV(cash offer) = 4,815,385
NPV(stock offer) = 3,634,616

Therefore, the acquisition should be attempted with a cash offer since it provides a higher NPV.

29.11　　(continued)

e.　　Recalculate the value found in part a for Portland, with a revised growth of 6%, instead of 7%:

$$Value = \frac{(\$1.80*250,000)1.06}{(0.1025-0.06)}$$
$$= \$11,223,529$$

This is the revised value of Portland Industries to Freeport.

Then, the revised NPV(cash offer) :

NPV 　　　= Gain-Cost

　　　　=$11,223,529 - ($40x250,000)
　　　　=$1,223,529

Now find the revised NPV(stock offer):
As with the 7% version, if Freeport offers stock, the value of Portland Industries to Freeport is the same, but the cost differs.

Value of the combined firm =

(Value of Freeport before merger) + (Value of Portland to Freeport)

= $15 * 1,000,000 + $11,223,529
= $26,223,529

Cost = (Fraction of combined firm owned by Portland's stockholders)

　　　* (Value of the combined firm)

$$Fraction\ of\ ownership = \frac{600,000}{1,000,000+600,000}$$
$$= 0.375$$

$$Cost = 0.375*\$26,223,529$$
$$= \$9,833,823$$
$$NPV = \$11,223,529 - \$9,833,823$$
$$= \$1,389,706$$

So, now we have

$$NPV(cash\ offer) = 1,223,529$$
$$NPV(stock\ offer) = 1,389,706$$

The acquisition should be attempted with a stock offer since it provides a higher NPV.

29.12 a.   Number of shares after acquisition (in millions)
$$= 30 + 15 = 45$$

Stock price of Harrods after acquisition:

$$Price = \frac{value}{\# \ shares} = \frac{1,000}{45} = 22.22 \ pounds$$

b.   Let α = fraction of ownership. Then,

$\alpha * 1 \ billion = 300 \ million$

$\alpha = 30\%$

$$Fractional \ ownership = \frac{New \ Shares \ Issued}{New \ Shares \ Issued + Old \ Shares}$$

$$30\% = \frac{New \ Shares \ Issued}{New \ Shares \ Issued + 30 \ million}$$

New Shares Issued =12.86 million

So, the exchange ratio is $\dfrac{new \ shares}{shares \ in \ acquired \ firm} = \dfrac{12.86}{20} = .643$

which we can also write as 12.86 : 20 = 0.643 : 1

The proper exchange ratio should be 0.643 to make the stock offer's value to Selfridge equivalent to the cash offer.

29.13   To evaluate this proposal, look at the present value of the incremental cash flows.

First, using the information in the problem and in the table for cash projections for Company B, fill in the table of Cash Flows to Company A (in $ million)

Year	0	1	2	3	4	5
Acquisition of B	-550					
Dividends from B	150	32	5	20	30	45
Tax-loss carryforwards			25	25		
Terminal value						600
Total	-400	32	30	45	30	645

The additional cash flows from the tax-loss carry forwards and the proposed level of debt should be discounted at the cost of debt because they are determined with very little uncertainty.

The after-tax cash flows are subject to normal business risk and must be discounted at a normal rate.

$$\beta_{bond} = \frac{8\% - 6\%}{8\%}$$
$$= 0.25$$

29.13   (continued)

$$\beta_{company} = 0.25^2 + 1.25*0.75$$
$$= 1$$

Discount rate for normal operations:

$$r = 6\% + 8\% (1)$$
$$= 14\%$$

To find the discount rate for dividends:
The new beta coefficient for the company, 1, must be the weighted average of the debt beta and the stock beta.

$$\beta_{company} = weight_{debt} * \beta_{debt} + weight_{stock} * \beta_{stock}$$
$$1 = 0.5(0.25) + 0.5(\beta_{stock})$$

so, solving for β_{stock}
$$\beta_{stock} = 1.75$$

and now we have:

$$r = 6\% + 8\%(1.75) = 20\%$$

Putting all this together for the total NPV (in millions):

$$NPV = -\$400 + \frac{\$32}{1.2} + \frac{\$5}{(1.2)^2} + \frac{\$20}{(1.2)^3} + \frac{\$30}{(1.2)^4} + \frac{\$45}{(1.2)^5} + \frac{\$25}{(1.08)^2} + \frac{\$25}{(1.08)^3} + \frac{\$900}{(1.14)^5} - \frac{\$300}{(1.08)^5}$$

$$= -\$400 + \$26.67 + \$3.47 + \$11.57 + \$14.47 + \$18.08 + \$21.43 + \$19.85 + \$467.43 - \$204.17$$

$$= -\$21.2$$

Because the NPV of the acquisition is negative, Company A should not acquire Company B.

29.14   The commonly used defensive tactics by target-firm managers include:

i.   corporate charter amendments like super-majority amendment or staggering the election of board members.

ii.   repurchase standstill agreements.

iii.   exclusionary self-tenders.

iv.   going private and leveraged buyouts.

v.   other devices like golden parachutes, scorched earth strategy, poison pill, ..., etc.

Mini Case: U.S.Steel's case.

You have 3 choices: tender, or do not tender or sell in the market. If you do sell your shares in the market, at some point somebody else would need to make a decision to "tender" or "not tender" as well.

It is important to recognize that the firm has about 60 million shares outstanding (since 30 million shares will give US Steel 50.1% of Marathon shares).
Let's consider the possible selling prices, which you will receive for each of the following scenarios:

US Steel Tender offer

	Succeeds	Fails
Tender	A pro-rated Price between $125 and $85	Market price
Do not Tender	$85	Market price

If US Steel's tender offer fails, you are equally well off since your share value is determined by the market price.

If you choose not to tender, and 30 million shares were tendered, US Steel succeeds to gain 50.1% control, you will only receive $85 a share.
If you do tender, the price you will receive will be no worse than $85 a share and can be as high as $125 a share.

Depending on the number of shares tendered, you will receive one of the following prices.

If only 50.1% tendered, you will get $125 per share.

If the shares tendered exceed 50.1% but less than 100%, you will get more than $105 a share.

If all 60 million shares were tendered, you will get $105 per share:

$$\frac{30}{60}(\$125) + \frac{30}{60}(\$85)$$

It is clear that, in the above 3 cases, when you are not sure about whether US Steel will succeed or not, you will be better off to tender your shares than not tender. This is because at best, you will only receive $85 per share if you choose not to tender.

Chapter 30: Financial Distress

30.1   Financial distress is often linked to insolvency. Stock-based insolvency occurs when a firm has a negative net worth. Flow-based insolvency occurs when operating cash flow is insufficient to meet current obligations.

30.2   Financial distress frequently can serve as firm's "early warning" sign for trouble. Thus, it can be beneficial since it may bring about new organizational forms and new operating strategies.

30.3   Under the absolute priority rule (APR), claims are paid out in full to the extent there are assets. In this case, assets are $5,000, so you should propose the follows.

	Original Claims	Distribution of liquidating value
Trade credit	1,000	1,000
Secured notes	1,000	1,000
Senior debenture	3,000	3,000
Junior debenture	1,000	0
Equity	0	0
Total	6,000	5,000

30.4   There are many possible reorganization plans. One that might work here is

Assets		Original Claims		Reorganized Claims	
Going concern value	15,000	Mortgage bonds	10,000	Senior debenture	10,000
		Senior debenture	6,000	Junior debenture	4,000
		Junior debenture	4,000	Equity	1,000
		Equity	-5,000		

The holders of mortgage bonds would receive senior debentures in original amounts. The holders of senior debentures would receive junior debentures at 66.67 cents on the dollar.
The holders of the junior debentures would receive equity at 25 cents on the dollar.

30.5   a.   APR: Absolute priority rule is the priority rule of the distribution of the proceeds of the liquidation. It begins with the first claim to the last, in the order : administrative expenses, unsecured claims after a filing of involuntary bankruptcy petition, wages, employee benefit plan, consumer claims, taxes, secured and unsecured loans, preferred stocks and common stocks.

       b.   DIP: Debtor in possession. Bankruptcy allows firms to issue new debt that is senior to all previously incurred debt. This new debt is called DIP debt.

30.6   There are four possible reasons why firms may choose legal bankruptcy over private workout.

     i.   It may be less expensive (although legal bankruptcy is usually more expensive.

     ii.   Equity investors can use legal bankruptcy to "hold out".

     iii.   A complicated capital structure makes private workouts more difficult.

     iv.   Conflicts of interest between creditors, equity investors and management can make private workouts impossible.

Chapter 31: International Corporate Finance

31.1   a.   In direct terms, $1.6317 / Pound
In European terms, DM1.8110 / $

        b.   The Japanese yen is selling at a premium to the U.S. dollar in the forward markets. Today, at the spot rate, U.S.$ 1 buys ¥143, while at the 90-day future rate, U.S.$ 1 buys only ¥142.01. Clearly, Yen are getting more expensive in dollar terms.

            This is even easier to see in direct terms:
At the spot rate, the yen cost just under 6 cents, while the 90-day yen costs over 7 cents.

        c.   It will be important to Japanese companies that will receive or make payments in dollars. It will also be important to other international companies outside Japan that must make or receive payments in yen. For these companies, future cash flows depend on the exchange rate.

        d.   The 3 month forward exchange rate is $0.6743 / SF. The amount of Swiss francs received will be

$$\text{SF148,301.94.} = \left[\frac{\$100,000}{\$0.6743 / SF} \right].$$

            We should sell dollars, because at the spot rate, it would be SF 149,454,49.

        e.   Let $S_{x/y}$ be the spot rate of currency X for Y

$$S_{Pound/DM} = S_{Pound/\$} \times S_{\$/DM}$$

$$= \left(\frac{Pound\ 0.6129}{1\ \$} \right) \left(\frac{\$0.5522}{DM\ 1} \right)$$

$$= \frac{Pound\ 0.3384}{DM\ 1}$$

$$S_{Yen/SF} = S_{Yen/\$} \times S_{\$/SF}$$

$$= \left(\frac{¥\ 0.6129}{1\ \$} \right) \left(\frac{\$0.6691}{SF\ 1} \right)$$

$$= \frac{¥\ 95.6813}{SF\ 1}$$

        f.   Both banks reduce their exposure to foreign exchange risk. If a bank finds another bank with a complimentary mismatch of cash flows in terms of foreign currencies, it should arrange a swap since both banks' cash flows would be more closely matched.

31.2   a.   It is easiest to see this by considering from the point of view of the DM:

$$DM\!\!\big/\!\!_\$ = 2 \text{ and } DM\!\!\big/\!\!_L = 4$$

and write as the inverse:

$$\$\!\!\big/\!\!_{DM} = 0.5 \text{ and } L\!\!\big/\!\!_{DM} = 0.25$$

Then write as a ratio:

$$\frac{\$\big/_{DM}}{L\big/_{DM}} = \frac{\$}{L} = \frac{0.5}{0.25} = 2.0$$

For no arbitrage, the quote for $\$\!\!\big/\!\!_L$ must be 2.0, but instead it is 1.8. Therefore, an arbitrage opportunity does exist.

   b.   Similarly, 100 / 2 = 50, and the quote is ¥50/DM, so arbitrage does not exist

   c.   and $100/7.8 = 12.8$, but the quote is ¥14/HKD, meaning arbitrage does exist

31.3   a.   False. On the contrary, according to Relative Purchasing Power Parity, an expectation of higher inflation in Japan should cause the yen to depreciate against the dollar.

   b.   False. Assuming that the forward market is efficient, any expectation of higher inflation in France should be reflected in discounted French francs in the forward market. Therefore, no protection from risk would be available by using forward contracts.

   c.   True. The fact that other participants in the market do not have information regarding the differences in the relative inflation rates in the two countries will make our knowledge of this fact a special factor that will make speculation in the forward market successful.

31.4   The approximation formula given in the text is:

$$S^* = \Pi_{BD} - \Pi_{WD}$$

where

S^* = rate of change in the BD/WD exchange rate

Π_{BD} = inflation rate in Empire Black

Π_{WD} = inflation rate in Empire White

Then,

$$S^* = 10\% - 5\% = 5\% = 0.05$$

So, the spot rate at year end is

31.4   (continued)

$$S_1 = S_0 \left(1 + S^*\right)$$
$$= 2.5(1 + .05)$$
$$= BD\ 2.625\!\!\Big/\!\!_{WD}$$

31.5   a.   The Interest-rate parity theorem specifies:

$$\frac{1+i}{1+i^*} = \frac{F(0,1)}{S(0)}$$

where:

       i = domestic interest rate

       i^* = foreign interest rate

     $F(0,1)$ = current price of a 1 month forward contract

       $S(0)$ = current domestic-currency price of spot foreign exchange

In this case, we have (and solving for the forward rate):

$$F(0,3) = \left[\frac{1+i_{US}}{1+i_{France}}\right] S(0)_{\$\!/\!FF}$$

Since $S(0)$ is \$/FF, we must take the inverse of the quote given in the problem, so

$$S(0) = \tfrac{1}{6} = 0.16667$$

Since i_{US} and i_{France} are specified in the problem annually and we want the 3-month forward rate, we must find the 3-month interest rates, so:

$$i_{US} = \left(\frac{5\%}{12}\right)3 = 1.25\%$$

$$i_{France} = \left(\frac{8\%}{12}\right)3 = 2\%$$

So, now we have:

$$F(0,3) = \left[\frac{1.0125}{1.02}\right] 0.16667$$
$$= 0.16544$$

Convert this back to FF/\$ (1/0.16544)
and we get FF 6.04/\$

     b.   Enter the buy-side position of a 3 month FF forward contract worth 1,000,000 x 6.04 = FF6.04 million. Then, when they buy the cosmetics 3 months from now, they will have the necessary French Francs, regardless of what happens to the FX markets during those 3 months.

31.6   a.   Compare the end-of-period investment value of each country:

Investment in the U.K.:
The treasurer can obtain 2.5 million Pounds [= $5 million / ($2 / Pound)]. After investing in the U.K. for three months at 9% he will have 2,556,250 pounds [= 2.5 million pounds x (1 + 0.09 / 4)]
The forward sale of pounds will provide $5,150,843.75 (= 2,556,250 Pounds x $2.015 / Pound).

Investment in the U.S.:
After investing in the U.S. for three months at 12%, the treasurer will have $5,150,000 [= $5,000,000 x (1 + 0.12 / 4)].

Since investing in the UK yields $843.75 more than investing in the US, the treasuere should invest in the UK.

b.   From the equation for interest-rate parity theorem:

$$\frac{1+i}{1+i^*} = \frac{F(0,1)}{S(0)}$$

where:

i = domestic interest rate

i^* = foreign interest rate

$F(0,1)$ = current price of a 1 period forward contract

$S(0)$ = current domestic-currency price of spot foreign exchange

Instead of interpreting the period as 1 month as before and in the text, we can interpret it as 1 year. Then we have

$$F(0,1) = \left(\frac{1+i_{US}}{1+i_{UK}}\right) S(0)$$

$$= \left(\frac{1.13}{1.08}\right) \$1.50/\text{Pound}$$

$$= \$1.57/\text{Pound}$$

c.   It all depends on whether the forward market expects the same appreciation over the period and whether the expectation is accurate. Assuming that the expectation is correct and that other traders do not have the same information, there will be value to hedging the currency exposure.

31.7　a.　One possible reason investment in the foreign subsidiary might be preferred is if this investment provides direct diversification that shareholders could not attain by investing on their own. Another reason could be if the political climate in the foreign country was more stable than in the home country.

Increased political risk can also be a reason you might prefer the home subsidiary investment.

Indonesia can serve as a great example of political risk. If it cannot be diversified away, investing in this type of foreign country will increase the systematic risk. As a result, it will raise the cost of the capital, and could actually decrease the NPV of the investment.

b.　First, we need to forecast the future spot rates for the next 3 years. From interest rate and purchasing power parity, the expected exchange rate is

$$E[S(1)_{\$/DM}] = \left(\frac{1+i_{US}}{1+i_{WG}} \right) \$/DM(0)$$

$$= \left(\frac{1.113}{1.06} \right) \$0.5/DM$$

$$= \$0.525/DM$$

Similarly,

$$E[S(2)_{\$/DM}] = \left(\frac{1.113}{1.06} \right)^2 (\$0.5/DM)$$

$$= \$0.5513/DM$$

$$E[S(3)_{\$/DM}] = \left(\frac{1.113}{1.06} \right)^3 (\$0.5/DM)$$

$$= \$0.5788/DM$$

Now, use these future spot rates to estimate the future cash flows in dollars, and discount those dollar cash flows:

$$NPV = (-DM10,000,000 \times \$0.5/DM) + \frac{DM4,000,000 \times \$0.525/DM}{1.15} +$$

$$\frac{DM3,000,000 \times \$0.5513/DM}{1.15^2} + \frac{(DM3,000,000 + DM2,100,000) \times \$0.5788/DM}{1.15^3}$$

$$= -\$5,000,000 + \$1,826,087 + \$1,250,586 + \$1,940,909$$

$$= \$17,582$$

c.　Yes, the firm should undertake the foreign investment. If, after taking into consideration all risks, a project in a foreign country has a positive NPV, the firm should undertake it. Note that in practice, the stated assumption (that the adjustment to the discount rate has taken into consideration all political and diversification issues) is a huge task. But once that has been addressed, the net present value principle holds for foreign operations, just as for domestic.

31.7   (continued)

  d.   If the foreign currency depreciates, the U.S. parent will experience an exchange rate loss when the foreign cash flow is remitted to the U.S. This problem could be overcome by selling forward contracts. Another way of overcoming this problem would be to borrow in the country where the project is located.

31.8 a.   Euroyen is yen deposited in a bank outside Japan.

  b.   False. If the financial markets are perfectly competitive, the difference between the Eurodollar rate and the U.S. rate will be due to differences in risk and government regulation. Therefore, speculating in those markets will not be beneficial.

  c.   The difference between a Eurobond and a foreign bond is that the foreign bond is denominated in the currency of the country of origin of the issuing company. Eurobonds are more popular than foreign bonds because of registration differences. Eurobonds are unregistered securities.

  d.   A foreign bond. In this particular case, a Yankee bond.

Selected Answers
to
Numeric Problems

Note to the student:

These Quick Answers are not intended to lead you to the solution to the questions and problems in your textbook. These are only to let you know if you have the correct final answer. In some cases (for long problems), a few key intermediate answers are given.

As such, most intermediate answers, and all questions requiring discussion are not included.

Note to the instructor:

If you want to use the textbook problems as assignments and you have the ability to selectively give students access to the Solutions and these Quick Answers (for example through WebCT), you might give students access to these Quick Answers to reduce anxiety without unduly compromising the value of the assignment. Then, after the assignment is due, you can give them access to the full Solution.

Chapter 2: Accounting Statements and Cash Flow

2.1   Common stock = 88,000
             Total liabilities&equity = 128,000

2.2   Total $212,000,000

2.3   Taxes = 51000
             Net income = 99,000

2.4   a. net income 20X1 = -94500; net income 20X2 = -53,200
             b. Operating CF 20X2 = $205,500; Operating CF 20X1 = $146,800

2.6   a. Net operating income = $400,000
             b. Earnings before taxes = $300,000
             c. Net income = $195,000
             d. Operating Cash flow = $395,000

2.7   Cash flows from the firm   -5000
             Cash flows to investors of the firm   -5000

Chapter 3: Long-term Financial Planning and Growth

3.1	Total Assets	$16,875,000
	Total Liabs & CS	$16,875,000

3.2   a. EFN = $3.24 million
      b. Total liabilities = $525 million
      c. Total liabilities = 574.26

3.3   a. sustainable growth = 5.26%

3.4   a. EFN = 2,880,000
      b. Total liabilities and equity = $38,400,000
      c. 3.45%

Chapter 4: Net Present Value

4.1   a. $1,628.89
       b. $1,967.15
       c. $2,653.30

4.2   a. $513.16
       b. $1,818.18
       c. $233.25

4.3   PV(C0) = $1,000
       PV(C10) = $926.39

4.4 $92.30

4.5 $187,780.23

4.6   a. PV(Alternative 1) = $10,000,000
         PV(Alternative 2) = $20,000,000
       b. PV(Alternative 1) = $9,090,909.10
         PV(Alternative 2) = $12,418,426.46
       c. PV(Alternative 1) = $8,333,333.33
         PV(Alternative 2) = $8,037,551.44
       d. The two alternatives are equally attractive when discounted at 18.921 percent.

4.7   PV(Smith) = $115,000
       PV(Jones) = $112,697.22

4.8   a. $214.55
       b. $463.20
       c. $680.59

4.9   The most she would be willing to pay for the property is $1,609,866.18.

4.10   a. PV(Investment) = $900,000
         PV(Cash Inflows) = $875,865.52
       b. NPV = -$24,134.48
       c. NPV = -$4,033.18

4.11   NPV @10% = -$2,619.97
       NPV @9% = $6,567.93

4.12   a. NPV = -$4,117.08
       b. The firm will break even on the item with an 8.447 percent discount rate.

4.13   PV(Aunt) = $3,571.43
       PV(Roommate) = $3,500

4.14   The interest rate required is 18.921%.

4.15   The value of the account at the end of seven years will be $6,714.61.

4.16   a. FV = $1,259.71
       b. FV = $1,265.32
       c. FV = $1,270.24
       d. FV = $1,271.25

4.17   a. FV = $1,822.12
       b. FV = $1,349.86
       c. FV = $1,648.72
       d. FV = $1,750.67

4.18   The PV of the cash flow is $1,528.36.

4.19   EAY(Bank America) = 4.16%
       eAY(Bank USA) = 4.13%

4.20   The price of the consol is $800.

4.21	a. $10,000
	b. $4,545.45.
	c. $20,000.
4.22	The PV as of the end of year 5 is $901.58.
4.23	The price of the stock is $45.
4.24	PV = $16.67
4.25	PV = $3,636,363.64
4.26	discount rate is 50%.
4.27	The price of the security is $333.33.
4.28	$13.25
4.29	NPV = $201.91
4.30	PV = $16,834.95
4.31	PV(Year 0) = $1,658.98
4.32	0.090626 = r
4.33	a.$4,347.27
	b. PV = $17,824.65
4.34	$11,980.88
4.35	PV = $1,201,180.55
	b.PV = $1,131,898.53
4.36	C = $2,544.79
4.37	NPV = -$545.88
4.38	PV(Lease) = -$120,283.16
4.39	FV = $440,011.02
4.40	NPV = $282.78
4.41	a. NPV(Engineer) = $352,535.14
	NPV(Accountant) = $345,958.20
	b. NPV(Engineer) = $292,418.30
	NPV(Accountant) = $292,947.73
4.42	PV(Offer) = $415,783.60
4.43	NPV = $3,041.91
4.44	Ian needs to save $58,396.23 annually from year 11 to year 30 in order to meet his objectives.
4.45	PV(Contract) = $174,276.73.
4.46	$293.18 = C
4.47	Repayment = $5,867.91.
4.48	PV = $3,429.38.
4.49	NPV(Contract) = $5,051,154.24.
	The equivalent annual salary from year 1984 through 1988 is $1,298,613.65.
4.50	PV(Balloon) = $291,439.54.
4.51	$186.43 = C
4.52	PV $4,352.43.

Chapter 5: How to Value Bonds and Stocks

5.1   a. $613.91
          b. $385.54
          c. $247.19

5.2   a. $1,000
          b. $828.41
          c. $1,231.15

5.3   a. $718.65
          b. $883.64

5.4 $846.33

5.5   0.09

5.6   a. 0.1236
          b. $748.49
          c. $906.15

5.7   a. PA = $1,000
             PB = $1,000
          b. PA = $850.61
             PB = $887.00
          c. PA = $1,196.36
             PB = $1,134.20

5.8   a. P = $1,000 / (1+i)
          b. (1+i) = (1+r) (1+Inflation)

5.9   a. r = 0.0622
          b. r = 0.0877

5.10   a. $18,033.86
          b. $3,888.89

5.11   a. True.
          b. True
          c. True.
          d. False.
          e. True.

5.12   a. True.
          b. False.
          c. True.
          d. True.

5.13 $28.89

5.14   a. True.
          b. False.
          c. True.
          d. True. EPS = $3.83

5.15   r = 0.084

5.16   2,754

5.17   a. $28.57
          b. $46.54

5.18 $26.93

5.19 $23.75

5.20 $47.62

5.21 $29.40

5.22	$14.09
5.23	$71.70
5.24	$2.49
5.25	a. 8.4%
	b. $21,680,000
5.26	0.1627
5.27	$4.82
5.28	a. $15.75
	b. NPVGO = $15.43.
5.29	a. $33.33
	b. $38,623,188.41
	c. $35.26
5.30	a. $28.57
	b. $64.30
5.31	a. 7.5
	b. 8.33

Appendix to Chapter 5

5A.1	a. $914.87
	b. 10.97%
5A.2	$945.66
5A.3	The one-year forward rate over the second year is 11.01%.
5A.4	a. f2 = 9.04%
	b. f3 = 16.25%

Chapter 6: Some Alternative Investment Rules

6.1   a. Project A has a payback period of two years.
        Project B has a payback period of three years.
        b. Project A= -$388.96
        Project B = $53.83

6.2   a. 6.67
        b. The discounted payback period is 12 years.
        c. NPV = $500,000

6.3   a. 56.25%

6.4   Average Accounting Return = 11.5%

6.5   44%.

6.6   IRR(Project A) = 0.1289
        IRR(Project B) = 0.1289

6.7   a. IRR = 0.0693
        b. No

6.8   IRR(Project A) = 1.88
        IRR(Project B) = 0.362

6.9   a. IRR = 0.1399
        b. Reject the offer when the discount rate is less than the IRR.
        c. Accept the offer when the discount rate is greater than the IRR.
        d. NPV(10%) = -$359.95
        NPV(20%) = $466.82
        e. Yes

6.10   a. IRR(Project A) = 0.2569
        IRR(Project B) = 0.1943
        d. The incremental IRR is 19.1%.
        f. NPV(Project A) = $689.98
        NPV(Project B) = $5,671.08

6.11   a. PV(A) = $49,824.62
        PV(B) = -$44,642.86
        b. IRR(Project C) = 0.1465

6.12   False.

6.13   a. PI(A) = 2.6
        PI(B) = 1.5

6.15   a. PI(A) = 1.183
        PI(B) = 1.099
        PI(C) = 1.148
        b. NPV (A) = $18,303.57
        NPV(B) = $19,706.63
        NPV(C) = $14,795.92
        d. PI(B − A) = 1.014

6.16   PI = 1.04

6.18 a. Payback Period Early Edition = 2.11
      Payback Period Late Edition =2.25
      b. New Sunday Early Edition IRR = 0.1676
      New Saturday Late Edition IRR = 0.1429
      c. IRR = 0.1102
      d. The average accounting return for the New Sunday Early Edition is 58.3%.
      The average accounting return for the New Saturday Late Edition is 66.7%.

6.19 a. The discounted payback period for deepwater fishing is three years.
      The discounted payback period for the submarine ride is three years.
      b. The IRR of the deepwater fishing project is 24.3%.
      The IRR of the submarine ride is 21.46%.
      c. IRR = 0.1992
      d. The NPV of the deepwater fishing project is $96,687.76.
      The NPV of the submarine ride project is $190,630.39.

6.20 a. 0.185565
      b. Yes.

Chapter 7: Net Present Value and Capital Budgeting

7.3   a. Incremental Net Income:
        Year 0 $0;   Year 1 $1,650; Year 2 $1,650; Year 3 $1,650; Year 4 $1,650
        b. Incremental cash flow :
        Year 0 -$10,200;   Year 1 $4,100; Year 2 $4,100; Year 3 $4,250; Year 4 $4,350
        c. NPV = $2,519

7.4 $13,348,256

7.5   NPVA = -$4,324
        NPVB = -$3,991

7.6   NPV = $129,870

7.7   NPV = -$11,232

7.8   NPV = $84,709

7.9   The least that the firm should charge for its initial lease payment is $523,117.

7.10   NPV = $89,514

7.11   The maximum price that MMC should be willing to pay for the equipment is $74,510.

7.12   a. Net Investment = -$16,200,000
        b. After-Tax Incremental Cash Flows: -16,200,000   13,029,600   15,028,800
                13,628,800   19,895,744
        c. IRR = 0.7948
        d. NPV = $27,772,577

7.13   NPVA = $1,446
        NPVB = $120

7.14   The nominal cash flow at year 5 is $158,226.

7.15   PV Project = -$20,576

7.16   PV = $705,882

7.17   NPV = $1,291,044

7.18   NPV = $45,614,647

7.19   Value of the firm = $91,520,000

7.20   NPV = $2,171,596

7.21   Headache-only medicine: NPV = $11,767,030
        Headache and Arthritis medicine: NPV = $27,226,206

7.22   PV = $150,100

7.23   EAC = -$22,344

7.24   EAC = -$16,286

7.25   EAC = -$14,980

7.26   The equivalent annual cost of model XX40 is $374.
        The equivalent annual cost of model RH45 is $339.

7.27   Facility 1: EAC = -$368,951
        Facility 2: EAC = -$426,487

7.28   NPV(Option 1) = -$1,606,950
        NPV(Option 2) = -631,636

7.29   SAL 5000 Total EAC = -$11,870
        DET 1000 Total EAC = -$14,920

7.30   EVF EAC = $47,456
        AEH EAC = $49,591

7.31   Mixer X EAB = $11,772
        Mixer Y EAB = $13,407

7.32   Tamper A EAC = -$276,446
        Tamper B EAC = -$254,338
7.33   The equivalent annual cost of the new autoclave is $615.
        The cost of the old autoclave in terms of end-of-year 1 dollars is $340.
        The cost of the old autoclave in terms of end-of-year 2 dollars is $435.
        The cost of the old autoclave in terms of end-of-year 3 dollars is $477.
        The cost of the old autoclave in terms of end-of-year 4 dollars is $620.

Chapter 8: Strategy and Analysis in Using Net Present Value

8.1   NPV(Test Market) = $12,130,434.78

8.2   NPV(Go Directly) = $600,000
NPV(Focus Group) = $720,000
NPV(Consulting Firm) = $680,000

8.3   NPV(Lower Prices) = -$1,547,500
NPV(Lobbyist) = -$1,300,000

8.4   The break-even sales price of the calculator is $66.

8.5   The distributor must sell 350 televisions per year to break even.

8.6   a. 281,250 abalones per year
b. Total Profit = $15,600

8.7   The present value break-even point is 297,657 abalones.

8.8   The present value break-even point is 20,532 units.

8.9   The break-even purchase price is $61,981.06.

8.10   a. Pessimistic: NPV = -$123,021.71
    expected: NPV = $247,814.18
    Optimistic: NPV = $653,146.42
b. NPV = $259,312.96

8.11   Pessimistic: NPV = -$675,701.68
expected: NPV = $399,304.88
Optimistic: NPV = $1,561,468.43
The expected NPV of the project is $428,357.21.

8.12   a. NPV = $608,425.33
b. The revised NPV is $699,334.42.
c. The option value of abandonment is $90,909.09.

8.13   a. NPV = $738,494,417.11
b. $12,403,973.08 = C1

Chapter 9: Capital Market Theory: An Overview

9.1   a. Capital Gain = $500
       b. Total Dollar Gain = $1,500
       c. R_{t+1} = 0.0811

9.2   a. Capital Gain = $450
       b. Total Dollar Gain = $1,050
       c. R_{t+1} = 0.1010
       e. Dividend Yield = 0.0577

9.3   The percentage return is –20.48%.

9.4 R_{t+2} = 0.0529

9.5   a. r = 0.0883
       b. r = 0.03
       c. r = 0.0262
       d. r = 0.00679

9.6   E(R) = 0.104

9.7   General Materials: (0.99) P0
       Standard Fixtures: (0.99) P0

9.8   The five-year holding-period return is 98.64 percent.

9.9   E(R) = 0.044

9.10   a. The expected return on the market is 10.55 percent.
        The expected return on Treasury bills is 3.5 percent.
       b. The expected risk premium is 7.05 percent.

9.11   a. The average return is 15.9 percent.
       b. The standard deviation of the portfolio is 0.1708.

9.12   b. The average risk premium is 8.49 percent.

9.13   a. E(R) = 0.088
       b. The standard deviation is 0.03311.

9.14   a. The expected return on the market is 15.3 percent.
       b. The expected return on Tribli stock is 6.28 percent.

9.15   a. The expected return on Belinkie Enterprises stock is 5.75 percent.
       The expected return on Overlake Company stock is 9 percent.
       b. The variance of Belinkie Enterprises stock is 0.000421.
       The variance of Overlake Company stock is 0.00115.

9.16   a. The average return on small-company stocks is 15.42 percent.
       The average return on the market index is 16.04 percent.
       b. The standard deviation of the small-company returns is 0.33249.
       The standard deviation of the market index is 0.47352.

9.17   The average return on common stocks is 18.33 percent.
       The variance of the common stock returns is 0.018372.
       The average return on small stocks is 20.90 percent.
       The variance of the small stock returns is 0.029734.
       The average return on long-term corporate bonds is 16.01 percent.
       The variance of the long-term corporate bond returns is 0.029522.
       The average return on long-term government bonds is 15.68 percent.
       The variance of the long-term government bond returns is 0.02868.
       The average return on the Treasury bills is 9.86 percent.
       The variance of the Treasury bill returns is 0.00075.

9.18   a. The average return on small-company stocks is 8.95 percent.
           The average return on U.S. Treasury bills is 6.63 percent.
        b. The standard deviation of small-company stocks is .2340.
           The standard deviation of the Treasury bill returns is 0.0119.
9.19   The range in which 95 percent of the returns will fall is between 0.5 percent and 34.5
           percent.

Chapter 10: Return and Risk: The Capital Asset Pricing Model (CAPM)

10.1   a. 10.57%

       b. Standard Deviation (s) = 7.20%

10.2   a. Expected ReturnA = 10.80%

       Expected ReturnB = 9.33%

       b. Standard DeviationA = 3.80%

       Standard DeviationB = 12.02%

       c. Covariance(RA, RB) = 0.004539

       Correlation(RA,RB) = 0.9937

10.3   a. Expected ReturnHB = 7.33%

       Expected ReturnSB = 6.08%

       b. The standard deviation of Highbear's stock returns is 5.80%.

       The standard deviation of Slowbear's stock returns is 0.75%.

       c. The covariance between the returns on Highbull's stock and Slowbear's stock is 0.000425.

       The correlation between the returns on Highbull's stock and Slowbear's stock is 0.9770.

10.4   The weight of Atlas stock in the portfolio is 2/3.

       The weight of Babcock stock in the portfolio is 1/3.

10.5   a. E(RP) = 16.20%

       b. The standard deviation of the portfolio equals 8.23%

10.6   a. E(RP) = 21%

       The standard deviation (sP) of the portfolio equals 14.42%

       b. sP = 10.58%

10.7   a. The expected return on her portfolio is 18%.

       The standard deviation of her portfolio is 13.54%.

       b. The expected return on her portfolio is 16.67%.

       The standard deviation of her portfolio is 10.00%.

10.8   a. The expected return on Stock A is 7%.

       The standard deviation of the returns on Stock A is 0%.

       The expected return on Stock B is 11.50%.

       The standard deviation of the returns on Stock B is 10.50%.

       b. The covariance between the returns on Stock A and Stock B is 0.

       The correlation between the returns on Stock A and Stock B is 0.

       c. The expected return of an equally weighted portfolio is 9.25%.

       The standard deviation of the returns on an equally weighted portfolio is 5.25%.

10.9   a. The expected return on the portfolio is 17%.

       The standard deviation of the portfolio is 10.61%.

       b. The expected return on the portfolio is 11%.

       The standard deviation of the portfolio is 4.74%.

10.11 a. The expected return on Security A is 10.20%.

       The standard deviation of the returns on Security A is 5.88%.

       The expected return on Security B is 6.50%.

       The standard deviation of the returns on Security B is 0%.

       b. The expected return of her portfolio is 8.04%.

       The standard deviation of her portfolio is 2.45%.

10.13   a. The expected return on Security 1 is 17.50%.
           The standard deviation of the returns on Security 1 is 4.03%.
           The expected return on Security 2 is 17.50%.
           The standard deviation of the returns on Security 2 is 4.03%.
           The expected return on Security 3 is 17.50%.
           The standard deviation of the returns on Security 3 is 4.03%.
       b. The covariance between the returns on Security 1 and Security 2 is 0.000625.
           The correlation between the returns on Security 1 and Security 2 is 0.3848.
           The covariance between the returns on Security 1 and Security 3 is -0.001625.
           The correlation between the returns on Security 1 and Security 3 is -1.
           The covariance between the returns on Security 2 and Security 3 is -0.000625.
           The correlation between the returns on Security 2 and Security 3 is –0.3848.
       c. The expected return of the portfolio is 17.50%.
           The standard deviation of the returns on the portfolio is 3.35%.
       d. The expected return on the portfolio is 17.50%.
           The standard deviation of the returns on the portfolio is 0%.
       e. The expected return of the portfolio is 17.50%.
           The standard deviation of the returns on the portfolio is 2.24%.

10.14   b. 13.5%

10.15   a. The expected return on an equally weighted portfolio containing all N securities is 10%.

10.19   a. $E(RP) = 9.9\%$
       b. standard deviation = 21.43%.

10.20   a. beta = 0.68

10.22   a. $E(RP) = 14.67\%$
       b. The beta of an equally weighted portfolio is 1.23.
       c. Slope between A and B = 0.08
          Slope between A and C = 0.091
          Slope between B and C = 0.10

10.23 $E(r) = 0.162$

10.24 $E(r) = 0.128$

10.25 $E(r) = 0.185$

10.26   beta = 1.4

10.27   The expected return on the market portfolio is 18.71%.
       rf = 0.03

10.28   a. $E(rA) = 0.075$
          $E(rB) = 0.05$
       b. The expected market risk premium is 10%.

10.29   b. $E(r) = 11\%$
       c. $E(r) = 22\%$

10.30 $E(r) = 0.194$

10.31   a. 0.1528
       b. 0.1586

10.32 $E(r) = 0.10$

10.33   a. The expected market risk premium is 5.35%.
       b. $E(r) = 0.1188$
       c. $E(r) = 0.1333$

10.34 $E(rP) = 0.1082$

10.35 a. $E(r) = 0.049 + b(0.094)$
       b. $E(r) = 0.1869$
10.36 The expected return on the market portfolio is 12%.
       The risk-free rate is 2%.
10.38 BetaPortfolio= 1.293
       $e(r) = 0.1822$
10.39 b. Firm A : $E(r) = 0.14$
          Firm B: $E(r) = 0.16$
          Firm C: $E(r) = 0.23$
10.40 a. Stock A has an expected return of 8% and a beta of 0.784.
          Stock B has an expected return of 9% and a beta of 0.24.
       b. $E(rP) = 0.083$
          $sP = 0.0947$
       c. BetaP = 0.6208
10.41 a. XB = 0.1875
          XA =0.8125
       b. $E(rP) = 0.0594$
       c. XB = 1/3
          XA = 2/3
       d. The variance of the portfolio is 0.01.

Chapter 11: An Alternative View of Risk and Return: The Arbitrage Pricing Theory

11.2 a. 0.53%
      b. 2.6%
      c. 6.37%

11.3 a. 0.372%
      b. 1.44%
      c. 11.81%

11.4 a. for Stock A:

$$R_A = \bar{R}_A + \beta_A \left(R_m - \bar{R}_m \right) + \varepsilon_A$$

$$= 10.5\% + 1.2 \left(R_m - 14.2\% \right) + \varepsilon_A$$

b. $R_P = 12.925\% + 1.1435 \left(R_m - 14.2\% \right) + 0.30\varepsilon_A + 0.45\varepsilon_B + 0.25\varepsilon_C$

c. i. R(a) = 11.46%, R(b) = 13.78%, R(c) = 16.8%
   ii. R(p) = 13.84%

11.5 a. $\bar{R}_p = 11.0 + 0.84F_1 + 1.69F_2 + \dfrac{1}{5} \left(\varepsilon_1 + \varepsilon_2 + \varepsilon_3 + \varepsilon_4 + \varepsilon_5 \right)$

b. $\bar{R}_p = 11.0 + 0.84F_1 + 1.69F_2$

11.6 a. var(r1) = .0225; var(r2) = .00225

b. var(r1) = .0585; var(r2) = .0025
c. var(r2) = .0225; var(r2) = .0225
d. $Corr \left(\varepsilon_{2i}, \varepsilon_{2j} \right) = Corr \left(\varepsilon_{1i}, \varepsilon_{1j} \right) + 0.5$

11.7 a. $s_A = 12.62\%$

$s_B = 17.84\%$

$s_C = 22.30\%$

b. i:

$s_A^2 = 0.5929\%$

$s_B^2 = 1.7424\%$

$s_C^2 = 2.7225\%$

ii.

$\bar{R}_A = 8.41\%$

$\bar{R}_B = 12.06\%$

$\bar{R}_C = 14.25\%$

11.8 a. E(Rp) = 20%; beta=2.5
      b. E(Rp) = 10%; beta = 0

Chapter 12: Risk, Return, and Capital Budgeting

12.1   NPV = -$20,016.52

12.2   a. The beta of Douglas stock is 0.864.

12.3   The beta of Ceramics Craftsman is 1.146.

12.4   a. The beta of Mercantile Banking Corporation is 1.0032.

12.5   b. i. The expected return on asset L is 18%.
              ii. The variance of asset L is 0.00016.
              iii. The standard deviation of asset L is 0.01265.
        d. i. The expected return on asset J is 20%.
              ii. The variance of asset J is 0.00048.
              iii. The standard deviation of asset J is 0.02191.
        e. The covariance of asset L's return with asset J's return is 0.000176.
           The correlation coefficient of asset L and J is 0.635.
        f. The beta of asset J is 1.10.

12.8   a. The beta of Compton Technology debt is 0.188.
        b. The beta of Compton Technology stock is 1.015.
        c. The asset beta of Compton Technology is 0.740.

12.11   a. The cost of equity is 17.5%.
        b. WACC = 0.1517

12.12   a. Adobe Online's cost of equity is 14.74%.
        b. WACC = 0.09645

12.13   WACC = 0.1423

12.14   WACC = 0.1643

12.15   WACC = 0.1108
        NPV = $819,299.04

12.16   WACC = 0.1725
        NPV = $240,608.65

Chapter 13: Corporate-Financing Decisions and Efficient Capital Markets

No numerical problems

Chapter 14: Long-Term Financing: An Introduction

14.1   a. 67,715
        b. $5 per share
        c.$40.

14.2   a. $150,500
        b. Capital surplus = 79,000

14.3   a. Capital Surplus = $195,000
          Retained earnings = 3,794,600
        b. Common stock =$1,750,000
          Capital Surplus = $170,000
          Retained earnings = 3,794,600

14.4   a. more than 1,000,000 shares
        b. You will need more than 250,000 shares.

14.5   Yes; No.

14.6   a. 20 additional shares
        b. it will cost you $2,500,000

Chapter 15: Capital Structure: Basic Concepts

15.1   a. $100,000

        b. $100,000.

        c. $75,000.

        d. $20,000 for Alpha; $15,000 for Beta

        e. dollar return to an investor who owns 20% of Alpha's equity is expected to be $70,000

           dollar return to an investor who owns 20% of Beta's equity is $69,400

           Strategy Summary:

           Borrow $5,000 at 12%.

           Purchase 20% of Alpha's stock for $15,000

15.2   a. Debt-Equity Ratio is ½.

           $r_S = 0.17$

           weighted average cost of capital is 16%.

        b. the cost of capital for an otherwise identical all-equity firm is 16%.

15.3   value of Unlevered is $800 million

           value of Levered, Inc. is $725 million

15.4   a. investor who owns 5% of Knight's stock expects to receive $12,000

           investor who borrows $34,300 to buy 5% of Veblen's stock expects $12,942.

15.6   a. weighted average cost of capital will be 18% after the restructuring.

        b. cost of equity after the restructuring will be 20%.

        c. $r_{wacc} = 0.18$

15.7   b. i. price will immediately rise to $22

           ii. The NPV of the buyout is $500,000.

           iii. Strom will need to issue 13,636.3636 shares

           iv. market value of the firm's equity increases to $5,800,000

           v. $PV_{NEW\ FACILITIES} = \$800,000$

           vi. expected return to Strom's equity holders is 15% (= $870,000 / $5,800,000).

           vii. $r_{wacc} = 0.15$

        c. ii. market value of the firm's debt will be $300,000

           iii. Total D+E = $5,800,000

           iv. expected return to Strom's equity holders is 15.27%

           v. $r_{wacc} = 0.15$

15.8   a. PV(Perpetuity)= $270,000,000

        b. i. $NPV_{NEW\ POWER\ PLANT} = \$10$ million

           ii. Gulf will need to issue 714,285.71 shares

           iii. increases to $300,000,000

           iv. $PV_{NEW\ POWER\ PLANT} = \$30$ million

           v. Gulf Power will be $300 million

        c. i. total market value of Gulf's equity will be $280 million

           ii. Gulf will receive $20 million in cash after the debt issue, and the market value of

               the firm's debt will be $20 million.

           iii. $PV_{POWER\ PLANT} = \$30$ million

           iv. value of Gulf Power will be $300 million

           v. $r_{wacc} = 0.10$

15.11 b. if Michael borrows 20%, expected return will be 16.25%

           if Michael borrows 40%, 18.33%

           if Michael borrows 60%, 22.50%

15.12   a. $V_L = \$26.25$ million
      b. expected return on Locomotive's levered equity is 16%
      c. $r_0 = 0.1429$
      d. $r_S = 0.1644$

15.13   a. $V_U = \$1,530,000$
      b. firm's annual after-tax earnings is $168,960

15.14 $S = \$2,800,000$

15.15   a. $V_U = \$8,250,000$
      b. $V_L = \$8,454,000$

15.16   a. $V_U = \$6,500,000$
         $V_L = \$7,375,000$

15.17   a. expected return on Green's unlevered equity is 9%
      b. market value of Green's equity is $10,000,000
      c. $V_L = \$10,800,000$
      d. stock price will rise to $21.60 per share.
      e. Green will have 407,407.41 shares of common stock outstanding after the repurchase.
      f. stock price will remain at $21.60 per share after the restructuring has taken place.
      g. $r_S = 0.941$

15.18   a. $V_L = \$20,833,333$
      b. $r_S = 0.18$
      c. $r_{wacc} = 0.1248$

15.19   a. $r_S = 0.3625$
      b. $r_0 = 0.20$
      c. $r_{wacc} = 0.17$ at DE .75
         $r_{wacc} = 0.158$ at DE 1.5

15.20   a. $V_U = \$240,000$
      b. $V_L = \$280,000$

15.21   b. market value of the firm is $487.5 million
      c. i. NPV(Purchase) = $20,000,000
         ii. Stephenson must issue 2,955,956 shares
         iii. stock price after the equity issue remains at $33.83 per share.
         iv. $PV_{PROJECT} = \$120$ million
      d. i. $V_L = \$647.5$ million
         ii. price after the debt issue will be $36.50 per share.

Chapter 16: Capital Structure: Limits to the Use of Debt

16.1   a. The value of Good Time's equity is $53.57 million.

       b. The promised return on Good Time's debt is 37.70%.

       c. The value of Good Time Company is $162.5 million.

       d. in a world with no bankruptcy costs, Good Time's debt would be worth $116.07 million.

       e. Good Time's debt indicates that the firm's bondholders expect to receive $80 million in the event of a recession.

       f. Good Time expects bankruptcy costs of $20 million, should bankruptcy occur at the end of the year.

16.2   a. The value of Steinberg's equity is $878,261.

         The value of Steinberg's debt is $652,174.

         The value of Dietrich's equity is $695,652.

         The value of Dietrich's debt is $834,783.

       b. The value of Steinberg is $1,530,435.

         The value of Dietrich is also $1,530,435.

16.10   a. i. $V_L = V_U + \$5,400,000$

         iii. The value of Fortune as an unlevered firm is $6.3 million.

           The value of Fortune as a levered firm is $11.7 million.

       b. i. The annual after-tax cash flow to equity holders under the unlevered plan is $1,440,000.

         The annual after-tax cash flow to equity holders under the levered plan is $792,000.

         ii. The annual after-tax cash flow to debt holders under the unlevered plan is $0.

           The annual after-tax cash flow to debt holder under the levered plan is $607,500

16. 11   c. Change in Value= $175,000

       d. Change in Value= -$0.25

16.12   a. $V_U = \$3,217,500$

       b. $V_L = \$3,657,500$

         The value of OPC will be $3,657,500 if it remains a levered firm.

16.13   a. $V_U = \$15,000$

       b. i. In a world without taxes, the value of Frodo will remain at $15,000.

         ii. S= $7,500

         iii. The required rate of return on Frodo's levered equity is 30%.

         iv. Frodo's weighted average cost of capital is 20%.

       c. ii. $V_L = \$12,000$

       d. $V_L = \$9,265$

16.14   a. $\Delta V = \$23.53$ million

16.15   a. $V_L = \$5,422,353$

       b. The added value of the firm's debt is $222,353.

16.16   a. NETC's overall cost of capital is 22%.

       b. The NPV of the Heavy-Duty Model is $265.27.

         The NPV of the Light-Weight Model is $389.84.

       c. i. The value of the NETC will be $10,680,000 if the CFO's plan adopted.

         ii. The value of NETC's levered equity is $8,680,000.

Chapter 16 Appendix: The Miller Model and the Graduated Income Tax

16.17 a. The equilibrium interest rate is 16.92%.

      b. Investors whose interest income is taxed at 10% will buy debt.
        Investors whose interest income is taxed at 20% will buy debt.
        Investors whose interest income is taxed at 40% will buy equity.

      c. The value of Firm A is $5.91 million.

16.18 a. The equilibrium market rate of interest is 12.46%.

      b. Group A will buy equity.
        Group B will buy debt.
        Group C will buy debt.

      d. The market value of all companies is $682.1 million.

      c. The total tax bill is $25,793,950.

16.19 a. The debt-equity ratio in the economy can range from 0.875 to 2.

      b. The debt-equity ratio in the economy is 2/3 (= $700 million / $1,050 million).

Chapter 17: Valuation and Capital Budgeting for the Levered Firm

17.1　a. P = $337,095
　　　b. APV = $30,688

17.2　APV = -$102,079

17.3　APV = $292,765

17.4　APV = $4,642,885

17.5　a. PV(Flows-to-Equity) = $2,351,571
　　　b. The value of Milano Pizza Club is $3,057,042.

17.6　a. $r_B = 0.10$
　　　b. $r_S = 0.1692$
　　　c. WWI's weighted average cost of capital is 13.48%.

17.7　a. Bolero has a capital structure with three parts: long-term debt, short-term debt, and equity.
　　　　i. If Bolero uses book value weights, WACC would be 10.47%.
　　　　　If Bolero uses market value weights, WACC would be 11.73%.
　　　　　If Bolero uses target weights, WACC would be 10.47%.

17.8　a. Neon's weighted average cost of capital is 14.42%,
　　　　NPV = $3,088,379

17.9　a. NEC's weighted average cost of capital is 11.07%.
　　　　NPV = $52,267,389

17.10　a. $V_U = $110,000,000
　　　　APV = $127,000,000
　　　d. r_S 0.2143
　　　　S = $77 million

17.11　a. $V_U = $29,610,000
　　　　b. $r_S = 0.184$
　　　　c. the value of Mojito Mint Company is $35,250,000.
　　　　d. value of Mojito's equity is $21,150,000.

17.12　a. Lone Star Industries is worth $456 as an unlevered firm.
　　　　b. APV = $656
　　　　c. required return on Lone Star's levered equity (r_S) is 39.23%.
　　　　d. value of Lone Star's equity is $156.

17.13　Blue Angel's weighted average cost of capital is 17.32%.
　　　　$NPV_{PROJECT} = $47,424

17.14　a. The NPV of the loan excluding flotation costs is $981,902.
　　　　b. NPV of the loan including flotation costs is $942,415.

17.15　a. North Pole's equity beta is 1.72.
　　　　　South Pole's equity beta is 2.37.
　　　　b. required return on North Pole's equity is 18.87%.
　　　　　required return on South Pole's equity is 24.40%.

Chapter 18: Dividend Policy: Why Does It Matter?

18.6   a. PV = 15

        b. you must sell 236.942 shares.

18.7   a. $1,412,000

        b. $138.00

        c. ii.76.67

18.8   a. $16.2

        b. Number of shares that Jeff needs to buy = 38

18.9   For either alternative, assume the $2,000,000 cash is after corporate tax.

        Alternative 1:

        If the firm invests in T-Bills: ATCF=1,577,070.82

        If the firm invests in preferred stock: ATCF = 1,829,026.37

        Alternative 2:

        ATCF = 1,589,775.66

18.11   a. the stock price will fall by the amount of the dividend.

        b. the stock price will fall by the after-tax proceeds from the dividend.

18.12   a. ordinary income tax rate=0.35

        c. 10.5%

18.22   a. Div_1 = 1.415

        b. Div_1 = 1.58

Chapter 19: Issuing Equity Securities to the Public

19.6   i. P=40

        ii. P=33.33

        iii. P = 30

19.10   a. 800,000

        b. 3

19.11   a. 24.55

        b. 0.45

19.12   The number of old shares = 800,000

19.13   a. price = \$36.25.

        b. 8.75

19.14   a. Price(ex-rights) = \$10

          Subscription price = \$4

          value of right = \$3

        b. Price(ex-rights) = \$12

          Subscription price = \$8

          value of right = \$1

        c. shareholder's wealth position is unchanged

Chapter 20: Long-Term Debt

20.1   a. $1,016.67.
        b. $1,025.
        c. $1,000.
        d. $1,012.50.

20.6   a. Value = 1,266.41

20.7   required coupon rate is 12.4%

20.8   a. Value = 1,164.61
        b. Value = 130.12

20.9   Value = 981.82

20.10   NPV = $17,857,143

20.11   Refinancing is a wise option if borrowing costs are below 7.42%.

20.12   8% perpetual bond: NPV= - $5,660,714
        9% perpetual bond: NPV = $808,190

Chapter 21: Leasing

21.2   The reservation payment is found by setting the NPV of the lease to $0, and then solving
            for the lease payment.
        a. L = $62,614.11
        b. L = $62,405.09
21.3   NPV = -$102.66 < $0
21.4   Maxwell's (the lessee) reservation price = $52,759.50
        Mercer's (the lessor) reservation price = $52,502.94
21.5   For Raymond Corp, L = $31,652.85
        For Liberty L = $24,962.04
21.6   a. L = $50.02
        c. Both parties have positive NPV for $50.02 < L < $50.05.
21.7   a. NPV of the lease-vs.-buy = -$3,177.78
        c. PV = $18,177.78
21.8   Redwood: L = $70,978.03
        American: L = $72,137
21.9   a. NPV of incremental cash flows= $77,339.09
        b. L = $1,246,002.96

Chapter 22: Options and Corporate Finance: Basic Concepts

22.5   a. max[0, S_T - K] = max[0, 55-50] = $5
        b. min[0, K- S_T] = min[0, 50-55] = -$5
        c. max[0, S_T - K] = max[0, 45-50] = $0
        d. min[0, K- S_T] = min[0, 50-45] = $0

22.6   a. max[0, K- S_T] = max[0, 50-55] = $0
        b. min[0, S_T- K] = min[0, 55-50] = $0
        c. max[0, K- S_T] = max[0, 50-45] = $5
        d. min[0, S_T- K] = min[0, 45-50] = -$5

22.8   a. Total Payoff if the stock price is $65 at expiration = $0 + $1000 = $1,000
          Total Payoff if the stock price is $72 at expiration = $400 + $300 = $700
          Total Payoff if the stock price is $80 at expiration = $2,000

22.9   a. cash flow at expiration is $3,000

22.13   The price of General Eclectic stock must be $42.36 per share in order to prevent
           arbitrage.

22.14   b. synthetic call position costs $25

22.15   a. a European call option with a strike price of $110 and one year until expiration is worth
           $7.32 today.
        b. Ken should purchase 1/3 of a share of Northwestern's stock and borrow $26.01

22.16   a. European put option with a strike price of $40 and six months until expiration is worth
           $13.64 today.
        b. Rob should short 5/9 of a share of Biolab's stock and lend $30.30
        c. total cost of the synthetic put option is $13.64

22.17   b. a European call option with a strike price of $375 and three months until expiration is
           worth $12.50 today.
        c. Maverick should buy 1/3 of an ounce of gold and borrow $104.17
        d. total cost of the synthetic call option is $12.50

22.18   d. Mark should short 2/7 of a share of the index fund and lend $467.29

22.19 $11.30.

22.20 $0.28.

22.21   a. The Black-Scholes Price of the call option is $16.13.
        b. P = $6.61

22.22   a. The Black-Scholes Price of the call option is $30.26.
        b. P = $0.04

22.23   a. The Black-Scholes Price of the call option is $4.95.
        b. The Black-Scholes Price of the call option is $6.69.
        d. The Black-Scholes Price of the call option is $0.16.

22.24   a. pay $80 per share.
        b. $2.76
        c. $77.91 to purchase a collar

22.26   a. value of the firm's equity is $67,289,720.
          value of the firm's debt is $332,710,280.
        b. price of Strudler's equity is $134.58 per share.
        d. current value of the firm's equity is $149,158,879.
          current value of the firm's debt is $250,841,121.

22.27   current value of the firm's equity is $335,891.
        current value of the firm's debt is $664,109.

Chapter 23: Options and Corporate Finance: Extensions and Applications

23.1   a. current value of his options package is $457,794
23.2   PV(Annual Salary Payments) = $1,243,426
        total value of Jared's compensation package is $1,332,726
23.3   right to build on office building is worth $975,610 today.
23.4   maximum bid that Jet Black should be willing to make at the auction is $370,237.
23.5   maximum amount that Sardano and Sons should be willing to pay for the lease of the
            warehouse is $81,904.

Chapter 24: Warrants and Convertibles

24.4   a. each share is worth $1,750
      b. value per share remains at $1,750
      c. stock price will rise to $1,986.67

24.5   a. lower bound on the price of the warrant is zero.
       upper bound on the price of the warrant is $8
      b. lower bound on the price of the warrant is $2 upper bound is 12

24.6   The price per share of Ricketti's common stock after exercise is $17.09

24.9   the value of each of Superior Clamp's warrants is $3.39.

24.10   Omega should issue 507,634 warrants today.

24.11   Scenario A is more likely.

24.12   a. convertible bond should sell for $960.

24.13   a. owns 12.5% of the firm's common stock.
      After conversion, Stevens will own 10%

24.14   a. conversion ratio is 28.
      b. one must surrender $35.71 to receive one share of Hannon's common stock.
      c. the conversion premium is 14.27%
      d. conversion value of the each bond is $875
      e. new conversion value of the bonds will be $931

24.15   a. straight value of the convertible bond is $385.54.
      b. conversion value of the bond is $300
      c. option value of the convertible bond is $14.46.

24.16   conversion value of this convertible bond is $333.33.

24.17   a. straight value of the convertible bond is $516.69.
      b. conversion value of this convertible bond is $280.
      c. $t = 9.79$

Chapter 25: Derivatives and Hedging Risk

25.4   a. $441.75.
       b. $532.06
25.8   a. Forward Price = $900.15
       b. Forward Price = $897.72
25.11 a. mortgage payment $35,238.
       d. i. Mortgage Value = $263,208
       e. i. Mortgage Value = $321,672
25.12 a. Price of Bond A = $900.90
          Price of Bond B = $593.45
          Price of Bond C = $352.18
       b. Price of Bond A = $877.19
          Price of Bond B= $519.37
          Price of Bond C= $269.74
       c. Percentage Change in Bond A = -2.63%
          Percentage Change in Bond B = -12.48%
          Percentage Change in Bond C = -23.41%
25.13 a. The price of Bond A is $904.90.
          The price of Bond B is $1,031.70.
          duration of Bond A is 3.6031 years
          The duration of Bond B is 3.4529 years
       b. Price of Bond A = $1,000
          Price of Bond B= $1,135.49
       d. Percentage Change in Bond A = 10.51%
          Percentage Change in Bond B= 10.06%
25.14 2.7591 years
25.15 3.5313 years
25.16 3.7008 years
25.17 4.3262 years.
25.18 a. duration of Blue Steel's assets is 2.94 years.
       b. duration of Blue Steel's liabilities is 2.75 years.
25.19 a. duration of Magnum's assets is 8.28 years.
       b. duration of Magnum's liabilities is 8.28 years.

Chapter 26: Short-Term Finance and Planning

26.3 change in cash balance $7,000

26.4 change in cash balance $13,000

26.5 a. Operating cycle = 152.1 days

  b. Cash cycle = 115.6 days

26.12 a. Sales = $42,857

  b. January: $44,143

  February: $66,000

  March: $76,000

26.13 Cash Collections from Sales   83   96.7   125.84

26.14 Ending cash balances $226,000 $282,000 $354,600

Chapter 27: Cash Management

27.3   Average annual earnings $2,298.72
27.4   a. $243,193 should be kept as cash. The balance, $556,807 should be invested in
        marketable securities.

        b. 17 times
27.5   avg weekly disbursement = $57.69 million
27.6   The target cash level is $34,536, and the upper limit is $63,608.
27.7   a. Z(gold) = 133,333; Z(silver) = 200,000
        b. variance for Gold Star: 6,444,251; for Silver Star: 15,733,333
27.8   Garden Groves daily float = $2,250,000
        Annual earnings = $506,250
        Net benefit of the lockbox= $398,875
27.9   at least 34 customers per day
27.10   Disbursement float = $60,000
        Collection float = -$45,000
        Net float = $15,000
        If funds are collected in four days Collection float would change to -$60,000.
27.11   a. Reduction in outstanding cash balances = $300,000
        b. Return on savings = $36,000
        c. Maximum monthly charge = $3,000
27.12 $6,240 per year.
27.13   annual net savings = $273,000
27.14   205,312.50: net benefit of concentration
        250,593.75: net benefit of lockbox

Chapter 28: Credit Management

28.1   PV(Old) = 26,954.18
             PV(New) = 26,901.49

28.2   Accounts receivable are 1,232,876.71

28.3   PV(Old) = 80,601.83
             PV(New) = 79,754.04

28.4   a. NPV(Current policy) = $20,000
                NPV(Credit policy) = 3,029.13
             b. 99.57%.

28.5   the price must increase at least $6.42

28.6   If the probability of payment is greater than 92.10%, Fast Typing should offer credit.

28.7   if Silver Spokes subscribes to the collection agency, the shop's net savings are $1,900

28.10   Average collection period = 30 days
             Average daily sales = $12,808.22
             Accounts receivable = $384.247

28.11   average investment $1.8 million

28.12   gross profit: $1.4 million

Chapter 29: Mergers and Acquisitions

29.1   The merger creates $100,000 of goodwill
29.2   goodwill is $60,000
29.3   assets are carried at the pre-merger levels
29.5   for Small Fry, the value is 50
        for the Benefits from acquisition; $i = 11.76\%$
        Value(Whale-Fry) = 292.5; $i = 11.28\%$
29.6   c. expected joint value is 580,000
        d. The bondholders are $10,000 better off after the merger.
29.8   a. Value = $3,500
        b. EPS =$1
        c. Price per share =$17.50
        d. EPS = $1.00
           Price = $25
           Value = $5,000
29.9   a. EPS will increase from $2.25 to $2.50.
        b. There will be no effect on the original Arcadia stockholders.
29.10   a. The synergy : $7.5 million
        b. $27.5 million
        c. cash: $15,000,000; stock: $15,625,000
        d. NPV(cash) = $12,500,000; NPV(stock) = $11,875,000
29.11   a. $14,815,385
        b. NPV = $4,815,385
        c. NPV = $3,634,616
        e. Value(PortlandIndustries) = 11,223,529
           NPV(cash offer) = 1,223,529
           NPV(stock offer) = 1,389,706
29.12   a. price = 22.22 pounds
        b. exchange ratio = 0.643 : 1
29.13   NPV = -$21.2 million

Chapter 30: Financial Distress

30.3   distribute $0 to holders of Junior debentures; Total distribution = $5,000
30.4   There are many possible reorganization plans. See solution set for one that might work.